The *Constitution* BEARING DOWN UPON THE *Guerrière*

From an Old Engraving

A HISTORY OF THE PEOPLE OF THE UNITED STATES

FROM THE REVOLUTION TO THE CIVIL WAR

BY

JOHN BACH McMASTER

Professor of History in the University of Pennsylvania

LIBRARY EDITION IN EIGHT VOLUMES

VOLUME IV. 1812–1821

NEW YORK AND LONDON

D. APPLETON AND COMPANY

1914

To the Memory of
my Mother.

CONTENTS OF VOLUME IV.

CHAPTER XXIV.

vi   CONTENTS.

CONTENTS.

viii   CONTENTS.

CHAPTER XXVIII.

CHAPTER XXXI.

CHAPTER XXXII.

CHAPTER XXXIII.

CHAPTER XXXIV.

CHAPTER XXXV.

CHAPTER XXXVI.

CHAPTER XXXVII.

CHAPTER XXXVIII.

CHAPTER XXXIX.

CONTENTS.

MAPS.

HISTORY

OF THE

PEOPLE OF THE UNITED STATES.

CHAPTER XXIV.

FIGHTING ON THE FRONTIER.

THE cause of the armistice so suddenly concluded by Dearborn and Prevost was the repeal of the orders in council. After five years of persistent effort the United States had triumphed. But she had triumphed not so much by reason of the justness of her cause as by reason of the distressed state of England. The long embargo and the Non-importation Act had inflicted a far deeper injury on Great Britain than Perceval and his ministry were willing to admit. Loss of the American market—a market worth to British manufacturers twelve million pounds a year—had brought commerce to the brink of ruin ; had depressed industries ; had closed workshops and factories ; and had driven thousands of operatives into idleness and want. Even Nature had been unkind, and to a winter of great severity had added a summer unfavorable to crops. The earth withheld her increase, and when the scanty harvests of 1811 were gathered, both wheat and barley rose very small from the flail. With the laboring classes of the manufacturing districts in idleness, with the warehouses filled to the roof with goods intended for the American market, with wheat at one hundred and forty shillings a quarter and flour at nineteen dollars a barrel, with the ports of the United States shut and no hope of exchanging manufactured goods for food, it needed no sagacity to foresee that the winter of 1812 would be one of great distress and suffering. Fully convinced that a crisis was at hand, the corporation of London, on the eve of the meeting of Parliament, carried up an address to the Prince Regent, asking that he would be pleased to cause a suspension of the use of grain in the distilleries, and to employ all means in his power to reopen trade with neutral nations.

Neutral nations meant the United States, with which no hope of an amicable arrangement remained. The newspapers brought in by every ship from Halifax or the West Indies made this plainer and plainer. The early meeting of Congress, the tone of the President's message, the comments of the press, the warlike report of the Committee of Foreign Relations, were known all over England before Parliament met, and left no doubt but that at last the patient and long-suffering Republic was really going to war. That such a war could end otherwise than in the complete prostration of the United States no Englishman for a moment believed. Yet it was not desired. Under no circumstances could England be the gainer. Under any circumstances she must be the loser. The United States was a continent. To her the war would be a stimulant, building up her manufactures, developing her resources, consolidating her Government, and making her independent of the whole world. Great Britain was a cluster of small islands, owning possessions scattered all over the face of the globe, and depending for her prosperity on the welfare of her manufactures and a world-wide commerce. To her war meant the idleness of every factory, every ship, every man engaged in the manufacture or the transportation of the sixty million dollars worth of goods, wares, and merchandise sent each year to the markets of the United States, and this price even Perceval was not prepared to pay. His American policy, therefore, seemed to the opposition to be a peculiarly fine subject for attack, and with the meeting of Parliament the attack began.

Success was won slowly. An attempt to have some strong language on the failure of the ministry to conciliate America inserted in the address to the Regent was defeated in the Commons. A motion calling for a statement of the value of goods sent to and brought from the United States for ten years past; for the number and tonnage of American ships taken into British ports in 1808 and 1809 under the orders in council; for a summary of the taxes levied as tonnage duties on American ships; and of the licenses granted since 1803—was carried. But a request for the papers relating to the orders in council was lost in the House, and motions for a Select Committee to consider the effects produced by orders in council and the license system were voted down, both by the Lords and the Commons.*

During the first two months of the session the disposition of the Commons not to meddle in American affairs was most manifest. The majorities against motions to take up such matters were never less than seventy-two, and often were one hundred. Had Parliament been left to do its will, such majorities would undoubtedly have continued to be polled to the end of the session. But Parliament was not left to do its will. Made reckless by idleness and want, and ignorant of the true causes of their distress, the workmen in the inland counties had turned upon their employers and opened the year with violent acts and the destruction of every kind of labor-saving machinery. To break stocking-frames and shears, spinning-jennies and mules, seize wheat and potatoes, and scatter the accumulations of speculators and forestallers, was the sole occupation of the laboring classes in many parts of England. Nottingham, Derbyshire, Birmingham, Sheffield, Manchester, Cheshire, Yorkshire, Cornwall, became the scenes of mob violence which the militia could hardly suppress. Seizing on this discontent and suffering, and on the well-known unwillingness of the ministry to incur the expense of an American war, the manufacturers in turn began to agitate, called meetings, passed resolutions, and drew up petitions for the repeal of the orders in council. The movement spread fast, and by March the northern, western, and midland counties were in open revolt, and petitions from the china and earthenware makers of Staffordshire; from the merchants and manufacturers engaged in the woollen trade in the West Riding of Yorkshire; from Lancaster, from Sheffield, from the frame-work

---

* The Parliamentary Debates from the Year 1803 to the Present Time. T. C. Hansard, vol. xxi.

knitters of Leicester, from York, Liverpool, Hull, Leeds, and Birmingham, were read in Parliament. The men who came up with the petition from Leicester declared that eleven thousand workmen had subscribed it. That from Leeds is said to have had seventeen thousand signatures. That from Birmingham bore twenty thousand names inscribed on a sheet of parchment one hundred and fifty feet long.*

The substance of these documents was invariably the same. The petitioners began with assurances of the love and loyalty they bore both king and country, and declared their perfect willingness to endure a reasonable amount of suffering, but entreated that they might not be driven to ruin and starvation. The closing of the European ports and the interruption of trade by the orders in council had wellnigh destroyed their business, and would have utterly destroyed it had not the American market remained. Should this be lost—and a further persistence in the orders would surely lose it—seventy thousand skilled workmen would be brought face to face with hunger, nakedness, and want. As each petition was read, the House had ordered it to lie upon the table. But as the usual motion for this purpose was about to be put in the case of the Birmingham memorial, Alexander Baring rose and protested against such treatment. He could not, he said, bear to see a petition signed by so many thousand men silently and carelessly laid aside. He could not think of the distress under which the signers labored without expressing the hope that their grievances would be speedily attended to. He was answered from the ministerial benches that the orders in council were not for retaliation, but for self-defence ; that they had not destroyed British commerce, nor produced distress in the manufacturing districts; and that they would in time be considered. Outwardly the ministry seemed firm in their determination to continue the orders, but secretly they had already begun to waver. The petitions, and, above all, the letters from the manufacturing counties, had greatly affected their followers. The burden of the letters was want of employment, scantiness of food, high price of provisions. The diet of the factory

---

* Hansard's Parliamentary Debates, vols. xxi and xxii.

hands was, the members were reminded, potatoes and oatmeal, both of which were now almost too costly to buy. Five years before, two hundred and forty pounds of potatoes sold for seven shillings, but could not then be purchased for seven teen. Forty-two shillings would once have bought two hundred and forty pounds of oatmeal, which could not then be had for less than sixty-seven. As provisions rose, wages fell and work became scarce. Two men out of three were idle; those who had occupation worked on short time, and were glad to take eleven shillings a week for skilled labor that had once commanded thirty-five. At Liverpool but sixty-six carts were busy about the docks, while one hundred and twenty-seven were idle. There as many as sixteen thousand persons had received relief in one week. Against statements such as these, and against the threatening attitude of the United States, the assertions of the ministers that the orders were beneficial went for nothing. Week after week the ranks of the administration party grew thinner and thinner, till the Prime Minister could with difficulty muster a majority of seventy-two in a House of three hundred and sixty. In the hope of getting relief, Perceval, on April tenth, bade Foster declare that if the United States would restore intercourse, Great Britain would grant no more licenses, and would resort to vigorous blockades; and the Prince Regent, on the twenty-first of April, proclaimed that whenever the French should issue an authentic act expressly and unconditionally repealing the Berlin and Milan decrees, the orders in council would be formally revoked. But the proclamation weakened rather than strengthened Perceval; and when, on April twenty-eighth, a motion was made in the Commons for a committee to hear the petitioners against the orders, the ministry gave way completely.

The committee began its session at once, and was still busy hearing testimony when, on May eleventh, a lunatic shot Perceval in the lobby of the House and killed him on the spot. The untimely death of the great defender of the orders served but to incite the opposition to push on the investigation with new energy. Witnesses from every part of England were examined, testimony was presented to show that great industries had been prostrated, mills and factories shut, merchants

embarrassed, and thousands of the working classes brought to
the verge of starvation by the loss of the American market.
Such evidence, coupled with the alarming news that Congress
had laid an embargo as the last step prior to war, was too much
for a weak ministry. They yielded, and when, toward the
middle of June, Brougham moved an address to the Regent
asking for the repeal of the orders and brought on another
debate, Lord Castlereagh rose and in the name of his colleagues
announced that the orders were to be immediately revoked.
Accordingly, on June twenty-third, the Prince Regent formally proclaimed that the orders of January seventh, 1807, and
April twenty-sixth, 1809, were no longer in force. They were,
however, to be revived if the United States should not repeal
the Non-importation Act or should resort to hostile acts.

So likely did it seem that the United States had resorted
to hostile acts that the next ship to sail for America carried
out instructions to Foster to conclude an armistice if war had
opened, and to Prevost to make no preparations beyond defence. These instructions met Foster at Halifax, whither he
had gone after war was formally declared. As he could not
carry them out himself, he persuaded John Borlase Warren,
admiral of the blue and commander of the station, to offer a
suspension of hostilities on the sea, while the Governor-General of Canada proposed an armistice on land. Prevost was
first to act, and despatched his Adjutant-General to Albany.
The orders of the American General were plain, distinct, and
positive. He was to support Hull by a vigorous offensive
movement on Canada at Niagara. He knew that Hull was in
Canada. He knew that every available British soldier in
Canada was hurrying toward Hull. He knew that time was
precious. Yet in the face of all this Dearborn, on August
ninth, gladly agreed with the agent of Prevost that the troops
along the frontier as far as he commanded should act on the
defensive till further orders came from Washington. Over
Hull, Dearborn had no command. He was not, therefore, included in the armistice ; but the stipulation was made that he
might come in if he wished, and a letter was sent off urging
him to do so. Had Dearborn been a man of action the letter
would have gone forward with all the speed a courier could

make. He sent it by the mail, and eight days were consumed in traversing the three hundred miles which separate Albany and Niagara. Indeed, it did not reach the banks of that river till Hull had been forty-eight hours a prisoner, till the news of the armistice had reached Washington, and till a letter disavowing the arrangement and bidding Dearborn push on with the utmost vigor and seize the British posts on the Niagara was half way on its journey to Albany.

The commanding officer on the Niagara frontier was Major-General Stephen Van Rensselaer, of the New York Militia. He was born at Albany, on the memorable November day when the Stamp Act went into force in America, and on the death of his father inherited the vast estate known as the Van Rensselaer Manor. Though the baronial rights of the family ceased on the establishment of independence, he was always known as the Patroon, and was the eighth in succession. After graduating at Harvard in 1782, he turned his attention to the improvement of his estates, and, favored by the stream of emigrants which soon swept across New York, and by the liberal terms he offered, had in time some nine hundred farms of one hundred and fifty acres each under cultivation. In 1789 he entered the Assembly of the State as a Federalist, and became in succession a State Senator, Lieutenant-Governor, and a Major-General of Militia. In 1812 he was a prominent candidate for Governor, in opposition to Daniel D. Tompkins. The story was current that when, in that year, the President called on Governor Tompkins to detach New York's quota of militia for the purposes of national defence, the Governor selected Van Rensselaer to command it, in the hope that he would decline to serve, and so injure his popularity and his chances of election. He accepted, however, and reached the frontier a few days after Hull's surrender, but utterly ignorant of that event. Almost immediately on arriving there he received the instructions of General Dearborn to conclude a cessation of hostilities with the enemy in his front. By the terms of the agreement thus made by Van Rensselaer and the British General Sheaffe, who commanded while Brock was at Malden, the armistice was to end four days after either party had notified the other of the receipt of orders to renew hostilities.   Orders so to do came to Van Rensselaer on September fourth, and at noon on September eighth war along the frontier began again.*

That it was now his plain duty to move into Canada and take the province was the opinion of everybody, and the substance of the orders of General Dearborn.   But to execute these orders was not possible, for of all the gatherings of men that ever bore the name of army, one of the worst was that to which the duty of invasion was assigned.   On assuming command at Niagara, Van Rensselaer found there about one thousand men, half clad and almost unarmed, scattered along the river from Black Rock to Fort Niagara.   Some had no shoes. The pay of all was much overdue, while there were not in the army ten rounds of powder per man, nor a single pound of lead, nor more than one heavy gun, and that had no gunners to serve it.†   With laudable zeal Van Rensselaer gathered the troops at Lewiston, drilled them and taught them the use of arms, and while so engaged the prisoners taken at Detroit were seen marching by on the other side of the narrow river.

Then the spirits of the troops rose high, and they cried out to be led into Canada at once.   Nothing but a battle would content them.   The winter must not set in, they must not think of going to their homes, till the disgrace of Hull had been wiped away.   For some weeks Van Rensselaer refused; but, the soldiers growing restless, the season being far advanced, some re-enforcements having come, and the Republicans openly accusing him of intentionally delaying the expedition because he was a Federalist, he decided to lose no more time, but cross the river and take Queenston.

No part of our northern frontier is so well known to the travelling Americans of our day as the little Niagara river about to become the seat of war.   Yet it has so changed since 1812 that it is well to recall the condition of the country as it was when Van Rensselaer reached Lewiston.   At the extreme northeastern end of Lake Erie, just where it narrows to form

---

* A Narrative of the Affair of Queenston in the War of 1812.   By Solomon Van Rensselaer.   Appendix No. II.

† Van Rensselaer to Governor Tompkins, August 19, 1812.

the Niagara, was Buffalo, which then stood on a low bluff a little back from the lake and from the marsh which bordered Buffalo Creek. The town was some six years old; but as it lay directly on the line of overland emigration, it already had a population of five hundred, and boasted of eight stores, four taverns, two schools, a weekly newspaper, and a fine trade with the West. At the entrance to Niagara on the Canadian side was Fort Erie, a strongly stockaded post, with a block-house and a barrack for troops. Two miles and a half north of Buffalo was the village of Black Rock, which might be regarded as a commercial rival, for not only was it deeply engaged in the salt trade, but by means of a ferry had carried on considerable commerce with Canada. At Black Rock the river was half a mile wide, clear as crystal, and flowed with a steady current, which interfered not a little with shipping, and so did much to favor the new lake port of Buffalo. Four miles below Black Rock the river divided, each branch passing around Grand Island and uniting again in a bay some two miles wide. On the west shore, at the mouth of Chippawa Creek, was the English village of the same name, numbering some thirty houses and deriving its importance from being the depot for the fur trade of Upper Canada. There, too, was a military station called Fort Welland, though no regular fortification existed. A mile or more below Chippawa the rapids began, the current growing swifter and swifter till the river reached Table Rock and made its plunge down the Falls of Niagara. Above the falls and on the banks of the rapids was the American village of Grand Niagara, or, as it was called by a few Anglomaniacs, Manchester. Here were a few houses, a grist-mill, a saw-mill, a fulling-mill, all moved by the fine water-power afforded by the river.

Once down the falls, the Niagara sweeps northward through a deep, narrow chasm it has worn in the rocks till it reaches a point some nine miles below Grand Niagara, where the rocky cliffs suddenly end, and the river, spreading out to a width of half a mile, flows on across an almost level plain to Lake Ontario, eight miles northward. Where the cliffs end and the plain begins were two villages. Lewiston, on the American side, was a thriving settlement where a great trade was carried

on. As the head of navigation from Lake Ontario, it was the
place to which all goods, wares, merchandise, and salt, coming
out from Albany by way of Oswego and intended for the
West, were brought by the lake craft, of which twenty-three
were owned in the town. As the beginning of the portage
round the falls to Lake Erie, it was the place from which the
ox teams, the "horn-breeze," set out for Black Rock and Buffalo. In it were many fine warehouses, constantly full of
grain, salt, flour, provisions, bound down the Ohio, and peltry
bound eastward. Across the river was the Canadian town of
Queenston, which in size, trade, and prosperity was a repro-
duction of its American rival. At the mouth of the Niagara
river on the Canadian side was Newark, which spread along
the shore of Lake Ontario for fully a mile, and, well laid out
and neatly built, contained over two hundred houses, two
churches, an academy, a jail, twenty dry-goods stores, and a
light-house. Behind Newark, on the river bank, was Fort
George, one of the strongest British posts in Upper Canada.
Under its guns in New York was Fort Niagara, built by the
French early in the eighteenth century.

It was just in the rear of Lewiston and at the foot of the
steep cliffs, some three hundred and forty feet high, which
form the end of the terrace through which the Niagara has
cut its deep gorge, that Van Rensselaer pitched his camp and
gathered the few troops which till that time had been scattered along the Niagara River from Black Rock to Fort
Niagara. While there encamped waiting for re-enforcements
he received, on the last day of September, a letter from Buffalo
announcing the arrival of Brigadier-General Alexander Smyth
and sixteen hundred and fifty regulars at Buffalo.

Smyth was a native of Ireland, where he was born in 1765,
but came to America when ten years old, and grew up and
was educated in Virginia. Having selected law as a profession, he read the few books necessary for admission to the bar,
and began practice in 1789. With law he joined politics, and
sat for several years in the State Legislature. But neither
law nor politics quite satisfied him, and when, in 1808, a regiment of infantry was raised for the United States army he
obtained the command, and did duty in the Southwest till, in

1811 he was ordered to Washington. At the opening of the war he was made Inspector-General with the rank of Brigadier-General, and at his own request was given command of the brigade of regulars ordered to Niagara. On reaching Buffalo, late in September, he reported to Van Rensselaer, and announced that, from what he heard of the character of the country to the north, he judged that Buffalo was the proper place from which to invade Canada, and would stay there. Van Rensselaer differed from him and asked him to name a day for a council of war. To this reasonable request not the least attention was paid, and, as Van Rensselaer could not force a regular army general to obey his orders, the preparations for invasion were made without his assistance.

At Queenston were then stationed some three hundred British troops, regulars and militia, and at Fort George, under the immediate command of Brock, were the regiment he brought back from Detroit and some Indians. Believing that he had force enough to contend with them, Van Rensselaer chose the night of October tenth for the attack, and just before daybreak on the eleventh the first boat shoved out from the New York shore. The lieutenant in command carelessly, or, as some said, traitorously, took with him all the oars. Not another boat could follow, and, after waiting till daylight in a blinding northeast storm for him to return, the troops were marched back to camp half mutinous.

On the morrow matters were better arranged. Colonel Solomon Van Rensselaer, a cousin of the general and a skilful officer, who had served under Wayne, was given the command. The troops were in two columns, the regulars led by Colonel Christie, the militia by Van Rensselaer, and in the early dusk of morning thirteen boats, bearing twenty-five men each, pushed off into the stream. The current was strong. The river was full of eddies. The enemy opened a rapid and well-aimed fire. But the beach was reached, a line formed, and the Canadians driven toward Queenston. The Americans now halted to rest. This display of courage was hailed with cheers from the American shore, and some four hundred more troops went joyfully over. But the English rallied, and began a severe engagement, in which Van Rensselaer was wounded four times.

Meantime, Christie having been carried down stream by the current, his command had devolved on Captain Wool, who, with a few companions, climbed the steep heights which over-hang the town. On the summit was a battery from which Brock looked down on what went on below.* As the river face of the cliff up which Wool had climbed was supposed to be impassable, his appearance on top was a complete sur-prise, and Brock and his soldiers barely escaped capture by a rapid flight down the hill toward Queenston. Once on the plain, the English general gathered a handful of troops and sent them to dislodge Wool. The first attack was beaten back. The second was also a failure, for it was led by Brock who fell dead at the foot of the slope, shot through the lungs.

The military importance of the heights, of which Wool was thus left in quiet possession, was the assistance the battery could give to the army in its advance on Queenston. But the army made no such advance. Indeed, save about six hun-dred militia and three hundred and fifty regulars, not a man crossed the river. Officer after officer came to the bank and shouted and beckoned to them to come over. Van Rensselaer, wounded though he was, crossed, and implored them to be men. Some well-known politicians, who were present, went about entreating them to fight. But it was of no avail.† No sooner did the militia behold a real battle, no sooner did they see the dead brought back in the boats, and hear the groans of the wounded, than fear overcame them, and they refused to cross. Soldiers who the day before were clamorous to be brought face to face with what they called the British hirelings now stood on their constitutional rights and refused to help their fighting countrymen. They were, they said, militia, and the only services for which the militia could be called out were to uphold the laws, to put down insurrection, to repel invasion. The Constitution did not give the President power to send them out of the United States, and they would not go.

Holding such views, they stood quietly on the American side, saw the British gather in force and march up the hill,

---

* Life of Brock, p. 330.
† Van Rensselaer to Dearborn, October 14, 1812.

saw their countrymen overwhelmed by numbers, driven back foot by foot to the edge of the cliff and down the side to the river bank, where, as no one would row a boat across, the little band of six hundred threw down their arms and surrendered. With them were captured some three hundred skulkers and cowards, who had been crouching at the river edge all day. The loss was serious, for among the officers taken were Winfield Scott, John E. Wool, and Joseph G. Totten. Van Rensselaer, who had crossed over to the New York bank to persuade the troops to fight, escaped. Enraged at such poltroonery, he asked to be relieved. Dearborn gladly consented, and, having denounced him to Eustis as an ignorant militia officer, jealous of the regular service, made over the command to Alexander Smyth.* Conceited and volatile, Smyth at once began to wage war by proclamation. In one handbill, which he issued early in November, he addressed the men of New York. " Our first army," said he, " has been disgracefully surrendered and lost. Another, led on by popular men, destitute alike of theory and experience in the art of war, has been sacrificed in an attempt to cross where the enemy is strongest. But in a few days the troops under my command will plant the American standard in Canada. They are men used to obedience, silence, and steadiness. They will conquer or they will die. Will you stand with arms folded and look on at the interesting struggle ? Are you not related to the men who fought at Bennington and Saratoga ? Has the race degenerated ? Or have you, under the baneful influence of contending factions, forgot your country ? Must I turn from you and ask the men of the Six Nations to support the Government of the United States ? Shall I imitate the officers of the British army and suffer our ungathered laurels to be tarnished by ruthless deeds ? Shame, where is thy blush ! No ! where I command, the peaceful man, the child, the maid, the matron shall be secure from wrong. Men of New York, the present is the hour of renown. Advance, then, to our aid. Come in companies, half-companies, or singly. But remember that every man who accompanies us places himself under my

---

* Dearborn to Eustis, October 21, 1812. War Department Manuscripts.

command and must submit to the salutary restraints of discipline." *

As Peter B. Porter was to command the volunteers, he
transmitted the address of Smyth in one of his own to the
people of the counties of Ontario and Genesee. He too
assured "the independent and high-minded yeomanry" that
Smyth had a powerful army; that it was under strict discipline; that it could, and in a few days would, occupy all the
British fortresses on the Niagara frontier; and that a vigorous
campaign of one month was all that was needed to "palsy the
savage hand then wielding the scalping knife," restore peace
to the frontier, and "redeem the tarnished reputation of the
nation." †

These appeals were so effective that within two weeks
upward of a thousand men had enrolled themselves in Ontario
County alone. Niagara, it was believed, would furnish as
many more, and Seneca and Cayuga each five hundred.
While these volunteers were enlisting and hurrying westward,
Smyth addressed himself to the army of the centre in much
the same style as he had addressed the men of New York, and
closed with an exhortation which the Federalists turned into
a byword. "Come on, my heroes," said he, "and when you
attack the enemy's batteries let your rallying word be ' The
cannon lost at Detroit—or death.' " ‡

Nothing now remained but to make these promises good,
for by this time there had been gathered at Black Rock a
band of forty-five hundred regulars and volunteers from New
York, Pennsylvania, and Baltimore, and a great fleet of scows
and long-boats. Smyth therefore decided to "plant the standard" in Canada, somewhere between Fort Erie and Chippawa Creek, and selected the night of November twenty-
seventh as the time for crossing. A party of regulars and
sailors was then ordered to go over and spike the guns of the
Canadian batteries while a second party of regulars and militia
descended the river some five miles, and hewed down the
bridge over the Chippawa. Scarcely had they started when a

---

* Niles's Weekly Register, vol. iii, p. 203.   ‡ Ibid., vol. iii, p. 216.
† Ibid., vol. iii, p. 233.

signal gun from the English batteries gave the alarm, and the boats returned. Next morning, however (November twenty-eighth), both parties made a landing. That against the bridge did litttle. That against the batteries spiked the guns; but the sailors, finishing their part first, brought back all the boats, and the soldiers thus deserted fell into the hands of the English. In spite of this, success seemed certain. The weather was good. The boats were ready. The troops were in the best of spirits. The guns on the Canadian side were silenced. The regulars were boarding their boats; indeed, some volunteers under General Porter had already pushed off from shore, when an adjutant rode to the river bank and cried out, "Fellow-soldiers, the expedition is given up," * and the troops were ordered to camp.

The whole army was furious. Some of the militia broke their muskets. Some threatened to go home instantly. Others said jeeringly that Smyth heard a bugle on the Canadian side, that the sound filled him with fear, and that if the sailors had only spiked the bugle instead of the guns, the expedition might have gone on successfully. The abuse which Smyth had heaped on Van Rensselaer and Hull was now in turn heaped on him. He was called on to make good his boasts. He was taunted with the cries, "Come on, my heroes," and "The cannon lost at Detroit." He was nicknamed Van Bladder, and heard the troops grow clamorous for Van Rensselaer as commander. Burning with rage, Smyth now named another day for the crossing. Again the army was drawn up. Again Porter led the way in a boat, and again the expedition was put off, the militia sent to their homes, and the regulars to winter quarters.† For this General Porter published him in the newspapers as a coward, and was promptly called out.‡ The challenge was accepted, and in the presence of the army the two generals, with surgeons and seconds and a party of invited friends, went over to Grand Island to fight. The ground was paced off; the seconds carefully drew the

---

* Canandaigua Repository, December 8, 1812.

† Smyth's account of his failure is given in a letter to Dearborn, December 8, 1812. Historical Register of the United States, Part II, vol. ii, pp. 118–122.

‡ Buffalo Gazette, December 8, 1812.

balls from the pistols; shots were exchanged; and the two came back to Black Rock unhurt.* Smyth was now hardly safe. Indeed, he fled for protection to the regulars, and pitched his tent in the midst of their camp. The mob hooted him wherever he appeared. A militiaman fired at him on the street at Buffalo. The Federalist press set upon him with scoffs and jeers. When asked by a committee of patriotic citizens of western New York to explain the cause of his failure to enter Canada, he took occasion in his answer to describe the army, and did so quite correctly. It was, he said, a crowd of men who had come to Niagara to look on a real battle as on a theatrical show; when the exhibition disappointed them they broke their muskets, and, when rations were short, went home.† This remark gave great offence, and his answer, printed on a handbill and headed "Reasons for not planting the American Standard on the Canadian Shore agreeable to the Late Proclamation," was spread all over the State of New York.

Smyth now asked Dearborn for leave to visit his family, and, having obtained permission, hastened by backroads and obscure villages to his home in Virginia, where he learned, some three months later, that Madison, without any legal right whatever, had stricken the name of Alexander Smyth from the roll of the United States Army. But his usefulness was not ended. His friends and neighbors still respected him, and, after sending him to the Virginia Legislature, elected him a member of Congress, and continued to do so till his death in 1830. In his old age his mind took on a theological bent, and he wrote and published a work which may yet be found in libraries, and is entitled "An Explanation of the Apocalypse, or Revelation of St. John."

The true state of the army now began to come out. Order and discipline, of which Smyth had boasted, had never existed. For months past the camp at Black Rock had been the scene of mutiny, desertion, riot, and race war. Some busybody having spread the report among the volunteers that if they went into Canada, even with their own consent, they would by that

---

* Niles's Weekly Register, vol. iii, pp. 283, 284.
† Ibid., vol. iii, pp. 263, 264.

act become "regulars" and be liable to five years' duty, seven hundred of the nine hundred "Proclamation Volunteers," five hundred of the Pennsylvania "Drafted Militia," all the Baltimore contingent known as the "mob-boys," and all but thirteen of the three hundred Irish Greens from New York city refused to cross. Mutiny, desertion, riot were of almost daily occurrence. On one occasion a race war opened between the Irish Greens from New York and some American volunteers, and became so serious that the regulars were summoned to put it down.*

While Smyth was issuing his proclamations and gathering his troops at Black Rock, the day of reckoning came for Dearborn. Early in the summer he had assumed command of the army of reserve, or, as it came to be called later, the army of the north, had fixed his headquarters at Albany, and had there collected some six thousand troops, regulars and militia. The wish of the President seems to have been that when Hull had taken Malden he should overrun Upper Canada and join Van Rensselaer on the Niagara frontier; that the two armies should then hurry to the St. Lawrence, and, uniting with Dearborn and the army of reserve, should move down the river and capture Montreal. But the surrender of Hull and the repulse of Van Rensselaer ruined the plan. The expedition did not take place, and Dearborn, left to himself, pushed down Lake Champlain and pitched his camp near the Canadian frontier. His orders were positive. The way to Mon-

---

* It was about this time that the phrase "Uncle Sam" became popular. Just when and where it originated is not known. The story, currently believed in 1812, is, that when a regiment of light dragoons was raised in 1808, the letters U. S. L. D. on their caps, were interpreted by some wag to mean Uncle Sam's Lazy Dogs. The contact of the militia with the regulars in 1812 gave the phrase greater currency, and it rapidly grew popular. The expression "Uncle Sam's men" occurs in Lansingburg Gazette, September, 1813; True American, October 7, 1813. The American Daily Advertiser of August 15, 1816, attributes the origin of "Uncle Sam" to the letters U. S. L. D. But just a year later, the Albany Gazette says it arose during the war from the letters U. S. on the soldiers' knapsacks, and "has come into general use." "The Indians at the West, from hearing it often used, have imbibed the idea that it is actually the name of the President, and while at Sackett's Harbor a considerable number of Indians and squaws crowded around the President, wishing, as they expressed it, to shake hands with Uncle Sam."—American Daily Advertiser, August 15, 1817.

treal was open, and the city might easily have been taken. But the militia once more refused to leave their native soil, and, after a couple of fruitless raids across the border, went into winter quarters at Burlington and Plattsburg.

The failure of Dearborn closed the list of disasters of 1812. But the end was not yet, for a disaster more terrible than all was near at hand. The fall of Detroit left the northwestern frontier at the mercy of the Indians, and was followed all over the country by vigorous calls for volunteers. At Albany, in New York city, at Baltimore, all through the western counties of Pennsylvania and Virginia, men were enlisted, money subscribed, and food, clothes, and gunpowder hastily collected. Alexandria raised two thousand dollars and a company of volunteers. At Richmond the women were asked to make tents and knapsacks for a company of fifteen hundred, and gladly did so. The State-House was thrown open to them, and for two days the rooms were full of women cutting, basting, and sewing with such industry that more tents and knapsacks were made than were wanted. Before the first of September three hundred men had gone from Fredericksburg and one hundred from Petersburg, and as many more from Baltimore. From every town and village where a score of able-bodied men could be collected came volunteers or tenders of service. Many were accepted, and in a few weeks the highways that led northward and westward were full of " Riflemen " and " Silver Greys," " Invincibles " and " Fencibles," " Irish Greens " and " Republican Blues." It was their boast that the spirit of the people was at last awake, and that the shameful surrender of Hull had done more to help on the war than could the capture of ten thousand British regulars.

Strong as was the war fever in the Middle States, it was stronger still in Kentucky. There age, politics, business, occupation, all were forgotten in the excitement of the moment, and men of every sort put down their names in the list of volunteers. Every man who sought for notoriety, or courted popularity, or bore a name famous in the annals of the State, who held an office or looked forward with longing to the day when he should, was eager to serve. Henry Clay went from muster to muster, rousing the patriotism of the troops and promising them victory. Two Kentucky Congressmen shouldered their muskets and joined the ranks. A third undertook to raise five hundred men. Fifteen thousand men are believed to have volunteered. Upward of ten thousand were enlisted, and the command of them given to William Henry Harrison, the hero of Tippecanoe. Harrison was then Governor of Indiana Territory; but so determined were the troops that he should command, that the Governor of Kentucky made him a Major-General in the militia of that State.

Placing himself at the head of the troops, which had gathered at Cincinnati, Harrison, on the twenty-eighth of August, set out for the Northwest. There his help was greatly needed, for the Indians had taken the war path, had besieged Fort Harrison on the Wabash and Fort Wayne on the Maumee, had threatened Vincennes, and had scalped and murdered men within thirty miles of Louisville. Pushing on with all the speed he could, he passed through Lebanon on August thirty-first, reached Dayton the next day, and on September third halted at Piqua. Want of gun-flints kept him at Piqua three days; but on September sixth he was again marching, and, driving the English and Indians before him, came in sight of Fort Wayne at dawn on the twelfth. Stopping there to punish the Indians, he laid waste the Little Turtle towns on Eel river, sacked the Pottawattamie villages on the Elkhart, and burned the lodges of the Miamis at the forks of the Wabash.

While so engaged, General Winchester, of the regular army, reached the fort. To him, as ranking officer, Harrison gave up the command, and started back to resume his duties as Governor of Indiana. But at Piqua he was overtaken by an express rider, who brought him a commission to be Commander-in-Chief of the Army of the Northwest. His first thought was to hasten back to the troops; but, before doing so, he drew up a handbill and sent a thousand copies into Kentucky to be scattered over the State. The bill announced his new command and called for help. The winter was coming; the campaign would be long, and the soldiers had not suitable clothing. Could any patriot, he asked, sleep easy on his bed of down, and think of the suffering of a sentinel exposed to the fury of a wild winter night in Canada?

Would " the amiable fair sex " suffer their brave defenders to
be mutilated by frost for want of the mittens and socks they
could so easily knit? Blankets, overalls, roundabout jackets,
shoes, socks, mittens—all were wanted and wanted at once.*

The answer was a supply of the needed clothing. While
it was being made ready, Harrison prepared a plan for the
campaign. The troops he proposed should gather at the rapids
of the Maumee, and, if the season were dry, move at once upon
Detroit. If the season were wet, he intended to wait till winter had frozen the vast swamp which spread from the Sandusky to the Auglaize rivers and cut him off from Detroit.
Toward the Maumee the troops were then moving in three
columns. The Virginians and the Pennsylvanians, making up
the right wing, had by October reached the Lower Sandusky.
The Ohioans, attempting to march along Hull's road, found it
impassable, and were stopped at Urbana, a hundred miles
from the Maumee. On the left the Kentuckians were at
Defiance, under the command of Brigadier-General Winchester. There they had been shut up since September, and, ill-
fed, ill-clothed, and idle, had grown mutinous.

The march northward from Dayton and Piqua had been
one of hardships and privations. But at Fort Winchester, as
the troops named the new camp built near Defiance, life became a desperate struggle with hunger and cold. Hundreds
of the men had no shoes and were forced to make moccasins
out of the green hides of hogs and steers. Provisions were
always scarce, but repeatedly the army was without flour for
many days, and on several occasions was almost without food.
In October, when Harrison reached the camp after his appointment as Commander of the Northwestern Army, he
found the troops had seen neither salt nor flour for five days,
and were on the verge of mutiny. Commanding the army to
be paraded, he assured the soldiers that food and clothing
were on their way to the St. Mary's river and would soon
arrive. A little did come. But the clothing covered few;
the food was soon consumed, and, as fever began to ravage
the camp, the suffering and discontent were greater than be-

---

* Nashville Whig, October 7, 1812.

fore. As the cold weather came on, the men, unable to keep
warm in the tents, began to build huts, and heard with dismay
that the boats with provisions and clothes sent from Kentucky were frozen in the St. Mary's river. A detachment
was instantly despatched to bring on the food by pack train,
and that night Winchester found in his hut a note informing
him that if the flour and salt, the clothes, and the shoes were
not in camp in two days the volunteers would march back
and get them. Next day the last ration of beef and pork was
drawn, and, had it not been for the fortunate arrival of a
drove of hogs, the army would probably have disbanded.

Yet the condition of affairs on the Maumee was not much
worse than on the Sandusky. By dint of great exertion and
great expense, hundreds of thousands of rations, thousands of
blankets, shoes, roundabout jackets, and pantaloons had been
gathered on the Sandusky river, to be sent thence to the
rapids of the Maumee, where the three parts of the army
were to meet. But none of the supplies ever arrived. The
wagons stuck fast in the mud and were abandoned. The
horses gave out, and, as they had been greatly overvalued
when taken into the service, the owners gladly destroyed
them. Now the water in the rivers was too low to use boats.
Now the boats were frozen hard and fast and could not be
moved. Not a ration ever came within fifty miles of the
Maumee.* Still, Harrison determined to push on, and in
December ordered Winchester to leave his camp and go
down the Maumee to the rapids. Sleds were made and the
few horses in the army hitched to them. Not one of the
animals had ever had a piece of harness on his back ; but
hunger had so tamed them that they submitted, and, fastened
by thongs of green hide, they dragged the sleds till they fell
and died by the wayside.† Two weeks of such marching,
now through slush, now through snow-drifts, brought the

---

* McAffee. History of the War in the Western Country, p. 184.

† A Journal containing an Accurate and Interesting Account of the Hardships, Sufferings, Battles, Defeat, and Captivity of those Heroic Kentucky Volunteers and Regulars commanded by General Winchester in the Year 1812–'13.
Elias Darnall, pp. 36, 38. Narrative of the Suffering and Defeat of the Northwestern Army under General Winchester. William Atherton, pp. 25–31.

army to the rapids.   While encamped there two Frenchmen came in to beg protection for a little village some thirty miles northward, called Frenchtown.*   It stood on the bank of the river Raisin, numbered about forty houses, and was then held by some three hundred Indians and Canadian militia.   As Winchester had with him thirteen hundred troops, and as the time of some of them was to expire in February, the whole camp became clamorous for a fight.   To go home without so much as exchanging shots with the enemy would, the soldiers said, be bad enough ; but to go home and tell the people of Kentucky that thirteen hundred men had remained quietly in their huts within thirty miles of three hundred British would be everlasting shame.   A council of war was called, and the decision reached to send six hundred and fifty men, the flower of the Kentucky troops, under Colonel William Lewis and Colonel John Allen, to the river Raisin.†

They started in high spirits on the morning of January seventeenth, and, marching on the ice that fringed the shores of Maumee Bay and Lake Erie, came to the south bank of the Raisin about two in the afternoon of January eighteenth.   On the north bank was a force of two hundred and fifty British and Indians, who offered so determined a resistance that it was dark when they were driven to the woods and Frenchtown occupied and held.

On hearing of this success, Winchester seems for the first time to have realized what a foolish act he had committed. Eighteen miles beyond the Raisin lay four thousand British and Indians.   Yet he had, in the presence of such numbers, divided his own feeble force into two equal parts, separated them by thirty miles, and sent one into the very hands of the enemy. Even the troops at the Maumee river saw the danger of their friends and demanded to be led to Frenchtown.   Winchester was so alarmed that he started at once, and was followed by two hundred and fifty regulars of the Seventeenth United States Infantry, who reached Frenchtown on the evening of the nineteenth.‡   Had the army been engaged in nothing more

---

* Atherton's Narrative, p. 32.   Darnall's Journal, p. 39.
† Winchester in the National Intelligencer, December 13, 1817.
‡ Ibid.

serious than a mock campaign, the condition of the camp
would have been shameful. Every man was suffered to select
such quarters as best pleased him on one side of the river,
while the general chose such as pleased him on the other. No
pickets were posted. No patrol went the rounds at night.
Order, regularity, system, were unknown. There was no
artillery and very little ammunition. The sole defence was a
line of high pickets, which surrounded the town on three
sides; and as all the troops could not find quarters behind this
rude protection, the United States Infantry lay in an open field.*

With such a general and such disregard of the simplest
principles of war, it is not amazing that in the broad daylight
of January twenty-first Proctor led a thousand Canadians and
Indians across the ice from Malden to Brownstown, marched
to within five miles of Frenchtown, camped, and at daybreak
on the twenty-second was within musket-shot of the picket
fence before his presence was so much as suspected. Had
Proctor dashed forward, the Americans would have been prisoners without the exchange of a shot, and perhaps without
the loss of a life. But he stopped, brought up his three-pound
guns, and while battering the picket fence saw the Kentuckians kill twenty-four and wound one hundred and sixty-one of
his soldiers.

In the open field beyond the picket fence, meantime, the
Seventeenth Regiment had been attacked by militia and Indians, had been flanked, and driven back toward the Raisin.
Seeing this, Colonel Allen's rifle regiment rushed out from behind the fence to help the regulars. But it was too late. The
British pressed steadily forward, the regulars went steadily
back, till once over the frozen river a panic seized the men and
they fled, with six hundred Indians in hot pursuit. Escape was
impossible. Colonel Allen was shot down. Nearly a hundred
Kentuckians fell near him and were scalped. Winchester and
Lewis and the few survivors surrendered and were taken before Proctor. By his advice Winchester now sent an order to
the men behind the picket fence to surrender. Hateful as
this was, there was nothing left but to obey or be massacred,

---

* McAffee's History of the War in the Western Country, p. 233,

for their ammunition was spent and their enemy outnumbered them three to one. Three hundred and eighty-four men accordingly threw down their arms. Their appearance, as they marched that day within the British lines, has been vividly described by one who saw them, and who some time afterward wrote a history of the war. They looked, he declares, miserable to the last degree, for their bodies were dirty, squalid, and covered with clothing that had long since reached the last stage of repair. On their heads were threadbare slouched hats, "from beneath which their long hair fell matted and uncombed over their cheeks." It was January, yet scarcely one had a great-coat, or a cloak, or a garment of wool. The dress of most of them were hunting shirts of colored cotton that came down to the knees, trousers of the same stuff, and blankets wrapped about the loins and fastened with a broad belt. For arms they carried tomahawks, axes, and those two weapons, the Bowie knife and the long Kentucky rifle, in the use of which they were the most expert of men.*

By the express terms of the surrender, Proctor agreed that private property should be respected; that sleds should be sent the following morning to move the sick and wounded across the lake to Amherstburg; that meantime they should be protected, and that side-arms should be returned to the officers at Malden. But no sooner had the prisoners paraded and given up their arms than the Indians began to destroy the tents and plunder the baggage. To this violation of the agreement Proctor paid no attention, for he stood in such fear of Harrison that he was most anxious to be off. All prisoners who could walk were therefore herded as quickly as possible and driven rather than marched to Malden. After they had left Frenchtown it became noticeable that Proctor had violated a second part of his agreement, and that two surgeons, a major, and three interpreters were all who were left to protect the wounded from the Indians. The night was passed by the prisoners in the greatest anxiety and fear of attack; but when the sun rose and no harm had come, their fears seemed groundless, and they had begun to make prepa-

---

* Richardson's War of 1812, p. 79.

rations for their removal, when, on a sudden, a horde of painted savages, drunk with whiskey and maddened by the recollections of past wrongs, rushed into the houses where the wounded lay, stripped them of clothing and blankets, and ordered them out of doors. Some, too badly injured to move, remained and were burned to death. The others, crawling and hobbling as best they could, came out into the yard, where the Indians shot and scalped them. Such as were not seriously wounded attempted to escape to Malden while the Indians were burning and plundering; but they were overtaken on the way and slain. A few were carried into captivity, but upward of thirty are known to have been massacred.*

The first intimation which Harrison received of Winchester's movement toward the Raisin came from the commanding officer at Lower Sandusky, on whom Winchester had called for a battalion to defend the camp on the Maumee. He instantly started for the front, and collecting all available forces as he went, had reached the Maumee, when he fell in with the fugitives from Frenchtown. The story they told was enough for Harrison, whose fear of Proctor was not one whit less than the fear in which Proctor stood of him. All thoughts of advancing on Malden were abandoned, and while the British general fled toward Canada, the American commander, having burned the post and stores at the rapids of the Maumee, turned his back and retreated to the Portage river, fifteen miles away. There he spent a week gathering troops and mustering courage to return to the rapids, where on February first he began the construction of a strong fortress which he called Fort Meigs. Fifteen hundred men would not have been enough to garrison the fort; yet the most he could retain behind its ramparts were five hundred regulars and militia of Pennsylvania and Virginia. Leaving them to make the best defence they could, Harrison, about the middle of March, went off to Chillicothe and Cincinnati, and was busy

---

* A Journal, etc., of the Sufferings of the Kentucky Volunteers and Regulars, commanded by General Winchester, in the Year 1812–1813. Elias Darnall, pp. 49–54. Narrative of the Suffering and Defeat of the Northwestern Army under General Winchester. William Atherton, pp. 56–67.

collecting re-enforcements, when the time of the Virginia militia at Fort Meigs expired and the troops marched home, reducing the garrison to a few half-sick regulars commanded by a major of artillery. Fearing an attack, Harrison hurried back with three hundred men, and reached the fort on April twelfth, just sixteen days before Proctor appeared at the mouth of the Maumee river. With Proctor were nine hundred and eighty-three whites, twelve hundred Indians, led by Tecumthe, plenty of artillery, and two gun-boats. Planting his guns on the north bank of the river, while the Indians surrounded the fort on the south, he opened fire, and during four days kept up a steady cannonade. Meantime a Kentucky brigade of twelve hundred men, under Brigadier-General Green Clay, which Harrison had left with orders to follow him, had come down the Auglaize river to Defiance. Learning there of the siege of Fort Meigs, eight hundred and sixty-six of them descended the rapids and surprised the battery from which the British had been cannonading the fort. Had they been supported, Proctor might easily have been driven from the ground. But General Clay did not come up. Harrison would not go over to aid them, and in the very face of the men they came to succor, seven hundred were killed, wounded, or taken prisoners.* The British loss did not exceed fifty.

The siege now went on four days more, by which time the Indians had deserted and half the Canadian militia had gone home.† Sickness was weakening those who remained, and Proctor, having no choice left, raised the siege and retreated unmolested to Malden. But he was very soon forced to return, for Prevost sent him word about the middle of July that no more rations and no more transports could be spared from Lower Canada, and that he must take his food from the American depots at Cleveland and at Erie. As Proctor's supplies were almost exhausted, he lost not a moment, and gathering a force of regulars, militia, and Indians, came by water to the mouth of the Maumee, and reappeared before Fort Meigs

---

* Harrison to Armstrong, May 13, 1813. War Department Archives,
† Proctor's report, May 14, 1813.

on July twentieth. But General Green Clay, who commanded, would not come out, and, as his Indians were growing restless, Proctor determined to attack Harrison's magazine on the Upper Sandusky. Sending the Indians on by land, he took to his boats, and coasting along the shore of the lake, landed at the mouth of the Sandusky river on August first. Between him and the magazines, just where the town of Fremont now stands, was a wretched stockade called Fort Stephenson, and ten miles behind it, at Seneca, was Harrison with eight hundred militia. The armament of Fort Stephenson consisted of one gun and the garrison of one hundred and sixty men, commanded by Major George Croghan, a young officer of twenty-two. He was born not far from Louisville, Kentucky, in 1791, and came of fighting stock, for his father had been an officer in the Continental army, and his mother was a sister of George Rogers Clark. Graduating from William and Mary College in 1810, he entered the army, was in the battle of Tippecanoe in 1811, and a year later was made captain in the Seventeenth Infantry. With this rank he served under Harrison in 1812 and 1813, and so distinguished himself in a sortie from Fort Meigs that he was appointed aide-de-camp with the rank of major, and assigned to the defence of Fort Stephenson. Lest Tecumthe and the Indians who were coming across country from Fort Meigs should make a flank attack, Harrison had ordered Croghan to burn the fort and retreat.* This he refused to do. "We are determined to maintain this place," said he, "and by Heaven we will." † Harrison thereupon despatched an officer to relieve him. But Croghan went to headquarters, carried his point, and when on August first Proctor summoned him to surrender, sent back a stout defiance. The next day the bombardment began, and toward afternoon, finding that the guns made no impression, Proctor ordered an assault. The soldiers, in three columns of one hundred and twenty men each, were to attack three sides. The Indians were to storm the fourth; but as they came out of the woods into the open a steady and well-directed fire from the fort drove them back. The troops,

---

* McAffee. Late War in the Western Country, p. 322.   † Ibid., p. 323.

thus left to fight alone, came on bravely to the very gates, made every possible effort to get into the fort for two hours, and then retreated with all the officers and one fifth of the men killed, wounded, or missing. That night Proctor fled a second time to Malden.

By the Americans the victory was hailed as a great one. Croghan's name was on every tongue. His praise was sounded in every newspaper. In speeches and in toasts he was declared to be the worthy companion of Bainbridge and of Hull. Nor was it forgotten that, while he contended so stubbornly against overwhelming odds, Harrison with eight hundred men sat quietly in camp, ten miles away, listening to the cannonade. At any other period in his career such conduct would have been his ruin; but, happily, no harm had come of it. The enemy had fled across the border. The time seemed most favorable for a naval demonstration which the administration had long been planning, and as in this the army was to play a minor part, Harrison was suffered to keep command.

The defeats of Hull, Van Rensselaer, Smyth, and Dearborn had been followed by the resignation of Eustis as Secretary of War.* Seizing on this as a fitting opportunity to strengthen the weak part of his Cabinet, Madison at once requested the resignation of Paul Hamilton as Secretary of the Navy, and early in January, 1813, sent to the Senate the names of two new Secretaries. For Secretary of War he chose John Armstrong, and for Secretary of the Navy William Jones. The Senate confirmed the nominations, and in February, 1813, the men were in office.

Armstrong fell to with a will, and before spring had fairly come had marked out the United States into nine military districts, had ordered Wilkinson to hasten from New Orleans to Sackett's Harbor, and had framed a plan for a vigorous campaign on the frontier. As part of the plan Harrison was commanded to make no offensive move, but defend the Maumee and wait till the fleet then building at Erie was ready to sail. The opening of the war found the United States navy with no armed vessel on Lake Erie, and with but one on the

---

* December 3, 1812.

waters of Lake Ontario. She was called the Oneida, carried a good crew and sixteen guns, and was commanded by Lieutenant Woolsey. Opposed to him, on the other hand, were the Royal George, the Prince Regent, the Earl of Moira, the Duke of Gloucester, the Seneca, and the Simcoe, carrying all told some eighty guns, and commanded by the Canadian Commodore Earle. Had Earle been a man fit for his place, the war on Lake Ontario would have quickly ended. He was most happily thoroughly incompetent, and suffered Woolsey to make several short cruises before he appeared, on July nineteenth, off Sackett's Harbor, and demanded the surrender of the Oneida, then at anchor near the town. Sackett's Harbor had been founded in 1801 by Augustus Sackett, and in 1812 numbered perhaps a score of houses facing the finest harbor on the lake. It was formed by a peninsula of limestone rock thirty feet high and in many places a rod wide, which jutted out from the lower end of the village, and enclosed and sheltered a sheet of deep water eight or ten acres in area. The land fronting the harbor rose to a height of thirty feet, while the two sides were of bare limestone rock, coming out of the water like the walls of a fortification. The place was a port of entry and the centre of a great trade in wheat and flour, beef and pork, lumber and potashes, which had been pouring through it since the days of the embargo, and which gave occupation to forty vessels in carrying the produce to Montreal, or to Kingston, with which before the war it was joined by a ferry.

Woolsey no sooner received the demands of Earle than he ran out and attempted to pass the fleet and make good his escape. But, failing in this, he beat back into the harbor, anchored close to the bluff, where his guns could rake the entrance, and whipping out those on the Oneida's off side, he mounted them on shore and then hurried away to take charge of a fort or battery at the end of the peninsula. It consisted of one long thirty-two-pound gun; but so well was it served that after a cannonade of an hour the British fleet drew off without having inflicted any damage.

Woolsey, acting under orders, now began to form a squadron by purchasing merchant ships and preparing them to carry guns. Commodore Isaac Chauncey, who had been selected to command the naval forces on Lakes Erie and Ontario, sent on guns, shot, stores, officers, shipwrights, and sailors from New York, and in October came on himself. A month sufficed to put the ships in war trim, and in November the fleet was on the lake. But, save a spirited attack on Kingston, nothing was done when winter closed navigation.

On Lake Erie better results were secured. When the war opened, the army at Detroit was in possession of a small brig called the Adams, armed with six guns throwing six-pound shot. But the department of the navy did not own an armed ship of any sort; so that when Hull surrendered and the Adams passed into British hands, the flag of the United States absolutely disappeared from Lake Erie. Re-naming their prize the Detroit, the British manned her, and in October, in company with a small two-gun brig, the Caledonia, she came down from Detroit and anchored close to Fort Erie.

Not long before this Lieutenant Jesse Duncan Elliott had come to Buffalo with instructions to construct a naval force by building two brigs and buying merchant schooners to act as gun-boats. Chauncey was to send on the crews, and on the very day the Detroit and the Caledonia came to Fort Erie, Elliott received word that a detachment of fifty-one men was but a few miles away. He at once determined to use them to cut out the ships, but when they arrived they had neither arms nor ammunition. Application for arms was therefore made to General Smyth, who not only furnished a supply of swords, pistols, and muskets, but detailed enough soldiers under Captain Nathan Towson and Lieutenant Isaac Roach to raise the force to one hundred and twenty-four men. These in two boats set off from Black Rock about midnight of October eighth, and after a row of two hours came alongside the enemy. A few minutes sufficed to board and capture the Detroit; but the noise of the fight having aroused the crew of the Caledonia, she was not carried so easily. As the wind was light and the current strong, the prizes could not beat out into the lake. The cables were therefore cut, and the two floated down stream till they stranded, the Caledonia on the

American side near Black Rock, and the Detroit on Squaw Island, where she was under the guns of the British batteries and was soon destroyed. In the creek at Black Rock were at that time four merchantmen which Elliott had purchased; but, as they could not be taken past the batteries, the existence of a navy on the lake depended on the success of the efforts then making to build ships at Erie.

In the late spring of 1812, before war was declared, three citizens of Erie made a trading voyage to Michilimackinaw, only to see the post fall into British hands and to find themselves prisoners of war. Their vessel was made a cartel and sent with the prisoners and non-combatants to Cleveland; but at Detroit it was stopped, and passed a second time to the British when Hull surrendered. Through the kindness of a British officer who knew them, the three men were suffered to escape and made their way back to Erie. Believing their experiences would be of value, one of them, Daniel Dobbins by name, was promptly sent to Washington with despatches by the militia officer commanding at Erie, and gave to the President and his Secretary of War the account of an eye witness of the capture of both places. It is said that Dobbins even urged the building of a powerful fleet to sweep the British from the lakes, and satisfied Madison that it could be done. It is certain, at all events, that he came back from Washington with the commission of a sailing master in the navy, and with orders to build two gun-boats and report to Commodore Chauncey at Sackett's Harbor. As no ship carpenters were to be had, he gathered a few house carpenters and began work late in October, and when Chauncey came to Erie in January, 1813, had made such progress that he was instructed to build two sloops of war. The winter was severe, and every stick of timber had to be cut from the stump. Yet in March, when a gang of twenty-five shipwrights from New York reached Erie, the keels and much of the timber for the ribs were ready on the ground. Gathering this up, they went hard to work and had the keels for the sloops nearly laid when a young man arrived from Buffalo, and, announcing himself as Oliver Hazard Perry, assumed command of naval operations on Lake Erie.

Perry was a native of Rhode Island. His father, when
little more than a lad, had been a privateersman during
the Revolution, had suffered in the Jersey prison ship at
New York, and after the war became master of a merchantman. The trouble with France in 1798 and the formation of
our navy brought him back in service, and with the rank of
post captain he was placed in command of the twenty-eight-
gun frigate General Greene. The son was then not fourteen
years old, yet succeeded in persuading his father to secure for
him the place of midshipman, and served on the General
Greene in the West Indian waters till the end of the war in
1800. Peace with France was followed by war with Tripoli,
and young Perry, first in the Adams and then in the Constellation, and next on the Nautilus as commander, began his
serious training in that grand school which gave to us so long
and so brilliant a list of naval heroes. By 1806 he was once
more at Newport charged with the duty of superintending
the building of seventeen of Jefferson's memorable gun-boats,
which he brought to New York, where for some time he did
duty in the harbor. During the embargo days he was at
Westerly building more gun-boats. But in 1809, as lieutenant
in command of the Revenge, he began a cruise along the coast
of the United States, which ended with the wreck of the vessel off Watch Hill Reef in 1811. The loss of the Revenge
left him without occupation till, in 1812, he obtained command of the gun flotilla at Newport. Service such as this
was not to his liking, and in his eagerness to be where fighting was to be done, he tendered his services for duty on the
lakes, first to the Secretary of the Navy, and then to Commodore Chauncey. The Secretary gave the application no
attention, for he attended to nothing; but Chauncey at once
wrote to Washington asking that Perry be sent to the lakes.
Orders to report at Sackett's Harbor with all the best men
under his command came to Perry on the seventeenth of
February, and before sunset fifty were on their way. One
hundred followed within four days, and Perry himself on the
twenty-second. On March third he entered Sackett's Harbor,
where he was detained by Chauncey for two weeks before he
was ordered to Erie.

At Erie he beheld a fine illustration of the utter incapacity of the Government for war. Sailing Master Dobbins and Master Shipwright Noah Brown, who brought the men from New York, had done their part, and on the ways were two gun-boats nearly planked, a third ready for planking, and the keels of two twenty-gun brigs. But not a gun had been provided for their armament, not a step had been taken to defend them from destruction by the British, not a musket or a bullet was to be had in Erie, nor had a rope or a yard of canvas been sent for sails and rigging. With characteristic energy Perry took up each of these matters at once. The day he arrived, some citizens of Erie were hired to guard the ships, which might easily have been fired by a British spy. Others were sent off to Buffalo for muskets, cartridges, and forty seamen from the navy yard, and as soon as possible he went himself to Pittsburg to hurry on the necessary supplies. Never were ships built under such disadvantages. The timber —white oak, black oak, chestnut, and pine—was cut on the spot, and many a piece which was put into the frame on an afternoon had been part of a standing tree that morning. Iron had to be gathered in scraps from stores, warehouses, shops, farm buildings, and was in every shape, from the tire of an old wheel to the hinge of a barn-door. About a thousand pounds were at last secured in Buffalo, and when navigation opened more came up from Pittsburg. From the same place were also forwarded ropes, cables, sails, guns and muskets, anchors, and all the many articles needed by the ships. A number of workmen and artisans came from Philadelphia to push on the work; a militia officer in the neighborhood furnished five hundred troops to defend the town which by the energy of Perry had been transformed into a navy yard; and early in May the three gun-boats were launched and equipped, and a few weeks thereafter the two sloops went off the stocks.

Perry now left Erie in order to take part in the attack of Dearborn and Chauncey on Fort George, and contributed more than any other naval officer present to its capture. His reward was most substantial, for, as the British immediately fell back from the Niagara river, he was enabled to add to his fleet at Erie the five vessels which had long been blockaded in Gonjaquade's Creek at Black Rock by the British batteries on the Canadian shore. To move them up the rapids was no easy matter; but, by the aid of ox-teams and the help of two hundred men furnished by Dearborn, the labor was accomplished in a fortnight, and on the evening of June fourteenth he sailed from Buffalo for Erie. Head winds baffled him, and the British fleet was a constant menace; but what the sailors called his luck did not desert him, and on the evening of the eighteenth the last of his five ships passed over the bar at Erie just as the sails of the British vessels hove in sight. There were now gathered in the harbor four little sloops and schooners mounting one gun each, two vessels with two guns each, one of three, one of four, and the Niagara and the Lawrence of twenty guns each.

Though his fleet was rigged and afloat, his troubles were not over. The Secretary, supposing that all was ready, sent order after order to Perry to aid General Harrison in a military movement which was to be made for the recovery of Michigan and the invasion of Canada. But the officers and men destined for the Erie fleet had been kept by Chauncey on Ontario, and Perry did not have more than one hundred and ten men fit for duty. Appeal after appeal was made to Chauncey and to the Secretary for commanders, gunners, seamen. "The enemy's fleet of six sail," said he on one occasion to the commodore, " are now off the bar of this harbor. . . . Give me men, sir, and I will gain both for you and myself honor and glory on this lake, or perish in the attempt." This appeal brought seventy men. "The enemy," said he on another occasion, "are now off this harbor. . . . My vessels are all ready. For God's sake, and yours and mine, send me men and officers, and I will have them all in a day or two." This brought sixty men; but before they came a despatch reached Perry from Harrison announcing that Proctor had a second time descended on Ohio and invested Fort Meigs. An attempt to enlist men at ten dollars a month for four months or till a battle had been fought gave him some forty volunteers and raised his effective force about August first to three hundred. On that day, which was Sunday, the fleet was moved to the bar, and on Monday the five small vessels

were sent across with orders to clear for action, and cover the
Lawrence and Niagara while they were lifted over. For
this purpose two "camels," or large scows, had been built just
the shape of the sides of the brigs and long enough to enclose
them from bow to stern. As soon as these were alongside of
the Lawrence the plugs were taken out and the water allowed
to run in and sink them till they were almost flush with the
lake surface. Spars were then passed through the port-holes
of the brig and, projecting out on each side, were made fast to
blocks resting on the camels. Plugs were next put in the
bottom of the scows, the water pumped out, the Lawrence
raised some four feet, and the attempt made to cross the bar.
But the water was shoaler than usual, and she stuck hard and
fast. Again the camels were sunk, more blocks inserted between them and the cross-timbers, the lifting process repeated,
and the ship slowly and by main strength hove across the bar.
The Niagara was carried over on the fourth, and the fleet was
about to put to sea on the eighth when an express arrived
with the news that Commander Jesse D. Elliott with one hundred and two officers and men was on his way to take command of the Niagara. By the twelfth all was ready, and
Perry with his fleet of ten vessels went up the lake in search
of the British. In time it anchored in Put-in Bay, where
Harrison sent on board a re-enforcement of one hundred regulars and Kentucky militia.

The wish to engage, so often shown by the British when
Perry's ships were at Erie, was no longer manifested now
that his fleet was on the lake. The English commander was
waiting till the Detroit, a fine new ship which was on the
stocks at Amherstburg, was in the water. Made, as were the
Lawrence and Niagara, of green timber, she was launched
rough and unfinished, was armed with guns of every calibre
taken from the ramparts, was manned by soldiers and frontiersmen unused to lake service, and early in September was
ready. On the ninth the British commander, almost driven
out by hunger, weighed anchor and sailed toward Perry,
then at anchor in Put-in Bay, where at sunrise on the tenth
his sails were seen by the lookout at the masthead of the
Lawrence. The squadron numbered six vessels—the Detroit

of nineteen guns, the Queen Charlotte of seventeen, the Lady
Prevost of thirteen, the Hunter of ten, and Little Belt of one
gun, all in command of Captain Robert Heriot Barclay, a
brave officer and skilful seaman, who had fought under
Nelson at Trafalgar, and in after days had lost an arm in
battle with the French. In number of guns the British fleet
was superior to the American. But in other respects—in
ships, in tonnage, in men, in weight of metal thrown in a
broadside, whether at long range or at short range—Perry had
a most decided advantage. Of this he made full use, and
leading the van in the Lawrence with the blue flag inscribed
" Don't give up the ship!" at her masthead, and supported by
two gun-boats on her weather bow, Perry bore down before a
light breeze and met the enemy's line of battle a few minutes
before noon. Barclay in the Detroit opened at long range,
where his advantage was great; but Perry, discovering this,
gave the signal for close action, passed on, gradually worked
his way to within canister range, and, accompanied by two gun-
boats and the Caledonia, became engaged in a desperate battle
with the Chippeway, Detroit, Queen Charlotte, and Hunter.
On each side the large ships were the targets for all guns, and
suffered dreadfully. The Queen Charlotte was almost disabled. The Detroit, raked by the fire of the gun-boats and
hulled by that of the Lawrence, was frightfully shattered; but
the Lawrence was reduced to a wreck. Not a brace, not a
bowline, not a gun on her engaged side remained; eighty-
three of her crew of one hundred and three had fallen;
her hull had repeatedly been pierced by shot which passed
through from side to side, killing or mangling the wounded
in the cockpit as they went. But the courage and resolution
of Perry never faltered. Assisted by the purser and the
chaplain, he fired the last effective gun, and finding the
Lawrence could no longer annoy the enemy, he leaped into
a boat, and with his brother and four seamen was rowed
to the Niagara. The best manned and best equipped of all
the fleet, she ought long before to have engaged the Queen
Charlotte; but Elliott, her commander, for some reason which
cannot now be known, had done his fighting with two long-
range guns quite out of reach of harm, and was imitated by

four of the gun-boats.   To the Niagara, therefore, Perry
transferred his flag, and having sent Elliott to bring up the
three schooners lagging in the rear, he bore down to break
the enemy's line.   Almost at the same moment the Lawrence
struck.   She had but fourteen unhurt men aboard.   With
the entrance of the Niagara into the fight, the day was
Perry's.   Firing her port guns into the Chippeway, the
Lady Prevost, and the Little Belt, and her starboard guns
into the Detroit, the Queen Charlotte, and the Hunter, she
came on, raking on both sides, and broke the line.   The Detroit and the Queen Charlotte, now reduced to helplessness,
fouled, and, swept by the Niagara, the Caledonia, and the
schooners at pistol-shot range, they surrendered about three
in the afternoon.   The Chippeway and Little Belt attempted
to escape, but were chased and
captured, and Perry, sitting
down while the smoke of battle was still in the air, dashed
off a message to Harrison, the
opening words of which, "We
have met the enemy, and they
are ours," were instantly taken
up by his grateful countrymen
and have never since been forgotten.†

Diagram of the Battle of
Lake Erie.*

The military and political
consequences of the battle were
immense.   It gave us the supremacy on Lake Erie ; it made
the evacuation of Malden and
Detroit necessary; it recovered
Michigan and all Hull had lost, and rendered it possible for
the American army once more to enter Canada.   But the effect on the people—what it soon became the custom to call
the moral consequences — outdid anything yet experienced.

---

* The Naval War of 1812.   Roosevelt.

† The despatch to Harrison was: "Dear General: We have met the enemy,
and they are ours.   Two ships, two brigs, one schooner, and one sloop.   Yours
with very great respect and esteem, O. H. Perry."

The almost unbroken series of naval victories on the sea had begun to pall. The charm of British invincibility was broken by Hull, Decatur, Bainbridge, and Burrows. Ship to ship, man to man, gun to gun, it had been proved over and over again that Great Britain was no match for America. But, till Perry met Barclay on Lake Erie, no fleet bearing the flag of the United States had ever encountered a fleet bearing the flag of England. In Perry, therefore, the people found a new sort of hero, a young Nelson, and, carried away by his youth, by the energy with which he built and manned his fleet, by the courage with which he bore the brunt of the fight, by the dramatic episode of the open boat, and by the skill with which, when all seemed lost by the mismanagement of Elliott, he brought up the Niagara and won the day, the people went wild with joy and in their ecstasy made him the hero of the war. All over the country bells were rung, cannon fired, towns and cities illuminated in his honor, and swords without number voted him. Albany gave him the freedom of the city, a sword, and a fine reception. Poughkeepsie was illuminated. Philadelphia took a day to rejoice and a night to illuminate. New York and Baltimore did the same. The people of Boston, in mass meeting assembled, voted a sword. The Constitution honored him with a salute. Both parties claimed him as their own. He became the toast of the hour at innumerable Democratic festivals held to celebrate " the triumph of the American arms over their enemies," and the chief theme of scores of naval songs, odes, verses, and impromptu lines. He deserved it all ; for if ever a battle was won by the obstinacy and courage of one man, it was the battle of Lake Erie.

Harrison, who was still at Seneca on the Sandusky river, received the despatch on September twelfth, and, knowing that it was now his turn to act, began to make ready. When Armstrong marked out the nine military districts he gave Harrison command of the eighth, and assigned him seven regiments of regular troops, which should have brought him seven thousand men, but did not bring him twenty-six hundred. Kentucky was therefore again appealed to and again responded most nobly. With the massacre of the Raisin fresh in mind, the opportunity to avenge it was seized right gladly, and three thousand Kentuckians, led on by Governor Shelby, joined him in September. These, with a mounted regiment of one thousand Kentuckians commanded by Richard Mentor Johnson, raised his army to sixty-five hundred men. Malden and Amherstburg having been selected as the points of attack, the mounted regiment was sent round to Detroit by land, while the main body embarked for Canada, and was carried by boat down the Sandusky and by way of Bass Island and Put-in-Bay Island to Middle Sister Island, some twelve miles from the Canadian side.* There they waited till Harrison and Perry had found a landing place, when they were put ashore three miles below Malden.†

Two days before Harrison left Seneca ‡ Proctor had assembled the Indian chiefs, had told them that he meant to abandon Malden and Detroit, had been denounced by Tecumthe, and, to the amusement of the army, had been likened to a fat animal that once carried its tail in the air, but, now that he was frightened, was about to run off with his tail between his legs.# But Proctor held to his determination, and when Harrison landed on Middle Sister Island he burned and destroyed the public property at Malden and Detroit, and retreated to Sandwich, whither Harrison followed and waited for the arrival of Johnson.‖ On October first Johnson crossed from Detroit, and then the pursuit began in earnest. The British were at a place called Dolson's, fifty miles away. But so quickly did the Americans move that on the third they came in sight of the British camp. Again the British fell back, first to a town called Chatham and then to the north bank of the Thames river, where, on October fifth, they halted and awaited the Americans. Toward the afternoon Harrison appeared and found them drawn up in two lines in a thick wood. On the left of the line was the river. Cutting through the middle

---

* Perry to the Secretary of the Navy, September 24, 1813.   Official Letters, p. 215.

† September 27, 1813.   ‡ September 18, 1813.

Life of Perry, by Alexander S. Mackenzie, vol. i, p. 299.   Richardson's War of 1812, p. 119.

‖ Harrison to the Secretary of War, September 27, October 9, 1813.   Official Letters, p. 233.

was a road. On the right behind a swamp were twelve or fifteen hundred Indians. Harrison ordered his troops arranged
according to the most approved methods, and while they were
forming was asked by Johnson for leave to charge.* He gave
it reluctantly, and Johnson, sending part of his horsemen
down the road to take the cannon, galloped off with the rest to
attack the Indians. Those sent by the road charged so furiously that they broke through the first line of the enemy and
penetrated to the rear of the second, where Proctor barely
escaped capture by flight, and made prisoners of the soldiers,
who only wanted an excuse to surrender. Meanwhile Johnson with his force crossed the swamp, dismounted his men,
and drove the Indians out of the underbrush and toward the
American line. Governor Shelby, seeing this, opened fire on
them and they fled, and so ended the fighting. To his dying
day Johnson maintained, and with good reason, that the battle
of the Thames was fought and won by his regiment of mounted
Kentuckians, and by his regiment alone.† That he should take
great pride in the conduct of his men was natural, for the results of the fight were most important and lasting. It finished
the work so well begun by Perry. It utterly crushed the
right division of the British army in Upper Canada. It put
an end to the Indian confederacy in the Northwest. From the
very first the heart and soul of that confederacy was Tecumthe. But Tecumthe was no more. When the Kentuckians,
after the flight of the Indians, came back over the field they
recognized the body of the Shawanee chief lying among three-
and-thirty slaughtered warriors. The sight of it roused a storm
of rage, and, stooping down, they cut long strips of skin from
the thighs for razor straps, to be kept, they said, in memory
of the massacre at the river Raisin.‡ As Johnson claimed
for the Kentuckians all the honor of the battle, the Kentuckians gave to him the glory of killing Tecumthe—a distinction

---

* Johnson to Armstrong, December 22, 1834. Armstrong's Notices of the
War of 1812, vol. i, p. 232.

† Johnson to the Secretary of War, November 21, 1813. Manuscripts, War
Department Archives.

‡ Richardson's War of 1812, p. 125. Lewis Cass to Armstrong, October 28,
1813. Manuscripts, War Department Archives.

which some years later, when he was a candidate for the Vice-Presidency of the United States, was seriously urged as a good reason for his election.

From the battle field of the Thames the shattered army of Proctor fled eastward a hundred miles to Ancaster, where the fugitives were stopped and two hundred mustered. Proctor laid all the blame for his crushing defeat on the troops, and Prevost, believing him, issued a severe reprimand; but after all the facts were placed before the Prince Regent, he reversed the judgment and disgraced both Proctor and Prevost.

So complete was the victory that when the American army returned to Sandwich, the Kentucky Volunteers and the mounted regiment were immediately discharged, and ten days after the battle were marching homeward. On their departure, Harrison and his regulars repaired to Sackett's Harbor, and the duty of protecting the region north of the Maumee was intrusted to two brigades of United States regulars. Perry returned to Newport, and in 1814 was assigned to duty at Baltimore.

As much of Armstrong's plan as depended for execution on the fleet of Perry and the troops of Harrison was thus entirely successful. As much as depended for execution on Dearborn, Chauncey, and Wilkinson resulted meantime in utter failure. The work assigned to Dearborn was to gather three thousand troops at Buffalo and four thousand at Sackett's Harbor and begin his campaign the moment Lake Ontario and the St. Lawrence were free of ice. His first move was to be against Kingston, at the source of the St. Lawrence. To this place his troops at Sackett's Harbor were to be carried in boats under convoy of the Ontario fleet commanded by Chauncey. Having captured Kingston, destroyed the magazines, the navy yard, the ships, and the public stores, the expedition was to sail to York, or, as we know it, Toronto, burn two ships on the stocks, hurry to Buffalo, and join the three thousand troops at that place. The entire army was then to attack the British on the Niagara river.*

---

* Armstrong to Dearborn, February 10, 1813. Armstrong's Notices, vol. i, p. 221.

Dearborn was at Albany when the orders reached him and promised to carry them out.* But Sir George Prevost coming unexpectedly to Prescott and Kingston, Dearborn repaired to Sackett's Harbor, fearing it was to be attacked, and there Chauncey persuaded him to disapprove Armstrong's plan and suggest a new one. There were then at Kingston less than four hundred and fifty British troops, officers and men.† But Dearborn magnified these to seven thousand,‡ and, despairing of taking the place with four thousand, he proposed to Armstrong that the campaign should be reversed and begin at York and end at Kingston. He would have Chauncey with twelve hundred soldiers under Zebulon M. Pike go first to York, and, when they had burned the ships, come back to the Niagara and lay siege to Fort George, take it, and wait there till the troops at Buffalo, having captured Fort Erie and Fort Chippawa, should join them. The whole army was then to move on Kingston.

Supposing that Dearborn knew the strength of the British at Kingston, Armstrong approved the plan, # and on April twenty-fifth the fleet, numbering fourteen ships, set sail. The winter and spring of 1813 was spent by the commanders on each side of Lake Ontario in vigorous preparations for the coming summer cruise. The British laid down the keels of two twenty-four-gun ships, and Earle, the Canadian commodore, having shown himself a man of small ability, was replaced by Sir James Lucas Yeo, who came out from England with captains, lieutenants, midshipmen, and four hundred and fifty sailors of the royal navy. By purchasing merchantmen, and building schooners and brigs, Chauncey succeeded about the middle of April in getting together a fleet of fourteen vessels of all sorts, carrying one hundred and twelve guns and

---

* Dearborn to Armstrong, February 18, 1813. American State Papers, Military Affairs, vol. i, p. 440.

† Distribution of Forces in Canada. Canadian Archives, Henry Adams. History of the United States, vol. vii, p. 151.

‡ Dearborn to Armstrong, March 9, 1813. American State Papers, Military Affairs, vol. i, p. 441.

Armstrong to Dearborn, March 29 and April 19, 1813. American State Papers, Military Affairs, vol. i, p. 442.

nine hundred and eighty sailors. Yeo's squadron numbered six vessels, with ninety-two guns and seven hundred and seventy sailors. Yet the difference between the two was by no means so great as these facts would seem to show. The British ships had all been built for war, were good sailers, were provided with quarters, and were fairly comfortable for the crews. The American ships were some of them war vessels and some of them merchantmen. The war ships had quarters, were weatherly, and sailed fast. The merchantmen had no quarters, were crank, and so loaded down with guns that what to the war ships was a good working breeze was to them a gale sufficient to upset them; and what to the schooners was wind enough was scarce sufficient to move the ships. In a word, while Yeo kept his squadron together in any weather, Chauncey could not keep his from straggling unless one half had the other half in tow.*

Such as they were, however, he got them ready for service before Yeo was on the lake, and, taking General Dearborn and sixteen hundred men on board, the armament set sail and favored by a good breeze appeared off York early on the morning of April twenty-seventh. The village contained, all told, some three thousand souls, was the capital of Upper Canada, was the place of residence of the Lieutenant-Governor, and boasted of two brick buildings within which the Legislature assembled. Yet the garrison was but six hundred regulars and Canadian militia, commanded by Major-General Sheaffe, the successor of General Brock in Upper Canada.

While the schooners beat up to the largest battery and opened with their long guns, the troops under Pike marched along the shore to storm it. The British, though outnumbered, made a good fight and then gave up the town, which the Americans proceeded to destroy. They burned one ship on the stocks, made prize of the brig Gloucester, sent off such stores as they wanted, destroyed the rest, and set fire to the two houses of Assembly. Happily this shameful act was done by some private soldiers acting without authority, was denounced by the press all over the country, and was pub-

---

* The Naval War of 1812, pp. 226, 227. Theodore Roosevelt.

licly disavowed by Dearborn.* Among the American dead was Pike, the ablest brigadier-general in the army.

Bad weather and contrary winds kept the fleet in port for a week. Some more time was then consumed in shipping the stores to Sackett's Harbor, so that it was not till the eighth of May that the troops were carried up the lake and landed at Fort Niagara on their way to Fort George. This post ought to have been taken at once, for it lay just over the river and was defended by not more than fifteen hundred men, while Dearborn, by stripping the garrisons within his district, had gathered at Niagara forty-five hundred soldiers and had, moreover, the aid of Chauncey and the fleet. But nothing was ready. Nor would the army have been ready for some time to come had not Dearborn fallen ill and made over the details of the expedition to Colonel Winfield Scott.

Scott was only chief of staff, but, though Major-General Morgan Lewis commanded Niagara, and Generals John Chandler, John P. Boyd, and William H. Winder the three brigades of the army, he became in reality the chief in command. His plan was to sail down the river and out on Lake Ontario and attack Fort George in the rear. Chauncey accordingly, on May twenty-sixth, in company with Perry, who came over from Erie to join him, made a careful reconnoissance, took soundings along shore in the night, set buoys to direct the small craft, and at three in the morning of the twenty-seventh the fleet weighed anchor, and when the mist cleared away was seen by the British standing toward the shore in a line two miles long. Taking the position marked out for them by Chauncey, the ships opened a terrible fire of grape; the troops landed, and the British General Vincent, having spiked his guns and destroyed his stores, fell back toward Queenston. Never was there a finer opportunity for a great and signal victory. Prevost was terror-stricken. The whole Niagara frontier was abandoned and Perry was suffered to take the Caledonia and the four schooners purchased by Elliott from Black Rock past the British batteries and into Lake Erie. For the moment it seemed likely that all of

* Letter of Dearborn, October 17, 1814. Niles's Weekly Register, vol. viii, p. 36.

Canada west of Kingston would fall into American hands. With an energetic general on the frontier this surely would have happened. But Dearborn waited five days before he ordered General Winder to follow the British with about a thousand men. Vincent had sixteen hundred. Winder, therefore, after marching twenty miles, stopped and sent back for more troops, which reached him on June fifth under General Chandler. Assuming command of the army, now two thousand strong, Chandler approached to within ten miles of the enemy, camped, and about two in the morning of June sixth was surprised and soundly beaten. So complete was the surprise, so utter was the demoralization, that in the darkness and confusion both Winder and Chandler walked into the British lines and were captured. The troops, abandoning the baggage and leaving their dead unburied, retreated ten miles. There the next afternoon Major-General Lewis took command. But the fleet of Sir James Yeo appeared at this moment on the lake, the rear of Lewis was threatened, and Dearborn, in great alarm, ordered him back to Fort George.

Matters now went from bad to worse. Dearborn was so broken in mind and body that it became necessary to issue orders placing General Lewis temporarily in command of the district. But Lewis soon went off to Sackett's Harbor and the command devolved on General Boyd. Burning with a desire to do something, Boyd despatched Colonel Boerstler with four hundred men and two guns to batter down a storehouse seventeen miles from Fort George. On reaching the place, he found himself in a wood surrounded by Indians and attempted to retreat. But some fifteen militiamen stopped him, and, though re-enforced by the arrival of one hundred and forty men, he was afraid to fight and surrendered. His own command numbered five hundred and forty; that of the British, two hundred and sixty.

While these things were happening at the head of the lake, a disaster which would have been ruinous had barely been averted at the foot of Ontario. The departure of the expedition against York and Fort George had reduced the garrison at Sackett's Harbor to four hundred regulars and two hundred and fifty volunteers. Prevost was far from being a bold and energetic commander. But the sight of Sackett's Harbor with its naval stores, its military stores, its ship-yard, with the twenty-eight-gun ship General Pike on the stocks almost ready to be launched, was too tempting, and he determined to attack the place. On the night of May twenty-sixth, accordingly, at the very time that Chauncey was making his soundings off Fort George, Prevost embarked eight hundred men on board the fleet of Sir James Yeo, sailed from Kingston, and soon after daybreak on May twenty-eighth sighted Sackett's Harbor. Had he entered the harbor boldly, landed his troops without a moment's delay, and stormed the forts, the place would have been his by noon. But he waited twenty-four hours; the militia of the neighborhood rushed in and, what was far more important, Jacob Brown had arrived and taken command.

Brown was of Quaker ancestry, and was born and raised in Bucks County, Pennsylvania. After a common-school education in his native State he began life as a school-teacher and surveyor, wandered off to Ohio where he passed two years surveying public lands, and at the close of the century came to New York city and taught school, studied law, and wrote political articles for the newspapers. The French War was then threatening, the country was busy with works of defence, and Brown became Military Secretary to Alexander Hamilton, one of the new major-generals. On the defeat of the Federalists in 1800 he emigrated to Jefferson County, New York. Having gathered a little money, he bought land and founded Brownsville, became county judge, colonel of militia, a brigadier-general of militia, and, at the opening of the war, was placed in command of the frontier from Oswego to Lake St. Francis on the northern boundary of New York. Of military affairs he knew nothing by education or experience; yet he was a man of marked military ability, and showed it plainly when he defeated the British in their attack on Ogdensburg in October, 1812, a service for which he was promptly offered a regiment in the regular army. This he declined, and was still in command of the State militia on the frontier when he was called to Sackett's Harbor and immediately made ready for battle. On the beach where he expected the British to land he posted the militia. Behind the militia he drew up the regulars. In rear of the regulars, at the edge of the village, was a block-house flanked by a log barrack and breastworks of fallen timber. About dawn on May twenty-ninth the British landed and moved rapidly forward without firing. The militia instantly fled. The regulars fell back to the barrack and the block-house, and there checked the British advance. Finding it impossible to storm the works, Prevost retreated to the beach with two hundred and fifty-nine men—one third his force—killed, wounded, or missing, re-embarked, and sailed for Kingston.* For this victory Brown was made a brigadier-general in the regular army. Yet it was but half a victory, for the naval lieutenant in charge of the ship-yards, hearing that Brown was falling back, supposed the day was lost and set fire to the storehouses, the marine barracks, and the two fine ships General Pike and Gloucester. Had these ships been consumed, our naval supremacy on Lake Ontario would have been ended. Fortunately, they were saved ; but the navy yard was ruined. As it was, till the Pike was afloat, Yeo ruled the lake. One day he came down upon a camp near Forty-Mile Creek and captured its stores, provisions, equipage, and batteaux.† On another he seized two schooners laden with supplies.‡ On a third he looted a depot of provision on the Genesee river,# and three days later took six hundred barrels of flour at Great Sodus.‖

Yeo now returned to Kingston, whence on August third he again sailed with his squadron, and after cruising up the lake came in sight of Chauncey's fleet at anchor off Fort Niagara. The day, August seventh, was just suited to the needs of the American vessels, for the wind was light and the water smooth. Yet the two fleets passed the day going through a series of manœuvres, which each commander afterward declared were intended to bring on a battle. With nightfall the wind came out squally, and about midnight a heavy gust striking two of Chauncey's schooners forced them to careen

---

* The Americans lost **twenty-three** killed and one hundred and fourteen wounded.

† June 8, 1813.   # June 16, 1813.

‡ June 13, 1813.   ‖ June 19, 1813.

till their guns broke loose and they foundered, drowning eighty men. After sunrise the wind went down, and two more days were spent in manœuvring, as each commander was quite ready to avoid a fight. At last, on the fourth day, a harmless exchange of shots began, and continued till two of Chauncey's schooners were cut off from the fleet and captured, when the two squadrons went down the lake, the British leading and the American following. A month later a second meeting took place off the mouth of Genesee river, and two weeks after a third in York Bay. On this occasion Yeo was beaten and fled to Kingston, where he remained blockaded while the army of Harrison, after its victory at the Thames, was brought in transports from Genesee to Sackett's Harbor, whence a month before Wilkinson led forth an expedition against Montreal and Quebec.

The long series of disasters which accompanied Dearborn had made his unfitness to command most manifest. Yet it was not till Congress and the whole people were crying out that Madison consented to remove him and bade Armstrong issue the order.* On the retirement of Dearborn the command of the Ninth Military District passed to James Wilkinson, a man more incompetent still.

When the war began Wilkinson was in command at New Orleans. But the people of the Mississippi Valley, who had formed a just estimate of his character, declared that New Orleans was not safe in his hands, and demanded, through the Senators of Louisiana, Tennessee, and Kentucky, that he be removed.† Madison, with great reluctance, consented, and one of the early official acts of Armstrong was an order bidding the general go immediately to the headquarters of Dearborn at Sackett's Harbor.‡ The order is dated March tenth, but some one took good care that it did not come to Wilkinson's hands till May nineteenth.# Three weeks passed before

---

* July 6, 1813.

† Strictures on General Wilkinson's Defence. Albany Argus.

‡ Armstrong to Wilkinson, March 10, 1813. Wilkinson's Memoirs, vol. iii, p. 341.

Wilkinson to Armstrong, May 23, 1813. Wilkinson's Memoirs, vol. iii, p. 341.

he found it convenient to start. He then went to Mobile, turned northward, crossed the Creek country, and, entering Washington almost five months * after the issuing of the order, found himself, by virtue of seniority, in command of the Ninth Military District.

Leaving Washington August eleventh, he travelled by easy stages to Sackett's Harbor, where he called a council of war. † To it came General Lewis, who commanded the troops after Dearborn was removed; Chauncey, who was in port with his fleet; Jacob Brown and the Quartermaster-General, Robert Swartwout, the brother of Burr's old friend. After discussing the various plans proposed by Armstrong, the council unanimously approved that called "Number Three." ‡ According to this, the army and navy were to gather at Sackett's Harbor, make a feint at Kingston, slip down the St. Lawrence, cut off the supplies of the enemy, sweep the river of armed craft, and, when joined by troops from Lake Champlain, attack Montreal.

As some weeks must elapse before the ships and troops would be ready to start, Wilkinson went off to Fort George. But he had hardly reached there when the Secretary of War appeared at Sackett's Harbor and established the War Department on the frontier. He had been brought thither by the seriousness of the situation, by the incapacity of the generals, and by a bitter feud between Wade Hampton and James Wilkinson, which threatened to be more troublesome than the enemy.

Wade Hampton was another of that small class of officers who, after serving with credit in the War for Independence, fought with discredit in the War of 1812. He was born in South Carolina in 1754, rode with the partisan bands of Marion and Sumter, and after our present Government was established was twice chosen a member of the House of Representatives. In embargo days he was appointed colonel in the regular army, and in 1809 was made a brigadier-general and sent to New Orleans. Hot-headed, proud, and stubborn,

---

* July 31, 1813.   † August 26, 1813.

‡ Armstrong's Notices, vol. ii, p. 33.   American State Papers, Military Affairs, vol. i, p. 463.

he found it impossible to agree with his subordinates, and in 1812 he was transferred to Burlington, on the northern frontier, and his command at New Orleans given to Wilkinson, whom he loathed and despised, and by whom his loathing and contempt were heartily and fully returned. No sooner, therefore, did Wilkinson find himself in command of the Ninth Military District than he determined to drive Hampton out of it. So eager was he that, on reaching Albany, he proceeded to embitter the old quarrel, and wrote letters distinctly setting forth that Hampton must obey his orders.* Hampton was furious, ignored the commanding general, and told Armstrong that if Wilkinson's conduct was approved he would resign.† The Secretary pacified Hampton as well as he could, consented that all orders and reports should go out from and be made to the Department of War, and with all possible haste transferred that department to the frontier. He reached Sackett's Harbor on September fifth, where his appearance instantly roused the jealous rage of Wilkinson. It was not, however, till October, when Wilkinson returned from Niagara, bringing with him General Boyd and all the regulars, that the trouble between the two became serious. Then began what under other circumstances would have been a ludicrous comedy. The general, having contracted the "lake fever," commenced by declaring that he was unfit to command, and offered to retire. The Secretary, who would gladly have been rid of him, replied that he could not be spared. As neither for a moment believed that Montreal could be taken, each next attempted to shift the responsibility for the future on the other. In August the general had been heartily in favor of attacking Kingston. But now, in October, finding that the Secretary also approved, he veered round and disapproved. Armstrong thereupon disapproved, and favored slipping by Kingston and hurrying on to Montreal. But Wilkinson again changed his mind, and declared that he would not abandon the attack on Kingston unless Armstrong expressly ordered him. In the midst of this unseemly contest

---

* Wilkinson's Memoirs, vol. iii. Appendix, xxxv, August 16, 1813.
† Hampton to Armstrong, August 23, 1813. Ibid., Appendix, xxxvi.

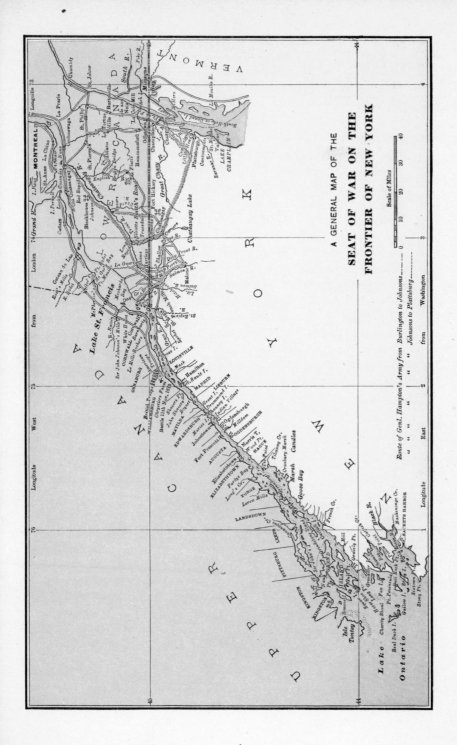

A GENERAL MAP OF THE

**SEAT OF WAR ON THE
FRONTIER OF NEW YORK**

Scale of Miles

Route of Genl. Hampton's Army from Burlington to Johnsons ————
Johnsons to Plattsburg ————

the expedition set sail, October seventeenth, from Henderson's Bay, and made for Grenadier Island, at the source of the St. Lawrence. The distance was eighteen miles. But a storm arose; the wind blew a gale, the batteaux were scattered far and wide, and two weeks passed before the last detachment reached the island. The moment it came the expedition set forth again, entered the St. Lawrence, passed the night not far from Ogdensburg, spent the next day in running by the British batteries at Prescott, and on the following evening reached White House, twenty miles below. A council of war was now called to consider what to do, for new dangers sprang up at every step. Chauncey, who had been left to blockade the entrance to the river, did his duty so badly that Captain Mulcaster, of the British navy, ran the blockade, and hung upon the rear of the army with his gun-boats. Joined by eight hundred men from Kingston and Prescott, who lined the bank at every narrow pass and fired on the flank of the army with musketry and artillery, while the gun-boats threatened its rear, Mulcaster became a dangerous enemy. At White House, therefore, twelve hundred men were landed on the Canadian shore, with orders to drive him away. The council meantime having decided to push on, General Brown with more troops was landed, and ordered to march ahead of the fleet and clear the bank, while General Boyd, with the reminder of the troops, protected the rear. In this manner the expedition went slowly down the river, making not more than twelve miles a day, till the night of November tenth, when it halted at a place called Chrystler's Farm. On the following morning, just as Brown sent word that the river bank was clear ahead, a messenger hurried in from Boyd, declaring that the British were advancing in column. But, as Wilkinson and Lewis were sick, and Brown and Scott far in the advance, Boyd was left to fight as he pleased, and after a stubborn resistance his force of two thousand men, beaten and almost routed by Mulcaster and his eight hundred, fled over the river in the dusk of the evening, and, without waiting for orders, clambered on board the ships. Next day the flotilla ran the Long Sault Rapids, joined Brown at Cornwall, and so terrified the army that within twenty-four hours the entire expedition had fled up the Salmon river and was safe within the United States.

Wilkinson was led to do this by a letter from Hampton. On taking command on Lake Champlain in July, Hampton made his headquarters at Burlington, where in the course of six weeks he succeeded in collecting four thousand men. While he was so engaged Wilkinson adopted plan " Number Three," and at once became anxious that Hampton should threaten Montreal. His wish was granted, and on September nineteenth the troops were moved down the lake and over the line into Canada. As he advanced he found the fields parched, the streams and springs dry, and saw on every hand unmistakable signs of a protracted drought. Fearing to go on, he turned back, struck the western road from Plattsburg, and followed it to Chateaugay Four Corners. It was on September twenty-sixth that he reached the Corners. As Wilkinson's expedition had not started, Hampton went into camp till orders came to march, when he passed down the Chateaugay river and on October twenty-second halted fifteen miles from its mouth. There, while bringing up his artillery, his ammunitions, and his stores, a most remarkable letter from the quartermaster-general was handed him. It bade him select some spot in Canada, and employ a brigade of militia in building as many huts as would shelter ten thousand men during the winter. Incredible as it may seem, the order on which this letter was based was written by Armstrong the day before the expedition left Henderson's Bay, three days before Wilkinson was expressly instructed to abandon Kingston and attack Montreal, and on the very day on which Hampton was bidden to move down the Chateaugay. Long after the war was over Armstrong explained his conduct by saying that "from the lateness of the season, the inclemency of the weather, and the continued indisposition of the commanding general," he suspected that the campaign would end as it did, "with the disgrace of doing nothing."

On Hampton the order had the effect of a command to do nothing. His hopes sank and he fell back slowly to Chateaugay, where he soon received a call for help from Wilkinson. The general, who was then at Ogdensburg, asked that supplies might be forwarded to him, and requested that Hampton would join him on the St. Lawrence somewhere below St. Regis.* Hampton answered that he had no supplies to send; that if Wilkinson needed supplies it would not be wise to increase the need by joining forces, and that he should under the circumstances return to Plattsburg.† This was the letter that Wilkinson received at Cornwall on November twelfth, and it immediately sent him into winter quarters at French Mills. As Wilkinson was hurrying up the Salmon river, Armstrong, who was at Albany, on his way back to Washington, again wrote to his old friend, and in the note had the face to say "I do so in the fulness of my faith that you are in Montreal." ‡

The spectacle of a secretary of war hastening to the frontier, planning an expedition which he knew must fail, yet collecting troops and stores at immense cost and sending forth his generals with assurances that he believed they would succeed, is humiliating enough. But what followed is more shameful still. To get soldiers for the expedition the whole frontier had been stripped of men. Harrison and his troops were at Sackett's Harbor. But from the harbor westward to Detroit not a post could be said to be defended. While the army continued to threaten Montreal, and the British forces were drawn to the St. Lawrence, the frontier might indeed be considered safe. But the moment the army went into winter quarters the plain duty of Armstrong was to hurry troops back to Niagara. No man ought for one moment to have supposed that even Sir George Prevost would suffer a handful of Americans to hold Fort George while their army was snowbound at French Mills and Plattsburg. Yet not a soldier was transferred. Indeed, the Secretary actually allowed the few garrisons that were on the frontier to be diminished! In November there were at Fort George and in the village of

---

* Wilkinson to Hampton, November 6, 1813. American State Papers, Military Affairs, vol. i, p. 462.

† Hampton to Wilkinson, November 8, 1813. American State Papers, Military Affairs, vol. i, p. 462.

‡ Armstrong to Wilkinson, November 12, 1813. American State Papers, Military Affairs, vol. i, p. 474.

Niagara several hundred volunteers commanded by Brigadier-General George McClure, of the New York militia. But as the winter came on the volunteers refused to serve,* and by December the whole number of troops scattered along the river from Fort George and Niagara on the north to Buffalo on the south was three hundred and twenty-four. Of these, one hundred were at Fort George when on December tenth McClure learned that a British force of five hundred men was within ten miles of him. He instantly burned the little village of Newark which lay under his guns, set fire to Queenston, and, leaving the tents and barracks standing in Fort George, fled over the river to the village of Niagara.† No re-enforcements coming, he continued his retreat to Buffalo. ‡ The burning of Newark was a wicked and cruel act and drove the British to take a swift and barbarous vengeance. During the night of December eighteenth, five hundred and fifty regulars crossed the river, crept up unseen to Fort Niagara, surprised the sentinels, rushed through the main gate, and captured the fort and three hundred and fifty prisoners. No surprise was ever more complete. No resistance was ever weaker. Lewiston, Niagara, and the country for miles around were now given up to plunder and devastation. That nothing might be wanting to complete the vengeance of the enemy, another force of fifteen hundred British and Indians crossed the river just above the falls on the night of December twenty-ninth and burned Black Rock and Buffalo. New Year's day found the cross of St. George floating over Fort Niagara, and the whole American side of the river a ruined country.

Had this series of shameful disasters been the purpose of the campaign, Armstrong could not have been more composed. That he was in anywise to blame for them never for a moment occurred to him. That it was his duty instantly to recover the lost forts he utterly failed to see, and leaving the British in quiet possession of the posts they had won, he al-

---

* McClure to Armstrong, December 10, 1813. American State Papers, Military Affairs, vol. i, p. 486.

† Ibid., vol. i, p. 486.

‡ McClure to Armstrong, December 22, 1813. Ibid., vol. i, p. 487.

lowed a month to pass before he disturbed the repose of Wilkinson at French Mills. When he did break up the camp it was not to drive the enemy from Niagara, but to send two thousand men with General Brown to Sackett's Harbor, while the rest marched with Wilkinson to Plattsburg. Every trace of the ancient friendship that had once existed between Wilkinson and Armstrong had by this time disappeared. The general was burning with wrath. To his mind, Armstrong was responsible for the failure of the expedition to reach Montreal and was guilty of a secret attempt to ruin him, and this blame and this guilt he determined should, in the most public manner, be fastened on the Secretary. At Plattsburg, therefore, Wilkinson, to use his own words, took " the bull by the horns," wrote a long letter, and with that sublime effrontery, that impudent assumption of injured innocence that had so often stood him in good stead, demanded arrest and court-martial. Meantime he would strike a blow against Montreal as a last proof of his military ability. The road to that city was then barred by small garrisons at St. Johns and Isle aux Noix, and by outposts at Lacadie and Lacolle. That at Lacolle Creek, a little stream flowing into the Sorel river, was not more than five miles over the border and did not number more than two hundred men. But it was stationed in a strong stone mill and, small as it was, would be hard to dislodge. Wilkinson took with him, therefore, the entire army and two field guns throwing twelve-pound shot, made his way through the deep snow to the mill, battered the stone walls for two hours, did no harm, lost two hundred men, retreated to Champlain, and there closed his military career. His request for a court of inquiry had been granted, and orders relieving him from duty having arrived, he made over the army to Major-General George Izard and departed. Once more the investigation was a sham ; once more Wilkinson was acquitted, but never again held command in the army, and passed the closing years of his life in Mexico.

George Izard was born in 1776 at London, where his father, Ralph Izard, was then living, but returned to Charleston in 1783, and, after attending many schools in many places, graduated from the University of Pennsylvania when not quite fifteen. Having shown a taste for a military life, he was sent back to Europe in 1792 under the care of Thomas Pinckney, who had just been made Minister to Great Britain. After studying by turns in the military schools of England and Germany, he succeeded in gaining admittance to the famous École du Génie, at Metz, where he was when in 1797 the trouble with France grew serious, and Charles Cotesworth Pinckney was forced to leave Paris. As the insolence of the Directory was not unlikely to be followed by war, young Izard was summoned to repair to the Hague, and in October sailed for Baltimore. The services of a trained engineer at that moment were most acceptable to the Secretary of War, who at once ordered Izard to Charleston, where he built Fort Pinckney, and commanded it till in 1800 he became aide-de-camp on the staff of Alexander Hamilton, who had just succeeded Washington in the command of the army of the United States. In 1803 he resigned, but again entered the army in 1812, and after service at Philadelphia and New York was sent at his own request, in October, 1813, to join General Hampton on Champlain.

And now the tide turned. At last the army was well rid of its incompetent generals. At last the command had passed to men of ability, energy, and decision, and under them it entered on a campaign which is one of the most remarkable in our military annals. The opening was far from propitious, for Armstrong was still possessed by the idea of taking Kingston, and ordered Brown, when he had not been many days at Sackett's Harbor, to make the attempt. But the troops could do nothing without the fleet; the fleet was not ready, and before it could be made so Yeo was scouring the lake, capturing schooners laden with supplies, and even destroying depots. On one of these expeditions he suddenly landed at Oswego, surprised and took the fort that was supposed to guard the entrance to the harbor, burned four schooners, and destroyed twenty-four hundred barrels of flour, pork, and salt. Had he gone twelve miles up the river—and he might safely have done so—he could have sacked the greatest depot of supplies on the whole northern frontier.

All these hindrances forced Armstrong to give up the old

plan of taking Kingston, and compelled him to form a new one which the Cabinet considered till June and then rejected. A third was accepted, and early in June General Brown was ordered, as soon as the fleet was ready, to cross above Niagara Falls and march to Burlington Heights and York. But the fleet could not be ready before the middle of July. Brown, therefore, in order to keep his troops' "blood from stagnating," was to take Fort Erie. He was to land in the night somewhere between Fort Erie and Point Abino, storm the fort, send a detachment to seize the bridge at Chippawa, and, if possible, go on farther. The general was only too glad to obey, and on the night of July third the troops crossed the river. They were in three brigades. Winfield Scott, who had just become a brigadier-general, commanded the first, made up of regiments he had himself drilled and trained most carefully. Eleazar Wheelock Ripley led the second brigade. Ripley was a native of New Hampshire. His father happening to be professor of divinity at Dartmouth, he graduated from that college in 1800, studied law, and began practice at Portland, Maine. There he soon rose into notice and became one of the representatives of the district in the General Court of Massachusetts. From 1810 to 1812 he was Speaker of the House, and then member of the Senate. When the war opened, Ripley joined the Twenty-first Infantry as lieutenant, and in 1813 was made its colonel.

The third brigade, composed of volunteer militia enlisted in Pennsylvania and of Indians belonging to the Six Nations, was commanded by Peter B. Porter. A battalion of artillery under Major Jacob Hindman raised the effective force of Brown's army to some thirty-five hundred men.

The British army numbered four thousand, commanded by Major-General P. Riall, and was scattered along the frontier in small garrisons. Some were at York and some at Burlington Heights. Others were in Newark, in Fort George, in Fort Niagara on the American side, at Queenston, at Chippawa, and in Fort Erie, which, at five o'clock in the afternoon of July third, after a weak resistance, surrendered to General Brown. According to instructions, Chippawa was next to be attacked, and toward it the army started bright and early on the morning of July fourth. Scott and his brigade went first. Though the distance was but sixteen miles, the enemy, by tearing up bridges, so delayed the march that it was not far from sunset when Scott reached Chippawa plains and found the British strongly posted on the banks of the Chippawa river. Falling back a mile or so to a stream called Street's Creek, he camped behind it in order to wait for Ripley and Porter, who came up during the night. Next morning Brown decided to build a bridge over the Chippawa above the British, cross the stream, and attack them. That Riall would quietly suffer this to be done was not likely, for even then the woods on the left of the Americans were full of his scouts and Indians. Porter's volunteers and some Indians were therefore sent to clear the woods that work on the bridge might begin. Driving the enemy before them, they soon came to the Chippawa river, where, to their amazement, they beheld the British crossing to attack, and instantly broke and fled.* As Ripley's brigade was in the rear of the camp and as Porter's brigade was in disorder, Scott with his troops was thus left to bear the brunt of the attack. So little did he expect a battle that he had set apart the day for the celebration of our national independence, had regaled his troops with as fine a dinner as the commissary could procure, and had formed them in order to cross Street's Creek and review them on an open plain. But just as he came to the bridge that spanned the creek General Brown, who had been to the front, galloped by and cried out, "You will have a battle." Scott answered that he did not believe the enemy numbered three hundred, pushed forward, and, as he crossed the bridge, received the fire of the British artillery. That the enemy was in force was certain; yet he would not turn back, but marched out on the plain, formed in line of battle under a heavy fire, and ordered an advance. At the same moment the British began a charge, and the two lines, stopping now and then to fire and load, came on till the flanks touched, when the British broke and fell back beyond the Chippawa. From their camp on the Chippawa they were dislodged two days later and followed by

---

* Stone's Life of Red Jacket, p. 352.

Brown as far as Queenston.   There Brown remained for two
weeks, when, finding that Riall had been strongly re-enforced
and that Chauncey did not come with the fleet, he suddenly
retreated to Chippawa and camped on the battle field.   That
same night Riall followed Brown as far as Lundy's Lane.
Meanwhile, not knowing that Riall had gone after Brown, a
detachment of six hundred men had been sent from Fort
George to Lewiston with orders to march up the American
side.   The morning of July twenty-fifth, therefore, found
Brown at Chippawa, Riall at Lundy's Lane, some two miles
away, and a small force of British at Lewiston.   Brown soon
heard of the troops on the American side, but of the near-
ness of Riall he knew nothing, when, about five in the afternoon, he sent Scott down the river to threaten the rear of the
British coming up from Lewiston.   Ere this General Drummond, alarmed for the safety of Riall, had recalled the detachment, and when Scott set out it had come back to the Canadian side and was about to march for Lundy's Lane.   Hastening along, suspecting nothing, Scott had almost reached the
falls when he was told that a strong body of the enemy was
in camp just below.   He was greatly surprised, but, with that
audacity which in later years carried him from Vera Cruz to
Mexico, he pushed forward, determined to attack.   Riall, hearing of his approach, ordered a retreat, and the troops had actually begun to march when Drummond came up, countermanded
the order, and formed line of battle.   The next moment Scott
was upon him.   From seven till near nine at night the fighting
was furious.   Both sides then stopped from sheer exhaustion
till, fresh troops arriving, the battle raged once more.   One
regiment of Americans in attempting to flank the British was
thrown into confusion and retired to reform; but another,
favored by the darkness, crept up the hill on which the British
battery was posted, rushed upon it, bayoneted the gunners,
and held the guns.   Not a hundred feet back of the guns was
the English line of battle, and this space between the two is
said to have become for some minutes a sheet of flame.   The
disorganized regiment having reformed, a second time fell on
the enemy's flank, and the whole British line went down the
hill and out of sight in the darkness.   Brown was now in pos-

session of the hill-top, the English guns, and Lundy's Lane—a
position from which the British three times attempted to dislodge him and three times failed.   In each of these attacks
the combatants came so near that in the flash of the musketry
the Americans could distinctly see the buttons on the British
coats.   So frightful was the slaughter that after the third attack not seven hundred men were in position.   To hold out
longer was impossible, and about midnight Brown led his
troops back in good order to camp.   His own guns he took
with him; but when horses were procured and sent back to
haul off the artillery captured in the battle, the British were
found once more in possession of the hill-top and of their guns.

Among the wounded were Brown and Scott.   As neither
was fit for active service, Ripley was practically in command.
He was a cautious man, and when, on the day following the
fight, Drummond moved his camp to Niagara Falls, Ripley retreated to Fort Erie.   The fort stood on the Canadian side
close to the shore, just where the waters of Lake Erie enter
Niagara river.   It was an unfinished work, open on the land
side, when the Americans captured it, and, as nothing had
been done to it since, the army was camped on the plain and
the labor of digging ditches and trenches and throwing up
heavy earthworks began.   While thus busy, General Gaines
arrived from Sackett's Harbor and took command.   He made
no change in the plans, and by August tenth the defences were
nearly completed.   One strong earthwork four hundred feet
long, with a ditch, ran from the fort eastward to the water's
edge, where it ended in a stone work named Battery Douglas.
Another entrenchment some two thousand feet long ran southward, parallel to the shore, to another battery called Towson's,
erected on Snake Hill close to the water.   The shore between
Snake Hill and Battery Douglas was undefended.

Hastily as the works had been constructed, they were,
nevertheless, so formidable that Drummond determined not to
make an assault until he had battered them, and accordingly
sent off for heavy guns.   On the thirteenth the siege guns
were in position, and the bombardment was begun and kept
up till midnight of the fourteenth, when the firing stopped.
Gaines understood this to mean that an assault was coming.

Nor was he mistaken; for about two o'clock in the afternoon the firing of the pickets announced that the British were at hand. They came on, as was expected, in three columns—one against Snake Hill, one against Fort Erie, and one against Battery Douglas. That against Snake Hill did nothing. Some were driven back by the hot fire from the battery. Others marching near the lake were thrown into disorder by the rocks and, unable to reform in the darkness, retreated. A few, wading out into the lake, made their way around the earthworks, came into camp, and were captured.

The column sent to assault Battery Douglas meantime having approached within a couple of hundred feet of the guns, was driven back, abandoned the attempt, and, turning off to the right, gained the ditch and made its way into the northeast bastion of Fort Erie. There the men of the third column quickly joined it, and for two hours the fighting was desperate. Every effort made by the Americans to drive the English out of the bastion was defeated. Every attempt of the British to drive the Americans out of the fort was futile. Had Drummond now brought up his reserves the victory would undoubtedly have been his. But no reserves came, and, about five in the morning, an ammunition chest having exploded under the platform of the bastion, the remains of the second and third attacking columns quit the fort and fled to their own intrenchments. In that midnight assault the English lost nine hundred and five men and the Americans eighty-four.

Drummond now ordered the bombardment of Fort Erie to go on; but no harm was done till August twenty-ninth, when Gaines was seriously wounded by the explosion of a shell. Ripley was then a second time put in command. But Brown, who distrusted him as a timid and over-cautious man, at once relieved him. General Brown would have been wise had he remained inactive, for everything that Nature could do was being done to discomfort the enemy. The season had set in cold and rainy. The English troops, having no tents, had put up rude huts, which afforded poor shelter against the drenching rains of autumn. The sick list grew larger each day. The roads became so deep that to get supplies was all but impossible. The ammunition gave out and Drummond only waited for better weather to retreat. Before better weather came, however, Brown's patience was exhausted, and he decided to attack the British in their intrenchments. These intrenchments consisted of a battery on the shore and a line of earthworks, which, protected by fallen trees, stretched inland half a mile from the lake to the dense forest, where it ended in another battery and block-house. Behind this were two more lines of intrenchments, and a mile farther in the rear the camp of the British army. As the defence of the first line was intrusted to a brigade, and not to the entire force under Drummond's command, the purpose of Brown was, as he expressed it, " to storm the batteries, spike the cannon, and roughly handle the brigade on duty before those in reserve could be brought into action."* About the middle of September, having obtained a thousand volunteers from New York, he felt strong enough to make the attempt. A day was then spent in cutting a path through the forest from Snake Hill to a point not five hundred feet from the right of the British line, and along this path General Porter was sent on the following day with some sixteen hundred men. He started at noon, and at three o'clock, in the midst of a pouring rain, fell upon the block-house and the battery nearest the forest, captured them, and, while a detachment spiked the guns and blew up the magazine, Porter hurried the rest of his troops to the next battery, known as No. 2. General Miller, whose men had been hidden in a ravine, now rushed upon the intrenchments between the two batteries, and in a few minutes No. 2 was taken, and the united forces of Porter and Miller then moved on No. 1, which stood near the lake shore. A fierce fight ensued ; but it could not be stormed, and Brown, thinking enough had been done, withdrew his troops.†

Drummond therefore claimed a victory. But he had, in the language of Brown, been so " roughly handled " that during the night of September twenty-first he retreated to Chippawa. A splendid opportunity now offered to destroy him.

---

* Brown's Report, September 29, 1814. Niles's Weekly Register, vol. viii, p. 100.

† The British lost 609 killed, wounded, and missing. The Americans lost 511.

But ere Brown could strike again General Izard arrived and took command.

Izard had reached Plattsburg on May first, and had scarcely had time to look about him when the British opened the campaign. . Neither during 1812 nor 1813 had anything of importance taken place on Lake Champlain. In 1813, it is true, some battles were fought, but they were small affairs. At the beginning of that year the American naval force consisted of two sloops, the Eagle and the Growler, of eleven guns each, and six gun-boats of one gun each. Taking the two sloops, Lieutenant Sydney Smith went down the lake to scatter the British gun-boats stationed at the head of the Sorel river, and, while cruising about the outlet of Champlain, he fell in with three which he chased down the river till he saw the flag on Fort Isle-aux-Noix, when he attempted to turn back. But the river was narrow, the current strong, and the wind so light that, before he had gone far, a large force of the enemy coming up on both banks overtook him. During three hours the crews fought stubbornly. Then, a shot from one of the British gun-boats having torn off a plank below the water-line of the Eagle, she sank and was taken. The Growler soon after had her rigging so badly cut that she became unmanageable and surrendered. The capture of the two sloops gave the supremacy on the lake to the British. The capture of Lieutenant Smith gave the command of the American flotilla to Lieutenant Macdonough.

This supremacy the British were quick to use, and, having refitted the Eagle and Growler and renamed them Finch and Chubb, they came up the lake late in July, landed at Plattsburg, plundered the magazines both there and at Saranac, and swept Champlain clear of shipping. Macdonough could do nothing, for the British were safe again in the Sorel river before his three new sloops were in the water. These were afloat August sixth, and, the mastery of the lake having passed to him, the British did no more plundering that year.

During the following winter and spring each side made serious efforts to put on the lake a naval force superior to the other, and many sloops, brigs, and gun-boats were constructed. The British, as usual, were first afloat, and early in May, 1814, came to the mouth of Otter Creek. The American squadron lay at anchor in the creek, and the aim of the British was to prevent its sailing by filling the channel. For this purpose two schooners laden with stone were brought along; but the enemy after a sharp encounter retired. Alarmed by this attempt, Armstrong ordered Izard to fortify Rouse's Point, or the mouth of Lacolle river, or Ash Island. As the river and the island were already in the hands of the British, Izard saw that to fortify Rouse's Point would be foolish, and occupied Plattsburg instead. There he gathered his troops, and while hard at work on his defences was informed by Armstrong of the plan of Brown's coming campaign on the Niagara. After Chippawa and Lundy's Lane Izard seems to have grown uneasy, and wrote to Armstrong suggesting that he should move northward and threaten Montreal, or make a demonstration against Kingston. Armstrong approved; but by the time the approval reached camp Izard had changed his mind. For weeks past troops from Wellington's army had been pouring into Canada, and when Izard, on August tenth, read the Secretary's letter, eleven thousand of the finest troops the English army could produce were camped on the Sorel river. That they were soon to take the field in an offensive campaign of no ordinary importance, that they were, in fact, merely waiting for the English naval force to get ready before they began the campaign, was quite clear to Izard, who remonstrated accordingly against any movement likely to take him away from Champlain. His letter, however, was passed on the way to Washington by one from the Secretary bidding him march with four thousand troops to Sackett's Harbor. In obedience to this, he set out on August twenty-ninth, went by easy stages across the state of New York, and in September entered Sackett's Harbor, where he heard with amazement of the great victory on Lake Champlain.

In his letter of remonstrance he had asserted that if the army went westward the British would, in three days' time, have possession of everything in northeastern New York save the works at Plattsburg and Cumberland Head.* The predic-

---

* Izard to Armstrong, August 11, 1814.

tion was fulfilled, for the troops had scarcely turned their faces westward when the British, eleven thousand strong, crossed the frontier under General Prevost, occupied Chazy, which Izard had just left, and on September fifth were within eight miles of the Saranac, at the mouth of which was Platts- burg, at that time a country village of fifteen hundred inhabi- tants. It stood partly on the north bank of the Saranac river and partly on the shore of Plattsburg Bay, one of the innumer- able indentations along the west coast of Lake Champlain, was of considerable importance in the trade with Canada, and con- tained four public buildings—a church, a jail, an inn, and a court-house, where the Court of Common Pleas and Quarter Sessions of the Peace sat twice a year. Its importance as a trading town made its possession especially valuable to the British. Ever since embargo days a stream of illicit trade had been rushing through Champlain into Canada, and from Canada back into the United States; and this stream, after the open- ing of the war, became enormous. Both Izard and Prevost agree in the statement that the British army were almost en- tirely fed on supplies drawn from New York and Vermont by way of Lake Champlain. " In fact, my Lord," wrote Pre- vost to Bathurst, " two thirds of the army in Canada are at this moment eating beef provided by American contractors, drawn principally from the States of Vermont and New York. This circumstance, as well as that of the introduction of large sums in specie into this province, being notorious in the United States, it is to be expected that Congress will take steps to de- prive us of those resources; and under that apprehension large droves are daily crossing the lines into Lower Canada." * Izard, who saw this from the American side, described it more fully. From the St. Lawrence to the ocean, he told Armstrong, the laws forbidding intercourse with the enemy were openly disregarded, and nothing but a cordon of troops from French Mills to Lake Memphremagog could stop the evil. The road to St. Regis was covered with droves of cattle and the river with rafts destined for the enemy. On the Vermont side of the lake

---

* Prevost to Bathurst, August 27, 1814. Adams's History of the United States, vol. viii, p. 94.

the highways were too narrow and too few to accommodate the herds of cattle that were pouring into Canada. "Like herds of buffaloes," said he, "they press through the forests, making paths for themselves. Were it not for these supplies, the British forces in Canada would soon be suffering from famine, or their Government be subjected to enormous expense for their maintenance." *

To protect this source of supply by getting military possession of the country was the duty assigned these veterans of Wellington, led by officers of distinction and commanded by Sir George Prevost. Opposed to them, after the march westward of Izard, was a body of fifteen hundred † fighting men under Brigadier-General Alexander Macomb. The main body was within the fortifications built at Plattsburg by Izard; but a few had been sent out by Macomb to skirmish and obstruct the road by which Prevost was advancing. To these he paid no attention whatever, but pushed on in solid column, never once deploying, and reached Plattsburg on September sixth, where, crowning a ridge just beyond the town, he beheld three redoubts, strong field works, and block-houses, and riding at anchor in the bay the little fleet of Macdonough. At the sight of these, confidence for the first time forsook him, and, sure that the place could not be taken by assault, he sat down to await the coming of Captain George Downie, of the Royal Navy, with the fleet. But five days passed before Downie sailed round Cumberland Head, which forms the eastern shore of Plattsburg Bay, and found the four ships and ten gun-boats of Macdonough anchored in line at the entrance. At the north end near Cumberland Head was the Eagle, flanked on either side by two gun-boats. Then came the Saratoga, then three gun-boats, then the Ticonderoga, then three more gun-boats, and the Preble, which closed the line. Downie's fleet numbered twelve gun-boats and four large ships —the Chubb, the Linnet, the Confiance, and Finch—one of which, the Confiance, he considered a match for the entire American flotilla. She was indeed a splendid vessel, for she

---

* Izard to Armstrong, July 31, 1814.
† Macomb to Armstrong, September 15, 1814,

was one hundred and forty-six feet long, was armed with thirty-seven guns, and carried a crew of three hundred officers and men. After pausing for a time at the entrance to the bay in order that his gun-boats might come up with him, Downie, with his four ships abreast and the twelve galleys to leeward, bore down on the American line. The Chubb and the Linnet singled out the Eagle. The Confiance dropped anchor before the Saratoga; the Finch with the galleys engaged the Ticonderoga and the Preble, and sought to turn the end of the American line. The battle which followed was fought long and well. At the head of the line the Chubb was quickly disabled by the Eagle, and, drifting past the Saratoga, received a shot that forced her to strike. She was then boarded by a prize crew and towed inshore and anchored off the mouth of the Saranac river. But the Eagle was soon forced from her position, and, running down the line, she anchored between the Saratoga and the Ticonderoga. The Ticonderoga meanwhile had been hotly engaged with the Finch, which, shattered and helpless, was, in her turn, driven from her anchorage, and, floating off toward Crab Island, grounded and was taken by the invalids from the hospital. The galleys now redoubled the fury of their attack on the Preble, and soon compelled her to cut her cables and take refuge inshore near the captured Chubb. On the Saratoga the day was going badly for Macdonough. The first broadside from the double-shotted guns of the Confiance, delivered at short range, almost blew the Saratoga out of the water. Such was the force of the shot that more than half the crew were thrown upon the deck and forty of them killed outright or wounded. Deprived of so many men, Macdonough began to fight like a sailor, and was busy sighting a gun when a round shot cut the spanker boom in two and threw a piece of it on his head, striking him senseless to the deck. Springing up, he went back to the gun, but a second shot, tearing off the head of the captain of the gun, flung it in his face with such force that he was hurled to the other side of the vessel. The Linnet, having driven off the Eagle, began to rake the bow of the Saratoga. But though his men fell thick around him, though his guns were one by one disabled, Macdonough fought manfully on till the navel-bolt of his last gun giving way, the piece leaped from its carriage and, plunging down the main hatch, left him without one carronade on his engaged side. Many a captain would have thought the time had now come to strike, but the emergency was one Macdonough had foreseen and had provided for, and, turning his vessel slowly round while the Linnet raked her, he brought his unused port battery to bear on the Confiance and forced her to surrender. Then, turning still farther round, Macdonough opened on the Linnet, and in fifteen minutes her commander hauled down her colors. A boarding officer was now sent to take possession of the Confiance, which, with every mast in splinters, with Downie and half the crew dead and wounded, and with one hundred and five shot-holes in her hull, lay a wreck on the water. As the lieutenant passed along her deck he ran foul of the lock-string of a gun, which immediately went off. It is believed that the report was understood by the British galleys to be a signal, for they at once began to move away slowly by the aid of the few sweeps left them. To follow was not possible, and they escaped with every ensign down.

The fight in Plattsburg Bay was undoubtedly the greatest naval battle of the war, and the victory stamped Macdonough as the ablest sea-captain our country produced down to the Rebellion. On land there was hardly any fighting. The moment the fleet came into sight Prevost sent a column to cross the Saranac and turn the American flank. But the troops lost their way, and, hearing the cheers which greeted the surrender of the fleet, halted and did nothing. The next day * the army fled to Champlain, a little town just south of the boundary line.

While these things were taking place in the east, Izard was slowly making his way westward. The distance which separated him from Ontario was two hundred and eighty miles; yet such were the difficulties that beset the way that twenty days passed before he entered Sackett's Harbor,† where a letter from Brown, asking help for Fort Erie, reached him, and he made ready to embark in the fleet of Chauncey. But vio-

---

* September 12, 1814.   † September 17, 1814.

lent storms and contrary winds hindered this movement till September twenty-first, when, at the very moment Drummond was in full retreat from Fort Erie, the fleet, with the troops on board, set sail. At the Genesee river the men were landed, and, marching inland, were met by Brown at Batavia,* where Izard learned for the first time of the retreat of Drummond to Chippawa. The opportunity of a lifetime was before him. The enemy, disheartened by defeat, had been reduced by sickness and by casualties to twenty-five hundred men. His own army numbered sixty-three hundred, and might with a little energy capture Drummond's entire force. For a time Izard seemed disposed to make the attempt, and having crossed the river, he moved against Chippawa on October thirteenth. Chauncey meantime, supposing his work to be over for the year, retired into port at Sackett's Harbor and began throwing up batteries to defend his ships. Never, even in the brightest moments of the campaign, had Izard any too much confidence in the success of the enterprise. Now that Chauncey was no longer on the lake, he had absolutely no confidence at all, and on October twenty-first broke camp and went back to a place just opposite Black Rock. There the army fell rapidly to pieces. Some of the troops were sent with Brown to Sackett's Harbor, some retired to winter quarters at Buffalo, and, our flag having been pulled down at Fort Erie, the works were blown up, and the Canadian side of the Niagara frontier passed once more into the control of the British.† Drummond, thus relieved from fear of attack, took to his boats ‡ and hurried to Kingston,# where he made preparations to besiege Sackett's Harbor the moment supplies could come over the winter roads from Quebec.

---

* September 27, 1814.   ‡ November 5, 1814.
† November 5, 1814.   # November 10, 1814.

CHAPTER XXV.

THE SHIP DUELS AND THE PRIVATEERS.

WHILE the army which the Republicans had expected would long since have taken Canada was meeting with disaster after disaster on land, the hated and neglected navy was winning victory after victory on the sea. Such was the neglect into which this arm of the service had been suffered to fall, that but five ships were ready for sea on the day war was declared. Two of these, by order of the Secretary, were riding at anchor in the lower bay at New York, where, on the twenty-first of June, the United States, the Congress, and the Argus, came in from the southward and joined them.* The arrival of the frigates was most timely; for they had hardly passed the Hook before Commodore John Rodgers, who commanded, received news of the declaration of war, and within an hour the fleet—composed of the President, the United States, the Congress, the Argus, and the Hornet—weighed anchor and stood out to sea. Rodgers had orders to strike any of the British cruisers that had so long been searching merchantmen off Sandy Hook and return to port. But information had been received that the homeward-bound plate fleet had left Jamaica late in May, and he went off in pursuit. For a while he ran southeast, till, falling in with an American brig that had seen the Jamaica fleet of eighty-five vessels,

---

* The Chesapeake was in Boston Harbor undergoing repairs. The Essex was in New York Harbor overhauling her rigging. The Constellation was in Chesapeake river unable to secure a crew. The Constitution was at Annapolis taking in stores. The Adams was at Washington, being turned from a frigate to a corvette. The Wasp was on her way home from France with despatches. The Nautilus was cruising off New Jersey, and the other brigs somewhere off the coast.

under convoy, in latitude 36° N., longitude 67° W., he set sail in that direction, and at six in the morning of June twenty-third made out a stranger in the northeast. She proved to be the British thirty-six-gun frigate Belvidera, Captain Richard Byron, which stood toward the fleet for a few minutes, and then turned and went off to the northeast, with the Americans in hot pursuit. The President, happening to be the best sailer, came up with her late in the afternoon, fired three shots into her stern, and was about to send a fourth when the gun exploded, killing and wounding sixteen men, and among them Captain Rodgers. Confusion and demoralization followed, the sailing became bad, the shots fell short, and the Belvidera, cutting away her anchors and throwing her barge, gig, yawl, and jolly-boat into the sea, and starting fourteen tons of water,* drew ahead and was soon out of danger. The fleet now went a second time in pursuit of the Jamaicamen, and kept up the chase till within a day's run of the English channel, when they stood to the southward and came back to Boston by way of Madeira, the Western Islands, and the Grand Banks.

While Rodgers was thus searching for the plate fleet, an English squadron was looking for him. Three days after her fight with the President the Belvidera reached Halifax with the news of war. Vice-Admiral Sawyer instantly dispatched Captain Philip Bowes Vere Broke with the Shannon, the Africa, the Æolus, and the Belvidera, to destroy Rodgers's fleet. Sweeping down the coast, the squadron was joined at Nantucket Island by the Guerrière, and on July sixteenth fell in with and took the brig Nautilus, then one day from port. Luck was with them, and twenty-four hours later the Constitution, Captain Isaac Hull, ran into their midst.

She had left Annapolis on the twelfth of July, and had experienced such light winds and strong currents that on the afternoon of the seventeenth she had gone no farther than Barnegat, on the coast of New Jersey, when the lookout about two o'clock in the afternoon descried four sail to the northward, and by and by a fifth in the northeast. Five was the number of Rodgers's fleet. But Hull, not feeling sure that

---

* Log of the Belvidera.

the strangers were friends, and finding that he was getting too near the coast, changed his course and went off due east toward the nearest ship, which was the Guerrière, Captain James Richards Dacres. Captain Dacres had parted from the squadron some time before, and, not expecting to meet it so soon, believed the vessels to be the fleet of Captain Rodgers. He would not join them, therefore, and, on sighting the Constitution coming toward him, kept away, so that it was half-past seven before Hull caught up with the Guerrière, and, clearing for action, ran on side by side with her, but not venturing to fire lest she might be a friend.

Captain Broke, meanwhile, seeing the two frigates near together, concluded they were Americans, and carefully abstained from making any signals lest they should be frightened away. The situation at nightfall was thus most complicated : the British fleet supposed the Guerrière and the Constitution were Americans; the Guerrière supposed the British fleet belonged to the United States and was not certain as to the Constitution, while Captain Hull was not sure as to the character of the Guerrière. He was not long in doubt, however, for about three in the morning the Guerrière fired two guns and a rocket and made off. Daylight showed that the fleet belonged to the enemy, and Hull turned to escape.

And now began the most exciting chase recorded in naval annals. During the night the Englishmen closed in about him, and when the mist and the darkness lifted the Shannon was some five miles astern ; two others were to leeward, and the rest of the fleet ten miles astern. The ocean being quite calm and no wind stirring, Hull put out his boats to tow the Constitution. Broke imitated him, and summoned all the boats of his squadron to tow the Shannon ; and having furled all sail was gaining steadily on the Constitution, when a little breeze swept over the water and sent her a few hundred yards ahead before the Shannon could shake out her sails and catch it. But the wind soon died out, and the Shannon, creeping up, got near enough to throw her shot over the Constitution. Fearing that this would soon destroy the rigging and so make her a prize to the fleet, Lieutenant Charles Morris suggested kedging. Hull took the suggestion, ordered all the spare rope to be payed down into the cutters, which were sent half a mile ahead, where a kedge was let go. The moment the anchor touched bottom a signal was given, the crew, in the language of the sailors, "clapped on," and the ship was warped ahead. Meantime a second kedge had been carried forward and dropped, so that when the first was tripped the second was ready to be hauled on. This device Broke also imitated, and all that day and till late the next night the Constitution and her pursuers kept on towing and kedging and occasionally exchanging harmless shots. A light breeze then sprang up, which freshened toward midnight, and the men were allowed to rest till two in the morning of the nineteenth, when the wind once more died out and kedging was again resorted to. By noon the breeze became light again, and about half-past six in the evening a squall of rain was seen coming over the ocean. For this, as for everything, Hull was ready, and keeping his sails taut till just before the squall struck, he then, in a moment, furled the light ones and double reefed the others, and so led the English captains to believe that a gust of unusual violence was near. Without waiting for it to strike them, they at once shortened sail and bore up before the wind, which compelled them to take a course just the opposite of that of the Constitution. The squall was really very light, and as soon as the rain hid him from his pursuers Hull made all sail, and, though the fleet continued the pursuit till the next morning, he escaped after a chase of three nights and two days, or sixty-six hours. Six days later he entered Boston Harbor.

There he stayed till August second, when he again put to sea. Having no orders, he ran down to the Bay of Fundy, sailed along the coast of Nova Scotia, passed Newfoundland, and took his station off Cape Race, captured some merchantmen, and, sailing southward, spoke a Salem privateer whose captain informed him that a frigate was not far distant. Taking the course indicated, Hull, on the afternoon of August nineteenth, sighted his old enemy the Guerrière. The order to clear the decks was instantly given; the boatswain's cry, "All hands clear ship for action!" sounded through the frigate; the fife and drum beat to quarters, and every man hurried to his place and work.   Marines and sailors climbed into

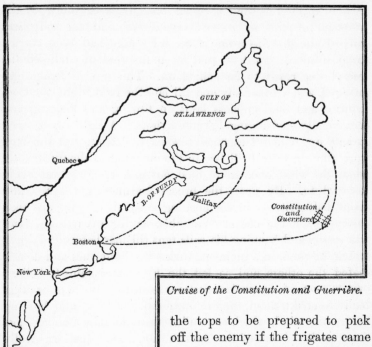

Cruise of the Constitution and Guerrière.

the tops to be prepared to pick off the enemy if the frigates came to close quarters, or trim the topsails if a sudden manœuvre became necessary, while below others stood ready to do the same with the lower sails.   The gun crews made haste to unlash the guns and load them; the powder boys ran about the deck piling up ammunition beside the carriages; a blanket soaked with water was hung over the entrance to the magazine; muskets, boarding-pikes, and cutlasses were stacked around the masts; buckets of loaded pistols were placed near at hand for the purpose of repelling boarders, and the deck sanded that it might not be made slippery by the blood shed by the killed and wounded.*   Each welcomed the other; for Dacres, who commanded the Guerrière, had just spread

---

* History of the United States Navy.   E. S. Maclay, vol. i, p. 369.

a challenge on the log of a merchantman and sent it into New York, offering to meet any frigate in the American navy off Sandy Hook,* and Hull was most anxious not to return to port without a fight.† For an hour the two ships wore and yawed and manœuvred, coming nearer and nearer till within pistol range, when the Guerrière bore up and went off with the wind on her quarter, as an indication of her willingness to engage in a yard-arm and yard-arm encounter. The Constitution immediately made sail, got alongside, and the two ran on together. As the battle must be at close quarters, Hull ordered all firing to stop, had his guns reloaded with round shot and grape, and quietly waited. Again and again Lieutenant Morris came to the quarter-deck and asked for orders to fire; but not till the frigates were at short pistol range was the command given, and a broadside delivered with unerring aim. For ten minutes the battle raged furiously. The mizzen-mast of the Guerrière was then shot away, and falling into the sea brought her up to the wind and so caused the Constitution to forge ahead. Fearing that he might be raked, Hull crossed the bows of the enemy, came about, raked her, and attempted to lay her on board. In doing so the Guerrière thrust her bowsprit diagonally across the Constitution's lea quarter. This afforded Dacres so fine a

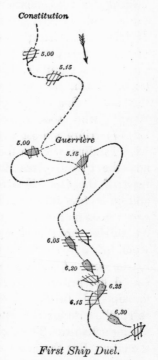

First Ship Duel.

* This challenge was written on the register of the brig John Adams, which reached New York some days after the battle was fought: "Captain Dacres, commander of his Britannic Majesty's frigate Guerrière, of forty-four guns, presents his compliments to Commodore Rodgers, of the United States frigate President, and will be very happy to meet him, or any other American frigate of equal force to the President, off Sandy Hook, for the purpose of having a few minutes' *tête-à-tête*."

† I am indebted to Mr. Theodore Roosevelt for permission to reproduce this and other diagrams from The Naval War of 1812.

chance to board that Lieutenant Morris sprang upon the taffrail to get a view of the enemy's deck, and beheld the men gathering on the forecastle and heard the officers instructing them how to board. Jumping down he reported this to Captain Hull, and in a minute the marines and seamen of the Constitution, armed with muskets and pistols, boarding-pikes and cutlasses, were mustered on the quarter-deck waiting for the enemy to come over the bulwarks. None came, and a terrible musketry fight began. Lieutenant Morris who, seizing a rope that dangled from the bowsprit of the Guerrière, had climbed up and was about to lash the frigates together, was laid on the deck by a bullet. Lieutenant Bush, of the marines, standing on the taffrail crying out, " Shall I board ? " was killed outright. Master Alwyn, who stood near by, was shot in the shoulder. On the Guerrière almost every man on the forecastle was picked off. Finding the sea too rough to board, the sails were filled and the two frigates drew apart. As they did so the foremast of the Guerrière fell, dragging the mainmast with it, and in a few minutes she struck. It was time she did, for every mast had gone by the board ; her hull had been pierced by thirty shot ; seventy-nine of her crew were dead or wounded, and she lay a helpless wreck, rolling her deck guns in the sea. As it was not possible to save her, Hull transferred his prisoners to the Constitution, gave his prize to the flames, and, turning homeward, reached Boston on August thirtieth, entered the lower harbor, and dropped anchor off the light-house. The day being Sunday, he did not go up to the city. But the news did, and when the people learned that the Constitution with Dacres and his crew was below they could not restrain their joy, though the day was the Sabbath. As Federalists they could not forget that it was a Federalist Congress and a Federalist President that established the navy ; that Federalists had always been its steady friends and stanch defenders ; that it had long been their boast that in the hour of trial the " wooden walls of Columbia " would prove the bulwark of the nation ; and now, when the hour of trial had come and a frigate built by Yankee shipwrights in a Boston shipyard and commanded by a Yankee captain had more than made that boast good, they could not find expression for their gratitude. The delight felt by every true American all over the country was intensified by local pride, and was made extravagant when on Wednesday morning the newspapers announced, side by side, the capture of the Guerrière and the surrender of Detroit.* On Monday, when Hull brought the Constitution up the bay, he was given a reception the like of which Boston had not yet accorded to any man. Every ship was gay with bunting. The whole population of the city stood on the wharves and crowded the windows and housetops overlooking the bay, and as Hull stepped ashore greeted him with a salute from the artillery and with deafening cheers and escorted him through the bunting-dressed streets to the Coffee-House, where he was received in " true Republican style." But now that the victory on the sea was made greater by contrast with defeat on land, men of both parties united to give Hull a naval dinner, to which Rodgers and the officers of his squadron, who had just returned, were invited. The old toast, " The Wooden Walls of Columbia," came again into use, and limners and engravers at once set to work to produce those representations of the great sea fight which, after hanging for a generation on the walls of our ancestors' houses and being copied by the makers of bad school-books, were consigned to the garrets by a less patriotic generation, and are now rarely to be met with.

As the handbills spread the news southward the pleasure of the people was expressed in innumerable ways. At New York money was raised to buy swords to be presented to Hull and his officers. At Philadelphia subscriptions were asked for a fund to purchase two fine pieces of plate for Hull and Lieutenant Morris. When the news reached Baltimore salutes were fired and every ship in the harbor ran up its flags. That same day, September seventh, the frigate Essex entered the Delaware and took part in the demonstrations of joy going on in every town along the river bank.

Her cruise had been short and generally uneventful. As Captain Porter was not ready to sail with Rodgers's fleet, he

---

* Boston Patriot, September 2, 1812. Columbian Sentinel, September 2, 1812.

finished his preparations, and, passing Sandy Hook on July third, began a cruise to the southward in search of the frigate Thetis, from South America with specie. After taking a few prizes of no great value, and failing to meet the Thetis, he turned northward, and on the night of July tenth sighted a convoy of British merchantmen. There was a moon, but clouds so obscured it that Porter determined to go close in, speak one of the ships, find out the strength of the escort, and, if possible, take her. To conceal his character the guns of the Essex were run in, the ports were closed, the top-gallant masts were housed, the sails trimmed in a slovenly manner, the men hidden, and everything done to give her the appearance of a merchant ship. Then, about three in the morning, the Essex drew cautiously in and spoke the sternmost vessel, and learned from her master that the fleet was carrying about a thousand soldiers from Barbadoes to Brock's army at Quebec, and that the escort was the thirty-two-gun frigate Minerva.

The success which so far attended his venture encouraged Porter to go in yet farther and speak a second. But her master was so alarmed by the appearance of the Essex, that he made ready to signal the presence of a stranger, when the ports were thrown open, the muzzles of twenty guns thrust out, and the transport ordered to follow in the frigate's wake or be blown to pieces. Taking his prize off a short distance, Porter found her to be a brig with one hundred and ninety-seven soldiers on board. Going in a second time, he was about to attempt to capture another transport, when dawn broke and the enemy discovered him. Whereupon, clearing for action, he offered battle to the Minerva. This offer was declined, and the Essex and her prize went off to the southward, meeting with nothing till August thirteenth, when a sail was seen which proved to be the sixteen-gun ship-sloop Alert, Captain Thomas Lamb Paulden Laugharne. Drags were at once put astern, the reefs shaken out, all sail made, and everything possible was done to persuade the enemy that the Essex was most anxious to escape. Completely deceived, the Alert ran down, and, with three cheers from her crew, opened fire. In eight minutes she was a prize, with seven feet of water in her hold.

This new lot of prisoners raised the number of Englishmen on board the frigate to five hundred. As they outnumbered the crew two to one, it was not long before a plan was
laid by the coxswain of the Alert's gig to capture the Essex
and take her to Halifax. By good fortune, however, on the
night the attempt was to be made, the coxswain, pistol in
hand, approached the hammock of Midshipman David Glasgow Farragut to see if he was asleep, and was discovered.
Pretending to be asleep, Farragut lay quiet till the coxswain
was gone, and then crept into the cabin and informed Captain
Porter. Rushing into the berth-deck, Porter shouted "Fire!"
The crew promptly went to the main hatch, where they were
armed, and the attempt was frustrated. But the warning was
not unheeded; and that he might be rid of his dangerous
prisoners, he now transferred them to the Alert, threw over
her guns, and sent the Englishmen to Nova Scotia on parole.
After a further cruise, during which he was chased by the
Shannon and another ship, Captain Porter was forced to put
in for water and stores. With her return every ship in the
navy was in port, and, taking advantage of this, the Secretary
formed such as were on the Atlantic seaboard into three squadrons. To the first, commanded by Rodgers, were assigned the
President, the Congress, and the Wasp. The second, under
Bainbridge, was composed of the Constitution, the Essex, and
the Hornet. To Decatur were intrusted the United States
and the Argus.

The orders of the three commanders bore date October
second, bade them sail without delay, and left to their judgment
where to go and what to do. Thus instructed, Rodgers and
Decatur sailed from Boston on October eighth with such ships
as were ready, but parted company when four days out.
Again ill luck attended Rodgers, who, after chasing the British frigates Nymph and Galatea, and cruising far and wide,
from the Grand Banks to 17° north latitude, returned to Boston on the last day of the year with nine small prizes. But
one, the Jamaica packet Swallow, was of any value, and on
her were two hundred thousand dollars in specie. To the
Wasp, the third ship of Rodgers's squadron, fate was both
kind and cruel. Master-Commandant Jacob Jones, her com-

mander, having received orders to join Rodgers at sea, set sail from the Delaware on October thirteenth, and ran off southward to get in the track of vessels passing from Halifax to Bermuda; and about eleven o'clock on the clear, moonlight night of Saturday, October seventeenth, he suddenly found himself near five strange sail steering eastward. They were part of a convoy of fourteen merchantmen on their way from Honduras to England under the protection of the eighteen-gun brig Frolic, Captain Thomas Whinyates. They had been scattered by a cyclone the day before, and had but just begun to rejoin their convoy. But some of them seeming in the moonlight to be ships of war, the Wasp drew to windward and followed them through the night. At daybreak on Sunday Master-Commandant Jones, perceiving that none but the Frolic was armed, bore down to attack her. She then showed Spanish colors. But the Wasp, undeceived, came on till within sixty yards and hailed, when the Frolic ran up the British ensign and opened with cannon and musketry. The sea, lashed into fury by a two-days' cyclone, was running mountain

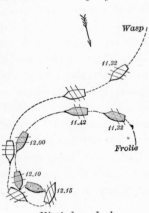

First sloop duel.

high. Wave after wave swept the deck and drenched the sailors. The two ships rolled till the muzzles of their guns dipped in the water. But the crews cheered loudly and the firing became incessant. The Americans discharged their guns as the Wasp went down the wave, so that the shot fell either on the deck or hull of the Frolic. The Englishmen fired as their ship went up the wave, and their shots struck the rigging of the Wasp or were wasted. The result was soon apparent. The slaughter on the Frolic became something terrible. The top-masts and rigging of the Wasp were so cut to pieces that when the last brace was carried away Master-Commandant Jones, fearing the masts would fall and the Frolic escape, determined to board her and end the battle. Wearing ship for this purpose, he ran down and struck her. As the side of the

Wasp rubbed across the bow of the Frolic her jib-boom came in between the main and mizzen rigging, and passed over the heads of Master-Commandant Jones and Lieutenant Biddle. She now lay so fair for raking that orders were given for another broadside. While loading, two of the guns of the Wasp went through the bow ports of the Frolic, and when discharged swept the deck.

At this moment a seaman named John Lang leaped upon a gun, cutlass in hand, and was about to board when he was called down; but he would not come, and, climbing on the bowsprit of the Frolic, was instantly followed by Lieutenant Biddle and the crew. Passing Lang and another sailor on the forecastle, Lieutenant Biddle was amazed to see that, save the man at the wheel and three officers who, as he came forward, threw down their swords at his feet, not a living soul was on the deck. The crew had gone below to avoid the terrible fire of the Wasp. As no one present was able to lower the flag, Lieutenant Biddle leaped into the rigging and hauled the ensign down. The sight which then met him was dreadful. The gun deck was strewn with bodies, and at every roll of the sloop water mingled with blood swept over it, splashing the dead and swirling about the feet of the victors. The berth deck was crowded with dead, wounded, and dying, for of a crew of one hundred and ten men, but twenty were unhurt. On the Wasp the loss was five killed and five wounded.

Master-Commandant Jones now ordered Lieutenant Biddle to take the prize into Charleston. But while he was busy attending the wounded, burying the dead, clearing away the wreck, and preparing the Frolic for the voyage, a strange ship under a press of canvas was seen coming toward him. The stranger was the British seventy-four-gun frigate Poictiers, Captain John Poer Beresford, who, throwing a shot across the Frolic as he sped by, ranged up near the Wasp and forced her to surrender. The two ships were then taken into Bermuda.

Just one week later another ship duel was fought with the usual result. After parting with the squadron of Rodgers, the United States, Captain Decatur, cruised off to the southward and eastward, and on Sunday, October twenty-fifth, when off the Azores, fell in with the British frigate Macedonian, Captain John Surnam Carden, who instantly made chase. But Decatur had no intention of escaping, and the action, like its predecessors, was short and decisive. In ninety minutes the

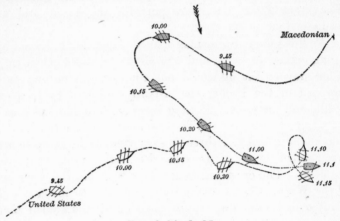

Second ship duel.*

United States had shot away the mizzen-mast of the Macedonian, had dismounted two of her main-deck guns and all but two of the carronades on her engaged side, had killed forty-three and wounded sixty-one of the crew, had put one hundred shot in her hull, and made her a prize. On the United States twelve men were killed or wounded. It was the old story of bull-dog courage, stubborn resistance, and frightful slaughter on the part of the British; and of splendid gunnery and perfect discipline and seamanship on the part of the Americans.

Placing his lieutenant on board the Macedonian as prize master, Decatur ended his cruise, convoyed her home and sent her into Newport, while he passed on to New London, which he reached December fourth. Lieutenant Hamilton, a son of the Secretary of the Navy, was then sent to Washington with letters and the captured flag. Reaching the Capital on the evening of December eighth, he learned that a great naval ball in honor of the capture of the Guerrière and the Alert was in progress at Tomlinson's Hotel, that the flags of these two

---

* Reproduced by permission from Roosevelt's The Naval War of 1812.

vessels were hanging on the wall of the ballroom, and that the President, the Secretaries, and a most distinguished company were there assembled. Hastening to the hotel, he announced himself, and in a few minutes was surrounded by every gentleman at the ball and escorted to the room, where, with cheers and singing, the flag of the Macedonian was hung beside those of the Guerrière and the Alert.*

Naval victories now had become of almost monthly occurrence. In August Hull had taken the Guerrière; in September Porter announced the capture of the Alert; in November came news of the splendid victory of the Wasp over the Frolic; in December Decatur brought the Macedonian into port; in February Bainbridge came in with the colors of the Java; and in March the people read with unspeakable delight of the capture of the Peacock by the Hornet.† Bainbridge, in the Constitution and accompanied by the Hornet, Master-Commandant James Lawrence, left Boston on October twenty-fifth, 1812. His third ship, the Essex, had sailed two days before from the Delaware with orders to seek him at a number of places, and not finding him, to cruise for herself. The first of these places was Porto Praya, and thither accordingly the Constitution and the Hornet went; but not finding the Essex there, nor at Fernando de Noronha, Brainbridge left a letter for Porter at the island and made for the coast of Brazil. It was arranged that while in these waters the Constitution and the Hornet should be known as his Britannic Majesty's frigates Acasta and Morgiana, while Captain Porter was to be known as Sir James Yeo, of the British frigate Southampton. The letter was therefore addressed to Sir James Yeo and left with the governor of Fernando de Noronha, while Bainbridge and Lawrence crossed the equator and put in at San Salvador, on

---

* National Intelligencer, December 10, 1812. A story was long current that the flag was laid, with much ceremony, at Mrs. Madison's feet, and has found its way into an excellent History of the United States under the Constitution. No such incident happened; the story was positively denied by many who were present.

† In the Boston Patriot of April 3, 1813, is a caricature of the fight. England is represented as part Bull, part Peacock. The Hornet has settled on the Bull, and, holding his horns, has thrust its sting through his neck.

the coast of Brazil. There they found the British eighteen-gun sloop-of-war Bonne Citoyenne, Captain Pitt Barnaby Greene, bound to England with half a million pounds in specie. The Hornet promptly challenged her, Lawrence pledging his honor that neither the Constitution nor any other American ship should interfere. But Captain Greene refused to fight. He was sure, he said, that if such a duel took place the victory would go to the sloop he had the honor to command, and he was equally sure that when it did Captain Bainbridge would not so far swerve from the duty he owed his country as to stand by and see a ship of his squadron fall into the hands of an enemy. To remove this doubt Bainbridge left the Hornet. But still Captain Greene would not come out, and finding him fixed in this determination the Constitution went on down the coast of Brazil, leaving the Hornet to blockade the enemy. About nine on the morning of De-

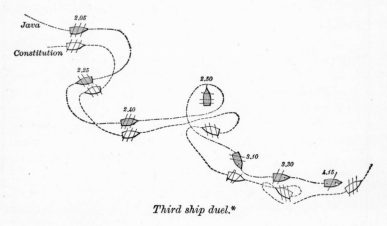

Third ship duel.*

cember twenty-ninth, when some thirty miles off shore, two strange sail were seen to windward. One was his Britannic Majesty's frigate Java, Captain Henry Lambert; the other was an American merchantman of which she had made prize. Recognizing the stranger as an enemy, the Constitution at once put to sea to draw her off a neutral coast. The Java

---

* Reproduced by permission from Roosevelt's The Naval War of 1812.

promptly followed, and, gaining on the Constitution, the fighting began at long range about two in the afternoon.   For
twenty-five minutes the two ran on side by side, giving and
taking a tremendous fire, when they passed each other on
opposite tacks, and in the course of manœuvring to get the
weather-gage a shot from the Java carried away the wheel
of the Constitution.   The mishap was most serious, and the
enemy, promptly taking advantage of it, ran across the stern
of the Constitution, poured in a broadside, luffed and again
raked her, but at too great a distance to do much harm.   This,
however, was enough for Captain Bainbridge, who, determined

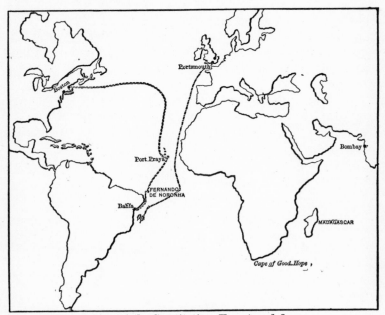

Cruises of the Constitution, Hornet, and Java.

to come to close quarters at any hazard, set his sails and boldly
headed for the Java.   He might easily have been raked from
stem to stern; but he was not, and when within short range
opened so terrible a fire that in a few minutes the jib-boom
and the bowsprit of the Java were shot away and the running
rigging almost destroyed.   Seizing this advantage and favored
by the dense cloud of smoke that hung over the ships, the

Constitution now wore without the enemy seeing the manœuvre till it was almost completed, when he attempted to imitate
it.   But he could not, and Bainbridge, taking a position off
the bow of the Java, swept her deck and shot away one by
one her foremast, main top-mast, and spanker boom.   The
slaughter on the Java at this time was terrible; but the crew
fought on, cheering lustily, till their commander was shot
down, and the frigate, riddled and dismantled, lay on the water
a wreck full of dead and wounded men, when they ceased
firing.   The Constitution thereupon drew off to repair damages, and while so engaged the Englishmen cleared away the
wreck of the masts from the guns, rigged a square sail to the
remains of the foremast, nailed a flag to the stump of the
mizzen-mast, and awaited another attack.   But when the Constitution came on to renew the fight, the Java struck.   Of her
crew, forty-eight had been killed and one hundred and two
wounded.

Taking out the prisoners and the baggage, Bainbridge destroyed the Java and made sail for San Salvador, where he
paroled the Englishmen and, leaving the Hornet still block-

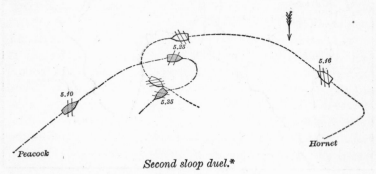

*Second sloop duel.**

ading the Bonne Citoyenne, set off for Boston.   During three
weeks the Hornet remained at her post.   Meanwhile Captain
Greene, knowing that he could not beat her, despatched a note
by a Portuguese fisherman to the commander of the seventy-
four-gun ship of the line Montagu, then at Rio de Janeiro, begging him to come and drive the Hornet away.   The Montagu

---

* Reproduced by permission from Roosevelt's The Naval War of 1812.

accordingly came, and came so suddenly that the Hornet was forced to run into the harbor to escape capture. But her stay was short, for that same night she slipped out in the darkness, and, running northeast, spent a month cruising off the coast and making prizes. About the close of February, happening to be off the mouth of the Demerara river, she fell in with the Peacock, Captain William Peake. The two ships stood for each other, and in a few moments the old story was repeated. The gunnery of the Peacock was bad; the gunnery of the Hornet was excellent, and just fourteen minutes from the firing of the first gun the Peacock was a shattered prize, with her ensign flying union down in the fore rigging as a signal of distress. She was sinking, and though everything was done to save her, though her guns were thrown over, her shot-holes plugged, the pumps worked, and even bailing resorted to, she went down suddenly, carrying with her nine of her own crew and three of the Hornet's, who were rummaging below. The Hornet was now so crowded with people and so short of water that Master-Commandant Lawrence made for home, ran through the West Indies, reached Holmes's Hole in Martha's Vineyard in safety, and came by way of Long Island Sound to New York.

The return of Bainbridge and Lawrence was greeted all over the land with salutes, processions, dinners, addresses of congratulation, votes of thanks, swords, medals, prize money, promotions—with every mark, in short, of the love and pride of a grateful people. The popular joy was not unreasonable, for never since England had ships had such a defeat been inflicted on her navy. As such she felt it keenly, and to the Americans of that time few things were more diverting than her attempts to explain it. For years past the armed vessels of the United States had been to Englishmen a never-ending theme of derision and contempt. Canning had described them as "a few fir-built things with bits of striped bunting at their mast-heads." The press never mentioned them, the people never spoke of them, save as "cock-boats." No merchantman ever returned from the West Indies but had a story to tell of the insolence of British naval captains and of their contempt for the "gridiron flag"; nor did a people who tamely submitted to impressment and search, and met the outrages of the Leander and the Cambrian, the Driver and the Leopard, with proclamations and embargoes, acts of non-intercourse and acts of non-importation, deserve any better treatment. The Little Belt, a corvette of twenty guns, attacking the President, a frigate of forty-four guns ; Dacres sending in his challenge defying any frigate of the United States to come out and fight him, were but feeble expressions of the estimation in which British seamen held the navy of the United States. Even when war actually began there was not a man in England who did not doom that navy to destruction within a month.   But when six months had passed, and the ships, still afloat, were busy inflicting on England a series of reverses without a parallel in her annals, when frigate after frigate had struck to the bit of striped bunting, it became clear to all the world that England had committed the most foolish, the most ruinous of all mistakes—that she had despised the enemy. To her the loss of five ships was not a matter of the slightest moment ; but the loss of her naval prestige which the destruction of these five ships produced was a matter of the very highest moment to the whole civilized world.   Never since the days of the contest in the Valley of Elah had there been a finer illustration of the everlasting truth that the race is not to the swift, nor the battle to the strong, but to him who by diligence earns it.   In the course of twenty years England had met and destroyed the navies of every maritime power in Europe.   The battle of Copenhagen, the battle of the Nile, the battle of Trafalgar, had given her a reputation for invincibility which a hundred smaller fights served but to justify.   But now, on a sudden, the captains of a people concerning whom the nations of Europe knew absolutely nothing had five times humbled her flag on the sea, and had demonstrated that her supremacy could not endure one hour longer than she continued to deserve it.   And this is the lasting value of the victories of Hull and Decatur, Bainbridge, Lawrence, and Jones.

Had Englishmen attributed their defeats to lack of discipline, to ignorance of gunnery, to the general demoralization of their sailors produced by uniform success, they would have done no more than trace back effects to their causes. But they did not, and nothing was more diverting to Americans than the attempts of the English press to explain the defeats. " The loss of a single frigate by us," said the London Times, referring to the Guerrière, " when we consider how the other navies of the world have been treated, is but a small matter. When viewed as a part of the British navy it is nothing ; yet it has cast a gloom over the city which it is painful to see. The superior weight of metal thrown by the Constitution, the greater number of men, the loss of the mizzen-mast at the very beginning of the action, were all urged. But people look only at the triumph of the Americans—a triumph small enough and of no importance, save as a reason for a rigorous scrutiny of the behavior of those responsible for it."* " This victory," said the London Star, " will conjure up a phantom of an American navy to frighten the tenants of the nursery, and will tend to procrastinate the war. America must be beaten into submission, and she will be. Her militia and her regulars are already disposed of. Her navy is bespoke by our cruisers, and will all be sent home to Britain in the spring."† This prediction, however, had scarcely been made when London heard with dismay of the loss of the Macedonian, and the press a second time attempted to explain. Those huge American frigates, the public were now assured, were ships of the line in disguise. They were fully equal to a British seventy-four. No wonder, then, that the Guerrière, whose masts were rotten, and the Macedonian, which was not fully manned, were forced to strike. It was no disgrace whatever for the largest British frigates to shun an engagement with these dangerous nondescripts. Captain Carden, it was said, had done his duty, and were it not that superficial people had so long been in the habit of boasting of the invincibility of the British seaman, nobody would have thought it strange that a vessel of superior force should capture an inferior foe. The Americans came of the same stock and were made of the same stuff as the British. They were equally active and bold, and, give them a trifling superiority, they would use it just as Englishmen would do.

---

* London Times, October 7, 1812. † London Star, December 15, 1812,

There was no disgrace, therefore, in the matter, except indeed such as attached to the Government for not providing vessels of such force as was necessary to meet the enemy.* "How," said the Courier, "is the Government to blame? It is true that the American carried more men and threw a heavier broadside. But have not English sailors been accustomed to contend against superior force and to conquer? The truth is, nobody ever supposed that one of our best frigates would not be a match for the American." †

When the Java struck, the cry of superior force could no longer be uttered with decency, for her decks were crowded with men on their way to join the crews of other ships. The Quebec Mercury ventured to cite the victory as evidence that British seamen were too brave; that their courage was greater than their physical powers, and impelled them to boldly meet and fight vessels much superior to them in every way. But no such language was heard in England. "This new defeat," said one journal, "calls for serious reflection—all the more serious when we put with it the fact that Lloyd's list shows five hundred British merchantmen taken by the Americans in seven months. Five hundred merchantmen and three frigates! Can this be true? Will the English people read this unmoved? Any man who foretold such disasters this day last year would have been treated as a madman or a traitor. He would have been told that ere seven months had gone by the American flag would have been swept from the ocean, the American navy destroyed, and the maritime arsenals of the United States reduced to ashes. Yet not one of the American frigates has struck. They leave their ports when they choose and return when it suits their convenience. They cross the Atlantic, they visit the West Indies, they come to the chops of the Channel, they parade along the coast of South America. Nothing chases them; nothing intercepts them—nay, nothing engages them but to yield in triumph." ‡ Smarting under these repeated defeats, the press now turned savagely on the Admiralty. It was ignorance and folly in fitting out the ships; it was want of plan and energy in naval administration that

---

* Examiner, January 8, 1813.   † Courier, December 26, 1812.   ‡ The Pilot.

had caused this series of reverses. The Admiralty denied each one of these charges; asserted that it had been fully prepared for war, and declared that when hostilities began the English ships on the American station were to the American ships in the ratio of eighty-five to fourteen. Yet the criticism was not without effect, and the Admiralty, having ordered the sailors on his Majesty's ships to be exercised at least once a day with the great guns, made vigorous preparations for the blockade of the American coast.

But there was in the British service one captain to whom neither the abuse of the press nor the caution of the Admiralty was applicable. Captain Philip Bowes Vere Broke, of his Majesty's frigate Shannon, was all that an officer ought to be, and had brought his crew to a state of proficiency in the use of the broadsword, pike, musket, and great guns which was most unusual in the British navy. To his lot it fell in the spring of 1813 to guard the coast east of Cape Cod with the Shannon and the Tenedos, and blockade the four American frigates Congress, President, Chesapeake, and Constitution, then in the harbor of Boston. But blockading was too tame a duty, and more than once he endeavored to persuade some one of them to come out and fight. For a time he was not successful, and Commodore Rodgers, declining the challenge, ran out on the night of April thirteenth with the President and Congress. Greatly disappointed, Broke thereupon sent away the Tenedos, and formally challenged Lawrence to meet him in the Chesapeake.

James Lawrence was a native of New Jersey, where he was born in 1781. At the age of seventeen, in the midst of the excitement produced by the X. Y. Z. despatches, he entered the navy then being formed, and saw service in the West Indies during the *quasi* French War, in the Mediterranean during the Tripolitan War, and by 1810 had reached the grade of commander. With this rank he had sailed in the Vixen, the Wasp, the Argus, and the Hornet, in which he fought that ever-memorable duel with the Peacock. For this signal victory he was promptly rewarded with command of the Chesapeake, whose old captain was too ill to go to sea. From the day when she struck to the Leopard the Chesapeake

had been looked on by both officers and men as a most un-
lucky ship, a superstition which no event in her career ever
tended to dispel.   On her return to port, April ninth, after an
unsuccessful cruise, her old crew left her, to seek for better
fortune in some more lucky ship, and such new men as could
be secured had been enlisted to fill their places.   Some were
British, a few were Portuguese ; others had never yet seen
service on an armed ship.   All were unknown to each other
and to their officers, and, having never been to sea together,
they were without discipline or training.   Indeed, it was not
till the anchor was about to be weighed that the last draft
came aboard, and these still had their hammocks and bags
stowed in the boats that brought them when the Chesapeake
surrendered.

The Shannon, on the other hand, was commanded by an
officer as courageous, as skilful, and as energetic as Lawrence,
and manned by a well-disciplined and well-practised crew.
Every day in the forenoon the men were exercised at training the guns, and in the afternoon in the use of the broadsword, the musket, and the pike.   Twice each week the crew
fired at targets with great guns and musketry, and on such
occasions the man who hit the bull's-eye received a pound of
tobacco.   At times Broke would order a cask thrown overboard and then suddenly command some particular gun to be
manned to sink it, a practice more than once witnessed by the
American officers at the Charlestown Navy Yard.   Save in
discipline and number of men (for the Chesapeake had forty-
nine more than the Shannon), the two frigates were not ill
matched, as in length, in breadth of beam, in guns, and weight
of metal they were almost exactly equal.

Considering the Chesapeake to be a fair match for the
Shannon, Broke had been most anxious to meet her.   Accordingly, on June first, seeing the Chesapeake riding at anchor
below Fort Independence as if waiting to put to sea, Broke
ran into the harbor and raised his flag.   Lawrence immediately
fired a gun and displayed his colors, mustered his crew, told
them he intended to fight, and when the tide turned went
down the harbor under a press of sail.

News of the coming duel spread fast and wide, and long

before Lawrence was under way thousands of people were hurrying toward every point likely to afford a view. The bay was covered with boats. Hundreds stood on Blue Hill and on the heights of Malden. Hundreds more went down to Nahant, Cohasset, and Scituate. Lynn, Salem, and Marblehead were full of strangers eager to see the fight.* All were disappointed, for the Chesapeake, having rounded the Boston Light, bore off to the eastward, and with the Shannon was soon lost to sight. The guns were heard, but almost three weeks passed before it was finally known how the fight ended. The pilot who left the Chesapeake at five in the afternoon reported to Commodore Bainbridge that the firing began at six ; that in twelve minutes both ships were laying alongside each other as if for boarding ; that at this moment a dreadful explosion occurred on the Chesapeake, and that when the smoke had blown away the British flag was seen flying over the American. His story was strictly true. But, though confirmed by a Cape Ann fishing boat and by some gentlemen who claimed to have been within two miles of the frigates in a packet, the people could not believe it. Even when a boat belonging to the Chesapeake was picked up at sea, and when word came from Bangor that the Tenedos had brought-to an American coaster and told the captain that the Chesapeake was a prize and Lawrence buried at Halifax, the public refused to give up hope. All over the country the greatest anxiety prevailed. Everywhere the post-offices were thronged ; everywhere travellers by stage were beset for information. In many places the citizens day after day would ride out for miles on the highway to meet the mail in hopes of getting news. Some earnestly urged that a flag of truce be sent to Halifax to find out what really had happened. At last, June eighteenth, Halifax newspapers with a long account of the funeral honors paid to Lawrence and Ludlow reached Boston, and all doubt was removed.

It then appeared that after passing the light-house at one o'clock the Chesapeake followed her enemy till five, when the Shannon luffed and waited for her to come up. The wind blowing fresh from the west, Lawrence might easily have

---

* Columbian Centinel, June 2, 1813.

chosen his position.   But he threw away this advantage, came
down on the Shannon's quarter, luffed, and ranged up some

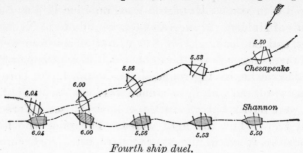

Fourth ship duel.

fifty yards from her starboard side.   At ten minutes before
six the firing began, and for seven minutes the frigates ran on
side by side.   Then, some shot from the Shannon having crippled the sails of the Chesapeake, she came up into the wind
and was taken aback, and drifted slowly stern foremost toward
the enemy.   Every gun on the Shannon's broadside swept her
from stem to stern.   Man after man was shot down at the
wheel.   A hand grenade blew up the arms chest, and the stern
of the Chesapeake, drifting helplessly, struck the Shannon
amidships.   A fluke of the Shannon's anchor caught in a port
of the Chesapeake.   A boatswain rushed forward to lash the
ships, and Broke, calling up his boarders, stepped on the muzzle
of one of the Chesapeake's guns and leaped over the bulwark to
her quarter-deck.   Just at this moment Captain Lawrence fell,
mortally wounded, and was carried below, crying out, "Don't
give up the ship!"   "Keep the guns going!"   "Fight her till
she sinks!"   Obedient to his orders, a few men on the quarter-deck made a desperate resistance.   In all, some fifty men
followed Broke, and, as they came forward, not a live man
was on the quarter-deck and not an officer on the spar-deck.
Lawrence and Ludlow, his first lieutenant, had been mortally
wounded and carried to the cockpit.   The second lieutenant
was stationed below.   The third lieutenant fled; whereupon
the foreigners and the raw sailors, seeing the British on the
spar-deck, deserted their quarters, and a Portuguese boatswain
having removed the gratings of the berth-deck the men rushed
headlong down the after-ladders.   Then was it that Lawrence,

hearing the men come down, cried out repeatedly, "Don't give up the ship! Blow her up!" But he was helpless. Broke was in possession of the spar-deck. Still the English captain might have been beaten, for at this moment the two frigates parted, leaving fifty Englishmen on the Chesapeake's deck. Seeing this, a few Americans of spirit made a desperate attack, in the course of which Broke almost lost his life. But resistance was useless. The guns ceased firing, the flag came down, and without any formal surrender the Chesapeake passed into British hands for the second time, and was taken into Halifax a prize. There Lawrence and Ludlow, having died of their wounds on the way in, were buried with military honors on the sixth of June. Their bodies were not, however, destined to rest long in foreign soil. Deeply as their countrymen felt the humiliation of the defeat, they did not forget the patriotism, the devotion, the inspiriting death of Lawrence. They put on mourning. They made of the injunction "Don't give up the ship!" a war cry which has never since been forgotten, and ten of them, all masters of vessels, under the lead of George Crowninshield, Jr., having obtained a flag of truce, brought back the bodies of Lawrence and Ludlow a few weeks later to Salem, whence they were carried by land to New York city and laid with all the honors of war in the yard of Trinity Church.

From Halifax news of the capture was carried to England by a brig which reached Plymouth on July seventh, and the next night the glad tidings were announced in Parliament, and received with boundless joy. So important was the victory in English eyes that the Tower guns were fired, and in time Captain Broke was made a baronet and a knight commander of the Bath, and received from London a sword and the freedom of the city. Concerning the fate of the frigate, whose history is bound up with so much that is shameful and so much that is heroic in our annals, it is worth while to recall that she was taken to England, and in 1820 was condemned and sold. Neither our Government nor our people had patriotism enough to buy her, and her shot-marked, blood-stained timbers were bought by a miller of Wickham, Hants, and were used to build a flour-mill, which is still standing.

Eight weeks after the mortal remains of Lawrence and Ludlow were placed in a common grave at Halifax, one of the pall-bearers on that sad occasion was buried side by side with an American officer at Portland, off whose harbor they had fought and perished. The whole coast of New Hampshire and Maine had yet escaped blockade. Every bay and harbor was, in consequence, alive with British privateers and smugglers engaged in trade with the British Provinces. To stop this trade the armed brig Enterprise had been ordered there to do duty as a revenue cutter. When she took part in the war with Tripoli she was a schooner carrying twelve guns and sixty men, but she had since been altered into a brig and given sixteen guns and one hundred and two men. Her commander was William Burrows, a young man of twenty-eight. He had just chased a suspicious schooner into Portland and was on his way to sea, when he espied* a brig getting under way near Penguin Point. She proved to be the English brig Boxer, Captain Samuel Blythe, carrying fourteen guns and sixty-six men. She was therefore no match for the Enterprise, and might well have declined a battle. But her commander, setting three English ensigns, ordered the colors nailed to the mast with the remark that they should never be struck while he had life in his body, and came on. The day was very calm, and so much time was spent in manœuvring that it was past

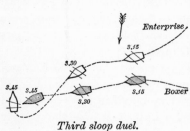

Third sloop duel.

three in the afternoon when the two crews, cheering loudly, exchanged broadsides within short pistol range of each other. Both commanders fell. Blythe was almost cut in two and died instantly. Burrows was mortally wounded and lay on the deck, crying out that the colors must never be struck. There was little danger of such a disaster, for the Enterprise, crossing the bow of the Boxer, raked the enemy till he surrendered. Though the Boxer was badly damaged, she was

---

* September 5, 1813.

brought to Portland. There the two commanders, wrapped in the flags they had so well defended, were borne with military honors to a grave in the Eastern Cemetery, which overlooks the bay.

The people were still mourning the loss of Lawrence and Burrows when they heard with renewed grief that the name of Master-Commandant Allen had been added to the list of dead, and the name of the Argus to the list of British captures.

William Henry Allen was born in Rhode Island in 1784, entered the navy in 1800, served under Bainbridge, Rodgers, Barron, and Decatur, and bore a part in some of the most memorable events in the sea annals of our country. As third officer of the Chesapeake he was present on that shameful day in 1807 when her flag was struck to the Leopard, and was the officer who, seizing a live coal from the cook's galley, held it in his fingers and fired the only gun discharged against the British. As first lieutenant of the United States he contributed not a little to that fine gunnery which overcame the Macedonian, and enjoyed the glory of bringing the prize to port. For these services he was promoted to the command of the gun brig Argus, and toward the middle of June, 1813, set sail for France with William Harris Crawford, the newly appointed Minister, on board. Having landed Crawford at L'Orient, the Argus made for the British Channel, cruised there a while, then passed around Land's End and took her station in the Irish Channel off the Welsh coast. The depredation which Allen there committed on English commerce was enormous. In a month twenty-seven ships were taken and burned. On board of one, according to the English journals, was a cargo of Irish linen worth one hundred thousand pounds. Never since the days when John Paul Jones and Gustavus Connyngham swept the Channel had the ship-owners and the underwriters of London been so alarmed. But the Admiralty came promptly to their aid, and the gun brig Pelican, Captain John Fordyce Maples, and the frigate Leonidas were soon in pursuit of the Argus. Now it so happened that on the night of August thirteenth Allen fell in with and burned a brig laden with wine from Oporto, and that the red glare was visible from the deck of the Pelican. Guided by the light, she came down under a press of canvas, and about six in the morning overtook the Argus. The battle began at once. For a time the Argus, having the best position, raked the Pelican at short range, but her guns were badly served and worse

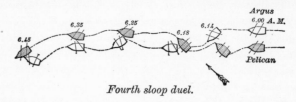

Fourth sloop duel.

aimed, and the fire did scarcely any damage. The gunnery of the Pelican, however, was excellent, and in twenty minutes the Argus was a helpless wreck. Taking advantage of this, the British captain chose a new position, and for twenty minutes more raked her without receiving one cannon shot in return. Then, just as boarders came over the bow, her flag was lowered. That so able a captain as Allen should have been beaten at gunnery at first seemed strange; for to him is to be ascribed the high degree of excellence reached by the crew of the United States. His lieutenant attributed defeat to fatigue, for the labors of three weeks had well-nigh worn out the crew. But there were not wanting those who declared that Oporto wine smuggled on board had much to do with the bad gunnery and the feeble defence, and that the crew of the Argus were too drunk, rather than too tired, to fight. How this might be Allen never lived to explain. The first broadside from the Pelican carried off his left leg, and, greatly weakened by the loss of blood, he was carried to the Mill Prison at Plymouth, where he died. His enemies admired his gallantry and buried him with all the honors of war.* His countrymen did not forget him, and in New York city there is to this day a thoroughfare which bears the name of Allen Street in his honor.

To a few despondent Federalists the loss of the Chesapeake and the Argus seemed to mark the end of American victories on the ocean. It was idle, according to them, to contend

---

* The True American, October 13, 1813.

further. Great Britain was mistress of the sea. The fate
which overtook all who contended with her on that element
had in our case been singularly delayed ; yet the hour would
surely come—nay, was at hand—when, putting forth her
enormous power, she would sweep our navy from the ocean
and lay our coast towns under contribution, if not in ashes.
To some extent the prediction seemed to have been accomplished. Of the gallant little navy, which a year before had
filled the world with the fame of its victories, scarcely a
vestige now remained upon the sea. The Chesapeake was
gone, the Wasp, the Argus, the Nautilus, the Vixen, were
captured ; the Constellation was shut in Chesapeake Bay ;
the United States and the Macedonian were blockaded at New
London ; the Adams and the Constitution were undergoing
repairs. On the day the Chesapeake struck to the Shannon,
the only frigates that carried our flag on the seas were the
President, the Essex, and the Congress.

No such despondency affected the people. To them the
loss of the brigs and the Chesapeake was no more than the
fortune of war ; and with an energy worthy of the pride the
people felt in their navy, the Government began at once to
repair losses. The keels of new frigates were laid down,
three fine sloops of war intended to supply the places of the
captured brigs were soon on the stocks, and early in the new
year (1814) another Wasp and another Frolic were at sea.
The new Argus was burned when Washington fell into British
hands ; but her place was well filled by the Peacock.

Profiting by the experience of the brigs, these new sloops
were large enough and strong enough to fight anything under
the smaller British frigates. They were rigged as ships, carried a crew of one hundred and sixty men, were armed with
twenty thirty-two-pound carronades and two long eighteen-
pounders, and threw at a broadside three hundred and thirty-
eight pounds of metal. Built to fight and run, they were expected to break the blockade with ease, and did not disappoint
the expectation. Commanded by daring officers, manned by
skilful sailors, no better opportunity than a dark night or a
heavy gale was wanted for making the attempt. Success
attended them, and once in the open they became the most

dreaded of commerce destroyers. Along the northern coast
the intense cold and heavy winter storms driving the British
cruisers off the shore, made the blockade far from rigorous
and easy to get through.

First to go was the frigate President. She ran out from
Portsmouth in December, 1813, and after an uneventful and
profitless cruise entered New York in February, 1814, and
there remained blockaded for the rest of the year. Next to
go was the corvette Adams. Originally a frigate, the Adams
had been cut down to a sloop of war at the Washington navy
yard, and, dropping down to Lynnhaven Bay, slipped by the
blockading fleet one dark night in January, 1814, and made
for the track of British merchantmen. For six months she
hung upon the Southern coast in search of Indiamen and the
Jamaica convoy ; but, meeting with little success, crossed the
Atlantic, cruised along the Irish coast, and, after many narrow
escapes and many hot pur-
suits, started for home. When
off the coast of Maine, in a
dense fog, she ran on the Isle
au Haut, and with great difficulty made the Penobscot
river, and in time was burned
there, to save her from capture by the British.

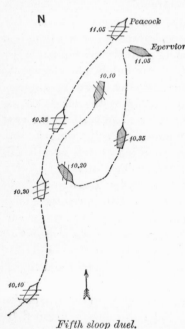

Fifth sloop duel.

The third cruiser to run
the blockade was the new
sloop-of-war Frolic. She had
been built at Boston, and,
quitting that port in February, fell a prey to the British
frigate Orpheus, when off
Matanzas, in April. Mean-
while the Peacock, Captain
Lewis Warrington, finding
the blockade growing lax, put
to sea from New York in
March, and ran down the coast to Florida, where, when off
the Indian river inlet, she made out three sail under convoy

of a brig of war. They proved to be merchantmen, on their way from Havana to Bermuda, guarded by the eighteen-gun brig Epervier. She was in no sense a match for the Peacock; but her captain brought her gallantly into action, and the two were soon at close range. For an hour they ran on side by side before the enemy struck and ended the duel in the old way. The fire of the Epervier was wild and reckless. The gunnery of the Peacock was steady and well aimed. The Epervier, therefore, was hulled forty-five times, had her masts and rigging badly cut, her guns dislodged, and her deck turned into a shambles. The Peacock was not once struck in the hull, and had but two of her crew slightly injured. The Epervier had twenty-three men killed and one hundred and twenty-eight wounded. So complete was the defeat that the British Admiralty did not dare to make the facts public. Captain Warrington brought his prize into Savannah, and after another cruise to the Faroe Islands and the Canaries ran into New York in October, having lost but one man of the crew, and having made fourteen prizes besides the Epervier.

More remarkable and more tragic was the cruise of the Wasp. She sailed for Portsmouth on the first of May, under the command of Johnston Blakely, and, making for the chops of the British Channel, began to repeat the ravages of the Argus by burning and sinking every British merchantman she met. While so engaged, on the morning of June twenty-eighth, the man-of-war brig Reindeer, Captain William Manners, bore down on her. But the enemy was no match for the American, either in armament, in gunnery, or in men, and after nineteen minutes of desperate fighting the duel

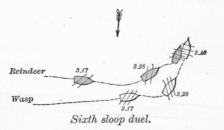

Sixth sloop duel.

was over and the British flag hauled down. Again the prize was literally shot to pieces and was blown up. But the Wasp did not escape unhurt. Six round shot and plenty of grape were in her hull. Her foremast was shot through and her rigging much cut.   Twice the British had tried to board her, and in repelling them her crew had suffered badly.*   Putting some of his prisoners on a neutral that passed by, Blakely carried the rest to L'Orient, refitted, and late in August went to sea.

On September first, when four days out, he encountered a convoy of ten sails in charge of a seventy-four-gun frigate, and, in spite of her, cut out a ship laden with guns and military stores.   On attempting to make prize of another he was driven away by the frigate, and while cruising along about half-past six in the evening descried four sail, two off the larboard and two off the weather bow.   They were the three British ships Castilian, Avon, and Tartarus, in hot pursuit of a privateer schooner. Blakely selected one, which proved to be the Avon, bore down upon her, and about half-past nine, having the chase directly under the Wasp's lea-bow, he hailed, and, receiving no answer, threw a shot across the enemy.   A broadside was returned, and a duel at short pistol range began in the darkness and continued for an hour as the two, under full sail, ran side by side

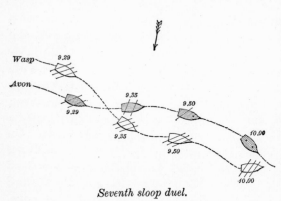

Seventh sloop duel.

before a strong wind.   At half-past ten the Avon struck. She had five guns dismounted and forty men dead or wounded, seven feet of water in her hold, her magazine flooded, and her masts and rigging well-nigh destroyed.   Yet she was not to be captured ; for, as Blakely was about to lower a boat to take possession of the enemy, a sail loomed up in the darkness and the crew once more went to quarters.   The heavy firing led the

---

* Eleven killed and 15 wounded.   The Reindeer lost 33 killed and 34 wounded in a crew of 118.

captain of the Castilian to abandon the chase, and, making all possible sail in the direction of the cannonading, he came on the scene just as the Avon surrendered. Almost immediately a second sail was seen, whereupon the Wasp, unable to cope with two, ran off before the wind. The Castilian pursued, came close up, fired into the Wasp, and was about to begin a new battle when signals of distress recalled her to the Avon. Her return was most timely, for, it is said, all the wounded had not been removed when the battered ship filled and sank.

Blakely now sailed to Madeira, where, later in September, he made prize of the brig Atlanta, which reached Savannah in safety. On October ninth the Wasp spoke a Swedish brig near the Cape de Verde Islands, and then disappeared forever. Since that day no piece, no sign, no token of her has ever been seen by man. What became of her no one knows; but it is likely that somewhere in the Atlantic Blakely and his gallant crew found a grave.

Of three smaller vessels, called the Siren, the Rattlesnake, and the Enterprise, two had by this time been captured, and the third, the Enterprise, had returned to port. The disappearance of the Wasp, therefore, left the United States without a war ship of any kind at sea, for even the Essex was then in British hands. She entered the Delaware in September, 1812, and after a short stay was ordered to join the Constitution and the Hornet and cruise in the Indian Ocean. On October twenty-eighth, 1812, accordingly, she passed the Capes of the Delaware, and with Captain David Porter in command put to sea never to return. For a while she ran off eastward to get in the track of British merchantmen, but finding none, went into Porto Praya. This was one of the places assigned for meeting the Constitution, but as she was not there, the Essex started for Fernando de Noronha, and in the afternoon of December twelfth, when a little south of the equator, sighted and after a long chase captured the English packet Nocton, of ten guns and thirty-one men, bound to Falmouth. The men were taken out, a prize crew put on board, and the prize sent to the nearest American port; but on the way she was retaken by the Belvidera.

Meantime the Essex, holding her course, reached Fernando

de Noronha, where Porter, disguising his ship as a merchantman
from London, sent Lieutenant John Downes ashore to report
to the Governor.   When he returned the lieutenant brought
word that the British frigate Acasta and gun-sloop-of-war
Morgiana had stopped there two weeks before, and had left a
letter addressed to Sir James Yeo, of the British frigate Southampton.   Convinced that the Acasta and the Morgiana were
the Constitution and the Hornet, Captain Porter again sent the
lieutenant ashore with a present and an offer to forward the
letter from Rio.   The letter was delivered, and Porter, holding

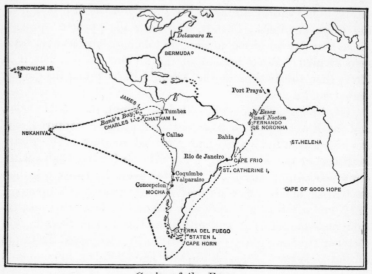

Cruise of the Essex.

it to the flame of a candle, saw this message, written in sym-
pathetic ink, become visible : " I am bound off Bahia, thence
off Cape Frio, where I intend to cruise till the first of January.
Go off Cape Frio, to the northward of Rio de Janeiro, and
keep a lookout for me."

 To Cape Frio the Essex accordingly went, and after cruising there a while started up the coast in pursuit of a convoy.
On the way Porter heard from a Portuguese that the Constitution and the Hornet had been off Bahia, and, on putting
into the island of St. Catherine, he learned that the Hornet

had been driven into Bahia by the Montagu and had gone to sea.

He was now free to choose his own course, and turning southward, made for Cape Horn, intending to double it, enter the Pacific, and destroy the British whalers. The season for doubling the Cape had long gone by, but Porter pushed fearlessly on, meeting with nothing of consequence till just as the Cape was sighted, when bad weather set in. Gale followed gale with such fury that more than once the ship seemed doomed to destruction. On one occasion a wave of enormous height broke over the Essex and all but wrecked her. But she came safely through the perils of the deep and early in March anchored off the island of Mocha. After laying in a supply of hog's meat and horse flesh, she proceeded to Valparaiso and remained five days. When again at sea she fell in with an American ship whose master reported that two American whalers had been captured off Coquimbo. Thither Porter went, and, about eight o'clock on the evening of March twenty-sixth, sighted a ship which, as he came near, showed Spanish colors. The Essex raised the English flag, and the stranger, bearing down, fired a gun and despatched an armed boat, which Porter sent back with orders for the ship to come under his lee, and when she did so ran out his guns and called on her to strike. She was a Peruvian cruiser named the Nereyda, and as she admitted having captured the American whalers, her guns, spars, and ammunition were thrown overboard before she was suffered to depart.

Porter now seized the opportunity as he sailed northward up the coast in search of whalers, to paint and trim his ship in such wise that she did not look unlike a Spanish merchantman, and while so engaged chased and captured a vessel named the Barclay, standing for the port of Callao. After cruising with her off Callao and meeting no more ships, he went with his prize to the island of Chatham, one of the Galapagos group, and sailed from island to island till April twenty-ninth, when the lookout sighted three sail, which when captured proved to be the British whaler Montezuma, a fine ship carrying fourteen hundred barrels of spermaceti oil, the Georgiana, a large whaler pierced for eighteen guns and carrying six; and the Policy, likewise a whaler, carrying ten guns. The Georgiana was so fine a ship that Porter took the guns from the Policy, mounted them on her deck, sent Lieutenant John Downes and a crew of forty-one men on board, raised and saluted the American flag, and transformed her, in a few hours, from a whaler to a cruiser. His squadron now numbered four vessels, and by their aid he ran down and captured, on May twenty-ninth, the British letter of marque Atlantic, carrying eight guns. Scarcely was this done when another sail was sighted, another chase begun, and another British letter of marque, the Greenwich, was a prize. Both were full of cordage, canvas, paint, tar, and fresh provisions, which were most acceptable. After this addition the fleet comprised the Essex, the Georgiana, the Greenwich, the Atlantic, the Montezuma, all armed, and the Policy and the Barclay unarmed,* seven ships in all, mounting eighty guns, carrying three hundred and forty men and eighty prisoners, and fully provided with naval stores taken from the enemy. The prisoners and the unarmed ships were so great an encumbrance that Porter made for a neutral harbor, and in June anchored in the river Tumbez. Meantime Lieutenant Downes was sent cruising in the Georgiana, and so well did he profit by experience that in a little while he was master of the Catherine, the Rose, and the Hector, mounting all told twenty-seven guns and carrying seventy-five men. The lieutenant in his turn was overburdened with prisoners, and converting the Rose into a cartel, he threw over her guns, destroyed her cargo, put the prisoners on board, and sent her to St. Helena, while he sailed for Tumbez.

Such conduct so richly deserved a reward that Porter raised

*	Guns.	Men.
Essex....................................	46	245
Georgiana...............................	16	42
Greenwich...............................	10	14
Atlantic	6	12
Montezuma..............................	2	10
	80	323
Barclay.................................	..	7
Policy..................................	..	10
	..	340

the armament of the Atlantic to twenty guns, named her Essex Junior, and after promoting Lieutenant Downes to the rank of master commandant, gave him command. On June thirtieth the squadron, thus reorganized, stood out to sea, where the ships soon parted. Essex Junior was sent to escort the Hector, Catherine, Montezuma, Policy, and Barclay to Valparaiso, and cruise till September. The Essex, the Greenwich, and the Georgiana sailed for the Galapagos, and when off Banks Bay sighted three strange sail. The Essex gave chase to one, which when captured proved to be the Charlton, of eight guns. The Georgiana went after the second, but the third, in place of being chased, stood for the Greenwich. She, however, taking some men from the Georgiana, bore down on her enemy, and after a few broadsides forced the Seringapatam, of fourteen guns and forty men to strike. The Essex made prize of the third, called the New Zealander. As these new captures could not be manned without reducing the crew of the Essex far below the limit of safety, the Charlton was stripped of her armament and ordered with the prisoners to Rio de Janeiro, while the Georgiana, having a full cargo of oil, was sent home to the United States. The fleet, again numbering four vessels, sailed for Albemarle Island; but after a long and fruitless chase of a stranger Porter put into James Island. There he repainted and utterly changed the appearance of the Essex and the Greenwich, and toward the close of August entered Banks Bay, where he left the prizes. Disguising his ship as a merchantman, he now sailed alone, and on September fifteenth descried a whaler lying-to " cutting in" blubber. So disguised was the Essex that she was within a few miles of the stranger before the alarm was taken, the whale cast off, and every effort made to escape. When at last the Essex overhauled her, Porter was delighted to hear that she was the letter of marque Sir Andrew Hammond, which led him the long chase six weeks before. On returning to Banks Bay with the prize, Porter was joined by the Essex Junior, which brought him word that several British frigates of force were searching for him. He determined, therefore, to sail to the Marquesas Islands, where, on the island of Nukahiva, he passed the winter overhauling the Essex.

As soon as the repairs were completed Porter, leaving his prizes at the island under a guard of twenty men, sailed with the Essex and the Essex Junior, for South America, and on February third entered the port of Valparaiso, where he was assured that the thirty-six-gun frigate Phœbe, Captain James Hillyar, was on the coast in search of him. The Phœbe had been despatched from England with orders to destroy the American fur station on the Columbia; but when she reached Rio de Janeiro she heard of the doings of the Essex, and taking the Cherub with her, went round the Horn to capture the American frigate. Porter knew nothing of the Cherub, and, as he had no desire to shun an encounter with the Phœbe, he waited quietly at Valparaiso, while the Essex Junior cruised in the offing keeping a lookout. The wait was not a long one, and on the morning of February eighth the Essex Junior was able to signal that two enemy's ships were in sight. They were, of course, the Phœbe and the Cherub, and the moment they entered the harbor the mate of an English merchantman hurried on board and told Captain Hillyar that Porter had given a ball on the Essex the night before, that the ship was still covered with awnings and buntings and decorations, that half the crew were on shore, and that she might easily be taken. Captain Hillyar thereupon got under way, and running into the harbor, luffed up within fifteen feet of the Essex. To his surprise she was completely ready. Every man had been recalled from shore; the decks had been cleared for action; the men had been sent to quarters; the powder boys were ready with lighted matches to fire the guns; and the boarders, cutlass in hand, were waiting to board in the smoke. Standing on an after-gun, Hillyar inquired after Captain Porter's health. He was answered, and warned not to fall aboard. If he did, it would, he said, be purely accidental. "Well," said Porter, "you have no business where you are. If you touch a rope yarn of this ship I shall board instantly." So close were the frigates that as the Phœbe passed by her jib-boom swept over the deck of the Essex, which could at that moment have raked her with an entire broadside.

During a few days the enemy lay at anchor half a mile away, and then went to sea and began a strict blockade of the port. For six weeks Porter submitted to this, but learning that several other frigates were searching for him, he had about made up his mind to run the blockade when, on March twenty-eighth, in a heavy gale, the Essex parted her port cable, and as she was dragging her starboard anchor to sea he determined then and there to make the attempt to escape. In doing so a squall struck the frigate, carried away the main top-mast, and forced him to seek shelter in a bay. But hardly was he there when the Phœbe and the Cherub bore down, and taking position, one under his stern and one under his starboard bow, opened fire at long range. Twice Porter succeeded in driving them off, but twice they returned, and, choosing their own positions, reduced him to helplessness at their pleasure. When at last, after a noble defence of two hours, he struck, the Essex was a wreck, and of her crew of two hundred and fifty-five men but seventy-five were able to do duty.

The Essex Junior was now made a cartel, and in it the survivors were sent to the United States. On the fifth of July, 1814, when off Sandy Hook, they were brought to by the Saturn, and, as the captain of the Saturn seemed little inclined to let them pass, Captain Porter and a few of his men dropped into a boat and pulled toward shore. The Saturn gave chase; but a dense sea-fog settled down, and after rowing all night long, Porter and his men reached Babylon, Long Island, where they were seized as spies. When he had convinced the people who he was they suffered him to go on by wagon to New York, where the Essex Junior had already arrived a few hours before.*

While the sloops and frigates of the United States navy had thus been acquiring imperishable renown on every sea, our flag was yet more widely displayed and as nobly defended by a class of vessels concerning whose exploits too little is known.

It may well be supposed that as the declaration of war was read in seaport after seaport, idle sailors and the owners of idle ships began to prepare for privateering. In happier days the sharp, fast-sailing, clipper-built ships so well fitted for the

---

* American Daily Advertiser, July 11, 1814.

work of commerce-destroying would have been few in number. But orders in council and French decrees had produced a class of vessels especially designed to escape the British cruisers sent to enforce the orders. That a merchant ship of the United States which had been to France, or to Holland, or to some West Indian port, and was on her way home with a cargo, should not be stopped and searched at sea was of the utmost importance. Search might give rise to a doubt as to the character of the ship and cargo. Such a doubt was sure to send her into a British port for examination, and such an examination, even if it ended in acquittal, broke up the voyage, lost the owners of the cargo a market, and ruined all concerned by the enormous costs of British litigation. Accordingly, long before the embargo was laid, ship-builders met this danger and constructed ships so swift that it was all but impossible for any single cruiser to overtake one. Now that fast sailers were wanted, they became greatly in demand, and, with the idle pilot-boats of the chief seaports, formed the first privateers. To gather fifty or sixty hardy and experienced seamen, purchase stores and ammunition and a sufficient number of sabres, muskets, and boarding pikes, mount a long-tom in the middle of the ship and perhaps half a dozen lighter guns in broadside, was a matter of a couple of weeks, after which the privateer—called by some saucy name as the " Orders in Council," or " Right of Search," the " Revenge," the " Yorktown," the " Saratoga," the " Fair Trader," or " Paul Jones"—was ready for sea.

Before the middle of July, 1812, sixty-five such privateers had sailed. Before the middle of October twenty-six had gone from New York and seventeen from Baltimore, in addition to twenty-five letters of marque. Those from New England coasted along Nova Scotia and Newfoundland; those from New York and Baltimore cruised down the Florida coast and in and out among the British Windward Islands in the Caribbean Sea, making prize of every merchantman they fell in with. If the cargo were valuable and the privateer could spare the men, the prize was sent in and became subject to examination in a District Court of the United States. The purpose of the examination was to inquire into the character

of the prize and see if it was really the property of the enemy
at the time of capture. If so, it was pronounced forfeited,
was sold, and the money distributed among the owners, the
officers and the crew of the privateer, according to the term
of the written agreement existing between them. The sale of
the ship and cargo was generally made by the United States
Marshal, who deducted one and a quarter per cent. from the
gross receipts and paid the remainder over to the clerk of the
Court, who, subtracting another one and a quarter per cent.,
distributed what was left to the claimants. When to these
commissions were added the duties, the costs of condemnation,
and a host of charges, many a prize became far more profitable
to the Court, the Government, and the officials than to any one
of the captors who had risked his life in taking it. That this
should be seemed most unreasonable and unjust, and became
the subject of a memorial to Congress by the owners of privateers fitted out in New York.

Light-armed craft had by that time fallen into disuse, for
vessels ready to surrender, even after a fight, to a privateer of
six or eight guns on the broadside, had either been swept from
the sea by the end of 1812 or sailed under strong convoy.
British merchantmen having a common destination, as the
East Indies, or the West Indies, or the South American coast,
would assemble at Portsmouth, Plymouth, or Cork, or, if
homeward bound, at Rio or Jamaica, and sail thence under
the protection of heavily armed ships of war. A large fleet
would have for escort a seventy-four in the van, a fast sailing
frigate in the rear, and on either side a gun-brig or sloop of
war. A smaller fleet was fortunate if beside a seventy-four it
secured a frigate or a couple of sloops of war. Such fleets,
laden as they usually were with sugar, coffee, molasses, rum,
and specie, were most tempting, and when the privateers sailed
in pairs some of the merchantmen were sure to be taken before the voyage ended. In spite of every effort on the part
of the convoy to drive off the privateersmen, they would hang
upon the fleet for days and weeks at a time, waiting for a
chance to run in and cut out a prize. This chance might happen when the merchantmen had become widely separated from
any cause, or when the slow sailers, by lagging, had stretched

the distance between the armed ship in the van and that in the rear to several miles.   To dash into the midst of the fleet, run alongside one of the vessels, take out the crew and the specie and apply the torch, or possibly throw a prize crew on board and make all sail, was, under such circumstances, no uncommon occurrence.   Should an attempt be made to drive the attacking ship away, its fellow was ready to run in while the frigate or the sloop of war was in pursuit.   In thick weather, or when a gale had scattered the fleet, the privateers had little more to do than select their prey.

But this system of convoy proved too slow for importers who owned ships, and who, to be first in port and reap the profits of an understocked market, were ready to take enormous risks.   By these men, therefore, private armed vessels called running sloops, which relied on their speed and their own guns for defence against the American privateers, were sent to sea in great numbers.   The cost of them was enormous, for insurance rates were high, and the great crews necessary to man the guns and repel boarders rolled up the expenses and reduced the freight-carrying capacity.

But the profits were also enormous, for they were always richly laden with costly goods.   They were accordingly most eagerly sought by privateers, and to capture them a new type of vessel was built in our ship-yards.   As specimens of naval architecture these ships had no equal on any sea.   In length on the spar deck they were not more than one hundred and twenty feet, and in extreme breadth were about thirty-one feet. They were rigged as ships or brigs, with long and slender masts and spars, had a light rail on the gunwale in place of solid bulwarks, carried a cloud of canvas, were armed with from six to eighteen guns—one of which, called "long-tom," was always mounted on a pivot amidships—and were manned by a crew of one hundred to one hundred and fifty sailors.   Intended to fight only as a last resort, the sailing qualities of the privateer were chiefly considered and developed by her builder.   Nothing so astonished her English enemies as the height and thinness of her masts, as the length of her spars, as the handiness with which she worked to windward, as the rapidity with which, at the very moment escape seemed hopeless, she would turn, almost within her own length, and, shaking out an immense spread of canvas, make off into the eye of the wind before her opponent could even come about.

Of the fights and adventures and hair-breadth escapes of the privateers but little is known. Many were owned by stockholders, and many more by firms and private citizens, who did not preserve and did not make public the reports of the captains. The records of the Admiralty Courts yield nothing, and, though the vessels bore something of a public character, their logs were never deposited in any public office for preservation. Now and then, after a desperate hand-to-hand fight, or a long chase and happy escape from overpowering force, the letter of a captain would find its way into the newspapers and be copied and preserved. Meagre as such material is, it contains the records of every famous sea fight in which the privateers were concerned, and is sufficient to form a rude idea of the great part they bore in the struggle for commercial independence.

The desperate nature of many of the cruises is well illus. trated by the experiences of the privateer-schooner Comet on the coast of Brazil and among the West India islands. The Comet, in command of Captain Thomas Boyle, was armed and fitted out at Baltimore in 1812, and in December, when ready for sea, ran down the bay, and on a dark and stormy night slipped through the British blockading squadron and made for the coast of Brazil. On the ninth of January, when off Pernambuco, he fell in with a coaster, and was told that some English vessels were to leave that port in a few days. Captain Boyle remained accordingly in the offing till the fourteenth, when, about noon, he sighted four sail standing out of the harbor, and laid by that they might get away from the coast before he cut them off. At three in the afternoon, when the ships were six leagues from land, he bore up and made all sail in chase. At six he was near enough to perceive that one of them was a large man-of-war brig, and, having called all hands to quarters and loaded the guns with round shot and grape, the decks were cleared and made ready for action. An hour later, being quite close to the enemy, the colors were displayed and the Comet sheered up to the brig, whose captain hoisted the Por-

tuguese flag, hailed, and said he would send a boat on board.
Boyle thereupon hove-to, received it, and was informed by
the officer that the brig of war was a Portuguese national ship
of twenty guns and one hundred and sixty-five men, and that
the others were British merchantmen bound for Europe under
his protection, and must not be molested.   Boyle replied that
he was an American cruiser, showed his commission, and said
he would take the Englishmen if he could.   The Portuguese
answered that he would be sorry if anything unpleasant occurred, but, as he was ordered to convoy the ships, he would
protect them.   The two then parted, and Boyle, finding the
officer did not return, made sail for the English vessels, consisting of a ship of fourteen guns and two brigs of ten guns
each.   A running fight of five hours now followed before the
three Englishmen struck.   Only one of the three was secured,
for so battered were the other two, and so persistent the attack
of the Portuguese man-of-war, that Captain Boyle suffered
them to make off, and contented himself with making prize
of a Scotch ship a few days after.   He was next met and
chased by the frigate Surprise ; but he easily outsailed her, and
continuing his cruise down the West Indies, discovered, one
morning in February, when near the island of St. John, two
sails to leeward and followed them.   The nearest was an armed
brig from Demerara, loaded with sugar, rum, coffee, and cotton, and as he came up she set her colors, fired a gun, and
struck.   Stopping just long enough to put a prize crew on
board, Captain Boyle went in pursuit of the second, which,
after an exchange of broadsides, lowered her flag and began to
cut away her rigging.   The purpose of this was to delay the
privateer till the man-of-war brig Swaggerer, then in plain
sight, could come down and drive him away.   But Captain
Boyle repaired the rigging of the prize as hastily as possible,
and sent her, in charge of a prize crew, through the passage
between St. John's and St. Thomas, while he sailed around
and about the Swaggerer till his prize had escaped, when he
steered for the Capes of the Chesapeake, again ran the blockade and reached Baltimore in safety.

At the very time our coast was declared blockaded—and, so
far as the frigates were concerned, really was—our privateers

were swarming around the British Islands. Such was their boldness that it was all but impossible to secure a shilling of insurance at Halifax for a homeward-bound voyage, or get a policy underwritten at Lloyd's for a trip across the Irish Channel. Thirteen shillings on the hundred pounds were asked and paid by vessels compelled to make the voyage. Three frigates and fourteen sloops of war were guarding the English seas, yet the capture of a privateersman was of rare occurrence. Such experiences were new to Englishmen, and on the twelfth of August the London Assurance Corporations petitioned for a naval force large enough and active enough to clear the British Islands of the privateers. They were assured by John Wilson Croker, Secretary of the Admiralty, that there was afloat a force adequate for the protection of trade both in St. George's Channel and the Northern Sea. But the capture of five brigs between the Smalls and the Tuskar ; * the absolute refusal of the underwriters to insure vessels bound for Ireland ; and the admission of the Morning Chronicle that " the whole coast of Ireland, from Wexford round by Cape Clear to Carrickfergus," was blockaded by " a few petty fly-by-nights," † made the assurance of Croker ridiculous. Now, at last, the sneer of the London Times in 1807, that Americans could not sail from New York to Staten Island without British leave, was reversed, and made applicable to Englishmen on their voyages from port to port of the British Islands. Even Croker was forced to admit this, and in an answer to a memorial from Bristol he told the merchants that if the masters of British ships " had availed themselves of the convoys appointed for their protection from foreign ports, or had not in other instances deserted from the convoys under whose protection they had sailed," there would not have been so many captures in the Irish and Bristol channels.‡

In the address made soon after by the Liverpool merchants to the Lords of the Admiralty, they complain of the burning and destroying of merchant vessels by privateers as " a new system of warfare," and call loudly for protection against

---

* Courier, August 22, 1814.   † Morning Chronicle, August 31, 1814.

‡ Niles's Weekly Register, vol. viii, Supplement, p. 186.

American capture. At Glasgow the merchants, ship-owners, and underwriters were so put out with the conduct of the Admiralty that an address was made to the Throne. The number of American privateers, said the address, with which our channels have been infested, the audacity with which they have approached our coast, and the success with which their enterprise has been attended, have ruined our commerce, humbled our pride, and discredited the naval power of Britain, whose flag, till of late, waved over every sea and triumphed over every enemy. In the short space of two years above eight hundred vessels have been taken by that power whose maritime strength we have hitherto held in contempt. It is distressing, it is mortifying, that, at a time when we are at peace with all the rest of the world, at a time when we have declared the whole American coast under blockade, when we pay so heavy a tax for protection in the form of convoy duty, and when our navy costs so great a sum, we cannot traverse our own channel in safety nor effect insurance without excessive premiums, and that a horde of American cruisers, unheeded, unresisted, unmolested, seize, burn, sink, destroy our ships in our own inlets and in sight of our own harbors. Lloyd's list for June third, 1814, gives the names of thirty-seven merchantmen captured in a few weeks. The privateer Perry, of Baltimore, took twenty-two in a cruise of three months. The Surprise destroyed thirteen ships and was chased sixteen times in the course of one hundred and three days. In another cruise of thirty days she captured twenty-one. The Governor Tompkins burned fourteen vessels in a cruise through the Channel. The Young Wasp was six months off the coasts of England and Spain, and the Harpy three months off the Irish coast and in the waters of the British Channel and the Bay of Biscay. Captain Thomas Boyle, who now commanded the Chasseur, was three months in British waters, and sent in a proclamation, to be posted at Lloyd's, blockading " all the ports, harbors, bays, creeks, rivers, inlets, outlets, islands, and sea-coast of the United Kingdom." The Prince of Neufchatel, Captain John Ordronaux, swept through the English Channel and sent six prizes into Havre de Grace, France.

Some months later, when homeward bound, laden with

the spoils of the enemy, Captain Ordronaux was sighted and chased, not far from Nantucket Island, by the British frigate Endymion. The experience was not new, for he had already, in the course of his cruise, been chased seventeen times, and might on this occasion have easily escaped had the wind been fair. It so happened, however, that just after sunset it fell calm, and Captain Ordronaux was forced to anchor, as the current was sweeping him on shore. The many prizes taken had reduced his crew from one hundred and fifty to thirty-three, and had burdened him with the care of thirty-seven prisoners. As these men, in the presence of the danger that now beset him, showed signs of an intention to rise against the crew, they were handcuffed and sent below, and every preparation made for a desperate resistance. The guns were overhauled; muskets, pistols, boarding-pikes, and sabres were brought out, and, as the gun-room was full of arms taken from the prizes, three hundred muskets were loaded and placed near at hand, while buckets of pistols were arranged behind the bulwarks, so that when the fight once began no time need be wasted in re-loading weapons. The shot lockers were next filled with heavy shot to be thrown into the enemy's boats to stave in their bottoms. Thus prepared, Captain Ordronaux waited anxiously for the first sign of the enemy, and about nine o'clock at night distinctly heard the sound of oars at a distance. So dark was the night that not a boat could be seen, till five, carrying one hundred and eleven men, closed in around the privateer. One was under each bow, one was on each side, and the fifth under her stern. The men from the two barges under the bows, meeting with the least resistance, cut through the nettings, clambered up, and had gained the forecastle, when Captain Ordronaux and a few followers trained a main-deck gun on them, and swept them off with canister shot and musket ball. At the stern and along the sides the fight was hand to hand with sabres, cutlasses, and boarding pikes. Again and again an attempt was made to board and was as often met with such a shower of heavy shot, musket and pistol balls that after twenty minutes of fighting the enemy cried for quarter. By that time one barge with forty-three men had been sunk, and three more had drifted away with apparently no living soul on board. The launch under the stern was taken possession of and contained but eight uninjured men in a crew of thirty-six. These, when deprived of arms and oars, were kept all night astern on the launch, for, as Captain Ordronaux had but nine of his own crew fit for duty, he did not dare bring his prisoners on deck. With daylight his situation grew more serious each moment. That the disabled condition of the privateer could long be hidden was not probable. To suppose that the thirty new prisoners, when they discovered it, would continue to be held in subjection by nine men on a ship whose deck was covered with fire-arms was irrational. The one hope for Captain Ordronaux was to adopt some *ruse* to conceal his plight, parole his prisoners, and put them ashore. This he did, and, hanging a sail near the main hatches in such wise as to screen the quarter-deck, and placing two boys behind it to beat a drum, play a fife, and stamp about as if a score of men were at quarters ready to obey his orders, he landed all his prisoners save five, who aided him in getting back to Boston.

Quite as desperate and far more famous was the defence made by the crew of the General Armstrong, a privateer schooner commanded by Captain Samuel C. Reid. She had run the blockade at Sandy Hook early in September, 1814, and after a long chase by two of the blockading squadron put into the harbor of Fayal for water and food. No ship of the enemy was there when she came, and none had been for many weeks past; but at sundown on the day of her arrival the British armed brig Carnation, Captain George Bentham, came in, and, learning what the General Armstrong was, anchored within pistol shot. Almost at the same moment the Plantagenet, a seventy-four-gun frigate commanded by Captain Robert Lloyd, and the thirty-eight-gun frigate Rota, Captain Philip Somerville, hove in sight, and the three began an exchange of signals. Sure that mischief was brewing, though Fayal was a neutral port, Captain Reid cleared for action, and by the aid of sweeps started to move in nearer shore. He had not gone far, however, when four barges put off from the brig and gave chase. As they drew near they were again and again warned away; but they rowed steadily on till close alongside, when, seeing that they were full of men well armed, Captain Reid opened so steady and well-aimed a fire that they soon cried out for quarter and withdrew. The General Armstrong was now brought within a few hundred feet of the shore, while the British in seven barges made ready for a second attack. At first they pulled in under shelter of a reef and lay there several hours; but at midnight they came out, and in the bright light of the moon pulled swiftly toward the privateer. The shower of bullets and shot of every sort that greeted them was dreadful; but they never faltered, and in a few minutes were engaged in a hand-to-hand conflict at the vessel's side, hacking at the boarding nettings and trying to climb on deck. The Americans plied musket and pistol with awful effect, clove the heads and limbs of the enemy with cutlasses, thrust them through with pikes, and so beat off the boats. Two were sunk, two more were captured, and three full of dead and wounded made their way back to the fleet. On the privateer two were killed and seven wounded. The British admitted thirty-four killed and eighty-six wounded, but the Americans placed the enemy's loss at two hundred and fifty.

After beating off the boats, Captain Reid received a note from the American Consul, telling him that the Governor of Fayal had remonstrated with Captain Lloyd, had asked that hostilities be suspended, and had been answered that the privateer should be taken if the town had to be battered down in doing so. The wounded on the General Armstrong were at once put ashore, damages were repaired, and the deck again cleared for action; and about daylight the English brig came close in and opened fire. A few broadsides sufficed to cut her rigging, wound her top-mast and hull, and force her to draw off. Then Captain Reid, thinking he had done enough for the honor of his flag, scuttled his vessel and went ashore with the crew. He had indeed done wonders, for so great was the damage he inflicted that the fleet was forced to stay a week at Fayal, burying the dead and caring for the wounded. That week's delay was most important; for the Rota, the Plantagenet, and the Carnation, on their way to Jamaica to join the expedition against New Orleans, were prevented, by the fight at Fayal, from arriving on time, and so delayed the fleet of Pakenham that Jackson had time to defend New Orleans. Captain Reid, by his splendid defence of the General Armstrong, may therefore justly be said to have contributed not a little to Jackson's great victory on the banks of the Mississippi.*

From Fayal Captain Reid was taken by a Portuguese ship to Amelia Island, whence he made his way by land to New York. Wherever he went he found that the news of the battle had preceded him, and that he was the hero of the hour. Poughkeepsie voted a sword to his lieutenant. Richmond gave him a public dinner. Most flattering comparisons were drawn between the loss he had inflicted on the British in a few minutes and the loss the great fleets of England had inflicted on her enemies at the end of engagements lasting many hours. But the finest compliment of all was the effort made in England to keep the details of the battle from the public and the false report of the British commander.

---

* The story of this famous fight is given by Captain Reid in a letter to the Mercantile Advertiser, in his protest made before the American Consul at Fayal, and in the letter of the Consul to the Secretary of State. Niles's Weekly Register, vol. vii, pp. 207, 253, 255, 319 ; and vol. vii, Supplement, pp. 167–170. A Collection of Sundry Publications and Other Documents, in Relation to the Attack made during the Late War upon the Private armed Brig, General Armstrong, of New York, commanded by S. C. Reid, on the Night of the 26th of September, 1814, at the Island of Fayal, by His Britannic Majesty's Ships Plantagenet, 74, Rota, Frigate, and Carnation, Sloop of War. New York, 1833.

CHAPTER XXVI.

THE COAST BLOCKADE.

RUMORS of the coming blockade began to be heard in the closing days of January, 1813, when the fishermen of Chesapeake and Delaware bays reported that little fleets of British ships were hovering off the coast. Early in February several expresses from different parts of the bay side of Princess Anne County, Virginia, confirmed these statements and alarmed the people of Norfolk with reports that a British squadron was in sight. It consisted, the riders said, of two seventy-fours, three frigates, and a schooner, and when last seen was standing in toward Hampton Roads. The story was true, for the fleet was that under the command of Admiral Sir John Borlase Warren and Rear-Admiral Cockburn. Now, it so happened that the day before the enemy appeared the Constellation, Captain Charles Stewart in command, had come down the bay from Washington on her way to sea, and had dropped anchor in the Roads. Her exposed position there afforded the British so fine an opportunity to cut her out, that the American commander at Norfolk ordered the drums beat to arms, and in an hour the Fifty-fourth Regiment was drawn up on Freemason Street ready to defend her. But a calm falling, the enemy's fleet anchored off Willoughby's Point and the Constellation was kedged up the bay till she grounded. When the tide turned she ran in and anchored off Norfolk, and remained blockaded till the end of the war.

Next day, as the ship Margaret, on her way from Madeira, was about to enter Delaware Bay she was boarded by an officer from the frigate San Domingo, who endorsed her register and sent her on to New York with the information that Delaware

Bay and river were closed to trade and closely blockaded by the San Domingo, the Dragon, and the Bellona. The blockade of the two bays was quickly followed by the report that a fleet of four vessels had cut off the coast trade with the Southern States; that a force had landed on Smith Island, near Cape Charles; that the Chesapeake was invested, and that Gallatin had ordered that the lamps in the light-houses on Cape Henry and along the shores of Chesapeake Bay should no longer be lit. Then the people of the seaboard cities and towns for the first time in their lives understood the dangers to which their defenceless condition exposed them, and made serious haste to protect their property. At Philadelphia the Common Council having twice called on the Select Council to meet with it and concoct measures of defence, and the Select Council having twice failed to respond, the citizens took up the matter, assembled at the Coffee-House, formed an association for the defence of the ports and harbors and of the Delaware, and named a committee to prepare a plan; a proceeding which so encouraged the Common Council that it called a mass meeting at the County Court rooms, where a grand committee of one from each ward was chosen and duly instructed. Their instructions bade them find out what Government was doing to protect the port of Philadelphia, how large a force there was at Fort Mifflin, and, if that force did not seem to be enough, draft a memorial to the Secretary of War and have it ready for a second meeting two days later. When the people again assembled, the committee reported that Government was doing all it could; that, considering the difficulty of navigating the Delaware without pilots, lights, and buoys, but little defence was needed, and that a floating battery between Fort Mifflin and Mud Island was all they had to recommend. Nevertheless, calls were made on the young men to form a corps of light infantry for defence of the city and the shores of the Delaware; for draymen who were willing to form a corps of light artillery to act with the First Regiment of Pennsylvania Cavalry, and for every man in the first division of the militia to mount the State cockade as evidence of his willingness to fight.

Farther down the river, at Wilmington, a similar gathering of the people was held at the Town Hall, and resolutions adopted to build a fort below the rocks, enroll and arm all the men, name a place of rendezvous, arrange signals, ask the Governor to call out the drafted militia, and remove the specie from the bank. Their action was none too soon, for the enemy was even then near at hand. The squadron blockading the Delaware was commanded by Captain John Poer Beresford, who, happening to need a supply of food, now made a demand for provisions on the Mayor of Lewiston. "Send me," said he, "twenty live bullocks with vegetables and hay. You shall be paid Philadelphia prices. If you do not send them I will destroy your town." The Mayor referred the letter to Governor Joseph Haslet, who replied that compliance with such a request was contrary to law, derogatory to him, and incompatible with his duty as a citizen. Beresford answered that his demand was a perfectly proper one. It was in his power to destroy Lewiston. The requisition was the price of its security, and whatever suffering might fall on the people of the town in consequence of the refusal must be laid at the door of the Governor and the Mayor. Few thought him serious; but he was, and with the Poictiers and two other frigates he moved up the river and anchored off the town. As the place stood so far back from the river as to be out of range of the Poictiers's guns, it would have to be attacked by landing parties, and to meet them the Governor hastily gathered some fifteen hundred militia and repaired to Lewiston in person. On April sixth the long-threatened attack was begun, and a bombardment opened which continued for twenty-two hours, when the ships drew off. The damage to Lewiston was estimated at two thousand dollars.

While Beresford was busy on the Delaware, Admiral Sir John Borlase Warren, who commanded the fleet in Lynnhaven Bay, despatched a little fleet of one frigate, two brigs, and four prize schooners to ravage the shores of the Chesapeake. Rear-Admiral Sir George Cockburn commanded the flotilla and made for the head of the bay, spreading consternation far and wide as he went. At Annapolis the drums beat to arms, the signal gun was fired, and the citizens were called out at three in the morning. When, a few hours later, Cockburn's seven sail were sighted from the steeple of the State-House, the citizens were sure they were to be bombarded, and began to carry away the records and public papers. But the enemy passed by and, having thrown Baltimore into a state of excitement, went on to the mouth of the Susquehanna river.

The presence so far inland of a British force numbering scarcely five hundred men—soldiers, sailors, and marines all told—was a deep disgrace to the men of Maryland and Virginia. But the people of these two States seem to have been alive to nothing but fear. They allowed Cockburn and his five hundred to take quiet possession of Spesutia Island at the mouth of the river, not far from Havre de Grace, live at free quarters on the farmers, and harry the country at his pleasure, while they spent their time, not in fighting, but in hiding and carrying away their property. At Elkton the few stores in the place were emptied and the goods hurried into the country. The specie was taken to Lancaster, in Pennsylvania. At Frenchtown, a little hamlet just coming into importance as a place of deposit for goods on their way to Baltimore or Philadelphia, the people worked day and night in the hope of getting every box, bale, and barrel to a place of safety. Hearing of this, Cockburn sent a party of one hundred and fifty men to Frenchtown, drove off the few militia who attempted to resist him, and burned five ships and great quantities of flour, clothing, saddles, and bridles intended for the use of the army.*

The raiders then went on to Havre de Grace to destroy a battery just erected. Reaching the place before daybreak on the morning of May third, they landed from eleven barges and surprised the earthwork, defended by three cannon and fifty men. The men fled to the woods, and the enemy, taking possession of the battery, made ready to sack the town. All day long on the roads leading inland were to be seen women and children loaded down with household goods and driving before them horses, cattle, and sheep. By night the British had burned four vessels, two taverns, thirteen houses, the ferry-boats, the stages, a bridge, a saw-mill, ten stables, a black-

* Admiral J. B. Warren's Report, May 28, 1813.

smith shop, and many stacks of hay.* It was said that the
soldiers, ripping up the feather beds, used the ticking to carry
off clothing, with which they went back loaded to their barges.
The purpose of this destruction of private houses was, Cockburn declared to Warren, "to cause the proprietors (who had
deserted them and formed part of the militia who had fled to
the woods) to understand and feel what they were liable to
bring upon themselves by building forts and acting toward us
with so much useless rancor." † Forty families were made
homeless and so destitute that funds were raised and a committee chosen at Baltimore to supply them with houses, food,
and clothes.‡

From Havre de Grace the troops moved up the Susquehanna and destroyed Cecil Furnace, where cannon were cast,
and by ten at night were again on board their ships, with one
man wounded and none killed. Two nights later Cockburn
sent another band in fifteen barges into Sassafras river, on
whose banks the militia for the first time made a respectable
defence. But they were soon dispersed and the villages of
Fredericktown and Georgetown pillaged and burned. This
ended the raid. Charlestown, on the North East river, overcome by terror, sent a deputation to assure Cockburn that the
village was at his mercy, and that neither guns nor troops
should be suffered to come there. The neighboring towns did
likewise, and the admiral, finding the upper part of the bay
cleared of vessels, militia, and warlike stores, went back lei-
surely to Lynnhaven. It was long, however, before the terror which he aroused subsided. For weeks the people of
the towns, even along the Potomac, continued to bury their
valuables and the banks to send off their specie. The Alexandria banks sent seven cart-loads to Winchester. Even Philadelphia felt the alarm and made ready for a more elaborate
defence of the city and river. But Warren kept his men inactive, and six weeks passed away before anything more important than the capture of a fishing vessel or a small privateer
was undertaken. Warren's attention was then drawn to Nor-

---

* Aurora, May 5, 1813. True American, May 6, 1813.

† Cockburn to Warren, May 3, 1813.

‡ True American, May 8, 1813.

folk. The city was of no little importance commercially; and, what concerned him far more, it was the chief obstacle that lay between him and the Gosport navy yard and the frigate Constellation. That he would have attacked it during the summer is quite likely, but when, just before daylight on June twentieth, fifteen of the gun-boats whose duty it was to close the mouth of the Elizabeth river came out into the Roads under cover of the darkness and attacked the frigate Junon, Warren seems to have thought that the time for action had arrived.

The gun-boats which composed the American flotilla were of the smallest kind. They were indeed provided with sails; but their chief motive power was derived from long sweeps. For armament each one, placed in the stern, had a long pivot gun, throwing a twelve- or eighteen-pound shot. When the water was smooth and no breeze stirring, these boats were at their best. But the moment a breeze sprang up they were utterly useless, for the sails and the gun then made them careen so far that it was difficult to keep them from capsizing, and quite impossible to use the gun. On the particular June morning in question, the water being quiet and no wind blowing, success seemed assured, and the boats, having come within long range, turned their sterns toward the Junon, pointed their guns, and dropped anchor. But the tide quickly swept their sterns down stream and made the guns useless. Sweeps were then used vigorously, the boats rowed to nearer range, and fire opened. In half an hour, however, a breeze sprang up, the flotilla grew unmanageable, and the Barossa, a frigate lying near the Junon, getting under way, the gun-boats were forced to retire.

The behavior of the flotilla afforded no little amusement to the British, but the impudence of it aroused Warren to the determination to inflict a speedy punishment by taking Norfolk.

The place and its approaches were well defended, for Captain Walker Keith Armistead, of the Engineers, had constructed two good forts on the river banks below the town, and General Wade Hampton was in command. Some five miles farther down, on the west bank just where the river entered Hampton Roads, was another line of works defended by General Robert Taylor, of the Virginia militia. Separated from these works by a few yards of water was Craney Island, on which was a battery of seven guns, manned by one hundred sailors from the Constellation and fifty marines,* and designed to cover the approach to a line of gun-boats anchored across the channel of Elizabeth river.

Before these defences the British appeared in force early on the morning of June twenty-second. The land division, made up of a battalion from the royal marine artillery, French prisoners of war who had enlisted in the English service, and a part of the One Hundred and Second Regiment of the line under Lieutenant-Colonel Charles James Napier, numbered some eight hundred, and were commanded by Major-General Sir Sydney Beckwith. The sailors, seven hundred strong, were led on by Captain Pechell, of the flag-ship San Domingo. As planned, the whole expedition was to go to the west of the island. Beckwith was then to land on the beach, march across country and attack the island battery in the rear, while Pechell's forces, rowing along close to shore, attacked the battery in front. Happily there was no concert between the officers, and long before Beckwith could reach the rear Pechell, with fifteen barges and seven hundred men, began the attack in front. As the water was very shallow, the leading boat grounded when two hundred yards from the beach. A sailor instantly thrust his boat-hook over the side and cried out that he found three or four feet of slimy mud under the boat. His statement was false, and was shown to be false by the fact that the launches had scarcely grounded when the battery opened on the flotilla and shattered three boats, which did not sink. Seeing this, Midshipman Tatnall, with some of the Constellation's crew, waded out and brought the barges safely to shore.† If the bottom was hard enough for Tatnall and his men to wade out to the barges, it was surely hard enough for Pechell and his men to wade ashore. This they were afraid to do, and the flotilla retired with the loss of ninety-one men.

---

* Letter of Captain John Cassin, June 23, 1813.

† Life of Commodore Josiah Tatnall, by Charles C. Jones, Jr., Savannah, 1878, p. 17. One of the captured barges was fifty feet long.

Beckwith's approach by land meantime had been stopped by creeks he might easily have gone around, but which, as they were too deep to ford, became insurmountable obstacles and forced him to abandoned the attack and lead the troops back to their barges.

For the movement against Norfolk there was much reason, but the wanton outrage at Hampton three days later can not be justified on any ground. The village stood on a little arm of James river and was of no commercial importance. The five hundred raw Virginia militia and the sand battery that defended the town were of no military importance. It could, however, be easily taken, and Warren now determined to take it as compensation for the defeat at Craney Island. Accordingly, at dawn on June twenty-fifth Beckwith and his troops were set ashore two miles above Hampton, with orders to attack in the rear, while Cockburn with the barges appeared in front. For a time the militia made a good fight, but they soon gave way, and the British, entering the town, proceeded to indulge in pillage, murder, and rape.

After staying two days at Hampton, Warren went back to Lynnhaven, where he divided his troops and ships, and while a part under Cockburn scoured the coast as far as Florida, the rest sailed into Chesapeake Bay, and on the first of July entered the Potomac. The outrages at Hampton added new terror to these raids, and as the ships came up the bay the people along its shores were panic-stricken. The news that Warren's sails were to be seen on the Potomac produced a panic in Washington, Alexandria, Georgetown, Fredericksburg, and Richmond ; business ceased, and half the male population, including the Secretary of War, hurried to the defence of Camp Monroe, some miles down the river. Such was the press for men at Washington that the editor of the National Intelligencer found his office so stripped of compositors that he was forced to reduce the size of his newspaper. When the express rode into Richmond at sunrise with the news that the enemy were in the Potomac, the Governor hurried on tents, powder, ball, and troops. But the fleet soon went back, and made as if for Baltimore and Annapolis. This, too, was a mere feint, and the rest of the year was passed in cruising on the bay.

North of the Chesapeake the blockade extended to Martha's Vineyard and Nantucket, and was everywhere vigorously enforced. To get in or out of the Delaware was impossible. At New York was Decatur with the United States, the Macedonian, and the Wasp; but so strict was the blockade that Decatur, despairing of running out by the Hook, took his fleet through the East river into Long Island Sound. Off Montauk Point he fell in with a seventy-four, a razee, and a frigate, which chased him back to New London, where the United States and the Macedonian stranded in the mud of the Thames, and remained till the end of the war. Beyond Cape Cod was Captain Philip Bowes Vere Broke, commanding the Shannon and the Tenedos.

Yet, despite this fine array of ships, Great Britain was never less mistress of the sea than at that very moment. The ports and harbors of New York and Charleston, Port Royal and Savannah, the Delaware, the Chesapeake, and the Mississippi had indeed been proclaimed blockaded, and some efforts had been put forth to make that blockade good. Cochrane had harried the farms along the Chesapeake; Beresford had bombarded the defenceless town of Lewiston; Sir Thomas Hardy had shut Decatur in the river Thames. The coast swarmed with vessels of war; yet Allen sailed from New York in the Argus in June. Porter quit the Delaware in the Essex in October, and began that cruise into the Pacific which had no parallel in naval history till the days of the Alabama and the Shenandoah. The President and the Adams twice went out and twice came back in safety. Little as was the attention their acts excited in the United States, they aroused much in England. The press dwelt upon them continually, and even in Parliament the question was asked how it happened that while great fleets of French ships, manned with the sailors of Holland, were blockaded by a few British frigates, the petty navy of the United States roamed the sea at will. Determined to stop it, the naval authorities of Great Britain now put forth renewed exertions, and in November, Admiral Warren extended the blockade to every port and har-

bor, bay and river, creek, inlet, outlet, island, and shore, from
Montauk Point to the Mississippi.* In April, 1814, Cochrane
proclaimed the whole coast from Eastport to New Orleans in
a state of blockade, and warned the ships of nations at peace
with England not to attempt to enter.† The proclamation
was not a paper blockade, and with all possible speed the
British carried it out. By June a frigate was harrying the
shores of Massachusetts Bay, frightening the fishermen and
burning the shipping at Wareham. By September all Maine
east of the Penobscot had been invaded, conquered, and formally annexed to New Brunswick. First to go was Moose
Island and the town of Eastport. The duty of reducing this
piece of territory was assigned to Sir Thomas Hardy, who
appeared off Eastport one fine evening in July ‡ with a fleet
and a force of twelve hundred men, and sent an officer with a
flag of truce on shore. To the astonishment of the townsfolk,
the officer made his way quickly to Fort Sullivan, delivered to
the major in command a written summons to surrender, and,
holding out a watch, announced that he would wait just five
minutes for an answer. At first the major stoutly refused ;
but, as the officer was being rowed back to his ship, the flag
on the fort came down, and within an hour a British flag was
in its place and a line of British troops surrounded the town.
Great as was the surprise of the people at their sudden capture, it was greater still when, a few days later, they beheld,
posted in every conspicuous place in town,# a proclamation
announcing that his Royal Highness the Prince Regent had
been pleased to signify his pleasure that the islands in Passamaquoddy Bay should be occupied by British forces ; and that
Moose Island and its dependencies, having surrendered and
been occupied by British troops, all the inhabitants were to appear on the school-house green on Sunday morning and swear
allegiance to the crown of Great Britain, or leave the island

---

* Proclamation dated Halifax, November 16, 1813.

† Bermuda, April 25, 1814. A copy of the proclamation is in the American
Daily Advertiser, May 9, 1814.

‡ July 14, 1814.

The proclamation is printed in the Daily American Advertiser, August 1,
1814.

within a week. Many submitted; a few held out; and these, by a second proclamation, were summoned to meet and be conducted to the main-land or be carried as prisoners to Halifax. As the news of the capture spread, the whole district of Maine was greatly excited. On every hand was heard the question, Why have the British invaded Maine? Some thought it was by way of retaliation for the capture of Erie and Queenston. Others gave it as their opinion that the capture of Eastport was necessary in order to stop smuggling and enforce the blockade. * But a letter from the British commander in New Brunswick, to General John Brewer, commanding the United States forces in Maine, was soon in print, and put all doubts at rest. " The chief reason for taking the islands in Passamaquoddy Bay is," said the letter, " that they belong to Great Britain by the treaty of 1783. This is all. His Majesty's Government has no intention of waging war on the people of the main-land so long as they remain quiet." †

Next to go was Nantucket. The people on the island had suffered greatly from the blockade, and at last, by July, were brought to such a state of destitution that famine seemed near. In this distress the selectmen convened a town meeting, for the purpose of getting authority to bring fuel and provisions to the island. Authority was gladly given, and a committee was at once despatched in a ship to find Admiral Cochrane and lay the case before him. Success attended the search. The admiral was found, and a ship of war sent to inform the islanders that if they would give up all public property and agree to be neutral during the war, they should be suffered to bring in food, clothes, and provisions, but would not be allowed to catch fish or whales.‡ The terms were accepted # and the promise made.

Castine now shared the fate of Moose Island and Nantucket. When the commandant in New Brunswick assured General Brewer that no attack would be made on the main-land, he

---

* Portland Gazette.

† Lieutenant-Colonel J. Fitzherbert to Brigadier-General John Brewer, July 12, 1814.

‡ American Daily Advertiser, September 1, 1814.

August 9, 1814.

promised what was not to be.   Whatever might be the reason
for seizing Moose Island, the British Government had really
begun a campaign of conquest in the Northeast, and on September first a fleet of twenty-five ships sailed into Penobscot
Bay and anchored off Castine.   Again the tactics so successful at Eastport were repeated.   A flag was sent on shore; a
demand was made for the surrender of the fort, and five minutes were given the officer in which to decide.   He answered
that he did not want one minute to decide; ordered the flag
back to the ship, fired off his four guns as the fleet came
nearer, blew up his magazine, and retreated.   Sir John Sherbrooke, Governor of Nova Scotia, then landed several thousand
men, took possession of Castine, and promptly despatched expeditions against Belfast and Hampden, a little shipping town
some thirty miles up the Penobscot, where the corvette Adams
was undergoing repairs.   The Adams, in command of Captain
Morris, had run the Chesapeake blockade in January, and in
August, while cruising off the Maine coast, struck on a reef
in the Isle au Haut and put into Hampden in a sinking condition.   Her guns were there taken out, and the work of repair-
ing her was far from completed, when the British entered the
Penobscot and sent off a party to destroy her.   Morris did his
best to defend her : arranged his twenty-eight guns in three
batteries, manned them with his crew, and begged the militia
general to protect the rear and flanks.   Though the two counties of Hancock and Kennebeck, through which the river
flowed, might easily have furnished twelve thousand fighting
men, but three hundred and seventy responded, and of these
many had neither arms nor ammunition.   As the crew of the
Adams was in the batteries, Morris ordered the ship's muskets to be distributed to the militia, and at daylight on September third received notice that the British were coming.
Hidden from view by a dense fog which overhung the country, they landed unseen, fell upon the militia, which instantly
fled, and attacked the batteries in the rear and flank.   Unable to hold out, the sailors spiked their guns, set fire to the
Adams, and retreated.   But, finding it impossible to subsist
his men in a body while passing through a country so
sparsely settled, he abandoned all attempt at organization,

and bade his men make their way as best they could to Portland.*

While Morris was fleeing through the woods, the British,
in four ships and seven barges, passed up the river, dropped
anchor off Bangor, and demanded the surrender of the town.
Terms were asked for, and were announced to be' an unconditional surrender, forty horses, provisions for the troops, and
quarters in private families for the officers. There was nothing to do but submit, and while some of the townsfolk fled to
the woods, the rest spent their time for several days driving in
sheep and bullocks, breaking down corn, and digging potatoes.
Every gun, every grain of powder, every old cutlass, every
boat in town was seized, and such shipping as was at the
wharves was burned. Vessels on the stocks were not destroyed, for fear they would set fire to the town. But the
selectmen were solemnly pledged to finish, launch, and deliver
every one of them at Castine before October thirtieth, or pay
thirty thousand dollars as a ransom. Belfast and Machias now
fell in rapid succession, and the whole of Maine, from the
Penobscot to Passamaquoddy Bay, was proclaimed English
territory.†

All New England by this time was in alarm. The inhabitants of Wiscasset hurried their goods and property into the
woods ; the banks at Portland buried their specie. The people
of Salem in one day sent away five hundred wagon-loads of
household goods, determined, as they said, that the British
should find nothing but empty houses. Nor was their alarm
causeless. Already two men-of-war were harrying the shores
of Cape Cod, plundering, destroying, and laying the towns of
Barnstable County under contribution. Wellfleet paid two
thousand dollars, Brewster paid four thousand, Eastham paid
twelve hundred, to save their salt works from destruction. The
officer commanding declared that his orders bade him destroy
every assailable town on the coast, but that such work was most
distasteful, and that he would on his own authority accept a ran-

---

* Morris to Secretary William Jones, September 20, 1814.

† Proclamation of Lieutenant-General Sir John Coope Sherbrooke, K. B.,
commanding a body of his Britannic Majesty's forces, and Edward Griffith, Esq.,
Rear Admiral of the White, etc.

som. Yet farther south was the fleet of Sir Thomas Master-
man Hardy. His work at Moose Island finished, he sailed
southward with two frigates, a bomb-ship and a gun-brig,
appeared off Stonington early in August* and sent to the
magistrates a brief and explicit message. " One hour," said
he, " is allowed you to remove unoffending inhabitants." The
excitement and commotion which followed the receipt of this
message outdid any the town had ever known. Goods
and valuables were buried in gardens, in the fields, and even
thrown down the wells ; women, children, and sick persons
were hurried off to New London or to the farms remote from
the shore ; expresses were sent off in every direction to summon help, and the batteries manned without delay.

When the hour had passed, and three more had been added
to it, yet no attack begun, many felt sure that none would be
made. The object of Hardy, they said, was to draw away
troops from New London, in order that he might destroy the
Macedonian and the Hornet, then lying in the Thames, some
ten miles above the town. But just before sunset the guns
of the ships opened, and kept up a steady fire till midnight.
Next day it was resumed, and went on till noon, when the
selectmen despatched a flag to ask Hardy what he wished them
to do. He answered : " Give assurances that no torpedoes
have been, and that none will be, fitted out at Stonington, and
send on board the family of the late British consul at New London." Receiving no reply, the ships again opened fire and
continued it for another day, when they all withdrew. Half
the houses in the village were damaged or in ruins.

The depredations along Cape Cod and Long Island Sound
were in obedience to strict orders from Vice-Admiral Sir Alexander Cochrane. He had lately succeeded Sir John Borlase Warren in the command of the fleets on the American
coast, and was at Bermuda when he received a letter from Sir
George Prevost urging him to punish the people of the seaboard for certain depredations committed by Americans on
the frontier.

It should seem that about the middle of May a small body

---

* August 9, 1814.

of American troops, having crossed Lake Erie from the New York shore to Long Point, made a raid into Canada, burned some mills, a distillery, and a few private houses, and returned. The raid was the work of the officer commanding, had not been authorized by the Government, and was promptly disavowed. Prevost, however, assumed that the Government was responsible, and, as he could not avenge the acts himself, he sat down and wrote to Cochrane at Bermuda, begging the vice-admiral to do so for him. Nothing suited Cochrane's temper better, and on July eighteenth he issued orders bidding every ship captain under his command from Maine to Florida destroy and lay waste such towns and districts on the coast as were assailable. The lives of unarmed citizens might he said be spared, but nothing more ; for it was only by such treatment that the Americans could be brought to realize the inhumanity of that system of plunder and devastation they must have learned from their allies the French.* The order was still recent when a chance to execute it was given to Cochrane himself.

It was part of the British plan for the campaign of 1814 that a diversion should be made somewhere on the Atlantic coast in favor of the army on the Canadian frontier. Major-General Robert Ross was chosen to make this diversion, and, duly instructed, he sailed from the Gironde on June twenty-seventh for Bermuda, which he reached July twenty-fourth. Just where the attack should be made was for Cochrane to decide. He decided in favor of the Chesapeake, and the expedition again set sail early in August. Ross and Cochrane passed the capes a few days in advance of the transports, and, going up the bay to the mouth of the Potomac, landed to consult with Rear-Admiral Cockburn and wait for the troops.

Three things, it was clear, might be done : they might capture and destroy the gun-boats of Captain Barney, which had taken refuge in the Patuxent river ; they might take Baltimore, or they might move against and possibly occupy the Federal capital. That Barney's flotilla should at once be de-

---

* Orders of Vice-Admiral Cochrane, July 18, 1814. Canadian Archives. Adams's History of the United States, vol. viii, p. 126.

stroyed seems to have been generally agreed to; what should then be done was doubtful. Cockburn insisted on a raid against Washington; but no decision had been made when the transports arrived, August seventeenth, and the fleet of forty-six sail stood on for the Patuxent river to attack Barney. At Benedict, a few miles up the river, the army was landed and marched in three divisions along the road, while Cockburn with the boats went off in search of the American flotilla. To prevent troops coming from Washington to cut off retreat, Captain Gordon was sent with a small squadron to bombard Fort Warburton on the Potomac, a few miles below Alexandria. To frighten the people of Baltimore and keep the troops in that city from moving to attack Ross in front, Sir Peter Parker was ordered to sail up the bay and make a demonstration in the Patapsco.

Never in the history of military movements had such a march been made. Had it been a pleasure excursion the discomforts could not have been much less nor the enjoyment very much greater. The road along which the army moved at leisure was a good one, and wound through dense woods which sheltered the men from the rays of the August sun. Not an enemy molested them, nor was anything more annoying than a thunderstorm encountered along the route from Benedict to Nottingham. At Nottingham the British spent the night, and about eight the next morning moved in the direction of Upper Marlboro, and heard on the way the heavy explosions which announced that Barney had blown up his flotilla.* As the work of the sailors was now done, Ross halted his army at Upper Marlboro while he made up his mind whether to attack Baltimore or Washington. After deliberating twenty-four hours he decided in favor of Washington, and at two in the afternoon of August twenty-third the army was once more in motion. Nothing of moment happened till five, when, about ten miles from Washington, they struck the American outposts and beheld a strong force posted on high ground a mile away, at Old Fields. The British instantly formed for battle, but the American force as promptly fled,

---

* Washington Gazette. American Daily Advertiser, August 25, 1814.

and the invaders camped that night nine miles from the capital.

The city was absolutely without defence. During the first two years of the war not so much as an attempt had been made to defend it. But by July of 1814 the blockade of the coast and the depredations along the Chesapeake had so alarmed the people that the President and his secretaries took up the matter, made a new military district on the Potomac, and placed Brigadier-General William H. Winder in command.* To have found a man less fitted for the place would, even for Madison, have been a hard task. Winder did, indeed, scour the country from Baltimore to Washington, and from the Potomac to the Patuxent, in search of spots on which to build great works for defence.† But on the August day when the ships of Cochrane and Ross dropped anchor off the Potomac not a spot had been selected, nor a ditch, nor an earthwork, nor an obstruction of any sort so much as planned on paper. It may well be supposed, therefore, that when the express brought the news to Washington ‡ that fifty British ships were off the mouth of the Potomac, the town and the Cabinet became greatly excited. Madison made a requisition for militia on the Governors of Pennsylvania, Maryland, and Virginia. Monroe rushed off to play the scout along the Patuxent. Armstrong offered advice. Winder was almost distracted by the letters, the orders, the consultations, the demands which crowded upon him from morning till night. The citizens seem to have been the only men who really acted wisely. At a public meeting held on the evening of Saturday they resolved to offer their services for the erection of works at Bladensburg, an offer Winder so gladly accepted that by Sunday night the first signs of defence began to appear.

By that time, too, the militia of the district was under arms, troops had come in from Alleghany, from Carlisle, from Alexandria, and these, to the number of two thousand, had been stationed at a place called the Wood-Yard, some twelve miles

---

* July 5, 1814.

† Winder to Armstrong, July 27, 1814. American State Papers, Military Affairs, vol. i, p. 546.

‡ August 18, 1814.

away. With them were Winder and Monroe. In the city, meantime, all was confusion. The whole of Sunday and Sunday night was spent by the citizens in secreting valuables, carting off furniture, and by the clerks in packing up the public books, papers, and documents. On Monday the banks sent off their specie to Winchester; numbers of families fled across the Potomac, and cart-loads of documents were hurried away. At the Wood-Yard the day was passed by Winder and Monroe in watching Ross. The place was at a cross-roads but a few miles from either Nottingham or Upper Marlboro, and by riding forward in the woods the British troops were plainly seen on their march to Marlboro.

Satisfied that Bladensburg would be the battle ground, Winder ordered his troops to go back to Old Fields, five miles in the rear of the Wood-Yard, whither about midnight came Madison, with Armstrong, the Secretary of War, with Jones, the Secretary of the Navy, and with the Attorney-General, Rush. Monroe was already there. Campbell was too busy with the affairs of the new loan to quit Washington. During the night the camp was a scene of confusion and disorder that beggars description. By morning, order having been partly restored, Madison reviewed the troops. They numbered three thousand two hundred. One thousand were regulars, four hundred were the sailors from Barney's gunboats, and the rest militia. Winder ought with such a force to have attacked Ross, who at that moment was deliberating what to do, and who might, by a vigorous assault, have been stopped and perhaps sent back to the Patuxent. But Winder spent the forenoon of Tuesday in scouting, and, convinced that the British would not march that day, he rode off about noon for Bladensburg. He had not, however, been gone from camp an hour, when Ross resumed his march and came suddenly on the Americans at Old Fields, where the two armies formed in line and made ready for battle, and where some resistance might have been made by the Americans had not Winder, unhappily, been summoned to return, and coming on the field about five o'clock, ordered a retreat. Had he known his duty he would have gone at once to Bladensburg. But he fell back to Washington by way of the bridge over the eastern branch of the Potomac and camped at the navy yard. The result of this was to carefully guard an approach already fully secured by the impassable eastern branch, by the length of the bridge which spanned it, by the guns and ships at the navy yard, and to leave the British free to march along the Bladensburg road direct to the capital. Toward Bladensburg, accordingly, the British moved early on the morning of Wednesday, August twenty-first. Ignorant of what Ross was doing, and uncertain what to do himself, Winder had written to Armstrong asking for the advice of the Cabinet. Thus summoned, every member promptly repaired to the navy yard, but they were hardly at headquarters when news came that Ross was marching. Camp was instantly broken, and in two hours a motley throng, made up of militia, regulars, volunteers, sailors, generals, secretaries, and the President, were racing across country to Bladensburg. Monroe, with some Maryland militia close upon his heels, came first on the spot, and found the field already occupied by General Stansbury and the Baltimore troops.

The eastern branch of the Potomac, which at the navy yard is broad and deep, is at Bladensburg a narrow, shallow stream, spanned by a bridge over which passes the road to Washington. Near the eastern bank of this stream in a ravine were the houses which made up the straggling village. The western bank is hilly, and it was on these hills that Stansbury had drawn up his troops shortly before the British were seen coming down the opposite hill behind the village. Almost at the same moment the troops of Winder began to appear and were assigned places wherever possible. But long before all of them reached the battlefield the British light brigade rushed over the bridge and made straight for the American centre. A deadly fire of musketry and artillery checked them for a moment, but they soon rallied and put the Maryland militia to flight with a discharge of Congreve rockets. The British were now in turn driven back to the bushes which lined the stream, and remained there till re-enforced, when they once more advanced, and the Americans once more took to flight. First went the Maryland riflemen, commanded by Pinkney, lately Minister to the Court of St. James; next went the artillerymen, who had not discharged their pieces twice; and then the Baltimore regiment, which, as it rushed from the field, swept Madison, Stansbury, and the Cabinet along in the rout, just as Barney and his sailors got into position. They had been left at the navy yard with orders to destroy the bridge in case of defeat, but the vigorous remonstrance of Barney had wrung from Secretary Jones a reluctant consent to join in the battle, and making all possible haste, they came in sight of the field as the flight began. With them were five guns, which Barney unlimbered on a hill-top a mile from Bladensburg, and calmly waited for the enemy to attack. His position commanded the main road, and down this road the British advanced, expecting no resistance, till they were almost upon the battery, which they three times attempted to take. In this effort they failed, till, entering a ravine they filed off by the right and left and attacked Barney on the flanks. Those on the left fell upon the Annapolis regiment, which fired and fled. Those on the right met some regulars, who likewise retreated, and the British, hurrying around behind the battery, opened on the sailors from the rear. Even then they stood their ground manfully, serving the guns with quickness and precision, till Barney fell and some of the gunners had been bayoneted with fuses in their hand. Then at last they fell back, leaving their guns and their leader with the British.

It was now four o'clock, and as not a vestige of the American army was in sight, the British, overcome with marching and fighting in the heat, rested on the field for two hours.

In the city the day had been one of intense anxiety and panic. Every man worthy of the name had gone to the front. The few that remained were either clerks and officials busy packing and removing the papers and documents of the Government, or servants or men too cowardly to fight. The dreadful quiet of the city; the lonely and deserted streets; the flying rumors that the British were at the Wood-Yard; that the troops were retreating; that a battle was near; the visible fear displayed by the Government officers in hurrying away their papers; above all, the recollection of the horrors perpetrated at Havre de Grace and Hampton, proved too much for the defenceless inhabitants, and all day long streams of women and children went over the bridge to Virginia. With a courage worthy of her high place, Mrs. Madison remained in the President's house keeping guard over the public property, and received from time to time brief despatches from the President. The last, which reached her late in the afternoon of August twenty-third, announced that the enemy was stronger than had been supposed, that he might possibly reach Washington and destroy it, and bade her be ready to go at a moment's notice. To her personal property she gave no thought, but gathering the Cabinet papers, packed them in as many trunks as would fill a carriage, and waited for the word to send them off, fully determined not to go herself till Mr. Madison came. The night was, if possible, a time of more anxiety than the day, and from sunrise till noon of the twenty-fourth she passed the hours, spyglass in hand, scanning the country in every direction in the hope of discovering the approach of her husband or friends. She saw " only groups of military wandering in all directions, as if there was a lack of arms or of spirit to fight for their own firesides." * At noon the sound of cannon was heard, and just before three in the afternoon two messengers covered with dust rushed in to bid her fly. By good fortune a wagon had been procured, and this, loaded with plate and valuable household goods, was sent to the Bank of Maryland. Still she lingered, till some good friends who had come to attend her almost forced her to the waiting carriage.

On the afternoon of the day before, Mr. George Washington Parke Custis had come over from Arlington for the purpose of saving the portrait of Washington by Gilbert Stuart, which then hung on the dining-room wall. He was assured that it should be well cared for, and now, when Mrs. Madison was about to leave, she insisted that the promise should be kept. As the great frame which held the picture was screwed to the wall, time did not suffice to admit of its being taken down, so she ordered it to be broken, and gave the canvas to Mr. Jacob Barker, who carried it to a place of safety.† This

---

* Memoirs and Letters of Dolly Madison, p. 110.

† That Mrs. Madison bore any part in the removal of the picture has been denied. (Gay's Life of Madison, American Statesmen Series, p. 330.) My state-

done, Mrs. Madison entered her carriage and drove to Georgetown. But anxiety for the safety of the President overcame
prudence, and she went back to Washington in search of him.

About two in the afternoon, while on the field at Bladensburg, Madison had remarked to Armstrong and Monroe that
"it will now be proper for us to retire in the rear, leaving the
military movements to military men." The next moment the
line broke, and the President, with Rush and Monroe, took
the road to Washington. By three he reached the city, where
he met Mrs. Madison near the lower bridge. At first she insisted on going with him into Virginia; but yielded to the
advice of friends, and, as the day was far spent, consented to
take refuge for the night in the house of an acquaintance some
two miles beyond Georgetown, and on the morrow join her
husband at a designated place. The President, accompanied
by his wife, after a short stay at the White House, crossed the
grounds to the river, went by boat to the Virginia shore, and,
in company with the Secretary of the Navy and the Attorney-
General, took a carriage and rode westward to a house a few
miles above the lower falls, where he passed the night. Mrs.
Madison, when he was out of sight, returned to Georgetown.

The night was a fearful one. The British, after a rest of
two hours on the field of battle, resumed their march at six
o'clock, and about dark camped a short distance east of the
Capitol. Up to the time when they reached the outskirts of
Washington the raid had been an eminently proper military
movement, and had been conducted in an eminently proper
way. Now, on a sudden, the character of the expedition
changed, and the orders of Cochrane began to be literally
executed. Hardly was the camp formed when Ross and Cockburn, at the head of a detachment of troops, entered the city,
made their way to the Capitol, fired a volley through the windows, entered, and gave the building to the flames. Among
the many fables which sprang from the capture of the city is
one, still to be found in school-books, which tells of a mock
session held by the British in the hall of the House of Repre-

---

ment rests on a letter of Mrs. Madison in Memoirs and Letters of Dolly Madison,
pp. 110, 111.

sentatives. Cockburn, the story sets forth, took his place at the Speaker's desk, and, while his men filled the members' seats, put the question, " Shall this harbor of Yankee democracy be burned ? " and when it was carried ordered chairs and desks to be piled in the centre of the chamber and the match applied. No such scene ever took place; the tale is pure fiction.

As soon as the fire began to burn brightly, Ross and Cockburn, with two hundred men, marched quietly along Pennsylvania Avenue to the President's house, or, as the Federalists delighted to call it, the Palace. The house of that time was indeed primitive : there was no lawn, no flowers, no enclosure; the front porch had not been built, nor had one room more than was absolutely necessary been furnished. Indeed, the East Room, since the scene of so many interesting events, was still in the same condition as it was when the wife of John Adams used it as a laundry. On entering the house to begin its destruction, the soldiers, by the British account, found that preparations had been made for a great dinner. The table was spread, the wine was cooling on the sideboard, the plates were in their holders by the fireplace, and the joints ready in the kitchen.* This, too, is false. When the troops had ransacked the rooms, the furniture was gathered in the parlor, and a live coal having been secured at a neighboring tavern, the building was soon wrapped in flames. The torch was next applied to the Treasury building. Commodore Tingey had already set fire to the navy yard, and the three conflagrations raged fiercely till after midnight, when a violent thunderstorm swept over the city and checked them. Next morning— which was that of Thursday, the twenty-fifth of August—the work of destruction was continued, and by noon the Departments of State, of War, two private dwellings, two rope-walks, a tavern,† and the office of the National Intelligencer were in ruins. The behavior of Admiral Cockburn at the sacking of the newspaper office was long remembered. Mounted on a

---

* Memoirs and Letters of Dolly Madison, pp. 105, 106. The Campaigns of the British Army at Washington and New Orleans in the years 1814–1815. London, 1836, pp. 134, 135.

† National Intelligencer, August 29, 1814.

white mare, with a black foal running at her side, he had been riding about all the morning displaying as trophies some trifling articles taken from the President's house,* inquiring after Mr. Madison, and joking with the citizens. Yet, high as his spirits were, one thought rankled in his mind, and, recalling the denunciations poured upon him by the Intelligencer for his conduct in the bay, he ordered that the office of that journal should be destroyed. As the soldiers were busy smashing presses and type, Cockburn became especially facetious, and shouted out, "Be sure that all the C's are destroyed, so that the rascals cannot any longer abuse my name!" At the navy yard such ships and stores as had been saved by the rain of the night before were again fired. At the arsenal at Greenleaf's Point the destroyers were driven off by an accidental explosion. Some barrels of powder which had been thrown into a dry well for concealment were exploded by a soldier throwing a lighted match into the well, supposing it was full of water. Numbers of his companions were blown to atoms and the rest retired, leaving hundreds of guns unspiked. Then Nature a second time came to the relief of the distressed city, and another cyclone swept over Washington, twisting off trees at their roots, unroofing houses, and forcing the enemy to seek shelter where he could. When the storm had spent itself, Ross, who had grown quite uneasy, began to make ready to retreat, and at nine that night departed. Leaving his camp-fires burning, he hurried to Bladensburg, where the dead were yet unburied, and where he now left his wounded; marched all that night and till seven in the morning of Friday, rested till noon, and at sunset was once more at Upper Marlboro.

On the morning after the capture of the city Mrs. Madison was astir before sunrise, and, bidding farewell to her host, set out to find the little tavern in an apple orchard, where the President was to meet her. The woods and lanes were full of straggling soldiers, sight-seers, and people fleeing for their lives. But she pushed on in the midst of a drenching rain and came at last to the tavern, only to find it full of refugees, who, pouring out imprecations on Mr. Madison as the author

---

* National Intelligencer, August 29, 1814.

of all their woes, refused her admittance. But when evening drew near and another thunderstorm swept over the country, they relented and took her in. Late in the night the President and his friends arrived; but even there he was doomed to find no rest, for, after midnight, a courier brought word that his hiding-place was discovered and that the British would soon be upon him, and, yielding to the entreaties of his wife, he fled to a little hovel in the woods. When morning came Mrs. Madison, in disguise, sought safety farther on, but hearing that Ross had retreated, she hurried back to the Long Bridge to find it burned at both ends, and with difficulty made her way into the city and through its deserted streets to the house of her sister. The President, meantime, obtaining an escort of dragoons, set off for Montgomery Court-House, where Monroe, Winder, and what remained of the army-had stopped running, and quietly waited while Ross destroyed the city.

As the British army hurried from Washington to the Patuxent, a British fleet, in command of Captain John A. Gordon, of the ship Sea Horse, worked its way up the Potomac toward Washington. The presence of a British force, however small, had now become so terrifying that at the first news of the coming of the fleet the officer commanding Fort Warburton blew up the fort and fled to Alexandria. This so alarmed the citizens that the town authorities determined to treat, sent off a deputation to ask for terms, and were soon informed by Gordon of the conditions on which their property would be spared. They must, he said, give up all naval and military stores, all their ships and ship furniture, and all their merchandise then in the place, together with all they had sent away for safety. They must supply the fleet with food at market price, and raise all vessels they had sunk to prevent capture.* Hard as were the terms, they were quickly accepted, and for three days the fleet lay off Alexandria, shipping flour, tobacco, and stores. One hundred thousand dollars, it was said, would not have purchased what was carried away. The citizens for a time sought for consolation in the

---

* Letter of the Mayor of Alexandria to the Mayor of Georgetown, August 28, 1814.

assurance that the ships were all worm-eaten, that the flour had soured, and that the tobacco had been purchased at half price. But the scorn of the whole country, and the jeers of the men of Georgetown, who declared they would see their homes in ashes and have their right arms cut off before they would endure such degrading terms, became galling, and in the search for some one on whom to vent their anger the citizens of Alexandria hit upon the Secretary of War.

When the secretaries scattered and fled it was understood that all should go to Frederick, in Maryland. Thither, accordingly, Armstrong and Campbell repaired, in hourly expectation of meeting the President. But Madison, hearing that the army was at Montgomery Court-House, crossed the Potomac and set off to join Winder and Monroe. Winder, however, learning that Ross had quit Washington, hurried the army toward Baltimore, so that when Madison reached the Court-House and found the troops gone, he too turned toward Washington, which he entered on Saturday morning, and summoning his secretaries began the work of restoring government. Offices were found for the departments in the houses of private citizens. The house lately occupied by the Minister of France became the home of the President. The home of the British Legation became the Treasury Department. What had once been Blodgett's Hotel, but had long been occupied by the Post-Office and the Patent-Office, was ordered to be fitted up for Congress. The hour for the meeting of that body being near, all good citizens who had boards were asked to loan them, and carpenters were detached from the army in order that the necessary alterations might not be delayed. As the enemy were on the Potomac and the Secretary of War still at Frederick, Madison assigned the war department to Monroe, who proceeded to prepare for the defence of Georgetown. Noticing that Colonel Wadsworth was placing some guns on the Virginia shore, he ordered him to desist. This the colonel flatly refused to do, and Monroe, riding over the bridge in great heat, bade him obey or leave the field. Wadsworth left the field, and, the story spreading, the militia met and resolved that they would not serve any longer under Armstrong. Two officers carried these resolutions to Madison the next morning, and brought back word that the President had promised that the Secretary should issue no more orders.* A few hours later Armstrong rode into town, and was visited by Madison that evening. When the two parted, it was agreed that Armstrong should quit Washington the following morning, which he did, and on reaching Baltimore sent back his resignation of the Secretaryship of War. For three weeks no formal appointment was made. Then Madison bestowed the place permanently on Monroe, and invited Governor Tompkins, of New York, to become Secretary of State. Tompkins declined, and Monroe continued to hold the two offices for almost a year.

One of the first acts of Monroe on taking up the duties of Secretary of War was to attempt to capture the fleet of Gordon. By order of the Secretary of the Navy, Porter and Perry and Rodgers, with all the marines and sailors at their command, were called to the Potomac and batteries were thrown up along the banks, to destroy the vessels as they passed down. But the guns were too light, and the fleet, little the worse for the cannonading, fought its way back to the Chesapeake. At the same time † the transports, with the army on board, came down the Patuxent and sailed up the Potomac,‡ as if to meet Gordon,# then suddenly changed their course, re-entered the bay, and under a great press of canvas ran for the mouth of the Patapsco. The movements of the squadron spread terror along the whole coast of the bay, from the Potomac to Baltimore. Wherever the sails were seen, alarm guns were fired, the beacon lights were burned, and the people fled inland. At Annapolis the inhabitants were panic-stricken, and, remembering the fate of Alexandria, threw the contents of their shops and warehouses into the nearest conveyances and hurried them away. The town, however, was not molested, and no stop was made till North Point was reached. There the troops were landed, and by eight in the morning of September twelfth were on their way to Balti-

---

* American Daily Advertiser, September 2, 1814.
† September 6, 1814.
‡ September 9, 1814.
# American Daily Advertiser, September 12, 1814.

more, while the fleet sailed up the Patapsco toward Fort
McHenry. All went well till the troops had marched about
five miles, when they found the way barred by the Americans.
There were then, in and around Baltimore, thirteen thousand
eight hundred and eighty-eight officers and men present for
duty. The British were not far from five thousand in number, and were veterans. But the battle of Bladensburg had
taught no lesson, and against these veterans General Samuel
Smith had despatched but three thousand two hundred raw
militia. To make matters worse, General Stricker, who commanded them, drew them up in close order in an open field,
with flanks unprotected. They did indeed make a stout fight,
in the course of which General Ross was killed; but they
were soon routed, and left the field to the enemy.

The day being then far spent, the British passed the night
where they were. Early the next morning they set forward,
but found the roads so obstructed with fallen trees and ditches
that evening came before they beheld the long line of intrenchments that crowned the heights about the city. To attack such works in broad daylight would have been most
foolish. It was determined, therefore, to wait till dark, and
then, when the fleet had silenced the river fort on the left
flank, try the fortunes of an assault. The delay, however,
was useless. All day long the fleet had been busy bombarding the forts and batteries that commanded the harbor, and
had accomplished nothing. The shallowness of the river and
a barrier of sunken boats kept the heavy ships out of range.
Without the protection of the frigates, the mortar-boats and
brigs could do nothing, and when, after midnight, Cochrane
sent word that he could do no more, the army instantly retreated to the transports. The ships followed, and with the
next fair wind the whole fleet stood down Chesapeake Bay.
The people of Richmond now in turn grew uneasy. But they
were safe, for Cochrane sailed immediately for Halifax.* The
troops a few weeks later † put out to sea, and the people of
the Chesapeake saw their enemies no more.

From the United States the army went straight to Jamaica.

---

* September 19, 1814.   † October 14, 1814.

Not long before his death Ross had been bidden to take his whole force to Jamaica as soon as his work in the Chesapeake was done, and join* an expedition led by Lord Hill, which it was expected would reach the west coast of the island by November twentieth. While the despatch was on its way to Ross, a long report from Cochrane reached Bathurst, which completely changed his plan. The subject of the report was the military condition of the gulf coast of the United States, and in the course of it the statement was made that three thousand men landed at Mobile could, with the help of the Indians, the Spaniards, and the French, drive the Americans out of Louisiana and the Floridas.† On the receipt of this, new orders were made ready, and Ross was duly instructed to carry out Cochrane's plan.‡ He was to return to Jamaica, where, with such re-enforcements as should be sent him, he was to move against our gulf coast, keeping two objects clearly in view. The first of these was to secure the mouth of the Mississippi and deprive the new States in the valley of that river of their outlet to the sea. The second was to occupy and hold some of the territory, the cession of which to Great Britain might be one of the conditions of peace.#

He was therefore to encourage the people to rebel against the United States, and when they had committed some overt act, aid them with arms, clothing, and military instruction. They were, moreover, to be encouraged to go back under the crown of Spain, but they were not to expect Great Britain to make such a cession to Spain "a *sine qua non* of peace."

A week after these instructions were written Ross was dead. News of his death reached London late in October, and without delay Major-General Sir Edward Pakenham ‖ and Major-General Sir Samuel Gibbs were despatched to the

---

* Bathurst to Ross, July 30, 1814. Manuscripts, British Archives. Henry Adams's History of the United States, vol. viii, p. 311.

† Cochrane to Croker, June 20, 1814. Manuscripts, British Archives. Henry Adams's History of the United States, vol. viii, p. 311.

‡ Bathurst to Ross, August, 1814. Manuscripts, British Archives.

Ibid., September 6, 1814. Manuscripts, British Archives.

‖ American Daily Advertiser, November 28, 1814.

West Indies to join Cochrane in Negril Bay and move against New Orleans.*

The death of Ross and the departure of Cochrane gave welcome relief to the whole Atlantic seaboard. The appearance of these men in the Chesapeake, and the boldness with which they sailed into the very heart of two States and sacked the national Capitol, spread terror through every city and town that lay near a navigable river. New York city, which had long been blockaded, was greatly excited. The deeds and the success of Cochrane, it was feared, would arouse every British naval commander to emulate him, and would bring down on the city all the horrors of a bombardment. Moreover, the arrival early in June of a French national brig,† with the lilies at her mast-head and the white cockade in the hats of her officers, reminded the people most forcibly that Napoleon was at Elba, that peace reigned in Europe, and that England was free to turn her army and her navy against the United States. That the autumn would witness such a vigorous prosecution of war as our country had never known was fully expected, and, much alarmed at the prospect, the Common Council chose a committee to examine the defences of the city and report.‡ The committee recommended that a deputation be sent to seek aid of the President; that the Governor call out three thousand men; that the city advance three hundred thousand dollars; that the citizens be asked to give money and labor, and that fortified camps be constructed around Brooklyn and on Harlem Heights. Each suggestion was heartily approved of, and a deputation despatched to Washington in such haste that in ten days it was home again and able to report that Madison had been most gracious, and had readily promised, if the city would pay the cost, to send officers and ammunition and call out the needed troops. The corporation thereupon appealed to the people. "The times," they said, "are portentous. Powerful fleets and armies have sailed from Europe to be used against the United States. Just where the attack will be made is

---

* American Daily Advertiser, November 29, 1814.
† The Olive Branch arrived June 9, 1814.   ‡ July 7, 1814.

a matter of doubt. It is wise, therefore, to protect every exposed point, and no point is more exposed than New York. Whether the war is necessary or unnecessary, just or unjust, is not the question. Our country, our city, our property, our families are in danger. Shall we, then, refuse to give our time, our labor, our money, our lives for the security of all we hold dear? No! Let every man who is exempt from military duty enroll himself without delay. Let every militia company drill, exercise, and be ready to move at a moment's notice. Let every citizen give his labor, that the defences already begun may be finished and yet others undertaken. Let every ship be removed without delay. They are dangerous. Their presence at our wharves will tempt the enemy to attack us, and if our city falls into British hands the ships will surely be burned, and perhaps set fire to our houses."

Many of these suggestions were already in the course of execution. The militia had begun to exercise so constantly that even the common affairs of daily life were seriously interfered with. Corps of exempts had begun to form in every ward, and the columns of the newspapers to teem with notices calling on men of the various trades and occupations to meet and organize for work on the intrenchments.

General Joseph G. Swift, of the Corps of Engineers, furnished the plan, which did not differ greatly from that adopted in revolutionary days by Washington. Along the hill-tops, in what is now the very heart of Brooklyn, was to run a line of defences stretching from the navy yard on the north to Gowanus Creek on the south, and made up of five strong forts * joined by intrenchments. A second line, drawn across Manhattan Island from the Hudson to the mouth of the Harlem river, was to protect the city on the north, while forts at Hell Gate and Williamsburg, Brooklyn Heights, Prince's Bay, and Sandy Hook, with such works as had already been constructed, completed the circle.

In the patriotic work of constructing these the officers of the militia led the way, and one morning in August crossed the ferry to Brooklyn, marched to the hill where the defences

---

* Forts Green, Cummings, Fireman, Masonic, and Lawrence,

were to be, and with a Federal salute and three hearty cheers fell to work with pickaxe, spade, and billhook. The patriotic journeymen cabinet-makers, the patriotic journeymen house-carpenters, the Society of Plumbers followed, and the custom became contagious. That no more should go over in any one day than could be conveniently handled, committees were chosen in each ward to notify the Committee of Defence of the number of men volunteering in their ward. The Committee of Defence then made selections and assigned days, and sent out the journeymen morocco-dressers and curriers, five hundred strong; the hands of the wire factory; the members of the Asbury African Church; citizens of every ward; citizens of Greenwich; the merchants' clerks; the Ugly Club; the stone-cutters; the printers; the masons and laborers at work on the new City Hall, and a thousand of the Patriotic Sons of Erin; the gilders and the framemakers; the gentlemen of the bar; the students of Columbia College; teachers, tallow chandlers, bakers, watchmakers; the free negroes; the Mayor and the corporation; the barbers; the tailors—but the list is too long to enumerate. It was said that not a man, old or young, in the city able to do a day's labor but went out cheerfully to the trenches. Banks, companies, firms, men who were not able to work, sent in money—one dollar and a quarter being considered as the equivalent of a day's labor.

When the forts and trenches were well under way along the hill-tops of Brooklyn the Committee of Defence turned its attention to Harlem Heights, and toward the close of August they too put on a most warlike appearance. The number of men volunteering for this work was so great, and time so precious, that the city authorities secured the use of one of the steam ferry-boats which since 1812 had been running on Paulus Hook, or, as travellers now know it, the Jersey City Ferry. As many as five hundred men were thus sent up each morning and brought back each night. Nor were the people of the region lying about the city less patriotic or less deeply concerned for the welfare of New York than were its own inhabitants. Every town for twenty miles around sent in its contingent of workers. East Chester, Westchester, Greenwich, Scarsdale, Newark, Paterson, Nyack, Bloomfield, Springfield, Yonkers, New Rochelle, Tarrytown, Rahway, Little Falls, Orange—all were represented. From the interior of the State came the Trojan Greens and the Albany Rifle Company, and some three thousand others sent down by the Governor to defend the city. Quarters were quickly found for them at the Battery and in the fortifications. With these men wandering about the streets in their fine uniforms, the going and returning each day of the working parties, and the drilling of the exempts and the militia, the city had much the appearance of a town in a state of siege.

To assemble at some wharf or before some tavern, and go in a body to dig in the trenches on Brooklyn Heights, or run up the Hudson on the steamboat for a day's labor at Harlem Heights, was, to journeymen barbers and shoemakers, cabinetmakers and draymen, a very pleasant outing and a very comfortable way of displaying patriotism. That the forts and trenches were ever to be used, that they were ever to become the scenes of bloodshed and slaughter, did not seriously enter their thoughts. These defences were prudent measures; they were menaces to deter the enemy. But when the news came that the British had actually sailed up the Chesapeake Bay, had marched overland to Washington, had burned the public buildings and were bombarding Baltimore, the feeling became general that New York would be the next place attacked, and the work of defence grew serious. Daylight was now all too short for the eager patriots, and, as it was late in August and the moon nearing the full, a call was made for volunteers to labor by moonlight. Thousands responded, and night after night, so long as the moon lasted, fatigue parties labored diligently on Brooklyn Heights. Fully aware that the General Government was now powerless, the Common Council called on the people to loan a million dollars to the city. The money was to bear seven per cent. interest, was to be paid back in one year, and be used solely for the defence of New York. Some croakers asserted that the city had no authority to make such a loan; but they were quickly silenced and the money raised. The defeat at Baltimore and the victory of Macdonough did much to quiet the public anxiety. But the work of defence went steadily on, and late in November the committee was still receiving subscriptions and still sending out parties to work on the forts. Indeed, the month ended before it ceased to act, and a year passed away before it reported to the Council.* By that report it appears that more than one hundred thousand days' labor was voluntarily expended by the citizens on the works, and that the cost to the city was repaid by the Federal Government.

The example thus set by New York was closely followed in Philadelphia. There, when it was known that Washington had been captured, the people met in the State Yard, chose a committee, organized for defence, formed a military association, and, under such names as the Philadelphia Volunteers, the Hamilton Guards, the Washington Guards, the Yankee Guards, the Rifle Corps, began active drilling. Calls were made for shipwrights and boat-builders to make gun-carriages; for draymen to form a company of artillery; for guns, blankets, clothing, and stores; and for volunteers to aid in throwing up works of defence on the hills bordering the west bank of the Schuylkill. There, too, the response was prompt, and in a few days the artists, the cordwainers, the cabinet-makers, the brick-makers, the printers, and the patriotic young men under twenty were applying to the committee to assign them a day. The people of color were reminded of what Pennsylvania had done to promote the abolition of slavery, and were summoned to defend her. The physicians were asked to be ready in the event of a battle to hurry to the field. "Pious men, whose conscientious views would deter them from joining other corps" made up of irreligious men, were urged to form one of their own kind. As fast as the citizens responded, the committee would form them into companies, each in charge of a captain, name some place of rendezvous, and select a day upon which the teachers or the Sons of Erin, the friendly aliens or the victuállers, or whoever they might be, would assemble at five in the morning with lunch in a knapsack or a handkerchief, march out to Fairmount

---

* Report of the Committee of Defence to the Common Council, November 6, 1815. The money borrowed and collected amounted to $1,204,326.25, "making a probable gain to the Corporation of about $150,000."

or Grey's Ferry, and fall to work. At ten, by order of the quartermaster, the drum would beat for grog, when each captain would hurry to the tent and receive the liquor for his company. At noon the drum would beat for dinner, and the captains attend a second time for grog. At five o'clock all work stopped, and at that hour " it is hoped," said the quartermaster in his rules, that " for the honor of the cause we are engaged in, every man will retire sober." * Before the works were finished fifteen thousand men had labored on them one day each.

Lest even these defences should prove insufficient, the committee called on the Governor to take measures of an extreme kind. He was asked the moment the enemy landed to despatch men to see that, in the region through which the British would pass, all horses, cattle, and wagons were sent inland; that every animal that could serve as food was killed or carried away; that the lower box and the spear of every pump were removed; that all roads and passes were impeded with fallen trees, and at least one indispensable wheel taken from every mill. The community was terror-stricken; and it is little to the credit of the men of the Middle States that they made so weak and timorous a defence. In Maryland, Virginia, and Pennsylvania there were then living not far from one and a half million of whites. Yet this great population remained in its towns and cities, and suffered five thousand Englishmen to spend five weeks in its midst without ever once attempting to drive the invaders from the soil.

---

* United States Gazette, September 12, 1814.

CHAPTER XXVII.

FIGHTING ON THE GULF COAST.

THE section of our country toward which Pakenham and Sir Alexander Cochrane were soon to move had already been the scene of military operations of a very serious kind. That Spain, after war began, would keep order in her possessions along the coast of the Gulf and do her duty as a neutral was not to be expected, for her King was still a prisoner and her throne in the hands of Napoleon. That the Floridas under these circumstances would be more than ever the resort of smugglers, of pirates, of privateers, and perhaps the landing place of British troops intent on the invasion of the United States, was certain. That it was the duty of the United States to remove so threatening a danger by occupying and holding the territory till the return of peace was so plain to Madison that he never doubted that Congress would order it done. Indeed, so sure was he, that during the autumn of 1812 troops were collected and preparations made for the seizure. By one despatch * the Governor of Tennessee was summoned to detail fifteen hundred militia for what the Secretary was pleased to call "the defence of the lower country." By another, General Pinckney was informed that, should Congress consent to the seizure of the Floridas, troops would be sent him for the capture of St. Augustine.† By a third, Wilkinson, then at New Orleans, was commanded to hold himself in readiness to lead an expedition against West Florida.‡

To have formed an enterprise into which the people of the

---

* October 12, 1812.

† Monroe to Pinckney, January 13, 1813. War Department Archives.

‡ Monroe to Wilkinson, January 30, 1813. War Department Archives.

Mississippi Valley would enter more gladly would not have been possible. They were not deceived by any pretence of defence. They were not afflicted with any such notions as troubled the militia on the banks of the Niagara. The war with them was to be one of conquest, and it would go hard with them if, when peace came, the flag of the Union did not fly over every fortress from the Sabine to the St. Mary. When, therefore, Governor Blount bade Andrew Jackson, Major-General of State Militia, call out two thousand men, every fighting man in Tennessee was ready to respond. Two thousand and seventy were accepted, and these, on the seventh of January, set out from Nashville. They were the very men for the purpose. "They are," wrote Jackson to Secretary Eustis, "the choicest of our citizens. . . . They go at our country's call to do the will of Government. No constitutional scruples trouble them. Nay, they will rejoice at the opportunity of placing the American eagle on the ramparts of Mobile, Pensacola, and Fort St. Augustine," and so forever end British influence along the Gulf coast.* Such as were mounted rode through the Indian country, while the infantry went by boat down the Cumberland, the Ohio, and the Mississippi. For more than a month they journeyed on without incident, when, on February fifteenth, in obedience to a request from Wilkinson, the flotilla stopped at Natchez, and the army camped on the bluffs to wait for further orders. By that time Congress had acted, and the Senate having refused to consent to the occupation of Florida east of the Perdido, an express was sent post haste after him as he floated down the Mississippi, with orders recalling him. "The cause," said the Secretary, "for marching the corps under your command to New Orleans no longer exists. You will therefore consider it as dismissed from public service." † Then the fiery temper of Jackson flamed high, and in his fury he disobeyed the order, marched his men back to Nashville, and made himself responsible for their rations and their pay.

Although Congress would not consent to the seizure of

---

* Life of Andrew Jackson. James Parton, vol. ii, p. 372.
† Armstrong to Jackson, February 6, 1813.

East Florida, no objection was made to the invasion of West Florida, and February twentieth Madison signed an act intended to accomplish it. The law provided that the President should occupy and hold so much of the province of West Florida as lay west of the Perdido, and should for that purpose make use of the army and navy. This was precisely what Madison wanted, and not an hour was lost in putting the law in force. Indeed, the rapidity with which it was executed was, for those days, astonishing. The law was not five days old when orders * were on their way to Wilkinson to seize West Florida. In four weeks they were in his hands.† In eight weeks he had organized an expedition at Pass Christian, had led it against Mobile, had captured Fort Charlotte and the city,‡ had begun the construction of Fort Bowyer at the entrance to the bay, and had returned to New Orleans.# There he found orders which sent him to the Canadian frontier. Almost at the same time Pinckney withdrew the troops from Amelia Island,‖ and all signs of war along the Gulf coast disappeared.

The disappearance was seeming; for just back of the coast line serious trouble was brewing with the Indians.

On the seventh day of August, 1786, the Continental Congress passed an ordinance for the regulation of Indian affairs, cut the country inhabited by Indians into two parts by the river Ohio, placed each district in charge of a superintendent, ordered that none but citizens of the United States should trade therein, and required even American citizens to first obtain a license. Such of the tribes as dwelt north of the Ohio and west of the Hudson formed the northern district; such as lived south of the Ohio and east of the Mississippi were included in the southern district. In the western part of this district, overrunning the whole country from the Ohio to the Gulf, were the Chickasaws and Choctaws; at the eastern end was the great confederation of the Creeks; and along the Florida border the Seminoles. The hunting grounds of the

---

* February 16, 1813.
† March 14, 1813.
‡ April 15, 1813.

May 19, 1813.
‖ May 16, 1813.

Creeks had once stretched across Georgia; but by treaties, first with Georgia and then with the United States, the bounds had been narrowed till in 1800 they were the Tennessee river, the western half of Georgia, and the present State of Mississippi. Over them, as agent for the United States, presided at that time Benjamin Hawkins. He had been appointed in 1796, had labored unremittingly for their good, and had done much to give them what little civilization they possessed. Following out the policy of the Government, he had taught them how to plough and sow, raise crops, spin cotton, and had persuaded them to adopt a sort of national organization for the purpose of preserving peace and enforcing law. His success was not as great as could have been wished. Nevertheless, while they clung tenaciously to their old habits of hunting, they dwelt in villages and owned farms, cattle, slaves, and knew the use of the humbler implements of agriculture. Most of these villages, perhaps two thirds of them, belonged to the Upper Creeks, and were scattered along the banks of the Coosa and Tallapoosa rivers, in the heart of what is now Alabama. The Lower Creek towns were on the Chattahoochee.

That such a people would take up the tomahawk and give serious trouble never for a moment occurred to Hawkins. He well knew, indeed, that the visit of Tecumthe in 1811 had greatly excited the young warriors, that the prophets were still busy, and that in many of the villages the young men were singing the songs and dancing the dances of the Indians of the Lake. But the old chiefs were peaceful and vigilant, and no one was more surprised than Hawkins when he heard that the whole Upper Creek country was rising for war. The remote cause was the visit of Tecumthe and the secret doings of the prophets. The immediate cause was a series of events it is now necessary to relate.

In 1812 the Creek nation despatched a half dozen Indians on a mission to the Chickasaws. Little Warrior, a headman of a town called Wewocan, led them.* Having delivered their talk, they ought to have come back to Alabama; but Little Warrior took them northward, joined Tecumthe at Malden,

---

* American State Papers, Indian Affairs, vol. i, p. 839.

and they were all present in the massacre at the river Raisin. Soon after this they started homeward, carrying talks from the British and the Shawanese, and a letter from a British officer at Malden to the Spanish officials at Pensacola. Crossing the present State of Illinois, Little Warrior and his band reached the Ohio early in February, and some seven miles above the mouth came upon the cabins of three families of settlers. The taste of blood shed at the Raisin was too much for them, and on February ninth the settlers were foully murdered.* Crossing the Ohio, the band hurried through the Chickasaw country, boasting of the deed as they went, and about the middle of March were once more on the Coosa.

As Little Warrior had talks from the British, the chiefs soon met at Tuckaubatchee to hear them, and were surprised to receive a letter from Hawkins complaining of the murders on the Ohio and demanding the delivery of the seven murderers. The accused men took to the woods ; the chiefs declared them guilty, decreed death, sent forth parties to carry out the sentence, and in a few days each of the seven was dead.†

Measures so rigorous produced much excitement, and the prophets became busier than ever. Noticing this, the old chiefs of Tuckaubatchee addressed a message to the Alabamas, a small tribe living about the junction of the Coosa and Tallapoosa rivers, and greatly under the influence of the prophets. "We have heard much," said they, "of what is going on among you, and how the Great Spirit comes in the sun and speaks to you. Let us see and hear some of these things, that we also may believe." ‡ The Alabamas, however, were in no state of mind to hear such a message, and, having killed the runner, sent his scalp about among their friends. In a week the whole Upper Creek country was aflame. The excitement pent up since the visit of Tecumthe instantly broke out. Every warrior who had borne a part in killing the murderers

---

* Hawkins to the Creek chiefs, March 29, 1813.

† Report of Big Warrior, April 26, 1813. American State Papers, Indian Affairs, vol. i, p. 843.

‡ Report of Alexander Corvello, June 22, 1813.

was driven from the country.   Even the Tuckaubatchee chiefs
fled to Coweta and sought protection of Hawkins.   In number the "Red Sticks," as the fighting Indians were called—
from their being armed chiefly with red sticks or war clubs—
were about two thousand.   Their purpose, as stated in a talk,
was to kill all who had aided in putting Little Warrior and
his band to death, destroy Tuckaubatchee and Coweta, march
against the whites, and not leave one living between the Chattahoochee and the sea.   For the accomplishment of this, they
had bows, arrows, "red sticks," and the magic of the prophets.
To the most fanatical these might seem arms sufficient; but
some who were cooler-headed determined to seek aid of the
Spaniards.   When Little Warrior fell, the letter he was carrying from the British at Malden to the Spaniards at Pensacola
came into the possession of another half-breed Creek named
Peter McQueen.   Gathering some three hundred warriors
about him, and collecting four hundred dollars, he set out
with the letter for Pensacola early in July.*   The Spanish
Governor was greatly alarmed, and, more from fear of the
Indians than from hostility to the United States, he gave them
guns, powder, and ball.   News of the visit of McQueen having
spread far and wide, the Americans settled above Mobile, determined to cut him off when on his way home, and, led on
by some half-breeds and a man whose wife McQueen had
taken prisoner, they met him in a place called Burnt Corn.
At first the Indians fled, and some pack-mules with powder
were captured.   But McQueen soon rallied his warriors, and
the whites in turn retreated.†   It was now the intention of
the leaders of the "Red Sticks" to hurry on and attack Hawkins at the Indian Agency at Coweta; but the families of
those killed and wounded at Burnt Corn cried out for vengeance.   McQueen was forced to yield, and gathering about a
thousand warriors from thirteen of the Upper Creek towns,
he turned southward in search of the men who had attacked
him at Burnt Corn.   As he marched along, he heard that the

---

* Hawkins to Armstrong, July 20, 1813.   American State Papers, Indian
Affairs, vol. i, p. 849.

† Big Warrior to Colonel Hawkins, August 4, 1813.   American State Papers,
Indian Affairs, vol. i, p. 851.

two half-breed leaders, Dixon Bailey and Daniel Beasley, were at Fort Mims,* and to this place the expedition repaired.

The reports that came from the Indian country of the doings of the prophets High-Head Jim and Josiah Francis, and the unhappy ending of the battle of Burnt Corn Creek, had terrified the Alabama settlers, who, abandoning homes and farms and driving their stock before them, fled for shelter to the houses of some well-known men and proceeded to fortify them. In a little while the whole country between the Alabama and Tombigbee rivers, from their junction northward, was dotted with such rude defences, behind which were often gathered several hundred men, women, children, and negro slaves. They were called forts; but they were in reality stockades hastily put up about a house, whose size, strength, and location made it capable of being defended.

Such a one was that of Samuel Mims, a well-to-do half-breed. It stood on what seemed to be a small lake, but what was in fact an old bend of the Alabama river, cut off by the movement of the river a mile westward. The house was a large frame building, and around this, as the centre, had been built a stockade enclosing an acre of ground. The stockade was in the form of a square, was pierced with five hundred loop-holes, and entered through two huge gates, and at one corner was to have been defended by a block-house. But this was never completed.

When the stockade was finished the Tensaw settlers began pouring in with their goods and cattle, till by August five hundred and fifty-three men, women, children, negroes, Indians, troops, and officers were in the fort. The troops were a few militia and some volunteers sent on by General Ferdinand Leigh Claiborne, who had come from Baton Rouge to defend Mobile. For commander the refugees chose Dixon Bailey, whose share in the Burnt Corn expedition had made him popular. He was a man of courage, and admirable as a leader in the field, but wanting in that eternal vigilance which is so often the price of success. Twice he was warned of what was to come, and twice the warning went by unheeded.

---

* Benjamin Hawkins to General Floyd, September 30, 1814. Ibid., p. 854.

Once it came from a negro who had escaped from a plantation destroyed by McQueen in his march, and once from two
negroes sent out from the fort to watch the herds.   Hardly
were they gone when they came running back, declaring that
twenty-four painted Indians had been seen in the canes.
Troops were sent to the spot, but, no Indian signs being visible, one of the wretched negroes was flogged.   Yet his story
was true ; and even while they beat him, the prophets—
painted and bedecked with feathers, and carrying red sticks
and rods of magic, and medicine bags curiously wrought—
lay in a ravine not four hundred yards from the stockade
gate, at the head of a thousand Indians, painted, naked, and
well armed.   Next day the same slave was again sent out and
again saw the Indians ; but this time he fled with the news to
Fort Pierce, two miles away, and the people in Fort Mims,
who would not trust the word of a negro, were left to destruction.   It came quickly, and at noon on August thirtieth,
when the drums beat for dinner, the Red Sticks, raising the
war whoop, rushed upon the fort.   The story of what followed is the old tale of Indian surprise and massacre.   Of the
five hundred and fifty-three inmates, a few negroes carried
off as slaves, and fifteen whites, who, in the confusion, broke
through the stockade and hid in the swamp, were all that
escaped.   Two hundred and fifty scalps are said to have been
carried to Pensacola on poles.   September ninth, when an
officer sent by General Claiborne, with a strong detachment,
to bury the dead, reached Fort Mims, he found a piece of the
stockade and the unfinished block-house alone remaining ; he
saw the plain about the fort strewn with carcasses ; he beheld
on the sites of the houses heaps of ashes mingled with bones ;
and looked with horror on mounds of bodies of white men and
black men, Indians, women, and children, all scalped and mutilated, from which flocks of buzzards and packs of dogs fled,
screaming and yelping, as he approached.*

Fort Mims destroyed, the Indians, in a high state of excitement, spread over the country.   They burned the deserted
houses, they destroyed the crops, and murdered every white

---

* History of Alabama.   Albert James Pickett, vol. ii, pp. 264–284.

man with whom they came in contact. A panic seized the whole population of Mississippi territory, and with one accord the settlers, abandoning everything, fled to the forts. At Fort Huron were three hundred and ninety, at Fort Rankin were five hundred and thirty, and at Fort St. Stephen were five hundred settlers. Two forts at Mount Vernon were literally packed with refugees. Help, if it came at all, must come quickly, and in a few days expresses were riding with urgent calls to the Governors of Louisiana, of Georgia, and of Tennessee.

Tennessee was first to respond. All over the State meetings were held, addresses and appeals made, with such success that on October twelfth twenty-five hundred infantry and a thousand cavalry had crossed the Tennessee and camped in what is now Alabama. Andrew Jackson, just from a sickbed, on which he had been laid by a wound received in a street brawl with Thomas Hart Benton, was in command. Nor is it uninteresting to note that serving under him were David Crockett and a young ensign named Samuel Houston.

Between him and the Hickory Ground, at the junction of the Coosa and Tallapoosa rivers, where were the villages of the fighting Creeks, was one hundred and sixty miles of wilderness. To plunge into it without provisions seemed madness; yet no provisions were to be had, for the river was low, and not a barrel of the food ordered could come down from East Tennessee. His disappointment was extreme. But turn back he would not, and, having sent his mounted men forward to forage, he broke camp and fairly dragged his troops over the roughest of countries to a spot where the Tennessee makes its great south bend, and there, in a mountain pass, established Fort Deposit. This done, he turned southward into the wilderness, determined to seek food as he went. It was on the twenty-fifth of October that he set out, and within ten days he had reached the head waters of the Coosa, sacked the Indian village of Talishatchee, and had begun the construction of a fort, which he called Strother, when an Indian came with word that the friendly Creek town of Talladega was besieged. On November seventh he marched to relieve it, and November eighth won a crushing victory over the Hillabees. At Talladega he was within sixty miles of the

Hickory Ground, and could, he firmly believed, have conquered the Indians in ten days' time had food and re-enforcements reached him.   But they did not, and in their place
came word that the Army of East Tennessee, which should

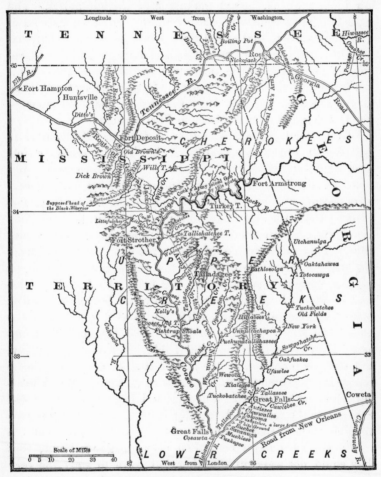

Seat of war among the Creek Indians.

have joined him, had turned and gone eastward.   This news
brought him back to Fort Strother on the tenth of November,
and there idleness and hunger began their work.   When it
seemed impossible to endure such hardships longer, the militia

mutinied. But Jackson called out the volunteers and restored
order, and had no sooner done so than the volunteers, ashamed
of their part in this affair, mutinied, and the next day started
homeward. But again Jackson met the emergency, and, calling out the militia, barred the march of the volunteers. The
grim humor of the thing, one of those earnest appeals he so
well knew how to make, and the solemn assurance that if supplies did not come in two days all should go home, restored
quiet. The supplies did not come, and Jackson, true to his
word, set out for Fort Deposit. Happily, he had not gone
twelve miles on the way when the supply train was encountered, and the army went back to Fort Strother.

Thenceforth there was no lack of food, and Jackson fully
intended to hurry southward. A few swift marches, a few
stout fights, and the Creek War would, he said, be over. But
again he was doomed to disappointment, for again the volunteers became unruly. They had enlisted on the tenth of December, 1812, for one year of service, and they would, they
now declared, start for home on the tenth day of December,
1813. This construction of the agreement Jackson stoutly
disputed. They had enlisted, he told them, not for one year,
but for one year of service on the field. Had such service
been rendered? By no means. They had been assembled at
Nashville, December tenth, 1812, had been discharged in the
same town May twenty-second, and called out again in October. They were therefore still liable for five months' duty,
and not one hour before the end of that time should they be
released. Arguments, appeals, commands were vain. A longing for home had seized the troops, and, growing stronger and
stronger as the tenth of December drew near, drove them into
open mutiny. Hearing on the evening of the ninth that the
volunteers were more bent than ever on going home, that
they could not wait till morning, but were to start the very
moment their time was out, Jackson was beside himself with
rage. It was long past eight o'clock, yet he ordered the volunteers to instantly parade in front of the fort, drew up the
militia in front of the volunteers, planted two cannon so as to
rake the line, abused the mutineers roundly, told them that
re-enforcements were coming, and that if they quit the fort

before that time they must cross their general's dead body.
The men yielded. Re-enforcements came December twelfth,
and the next day the volunteers went off in a body. But matters were not mended. The new arrivals were three-months'
men from East Tennessee, had but one month more to serve,
and could not be induced to lengthen their stay long enough
to make even a short raid against the enemy. During a month,
therefore, they guarded the fort, and were in turn followed *
by nine hundred recruits bound to serve for sixty days. They
were raw, insubordinate, and unsteady. Nevertheless, they
were troops, and with them, such as they were, Jackson at
once set off for the Indian country. January seventeenth he
left Fort Strother, reached Talladega the next day, and on the
twentieth was encamped on a creek named Enotachopco, twelve
miles from the Indian village of Emuckfaw. He was now
well in the country of the Red Sticks, and, advancing with
great caution, he soon fell upon a large trail which led to a
new road well beaten and lately travelled, and clearly showing
that a strong force of the enemy was near. The day being far
spent, a camp was formed and carefully guarded, and just at
dawn it was hotly attacked by the Indians. They were beaten
off; but Jackson, after passing one more night on the ground,
turned back, and at the end of January was again in Fort
Strother.

The purpose of his raid was to draw the attention of the
Indians from General John Floyd. Floyd commanded a troop
of Georgia militia, about nine hundred and thirty in number,
and with these and a few hundred Indians he had crossed the
Chattahoochee on November twenty-fourth. Marching direct
for the Creek village of Autossee, he drove out the Indians,
burned some four hundred houses,† and immediately retreated
to Fort Mitchell on the Chattahoochee. There he stayed till
January,‡ when he once more took the field, marched toward
Tuckaubatchee, and, when eight miles from the town, built
on Calibee Creek a fortified camp which he named Defiance.
There, just at daybreak,# the Creeks attacked him. They

---

* January 14, 1814.   ‡ January 18, 1814.
† November 29, 1813.   # January 22, 1814.

were driven off; but the militia had now enough of Indian warfare, insisted on going home, and forced Floyd to retire so hastily that four days after the fight they were again on Georgia soil at Fort Mitchell.

Thus, while Jackson was fleeing toward Fort Strother in one direction, Floyd was fleeing toward Fort Mitchell in the other, and January closed with the Creeks triumphant. Six months had passed since they took up the war club. Three armies, led by men of no mean ability, had marched against them. Some villages had been burned and nearly one quarter of the warriors in arms had been slain, but not a town in the heart of their country had been molested. This, however, was not to continue. When, in December, 1813, the volunteers left Fort Strother for home, Jackson had appealed most earnestly to Governor Blount, of Tennessee, for more men. The Governor would willingly have complied, but he had already called out all the troops authorized by law, and more than this he feared to do. In a long letter,* therefore, he stated these facts to Jackson, told him that the campaign had failed through no fault of his, and advised the general to give up the struggle and come home. But he knew not the man, and received in reply such a letter as it has rarely been the lot of any governor to read. Blount was told that such a suggestion could only come from the bad advisers with whom he was surrounded; that Jackson would not go home; that he would perish first; that he would hold the forts he had built till ordered away by the general commanding; that the proper thing for Blount to do was to act with the energy and decision the crisis demanded, and send on troops enlisted for six months.† The letter had its effect. Blount put aside his scruples, and ordered a new levy of four thousand militia. Two thousand of them from East Tennessee set out from Knoxville under General Cocke. They had been mustered in for six months, but hearing as they marched along that the militia of West Tennessee were to serve but three months, they instantly mutinied. General Cocke did his best to allay it, but before he succeeded orders

---

* Governor Willie Blount to Jackson, December 22, 1813. Life of Andrew Jackson, by James Parton, vol. i, pp. 479, 480.

† Ibid., pp. 480-484.

came from Jackson to one of the brigadiers to arrest and send to Fort Strother any officer of whatever rank found exciting the men to mutiny; whereupon he was arrested, his sword taken from him, and his troops brought on quietly to Fort Strother.

The cause of the disturbance was the refusal of a company of the Twenty-eighth Regiment, mustered in at Fayetteville, to serve for more than three months; a demand to which the commanding officer, finding them determined, yielded, and no more was heard of the matter till the company was near Fort Strother. That there might be no possible chance for misunderstanding, the men then halted and sent on their commander to see Jackson and get his acceptance of the terms. They might have spared themselves the trouble, for Jackson went into a towering rage, accused them of attempting to bargain with him, and dismissed the officer with a flat refusal. On returning to camp, he found it deserted and his troops twenty miles off on their way home. After reporting this to Jackson, he was ordered to return, offer pardon to all who would come back, and arrest as a deserter every man who would not, and, if necessary, lodge him in the nearest jail. Measures so vigorous had the desired effect. Once more the company mustered, and this time marched to Fort Strother. There Jackson felt he had them at his mercy, for the Thirty-ninth Regiment of regulars had joined him, and he was fully determined that if the regulars did nothing else they should keep the militia in order. How serious he was became very apparent when, not long after, a private in the Twenty-eighth named John Woods was court-martialed, tried, found guilty, and shot for refusing to obey the officer of the day.

As many of the men had but one month more to serve, he broke camp at once, and on March sixteenth dropped down the Coosa river some thirty miles and then started eastward for the Tallapoosa. In a great loop of that river, called the Horseshoe, some eight hundred Ocfuskee Indians had taken refuge with their women and children, and had built a rude fort. Across the neck of the Horseshoe was a breastwork five logs high, provided with two rows of loop-holes and arranged in the form of a crescent, so as to expose the assailants to a cross-fire. The space enclosed by the river and the breast-work was some eighty acres, was well wooded, and made stronger still by the fringe of matted bushes and fallen trees which lined the river banks. At the bottom of the loop on a flat were the Indian huts, and on shore, just at the water edge, were hundreds of canoes ready for use in case flight became necessary. But Jackson no sooner saw the place than he determined there should be no escape, and while he arranged his infantry and brought up his two guns and bombarded the breastwork, General Coffee, with the mounted men and the friendly Cherokees, crossed the river and surrounded the bend. This done, General Coffee, seeing the canoes on the opposite bank, sent over some Indians, who brought back so many that a detachment of his force soon landed on the Horseshoe, set fire to the Indian huts, and began an attack on the rear of the breastwork.

The smoke and the firing made known to Jackson what had happened, and he ordered the breastwork to be assaulted. The fighting now became terrible. Not an Indian would ask for quarter, but from fallen trees, mounds of brush, and piles of logs they kept up a hopeless resistance till darkness ended it. Of the nine hundred Red Stick warriors who began the battle, five hundred and fifty-seven were found dead in the Horse-shoe, and among them, resplendent with paint and feathers, were the three great prophets. As many of the Creeks were shot while attempting to swim the river, it is believed that not more than two hundred escaped. In Jackson's army the killed were fifty-one and the wounded one hundred and fifty-eight. Among the killed was Major Lemuel Pennell Montgomery, whose name is still borne by the county within which the battle ground lies. Among the desperately wounded was Samuel Houston, the young ensign of the regulars, of whom the country was yet to hear more.

The day after the battle Jackson fell back to a fort he had built on the Coosa, spent five days in refitting his army, and then marched southward, harrying the country as he went. Heavy rains and floods retarded him, but on April seventeenth he reached the Hickory Ground and pitched his camp at a point four miles from the junction of the Coosa and Tallapoosa, where the old French Governor Bienville had built Fort Toulouse. More than a century had elapsed since that day, but the remains of the ancient fort were still visible, and, taking possession of these, the army planted the American flag, cleared out the old trenches, put up an American block-house and stockade, and named the works Fort Jackson.

His presence spread terror among the Red Sticks, and though a few chiefs came in and made submission, McQueen and many of the inhabitants of the Coosa, Tallapoosa, and Alabama fled over the boundary to Florida and sought aid of England. The campaign ended and the Indian power destroyed, Pinckney dismissed the volunteers and Jackson gladly led his men back to Tennessee. But his stay at the Hermitage, as he called his home, was short, for William Henry Harrison now resigned, and Jackson was immediately appointed major-general in the regular army, in Harrison's place, and put in command of the Seventh Military District.

His orders bade him take command of the three half-filled regiments which formed the Army of the South, make his headquarters at Mobile, and, as he went thither, sign a definitive treaty with the conquered Creeks. On this duty he set out immediately, and, July tenth was once more at Fort Jackson, on the Hickory Ground. There he took command of his troops, there he soon met the friendly chief, and there he perpetrated one of the many gross and shameless wrongs on the Indians which disgrace the American people. Not a prophet, not a Red Stick, not an Indian in arms was north of the Florida boundary. The chiefs who met him in council were those whose friendship had been sorely tried and not found wanting, who had suffered for keeping the faith, who had fought in the service of the Government, and who in common justice ought to have been rewarded, not punished. Yet the terms which Jackson now dictated could not have been harder had he been dealing with McQueen and the Red Sticks. There must be, he said, in the first place, a land cession as indemnity for the cost of the war; there must be, in the second place, a stipulation that the Creeks would have no communication with any Spanish garrison or town, nor deal with any trader who did not have a license from the United States;

there must, in the third place, be an acknowledgment of the right of the United States to open roads, build forts, and put up trading posts in any part of the Creek territory that might seem best ; in the fourth place, the prophets and stirrers-up of the war must be surrendered. To give up the prophets was not possible, for they were dead or in Florida. To the requirements regarding the roads, the forts, the Spanish towns, and unlicensed traders, no objections were made. But when they heard that they must give up all southern and western Alabama and live henceforth between the Chattahoochee and the Coosa, they unanimously refused to sign. Jackson, however, stood firm. He told them that the land demanded had belonged to the Red Sticks, and would be taken whether they consented or not. He told them that such as refused to sign would be enemies of the United States, and would do well to join their friends at Pensacola. He told them that if they went it would be his duty to overtake and destroy them ; and when he had told them this, the Creeks, knowing that they were powerless, yielded, and on August ninth, 1814, signed the treaty at Fort Jackson. When this formality was over the journey was resumed, and the troops, floating down the Alabama river, reached Mobile on August fifteenth, and at once began to prepare for the invasion of Florida. The intense longing for that strip of territory, which had always been felt by the people of the Southwest, was in Jackson an overmastering passion. To his mind, the Revolution was not complete, the Republic was not safe, the Southwest was a retarded country, while a single Spanish garrison or a single Spanish flag could be seen anywhere along the north coast of the Gulf of Mexico. When he began his first campaign against the Creeks, Pensacola was the place where he hoped to end it. When he was made major-general and ordered to Mobile, he at once begged hard for orders to take Pensacola. "Only say to me," he wrote to Armstrong, " raise a few hundred militia, and, with such a regular force as can be conveniently collected, make a descent upon Pensacola and reduce it." *

---

* The Life of Andrew Jackson, Major-General, etc. By John Henry Eaton, p. 212.

Orders did not come, and when he reached Fort Jackson, in July, he did his best to provoke a quarrel with the Spanish Governor of Pensacola by demanding the delivery of the Red Sticks who had fled to Florida.   In August, when he reached Mobile, he was more eager than ever to see the Spanish flag come down at Pensacola, for the British were already there.

The old Spanish town of Pensacola, or Santa Maria de Galve, was founded as early as 1693 by Andres de Pes, and under Spanish rule had grown to be a place of no little beauty and note.   Its harbor was the finest in all Florida. The overland trade between it and St. Augustine was great enough to build up more than one mission, whose rusting church bells, half-buried cannon, and mouldering walls still mark the route.   The gardens, the public buildings, the fortifications, impregnable in those days, were no mean representatives of Spanish greatness.   But, long before Jackson ever beheld the place, all this splendor had passed away, and Pensacola had become a town of no importance whatsoever.   The Governor still lived there, and had with him a few troops, with which to maintain his dignity and garrison Fort Barrancas, which, six miles from town, barred the entrance to the bay.   But the inhabitants of the few unsightly houses were West Indian traders, smugglers—pirates, as the Governor called them—privateersmen, Indians, half-breeds, runaway negroes, and white men who had fled the States for cause. Before this place, however, such as it was, appeared late in July Major Edward Nicholls, with four officers, eleven non-commissioned officers, ninety-seven privates of the Royal Marines, two howitzers, a thousand stand of arms, and three hundred suits of clothing, and Captain W. H. Percy, in command of the sloops of war Hermes and Carron.   The town and the territory were dependencies of the Spanish Crown, yet Nicholls landed without the slightest ceremony, seized Forts Barrancas and St. Michael, raised the English flag beside that of Spain, put arms and ammunition on shore, took up his abode in the house of the Governor, and issued a proclamation, addressed to the people of Kentucky and Louisiana.   "Natives of Louisiana," said he, " on you the first call is made to assist in liberating your paternal soil from a faithless, imbecile Government. The American usurpation of this country must be abolished. I am at the head of a large body of Indians, well armed, well disciplined, and commanded by British officers. But be not alarmed at our approach. The same good faith which distinguished the Britons in Europe accompanies them here. A flag over any door, whether Spanish, French, or English, will be a sure protection; nor dare any Indian put his foot on the threshold thereof under penalty of death. Inhabitants of Kentucky! you have too long borne with grievous impositions. The whole brunt of the war has fallen on your brave sons. Be imposed on no longer. Range yourselves under the standard of your forefathers or be neutral. After the experience of twenty-one years can any of you longer support those brawlers for liberty who call it freedom when they themselves are free ?"

While waiting for this appeal to take effect, Nicholls set about collecting the large body of Indians mentioned in the proclamation, and as some of the Red Sticks had flocked to town, on hearing of his arrival, they were gathered, and, dressed up in red coats and armed with muskets, were drilled every day on the streets of Pensacola. Not to appear idle in the midst of such activity, Captain Percy was next to act, and on September first despatched a ship bearing a letter to the man known to our countrymen of that day as "Jean Lafitte, the Pirate of the Gulf."

During her long and desperate struggle with England it had been the custom of France to sell letters of marque and reprisal to any adventurers who cared to buy them. Sharpers, lawless men, and men led astray by the thirst for gain, were quick to see the use to which such letters might be put, and in a few years the Spanish main swarmed with wretches who, claiming to be privateersmen of France and showing commissions from that Government, made Guadeloupe and Martinique their island haunts, and sallied forth to prey upon the commerce of all nations. As England spread her conquests in the West Indies, she broke up these nests of pirates, till, with the fall of Guadeloupe in February, 1810, their last refuge was taken from them, and they sought new homes along the borders of the United States. Some turned smugglers and brought their plunder to Amelia Island; but scores of others found safety in the bays and marshes of the Louisiana coast, and there followed their shameful calling more openly than ever. Nor could another spot be found on earth better suited to their needs. The whole coast of Louisiana is a vast sea marsh; for fifty miles on either side of the delta the country is low, flat, and wet, covered with marsh grasses growing higher than a man's head, and deeply indented with innumerable bays. Across the entrance to the bays lie long and narrow islands, sometimes of white sand thrown up by the waves of the Gulf, and sometimes of rich earth brought down by the rivers and bayous. Behind these outlying islands, in the brown waters of the bays, are hundreds of smaller islands separated by narrow passes, winding and twisting as they come down from the interior, and almost hidden by the rank growth of bulrushes and shining reeds that rise twelve feet in the air. It was in such a bay, called Barataria, that the pirates, when driven from Guadeloupe, found refuge.

This great sheet of water lies to the west of the delta and some sixty miles south of New Orleans. Stretching across two thirds of its entrance is Grande-Terre, an island two miles long by a quarter of a mile wide. Just west of this is a pass a mile in width, separating Grande-Terre from another island called Grande Isle, and affording an easy entrance from the Gulf to the deep and quiet harbor of Barataria. On the western side are a multitude of small islands, parted by little lakes and passes which lead to the bayous Terre Bonne and La Fourche. Toward the north the bay stretches away for sixteen miles before it again breaks up into lakes and bayous, through which obscure water ways lead to the levee opposite New Orleans. Barataria was the very place for a pirate colony, and, taking possession of Grande-Terre, the exiled privateers fortified the island, built store-houses and dwellings, laid out farms and orangeries on Grande Isle, and sold their plunder at auction on one of the neighboring islands, whence the buyers smuggled it up the bayou Barataria and the lakes Salvador and Des Allemands to New Orleans.

At New Orleans were then living two brothers, Jean and Pierre Lafitte. They were natives of Bordeaux, had seen

much of the world, and spoke English, French, Spanish, and
Italian fluently. Pierre was a seafaring man, who had once
been in the French navy, and was well known in the city as a
fencing-master. Jean derived support for some years from a
blacksmith shop, in which the work was done by his negroes.
But in 1808 a far more lucrative occupation presented itself.
On the first of January of that year the law forbidding the
importation of slaves into the United States went into force.
A few weeks later news of the embargo reached New Orleans,
and the brothers Lafitte instantly turned merchants, opened a
shop, and under this thin disguise began to smuggle in negroes
and British goods. Such was their success that when the
West Indian refugees and the privateers from Guadeloupe
made their settlement at Grand Isle in 1810, Jean and Pierre
Lafitte became first their commercial agents and then their
chiefs. The laws of the land were now set at naught. Custom inspectors and revenue officers were defied, and orders
were given and taken openly in New Orleans for their prize
goods and their cargoes of slaves. That the ships which
brought these cargoes to "The Temple" were pirates of the
genuine sort, and not privateers, was never for a moment
doubted. More than once the Government sought to dislodge
them; but the Baratarians were too strongly armed, and the
attacks served but to induce them, when Venezuela revolted
in 1811, to take out letters of marque from the patriots
and run up the flag of Cartagena. Thenceforth they grew
bolder and more outrageous than ever, and with the opening
of the war reached the very summit of lawless power and
appeared daily in the public resorts of New Orleans. This
was too much for even the apathetic Creole, and in July,
1814, a grand jury denounced the Baratarians as pirates and
indicted Pierre Lafitte, who was soon shut up in the calaboza
with one of his captains named Dominique You.

It was while affairs were in this condition that Captain
Lockyer, in the Sophie, came in sight of Barataria on September third, and, after firing on an inbound vessel and forcing her to run aground, dropped anchor some six miles off
shore. The cannonading brought the whole population of
the island to the beach, whence Jean Lafitte promptly set off

in his boat to inspect the stranger, from whose side, as he was rowed along, he beheld a pinnace put off with a white flag in the bow and the British flag astern. In the boat were Captain Lockyer and two officers, who soon made known their name and asked for Lafitte. Jean, announcing himself to be the man they sought, received a packet, led the way to shore, and, while entertaining his visitors most royally, proceeded to read the documents. They were four in number. One was the proclamation of Nicholls to the people of Louisiana and Kentucky; another was an address to the people of Barataria, warning them that if they did not join Great Britain in her just and unprovoked war against the United States, stop hostilities against Spain, and put their armed ships under the command of Nicholls, Captain Lockyer would destroy the place, in return for the depredations they had committed on British merchantmen; the third was addressed to Jean Lafitte, offered him the rank of captain in the British service, and protection to person and property; the fourth was a part of the instructions of Percy to Lockyer, and was to the effect that if Lafitte agreed to serve England his ship should be made ready for an attack on Mobile.

After reading the letters, Lafitte retired to consider. But he was scarcely out of the room when the pirates rushed in, seized the officers and the crew of the pinnace, and held them prisoners all night. In the morning Lafitte appeared, and, with a profusion of apologies for the rudeness of his men, escorted his visitors to their boat. A few hours later he addressed Captain Lockyer, gave assurance of a full determination to accept the offer, and asked for two weeks in which to put his affairs in order. To this Lockyer answered that he would return in fifteen days.

The next step of Lafitte was to gather up his letters and send them to an old friend, then a member of the Legislature, asking in return for this information but one favor—the amelioration of the lot of his unhappy brother. That the request was granted seems quite likely, for in the New Orleans newspapers of the following day a reward of one thousand dollars is offered for the capture of Pierre Lafitte, who broke jail the night before. Jean now wrote to his friend a second time. The armed brig and two sloops of war were still in the offing; should he, therefore, make overtures to the United States? What advice was given is not known; but on September tenth Claiborne received a formal tender of service from the pirate chief.

"This point of Louisiana," said he, "which I occupy is of great importance in the present crisis. I tender my services to defend it, and the only reward I ask is that a stop be put to the proscription against me by an act of oblivion for all that has been done." Never, at any time, had he sailed under any flag but that of Cartagena. His vessels were therefore, he held, perfectly regular, and, could he have brought his prizes into the ports of the United States, he would not have used the illicit means to which proscription had driven him.

Claiborne knew not what to do; so, gathering about him an officer of the army, of the navy, and the militia, he laid the letters before them and asked for advice. Were the letters genuine, or a mere ruse of Lafitte to ward off the doom so soon to fall upon him? If genuine, was it proper for the Governor of Louisiana to hold communication with a pirate? One of the officers—General Villeré, of the militia—voted Yea! But the two others—Colonel George T. Ross, of the regular army, and Master-Commandant Daniel T. Patterson, of the navy—voted Nay, for they were at that very moment engaged in making ready an expedition to destroy Lafitte.

Once before a like attempt had been made, but with no success. The impudence of Lafitte's conduct having become a scandal to the State, Claiborne in 1813 set a price on the pirate chief, and offered five hundred dollars for his head. Lafitte answered with a reward of five thousand dollars for the Governor's head, which so angered Claiborne that he ordered out a few militia, and sent them by land to Barataria, to destroy the settlement and scatter the banditti. The troops had almost reached the place without seeing a human being, when suddenly, at the sound of a boatswain's call, they found themselves surrounded by armed men, who came swarming from every hidden pass of the bayou. Then was enacted the scene with which every reader of the literature of pirates and high-waymen is familiar. Tempting offers are made the militia captain. The officer spurns them, and Lafitte, with great courtesy, sends the honest soldier home unhurt.

But the expedition which went out in 1814 was of a very different sort. At the head of it was Commander Daniel T. Patterson, who, when he dropped down the river on September eleventh, had with him three barges full of troops.* At the Balize he was joined by six gun-boats and a schooner, and before sunset of September sixteenth Grande Isle and Grande-Terre, seven piratical cruisers, and three armed schooners, under the flag of Cartagena, were in his hands.† At Barataria Patterson spent a week destroying houses, stores, and property, and about the end of the month he returned with his prizes to New Orleans. Meantime, the day for the return of Lockyer to Barataria arrived. But he came not, for the little fleet of which his vessel formed a part had been badly worsted at Mobile.

Lockyer had been ordered by Percy to bring the ships of Lafitte with him for an attack on Mobile ; but if he could not, he was to return with all haste to Pensacola and report. This he did ; whereupon Nicholls, though disappointed in his attempt to win over the pirates of Barataria, decided to attack Jackson without the help of Lafitte, and set out, with Captain Percy and the ships, to bombard Fort Bowyer, a small earth fort built by Wilkinson in 1813, on a low, barren sands-pit at the entrance to Mobile Bay. Its armament consisted of twenty guns, of which but eight were serviceable, and its garrison, of one hundred and sixty men, of the second infantry, commanded by Major William Lawrence. To reduce this redoubt, Percy took with him the Hermes, of twenty-two guns, the Sophie, of twenty guns, the Carron and Childers, each of eighteen guns, and a large force of marines and Indians, under Colonel Woodbine.

The marines and the Indians, with two light guns, were landed on the beach far in the rear of the fort, and took position behind the sand-hills on the morning of September twelfth. But the ships lay at anchor in the Gulf for three days,

---

* J. K. Smith to the Secretary of the Navy, September 23, 1814.
† Daniel T. Patterson to Governor Claiborne, September 25, 1814.

and the fifteenth came before any serious attack was made on
Fort Bowyer. On that day, however, the fleet, with the
Hermes in the lead, was seen coming on in line of battle.
Lawrence instantly announced the war-cry for the day to be,
"Don't give up the fort!" The officers solemnly bound
themselves under oath never to surrender till the ramparts
had been battered down and the garrison almost destroyed;
and not even then unless fully assured that no Indian outrages should be allowed. The men took their places at the
guns, and about four in the afternoon the Hermes, with the
fleet in line behind her, ran into the narrow channel that led
to the bay, and dropped anchor off the fort. During an hour
the firing from the ships, the fort, and the little battery behind the sand-hills was incessant. Then the superiority of
the American gunnery began to tell. The cable of the
Hermes was cut, and the current, swinging her bow toward
the fort, swept her slowly down stream, the Americans raking
her from stem to stern as she went, till she grounded, when
Percy, fleeing with his wounded to the other ships, set her on
fire. The Sophie, which by this time had six killed and sixteen wounded, drew off, the Carron and the Childers followed,
and about ten at night the Hermes blew up. At daybreak
the fleet was on its way back to Pensacola, while the marines
and Indians, having put their guns on board the vessels, went
by land with all the speed they could to the same place.

To Pensacola Jackson would gladly have followed the
enemy, but he had not troops enough, and was forced to wait
till the twenty-five hundred men he had summoned from Tennessee reached him. Meantime he issued one proclamation to
the Louisianians much in the style of that of Nicholls, and
another to the free negroes, calling on them to enlist, and received a warning from Monroe that New Orleans would surely
be attacked. He was told by the Secretary, in September,* that
there was reason to believe that the enemy had set on foot an
expedition against Louisiana; that the President had therefore
ordered five thousand troops to be sent from Tennessee, and
twenty-five hundred to be raised in Georgia and held ready to

---

* Monroe to Jackson, September 25, 1814.   Mss. War Department archives.

march ; and that one hundred thousand dollars in treasury notes had been given to Governor Blount, of Tennessee, to pay the cost of the campaign. Lest this should not be sufficient, Monroe wrote again in October that a force of fifteen thousand men had sailed from Ireland early in September for New Orleans and Mobile, and that twelve thousand five hundred men were subject to Jackson's orders in Kentucky, Tennessee, and Georgia.* But he gave the letter of September no heed. His mind was set on taking Pensacola, and toward it, as soon as the Tennessee troops arrived, he marched with four thousand one hundred men.

The expedition was marked by all the zeal, by all the impetuosity, by all the burning energy for which Jackson is so justly famous. He left Mobile on November third, demanded the surrender of Pensacola on the night of the sixth, carried it by storm on the seventh, saw Fort Barrancas blown up by the British on the morning of the eighth, and was back again at Mobile on the eleventh. But there his activity ended. The object for which he had striven so long having been accomplished, he might well have turned with the same energy to the defence of New Orleans, against which the long-predicted expedition had sailed. But had it been his settled purpose to suffer the city to fall into British hands, he could not have been more negligent. Twelve hundred of his men he left at Mobile. A thousand more he sent to chase Indians and British on the Yellow Water and the Escambia. Two thousand under General Coffee he ordered to march by the most comfortable route to Baton Rouge. One regiment he sent direct to New Orleans, while he himself, sick and suffering greatly, went by easy stages to the same city, where he arrived December second. If Jackson was negligent, the Government and the people of Louisiana were shamefully indifferent. The letters of Lafitte to Claiborne had been published in New Orleans in September, and would in a week have been forgotten had it not been for the exertions of Edward Livingston.

Livingston was a native of New York and a brother of Robert R. Livingston, whose name is bound up with so many

---

* Monroe to Jackson, October 10, 1814. Mss. War Department archives.

of the ever-memorable events of our early history. He was bred a lawyer, but in the exciting days of the struggle for neutrality he turned to politics, entered the House of Representatives in 1795, and, with Madison and Gallatin, led the opposition to the administrations of Washington and of Adams. As a reward for these services, and for the yet greater service rendered in the contested election of 1801, Jefferson made him United States District Attorney, and the Council of Appointment sitting at Albany made him Mayor of the city of New York. Though an earnest Democrat, he did not consider it improper to hold two offices at the same time, and continued to serve as Mayor and Attorney till, in 1803, by gross neglect of duty, he became a defaulter to the United States. Having confessed judgment, and made over all his property to a trustee to sell for the purpose of paying his debts, he fled to New Orleans, and once more began the practice of law. The Province of Louisiana had just been delivered to the United States, and Livingston, finding the old French and Spanish law in dreadful confusion, set himself to draw up a code of practice, which the Assembly of the Territory of Orleans adopted. At the bar his success was rapid, and among his clients he soon numbered no less a person than Jean Lafitte. As he thus knew the pirate chief well, Livingston never for a moment doubted the genuineness of the letters sent to Claiborne, and took the lead in a call for a meeting of citizens at the Coffee-House to consider the danger which threatened the city.

The meeting passed some resolutions and chose a Committee of Defence. But the committee, after framing an address and voting a sword to Major Lawrence for his conduct at Fort Bowyer, did nothing. The Governor was next to act, and called a special session of the Legislature. But the Legislature voted no money, raised no troops, adopted no plan of defence, and on the December day when Jackson entered New Orleans the city was utterly unprepared to resist, though the British fleet was then off the coast of Cuba.

Of all the combined fleets and armies Great Britain ever sent against a foe, few had equalled that which, toward the close of November, 1814, was assembled in Negril Bay. There, riding at anchor, were fifty of the finest ships the English navy could furnish, armed with a thousand guns and carrying on their decks nearly twenty thousand soldiers and sailors who had fought with Wellington on the Peninsula and with Nelson at the Nile. One, the Toussaint, a ship taken by Nelson at the Nile, was of eighty guns, and carried the flag of Sir Alexander Cochrane, commander of the fleet. Five others were seventy-fours, each one commanded by a man of famous memory, more than one of whom was well known in America, for among them was Sir Thomas Hardy, who had captured Eastport and bombarded Stonington, and James Alexander Gordon, who had plundered the people of Alexandria. Of the rest, sixteen were transports. Twenty were ships carrying from sixteen to fifty guns apiece. On the transports were the men who fought at Bladensburg and Baltimore and laid the buildings at Washington in ashes; two negro regiments raised in the West Indies; some Highlanders fresh from the Cape of Good Hope, and four regiments which had served in the Peninsula campaign, all under the command of Sir Edward Pakenham, the brother-in-law of Wellington and the ablest of his lieutenants. That the expedition could fail had not entered the mind of any one; and as the country was to be occupied and held, there were on board, besides the troops, not only the wives of several of the officers, but a collector for the port of New Orleans and many civil officers and their families.

It was on the morning of November twenty-sixth that the ships of the fleet shook out their sails, and, after a run of two weeks, made land at Chandeleur Island, at the entrance to Lake Borgne, on December tenth. Troops were at once transferred from the heavy ships to the light, and these, under convoy of such gun brigs as the shallow water would float, entered the lake, where they beheld six gun-boats draw up, as if to meet them. As they came on, however, the gun-boats weighed anchor and fled toward the city, whither a flotilla of fifty launches and barges, led by Captain Lockyer, followed, and, after a desperate hand-to-hand fight, captured and destroyed all six at noon on December fourteenth.

News of the disaster reached Jackson as he was returning to New Orleans from a tour of inspection down the river.

In an instant he was the Jackson of the Hickory Ground and Pensacola, and in a few hours riders with orders were speeding over the country in every direction. The officer in charge of Fort St. Philip was commanded to hold the fort while a man remained alive to point a gun. General Coffee, at Baton Rouge, was bidden not to sleep till he reached New Orleans. General Winchester was enjoined to be watchful, to guard the route to Fort Jackson, and defend Mobile Point at all hazard. The citizens were told in a proclamation that the district must and would be defended; that all who were not with the cause were against it; and that every man who did not appear with arms in his hands, ready to dispute each inch of ground with the British, should be dealt with accordingly. Nor was this threat an idle one; for, when the Legislature hesitated to suspend the writ of habeas corpus, Jackson proclaimed martial law and turned the city into a camp.

And now re-enforcements began to arrive. First came Lafitte, tendering the services of himself and his men, an offer which was gladly accepted. Next came General Coffee, and then General Carroll, with the Tennessee brigade, promised a month before by Monroe. Meantime the British brought their ships up the lake as far as the shallow water would allow, and put the troops ashore. The traveller who, in our day, comes to New Orleans from Mobile by railroad, just as he reaches the extreme southeastern corner of Louisiana is hurried across an island formed by the two mouths of the Pearl river. Rising a few feet above the surrounding marsh, it is at times dry ground, and it was on this, the Isle aux Poix of the Creoles, that the British forces were landed. But so difficult was the undertaking that a week was spent in carrying seven thousand men in small boats over the thirty miles between the ships and the island. While this was going on, two officers who were sent to examine the head of the lake made their way in the night to a village of Spanish fishermen just at the mouth of Bayou Bienvenue, where they were well received and carried in canoes up the bayou and through one of its branches to the Villeré plantation, not six miles from the city. There at their leisure they chose the line of advance, and then

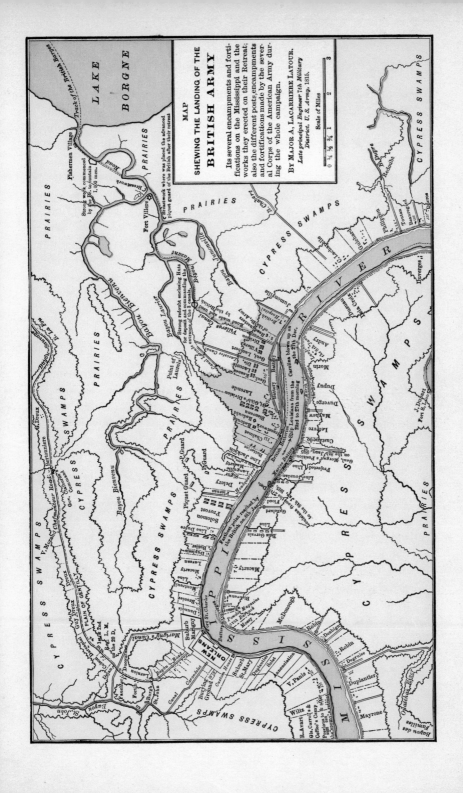

MAP
SHEWING THE LANDING OF THE
BRITISH ARMY

Its several encampments and fortifications on the Mississippi and the
works they erected on their Retreat;
also the different posts, encampments
and fortifications made by the several Corps of the American Army during the whole campaign.

By MAJOR A. LACARRIERE LATOUR,
Late principal Engineer 7th Military
District, U. S. Army, 1815.

Scale of Miles

LAKE
BORGNE

went back unmolested to the island.*   They departed just in time, for, forty-eight hours later, a sergeant and eight men reached the village to do duty as pickets.

As soon as the troops had all been landed on Isle aux Poix, sixteen hundred and eighty-eight of them were despatched to make their way to the Mississippi.   They set out on the morning of the twenty-second, surprised the picket at the fishing village on the morning of the twenty-third, and pushed up the Bayou Bienvenue to the little Bayou Mazant, and so to the mouth of a draining canal, where they landed, and, marching along its bank through a wood, came suddenly upon the house of Major Villeré and made him and all his family prisoners.   They were then but six miles from New Orleans, without a fortification of any kind between them and the city.

Happily Major Villeré broke from his captors, reached New Orleans in safety, and reported to Jackson what had happened.   It was long past noon, and, the people having retired to their houses for their mid-day dinner, the levee and the streets were quite deserted.   But the great bell of the cathedral no sooner rang out the alarm, the drummers no sooner began to beat the long roll, than Creoles and Americans, negroes, regulars, and San Domingans poured into the Place d'Armes from every quarter.   In half an hour the regulars were on the march.   In two hours the Tennesseeans were posted behind the Rodriguez canal, and by sundown Jackson, with twenty-one hundred men and two guns, was on his way toward the British camp.   As darkness came on, the war schooner Carolina, of fourteen guns, dropped down the river, ran close inshore, and about seven o'clock opened on the camp with her broadside.   Her firing was the signal for the land attack to begin, and Jackson, who was waiting two miles above, moved down the levee, while General Coffee, who was marching along the cypress swamp, wheeled to the right and advanced on the British flank just as a thick fog settled over the marsh and river.   So complete was the surprise that Cof-

---

* Vice-Admiral Cochrane to Mr. Croker, January 18, 1815.   James's Naval Occurrences, vol. ii, p. 550.

fee found nothing but squads of men gathered about their officers to oppose him. The thickening fog, the smoke of battle, the darkness, added to the confusion, and squads of men—red-coats and Tennesseeans, Creoles and Highlanders—swept over the field, here advancing, there retreating, firing alike into friend and foe, and fighting often with fists, knives, and musket butts. Little by little the British fell back till a place of refuge was found behind an old levee about three hundred yards from the river. Here they were sheltered by the new levee in their rear from the fire of the Carolina, and, as re-enforcements came up, Coffee withdrew his men. Jackson had done the same thing on the levee an hour before, and next morning took position two miles away, behind the Rodriguez canal, which stretched from the levee to the swamps.

If the material gain of the battle was small, the moral gain was great. Not a moment was lost by the British in hurrying forward the troops, till, by the morning of Christmas day, upward of six thousand were gathered on the Villeré plantation, with Sir Edward Pakenham in command. Even then he would not attack till the two schooners in the river, the Carolina and Louisiana, had been driven away. This required artillery, and two days were spent by the sailors in dragging nine field pieces, two howitzers, and a mortar across the swamps to the levee. Once there, they quickly destroyed the Carolina with red-hot shot, drove away the Louisiana, and enabled the army to move forward on the morning of the twenty-eighth. But the march was a short one, for no sooner did Pakenham behold the half-finished breastworks of Jackson than he halted, fell back out of range, and ordered the troops to tent themselves. Once more the sailors were put to work. Once more cannon were brought with infinite labor from the ships and tugged over marsh and bog to the British camp on the river, till, on January first, 1815, thirty had been planted in eight batteries. The day dawned so foggy and hazy that the American position could not be seen. But toward eight o'clock the mist cleared away, Jackson's line stood out, and the British poured upon it a heavy fire of shot and Congreve rockets. The Americans answered, and with such precision that by noon the British gunners were driven

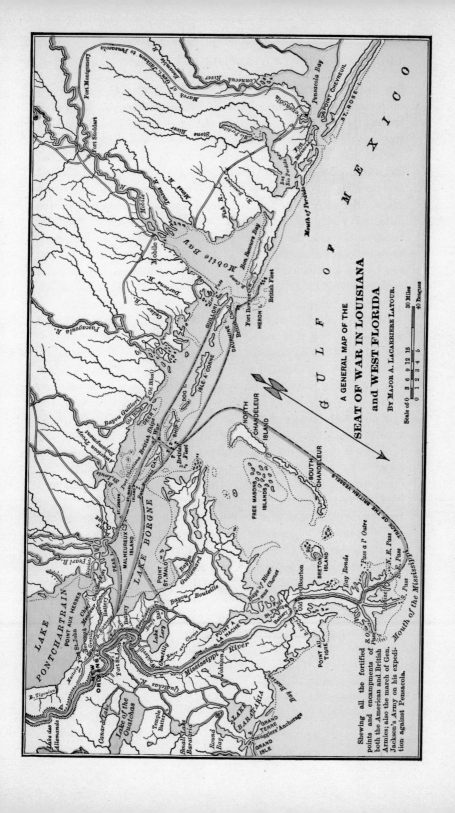

A GENERAL MAP OF THE

SEAT OF WAR IN LOUISIANA
and WEST FLORIDA

By Major A. Lacarriere Latour.

Scale of 0 3 6 9 12 15   30 Miles
          0 1 2 3 4 5   40 Leagues

Shewing all the fortified
points and encampments of
both the American and British
Armies; also the march of Gen.
Jackson's Army on his expedition against Pensacola.

from their pieces and the batteries completely silenced. Again the moral effects of victory surpassed the material, and Pakenham, fearing to storm the American line, waited one week for re-enforcements which raised his army to more than eight thousand men. Then the attack was renewed.

Across the Mississippi, opposite the British, was a battery put up by Master-Commandant Patterson before the Carolina was destroyed. To this, after the destruction of his ship, he retired, and against this the British now made preparations to move. The draining canal, up which the English had come to its head in the rear of the Villeré plantation, was therefore continued across the plantation to the levee. By means of this work, which to this day is called the Canal Pakenham, the boats were to be floated to the back of the levee, dragged over its top, and launched on the Mississippi. Troops were then to be sent across to silence the battery, while the army in three columns, unhindered by a fire on their flank, fell upon Jackson's line. But the canal was discovered, the object suspected, and on the afternoon of January seventh some Kentuckians were ordered to hurry to New Orleans, cross the river by the ferry, march down the west bank, and defend the batteries. The order was executed, and about four in the morning they reached a small redoubt, where General David Morgan, with some Louisiana militia, was encamped, just as the British on the eastern shore were forming to begin the assault. The purpose of Pakenham was to keep one division in reserve, and before dawn to attack with two. But Colonel Thornton, who, with some twelve hundred men, was to cross the river, was long getting the boats afloat, and dawn came before the first detachment pushed off from the levee. Swept down by the current, the men landed on the west bank, far below the battery, about six in the morning, and formed as rapidly as possible.

On the eastern bank, meantime, Pakenham, having drawn up his troops, was listening for the first sound of Thornton's attack. But when dawn turned to day, when the sun rose and the fog began to lift, and no sound came, Pakenham could wait no longer. The order was given; a rocket went up from the edge of the swamp, a single cannon answered from the

American line, and the artillery on each side opened with a roar.

Jackson's line of defence ran along the inner edge of the Rodriguez canal from the levee to the woods, and on through the woods to the swamp. Where it crossed the open it was a rude, uneven earthwork; but in the forest it was a double row of logs two feet apart, filled in with earth.* Behind the line—which, that nothing might be wanting to make it hard to defend, was a straight one—were gathered as motley an array of men as ever at any time fought under one banner. On the extreme right, just where the line joined the levee, were some regulars, a company of New Orleans Rifles, some dragoons grouped about a howitzer, some sailors from the Carolina who served a small battery, and a battalion of Louisiana Creoles resplendent in gay uniforms. In the midst of the battalion were Dominique You and Beluche, with the swarthy crews of their pirate ships serving two twenty-fours Then came a battalion of free negroes, more sailors with a thirty-two-pound gun, a battalion of San Domingans, more regulars, some old French soldiers under one of Napoleon's gunners named Flaujeac tending a brass gun, a long line of Carroll's Tennesseeans in brown homespun hunting shirts, some more sailors, some more regulars with a long brass culverin, then John Adair and his Kentuckians, and last of all, standing knee-deep in the water of the swamp, Coffee's Tennesseeans.

Against this array of magnificent marksmen, backwoodsmen, frontiersmen, Indian fighters—men who never fired till sure of their aim—the British army now advanced joyfully. Far on the left some West Indians made an attack and were driven back immediately. Far on the right a detachment in solid column charged a redoubt a few yards in front of the line, stormed it, and were rushing forward when a dreadful fire opened on them, and the veterans of the Peninsula, cut to pieces, retreated in disorder. The main attack was made near the swamp, where the line was defended by the riflemen of

---

* It is still the popular belief that Jackson and his men fought behind cotton bales. This was not the case. A very few bales were used at one part of the line, but on January first the British cannon-shot scattered them in every direction and set them on fire, and no further attempt to use cotton was made.

Kentucky and Tennessee. Four hundred yards in front was a ditch, and behind this the British, loaded down with knapsacks, muskets, scaling ladders, and fascines of ripe sugar-cane for filling up the ditch, had formed in solid column of sixty men front. As the signal rocket shot into the air these doomed and wretched men, cheering lustily, moved steadily forward under a shower of Congreve rockets to the slaughter. Veterans though they were, the precision of the fire poured upon them was too much. They fell, said an eye-witness, like blades of grass beneath the scythe of the mower, and before the head had reached the canal the column faltered, broke, and fled back to the ditch where it had formed. There knapsacks were thrown aside, re-enforcements secured, and a new column started forward on the run. General Gibbs, who led it, fell within twenty yards of the glacis. General Pak-enham, who came forward waving his hat and cheering the onset, was struck by a cannon ball, and the whole line a second time fell back in confusion. The command of the army now passed to Major-General Lambert, who during the battle led the reserves, and who instantly withdrew his troops.

Scarcely had he done so when fighting began on the west bank. Though the first detachment of Colonel Thornton's men landed about four in the morning, the troops came over so slowly that when the assault on Jackson's lines began but six hundred had crossed the river. Without waiting for more, Thornton led these, supported by three gun-boats, up the levee at double-quick, struck General Morgan's line, routed it, and fell wounded. But his troops advanced against Patterson's battery of heavy guns, forced him to spike them, and pushed their way up the river to a point a mile in Jackson's rear. That night, however, Lambert recalled them to the east bank and Jackson was safe.

On the morrow an armistice was concluded, and the day spent in gathering the dead and digging shallow trenches for graves. When night came the dead thus gathered were buried by torchlight, in the presence of the whole British army. They numbered, it is said, almost seven hundred, of whom three were generals, seven colonels, and seventy-five officers of lesser rank.

So shallow were the graves and so thin the covering of earth that arms and feet and heads soon began to be visible, and for months afterward every south wind that swept across the field came to New Orleans laden with the stench of dissolving bodies. Nor since that day has a plough or a spade disturbed the soil, which long ago was covered by a dense grove of stunted cypress.

Though beaten and well-nigh cut to pieces, the British were in no haste to depart, nor did Jackson show any disposition to force them. Some artillery fire was indulged in, but it was not till the eighteenth that Lambert, leaving the guns that had covered the river, withdrew to the mouth of the bayou, and not till the twenty-seventh that he boarded the ships off Chandeleur Island. Even then he seemed loath to depart, and the seventh of February came before the fleet, taking advantage of a favoring breeze, quit Lake Borgne, put to sea, and, heading for Mobile, was soon off Fort Bowyer. On the twelfth the garrison, after a manly defence, marched out with all the honors of war and laid down their arms on the glacis. Two days later both soldiers and sailors heard with unfeigned joy that war had ended and peace returned.

CHAPTER XXVIII.

THE STRESS OF WAR.

THE opening of the war found the people on the eve of a presidential election. The campaign may be said to have opened in February, for in that month the members of both branches of the Virginia Legislature, in caucus assembled, chose five-and-twenty men to be the Virginia electors of President and Vice-President.* No presidential candidate was formally named; but, as each elector was pledged to vote for Madison, a nomination, to all intents and purposes, was made. Against this action of the Legislature not a few earnest Republicans protested. Virginia, said they, is arrogating too much to herself. She is impudently seeking to forestall public opinion and drive Congress to a nomination of Madison. This was denied. Congress said the friends of Madison has enough to do without meddling with the President and his electors. Virginia has but used a right she enjoys in common with every State in the Union. New York, Pennsylvania, Massachusetts—any State—may do as she has done. Whether they agree or disagree it matters little, for the electors are free to act as they please, and they will choose the President. A caucus of the Pennsylvania Legislature did follow the example set by that of Virginia, and went one step farther and formally renominated James Madison and George Clinton. Even then congressmen hesitated to act; nor was it till Madison had formally committed himself to the policy of war that a call for the regular Republican congressional caucus went out.

There were then in the House and Senate two hundred and

---

* True American, February 28, 1812.

eighteen men, of whom one hundred and seventy-eight called themselves Republicans. When, however, the caucus met on the evening of May eighteenth, but eighty-three were present. Of these, all save one voted for Madison, and as Clinton was dead, John Langdon, of New Hampshire, was given his place. A resolution was then passed setting forth the reason for their action. In recommending Madison and Langdon to their fellow-citizens they acted, the resolution stated, not as congressmen but as citizens, led not by a desire to dictate, but animated by a deep conviction of the importance of Republican union throughout all parts of the United States. Langdon, however, declined to serve, and at a second caucus Elbridge Gerry was chosen in his stead, for it was thought most advisable to have an Eastern man.

The Federalists, true to their ancient policy, held no caucus and named no candidates, but contented themselves with a hearty support of the men put forward by the discontented Republicans and the Friends of Peace. Quite early in the year, such members of the Legislature of New York as hated Madison and what they called Virginia rule, held a secret caucus and appointed a committee to examine the condition of politics in the sister States. Just what the committee did is not known. But it is known that the Republicans were about to hold a caucus when the Legislature was suddenly prorogued by the Governor because of the prospective passage of the Six Million Dollar Bank Bill. On reassembling, however, toward the end of May, a caucus was promptly held, and De Witt Clinton unanimously nominated. No candidate for the Vice-Presidency was selected, for that office was in those days regarded as of no importance.

To this course of action the discontented Republicans were moved by the strong anti-war feeling rising in every part of the North and East, by the growing demand for a Northern President, and by the great success of the Friends of Peace, Union, and Commerce, in the spring elections just closed. In New Hampshire and Rhode Island they had triumphed signally. In Massachusetts they had carried the Lower House, had defeated Gerry, and had chosen a Federalist Governor. In New York they had secured the Assembly, and made such gains in the Senate that, on joint ballot, their majority in the Legislature was two.

The Massachusetts election was no ordinary one. It marked an epoch in the political annals of our country, for then it was that the people for the first time in history were called on to condemn that unjust and infamous system of apportionment known as Gerrymandering. At the last session of the General Court the Republicans, happening to have both branches of the Legislature, passed an act * rearranging the senatorial districts in such wise that a large majority of them should thenceforth be Republican.† The story is told that a map of one of these new districts, that of Essex, was hanging on the office wall of the Columbian Centinel one day, when the artist Stuart came in. Struck by the peculiar outline of the towns making the district, he added a head, wings, and claws with his pencil, and, turning to the editor, said, " There, that will do for a Salamander." " Better say a Gerrymander," replied the editor, punning on the name of the then Republican Governor, Elbridge Gerry. That the story is true may well be doubted ; nevertheless, the nickname " Gerrymander " was applied to the odious law,‡ came rapidly into current use, and has remained in our political vocabulary ever since. Indeed, a huge cut of the monster was prepared, and the next year was scattered as a broadside all over the Commonwealth, and so thoroughly aroused the people that, in the spring of 1813, despite the Gerrymander, the Federalists regained control of the Senate and repealed the law ; but not before the progeny of the monster had sprung up in New Jersey.

In the October election in that State the Republicans had a majority of all the votes cast at the polls. But, by a loss of twenty-six votes in Monmouth County and of four in Hunterdon, both branches of the Legislature passed to the Federalists. Carried away by such unexpected good fortune, the Legislature had no sooner assembled at Trenton than the Federalists most wantonly abused their power.

---

* February 11, 1812.

† History of the People of the United States, vol. iii, pp. 452, 453.

‡ For some remarks on " The Gerrymander," see Columbian Centinel, May 23, 1812, and October 21, 1812.

Although they had a majority of the votes in the Legislature, the Republicans had a majority of twenty-five hundred votes of the people. Now it happened that in 1807 the law requiring the choice of electors of President and Vice-President of the United States to be made in districts was changed, and an act was passed providing for a general ticket to be voted on by the people all over the States. It was quite certain that, as the Republicans had a majority of the votes of the people, the electoral ticket of New Jersey would be Republican. But this the Federalists, having the power, determined to prevent, and six days before the election was to take place brought in a bill giving the choice of electors to the Legislature. The Republican minority protested vigorously against the change, urged that a choice by the people at large was a mode most agreeable to their wishes, was most consonant with a Republican form of government, and was quite in accord with the spirit of the Federal Constitution; said that the old law had already been in part executed, that nominations had been made, transmitted to the Secretary of State, and by him published, and that, as a majority of the people of the State were stanch supporters of the measures of the General Government, to wrest from them the privilege of expressing their approbation by the choice of Republican electors was an act of oppression and tyranny they would not quietly submit to.

The answer was a loud call for the question and the passage of the bill, and the choice of eight Federalist electors. The next step was to Gerrymander the congressional districts. The custom so familiar to us—the custom of each State having as many congressional districts as it has members of the House—was not then in universal use, and the six representatives from New Jersey were chosen by a general ticket. Here again the Republican majority would have caused the election of a Republican delegation, to prevent which a bill was brought in to establish congressional districts. After considering the manner of division, it was found that by no honest system could the Federalists secure more than two of the six. A recourse was therefore had to the new Republican institution of Gerrymandering, and three districts sending two representatives each were so marked out that two were Federalist and one Republican.* No attention was paid to population, so that while in the first district, where the Republicans were strong and into which many Federalists had to be brought to overcome them, the population was eighty-eight thousand, in the third district there were but seventy-three thousand, or three thousand more than, by act of Congress, it must contain.†

Another contest, quite as unseemly, took place in the General Court of Massachusetts during the June session. As the result of the first election under the Gerrymandering law the Senate was heavily Republican and the Assembly heavily Federalist. The late election had clearly shown that if the old method of choosing presidential electors by a general ticket was continued, the twenty-two votes of Massachusetts would go to Clinton. The Republicans in the Senate therefore determined to change the custom, and, when the time came to take up the business, sent a resolution to the Assembly providing for the choice of twenty electors in the twenty congressional districts and two by general ticket. The Assembly returned it so amended as to provide for an election in twenty-two districts. To this the Senate would not agree; and though conference after conference followed, and offer after offer was made by the Assembly, the Senate stood firm, and the General Court rose with nothing done. A special session in October thereupon became necessary. Once more the Federalists offered to agree to a choice of electors by a general ticket, or by concurrent ballot of the two houses, or by the district system. Once more the Republicans refused to yield till the plan of choosing electors in districts formed of the Court of Common Pleas circuits was suggested. Then they gave way, and a law making such provision was passed. The cost to the State of this extra session was some thirty thousand dollars.

In other States where the people had a presidential vote the men to be electors were either named by the legislative caucus or by the people in convention. Thus, in Massachusetts the towns of each district sent delegates to a district convention. In New Jersey, not knowing that a Gerrymandering

---

* The protest of the minority, giving all the details of these proceedings, is published in the Aurora, November 17, 1812, and January 4, 1813.

† The ratio of representation was 1 to 35,000.

law would be passed, the " Peace-makers " held a State convention at Trenton ; in New York delegates from thirty-four
counties met at Albany ; in Pennsylvania the Peace Democrats assembled at Lancaster, and, having selected electors,
bade them vote for Clinton and Jared Ingersoll, "the people's nomination " ; in Virginia representatives from eighteen
counties gathered at Staunton and declared for peace, commerce, union, and no foreign alliance, but gave no instructions
to the electors.   The legislative caucus having now become a
part of the political machinery of the Republicans, such conventions were not used by them, and the duty of framing the
electoral ticket was performed by the caucus or laid on the
General Committee of Correspondence.

Chief among the many duties of a general committee of
correspondence was the appointment of local committees
throughout the State, the preparation of campaign literature,
and the issuing of addresses—for the stump orator of our day
had no existence.   From these addresses it appears that the
nomination of Clinton was denounced by the Republicans as
irregular, unprecedented, and dangerous ; as a departure from
the custom of confiding to Republican congressmen the
power to nominate a presidential candidate ; and as a mark of
public disapprobation of the conduct of Madison.   Such a
mark he did not, in their opinion, deserve.   He had been
selected by a meeting of Republicans from all parts of the
country as the one man most likely to be acceptable to the
people in an hour of great peril.   The manner of selection
was not new.   The people were familiar with it, and, by
twice electing the candidates so nominated, had approved it.
Nay, more ; it had within a few weeks been approved and
confirmed by the Republican members of the Legislatures of
nine States.   Was not this equivalent to nine such nominations as that of Mr. Clinton ?   How, then, could the nondescripts cry, "Caucus nomination"?   If they did not like the
actions of their brothers in Congress, what objection could
they consistently bring to the action of their brothers in the
Legislature of Pennsylvania, of Rhode Island, of Massachusetts, of every State that had nominated Madison ?

The manner of his nomination, unconstitutional as it is,

said the New York committee, is but one of our many objections to James Madison. We are opposed to Virginia influence and Virginia control. If we are asked who is to nominate, we answer, A State, but not always and forever the same State. New York now brings forward her claims for the first time. Her population and her resources put her in the front rank. She is a Middle State. Her position makes her, therefore, a fit depository of power until the jealousy and distrust existing between the Northern and the Southern States has gone down. Eminently commercial, she understands the sentiments of the Eastern States. Extremely agricultural, she sympathizes with the South. She is therefore, of all States, most likely to hold an even balance, and in times like these is well qualified to name a President. This she has done in the person of DeWitt Clinton. Should Mr. Clinton be elected, said the " Friends of Union, Peace, and Commerce," as the supporters of Clinton called themselves, we do verily believe that in six months the war will end, our rights on the ocean be respected, and our impressed sailors given up. Should James Madison be elected, we see nothing before us but a long war— a weak, an inefficient, a disastrous war—heavy taxes, enormous loans, standing armies, poverty, misery, and an alliance with the French.

DeWitt Clinton, a nephew of the late Vice-President, was born in Little Britain, New York, in 1769, was graduated at Columbia College in 1786, and began the practice of law two years later. The proposed Constitution of the United States was then before the people for adoption or rejection ; the feeling in New York ran high, and young Clinton quickly drifted from law to politics. That he should follow the traditions of his family was natural, and under the signature of " A Countryman " he opposed the Constitution and replied to the Federalist, just then appearing in the Independent Gazetteer. For this the uncle rewarded him with the secretaryships of a number of boards, and in 1797, by his influence, sent him to the Legislature, and in 1798 to the State Senate. There his career marked him out as a man of liberal views, and joined his name with the beginning of more than one great reform—with the abolition of imprisonment for debt, with the abolition of slavery in New York, with the establishment of sanitary laws, and with the encouragement of agriculture, manufactures, steam navigation, and internal improvements.   In 1800 the Assembly, happening to be Republican, chose a Republican Council of Appointment and made Clinton a member.   This famous body was one of many reminders of the deep and lasting dread of the one-man power, with which the rule of George III had filled our ancestors.   It was composed of the Governor and four senators chosen by the Assembly, one from each of the four senatorial districts into which the State was then divided, and had at its disposal every office, not elective, in the State.   As the officers elected by the people were the Governor, Lieutenant-Governor, members of the Legislature, and a few county and town officials, the list of appointments was a long one, and included the Secretary of State, the Comptroller, the judges, the Attorney-General, the district-attorneys, the coroners, the mayors of New York city, the sheriffs, the justices of the peace, and all the higher officers of the militia.   In making these appointments the Governor had merely the casting vote; but, as the State Constitution said, he must, " with the advice and consent of the said Council, appoint the said officers," the Governor held that he could not be said to appoint unless he nominated, and had always claimed sole right to nominate.   So long as the Council and the Governor were of the same party the claim was allowed. But in 1794 the revolt against George Clinton made the Council of Appointment a Federalist body, which declined to pass its time putting Republicans into office, and asserted an equal right to nominate.   Clinton protested, and there the dispute ended till the sweeping Republican victory of 1800 gave the Council of Appointment to the Republicans and put the Federalist Governor, John Jay, in the same condition in 1801 that George Clinton had been in 1794.   When, therefore, Jay summoned the Council in February, 1801, and announced that the civil commissions in eleven counties and of the mayors of four cities had expired, the board, led on by DeWitt Clinton, rejected in rapid succession eleven of the Governor's nominations, refused to vote on several more, and then began to consider nominations made by members.   Of this Jay would hear nothing, and, dismissing the Council, he appealed to the Legislature, which called a convention which so amended the Constitution of the State that any member of the Council could make nominations, the appointments being made by the majority. This was in 1801. The date and the amendment are important, for under that amendment and in that year DeWitt Clinton introduced "the spoils system" into New York politics.

The doctrine which he asserted was one which had been announced and practised by every President from Washington down to Jefferson, then recently inaugurated—the doctrine that it is suicidal to have in any office of consequence a man hostile to the measures of the government he serves. No sooner, therefore, was the Council summoned by George Clinton, who succeeded Jay as Governor in 1801, than DeWitt Clinton put his theory into practice and the work of proscription began. At the Council Board, beside the Governor and his nephew, sat a Federalist, a Republican named Roseboom, and Ambrose Spencer, a man of great parts and already entering on a great career. Clinton and Spencer easily led Roseboom, and the three, making a majority of the Council, began the first political proscription of office-holders in the history of the State. The Secretary of State, the Comptroller, the District Attorney, the Recorder of New York, the Clerk of the Circuit Court, every one of the puisne judges of the County Courts, and every one of the justices of the peace who was not a Republican, were instantly turned out of office. The Governor, George Clinton, filled with honest indignation, cast his vote and entered his protest in the journal against these acts. But he protested in vain. The school to which he belonged was of the past. The party heartily approved, and by way of reward sent Clinton to the United States Senate and raised Spencer to the bench of the Supreme Court. His term in the Senate was short, for in 1803 the Council of Appointment made him Mayor of the city of New York, a post he held almost continuously till 1815. In theory the Republicans were bitterly opposed to the multiplicity of office-holding, and had soundly berated Jay for retaining the office of Chief-Justice of the United States while he was Minister to England. But few ever put the theory into practice, and neither Clinton nor his friends thought it strange that he should be at one and the same time Mayor of New York, a member of the Council of Appointment, a member of the State Senate, and a commissioner to examine a route for the Erie Canal. In 1811 he was chosen Lieutenant-Governor, and was acting as such when nominated for the Presidency by the Republicans of the Legislature in 1812. From that hour he descended to the level of Burr and became all things to all men. Beyond the borders of his native State he did not, in all likelihood, have one follower. But he knew men and the ways of men, and was soon at work building up a party by every means known to the primitive political machine of his day. War Republicans were assured by the journals that supported him that he was for a most vigorous prosecution of the war. Peace Republicans were told that he was eager for peace without dishonor. Federalists whom he had for years proscribed he now bribed with bank charters. To bring to his support the Federalists of other States was a very different matter, and for a time indeed it seemed impossible. But, by a piece of skilful management, which may well be ascribed to Martin Van Buren, a great caucus of Federalist leaders from eleven States was held at New York in September. What influence was used, what bribes were offered, what pledges were given, cannot be known; but after a secret, and it is said a stormy, session of three days, during which Rufus King denounced Clinton as bitterly as, in a like caucus, Hamilton once denounced Burr, the electoral votes of the Federalist States were guaranteed to Clinton. The Republicans instantly raised the cry of " Coalition," and spread the story that Clinton had solemnly assured the Federalists that all connection with his old party was severed. Both Federalists and nondescripts denied that any coalition had been formed, denied that Clinton had ever given such assurances, and bet one thousand dollars that the charges could not be proved. Nevertheless, there is reason to believe them true.

From the first the Republicans had conceded to Mr. Clinton twenty electoral votes, and had put down as doubtful fifty-nine more. When the October election came on, however, State after State, to their dismay, passed from the doubtful column to the side of Clinton. Delaware, which in 1810 chose a Republican Governor, now went Federalist by a great majority. Four counties in Maryland, which in 1811 sent Republicans to the Legislature, now chose Friends of Union, Peace, and Commerce, and made the Legislature Federalist. New Jersey was lost. Even in Pennsylvania the Peace ticket made great gains. This reduced the doubtful States to two and emboldened the supporters of Clinton to claim his election.

There are, said they, two hundred and eighteen presidential electors.* One hundred and ten are necessary for a choice. The late triumphs at the polls assure him of the vote of States which in December will cast one hundred and eleven votes. He will therefore be elected. For a while the returns, as they came slowly in, encouraged this belief, and even so late as the middle of December, when the vote stood eighty-nine for Clinton and one hundred and one for Madison, all hope of the election of Clinton was not abandoned. Ohio, it seems, had lost one vote through absence of one elector. In Pennsylvania four vacancies had occurred and had been filled by the Legislature after the first Wednesday in December, before which date the law required that all electors must be chosen. Their choice was therefore held to be illegal. Indeed, it was a question whether their voting with the other electors had not cost

* STATE.	Electoral vote.	Manner of choosing electors.	PRESIDENT.		VICE-PRESIDENT.	
			Madison.	Clinton.	Gerry.	Ingersoll.
New Hampshire	8	General ticket..........	..	8	1	7
Vermont......	8	Legislature............	8	..	8	..
Massachusetts..	22	Six Circuit Court districts	..	22	2	20
Rhode Island...	4	General ticket.........	..	4	..	4
Connecticut....	9	Legislature............	..	9	..	9
New York.....	29	Legislature............	..	29	..	29
New Jersey....	8	Legislature............	..	8	..	8
Pennsylvania...	25	General ticket.........	25	..	25	..
Delaware......	4	Legislature............	..	4	..	4
Maryland......	11	Districts..............	6	5	6	5
Virginia.......	25	General ticket.........	25	..	25	..
North Carolina.	15	Legislature............	15	..	15	..
South Carolina.	11	Legislature............	11	..	11	..
Georgia.......	8	Legislature............	8	..	8	..
Ohio..........	8	General ticket.........	7	..	7	..
Kentucky......	12	Districts..............	12	..	12	..
Tennessee.....	8	Districts..............	8	..	8	..
Louisiana......	3	Legislature............	3	..	3	..
Total.......	218	....	128	89	131	86

Pennsylvania her entire vote. Be this as it might, it was clear to the " Peace-makers " that five votes must be taken from the one hundred and one already secured by Madison. This would give him ninety-six. Clinton had eighty-nine, and as they claimed the three of Louisiana and one of the four districts of Kentucky, which had three votes, he also would have ninety-six. They were too hopeful, for when all the returns were in it appeared that the election had been strictly sectional. Every State east of the Delaware river, save Vermont, had given her undivided vote to Clinton. Every State south and west of the Delaware, save Delaware, had been carried by Madison. Maryland was divided.

The meaning of this, said the New England Federalists, is, that the South again rules ; that the freemen of the North are at the mercy of the slaves of the South. In the seven States that have voted for Madison and war there are more than nine hundred and eighty thousand slaves. As is well known, they have no more voice or share in government than so many black cattle of New England. Yet, as each forty-five thousand of them is entitled to one elector, they have given Madison and his war twenty-one electoral votes. They are, we are told, constitutional votes. Very true ; but have not all the parts of the Constitution which were offsets for this degrading concession been obliterated by their continued violation ? Was the manufacture of new slave States in the South from foreign soil ever contemplated by the framers of the Constitution ? For the next four years the people of New England, New York, New Jersey, and Delaware will be under a government as foreign in fact to this great section of the Union as that of any European power. Its measures, too, without a change of system, will bear on us as heavily and in much the same mode as the policy of France on Holland and the Hanse towns. We do not insist that any remedy is to be applied to this great grievance ; nor is it asserted that the free people of these States are not bound by the Federal compact to endure and support measures clothed in the form of the Constitution. We only say it is a new case, and not foreseen and not provided for when these States acceded to the compact.

If the result of this election teaches anything, it teaches

that we are a divided people, and that the lines of our political
and geographical division are nearly coincident.   North of
Delaware there is, among all who do not bask in the executive sunshine, but one voice for peace.   South of that river
the general cry is war!   There are not on earth two hostile
nations with political views more discordant than these
two great divisions.   The sentiment is hourly extending,
and will soon be universal in these Northern States, that we
are no better in relation to the Southern States than a conquered people.   We have been forced, without the least necessity, to renounce our habits, occupations, means of happiness, and subsistence.   We are plunged into a war without
a sense of enmity or a perception of sufficient provocation,
and made to fight the battles of a cabal.   We, whose soil was
the hotbed and whose ships were the nursery of sailors, are
insulted with the hypocrisy of a devotion to sailors' rights
and of pretended skill in maritime jurisprudence by those
whose country furnishes no navigation beyond the size of a
ferry-boat or an Indian canoe   The consequence of this state
of things must be that either the Southern States must drag
the Northern States yet further into the war, or we must drag
them out of it, or the chain must break.   We must no longer
be deafened by the senseless clamor over a separation of the
States.   The States are separated in fact when one section
with a high hand perseveres in measures fatal to the interests
and repugnant to the opinions of another section by dint of a
geographical majority.   This would be another case not contemplated by the parties to the original compact.

Just as the presidential election was about to begin in the
States, the twelfth Congress met and opened its second session.   The disastrous experiences of the last few months
seemed to have aroused the members to energetic action, and,
throwing aside all considerations of party consistency, the
Republicans became eager for a vigorous prosecution of the
war.   By one act they raised the pay of the troops, exempted
every soldier from arrest for debt contracted before or after enlistment, and attempted to allow the enlistment of minors above
the age of eighteen without the consent of parents, guardians,
or masters.   The clause exempting soldiers from arrest for

debt met with small resistance. It was necessary to prevent gross frauds. A member of the House assured his hearers that in the Massachusetts town where he lived a man would no sooner enlist than he would contract a fictitious debt above the sum of twenty dollars and have himself arrested. After arrest, on giving bail, he would be set free, but would not return to camp. Should the commanding officer, as had often been done, send and have him seized, a writ of *habeas corpus* would be taken out, and the soldier be at liberty again, for the courts had decided that a debtor was the property of his bail until the suit was decided. But such a decision would never take place, for the suit would be continued from term to term, so long as the time of enlistment lasted. Meanwhile the man drew pay and bounty.

To the clause enlisting minors without the consent of parents, guardians, or masters, most vigorous resistance was made—a resistance which found its best spokesman in Josiah Quincy. "The absurdity of this bill," said he, "consists in supposing these provisions to be the remedy for the evil of which the President complains. The difficulty is that men cannot be enlisted. The remedy proposed is more money and legislative authority to corrupt our youth. In this lies the error. It is not pecuniary motive that is wanting to fill your armies. It is moral motive in which you are deficient. Sir, while some difference of opinion may exist among the happy and wise yeomanry of New England in relation to the principle and necessity of this war; there is very little concerning the invasion of Canada as a means of preventing it. Abandon your project of invasion; throw your shield over the seaboard and the frontier; awe into silence the Indians on your territory; fortify your cities; take the shackles from your commerce; give us ships and seamen, and there will be no want of men, money, or spirit.

"It must never be forgotten in the conduct of government that these United States form a political association of independent sovereignties, greatly differing in wealth, resources, enterprise, extent of territory, and preparation to arms. Now, sir, wise men, conducting an association thus formed, will not disgust any of the great sections of the country either in regard to its interests, habits, or prejudices. But, of all the distinctions which exist in these States, that which results from the character of labor is the most obvious and critical. In the Southern States all the industry of the country is conducted by slaves. In the Northern States it is conducted by the yeomanry, their apprentices, and their children. The planter of the South can look around on his fifty, his hundred, his thousand of human beings and say, ' These are my property.' The farmer of the North has only one or two ewe lambs—his children—of whom he can say, and say with pride, ' These are my ornaments.' Yet these this bill proposes to take from him, or, what is the same thing, bribe them out of his service, and that, too, at the very age when the desire for freedom is the most active and the splendor of false glory the most enticing. Yet your slaves are safe. There is no project for their manumission in the bill. Take a slave from his master on any general and novel principle and there would be an earthquake from the Potomac to the St. Mary's. Bribe an apprentice from his master, seduce a son— worth all the slaves Africa ever produced—from a father, and we are told it is only a common affair. Mr. Speaker, I hope what I am now about to say will not be construed into a threat. It is not uttered in that spirit. But pass this law, and if the Legislatures of the injured States do not come down upon your recruiting officers with the old laws against kidnapping and man-stealing, they are false to themselves, to their posterity, and to their country."

The speech stirred up much ill feeling. Randolph praised it and likened the attitude of Massachusetts to that of Virginia in 1798 and 1800. David Williams, of North Carolina, declared that if Massachusetts carried out the threat and arrayed herself against the Federal Government, he, for one, would not hesitate to use force to put her down. But it produced no effect, and the House passed the bill with the clause intact. The Senate, however, struck it out, and in this form the bill finally became law. Other bills, to increase the bounty; to build more seventy-fours and forty-fours; to give pensions to naval officers; to improve the organization of the army; to raise more rangers for use along the frontier, and to increase the navy on the Lakes, were readily agreed to. Another to raise an additional force of twenty thousand men took up the time of Congress for a fortnight, and provoked a bitter debate, in which the cause of the war, the necessity of the war, the cost of the war, the opposition of the Peace-makers, British influence and French influence, the disasters on the land, the triumphs on the sea, the iniquity of invading Canada for conquest and plunder, Virginia influence, the orders in council, the Berlin decrees, the wickedness of Napoleon—the whole history, in short, of the Federalists and the Republicans, of Great Britain, of France, and of the Indians, from the day the Bastile fell to the day Hull surrendered at Detroit, was reviewed most elaborately. But again opposition was fruitless and the bill passed.

The House next turned its attention to means of providing money to meet these new expenses. Gallatin's report on the state of treasury at the opening of the session was far from encouraging. The total expenses for 1813 would, he said, be upward of thirty-two millions, the total receipts some twelve millions, and the deficit to be made good twenty millions. Just how it should be made good he did not suggest in the report, but in a letter accompanying it he set forth a most tempting scheme of confiscation. A clause in the Non-intercourse Act of 1811 provided that if Great Britain should recall or so change her orders in council that they no longer injured the neutral commerce of the United States, the President should proclaim the fact and intercourse be instantly restored. On the twenty-third of June, 1812, Great Britain did recall the orders in council. Supposing that the arrival of the news in America would be promptly followed by the restoration of commercial relations, every American ship captain in England, and not a few British, loaded their ships with hardware and crockery, woollens, linens, and dry goods of every sort, all of British make, and set sail for America. As the declaration of war was not known in London till the thirtieth of July, the captains knew nothing of what had happened till some privateers made prize of them on the sea, or the officers of the Custom-House seized and libelled them as they entered the ports of the United States. The position taken by Gallatin was a sound one; for the law expressly stated that the proclamation of the President should be the evidence and the only evidence of the repeal of the orders and the opening of the ports, and as no proclamation had issued, he held that the trade was illegal.

The importers appealed to the courts and the courts took different views. Some ordered the goods restored, provided the owner gave bonds equal to the appraised value; some ordered the cargoes to be held. That all might be treated alike, Gallatin bade the collectors admit the goods under bond and exact payment of duties, and had thus come into the possession of eighteen millions of merchant bonds and some five millions of dollars of duties. The matter was brought before the House by a report of the Committee of Ways and Means on so much of the President's message as related to the importation of the goods, and by the petition of the merchants concerned. The report recommended no legislation, but a reference of the petitions to the Secretary of the Treasury, who explained his views in the letter which the committee by their action indorsed. If, he said, he were to enforce the law of forfeiture, half the value of the goods would go to the collectors or informers and half to the United States. But he did not propose to enforce it. He would prefer instead to remit the half that would fall to the collectors and exact for the Treasury a share of the extraordinary war profits which the merchants did not expect to make when the goods were shipped, and to which under the law they had no claim whatever. Were the House to accept the report of the committee and send the petitions to the Secretary, he would, it was understood, compound with the merchants in some way and so add a few more millions to the bankrupt Treasury. The debate on the acceptance or rejection of the report was therefore a debate on the question, Shall the law of forfeiture be enforced, and commercial ruin spread over the country, or shall the violators of the Non-intercourse Act be suffered to buy indemnity by giving up a part of their unexpected war profits? The scene which the long discussion produced was such as had never before been witnessed in Congress. For the first time in our history a Secretary of the Treasury found himself assailed by the leaders and the followers of every party and of every faction, by Federalists, by war Republicans and by peace Republicans, by Josiah Quincy, by John Randolph, by Langdon Cheves, Calhoun, and Clay. Yet, in spite of this opposition, Gallatin all but had his way. The prospect of bringing money into the Treasury and so putting off still further the evil day of loans and taxes was so alluring, that the majority for disagreement with the report was three. From the Committee of the Whole the report now passed to the House, where it was again being debated when a bill came down from the Senate legalizing the importation. Once more all parties rallied and by the same majority of three passed the bill.

Nothing now remained but taxation or loans. Of taxes the war leaders would hear nothing; for, by this time the presidential election had taken place, the members of the thirteenth Congress had been chosen and the fact made most plain that, save in the South and Southwest, the war had no supporters. That was precisely the region where internal taxation would be most unpopular and most likely to be resisted. Recourse was accordingly had to a loan, and the President bidden to borrow sixteen millions of dollars, allowing such discount and paying such interest as the purchasers demanded. That this great sum could be borrowed on any terms seemed doubtful, but as a provision in the law for such a contingency would invite defeat, the provision was quietly inserted in another law for the issue of Treasury notes. The total amount authorized by the act was ten millions of dollars ; but, if this sum were issued, five millions were to be considered as part of the sixteen-million loan, which was then to be reduced to eleven millions.

These notes were to be redeemed at the end of one year from the day on which they were issued, were to bear five and two-fifths per centum interest, were to be transferable by delivery and assignment when endorsed by the person to whom they were issued, and to whose order they were made payable, and were to be taken in payment of all taxes and duties laid by Congress, and of all public land sold by order of Congress. That even this source of revenue would be found sufficient seemed so doubtful that before the session ended an attempt was made to repeal the Non-importation Act and resort to taxation. Indeed, the House went so far as to order a war-tax bill to be framed by the Committee of Ways and Means, but it was then so late in February that nothing could be done, for the term of the House expired on the fourth of March. An extra session was therefore called for the fourth Monday in May. Earlier than that it could not be; for in Virginia, in North Carolina, and in Tennessee the members of the thirteenth Congress would not be elected before April.

As the Treasury was now on the verge of bankruptcy, not a moment was lost in putting the loan act in force. Notices were published in the newspapers and subscription books opened in eleven seaboard cities and towns. Everything seemed favorable for a liberal subscription. The long series of splendid naval victories, the news of the Russian triumphs, of the defeat of Napoleon, of the retreat of the French from Russia and Poland, above all, the appearance of the English fleets on our coast and the rigorous blockade of our harbors, would, it was hoped, rouse the people to a vigorous prosecution of the war and to a liberal provision of the money, without which no vigorous prosecution could be hoped for. But when the books were closed,* not four millions † had been taken in the whole country. Once more the books were opened, ‡ and proposals asked for the purchase of so much of the loan as should remain untaken on April first. The new subscription did not yield two millions.# But the Secretary having laid the Treasury at the feet of the men of wealth, they came forward eager for plunder, and sent in proposals for almost a million more of the loan than remained to be taken.‖ And well they might, for they demanded for each eighty-eight dollars subscribed one hundred dollars in stock, bearing six per cent. interest—a premium of thirteen dollars and sixty-four cents △ on each hundred dollars loaned. This was accepted

---

* March 12 and 13, 1813.   ‡ From March 25 to 31, 1813.
† $3,956,400.   # $1,881,000.
‖ $944,200. This was over and above $1,000,000 subscribed too late by the Legislature of Pennsylvania.
△ 13.63\frac{7}{11}$.

by Gallatin, and seven millions were then taken by Parish and Girard, of Philadelphia, and two millions by John Jacob Astor, of New York. Half a million was taken at par. But, for doing so, the buyers demanded and received for thirteen years an annuity of one and a half per cent. over and above the six per cent. interest. The bargain was a hard one; but the needs of the Government were pressing. Indeed, on the seventh of April, when the sales were made, the coffers were empty, and the drafts on the Treasury could not be paid. Under such circumstances, money must be had at any price. New England, where it was more plentiful than elsewhere, would do nothing, and in that whole region less than half a million was subscribed. Federalist newspapers gloated over the fact that in Boston but seventy-five thousand dollars were given for "heating the war poker." That such capitalists as would loan to a Government afraid to tax its people, to a Government with nothing to pledge as security but paper money and promises, should be content with the terms thus offered was much to their credit, for the Treasury was at their mercy. When the next Congress met, and the conditions of the loan were reported, a great outcry went up. But the men who clamored were those who, in the hour of need, gave neither their money nor their services to their country.

The refusal of the people of New England in general and of Massachusetts in particular to loan the Government money was not the only way in which the dissatisfaction of that section with the war found expression. The astonishing naval victories of 1812 had encouraged the legislatures of many States during their sessions in 1813 to consider the expediency of building, equipping, and presenting to the Government a frigate or a ship of the line, and among them was that of Massachusetts. In her House of Representatives the question was referred to a committee, whose adverse report expressed the sentiments of the people. The need, said the committee, of a navy for the defence of the extensive commerce of the United States has always been urged by the statesmen of the North, and had the wise and prudent means adopted by them for this purpose more than twelve years ago been followed out, had the materials collected for building six seventy-four-gun ships been used for that purpose, had a small part of the revenue derived from commerce been annually applied for the protection of commerce, a very respectable naval force would now exist without any heavy taxation of the people. But great as is the need for a navy, it is very doubtful whether the Legislature of Massachusetts has the constitutional right to levy taxes on its constituents for the purpose of aiding the General Government in the prosecution of the war. The people of the Commonwealth have given Congress sole power to declare war, to raise and maintain armies and navies, and for this purpose to impose taxes, duties, imposts, and excises. It is the plain duty of Congress, then, to lay such taxes as may be necessary to construct the needed vessels, and it is not expedient for Massachusetts to build, equip, and loan the Government a ship of the line.*

A few months later some resolutions were presented to the Senate praising the meritorious conduct of James Lawrence and of his officers and crew in the destruction of the Peacock. But, recollecting the indignation expressed by the people over a like set on another occasion the Senate refused to act. Lest this might be construed into a slight upon a most deserving officer, a resolution was presented and adopted declaring that it was the sense of the Senate that in a war like the present, waged without just cause and prosecuted in a manner which showed that conquest and ambition were its motives, it was not becoming in a moral and religious people to express any approbation of military or naval exploits not immediately connected with the defence of their sea-coast and their soil. The resolution was cruel, for the Chesapeake-Shannon duel had lately been fought off Boston Harbor, and though the Senate knew it not, the brave and gallant Lawrence at that very moment lay in his grave at Halifax.

In the expression of such sentiment the House was not one whit behind the Senate, and willingly joined with it in a remonstrance to Congress against the war. After some remarks on the character of the "national compact," the reserved rights of the States, the alleged causes of the war, and

---

* Journal of the Massachusetts House of Representatives, February 16, 1813.

the conduct of France and England toward us, the General Court declared its opinion to be that the war was premature and that perseverance in it after the repeal of the orders in council was improper, impolitic, and unjust. It was improper, said the protest, because it showed a distrust of the good faith and disposition to peace on the part of a nation which had just given signal proofs of both; impolitic, because it lent color to the charges of subserviency to the views of France, and tended to unite all descriptions of people in England in favor of war; unjust, because the repeal of the orders in council ought to have satisfied us, and because the whole history of our diplomatic relations with England proves that we never induced her to believe that we considered the impressment of her own subjects on board our merchant ships a sufficient cause for war. No State in the Union has a stronger motive to protect commerce and maintain the rights of sailors than Massachusetts. Her people own one third of all the shipping, and furnish one half of all the native seamen of the United States; yet we are constrained to say that the evil of impressment has been grossly exaggerated, and that the interest of the United States would have been better served by an honest exclusion of English subjects from our ships than by a resort to bloodshed.

As the avowed causes are thus wholly insufficient to justify an appeal to arms, what are the secret and concealed motives? They are ambition and a lust of conquest. Were not the Territories of the United States extensive enough before the annexation of Louisiana, the projected reduction of Canada, and the seizure of West Florida? Had we not millions and millions of acres of uncultivated wilderness scarcely explored by civilized man? Could these acquisitions be held as conquered provinces without powerful and standing armies? Or is it intended to form them into new States and admit them into the Union without the express consent of every member of the original Confederacy? Already we have seen the formation and admission of one State beyond the limits of the United States and against a practice so hostile to the rights and safety of this State, so destructive of her political power, so subversive of the spirit of the Constitution, Massachusetts enters her most deliberate and solemn protest.

The Congress to which this remonstrance was addressed assembled in extra session on May twenty-fourth. The war Republicans still had a great majority of the House, and again made Henry Clay their Speaker. Nevertheless, at the last election many changes had been made in the membership, and as Clay looked down from the Speaker's chair he missed for the first time the familiar face and figure of John Randolph, and beheld for the first time the magnificent head and lofty brow of Daniel Webster. The refusal of Randolph to support the administration had induced the son-in-law of Jefferson to take residence within his district and contest his election. Success attended the attempt, and for the only time in his long career Randolph lost the election and John W. Eppes took his seat.

Daniel Webster was born at Salisbury, a frontier town in New Hampshire, on the eighteenth of January, 1782. He was the ninth in a family of ten children, and gave little promise in his early years of ever reaching manhood. So delicate and sickly was he that none of the farm work exacted of the other sons was assigned to him. Left to himself, he passed his days playing in the woods and fields and reading such books and picking up such rudiments of education as came in his way. His memory, he declared in later years, did not go back to a time when he could not read ; but his knowledge of ciphering and spelling was acquired at the district schools held now in his native town and now at some neighboring village, as the schoolmaster wandered from place to place in his itinerancy. With this smattering, Webster's education would probably have ended had not his father been made judge of a local court, a place which yielded a salary of a few hundred dollars a year, and enabled him to send Daniel to Exeter Academy, where the boy passed nine months. At the end of that time he was confided to the care of a minister at Boscawen, who with the help of another tutor imparted a sufficient knowledge of Latin and Greek to enable him to enter Dartmouth College in August, 1797. So bad was his preparation, even in that day of low-grade scholarship, that he had little else

than his own extraordinary natural gifts to depend on ; and as
such gifts are developed slowly, his career at college forms no
exception to the general rule of extraordinary men in the process of education.   The prizes, the honors, the high places in
the class went to those the world has never heard of, while he
was merely admired for the qualities of mind and body which
afterward gave him fame and power.   His personal appearance, his crag-like brow overhanging the cavernous dark
black eyes, the mastiff mouth closed like a vice, the deep tones
of his voice, his memory, his clearness of statement, and above
all his eloquence, seem to have been his distinguishing charac-
teristics.   It is not surprising, therefore, that on the fourth of
July, 1800, while still a member of the Junior Class, he delivered, by invitation, an oration in honor of independence
before the citizens of Hanover, the college town.   In 1801 he
took his degree, went back to Salisbury, and had begun to
read law, when lack of money forced him to drop his studies
and become the schoolmaster in the town of Fryeburg, Maine.
His engagement was for six months, and, when completed,
Webster once more returned to Salisbury and his study of law,
which he followed for two years, when he entered the office of
Christopher Gore, at Boston, and the next year was admitted
to the bar.   From Boston he went first to Boscawen and then
to Portsmouth, where in 1812 he was called on to deliver the
Fourth of July oration before the Washington Benevolent
Society of that town.   His reputation as a public speaker was
by that time well known through all southern New Hampshire ; but his speech on this occasion was considered remarkable, and secured his election as delegate from Portsmouth to
the Rockingham County Convention, a convention whose
duty it was to frame a memorial condemning the war and to
nominate a member of Congress.   That the opportunity of a
lifetime was now before him he seems to have fully realized,
and before the convention adjourned he so impressed the
fifteen hundred men assembled at Rockingham that they
chose him to write their memorial and nominated him for
Congress.   Election followed as a matter of course, and, as he
came to Washington a strong opposer of the war, he began his
attack on the measures of the administration without delay,

and before the session was three weeks old threw the House into violent commotion by a series of resolutions on the French decrees. In substance they called on the President to inform the House when, by whom, and in what manner the first intelligence of the decree * purporting to be a repeal of those of Berlin and Milan had been received by Government; they asked if the first news of that decree was the statement of the Duke of Bassano to Joel Barlow, May twelfth, 1812; and whether the Government had ever demanded of France why that decree had been so long concealed. The history of the affair is this: On the twelfth of May, 1812, the Duke of Bassano communicated to Joel Barlow, the American Minister, a decree purporting to repeal those of Berlin and Milan, and dated April twenty-eighth, 1811. Barlow, amazed at the concealment for more than a year of a decree which, had it issued on the day of its date, would have saved the country from untold evils, asked Bassano if the paper had ever been published. The Duke replied that it had been made known to the predecessor of Barlow, and had been sent to the French Minister at Washington to be communicated to the Government of the United States. If this statement was true, then Madison was guilty of the concealment. Yet this charge, made in the face of the world, had never been affirmed or denied by the President. The purpose of the resolutions, Webster held, was to find out the truth. That Bassano lied no man now doubts for a moment. But such was the turpitude of politics in those days that the Republicans durst not fling back the falsehood, and a fierce debate went on day after day for four days before the resolutions were sent to Madison.

It was in such debates that the two months of the session wore away. Save the passage of the tax bills, no business of any importance was done. The passage of those bills, however, was of the utmost importance. It forms an epoch not only in the history of the Republican party, but in the history of our country; for at last Democracy was reconciled to internal taxation, and in a single session the Republicans replaced on the statute-book every one of the Federalist taxes they wiped

---

* That of April 28, 1811.

away in 1802, and against which they had sturggled for ten years.

The system of internal taxation by the Federal Government began on the memorable day in 1791 when Washington signed the bill laying a duty on domestic distilled spirits; a tax which, proving more harsh in its operations than was expected, was amended in 1792, and after being denounced by legislatures and by mass meetings as oppressive, unequal, and unjust, was openly resisted by the people of western Pennsylvania, who rose in armed rebellion in 1794. In that same year taxes were laid on licenses for retailing wine and liquor, and on the manufacture of snuff, tobacco, and refined sugar, on carriages, and on sales at auction.* This closed the list in Washington's two terms, during which a stamp tax and a direct land tax had both been proposed and rejected. But they came soon after; for on March fourth, 1797, Adams began his administration, and on July sixth, 1797, signed the stamp-act, and almost precisely a year later † the law imposing a direct tax on lands, houses, and negro slaves. Against this a little community of eastern Pennsylvania, under the lead of Fries, rose in rebellion, and the Republican press all over the country cried out most vigorously. The South and West resisted more quietly and effectually, and in June, 1812, when war was declared, much of this tax were still due and uncollected in States south of the Potomac. In 1799 the stamp tax was slightly altered. In 1800 the general stamp office was established and the tax on snuff mills repealed. In 1801 the taxes on carriages, on licenses for retailing liquor, on snuff and refined sugar, on sales at auction, when about to expire, were continued without a time limit; but the next year the Republicans were in control, and every kind of internal tax was abolished with exultation.

With this record behind them the two parties met in the extra session of the thirteenth Congress and changed places. The Federalists became the enemies of taxation; the Republicans became its advocates, and before the session ended taxed pleasure carriages, sales at auction, sugar refineries, salt, licenses

---

* June 5 and 9, 1794.   † July 14, 1798.

to sell liquor at retail; laid a stamp tax on all kinds of legal document, taxed whiskey stills, imposed a direct tax of three millions, and brought back all the machinery of assessment and collection, and again turned loose in the land the tax-gatherer and what they had once called his minions. As some months must necessarily pass by before any money could be raised from these sources, another loan of seven millions and a half was authorized.

Though the Republican party was thus leaving, one by one, the fundamental principles on which Jefferson had founded it, a faction of its senators showed that, when spite moved them, they could exhibit a singular concern for the preservation of those principles. The appointment of Adams, Gallatin, and Bayard as peace commissioners had been made during a recess of Congress. Madison, therefore, as in duty bound, sent in their names for confirmation soon after the Senate met. But the disaffected Republicans, joining with the Federalists, de-manded to know who was to discharge the duties of Gallatin in his absence. Madison answered that the Secretary of the Navy was acting Secretary of the Treasury under authority of an act of Congress, whereupon the Senate referred the matter to a select committee, and, on the President refusing to confer with the committee, voted that the duties of a Secretary of the Treasury were incompatible with those of an Envoy Extraor-dinary. Madison now fell ill, and nothing more was done till late in July. He was then well enough to receive the com-mittee, but, as he still refused to discuss the appointment, the Senate, in a fit of childish anger, confirmed Adams and Bayard and rejected Gallatin * almost on the very July day on which he reached St. Petersburg.

At the time of making the rejection the Senate was in hourly fear of being forced to fly from Washington, for then it was that a British fleet entered the Potomac and threw the city into violent commotion. Long ere this, however, the whole seaboard had begun to feel the consequences of a rig-orous blockade. At Charleston flour rose rapidly to nineteen dollars a barrel. At Baltimore, Virginia coal, which had been

---

* Executive Proceedings.   Annals of Congress, 1813–1814, vol. i, pp. 83–90.

selling at thirty-three cents a bushel, now brought seventy-five.
At New York the people, deprived of the supply of fish which
came from New England, were forced to be content with such
chub and mackerel as could be caught in the Sound.

The interruption of the coasting trade was indeed a very
serious affair. For years past that trade had given occupation
to thousands of coasters and tens of thousands of sailors. The
shoes made at Lynn, the Yankee notions of Connecticut, the
cotton cards, the domestic cottons, the playing cards, produced in New England, the flour of the Middle States, the
East India goods brought in from abroad, had found a ready
market at Charleston, Savannah, and Augusta, whence great
quantities of rice and cotton were brought North. On the
arrival of the British fleet this trade, no longer to be carried
on in safety by water, began, of necessity, to be carried on by
land. At first some merchants at Boston, having chartered a
few wagons, despatched them with loads to Philadelphia, and
even to Baltimore. This was enough. The hint was taken.
A new industry sprang up, and by the early summer the roads
leading southward exhibited one continuous stream of huge
canvas-covered wagons tugged along by double and triple
teams of horses or of oxen. No distance was then too great,
and hundreds of them wound their way from Salem and Boston to Augusta and Savannah. An estimate made toward the
close of the year places the number of wagons thus employed
at four thousand, and the number of cattle, horses, and oxen
at twenty thousand. Nor does this seem excessive; for a
traveller who drove from New York to Richmond declares
that he passed two hundred and sixty wagons on the way.

Such was the stream that the good people of the New England towns along the post road from Boston to New York,
scandalized at the wagons that went creaking through their
streets every Sabbath, cried out that the tithing-men must do
their duty. Since the days of the turnpike and quick packet
stage the laws against travelling on the Sabbath had, even in
Connecticut, been suffered to go unenforced. Here and there,
indeed, a tithing-man of the old school would quiet his conscience by calling out, Sunday after Sunday, to the driver of
the regular four-horse Boston packet as, loaded with passen-

gers and with steeds at full gallop, it came clattering down
the main street of his native village. But no driver was foolish enough to heed him, and the matter was forgotten by the
time the cloud of dust raised by the coach had settled. His
inability to cope, single-handed, with a coach and four at full
speed satisfied the town that he had done his utmost to enforce
the law. But no such excuse applied to a heavily loaded wagon
drawn by six oxen, driven by one man on foot, and the law
began to be rigorously applied. In Fairfield and Weathersfield this was especially the case, and these two towns soon
became the dread of every wagoner whom Fate brought to
them on Sunday.

Delays of this sort, coupled with the more serious deten-
tions caused by the unfitness of the wretched ferry-boats on
the great rivers to do the work they were thus suddenly called
on to perform, did much to prolong the journey, which must
at best have been slow. Even at New York, which now boasted
of a steam ferry-boat to Paulus Hook, as many as eight and fifteen wagons were often to be seen drawn up in line at the ferry
waiting a chance to cross. On several occasions the wagons
stood for three days in the street, and so obstructed travel
that the teamsters were arrested and fined ten dollars each for
blocking the highways. During the summer, when the roads
were at their best, the trip from Boston to Baltimore was made
in twenty-six days, from Baltimore to Richmond in ten days,
and from Baltimore to Augusta in thirty-three days. Two
months were thus consumed on the road between Boston and
Augusta. From New York to Augusta the journey was usually
made in fifty days, and from Philadelphia in forty-five. That
merchants whose cargoes of boots and shoes, whose boxes of
India goods, cotton goods, tinware, hardware, and fancy goods
were thus intrusted to the honesty of unknown wagoners
should be most anxious to follow them in their slow progress
southward, was most natural. It was seriously suggested,
therefore, that the owners of the wagons should name them as
in the case of ships, keep a rough log in which to enter the
names of other wagons met on the road, their destination and
their condition, and report to the newspapers of each town and
city they passed through. All this information should then

be published and copied by newspaper after newspaper for the benefit of shippers. This was done, and in a few weeks every wagon had a name, serious or humorous, according to the temper of the owner. There was Teazer and Split-Log, Commerce Renewed and Old Times, Neptune Metamorphosed, Toe-the-Mark, Mud-Clipper, Sailor's Misery, Cleopatra, Tecumthe, Serveall, Jefferson's Pride, and Don't give up the Ship. Entering into the humor of the thing, others procured great streamers bearing the words, " Free Trade and Teamsters' Rights," " Free Trade and Oxen's Rights," " No Impressment," and hung them to the sides of their wagons. Taking up the jest, the newspapers now began to record the arrival and departure of the wagons in the columns once devoted to ship news, under the headings, " Horse-Marine Intelligence," " Horse-and-Ox Marine News," " Jeffersonian Commerce." Every wagon team was a " fleet of fast-sailing wagons," to be regularly " cleared " at each city on its route. Every teamster now became a " captain," whose adventures on the way were duly published as a log in some such form as this : " Port of Salem. Arrived the three-horse-ship Dreadnaught, Captain David Allen, sixteen days from New York. Spoke in the latitude of Weathersfield the Crispin, Friend Alley master, from New York, bound homeward to Lynn, but detained and waiting trial for breach of the Sabbath." " The late northeaster has laid an embargo on many wagons. Saw several scudding under bare poles." " Sunday, seventeenth instant, at eleven A. M., Weathersfield meeting-house bearing west, northerly twenty rods, the graves just under our lee, was boarded from a Government cutter called The Tithing-man, who put a prize master on board and ordered us to the first tavern. There, notwithstanding the law that free gigs make free passengers, was detained till midnight, when, upon paying the innkeeper's fees, was released." Others contain accounts of " boardings" and " overhaulings" and " searchings" by Custom-House officers, who are invariably called " *douaniers* " by the Federalists' prints. If the cargo was not of English make and smuggled, the teamster would submit with a good grace, and perhaps even court investigation. Thus a story was told of a wagoner who, when stopped and asked, " What are you loaded with ? " replied, "Quintals of pollock, casks of oil, and dry goods from Eastport." "Dry goods from Eastport!" exclaimed the *douanier;* "they must be smuggled!" The wagoner protested that they were of American make; but the boxes were broken open, and were found to contain, not Yorkshire broadcloth and Irish linens, but dried herrings.

That all these things should go unnoticed by the verse-makers and ballad-writers of the day was impossible. Indeed, they seized on the opportunity with eagerness, and provided the new captains with as fine a set of catches as had ever belonged to their brethren of the sea.* The favorite was a parody of that stirring hymn of Campbell which begins, "Ye mariners of England, that guard our native seas!" †

Great as was the trade carried on in this manner, it nevertheless was impossible to keep down war prices. Speculators laid hands on everything that had come to be a necessity and held it. By October flour was selling at seventeen dollars a barrel at Boston, and salt at three dollars a bushel. By Novem-

---

* One refrain ran:
> "Our march is on the turnpike road,
> Our home is at the Inn."

Another begins:
> "Tho' Neptune's trident is laid by,
> From north to south our coasters ply.
> No sail or rudder need these ships,
> Which Freemen drive with wagon whips."

† Ye wagoners of Freedom,
> Whose chargers chew the cud,
> Whose wheels have braved a dozen years,
> The gravel and the mud;
> Your glorious hawbucks yoke again
> To take another jag,
> And scud through the mud,
> Where the heavy wheels do drag;
> Where the wagon creak is long and low,
> And the jaded oxen lag.
> Columbia needs no wooden walls,
> No ships where billows swell;
> Her march is like a terrapin's,
> Her home is in her shell.
> To guard her trade and sailors' rights,
> In woods she spreads her flag.

ber, tea, coffee, butter, molasses, and sugar were far beyond the reach of the poor man, and were bought by none save the very rich. In December coffee was forty-five cents a pound, sugar thirty cents a pound, molasses two dollars a gallon. To make matters worse, an embargo was laid by Congress on December seventeenth, and immediately every foreign food product rose to a fabulous price. Sugar was then sold at fifty cents a pound. For hyson tea by the chest four dollars a pound was offered and refused. At Alexandria salt sold by the quantity at five dollars a bushel. At Portsmouth a case of English hardware, mostly awl-blades and tacks, which cost two hundred pounds sterling, sold at auction for five thousand dollars. Everybody who had money to spare made haste to buy something and held it for a rise in price. Never since revolutionary days had the country experienced such a fever of speculation. Against this the people cried out lustily. They were willing, they said, to pay high prices when such were the result of the pressure of the enemy, but they were not willing to have the embargo, a measure taken to injure the enemy, used to injure and plunder the people of the United States. In Philadelphia the feeling was so strong that the citizens formed non-consumption associations, each member of which pledged himself not to buy coffee at more than twenty-five cents, nor sugar at more than twenty cents a pound; not to use articles made in foreign lands if similar goods were made in America, and not to consume any tea not already in the country.

This new restrictive measure, the last of the many embargoes, went into force on the seventeenth of December. That it was really aimed against Great Britain no sane man could believe. The ports of Russia and Prussia, of Denmark and Sweden, of Spain, and of the countries of South America, were at that moment open to her commerce. That she could, in spite of this, be distressed by shutting the few ports of the United States which she still left unblockaded, was preposterous. All these ports were in New England. To them came, in considerable numbers, the merchant ships of Spain and Sweden, and British ships under Swedish flags, with cargoes of Spanish wool and Muscovado sugar, Campeachy logwood, Havana segars, cocoa, hides, and Lisbon salt. From New

England, again, as was well known, went out no inconsidera-
ble part of the supplies on which the British troops in Canada
and in the West Indies subsisted.   That Boston and Salem
should enjoy all this trade, while Philadelphia and Baltimore
were deprived of their usual share of it by a rigorous blockade,
and should enjoy it as the reward of downright hostility to the
war, was too much for Republican patience.   Justly indignant
that such a traffic should go on openly, Madison undertook to
stop it, and early in December made it the subject of a special
message.   In it he complained that the laws relating to trade
and commerce had produced a state of things most helpful to
the enemy and most hurtful to the United States.   British
products and fabrics daily came into the ports in neutral ships,
and in British ships disguised as neutrals by false papers and
flags.   American products daily went out of the ports to supply the armies of the enemy in distant lands.   Nay, the very
fleets and troops that infested the coast, harried the shores,
and sacked the towns, and the very armies against which his
fellow-citizens were contending in Canada, obtained from the
United States supplies of food which could not be had elsewhere.   All this encouraged the enemy in their predatory and
incursive warfare, and did much to prolong the struggle.   He
would therefore suggest, as a remedy, that an embargo be laid
at once, and that articles known to be derived almost entirely
from Great Britain be excluded from the ports, even when
brought in neutral vessels.

To this the House readily consented.   The Senate was less
hasty; but on the afternoon of December seventeenth a bill
laying an embargo was signed by the President of the Senate,
and a few hours later by the President of the United States.
Long before that time news of what was coming had gone
abroad, and all neutral ships in the ports of New England that
could possibly do so had put to sea.   It was well they did, for
the law embargoed every merchant ship, cleared or not cleared,
within the jurisdiction of the United States, unless each one
of its officers and each one of its crew was a subject of a nation
in amity with the United States.

Had Madison been a little more patient, had he waited
but three weeks longer, the embargo in all probability would

not have been even proposed; for, on the thirtieth of December, before it had gone into force along the frontier and on the gulf coast, the British flag of truce Bramble, forty-two days out from Plymouth, reached Annapolis with newspapers and a despatch. The despatch was from Lord Castlereagh, and informed Monroe that, while Great Britain could not accept the mediation of Russia, she would willingly treat with the United States directly at Gothenburg or London. The newspapers were from London, and contained information which startled the whole country and aroused the wildest desire for peace.

The splendid host which, a few months before, had assembled on the banks of the Elbe under the eagles of France—the finest army which Europe had ever beheld—had been discomfited, beaten, and overthrown. The battles fought around Leipsic in October and the victories won by the allies had overwhelmed Napoleon in disaster so irreparable that all hope of conquering Germany was ended. Save France, the whole Continent of Europe was now open to British ships and British goods, and it might be that the next vessels from abroad would bring word that France herself was in possession of the allies. Convinced that Napoleon was doomed and that peace was near, the opponents of war forgot for the moment the dreadful news from the Niagara frontier—forgot that Canada had been abandoned, that Fort Niagara had fallen, that Black Rock and Buffalo were in ashes—and rejoiced over Leipsic as if it had been won by American generals on American soil. The downfall of the tyrant of the world, they would say, must give consolation to every virtuous American. The nations of the earth can have no hope for repose till the power of France is effectually crippled. Had Bonaparte defeated and scattered the allies, he would have commanded the administration to make no peace with England, and it would have obeyed. He is the real author of our present war. He dragged us into it with a cord about our necks—a cord which the allies alone can cut, and which there is every reason to believe they have cut.

As a fitting mode of expressing such feelings it was decided, at a great meeting of citizens in Philadelphia, to have a public dinner, which was to be given, it was announced, in honor of the Emperor Alexander and the King of Sweden and of the splendid victories which their arms had won in defence of the rights of man ; in honor of the heroic courage of the people of Germany ; in honor of the successful efforts of the patriots of Spain and Portugal in repelling their cruel invaders ; and in exultation over the final overthrow of a system fatal to peace, liberty, commerce, and universal happiness. In the midst of the preparations news came that Holland was free, or, as her friends delighted to express it, that " the Dutch have taken Holland," and immediately a second dinner was given by " the native Germans, Hollanders, and Swiss," to celebrate their heartfelt satisfaction at again seeing their native lands " freed from foreign despotism."

Soon after this the ship Ann-Alexander, from Liverpool, entered Boston with newspapers as late as December twenty-fifth containing long accounts of the surrender of Dantzic, of the overtures of peace made by the allies, and of their acceptance by Napoleon. Again the commercial cities were full of excitement. Prices fell rapidly, and rumors of the wildest sort were started to affect the market—Napoleon was said to be dead ; it was reported that an armistice had been concluded with England ; that the Continent was at peace, and that an express had been sent from Boston with despatches from Mr. Adams. That Holland was free was now certain, and " in honor of her emancipation " the descendants of the Dutch settlers at Albany held divine service in the North Dutch Church and toasted all the allied kings and all their distinguished generals at a dinner at the Eagle Inn. At New Brunswick the descendants of Dutch ancestors commemorated " the emancipation of Holland from the fangs of French despotism " with a street parade, a solemn thanksgiving service in the Dutch Church, and a public dinner.

Under the influence of these popular rejoicings, of the hope for peace, and of the changed conditions of Europe, men who were earnest supporters of the administration began to question the wisdom of the embargo. It was right, they admitted, that the shameful trade New England was carrying on with the enemy should be stopped. But now that a fair trade would soon be opened with Holland, with Germany, and per-

haps with France, was it just to punish honest men for the
sins committed by rogues? Must the whole country be deprived of tea and coffee, sugar and Havana cigars, china and
hardware, because men in New England drove cattle into
Canada and bought English bills of exchange? Such a policy
was distressing to America and the subject of derision in England, which had the markets of Europe at her command. But
even before such reasoning the administration could not bear
to yield, for New England was every day growing more hostile, more defiant.

To the people of that section the embargo was a blow
struck directly at them. They met it accordingly, and from
the moment the fall of Bonaparte seemed assured, their leaders,
their representatives, their press, their town meetings, began
seriously to discuss the propriety of withdrawing from all
share in the war and making their own terms with England.

In this form of resistance the Governor of Vermont had
already led the way by ordering a brigade of militia, which
had been placed under the command of an officer of the United
States and marched to the defence of New York, to return to
their homes and there hold themselves in readiness to defend
Vermont. But when the proclamation was read to the troops
they refused to obey. Indeed, the officers sent back a most
insolent, defiant, and mutinous reply. "We are," said they,
"in the service of the United States, and your power over us
as Governor of Vermont is suspended. We will not obey,
but will continue in the service of our country till discharged.
We consider your proclamation an unwarranted stretch of
authority, and as issued from the worst of motives, to effect
the basest of purposes. We regard it with mingled emotions
of pity and contempt for its author, and as a striking monument of his folly." Here it would have been well to have let
the matter rest; but as the Governor or his agent seemed to
be liable to punishment under the law of 1795, a set of resolutions were moved in Congress declaring that the Governor of
Vermont had violated the law of 1795, had enticed soldiers to
desert, and instructing the Attorney-General of the United
States to prosecute him. They were laid over for future consideration, but when they were known in New England, the

Legislature of Massachusetts passed a resolution whose meaning was not to be mistaken. Respect due to Congress, it read, forbade the belief that so flagrant an indignity to an independent State would ever be sanctioned by the National Legislature. Yet every attempt to make the Governor of a State amenable to any other tribunal than that of the State over which he presided was to be repelled promptly; and as it was the duty of Massachusetts to aid the Governor of Vermont with her full power in any effort to support his constitutional rights, she would, when requested by Vermont, " make provision by law for effectual support." As the resolutions had not passed Congress, that offered in the Massachusetts House was laid on the table to await results in Washington, and was never heard from again. But a law passed soon after this, ordering the sheriffs to discharge all Federal prisoners confined in the county jails, showed that the opposition of Massachusetts was not confined to threats.

Though the new trade restriction applied with equal force to every port in the United States, it fell with especial severity on those of Massachusetts. The blockade which, during 1813, extended from Rhode Island to New Orleans, had long since stopped all coasting south of Cape Cod. Trade by sea with the Southern States was not, therefore, affected by the embargo. But from Boston to Eastport there had gone on, as usual, a legitimate and proper coasting trade, and this in one moment was destroyed. Ships from Nantucket, from Eastport, from Portland, from any port in Maine that happened to be at Salem or Boston or New Bedford on the fatal day when the law went into operation, were stopped and their crews left, hundreds of miles from home, to shift as best they could. Early in January, as a consequence, the roads from Boston to Maine were dotted with bands of sailors, on foot, with packs on their backs, begging their way homeward. Two hundred went off in one week, and among them were two crews from Eastport, four hundred and sixty miles distant. Others, who lived at Nantucket, were forced to subsist by charity. Yet, strange as it may seem, the members of Congress who resisted any modification and finally voted against the repeal of the embargo were the Federalists from New England. The Constitution, they argued, gives Congress no power to prevent trade by sea between towns and cities in the same State, nor between the ports of one State and those on the seacoast or navigable rivers of an adjoining State. The law imposing the embargo is therefore unconstitutional. But when a resolution was offered to instruct the Committee on Foreign Relations to report a bill repealing it, the House refused to even consider the motion. An effort was then made to secure a slight modification, in order that ships away from home when the embargo was laid might be permitted to return. Numbers of masters and crews, it was stated, who had been guilty of no offence whatever, who had gone from Boston or from Salem to some port in Maine long before the President had suggested the measure—nay, before Congress had assembled—had been forced to abandon their ships and go on foot, in the depth of winter, two hundred miles or more to their homes, or suffer all the privations imposed by idleness and poverty in a place where they were strangers. To Congress it could surely make no difference whether the ships were tied to the wharves of one port or another; but to those who owned and to those who sailed the ships it was a matter of very serious importance where they were embargoed. This seemed so reasonable that, when a resolution was moved to bid the committee inquire into the expediency of permitting coasting vessels absent on December seventeenth to return to the ports where the voyage began, the House consented, though almost every Federalist present voted No. That they would have done so had the suffering really been as great as was depicted, or had their vote been needed to pass the resolution, is by no means probable. They objected because the motion was for an inquiry into the expediency of granting the liberty to do an act from which, under the Constitution, their constituents, they held, could not legally be debarred. Their conduct in regard to the Nantucket bill, which came down from the Senate just before the resolution passed, was therefore very different.

The people in Nantucket had been the chief sufferers. Many of the inhabitants who happened to be in Massachusetts on business found themselves, without a moment's warning, cut off from home and family, while those on the island were quickly brought to a state bordering on starvation, for it was from the main-land that they drew their supply of fuel, flour, and provisions. On the arrival, therefore, of the Senate bill giving the President authority to allow the islanders to carry from Massachusetts such quantities of fuel and food as were necessary, the Federalists gave it a hearty support and it passed with but eight votes cast against it. One of the eight was given by Webster, who declared that he considered the embargo law unconstitutional, null, and void, and that he would not vote for a bill granting his fellow-citizens a right of which they were not, and could not be, deprived.

The success in the case of Nantucket encouraged the introduction of motions to inquire into the expediency of allowing vessels with firewood, lime, and bark to go from port to port within the same State; to suspend the embargo during the negotiations for peace; to inquire into the expediency of repeal; but the House seemed determined that, as the administration had asked for the measure, the administration must propose its repeal, and refused to consider the motions. To accept this situation was hard indeed; but, as every newspaper that found its way to our shores from England confirmed the first reports of the signal victories of the allies, Madison yielded, and on March thirty-first asked for the repeal both of the embargo and the Non-importation Act, which had been in force against Great Britain since 1811. He gave as his reasons the importance of commercial intercourse between the United States and the nations at peace with her; the extensive changes, so favorable to a renewal of commerce, which had lately taken place in Europe; and the belief that important advantages would result from adapting our commercial laws to the new conditions.

Lest so sudden a change of policy should be ruinous to the manufactures the restrictive system had produced, he further suggested that the double duties on imports, which were to expire one year after peace with Great Britain, should be continued till two years after that event, and, that the banks might not be embarrassed, he asked that the exportation of specie be forbidden. So much as concerned the embargo and the Non-intercourse Act was quickly reported on by the Committee on

Foreign Relations, and a repealing act presented. To the surprise of the people, the very men who, a few months before, had been denouncing the law as unconstitutional, now cried out against its repeal. The whole system of restriction, said they, is wrong and bad, but the present is no time to abolish it. A negotiation for peace is pending. At such a moment, to appear vacillating will weaken our demands and lessen the inducement of the enemy to make peace. Moreover, the opening of the ports will bring in a flood of foreign goods, will destroy our carrying trade, break down our growing manufactures, and strip the country of specie as effectually as in 1786. But their resistance availed nothing, and the House, by a vote of one hundred and fifteen to thirty-seven, sent the bill to the Senate. There some amendments were made, to which the House reluctantly agreed, and on April fourteenth it was signed by Madison and became law at once. With this effort the administration again settled down in a state of torpor and suffered the people to nurse the idle hope of an armistice and a peace, while the enemy gathered in force on the frontier and off the coast. In May came the proclamation of Sir Alexander Cochrane, extending the blockade over New England, from Block Point at the eastern entrance to Long Island Sound to Eastport, and warning neutrals not to break through. Then followed the capture of Eastport, Castine, Nantucket, the depredations along the coast, the arrival of the fleet in Chesapeake Bay—and it mattered little that the embargo was no longer in force. In June came the news that Paris was captured, that Napoleon had been dethroned and banished to Elba, and a new series of dinners and festivals, " to celebrate the deliverance of Europe from a relentless tyranny which threatened to exterminate freedom from the world," swept over the country. The French Minister, by proclamation, informed all Frenchmen that they were absolved from allegiance to the late Emperor; that their new master was Louis Stanislas Xavier; that the consuls would receive their oaths of allegiance; * and immediately the white cockade, after an absence of twenty-one years, reappeared on the streets of our cities, and the white flag

* " Avis aux Français," American Daily Advertiser, June 16, 1814.

on the ships in our harbors.   The Te Deum was sung in the
Catholic churches to celebrate the deliverance of the Pope
from his six years of imprisonment.   When the Fourth of July
came round the Washington Benevolent Societies, the Washington Guards, the Federalists everywhere, were loud in the
demonstrations of joy over the fall of tyranny, the emancipation of Europe, the revival of commerce, and the prospect of
a speedy end to the war.

From this dream of peace the country was rudely awakened
before the orations and the toasts were half forgotten.   The same
newspapers which reported the Fourth-of-July festivities were
full of extracts from the Quebec papers announcing the arrival
from Bordeaux of a large part of Wellington's army, and contained a new circular from the War Department to the Governors of the States and Territories calling for more troops.
The late pacification of Europe, the letter said, afforded the
enemy a large land and naval force with which to carry on the
war against the United States more vigorously and more widely
than ever.   That it would be so used was impossible to say.
Yet it was well to be prepared, and for the purpose of defending the Atlantic coast the President thought it necessary to call
for ninety-three thousand five hundred men, to be organized
and held for instant service.   Even then, for a moment, the
people allowed themselves to be lulled into repose by another
rumor of an armistice that came from the northern frontier.
But the next mail from the South announced that the British
were in force on the Chesapeake, that they had landed at the
mouth of the Patuxent, that the war was raging again, and
that Madison, for " great and weighty " reasons, had summoned
Congress to meet on the nineteenth of September.*   When the
appointed day arrived the Capitol was in ruins, and the members assembled in the quarters hastily prepared for them in
what, before the British invasion, had been the Patent-Office.

They had been summoned in extraordinary session to provide for the wants of the Treasury.   But their own condition
claimed their first attention.   The House in particular was
most uncomfortably provided for.   The old patent-office room

---

* The proclamation is dated August 8, 1814.

in which it sat was too small. Every inch of floor space up to the windows and even to the fireplace was occupied with chairs. Yet the members were more numerous than the seats, and, had a full House attended, many gentlemen would not have found standing room. The prospect of the discomfort and the unhealthfulness of a long winter, and, it might be, a long summer session in such a room, was far from pleasant. The members became eager to get away, and in a little while had appointed a committee to consider the matter, had approved a report recommending removal, and had under debate a bill to transfer the seat of government to Philadelphia, there to stay till the beginning of the next session after the war. By this time, however, a month had slipped away. The enemy had burned their barracks on Tangier Island, and had left the Chesapeake without showing any intention of coming back. Members were growing used to the hardships and discomforts that surrounded them. A tender regard, too, began to prevail for the injury such a removal would do to private property, and grew so strong that the bill was rejected by a majority of nine.

Having decided to stay in Washington, Congress took the first step toward regeneration and ordered the purchase of Jefferson's library. The books were the accumulation of fifty years, and had been gathered with no small industry and much good sense from every quarter of Europe. Need of money and a real desire to aid the Government in its embarrassed state moved Jefferson to offer them to Congress as the beginning of a new collection. No other such collection could then be purchased in bulk in the United States, and Congress bought them for fifty thousand dollars. Against this a great outcry was made by Federalists, and by men who were not Federalists, as a piece of shameful extravagance; and considering the condition of the Treasury, there was much justice in the complaint, for the Government was bankrupt.

On receiving the offer of England to treat at Gothenburg, Madison accepted the conditions forced on him by the Senate in July, and, desiring to renominate Gallatin a peace commissioner, declared the office of Secretary of the Treasury vacant, and sent the name of George W. Campbell to the Senate as that of a proper man to fill the vacancy.* The Senate approved, and from Campbell, at the opening of the session, came a most disheartening report. Between January first and July first, 1814, he had, he said, paid out nearly twenty millions of dollars. Twenty-seven millions more would be needed before the end of the year. To meet this he could, he thought, count with safety on thirteen millions. This would leave a deficit of fourteen millions, which, added to the deficit sure to occur in 1815, would make some fifty millions to be provided for if war went on till January first, 1816.

How this vast sum should be raised he did not venture to say. It mattered little, however, for with his report went his resignation, and Alexander James Dallas was almost immediately appointed Secretary in his place. But before Dallas had time to look about him in his new office and frame a plan for the relief of the Treasury, the Committee of Ways and Means reported one of their own to the House of Representatives. Taxes, loans, and Treasury notes were, they said, the only means at hand for meeting the cost of war. The product of taxation was too slow to meet the immediate demand of the Treasury. Loans could no longer be relied on. Treasury notes were therefore the only resource left; nor did it seem a fruitless one. The want of a circulating medium was felt by every one. The suspension of specie payments by the banks of the Middle States had embarrassed the Treasury, and, by confining the circulation of bank-notes to the limits of the States in which they were issued, had stopped the transmission of money. This was the time, then, to so modify the Treasury notes that they should become a national circulating medium. To turn them into such a medium it was only necessary to issue them in denominations small enough to meet the wants of daily life, permit holders to fund them at any loan office for eight per cent. stock, make them receivable in payment of public lands and taxes, pledge the internal revenue for the interest, and raise the revenue by increasing existing taxes.

The report of the Committee of Ways and Means was on

* The Federalists declared he was just the man for the emergency, as his initials, G. W. C., exactly expressed the state of affairs—Government Wants Cash.

so much of the President's message as related to finance. But, realizing that the new Secretary might wish to be heard, the chairman now informed him that proceedings would be suspended on the report that he might have a chance to suggest a scheme of his own. Dallas promptly undertook the task of preparing a plan, and in a few days sent back a most formidable document. There should, in the first place, he thought, be a permanent annual revenue of twenty-one million dollars raised by taxes, duties, imposts, and excises. There should, in the next place, be a temporary or war revenue of twenty-one million dollars raised yearly by doubling the direct tax, doubling the rates of postage, doubling the old taxes on licenses, on auction sales, on carriages, and by laying new ones on snuff and tobacco, on iron and leather, on paper, mortgages, playing cards, and on counsellors and attorneys-at-law; and there should, in the third place, be a national bank to supply a national circulating medium and facilitate exchange.

The letter was duly presented to the House, and when the House took the matter into consideration the Committee of Ways and Means requested that their report might be so amended as to conform to the ideas of the Secretary. This was done. The suggestions of Dallas and the committee were then put in the form of resolutions, were adopted, and the committee ordered to bring in bills establishing such a system of taxation as the people of the United States had never known before. First came the bill to incorporate sundry subscribers to a Bank of the United States.

That the disorders of the currency were now past all endurance was universally admitted. That Congress had power to regulate the currency was not to be questioned, as it was granted in so many words in the Constitution. That the best way to regulate it was by means of a national bank was very generally admitted even by old Republicans. But there were a few who could not forget that hatred of banks had always been good democratic doctrine, and that they had themselves raised their voices and cast their votes in favor of a refusal of a charter to the old Bank of the United States. These, for the sake of consistency, refused to support the plan of Dallas. Nevertheless, the House, by a great majority, voted that it was expedient to found a bank, and early in November the bill based on the plan of Dallas was reported.

The location of the bank was to be Philadelphia. The capital was to be fifty millions, of which three fifths was to be subscribed by companies, corporations, or individuals, and two fifths by the United States. The Federal Government might pay its subscription in six-per-cent. stock. But companies, corporations, and individuals must pay one fifth in gold or silver, and the rest in specie or Treasury notes and stock, in the proportion of one dollar in notes to three dollars in stock.*

Had the friends of the bank been in need of new arguments to support their measure, they might easily have drawn them from the state of the Treasury on that day. The capture of Washington and the attack on Baltimore had been succeeded by a suspension of specie payments by every bank along the seaboard from New York to Georgia. A panic followed. Bank-notes first depreciated and then almost ceased to circulate. Banks in the same State, in the same neighborhood—nay, in some instances in the same city—would not take each other's paper. Exchange rose to an enormous figure, and the Secretary of the Treasury found it impossible to move the revenue of the Government from the banks of the ports where it was collected to the towns and cities where creditors were to be paid. Indeed, even the New England banks, which had not suspended specie, now refused to pay it out on Treasury drafts. Thus, on the first of October the quarterly interest on the United States stock fell due. To meet so much as was payable at Boston a draft on the State Bank at Boston was sent to the Commissioner of Loans for Massachusetts. There was then on deposit in the bank to the credit of the United States a sum far in excess of that needed to pay the interest. But when the public creditors came to the bank all whose dividends exceeded

---

* The capital as thus arranged was to consist of—

United States Government stock	$20.000,000
Subscriptions of companies and individuals in Treasury notes	6,000,000
Subscriptions of companies, etc., in United States stock	18,000,000
Specie	6,000,000
Total	$50,000,000

one hundred dollars were refused cash and tendered Treasury notes at par. These the majority of the creditors refused to take, because they were not a legal tender, and because, while offered at par, they did not bring seventy-five cents on the dollar in the market.

By the time news of this reached Washington Dallas was Secretary of the Treasury. Pressure of new duties made it impossible to give the matter immediate attention. But on November ninth, two days after his bank bill was reported to the House, he wrote to the commissioner at Boston that the Treasury was bankrupt; that the suspension of specie payment made it impossible to pay the public creditor his interest money in specie; and that if he would not take Treasury notes he must either take some of the six million loan yet unsubscribed for, receive drafts on banks south and west of Philadelphia, or wait for payment till better days.

Desperate as was now the state of the National Treasury, the Federalists had nothing but ridicule for the bank bill. This bank, said they, is to have a capital of fifty million dollars. Thirty millions is to be subscribed by corporations, companies, and individuals who may have that much to throw away, and twenty millions by the Government. Of the popular subscription, six millions is to be in specie and twenty-four in Treasury notes and six-per-cent. stock of the United States at par, though both of them are now floating on the market at very depreciated values. The twenty millions of Government subscription is to be paid in its own stock, on which it can not now raise a dollar. The bank in return is to loan the Treasury thirty millions. The banking capital of this institution then will consist of six millions of specie, forty-four millions of Treasury notes and six-per-cent. stock, and a Government promise to pay of thirty millions more. On this handful of specie, and this seventy-four millions of Government debt as security, fifty millions of bank-notes are to be issued as regulators of the currency. Was there ever such an attempt to gull people out of their money? The national loan will not bring seventy-five per cent. Treasury notes are not much better. Yet such stuff as this is to form the bulk of the capital! A note of the new bank, instead of representing gold or silver, will represent so much loan or so many Treasury notes. And does anybody suppose such paper will pass at par? Will any sane man take a bank-note at par which represents another piece of paper which he can buy in the market twenty-five cents on the dollar cheaper? And if not taken at par, how will the notes of the United States Bank be any better than the notes of the State's bank? The true state of the case is this: A is in debt for bonds, notes, and bank debts. If he should issue more notes with which to pay his liabilities his credit would be injured, so he establishes B in a banking house with a stock of his bonds as capital, and then borrows B's notes, which bear no interest, and with them pays his own notes, which do bear interest. Creditors who will not take A's bonds at twenty per cent. discount are expected to readily take B's notes, bottomed on those bonds, at par. Hence it follows that a bankrupt administration may pay its debts by creating a new firm with a capital of insolvency.

Discussion of the bill had scarcely begun in the House when Calhoun brought in yet another scheme, which provided for a huge private bank in which the Government should own no stock, over which it should have no direction, and from which it could not borrow one cent. The capital was to be fifty millions, might be subscribed in certain proportions on the last three days of each month, and was to consist of six millions of specie and forty-four millions of Treasury notes to be issued for that purpose.

On this scheme the House in committee seized with eagerness, and, substituting it for the plan of Dallas, proceeded to discuss it. Meantime the Federalist press made merry with Calhoun's bank. The struggle in the House, said one, seems to be whether the stock jobbers shall fill up the subscription with depreciated paper they have on hand, or let Government do so with worthless paper especially issued for the occasion. How, said another, can Mr. Dallas keep his place? Now that the House has declared, by a two-thirds vote, that Mr. Calhoun is the better financier, must not the Secretary resign? The plan, said a third, is not the work of Mr. Calhoun, but of a theorist who has been crazy these twenty years.

In the House, however, Calhoun's bill was much preferred,

was accepted, and sent to the committee. As soon as the committee received it, Lowndes, who was chairman, wrote to Dallas asking two questions. "What effect," said he, "will a new issue of forty-four million dollars in Treasury notes— receivable in payment of subscriptions to a national bank— have on the market value of notes already out and not receivable in payment of such subscriptions, and on the sale of the proposed loan for 1815?" The second question was, Could the new notes be put in circulation without depreciation?

To the first Dallas replied that the effect would be bad, because the new creditors would thus enjoy a privilege not granted to the old and equally meritorious creditors; because this discrimination would arouse discontent and depreciate Government paper already out; and because, unless the Government could borrow from the bank (a privilege the proposed charter expressly forbade), the prospect of placing the loan of 1815 was small indeed. To the second question the Secretary replied that to put the notes in general circulation would be. quite impossible. If a desire to subscribe to the bank became general, the notes would be seized by speculators and held for a premium. If such a desire did not become general, the people would not take forty-four millions of notes on any terms.*

The committee, feeling the weight of his argument, came back to the House, told it they did not know what to do, and reported the bill without amendment.† The House thereupon took the bill into consideration, cut down the capital to thirty millions, and listened to a fierce debate on a motion to strike out the first section. At no time during the session had the members been so angry. Again and again the Speaker was forced to call for order. Not till the previous question was put could the debate be stopped. Then, by a great majority, the bill was refused a third reading and so was rejected.‡

That it might not pass out of the possession of the House, a member who had voted against it now moved a reconsideration, in order, as he said, to recommit the bill and so keep the

---

* Letter of A. J. Dallas to William Lowndes. Annals of Congress, 1814–1815, vol. iii, pp. 652–654.

† November 28, 1814.   ‡ Ibid.

bank question open for discussion. But he soon withdrew the motion and no more was heard of the matter for some weeks, when a bill to establish a national bank came down from the Senate. More debating, more amending, more quarrelling now followed till the second of January, when, the vote having been taken on the passage of the bill, the nays were found to be eighty and the yeas eighty-one. Thereupon the Speaker— Langdon Cheves, of South Carolina—rose, and, having reminded the House of the rule which made it the duty and the right of the Speaker to vote in two cases, spoke strongly against the bill and voted in the negative. This made a tie; whereupon he gave his casting vote, also in the negative, and the bill was rejected.

On the morrow this vote was reconsidered and the bill sent to a select committee, which soon reported it with amendments, which the House accepted. But the troubles which beset it on every hand were not yet ended, and it quickly came back to the Senate with Madison's veto. He objected because the amount of stock subscribable was not enough to raise the price of that stock in the market; because the amount of Treasury notes subscribable would not benefit the public credit in the least; because the bank could furnish no real aid in the way of loans;* and because during the war it could not be relied on to provide a circulating medium. Once back in the Senate, a feeble attempt was made to pass it over the veto; and failing in this, a new bill providing for a bank with fifty millions of capital, from which the Government might borrow thirty millions, was hurried through three readings and sent to the House, where it was at once taken up. But news of peace came a few days later, and the whole matter was postponed indefinitely.

The failure of Congress to provide the country with a currency followed hard on its failure to raise and equip an army. On the day it assembled in the Patent-Office the military condition was, if possible, more desperate than the financial. One hundred miles of the coast of Maine were in the hands

---

* The bank was never to loan the Government more than $500,000 in any one year, and must redeem its notes in specie or lose its charter.

of the British.   A great naval and military force was known to be on its way to the gulf coast.   A fleet of five ships and twenty thousand men were gathering at Kingston to attack Sackett's Harbor.   A third force had laid the capital in ashes. That so desperate a condition made desperate remedies necessary seemed certain to even so timid an administrator as Monroe.   Indeed, the measures which he now urged were such as ten years before he would have considered " a deliberate, dangerous, and palpable " violation of the Constitution. But he, too, had learned that the theoretical administration of the Constitution is one thing and the actual conduct of affairs in the hour of danger is a very different thing, and was now ready to advocate measures which, a little earlier, he would have thought most shocking.   The military committee of the House had called on him, as Secretary of War, for suggestions for the betterment of the army, and in return received a plan and an interpretation of the Constitution.

Let there, said he, be an army for the field and an army for defence of the cities and the frontier.   Let the field army, which on the first of October numbered less than thirty-four, be raised at once to the legal limit of sixty-two thousand men, let the army of defence consist of forty thousand more, and let the next campaign open with one hundred thousand regular troops in the field.   That so great a number could be gathered by enlistment in a few weeks, when the utmost exertions of two years had never been able to put forty thousand under arms, was beyond belief.   Monroe therefore suggested four plans of raising them : The first was a general and sweeping draft.   The entire free male population of the country, from eighteen to forty-five years old, was to be enrolled and divided into classes of one hundred.   Each hundred within thirty days was to furnish a certain number of men for the war, and if any of them were killed, wounded, or taken, fill their places. Should any class fail to supply its quota, the men needed should be drafted from it and the bounty money assessed on the property of the class from which they were drawn.   His second plan was to divide the militia into three classes, according to age, and suffer the President to call any part of either class into service for two years.   The third was to exempt

every five men from militia service who would find one to
enlist for the war. The fourth was to give the recruit one
hundred and sixty acres of bounty land at the time of enlistment and one hundred more for each year of service.

Taking up the matter at once, the military committees of
the House and Senate began a careful canvass to ascertain the
strongest measures Congress would support. The result in
the House showed that there was not the slightest disposition
to act finally on the subject, and that no strong and energetic
measure had the least chance of success. The committee
therefore refused to report a bill. But in the Senate a better
feeling existed, and two bills were soon passed and sent down
to the House: the one proposing to fill the ranks of the regular army by enlisting minors without the consent of their
guardians or parents, and by doubling the bounty and exempting from duty every militia-man who should find a regular
recruit; the other proposing to supply an army of defence by
authorizing a draft of eighty thousand militia to serve in
their own or an adjoining State.

In the Senate the Militia Bill had passed by a small majority, had been bitterly opposed by the members from the eastward, and had caused a debate during which the senators from
New England used language high and menacing. "The bill,"
said they, "is unconstitutional, unequal, unjust, oppressive, and
cannot be executed. It is unconstitutional because it supposes
an unlimited power of Congress over the militia in time of
war. Nothing can be more absurd. That the powers of this
Government are limited, that powers not expressly delegated
are reserved, is universally admitted. Before the Constitution
was made each State had entire control over its militia. All
control save what has been expressly delegated is therefore still
retained. And what power has been delegated? Power to
call forth the militia to repel invasion, to execute the laws, to
suppress insurrection; and power to provide for organizing,
arming, disciplining, and governing such part as may be in the
service of the United States, have been expressly delegated.
Is there any delegation of the right to govern them before
they are called into the service of the United States? No,
there is not. What right, then, has Congress to pass a bill

prescribing the way the militia shall be raised, dividing it when raised into classes, and forcing each class to provide a man or submit to a draft? It has no such right. The Government of the United States cannot control the militia, cannot even train it till actually in service. The bill before us is therefore unconstitutional. It is the first step on the odious ground of conscription, which never will and never ought to be submitted to by the people of this country while they retain one idea of civil freedom—a plan which if attempted will be resisted by many States and at every hazard, and should be resisted by all who have any regard for public liberty or the rights of the States." *

"This system of military conscription is not only inconsistent with the spirit and provisions of the Constitution, but also with all the principles of civil liberty. In atrocity it exceeds the conscriptions of the late Emperor of France. He allowed exemptions to fathers of families. But this bill allows none except to the President of the United States and the Governors of the States. All others within the prescribed limits, whatever their pursuits, whatever their condition of life, must submit to the iron yoke. Priests must be taken from the altar, judges must be taken from the bench, seminaries of learning are to be robbed of their professors and scholars. The highest officers, both civil and military, must be forced into the ranks of the army. Such a measure cannot and ought not to be submitted to. It ought to be resisted.†

" But the unconstitutionality of this bill, though it is bad enough to justify opposition, is not the only defect. There is in it a rigor and a severity never before made use of which the people of this country will not endure. On whom, pray, does this severity fall? On the middling ranks of society; on your tenantry, your mechanics, your manufacturers; on the men who constitute the very bone and muscle of your population. The rich man will find his substitute, but the apprentice is to be forced from his workshop and the farmer from his fields; the mechanic is to be made to abandon his business and

* Speech of Senator Gore. Annals of Congress, 1814–'15, p. 100.

† Speech of Senator Mason [New Hampshire]. Annals of Congress, 1814–'15, p. 84.

the poor man his family for the space, if needs be, of two long years. Is this justice? Is this equality? Is it not tyranny and oppression of no common sort? Sir, you dare not—at least I hope you dare not—attempt a conscription to fill the ranks of your regular army."

To all such arguments and appeals the Senate was deaf, and sent the bill down to the House in November. The bill to provide for filling the ranks of the army by doubling bounties and enlisting minors had already passed the Senate with little debate. It was now, however, vigorously attacked by the House. The right to enlist minors without the consent of parents or guardians, and apprentices without the consent of their masters, was loudly denounced as a violation of contract and unconstitutional. Amendments were therefore made giving the minor four days after enlistment in which to think over his action. If at the end of that time he had not withdrawn, his enlistment became binding. This the Senate accepted and the bill became law. But the amendments made by the House to the Conscription Bill, and an amendment reducing the term of military service from two years to one, were not accepted and the bill was lost.

Failure to provide an army left the administration to fight on as best it could with thirty-two thousand regular troops, the six-months militia, and such others as might be tempted into the ranks by the great bounty payable in land or by a desire to get rid of a harsh master. That every soldier of the thirty thousand would be needed on the frontier, that the Government was utterly unable to provide for the common defence, that the time had come for the States to defend themselves, was now admitted, and one by one State armies began to be formed. No ill-will toward the Government prompted this. No State in the Union was then more warmly supporting the war than New York; yet at a special session in the autumn of 1814 the Legislature, with the reports of the burning of Washington fresh in mind, passed a bill authorizing the raising of twelve thousand men for the defence of the State. As the troops were to be gathered by a sweeping conscription, Chancellor Kent, when the bill came before the Council of Revision, declared it to be against the spirit of the Constitution and the

public good.   Individual States, as States, he said, had nothing
whatever to do with the war.   Power to make war, raise and
support armies, and levy taxes, duties, and excises, in order to
pay for the common defence and general welfare, had been
expressly given to Congress.   After such a grant the State
had no right to raise twelve thousand men, arm, equip, and
give them bounties at a cost of two and a half millions of dollars, for such an outlay was an undue, disproportionate, and
burdensome tax to provide for the common defence and general welfare.   But the council overruled his objection, approved the bill, made it a law amid the hearty condemnation
of the people and the vigorous denunciations of town-meeting
after town-meeting all over the State.*   Connecticut bade her
Governor borrow four hundred thousand dollars, buy two
thousand muskets, use any part of the militia he saw fit in the
defence of any adjoining State when invaded, and, if Congress should pass the Conscription Bill, convene the Legislature immediately.

Massachusetts came next.   The Governor in his message
had called attention to the defenceless condition of the State,
and a committee appointed to consider it made strong recommendations.   The unhappy and ruinous war against Great
Britain, the committee reported, had at last assumed an aspect of great and immediate danger to the Commonwealth.
Repeated invasions of Canada had produced the invasion of
the seaboard and river towns of Massachusetts.   A portion of
her territory was at that moment in the possession of the
enemy, and her whole sea-coast, wherever assailable, was men-
aced with desolation.   No means bearing any proportion to
the emergency had been provided by the General Government
to defend her soil and repel the invader.   By far the larger
part of the regular troops raised or at any time quartered in
the State had been drawn away to wage war on the Canadian
border.   There remained, therefore, no alternative but submission to the enemy or self-defence.   But the people of
Massachusetts were not yet ready for conquest and submission.
They must and would defend themselves, and with this in

---

* New York Evening Post, October 29, 1814.

view, provision ought to be made for a military force independent of the militia. It was resolved, therefore, that ten thousand men should be raised by voluntary enlistment to serve for a year or during the war; that they should be organized and officered by the Governor for the defence of the State; that a part should take the field at once, and that all should be ready to move at a moment's notice, and that a million dollars should be borrowed to pay expenses. Maryland ordered five thousand State troops to be raised, and when word came that the Conscription Bill had passed the House of Representatives, her own House of Delegates ordered a committee to report "what measures it may be competent and proper for this House to take for maintaining the sovereign rights of this State, and protecting the liberties of its citizens against the operations of arbitrary and unconstitutional acts of the General Government." * Virginia made preparations to gather a State army, and South Carolina a State brigade. Kentucky ordered ten thousand men to be enlisted, and Pennsylvania, when peace came, had under consideration a bill to raise a military force to be used for the defence of herself, New Jersey, Delaware, and Maryland. In the opinion of many who took the view of Chancellor Kent, these State armies were unconstitutional. But the administration was in no condition to discuss the question of right. The situation was accepted, and, treating them as State levies, an act was passed permitting the President to muster them into the service of the United States in case of need.†

The Government was now on the brink of ruin. Without an army, without money, without a currency, hard pressed by the enemy on every hand and sitting in the ashes of its former home, it did indeed seem as if it must soon collapse, and, abandoning the duties it was created to perform, leave their execution to the States; a condition the people to the eastward were preparing to meet by the formation, if necessary, of a new federation out of the fragments of the old.

Ever since the defeat of Adams, New England in general and Massachusetts in particular had been ill-disposed toward

---

* December 17, 1814. † January 27, 1815.

the Government. The purchase of Louisiana, the representation of slaves, the admission of new States in the South and West, the embargo, the whole restrictive system, the attack on the Federal judiciary, the seeming hatred of England manifested by the Republicans, and their seeming devotion to Napoleon and France, had been grievances of no common sort to the people of New England. Twice their extreme partisan leaders had planned and considered a movement for secession. But it was not till 1814, when the Federal Government was tottering under a load of troubles, that the people began to do their part.

The seizure of eastern Maine had been followed by a call from Governor Strong, of Massachusetts, for a special session of the Legislature. On assembling, the members were told that when Castine fell, General Dearborn, who commanded the military district, had asked that the militia be called out ; that the request had been granted; that because of the great number of troops wanted they had been placed in command of a general of the State ; and that in consequence the President had refused to assume the cost of maintaining them. As the regular troops had been drawn away to the Canadian border, the Commonwealth was left to defend herself as best she could at her own cost. "The situation," said the Governor, "is dangerous and perplexing. We have been led by the terms of the Constitution to suppose that the Government of the Union would provide for our defence. We have resigned to that Government the revenues of the State with the expectation that this object would not be neglected. But the Government has declared war against the most powerful maritime nation, whose fleets can approach every section of our extended sea-coast, and we are disappointed in our expectation of national defence. Let us, then, relying on the support and direction of Providence, unite in such measures for our safety as the times demand and the principles of justice and the law of self-preservation will justify."

The Senate told the Governor in reply that it should never be forgotten that the dreadful condition of public affairs of which he spoke had been forced on the Commonwealth not merely against her consent, but in opposition to her most earnest protestations. From the moment the administration, yielding to its own passions, began its system of commercial hostility to England and its subservience to the late tyrant of France, the needless and cruel embarrassments that must follow were distinctly foreseen and plainly foretold by former Legislatures. "Never at any time," said the Senate, "was it doubted that a war with Great Britain would be attended by the extinction of our commerce, by the banishment of our sailors, by the desolation of our coast, by the blockade of our sea towns, by failure of our national credit, by new taxes, and by an alliance with the despot of France, from which, greatest of all calamities, we have been saved only by his fall. Of all these evils the Government was forewarned. But it was deaf to the warning, and, affecting to believe the citizens of Massachusetts disloyal to the Union, lavished the public money in the vain attempt to fix by evidence this odious imputation." It was therefore with great concern that the Senate felt forced to declare that the Constitution of the United States, under the administration of the persons then in power, had failed to secure to New England the rights and benefits which were the great object of its formation. The people, however, had a certain means of redress. They could, at their will, amend the Federal Constitution. But, knowing that a proposition for such a convention, if made by a single State, would not be successful, the Senate would suggest that a conference of New England States be held, and that this conference, if it seemed wise, should lay the foundation for a radical reform in the national compact by inviting to a future convention a deputation from each State in the Union.*

A resolution embodying a call for the convention to meet at Hartford on the fifteenth of December was then introduced, and after a sharp debate was passed in each branch by a great majority. The minority protested vigorously. That in the Senate declared it to be their belief that propositions for a separate peace might grow out of the proposed meeting; that if such offers were made and were highly favorable—and undoubtedly they would be—a compact might be made with

---

* Synopsis of debates in the Massachusetts Legislature.

the enemy, an army of foreign emissaries might be introduced, and a civil war result.*

In the House the minority were yet more outspoken. There must, they said, be more designed than was openly avowed. The report assumed that the Constitution had failed of its object, and that the people of Massachusetts were absolved from all allegiance and free to adopt another. In debate it had been reiterated that the Constitution was no longer to be respected and that revolution was not to be deprecated. They felt sure that other States would see in these things and in the resolutions a determination that "Massachusetts shall govern the administration or the Government shall not be administered in Massachusetts." † At this the House took offence, declared the protest disrespectful, and refused to receive it. Thereupon the minority left the House, and the majority, a few days later, chose twelve men to represent Massachusetts at Hartford.

In obedience to the commands of the General Court, the Governor sent forth his letter of invitation, and one by one the replies began to come in. Connecticut at once accepted, and chose seven delegates, but limited them to "such measures for the safety and welfare of these States as may consist with our obligations as members of the national Union." Rhode Island chose four delegates, and bade them do nothing they could not do "consistently with our obligations." Vermont declined. It was, she said, inexpedient to send delegates. New Hampshire was prevented from joining by the firm stand of her Council.

The result was a little disheartening, and was hailed by the Republican press with scoffs, jeers, and angry taunts. The adhesion of Connecticut and Rhode Island had been welcomed by a Federalist newspaper with the heading, "Second and Third Pillars of a New Federal Edifice Reared." ‡ The Republican press now warned the delegates to beware lest the three-legged structure toppled over, and called upon the

---

* Protest of the minority of the Senate, October 15, 1814.

† Protest of the minority of the House of Representatives, signed by seventy-six members.

‡ Columbian Centinel, November 9, 1814.

mountain to make haste and bring forth its mouse.   The Federalists flung back the taunts, pointed to the Conscription
Bill then before Congress as new evidence of the need of
Constitutional revision, warned its supporters that "the
hardy sons of the North would not thus be fettered," and
spent the interval before the convention met discussing what
it ought to do.

At the appointed time, December fifteenth, twenty-three
gentlemen took their seats in the Council Chamber of the
State-House at Hartford and proceeded to organize.   George
Cabot, of Massachusetts, was put in the chair, Theodore
Dwight was made secretary, chaplains were appointed, and a
committee named to examine credentials.   The committee reported that there were present two gentlemen chosen by popular conventions in the counties of Grafton and Cheshire, New
Hampshire, and that they were entitled to seats.*   The doors
were then closed, and for three weeks the members deliberated
in secret.   Meanwhile speculation ran rife.   To the southward
the belief was strong that New England, imitating Nantucket,
would declare herself neutral and open her ports to Great
Britain.   Some even believed that a separate confederation of
New England States was meditated and that the Hartford
Convention was framing the Constitution.

Eastward the fear seemed to be that the convention would
not do enough, and as not one of the delegates was such a
man as the malcontents would have selected, a vigorous effort
was made through the press to rouse the people to call for the
instant stoppage of the war.   "Throwing off all connection
with this wasteful war," wrote one of them, "making peace
with our enemy and opening once more our commerce with
the world, would be a wise and manly course.   The occasion
demands it of us, and the people at large are ready to meet
it."   How eager the people were for peace at any price was
well illustrated by an incident of recent occurrence.   On the
day Governor Strong sent forth his call for the convention the
terms offered by the British peace commissioners were pub-

---

* Later in the session a member from Windham County, Vermont, was given
a seat.

lished in the newspapers. Among the demands was that for
a cession of a piece of New England soil and the abandonment
of our rights to the fisheries. Yet such was the state of the
popular mind that the commissioners were loudly blamed for
not accepting them. Sixteen years later a renewal of the
proposition drove both Maine and Massachusetts into threats
of nullification. "At your hands," wrote another, addressing
the convention, "we demand deliverance; New England is
unanimous; and we announce our irrevocable decree that the
tyrannical oppression of those who at present usurp the powers of the Constitution is beyond endurance, and that we will
resist it." At Reading, in Massachusetts, the people voted to
make no returns for national taxation and pay no more national taxes till the State should decide what to do.

At last, on the fifth of January, the convention adjourned,
subject to the call of its president, and all suspense was ended.
The report began by urging patience and firmness. To urge
patience on a people already exhausted by distress was admitted to be likely to drive them at once to summary measures of
relief. But when abuses, reduced to a system and accumulated
through a long course of years, had entered every department
of Government; when they were clothed in the form of law
and enforced by an executive whose will was their source, no
summary means of relief remained save open resistance. For
this the time was not ripe. Under a wise and virtuous administration the Constitution had accomplished all its framers
wished, and had turned a few weak and disjointed republics
into a great, united, and prosperous nation. True it was, this
high state of public happiness had undergone a miserable and
afflicting reverse. But the lust of power, the corruption of
patronage, the wasteful expenditures, the heavy taxes, the unjust and ruinous war which had caused this reverse, were not
peculiar to any form of government. They were the natural
offspring of bad administration, and with a change of administration might pass away. Should events prove these evils to
be permanent, and due to implacable combinations of men or
of States to monopolize power and trample on the rights of
the commercial sections of the country, a separation would
then be better than a union by constraint of seeming friends

but real enemies.   Even then the separation should take place in peaceful times and by deliberate consent.

Having thus dismissed the question of immediate secession, the convention passed in review the right of the President to call out the Militia and the Conscription Bill then before Congress.   In the behavior of the President and in the plan of the Secretary of War the convention beheld a total disregard of the Constitution and a disposition to violate its provisions, which demanded a firm stand from the States.   It did not, however, comport with the forbearance due from a State toward the General Government to fly to open resistance on every infraction of the Constitution.   The mode and energy of the opposition should always conform to the nature of the violation, the intention of the authors, the extent of the injury inflicted, the determination manifested to persist in it, and the danger of delay.   " But in cases of deliberate, dangerous, and palpable infractions of the Constitution affecting the sovereignty of a State and the liberties of a people, it is not only the right but the duty of such a State to interpose its authority for their protection in the manner best calculated to secure that end.   When emergencies occur which are either beyond the reach of the judicial tribunals or too pressing to admit of the delay incident to their forms, States which have no common umpire must be their own judges and execute their own decisions."   It would therefore be well to wait till Congress had disposed of the Conscription Bill before the State decided what to do.

The convention next reviewed the whole course of Republican administration since the fourth of March, 1801, and having done this, made four recommendations to the States.   The first was that Congress be asked not only to suffer each State to defend itself, but to permit a part of the Federal taxes gathered within each State to be used to meet the cost of defending itself.   The second was that State armies be raised.   The third proposed seven amendments to the Federal Constitution. On these, immediate action could not be expected and was not asked.   But on the first and second recommendations speedy action was expected.   The fourth recommendation, therefore, urged that if Congress did not act, if peace was not concluded, if New England was neither defended by the General Government nor given leave to defend herself and pay the cost with the receipts of Federal taxes laid on her people, a second convention should meet in Boston on the third Thursday in June.

Before the report was two weeks old the Massachusetts General Court assembled and within a few days adopted it, approved each recommendation, and selected three commissioners to carry her complaints to Washington. They were bidden to go with all speed to the capital and there demand of the Government of the United States that Massachusetts be allowed to defend herself, enter into defensive alliances with her neighbors, and retain a reasonable share of the Federal revenues gathered within her boundary and use it to pay her State army. Connecticut added two more commissioners, and early in February the five set out.

It was now the very darkest period of the war. A long series of misfortunes, disasters, and disappointments had exhausted the resources of the country and depressed the spirits of the people. The capture of Washington was keenly felt. The campaign along the Niagara and on the Lakes, from which so much had been expected, had ended disastrously. Every bank along the seaboard, from Albany to Savannah, had suspended specie payment. The coast was closely blockaded. Business was paralyzed. Taxes were doubled. Prices were quadrupled. Exchange had risen to an enormous figure. The Government, unable to move its revenue from place to place, was reduced to bankruptcy and had defaulted. In the East, half of Maine was in possession of the enemy. On the Atlantic coast a force under Cockburn had seized Cumberland Island, had captured the fort at the mouth of St. Mary's river, had taken the town of St. Mary's with all its shops and goods, and was only awaiting the coming of a brigade to make an attack on Savannah. Worst of all, the favorite naval hero of the war had, after a feeble resistance, struck his flag and given up his ship within fifty miles of Sandy Hook.

For some weeks past a little squadron, consisting of the Peacock, the Hornet, a store-ship, and the forty-four-gun frigate President, had been waiting in New York Harbor for a chance to run the blockade. Their destination was the Indian seas, where they were to destroy British merchantmen engaged in the China and East Indian trade. But so closely was the port watched that it was not till the middle of January, when a strong west wind drove the blockading fleet out of sight, that Decatur ventured to cross the bar and make for the open with the President. It was night, and, keeping close to the Long Island shore, he ran on for some fifty miles, when, thinking he had passed the blockaders, he turned southward, and an hour before the break of day fell in with the fleet. The English ships were four in number and named Majestic, Pomone, Tenedos, and Endymion. The chase began at once, but by two in the afternoon the Endymion, proving the fastest sailer of the four, came so near the President that shots were exchanged from the stern and bow chasers. About five the wind fell off, and, the Endymion creeping slowly up, the fight began at short range and continued for two hours and a half, when the Endymion was silenced and beaten off. The President now made every effort to escape under cover of the night; but about eleven o'clock the Pomone came within range and fired a broadside. The President returned it. The Pomone fired a second and was about to fire a third, when the light abaft, which in night actions stands for the ensign, was hauled down and the President was a prize.

Though firing had been heard off Stonington and Newport, nothing was believed to have gone ill with the President. The people therefore were deeply chagrined when, a week later, a boy came up from the squadron blockading New London and delivered to the commanding officer at Fort Trumbull a letter from Decatur to his wife, announcing his capture. But no shame attached to Decatur. He was in the popular estimation the victim of traitors. It was remembered that the President had sailed on a Saturday night, and that long before sunrise on Sunday the Majestic, which lay near Plumb Island, got under way in great haste and put to sea so hurriedly that her water-casks were left on shore. That Decatur had been foully dealt with seemed certain. "What," it was asked, "did this haste mean? Could any sane man doubt that it was the consequence of information conveyed by some traitor— some blue-light wretch who still defrauded the gallows of its dues?" Happily the scheme had in part miscarried. The Endymion had been beaten off and a splendid victory won before Decatur, overpowered by numbers, was forced to strike. The loss of the brave men killed and wounded was indeed to be regretted. But our naval glory was untarnished, and on the sea we were still the masters of Great Britain man to man and ship to ship. A court of inquiry took much the same view and was loud in its praise of Decatur, his officers, and crew. Yet it is impossible to believe that he would have been taken had he been less eager to escape and more eager to fight, or, when forced to fight, had he displayed the energy and spirit which so distinguished him in the great battle with the Macedonian.

On every hand the outlook in January was most dismal. But the darkest hour is just before the break of day, and with February the dawn began to break. Since the end of the year rumors of peace had been rife. One came up from the Capes of Delaware about the middle of January. A British seventy-four-gun frigate, the Spencer, report said, entered the Delaware on the last day of December, ran up a white flag, and announced to those who went out to her that preliminary articles of peace had been signed at Ghent. Another report came to Boston by way of Long Island. A sea-captain who had visited the blockading squadron on the Sound had returned with word that a vessel just from Halifax reported the arrival of a fast ship from England with news that peace was hourly expected. The privateer Harpy brought a third version. From Castine, from Salem, came stories still more reliable. But the journals of both parties warned the people not to believe such groundless rumors. More than one hundred days, it was said, have elapsed since a word of any kind has been received from the envoys at Ghent. This is most discouraging and forebodes no good. No man can recall the conduct of Congress during the session so soon to end and not see that public measures have been greatly affected by the hopes, the fears, the tormenting doubts which grew out of ignorance concerning affairs at Ghent. The lack of money, the invasion of the country, the burning of the capital, the disorders of the currency, the need of troops—all grave and weighty matters—

made a call for an early meeting of Congress necessary. Yet what, after a session of five months, has been done? Hopes of an early peace have destroyed all vigor of action, and, while the enemy is preparing for the renewal of hostilities in a manner more brutal than ever, we are relying on negotiation, nursing the rumor of a peace, and doing nothing. Better, infinitely better than this, would be the arrival on our shores of the commissioners with news that they had utterly failed.

This, most happily, was not to be. For weeks past messengers had been riding post-haste up the Mississippi Valley, and on the fourth of February startled Washington with the news of the glorious victory of New Orleans. But this was not all. The illuminations, the bonfires, the bell-ringing, the dinners, the wild outburst of joy which followed, were still in progress when, one Saturday night in February, the sloop Favorite entered the harbor of New York, and sent off a boat bearing a gentleman who, landing at the battery, hurried to the City Hotel, where he declared himself to be Henry Carroll, one of the secretaries of the commission and the bearer of the treaty of peace.

CHAPTER XXIX.

THE RETURN OF PEACE.

THE long and tedious negotiation which ended with the treaty of Ghent was begun by Russia in the early autumn of 1812. She was herself then hard pressed by France, for Napoleon had declared war against the Czar on the twenty-second of June, had crossed the Niemen on the twenty-fourth, had reached the banks of the Dneiper by August fifteenth, had taken Smolensk three days later, and, following the retreating Russians toward Moscow, had fought the battle of Borodino on the sixth of September and had entered the city of Moscow on the fourteenth. Yet, desperate as were his own affairs, the Emperor Alexander found time to think of those of the United States, and at the very moment when the enemy were in the heart of his country he bade the Chancellor, Count Roumanzoff, send for Mr. Adams, assure the American Minister that he was greatly disturbed by the new war, and ask if an offer of mediation on his part would be acceptable to the United States. The answer of Adams was to the effect that such an act could not fail to be considered a new indication of the friendship of the Czar; but that it would be well to consult England. Roumanzoff replied that she had been consulted; that her Minister had already written to London; and, regarding the response of Adams as favorable, he drew up the proposal and sent it off to Washington without waiting to hear from England. Many months, however, went by ere the despatch found its way across the ocean, and under date of March eighth was communicated by the Russian *chargé d'affaires*, Daschkoff, to Monroe, who formally accepted the offer in a note full of compliments to the Czar. Who should be the commissioners on the part of the United States, when they should set out, and what instructions they should receive, were questions to be decided with more deliberation. The work of negotiation might with perfect safety have been intrusted to Adams alone, but it seemed best to follow the precedent set by John Adams in the days of our dispute with France and appoint a commission in which each party, and so far as possible each section of the country, should be represented, and two new envoys—one a Federalist and one a Republican—were chosen to serve with Adams. The Federalist was James A. Bayard. The Republican was to have been a Western man, and would undoubtedly have been Henry Clay, but this part of the plan was defeated by Gallatin, who asked for and received the appointment himself. Gallatin was, it is true, Secretary of the Treasury ; but as John Jay while Chief-Justice had been sent to England in 1794, and Oliver Ellsworth while Chief-Justice had been sent to France in 1800, Madison was merely following Federalist precedents when in 1813 he sent Gallatin to Russia.

The fact that he was Secretary of the Treasury greatly delayed the day of departure, for at the time of his appointment he was engaged in placing the sixteen-million-dollar loan, and in preparing all the financial measures on which Congress was expected to act. It was May ninth, therefore, when the two envoys sailed down the Delaware on their way to St. Petersburg. Their instructions were long, but the substance was that no treaty should be signed which did not contain a clear and distinct provision against impressment and the right of search.

While the travellers thus instructed were still at sea, complications began in Europe. Hardly were they well out of sight of land when Castlereagh, with many expressions of high regard for the Emperor, informed the Russian Minister at London that the proffered mediation could not be accepted. This information reached St. Petersburg about the middle of June, and was made known to Adams on the twenty-second of the month, when he called to tell Roumanzoff that Bayard and Gallatin had been appointed peace commissioners and were then on their way. To Adams the refusal of Great Britain seemed to end the whole matter, but the Chancellor declared that it did not; insisted that the appointment of the American commissioners put an entirely new face on the affair; said that he believed it would now be well to renew the offer of mediation, and announced his determination to ask leave so to do of the Emperor, whom the fortunes of war had then brought to Gitschin, in Bohemia, nine hundred miles or more from St. Petersburg. Though Roumanzoff kept his word and wrote promptly, it was not till August tenth that a favorable answer reached him, before which time Bayard and Gallatin had landed at Gothenburg, whence news of their arrival was quickly carried to London. At London the report seems to have given Castlereagh no little uneasiness. Up to this moment he had been content to announce the refusal of England to the Russian Minister. He now in quick succession sent off two despatches to the English Minister at St. Petersburg. In the first he bade Lord Cathcart urge the Emperor in the strongest manner not to press his offer of mediation further. In the second, written one week later, he bade the Minister assure the Czar that England was ready to name plenipotentiaries to treat with those from America at Gothenburg or London, but not at any place which would seem to imply the interference of a third power. The mere knowledge of such intervention would, he declared in a private letter to Lord Cathcart, be enough to turn the people of Great Britain against any arrangement with the United States which might result from it. By this time Alexander, at Gitschin, had received the declination of England made to his Minister in London in May, and had formally expressed his full satisfaction with the reason and conduct of Great Britain. But he had scarcely done so when he received the note of Roumanzoff telling him that his mediation had been accepted by the United States, and that her commissioners were on their way to Europe. Though he had but a few days before declared that he concurred in the refusal of England, he now changed his mind, and with great promptness told Roumanzoff to write to London and renew the offer. This was the instruction which the Chancellor read to Adams on the tenth of August, and which with no little alacrity he hastened to obey. Before, however, the instructions to Count Lieven could be written, the letter of Castlereagh announcing the willingness of England to treat directly with the United States reached Cathcart at the headquarters of the army in Bohemia. As the armistice had ended and a new campaign was about to begin, the despatch was not formally communicated to the Emperor till the allies had been beaten and Alexander had fled to Töplitz. There, September first, Cathcart addressed a note to Count Nesselrode. Although the Prince Regent, the ambassador said, had not been able to accept the mediation of his Imperial Majesty, he greatly desired, nevertheless, to see the beneficent wishes of his Majesty carried into effect; and having heard that the American plenipotentiaries had arrived in Russia, he was ready to nominate ministers to treat directly with them at London or at Gothenburg.* A copy of this note having been duly sent to London, was transmitted under cover of another, dated November fourth, to Monroe, at Washington.†

To say that the offer was eagerly seized on by both President and Congress but feebly expresses what then took place. On the third of January, 1814, the note was received; on the fifth the overture was formally accepted; ‡ on the seventh the note and the answer were laid before Congress; # on the eighth new instructions were hurried off to Bayard and Gallatin bidding them go without delay to Gothenburg.|| Not a line had come from them since they sailed for Europe.▲ That they had reached St. Petersburg on the twenty-first of July; that Roumanzoff had informed them of the refusal of England to accept mediation; that the Czar had authorized Roumanzoff to renew the offer; that Gallatin had received a letter from Alexander Baring announcing that England would treat directly; and that, after waiting many weeks for the Emperor to close the mission, or for Madison to call them home, they were at that moment on the point of leaving—was all unknown to Monroe. He addressed them, therefore, at St. Petersburg, told them that their new duties would require new commissions, assured

---

* American State Papers, Foreign Relations, vol. iii, pp. 621, 622.

† Ibid., p. 621.

‡ Ibid., p. 622.

Ibid., p. 621.

|| Ibid., p. 701.

▲ Ibid., p. 701.

them that the name of each of them should be sent to the Senate, and bade them, after expressing the sensibility of the President of the friendly act of the Emperor, go at once to the rendezvous at Gothenburg and there await further orders. Before the letter reached its destination part of these commands had been executed, for Bayard and Gallatin, on the twenty-fifth of January, left St. Petersburg for Amsterdam, where they arrived on the fourth of March.

As they made their way slowly across northern Europe, they found the people of every city and village through which they passed wild with ideas of resistance to France and the restoration of the ancient monarchies. At Amsterdam, where a few weeks were spent, nothing was so unpopular as hostility to England and English principles. Crossing the Channel, they landed at Harwich in April, and entered London, to find its streets and houses a blaze of light and its people carried away with joy over the capture of Paris and the downfall of the Corsican monster. Napoleon was a captive. The Bourbons were about to be restored, and the whole of Europe, after more than twenty years of strife, was once more at peace. In one part of the civilized world, and in that part alone, was the power and authority of England defied. That she would, under these circumstances, be little disposed to peace till she had, by some signal victories, wiped out the record of defeats met with on Lake Erie, at the river Thames, and on the ocean, seemed almost certain to Gallatin. The entire press of England called for this and predicted it. The London Times, the Morning Post, the Sun, the Courier, were incessant in their demands, and beyond all others abusive in their language. James Madison, according to these journals, was a despot in disguise, a liar, an impostor, and the most abject of the many abject tools of Napoleon. The Government of the United States was, in the opinions of their editors, the most unprincipled, the most despicable, the most incapable on the face of the earth— a Government not only insensible to shame, but destitute of that brutish quality of being beaten into a sense of its worthlessness and incapacity. The people of the United States were a base and ignorant set, who had not added one work to literature nor one discovery to science; who had not produced so

1814.   CONDITIONS OF PEACE.   261

much as one good poet or one celebrated historian, or made the world one whit better for their having lived in it.

With such a government, headed by such a man and supported by such a people, peace was not to be made too hastily. It must first be taught that no nation could make war on Great Britain with impunity. The thunder of British cannon must first be heard along the whole Atlantic coast. The American title to Louisiana must be inquired into. " The dirty, swindling manœuvres" of Madison in respect to Florida must be punished. After all this was done it would be time, not to negotiate, but to dictate terms of submission, at Philadelphia or New York. When Paris was captured, when the Ministry had seriously turned its attention to the United States, when thousands of the best troops of Wellington had embarked, the court journal began to set forth the conditions on which peace should be granted. The right of Great Britain to search American ships for British subjects was to be acknowledged in so many words. The ancient right of Americans to take fish in Canadian waters was to be given up. Spain was to be supported in her effort to get back Louisiana. Canadian interests so ignorantly sacrificed in the treaty of 1783 were to be recovered and protected.

Just what these interests were had been fully, repeatedly, and clearly set before the Ministry by Canada herself. Had our country been in the position of France, had Madison been a prisoner, and Washington in quiet possession of an armed enemy, the demands of Canada could not have been more humiliating. No Yankee must ever again be allowed to catch a fish or dry it on the coasts of Nova Scotia, or Labrador, or the Magdalen Islands, or of Newfoundland. Louisiana must be given up. A large piece of Maine must be ceded. Control of the St. Lawrence river must be secured to Canada by surrendering a strip of New York north of a line drawn from Plattsburg to Sackett's Harbor. Troops must be withdrawn from the posts in the Northwest, and the safety of Canada yet further secured by the acquisition of the eastern bank of the Niagara river and the formation of an Indian territory reaching from Sandusky to the Kaskaskia. Extravagant and unreasonable as were these demands, there was not a particle of doubt that England was determined to insist on them. Gallatin, far more disposed to be hopeful than despondent, wrote to Monroe in June that a great land and naval force was soon to depart for America, that war was to be prosecuted with vigor, that peace would not be made till another campaign was ended, and that then, even if the United States held her own, the best that could be expected was "the *status ante bellum.*" On neither the question of blockade nor the question of impressment was a settlement to be expected. So dark did the future seem that a few days after writing to Monroe he obtained an audience of the Czar, then in London, and asked Alexander to persuade the Regent to moderate his demand. The Czar could hold out no hope, and a few days later Gallatin and Bayard set off for France and joined the other members of the commission at Paris.

For the difficult work that lay before the commission the President had selected and the Senate had confirmed John Quincy Adams, James A. Bayard, Henry Clay, Albert Gallatin, and Jonathan Russell, who after serving as *chargé d'affaires* at Paris and at London had just been appointed Minister to Sweden. As Adams, Bayard, and Gallatin were already abroad, Clay and Russell, with a little retinue of official and unofficial secretaries, set sail on February twenty-seventh in the sloop of war John Adams for Europe. The voyage was long and tempestuous, but the Texel was reached in safety, and the party soon after were landed at Gothenburg.

Had England been so disposed, negotiations might have begun at once. But as the war was popular and Castlereagh determined to take no steps toward peace till the troops despatched in May had reached America and the campaign had begun in earnest, August came before her commissioners quit London for Ghent, which had been selected in place of Gothenburg. It was at Ghent, therefore, on the evening of the first Sunday in August—when the three fine armies soon to be so signally defeated at Baltimore, at Plattsburg, and at New Orleans were well on their way to expected victory—that the secretary of the British commission called at the house where the American commissioners were lodged. Bayard alone was at home; and with him the morrow was fixed

as the time and the house of the British Legation as the place
for the first joint meeting. To this plan the associates of
Bayard when they returned would not agree. "Meet the
English Ministers who have kept us here so long waiting their
coming!" exclaimed Adams; "meet them at their bidding, at
their own time, at their own place, and become the laughing-
stock of Europe, of London, of Ghent!" "Never," said Gallatin; "I would rather break up the mission and go home!"
The place was accordingly changed to the Hôtel des Pays
Bas, where at one o'clock on the eighth of August the first
conference took place.

The Englishmen were three in number, and were, in rank,
in notoriety, and ability, a good indication of the contempt
with which Castlereagh regarded America. At the head of
the legation was Lord Gambier, a man whose appointment
had called forth expressions of surprise even in London.
Twenty years before as a post captain he had commanded his
ship, the *Defence*, with ability, had been made a Junior Lord
of the Admiralty, had charge of the expedition that bombarded and burned Copenhagen, and for this infamous act
had been raised to the peerage and made a lord. Next to
Gambier was Henry Goulburn, a very young man who had
learned what little he knew of American affairs and of diplo-
macy as Under Secretary of State to Lord Bathurst. Associ-
ated with these two was William Adams, a Doctor of Civil
Law, and a man of whom the public knew nothing then and
nothing afterward. When the usual powers had been exhibited and the usual forms and ceremonies had been passed,
the British members led the way, and Goulburn plainly stated
the questions they were authorized to discuss. These were,
first, impressment, and in connection with it the right of his
Majesty to the allegiance of all native-born subjects of Great
Britain; second, the determination of an Indian boundary line
and the admission of the Indians to the general pacification;
third, a revision of the boundary line between the United
States and Canada; fourth, the fisheries. Goulburn was careful to state that the matter of the Indians and their territory
was a *sine qua non;* that the revision of the Canadian boundary was not an attempt to acquire territory; and that in with-

drawing the privilege so long enjoyed by Americans of fishing within British jurisdiction, and of landing and drying fish on British soil, no denial was made of their right to fish in the deep sea.*

Having heard these demands, our commissioners retired, and the following day made answer. Concerning the Indians and the fisheries, no instructions, they said, had been given them, for these matters had never been in dispute between the two countries and nobody had ever supposed they would be. Concerning impressment, allegiance, and the Canadian boundary they had very specific instructions, as also on many other matters not mentioned by the British commissioners. They then brought forward as proper for discussion, the definition of a blockade; certain claims of private citizens for indemnity for captures and seizures of property, and announced that their instructions covered other points to be considered later. Conversation of a general nature then followed, in the course of which it came out that the Indian territory was to be made a barrier between the United States and the possessions of Great Britain, and that each government was to be forbidden to buy any of the soil so set apart, though the Indians might sell to a third party. This demand for a cession of soil and sovereignty over it so enraged our commissioners that, despite assurances that it was a *sine qua non*, they refused to even consider it. Finding them firm, the British commissioners then asked for a suspension of the conferences till further instructions could come from London.

After waiting ten days they came, and came by the hand of Lord Castlereagh, who, with an immense suite in twenty carriages, reached Ghent on the evening of the eighteenth, on his way to the Congress of Sovereigns at Vienna. A notice was immediately sent off to the Americans, who on the afternoon of the next day listened to new demands more impudent and more humiliating than ever. His Majesty's Government, they were told, was surprised that they were not instructed regarding the Indians. As this had not been done,

---

* The Commissioners to Monroe, August 12, 1814. American State Papers, Foreign Relations, vol. iii, p. 705.

it was hoped—the settlement of the boundary being absolutely necessary to a peace—that at least a provisional article would be signed. They would therefore frankly state the purpose and basis of such an article. The purpose was to erect a permanent barrier between the Western settlements of the United States and the possessions of Great Britain, and prevent the two from ever touching. With regard to the southern boundary of this dividing strip they would propose the line of the Greenville treaty of 1795. The Americans were dumfounded, and when Gallatin asked what was to be done with the hundred thousand citizens already settled beyond the Greenville line in Ohio, in Indiana, in Michigan, and Illinois, Goulburn and Dr. Adams coolly replied that they must shift for themselves.

Continuing to read, Goulburn passed on to the next matter —the revision of the boundary line between the United States and Canada. This contained three distinct demands : First, a cession of so much of the district of Maine as lay between New Brunswick and the Quebec line, in order that direct communication might be secured from Halifax to the city of Quebec. Second, a revision of the line from Lake Superior to the Mississippi. When asked if they did not mean from the Lake of the Woods, they answered, No, from the Mississippi. Third, the dismantling of Fort Niagara and Sackett's Harbor, and the agreement that the United States would never again maintain an armed force either along the shores or on the waters of the Great Lakes or any of the rivers emptying into them. Great Britain, however, was to have as many ships and as many ports as she desired. Experience had proved that joint possession of the lakes and the common right to keep on them ships of war made peace insecure. As Great Britain was the weaker in Western North America, her possessions were the more exposed, and it was only reasonable that the United States should disarm.

The Americans, quite overcome, now asked if this was all, and if his Majesty's Government had nothing to say as to the ownership of Moose Island and such other bits of land in Passamaquoddy Bay as had recently been captured. They were answered that nothing need be said. The islands in question always had belonged to Great Britain, were at that moment as much a part of England as Northampton, would certainly be kept, and the ownership of them was not a subject for discussion. Once more the Americans ventured to ask a question, and begged to know if the demand that the United States should garrison no ports along the shores and keep no ships on the waters of the Great Lakes was a *sine qua non*. This was somewhat rudely answered by the remark that one *sine qua non* had been given them, and that when this had been disposed of it would be time enough to talk of another.

Not one of the five gentlemen who listened quietly to these demands even for a moment thought of yielding to them. The British commissioners, however, were asked to put them in writing, and John Quincy Adams undertook the task of framing the answer. On August twenty-fourth the draught was ready, and the five commissioners sat till almost midnight " sifting, erasing, patching, and amending." The result was a note which, in dignity, in temper, in force of reasoning, and in clearness of statement, is not unworthy to rank with the papers of the Revolution, and this is high merit indeed. In that note, after answering one by one the various demands, the commissioners closed with a few paragraphs which well described the conditions offered by Great Britain. They have, said the Americans, no relations to the causes which produced the war, are inconsistent with every principle of public law, and are not founded either on reciprocity or any of the usual bases of negotiation as that of *uti possidetis* or of *status ante bellum*. Acceptance of them would inflict most vital injury on the United States, would dismember her territory, would arrest the natural increase of her population, would leave her Northern and Western frontiers exposed to British invasion and Indian depredation, and would, above all, load the United States with infamy by forcing her to give up a part of her territory, abandon thousands of her citizens, and cease to exercise her natural rights on her own shores and her own waters. A treaty made on such terms would be but an armistice. To refer such demands to the American Government for instructions was useless. They could never become the subject of consideration till the people of the United States were ready to give up their liberty and their independence.

After such conditions had been offered as a *sine qua non* and flatly refused, it seemed idle to expect that negotiation could go on. The commissioners accordingly made ready to leave Ghent at once. Clay accepted an invitation to visit our Minister at Paris. Adams proposed to return to St. Petersburg. Russell fully expected to set off for Stockholm. The ship Neptune at Brest was put in readiness to carry Bayard and Gallatin back to the United States, and on the last day of August George Mifflin Dallas sailed from the Texel in the cartel John Adams with despatches announcing that the mission had failed.

The run across the Atlantic was a fair one, and landing at New York early in October, Dallas made all possible speed to Washington. If the news he bore was bad, that which greeted him was most encouraging. Much of Washington was indeed in ashes. But Baltimore was safe; Ross was dead; the British army was about to sail discomfited from the Chesapeake; and the whole country was rejoicing heartily in the splendid victories of Scott, Brown, Gaines, Macomb, and Macdonough. For the announcement of such intelligence as Dallas bore no time could have been more opportune, and on October tenth, just after the House had received a joint resolution from the Senate thanking Macdonough and his men for the great things done on Lake Champlain, and at the very moment when, in Committee of the Whole, the representatives were considering resolutions expressing a due sense of the gallantry of Scott and Brown, Gaines and Macomb, the Secretary of the President appeared at the door of the House and delivered a copy of the papers brought by Dallas. The committee instantly rose, the House ordered ten thousand copies to be printed, and the insolent demands of England were spread broadcast over the land.

Meantime a copy of the answer of the Americans to the British note of August nineteenth was sent with all haste to Lord Castlereagh at Paris, who in reply commanded the British commissioners to await instructions from London. Both he and the Ministry were far from pleased at what had been done. The policy of the British Government, they declared, was greatly misunderstood by the English

commissioners.   To suffer negotiations to be broken off on
the two notes presented would make the war most popular
in America, and, what was more serious still, most unpopular in England.*   The Americans must not be allowed to
say that points were brought forward as ultimata, which
were really brought forward to prolong discussion.†   That
some concession must be made was manifest, and Lord Bathurst, who, during the absence of Castlereagh, took charge
of affairs at Ghent, sent off new instructions which the commissioners made known to the Americans on the fourth of
September.   It was true, the note admitted, that the demands
regarding the Indians, the boundary of Canada, and the occupancy of the lakes had nothing to do with maritime rights.
It was true that the United States had begun the war in defence of maritime rights.   But it was also true that the alleged
defence of maritime rights was largely a pretence, and that a
spirit of conquest and aggrandizement—a spirit displayed in
the progressive occupation of the Indian lands, in the purchase of Louisiana, in the attempt to wrest the Floridas from
Spain, and, above all, in the avowed purpose to conquer and
annex Canada—had much more to do with the outbreak of hostilities than impressment and search.   Under these circumstances the plain duty of Great Britain was to protect her
dominions against all future attempts at conquest by securing military possession of the lakes and by founding a neutral
Indian power between her and the United States.   In each
note and at each conference the British commissioners had distinctly stated that the establishment of such a territory with
the Greenville treaty line as a boundary was a *sine qua non*,
and was not open to discussion.   Now, however, Great Britain
gave way, and her commissioners declared the proposition was
not a *sine qua non*, and was especially designed to invite discussion.   The answer of the Americans was that both these
demands—that for military possession of the lakes and that
for an Indian boundary—were utterly inadmissible, could not

---

* Liverpool to Castlereagh, September 2, 1814.   Henry Adams, History of
the United States, vol. ix, p. 26.

† Liverpool to Wellington, September 2, 1814.   Ibid., vol. ix, p. 26.

be discussed, could not be put in the form of a provisional article, could not even be referred to Washington.

Once more the answer was sent to London, and once more instructions to make yet further concessions came back to Ghent. The propositions for the exclusive control of the lakes and for an Indian territory were now dropped, and in their reply the British informed the American commissioners that the *sine qua non* was the admission of the Indians as parties to the treaty of peace. This, too, was firmly refused, and in its place an offer of a general amnesty for all Indians who had taken up arms in behalf of Great Britain was tendered by the Americans. In the eyes of the Englishmen such an offer was a flat rejection of their ultimatum, and a good and sufficient reason for breaking off all negotiations at once. It had, however, to be referred to London, and from London came orders to accept it and transmit to the Americans an article in which the proposition was formally reduced to writing. A ready acceptance followed and the first serious struggle was won by the United States. After two months spent in writing long notes and holding long conferences, the demands for an Indian boundary line, for a strip of neutral Indian territory, for the military and naval supremacy of England on the lakes, and for the inclusion of the Indians as parties to the treaty, were all quietly dropped.

The same note which informed the Englishmen that their offer of amnesty was accepted contained a hint that it was now high time to present the heads of a treaty. Before such an outline could be framed it was necessary to decide which of the two bases on which treaties of peace were usually made— the *status ante bellum* or the *status uti possidetis*, the state before the war, or the state of possession—should be adopted on this occasion. Great Britain chose that of *uti possidetis*, and presented it on the very day * whereon the Americans heard, with feelings of pride and joy, of the triumph at Baltimore, of the death of Ross, of the splendid victory on the waters and shores of Lake Champlain, and of the hasty retreat of Prevost's great army into Canada. A time more inauspicious for such

---

* October 21, 1814.

a demand could not have been found, and it was without hesitation rejected.* The Ministers for a moment were appalled. The rejection of the offer seemed to render further negotiation impossible. Smarting under the defeats at Baltimore, at Plattsburg, at Fort Erie, the British press and the British people were crying out for a vigorous prosecution of the war. To fight on would cost ten millions of pounds, and to raise ten millions of pounds would prevent the reduction of taxation, for which the English public were as clamorous as they were for glory. In its distress the Cabinet now turned to Wellington and begged him to go to Canada, take supreme command, and bring the war to an honorable ending. Wellington was then at Paris, and from Paris he wrote that while he would go if ordered, he did not expect success; that the great want in Canada was neither troops nor a general, but naval superiority on the lakes; and that, in his opinion, the success of the British armies did not justify the demand for territory and the *status uti possidetis.*

Thus advised, the Cabinet yielded. Negotiations were not interrupted, and on the last day of October the British commissioners asked for the heads of a treaty from the Americans, since that offered by them was not acceptable. Adams and Gallatin fell to work on a draught without delay. But they had not gone far when what little harmony had hitherto existed between the American commissioners was rudely broken, when they were parted on geographical lines, when a dispute began which, after threatening the utter ruin of the treaty, was compromised, to the lasting injury of more than one of the little band of men who represented our country at Ghent.

The cause of the dispute was the existence in the definitive treaty of 1783 of two articles, one of which recognized the liberty of the people of the United States to use the northeastern fisheries as freely as they had ever done when subjects of the Crown, while the other gave to the people of Great Britain the right to navigate the Mississippi river. The one was essentially a New England interest, and had been won in 1783 by the stubborn persistence of John Adams, who suc-

---

* American State Papers, Foreign Relations, vol. iii, p. 725.

ceeded in making it the ultimatum of peace. The other was essentially a Western interest, and had been granted at a time when the Mississippi was supposed to rise in Canada, when the United States claimed but one bank of the river, when she did not own its mouth, and when the country through which it ran was not much better than a wilderness. But times had greatly changed in the course of thirty years. The sight of a large fleet of American vessels fishing in British waters, and dealing out tea, coffee, clothing, and a hundred other articles on which no duty was ever paid, had long been most offensive to the people of the provinces, and had more than once been made the subject of earnest appeals to the Crown. By these men, therefore, the war had been hailed with delight as sure to put an end to American use of the fisheries, and it was in their interests that Great Britain now declared American fishing rights were ended. Her argument was: The liberty to catch fish off the coast of Newfoundland, and dry and cure them on the unsettled shores of the creeks, bays, and harbors of Nova Scotia, the Magdalen Islands, and Labrador, was a privilege secured to the United States by the treaty of 1783. A war between two parties ends all treaties between those parties. The declaration of war by the United States ended the treaty of 1783, and consequently the fishing rights created by it. The position taken by the United States was that the treaty of 1783 defined boundaries and recognized independence, and belonged, therefore, to that class of treaties which are permanent, and not affected by any suspension of friendly relations; that the treaty was a unity, and that the article respecting the fisheries was therefore no more affected by the war than those which recognized independence and defined the boundaries. If this were true it must also follow that, the treaty being a unity and permanent, the British right to navigate the Mississippi was unimpaired and not to be got rid of. But Clay was most anxious to get rid of it, for nowhere outside of Pennsylvania was Great Britain and her ways so hated as in the valley of the Mississippi. The Legislature of Pennsylvania by one act had decreed that no British law book written since the fourth of July, 1776, and no English decision—admiralty cases alone excepted—made since independence was declared, should ever be quoted or cited before any court of the Commonwealth. A large faction of her Legislature would gladly have seen the common law of England swept away, and did actually succeed in carrying a resolution which bade the sergeant-at-arms take the mace and cast it out the door of the House of Representatives, as an English symbol hateful to Republicans. But the feeling of which these acts were the expression was lukewarm in comparison with that which animated the constituents of Clay. That England would ever use her right to navigate the Mississippi seemed to the people in the East far from likely. A few enthusiasts, who had faith in the future of the steamboat, did, indeed, believe most firmly that she would. But to the people in the West the question of the navigation of the river was one of immense importance. The moment, therefore, that Gallatin brought forward the draught of an article recognizing and confirming the right of Englishmen to navigate the Mississippi and the right of Americans to use the fisheries, Clay and Adams took opposite sides. In the opposition Clay was joined by Russell, so that, when the vote was taken on inserting the article in the project, two said Yes and three said No. This should have settled the matter. But on Clay's solemnly declaring that he would never sign the project with the article in, the question was reconsidered, and five days were spent by Gallatin in the attempt to persuade Clay to change his mind. Change he would not, but in the way so characteristic of him he offered a compromise. His associates accepted it, and on the tenth of November the treaty project went to the commissioners for Great Britain. Not a word was said in the instrument about the fisheries or the Mississippi; but in the note which accompanied the paper was the statement that, from the nature of the treaty of 1783, no further stipulation regarding the fisheries was thought necessary.

A fortnight sped by before the commissioners were thrown into a state of new excitement by the return of the project with its margin full of alterations. Neither in it nor in the note that came with it was the slightest notice taken of the fisheries, or of the compromise which had caused the Americans so much heartburning and strife. But in place of the eighth article was a new one containing the hated provision that the subjects of his Britannic Majesty should enjoy the free navigation of the Mississippi river. Adams would gladly have accepted this; but Clay grew more angry and determined than ever, and boldly announced his willingness to let Massachusetts pay for the peace she so eagerly wanted. On Gallatin again fell the task of reconciling these two men—a task which he so well performed that on the first of December, at a conference, the Americans formally tendered the navigation of the Mississippi in exchange for the use of the fisheries. By this time the British Cabinet were bent on peace, and, yielding to the persistence of the Americans, bade their commissioners offer to leave the question of the fisheries and the river for negotiation in the future. Considering this an abandonment of a right, it was refused. In place of it an offer was made to be silent on the two matters which had so long delayed a peace, an offer which Great Britain accepted, and on Christmas eve, 1814, the commissioners met for the last time to sign the treaty. The document which, in triplicate, then lay upon the table provided for a cessation of hostilities by land and sea; for a speedy release of prisoners; for the surrender of all territory captured during the war by either party, save such islands in Passamaquoddy Bay as were then in dispute; for the pacification of the Indians; for a better definition of the boundaries; and contained a pledge that the two nations would do their best to help on the abolition of the slave-trade. The labor of determining and defining the boundary was assigned to three boards of commissioners. The first was to meet at St. Andrews, in New Brunswick, and decide whether the United States or Great Britain owned the islands of Deer, Moose, Dudley, and Grand Menan. The second was to assemble at the same place, and after deciding what was meant in the treaty of 1783 by the terms "northwest angle of Nova Scotia," "northwesternmost head of the Connecticut river," "the highlands," were to survey, monument, and map the boundary line from the source of the St. Croix river to the point where the forty-fifth degree of latitude meets the St. Lawrence. Taking up the boundary at this point, the third commission was to run the line on to the "most northern point of the Lake of the Woods," and determine its latitude and longitude.

Concerning the great issues which had produced the war the treaty was silent. Yet silence was not dishonorable. Our countrymen did indeed fail to extort from Great Britain damages for the spoliation inflicted on their commerce. They did indeed fail to make good their claim to the islands in the Bay of Fundy, and to a natural right to fish in British waters. But it must also be remembered that Great Britain failed to extort from them any admission of her right to search their ships, to impress their seamen, or to lay paper blockades on the coasts of Europe.

That same night Mr. Hughes went off with one copy of the treaty for Bordeaux, where a ship stood ready to carry him to America. On Monday, the twenty-sixth of the month, Mr. Carroll, with a second copy, started for London, and on the second of January, 1815, sailed in the sloop of war Favorite for New York. Handbills announcing his arrival and the joyful news he brought were instantly struck off at the printing-office of the Gazette and scattered broadcast. But long before this the news had spread, and in half an hour after he reached the City Hotel the bells were ringing in every spire, candles were appearing in the windows of every house, while the streets resounded with cheers and the joyful cry of " A peace ! A peace ! "

Early on Sunday morning, while expresses were riding in every direction, Mr. Carroll took horse for Washington. At noon he passed through Philadelphia, and by nightfall was well on toward Baltimore. Monday was a day long remembered. In New York and in Philadelphia the Government stocks rose ten per cent., while the premium on specie and exchange on Boston fell off fifteen per cent. The Common Council of New York called on the citizens to illuminate. At Philadelphia the Aurora would not believe the news, and on Monday, while every other paper in the city announced it with delight, called on its readers to be doubtful. The tidings had come in a British ship and near the close of a session of Congress. So did the British sloop Bramble bring pacific despatches two years before, and had any one forgotten the effect of the hoax ? It would be full time to rejoice over peace when the constituted authorities announced that a just and honorable peace had been concluded. Till then rumors brought by British ships were not to be regarded. The Mayor was not so sceptical, and issued a proclamation urging the people to illuminate on a certain night, but requiring that all lights should be out by ten o'clock, and warning thoughtless people not to molest any Friend whose religious scruples would not permit him to light and decorate his house. By seven on Sunday morning the news reached the people of New Haven, and at four was cried in the streets of Hartford. At one that same day a rider startled the people of Albany, and twenty hours later another reached Vergennes. On Monday a rider entered Boston. The moment he announced the return of peace a rush was made for the churches and every bell set ringing. The schools were dismissed, the flags were run up on the long-deserted ships, and the streets filled with men shouting, cheering, and shaking hands. At the Exchange Coffee-House a purse of two hundred and twenty-five dollars was made up to pay the expenses of the express who brought the news from New York. The Legislature adjourned, all business stopped, the troops turned out to fire a salute, and the cartmen, forming a procession of sleighs, drove about the city with their hats labelled "Peace." On Monday night an express rode into Washington just as the commissioners from Massachusetts and Connecticut reached the capitol. They were charged with the duty of making an earnest appeal to Congress to grant their States leave to form State armies and give them a reasonable part of the Federal taxes collected within their boundaries; but though few were inclined to credit the rumor of peace, the city was so greatly excited that the commissioners, calling the representatives from Massachusetts into consultation, decided to do nothing till the rumor was fully confirmed or shown to be false. Twenty-four hours later it was confirmed by the arrival of Mr. Carroll, and, the war having ended, their mission was useless. Without showing their credentials to a living soul or making any formal announcement of their presence in Washington, they now went back to New England, followed by shouts of derision from the whole Republican press. To approve the treaty was a matter of a few days, and on February eighteenth it was proclaimed the supreme law of the land.

While the bells were ringing and the cannon booming, none, save a few old Federalists, thought it necessary to stop and inquire what the terms of the treaty might be. The feelings of the people, as expressed in their actions, were, We have peace, and peace is all we want. But now that the treaty was made public and the first outburst of joy had subsided, the terms were read by the Federalists with shouts of exultation, by the Republicans with humiliation and with shame. "Bad as it is," said the Federalist journals, "we hail it with delight. To our country pining for peace it is a sweet restorative. To our people harassed by war and impoverished by taxes it is a welcome relief. To our bankrupt treasury whose every resource was gone it is a happy escape. In truth, it is not too much to say that the coming of peace has saved the country and the Government from disunion. But when the sweet delirium we all now enjoy has passed away the day of reckoning will come, and we shall then hear asked on every hand, What have we gained by war? Can Mr. Madison tell us? Into that war he dragged us in defence of Free Trade and Sailors' Rights. Have they been secured? No! Are they reserved for future negotiation? No! Are they silently surrendered and with them, according to the declaration of war, the honor and independence of the nation? They are indeed. But we also fought against certain doctrines of Great Britain in the matter of paper blockades, which were too outrageous to be borne any longer. These surely have been settled in our favor? No, not a word is said about them. But those impressed sailors, those sixty-two hundred and fifty-seven American citizens shut up in 'the floating hells of England,' have they been released and compensated? No, they are not even alluded to. Well, at all events, we have lost nothing. Not so; we have lost much. We have lost Moose Island; we have lost our right to the fisheries claimed by us in the treaty of 1783 and recognized by it; we have lost the West Indian trade, and, most shameful of all, we have submitted the boundaries of the United States to the revision of monarchical umpires, sceptred brothers of the British King. The limits of our republic now depend on the honesty of kings!"

The Republicans, on the other hand, had nothing to say in defence. They contented themselves, therefore, with dwelling on the blessings of peace, on the happy result of the war, on the great lessons it had taught the people and the world, and on the bright era of prosperity that seemed to be at hand.

In the midst of the general rejoicing not a little anxiety was felt for the safety of the three national ships yet at sea. On the night the President ran the blockade she left the Peacock and the Hornet behind at New York. But they did not tarry long, and on the twenty-second of January, while the President was on her way to Bermuda, a prize, they, too, crossed the bar in a gale of wind and made for the rendezvous at Tristan d'Acunha. The Hornet was first to arrive, but had not time to anchor when Captain Biddle sighted the English sloop of war Penguin. Chase was made at once, and the two were soon alongside, for Captain Dickinson, of the Penguin, was nothing loath to fight. In size, in armament, and in men the sloops were well matched. But again the gunnery of the Americans surpassed that of the enemy, and in twenty minutes the Penguin, in the language of her officer, lay in the water a perfect wreck. Her bowsprit was gone. Her foremast was shot away. Her captain was dead, and eight-and-thirty of her crew killed or wounded.

After the capture and destruction of the Penguin the Hornet waited for the Peacock, and then continued the cruise till late in April, when a sail was seen and followed. In the thick and smoky haze that covered the sea she seemed to be an Indiaman, but when the chase had gone on for a day and a half the Peacock signalled that the enemy was a ship of the line. The two sloops thereupon made off, with the Cornwallis, a seventy-four-gun frigate, in hot pursuit of the Hornet. The only hope of Biddle was to escape in the darkness; but finding the enemy drew nearer each hour, he threw over twelve tons of kentledge, part of his shot, some heavy spars, cut away the sheet anchor and cable, and started the wedges of his masts. Even this was not enough. The frigate still came nearer and nearer, and by noon of the next day the remaining anchor and cable, the launch, more shot, all of the guns save one, all the spars, every heavy article on deck or below, had gone by the board. Then the sloop began to draw away, and, the wind freshening, Captain Biddle made for San Salvador, where, on June ninth, 1815, he heard of peace.

The Peacock alone reached the Indian Ocean and made a short and successful cruise; but on June thirtieth, while in the Strait of Sunda, she fell in with a cruiser whose captain hailed and announced peace. Warrington would not believe it, and bade the Englishman, if it were true, pull down his flag. He refused, and a moment later received a broadside from the Peacock which well-nigh wrecked his vessel.

One other frigate of our navy was at sea on the day peace was signed at Ghent. Late in December, 1814, the Constitution had slipped out of Boston Harbor, and crossing the Atlantic, had begun a cruise between Gibraltar and Madeira. Captain Charles Stewart was in command, and toward noon of the twentieth of February descried two sails some sixty miles from Madeira. They proved to be the Cyane and Levant. Though sloops of war of the largest size, they were, even when taken together, much inferior to the Constitution. That they should have made all sail to escape was to be expected, but to the surprise of Stewart they drew together and awaited the battle. The resistance was most spirited and stubborn, and three quarters of an hour passed before the Cyane struck. The Levant was then some miles to leeward, and might well have run off. But she bore down upon the Constitution and fired a broadside at short range before attempting to escape. It was then too late, and after a chase of two hours she too struck her colors.

Next morning the three ships set sail together, and on the evening of the eighth of March anchored in the harbor of Porto Praya, on the island of St. Jago. The island belonged to the Cape de Verde group, and was a dependency of the Portuguese Crown. Porto Praya, therefore, was neutral water. But when, on the morning of March twelfth, Captain Stewart descried three British frigates standing in, he instantly spread his sails, cut his cables, and signalled to his prizes to follow, for he had no faith in British respect for neutral waters. As he expected, the English squadron tacked and gave chase. A run of half an hour showed that the Cyane could not keep up,

for she was fast falling behind and to leeward. She was signalled, therefore, to tack ship. Stewart had hoped that one of
the frigates would follow, but much to his amazement the
squadron kept on in hot pursuit of the Constitution and the
Levant for ten hours. Then the Levant was in much the same
condition as the Cyane had been. She was far in the rear,
and was in turn ordered to tack and make off. The order was
promptly obeyed, and to the utter astonishment of Stewart the
entire English squadron also tacked and stood after the Levant.
Some firing now took place, but with all sails spread she
reached Porto Praya, and took refuge under the guns of a
Portuguese fort. Then was the wisdom of Stewart's action
made manifest, for with that disregard for neutral waters
which distinguished British captains, the Acarta and the Newcastle followed, fired on the Levant, and made her a prize.

Sailing westward, Stewart reached the coast of Brazil,
heard the news of peace at Porto Rico, and entered New
York Harbor on the tenth of May, to find the people busy
obliterating every trace of war.

CHAPTER XXX.

DISORDERS OF THE CURRENCY.

FROM the long story of battles and sieges and civil strife it is delightful to be able to turn once more to the narration of the triumphs of peace. At last, after a period of five-and-twenty years, the people of the United States were free to attend to their own concerns in their own way, unmolested by foreign nations. For a few months after the adoption of the Federal Constitution such a time existed; but it was of short duration, and from the unhappy day when Genet landed on our shores the history of our country is in large part the history of a protracted and desperate struggle for commercial independence and the freedom of the seas. From 1793 to 1815 the questions which occupied the public mind were our neutral rights, orders in council, French decrees, impressment, embargoes, treaties, non-intercourse acts, admiralty decisions, blockades, the conduct of England, the conduct of France, the insolence of the French Directory, the triumphs, the ambition, and the treachery of Napoleon. Henceforth, for many years to come, the questions of the day were to be the state of the currency, the national bank, manufactures, the tariff, internal improvements, interstate commerce, the public lands, the astonishing growth of the West, the rights of the States, extension of slavery, and the true place of the Supreme Court in our system of government.

On the day, therefore, when Madison issued his proclamation announcing peace, a new era in our national history was opened. For a while it was pre-eminently a period of reorganization, reconstruction, consolidation. Old conditions had passed away. New conditions were to be met and adjusted, and in the effort to effect this adjustment our country passed through a period during which government of the people by the people was sorely tried, but not found wanting.

Of the many public matters which, at the opening of this new era, sadly needed immediate attention, the disordered condition of the currency was most pressing. The state into which it had fallen was indeed serious and alarming, and was due in part to the evils of war and in part to the mania for State banks which then afflicted the entire country. These institutions were of recent appearance and may be said to have come in with the adoption of the Federal Constitution. On the day the old Confederation expired, three banks, it is true, were doing business in the United States.* But it was in the flush times of 1791 that the system took root and began to flourish. The adoption and establishment of a strong and vigorous government on the ruins of the Confederation, the stripping from the States of the power to coin money and issue paper, and, above all, the funding of the revolutionary debt, had restored credit. The restoration of credit called out from attic floors and old stockings hundreds of thousands of dollars which had long lain hidden and unused ; and these, in addition to the millions of new capital created by the Government funding at their face value the indents, the final settlements, the loan-office certificates, the commissary certificates, the quartermasters' certificates, the thousand and one forms of the revolutionary indebtedness which till then had not been worth three shillings to the pound, provided an enormous fund, whose owners were eagerly seeking investment. This eagerness to invest was well displayed when, on the fourth of July, 1791, the books of the National Bank were opened at the old State-House in Philadelphia, and in half an hour every penny of the eight million dollars of stock offered the public was taken.† The people were astonished, and an era of wild speculation began. Stock-issuing corporations sprang up on every hand. The cities abounded with the projectors of canal companies, turnpike companies, manufacturing companies, and State banks.

---

* History of the People of the United States, vol. ii, p. 29,
† Ibid., vol. ii, p. 37.

In the course of a twelvemonth eight were chartered, and the State bank as a financial institution may be said to have been introduced.

Thus started, the banking system spread rapidly over the seaboard portion of the commercial States, and along the great routes of emigration westward, till by the end of the century twenty-six banks existed, and of these, fourteen were in New England and two south of the Potomac. Five years later thirty-eight others had been established, almost three fourths of which were again to be found in New England. But the movement of population westward was filling up the region beyond the Alleghanies, and when, in 1811, the charter of the United States Bank expired, State banks were to be found along the Mohawk, in central Pennsylvania, in western Maryland, at Steubenville, at Marietta, at Cincinnati, at Chillicothe, in Kentucky, in Tennessee, and in the Territory of Orleans. Eighty-eight were then doing business.

In the main they differed but little one from another. Their capital was any sum from one hundred thousand to two millions of dollars. Each could receive deposits, discount notes, contract debts, and issue bills to an amount equal to three times its capital, which were always taken in payment of State taxes and dues. Some had power to establish branches, others had not. Some paid the State a bonus for the charter. Some had the State for a stockholder. Others were nothing more than the State treasury put in commission and incorporated, and provided with a capital made up of all the stocks owned by the State, all the bonds and notes due the State, and all the unexpended money derived from taxation. Nominally the notes of such institutions were redeemable on demand in gold or silver. But no penalty was attached to a refusal to redeem, nor did any real check exist to prevent an issue of bills far beyond the legal limit. None could circulate notes of denomination less than a dollar. Generally the limit was two or five dollars. The small change of the country was supposed to be specie, and in the great seaboard cities it was; but in many inland towns and cities specie was never seen, and the small change was made up of due bills, tickets, promissory notes, issued by individuals, by unincorporated associations, by bodies corporate, and by private bankers. In the States beyond the Alleghanies, where banks were few and specie scarce, the small change was "cut money," which was but another name for Spanish dollars cut with a shears into quarters, eighths, and sixteenths.

The circulating medium of the United States in 1811 may then be said to have consisted of the small notes and bills of individuals and corporations; of State bank paper, which did not circulate far from the bank that issued it; of here and there the remains of the old State paper money of 1785; of such gold and silver coin of foreign countries as Congress had made legal tender; of cut money, and of such coins of United States mintage as had not been shipped abroad as bullion. The five million dollars of notes of the Bank of the United States were called in and redeemed after 1811 and need not be considered.

Of these many kinds of currency the coins of the United States were the rarest. Many efforts had been made under the Confederation to create a national coinage; but they had all ended in failure, and save a few copper cents manufactured by contractors and now to be found in the cabinets of collectors under the name of "Fugios," not a piece was struck. On the establishment of government under the Constitution, however, Congress once more returned to the subject of a national coinage, and in 1791, after listening to the famous report of Hamilton, ordered that a mint be established and that Washington secure such artists and buy such machines as might be necessary. One year later a second law specified the officers of the mint, established the mint, fixed the standard of fineness, and named the coins to be struck. Gold, silver, and copper, the law provided, were to be coined without charge for all comers in the order of their arrival at the mint: the gold into eagles, half-eagles, and quarter-eagles; the silver into dollars, half-dollars, quarter-dollars, dimes, and half-dimes; the copper into cents and half-cents. Having thus provided for a bimetallic currency, the law further ordered that the ratio between the two precious metals should be fifteen to one, or that fifteen pounds' weight of pure silver should have the same legal value as one pound of pure gold. The unit was the dollar, and into it were to go three hundred and seventy-one and a quarter grains of pure, or four hundred and sixteen grains of standard silver.

Although the law was passed in April, such haste was made to carry it out that when October came a site had been purchased in Philadelphia, a mint (the first public building ever erected by the new Federal Government) had been built, and the coinage of silver half-dimes had begun. Some cents and half-cents were made in 1793, but the serious work of coining did not begin till October, 1794. The Secretary of the Treasury having no authority to purchase bullion, the mint was forced to depend on the Treasury, the banks, and the merchants for a supply of gold and silver in the form of foreign coin; sources which proved trivial and uncertain. As neither metal was mined in the country, no private interest existed eager to avail itself of the free coinage provided by law. As joes and guineas, doubloons and dollars, indeed every sort of foreign coin, circulated freely from hand to hand, and were still legal tender for Government dues, merchants were under no inducement to turn them in for recoinage. The Secretary of the Treasury was, it is true, in duty bound to send each foreign coin received in payment of taxes or duties to the mint, there to be made into national currency. But each succeeding Secretary so flatly refused to obey the law that when the mint was ten years old the director reported that not one dollar had been coined on Government account. The State banks were the great sources of supply. Indeed, it was from one of them —the Bank of Maryland—that the first deposit of silver was received in July, 1794. It consisted of French guineas and crowns worth eighty thousand seven hundred and fifteen dollars, and from these pieces dollars and half-dollars were struck and returned to the Treasury in October. In making them the director deliberately and wilfully disobeyed the law. He was convinced that the standard of fineness prescribed by law would debase the coin and cause the pieces to turn black when used, and had recommended that for nine parts pure silver there should be one part alloy. Sure that his suggestions would be approved, he had ordered the dollars to be made in accordance with the proposed standard, and was not a little chagrined when, a year later—Congress having given no heed to his request—he was forced to coin according to the old law. Meantime, every depositor whose silver had been used suffered a loss ; for, although he got back all his deposit, he did not receive as many dollars as he was legally entitled to.

The first silver piece having been struck, the President, as the law required, put forth a proclamation declaring that on the fifteenth day of October, 1797, all foreign silver coins, the Spanish milled dollar excepted, should cease to be legal tender for debts. Some half-eagles made from gold deposited by a Boston merchant having been sent to the Treasury in July, 1795, a like proclamation was issued concerning gold coins, and the people informed that in July, 1798, all gold pieces of foreign nations would cease to circulate. The day then seemed near when the United States would have a national specie currency of their own. But when the three years expired eagles and half-eagles, dollars, dimes, and half-dimes were as scarce as if no mint existed. The reason is plain. The administration was trying to do what no power has ever yet succeeded in doing—it was trying to put in circulation side by side a sound and an unsound currency. The foreign coin, old, worn, clipped, and light of weight, drove out the new American dollars and quarters which, sound and of full weight, were of far more value as a commodity in foreign markets than as a circulating medium at home. They were therefore exported in such numbers that enough could not be had to pay the dues of merchants at the custom-houses, and in 1798 the law was suspended and foreign coins continued to be a legal tender at specified rates for three years more. But the exportation of the coin still went on, and when 1802 came the people were as far as ever from enjoying a metallic currency of their own. Popular sentiment meantime had turned strongly against the mint. It was denounced as another of the many costly and useless pieces of political machinery saddled on the country by the Federalist party. This mint, it was said in 1800, has been seven years in operation, yet the entire output of coins—gold, silver, and copper—is short of two million six hundred thousand dollars, while the cost of making them exceeds two hundred thousand dollars. To coin ten dollars entails an outlay of one dollar, and when the ten are coined half of them are shipped to London. For the half locked up by the banks we pay accordingly twenty per cent. of their value for the privilege of trying to have a national coinage. The game is not worth the candle. The burden is too heavy to be borne. In the House of Representatives this feeling was so general that a committee reported in favor of abolishing the mint, and in 1802 a bill passed closing it. To this the Senate would not agree, and for twenty-six years it was continued from time to time by a series of acts running from one to five years.

An examination of the work done by the mint during the first ten years of its existence will give no mean idea of the condition of the specie currency. In the course of this decade there were coined a little over twelve thousand dollars in half-dimes, a little over seventeen thousand in dimes, fifteen hundred in quarters, two hundred and nine thousand in half-dollars, and nearly a million and a half of dollars. But it must not be supposed that even a large part of these dollar pieces remained in the country. Indeed, so many were exported that the director of the mint, without any legal authority, stopped the coinage of the dollar, and not one was struck from 1805 till 1836. No quarters were made between 1797 and 1803, nor between 1807 and 1815. No half-dimes were struck after 1805. When the director ceased to coin the dollar he seems to have turned in serious earnest to the manufacture of half-dollars, and raised the output from sixteen thousand in 1803 to eight hundred thousand in 1812, when they were by far the commonest of our silver as the half-eagles were the commonest of our gold coins. Half-eagles had been struck regularly year by year. But no eagles were made after 1804 and no quarter-eagles after 1807, for they could not be kept in the country.

That the business of the Union was transacted with so small a specie currency is due, and largely due, to the enormous credit currency supplied by the State banks, to the issue of small change notes by private bankers and unchartered banking associations, and to the remonetization in 1816 of foreign coins then passing through the banks on their way from South America to Europe.

The change bills and notes put out by individuals and corporations had long been a steadily growing evil, and as early as 1809 two States attempted to suppress it. North Carolina, in that year, after declaring that promissory notes and due bills for small sums had become so plentiful as to be "injurious to travellers," fixed a limited time during which none should be drawn for less than ten shillings, and named a day after which they should not pass current as money at all.

In Pennsylvania a like condition existed. The Bank of the United States issued no bills under ten dollars in value; the State banks could issue none under five; and, as the specie (composed largely of foreign coin) was drawn to the seaports to meet the needs of importers, the inhabitants of the inland towns and villages were often in great straits for change. To supply this, numbers of individuals and associations of individuals had gone into the banking business without charters, and, procuring plates and paper, had issued notes of all denominations far beyond their ability to redeem. But the Legislature, in 1810, forbade unincorporated banking associations to issue notes or bills, or to make loans, or to receive deposits, and so ruined the business that six associations sought for charters during the same session. Five were refused. But the petitioners were not discouraged, and at the next session nine, and in 1812 fourteen applications were made to the Legislature.

One of the fourteen deserves especial mention, for those who made it were none other than the Pennsylvania stockholders of the Bank of the United States, whose charter had now expired. Taking the name American Bank, these gentlemen asked for a twenty years' charter, with a capital of five million dollars, and offered in return to give the State three hundred and seventy-five thousand dollars, to be used for building roads and bridges. As the session wore on, and the Legislature seemed loath to act, the cash bonus was raised to five hundred thousand dollars, and an offer was made to loan the State another five hundred thousand dollars for internal improvements. This was indeed tempting. But the feeling was general that if the petitioners could make such a bid the profits of the business must be immense, and ought to be enjoyed, not by one great bank, but by many small ones, and the prayer was not granted.

Nevertheless it bore fruit, and aroused such eagerness for local banks as alarmed the Governor. In his message at the opening of the session of 1812–'13 he cautioned the Legislature against what he saw was coming; told it that the banking capital in the State was all sufficient; cited in evidence the fact that within six months the Philadelphia banks had subscribed two million four hundred thousand dollars to the United States war loan, and had taken in addition one million dollars in treasury notes bearing less than bank interest; and reminded the members that in the Harrisburg institution one hundred thousand dollars had long been lying idle for want of a good investment. The people, however, were determined to have their way, and before the Legislature arose applications were received for thirty-one charters, and a bill establishing a general banking system for the whole State, and calling for five-and twenty new banks, was laid before the Governor. Each of the twenty-three congressional districts was to be a banking district, and contain at least one of the new institutions. They were to be the people's banks; and that the farmers and mechanics might have a chance to subscribe and enjoy some of the riches about to be scattered broadcast, great care was taken to keep the stock out of the hands of capitalists. Nobody, therefore, could subscribe for more than one share on the day the subscription books were opened, nor for more than two shares on the second day, nor for more than three shares on the third day; and so on to the sixth day, when for the first time the subscriber could buy all the stock he wanted. One per cent. on the amount of stock sold was to be paid each year to the State, a sum which, as the capital of the twenty-five banks was to be nine million five hundred and twenty-five thousand dollars, was far from trifling.

Unhappily for the scheme, the Governor vetoed the bill, and gave nine good reasons. The people now grew more determined than ever; and when the Legislature met again, it laid on the table of the Governor a bill establishing forty-one new banks in twenty-seven districts. Once more he vetoed the bill, but this time it was passed over his veto, and thirty-seven of them went into business in 1814.

In New York the struggle was still more exciting. There, when it was known that the Bank of the United States was not to be rechartered, some capitalists bought out the foreign and such resident holders of the stock as would sell, and in 1812 applied to the Legislature for a charter. The name of the new institution was to be the Bank of America, the capital was to be six million dollars, and no foreign share-holder was to vote. As it had now become the custom to buy charters, a most liberal and tempting offer was made. For a thirty years' grant the bank would pay four hundred thousand dollars, in four annual and equal payments. If during ten years no rivals were chartered to do business in New York city, another one hundred thousand would be paid the State at the end of that period; and yet another one hundred thousand dollars if, at the end of twenty more years, no other bank had been established in the city. One million was offered to the State at five per cent., to be used in building the Erie Canal, and another million at six per cent., to be loaned by the State to the farmers on landed security. In the Assembly the measure found many warm and earnest friends, was passed after a vigorous struggle, and was about to be voted on by the Senate when the Governor, to the amazement of the whole community, prorogued the Legislature for fifty-five days. Many reasons for the act were given, but the chief one was that from the journals of both Houses it appeared that attempts had been made to bribe four assemblymen and one senator to vote for the bill. "Far be it from me," said the Governor, "to assert that the charges are true. Yet before the bill passes it would be well to examine and refute them." Thinking that the honor and morals of the State required it, and wishing to give time for reflection, he felt it to be his duty to send the members home for a few weeks.

No good came of the dismissal, for the moment the senators were back in their seats the bank bill was passed and sent to the Council of Revision. The Council of Revision was a body made up of the Governor, the Chancellor, and the Judges of the Supreme Court of the State, and possessed that veto power which in many other States was given to the Governor. To it went every bill passed by the Legislature. If, in the opinion of a majority of the council, the bill was an improper one, it was vetoed, and returned to the House in which it originated. If it was approved, or for any reason failed to be considered within ten days, it became law.

When the six-million bank bill reached the council the Chancellor was absent, and the six remaining members were equally divided. What should be its fate rested, therefore, with the Chancellor, who, to the joy of the bank men, hastened back to Albany and cast his vote in their favor.

In Massachusetts the bank question was brought up by the approach of the October day, 1812, when the charters of sixteen of the existing banks would expire. For a time the idea of replacing them by one great institution, with capital enough and branches enough to transact the banking business of the whole State, was a favorite one. But the closing of the Bank of the United States brought on the mania for local banks, and in 1812 twenty were founded and located in eighteen towns.

New Jersey established six, and, by way of bonus, the State reserved the right to subscribe to half the capital stock, and to appoint the president and six of the directors of each. But the law was hardly a year old when the Federalists secured control of the Legislature; and, determined that the benefits of the banks should not be enjoyed by the Democrats alone, they passed a law for the sale of the stock owned by the State. In twenty-four hours not a share of five of them was in the hands of the Governor. Delaware chartered three banks. Ohio did the same. In Virginia an attempt to add one million five hundred thousand dollars to the capital of one of the two banks was defeated.

Thus in the course of two years did the craze spread over the seaboard States, and raise the number of banks from eighty-eight to two hundred and eight. As each possessed the right of issuing bills, and issued them to at least three times the amount of its capital, the country entered once more upon an era of paper money. Had they been able to obtain enough specie to redeem even a small proportion of their paper, all would have gone well. But, unfortunately for them, much of the specie on which their circulation depended was at that moment in New England. For this the long embargo, the days of non-importation, and the war were chiefly responsible. Under the restrictive system, which began in 1807 and had not yet ended, manufactures were growing. Greatly against their will, the people of New England had turned their attention to spinning and weaving, and, favored by the exclusion of English competitors, were supplying the domestic market with many articles. As early as 1811 the effect of this was apparent in the slow and steady flow of specie from the South and West to New England; a movement which, with the opening of the war and the rigorous blockade of the coast south of Newport, became more marked and rapid. The only outlet for the cotton, rice, tar, pitch, and hemp of the South, and the tobacco and flour of Virginia, was through Massachusetts, whose ports were still open to neutrals, and to the enemy disguised as neutrals. Into them came the hardware and the crockery of England, the wines and spices of the West Indies, which, with the boots and shoes, the negro cloth, the woollens, and the cotton cards made in New England, were carried by wagon to Richmond and Augusta, to be distributed over the South and West. So enormous did this trade become, that, during 1813, employment was given to more than four thousand four-horse wagons. As the needs of the South forced it to buy of the East more largely than the opportunities of the East enabled it to buy of the South, the bales of cotton the teams brought North did not begin to settle the balance, which had, in consequence, to be paid in specie. Bad as this was, it became much worse when Congress, in December, 1813, laid an embargo and stopped the trade of New England with the enemy and with neutrals. The South had then no market for its produce, and its banks were quickly stripped of every available dollar of specie.

In effecting this settlement the banks of Boston called on those of New York, which called on those of Philadelphia and Baltimore, which in their turn called on the banks yet farther South. So great was the drain that, in spite of sums used to pay for foreign merchandise, in spite of sums used to pay for British bills of exchange, in spite of sums smuggled out of the country to be sold at a high premium to the enemy, the specie in the Boston banks swelled from less than eight hundred thousand dollars in 1812 to more than seven million dollars in 1814.

That this state of affairs had brought the banks of the Middle and Southern States to a desperate condition was made apparent by several incidents: by the attempt in Congress to charter another national bank with thirty millions of dollars as capital; by the refusal of the banks of Philadelphia to any longer receive, as deposits, the notes of Southern and Western banks; and by the seizure in New York of specie on its way to Boston. Early in the year a petition from well-known men in New York city had been laid before the House. The petitioners prayed for the incorporation of a national bank with thirty millions of dollars of capital, and offered in return to loan the Government half that sum; they reminded Congress that the whole circulating medium of the United States had been seized on by the State banks, which, in lieu thereof, circulated their own paper to the amount of fifty millions of dollars, to the exclusive benefit of their stockholders, and they hinted that much political good would come from having moneyed men of all parties concerned in a bank whose existence depended on the stability of Government.

The petition went to the Committee of Ways and Means, who soon reported that power to charter a bank within the limits of the States, without consent of the States, was not granted by the Constitution. Regarding this as of small moment, so far as the practical workings of a bank were concerned, Calhoun moved that the Committee of Ways and Means be instructed to inquire into the expediency of establishing a national bank in the District of Columbia. To this the House gladly agreed, and in due time a bill to incorporate a national bank in the District of Columbia was read twice and committed. There it remained, and no more was heard of the matter till, in the closing days of the session, Felix Grundy, of Tennessee, asked for a special committee to inquire into the expediency of founding a bank. This was granted. But, just before the House rose, the committee was discharged, and consideration of the old bill, which for weeks past had been lying on the Speaker's table, was postponed indefinitely.

The seizure of specie in New York was a most high-handed act. In the regular course of business several of the Boston banks had received from their depositors bills on New York city banks amounting, in round numbers, to one hundred and thirty-nine thousand dollars. As was usual in such cases, a messenger was sent with the bills to New York to receive payment and send the specie to Boston by land. On presenting them he found not the slightest difficulty in having them cashed, and loading his silver on three wagons he set off for home. At Chester, however, some fourteen miles from New York, he was stopped by order of the Collector of Customs, and the silver seized and brought back to the city; for the embargo was in force, and by it collectors of the ports were empowered to stop and seize any wagon loaded with specie when on its way toward the territory of any foreign power, or the vicinity thereof, or when going toward a place where specie was usually exported.

That this provision was never intended to apply to such shipments of specie is certain, for, had it been so intended, the Government would not have been able to move its own money from bank to bank, or city to city, in order to pay its debts and the interests on its stocks and loans. The purpose of the seizure was to keep the specie in New York, for the collector was a director in one of the banks from which the money had been taken, and was also a director in another bank in which the silver, after seizure, was deposited.

Nothing but a crisis, or the first symptom of public discredit, was now needed to send every bank from New York to Savannah into bankruptcy. Both these things came to pass toward the close of August, 1814, when the British landing on the shores of Chesapeake Bay marched to Washington, burned the public buildings, cut off communication with the South, and attacked the city of Baltimore. That depositors, in such a time of excitement, should hasten to withdraw their money, and that people having bank-notes should be eager to exchange them for specie, was no more than was to be expected. The banks along the seaboard south of Baltimore, gathering what little coin they still had, packed it in boxes, carried it far into the interior, buried it, ceased to redeem their notes, and forced those in Baltimore to do the same. Those in Philadelphia held out a few days longer. But the run began, and on the twenty-eighth of August the presidents of six in the city ordered specie payment to be suspended, and gave the public the reasons.

"From the moment," said they in their circular, "the rigorous blockade of the ports stopped the exportation of our products, foreign goods had to be paid for with coin. As the importation of foreign goods and wares into New England has been very great, there is a heavy drain on the banks—a drain swelled yet more by a trade in British Government bills of exchange which has taken great sums out of the country. To meet this demand, the course of trade has enabled us heretofore to draw from the South. But the unhappy state of affairs there cut off that source of supply, and the question arose, Shall we continue to gather all the specie of the country into our vaults merely in order that it may be sent out of the country, or suspend specie and save the coin? Believing that the public interest is best served by taking the latter course, we have unanimously agreed to suspend, and appeal to our fellow-citizens to support us."

The appeal was not in vain. The friends of both political parties pleaded vigorously in its behalf; the merchants, who were deeply indebted to the banks, assembled at the Coffee-House, and agreed to take the bills of the institutions suspending payment; the committee of defence publicly indorsed the action as a wise measure of precaution, and the people quietly submitted.

At New York, while the British were burning Washington, committees from the eight banks met and passed a set of resolutions declaring that no reason existed for suspending payments in specie, and that they would make every effort and suffer any sacrifice necessary to prevent such a catastrophe. But when the news came from Baltimore matters wore a very different aspect, and believing that a necessity did exist, they suspended, and assured the people that, till specie was again in circulation, they would not increase the amount of their notes then outstanding, and would take one another's notes in all payments. On hearing this, the merchants and traders met at the Tontine Coffee-House, and unanimously resolved to avoid all negotiation requiring specie payment, to take the notes of the banks as freely in the future as they had in the past, and to do their utmost to maintain bank credit. The city, in its corporate capacity, agreed to issue bills of a penny and upward to replace the small silver and the cents. When these things became known at Albany, the banks of that city suspended, and in a few days not one in any of the seaboard States, from New York to Georgia, was making specie payments.

The chief sufferer from this state of things was the Government. Millions of its revenue were at that moment deposited with the Southern banks. But the suspension having prevented the movement of a dollar to the frontier, where the troops, the army contractors, the thousand and one creditors, were to be paid, the Treasury was practically bankrupt. In a little while numbers of acceptances for large amounts were protested. More than once the paymaster of the army was unable to meet demands for sums so trifling as thirty dollars. The War Department was in such distress that the Secretary of the Treasury was forced to ask a bank at Georgetown to pay a debt of thirty-five hundred dollars.

At some places along the frontier, when the terms of service of the troops expired, they were paid in certificates. On attempting to sell these bits of paper for one half the face value, the soldiers could not find a man who would take them, and were forced to beg their way home. At Plattsburg, where some New York militia were discharged, not even certificates were to be had, and they, too, went about begging food and money from the citizens. When, on the first of December, certain Treasury notes fell due at Philadelphia and were presented for payment, the Loan Commissioner offered new stock of the United States or bills of Southern banks. As no specie of any denomination was to be had, the Secretary was now forced to take another step, and order the collectors of revenue not to receive Treasury notes in payment of taxes or dues when the amount of the note was greater than the sum due. Thus, if the debt were nineteen dollars and ninety-nine cents, the collector must not accept a twenty-dollar Treasury note. This order was construed with great strictness, and when some New Bedford liquor dealers applied to the collector for licenses, and offered a note greater in value than the sum total of all their respective dues, it was refused. Thereupon the dealers declared they would go on without licenses, and told the collector to go to law if he dared. At New York, three men, whose combined taxes footed up twenty-one dollars and fifty-one cents, offered a twenty-dollar Treasury note and the rest in specie; but this, too, was rejected, because, while the bill was less than the amount due from the three, it was greater than the amount due from any one.

Unable to get a dollar in specie or move a cent from one city to another, the Secretary of the Treasury, toward the close of the year, addressed a circular to the public creditors at Boston, in which he openly admitted that the Treasury was empty. " The suspension of specie payments," said he, " by the greater part of the banks in the United States, and among them those in which the Government's money lies, makes it no longer possible to apply money collected in one part of the country to the payment of debts incurred in another. The public creditors, therefore, must be content to receive Treasury notes in place of specie, or wait patiently till such time as the Secretary has specie with which to pay them." Some took Treasury notes, but they were few in number; and when the first day of 1815 arrived, the Treasury had defaulted in the payment of dividends on the funded debt due in Boston, had defaulted in the payment of two million eight hundred thousand dollars of Treasury notes due in many places, and had failed to take up two temporary loans of two hundred and fifty thousand dollars each made by the State Bank of Boston.

Up to this time the Western banks had escaped the financial trouble which beset those in the East, for they had small dealings with them. But when a Spanish joe brought nine per cent., and an American dollar six-per-cent. premium in any seaboard city, it may well be supposed that great efforts were made to bring over the mountains what little specie the

Mississippi Valley contained. So serious were these efforts that, early in the new year, the Miami Exporting Company, the Farmers' and Mechanics' Bank, and the Bank of Cincinnati, all doing business in Ohio, were forced to suspend specie payments. The high price of specie in the East, the presidents stated in their circular, had directed the attention of "moneyed emissaries" to the West, and the refusal of the Ohio banks to pay gold or silver was a measure of self-protection.

Locking up the coin by the banks bore heavily not only on the Treasury Department and the public creditors, but on the great body of the people as well. It stripped the country of small change; not a sixpence, not a shilling, not a pistareen, was anywhere to be seen in the region of the suspending banks. As no financial institution could, at that time, legally issue bills of a lower denomination than one dollar, the place of the silver pieces had to be supplied by an illegal issue of small paper bills. The cities, in their corporate capacity, printed thousands of dollars' worth of cent, two-cent, and six-cent notes, which their treasurers sold in sums of five or ten dollars to such as needed change, with the assurance that they would at any moment be redeemed in bank bills, and would be taken in payment of taxes. Thus the city of New York, in a few months, put out in this manner one hundred and ninety thousand dollars, of which one hundred and fifty thousand dollars were in constant circulation. The banks did likewise; but, as they could not legally issue in their own name, they generally appointed some honest man to sign the bills for them.* Merchants, tradesmen, manufacturers, stage-owners, tavern-keepers,

---

* The following is a specimen of the ordinary change bill :

Two Cents.   Two Cents.

I promise to pay the Bearer

TWO CENTS

On demand at the

SCHUYLKILL BANK,

When a sum amounting to one dollar shall be presented.

RICH'D BACHE.

Philad'a, July 4, 1815.

ferrymen, and unchartered banks followed, and before spring came the whole seaboard south of New England was flooded with paper money of the worst description.*

When peace returned, when the ports were opened in March, and a brisk trade began with foreign nations and along the coast, the evils of this kind of currency were felt most severely. The prices of all commodities instantly declined, and among them that of specie, which fell in a few days from a premium of fourteen to a premium of three per cent. Everybody was sure that coin payments would at once be resumed. But the fond hopes of the public were not realized. The revival of commerce increased tenfold the demands for money; the banks gladly made the loans, and, as they could not possibly redeem their paper in specie, gave up all idea of attempting to do so. This unexpected, this wilful, this unnecessary perseverance in the non-paying system first astonished and then angered the people, and in time aroused the legislatures to take measures of force. In New York a bill was promptly brought into the Assembly laying a tax of fourteen per cent. per annum on all bank-notes not redeemable in coin after January first, 1816, and so alarmed the banks that the General Committee of those in New York city met in haste, resolved that debtor banks should reduce their loans till the balance due the creditor banks was paid, and that the banks of New York city should pledge themselves to the public and to each other, to spare no pains or cost to hasten the resumption of specie payments. These resolutions, sent post-haste to Albany, were read in the Assembly, and stopped all further action on the

---

* The following is a specimen of the tradesmen's change bills:

SIX-AND-A-QUARTER CENTS.	A GENERAL ASSORTMENT OF GROCERIES.			SIXTEEN FOR ONE DOLLAR.
	6¼ cts.	Chest of tea and hogshead.	No. 233.	
	I promise to pay the bearer on demand, in groceries, or Philadelphia bank-notes, at No. 130 North Water Street, six-and-a-quarter cents. JOHN THOMPSON. Phila., December 10, 1814.			

bill. But they were a mere blind, and, relieved of the danger of legislative interference, the banks went on in their old way and made no reductions, no attempt to return to a specie basis. On noticing this, the banks in Connecticut met in convention at Middletown in July, addressed those in New York on the subject, and asked them to redeem their loans at the rate of two per cent. a month till specie payment was resumed. The answer was that, in the opinion of the committee, "the banks in this city are alone competent to decide upon the rate of reduction ; and it is therefore unanimously resolved that it is inexpedient to make any specific pledge on the subject of a reduction of loans." *

In consequence of this refusal of the banks to resume specie payments, their notes immediately began to depreciate again, so that by October, American dollars, which in March brought six-per-cent. premium, sold at sixteen per cent. advance, and Spanish coin at twenty-one. Around each city were drawn a series of imaginary rings, representing so many zones of varying discount. At Philadelphia, notes of the Delaware banks were taken at two-per-cent. discount; those of Baltimore at three ; those of Richmond, if of chartered banks, at three ; those of Pennsylvania and Ohio at seven.

Northward and eastward a better state of affairs existed, and Jersey bills were taken in Philadelphia at par, New York bills at four, and Boston bills at nine-per-cent. premium. At Boston, all the notes issued by New York State banks passed at a discount of twenty per cent., those of Philadelphia at

---

* An Appeal to the Public on the Conduct of the Banks in the City of New York. By a Citizen. New York, December, 1815.

The other pamphlets called forth at this time were:

Reflections on the Consequences of the Refusal of the Banks to receive on Deposit Southern and Western Bank-Notes. Philadelphia, 1815.

Letter to Albert Gallatin, Esq., on the Doctrine of Gold and Silver, and the Evils of the Present Banking System, in Effect and Tendency. By Publicola. New York.

The History of a Little Frenchman and his Bank-Notes, "Rags! Rags! Rags!" Philadelphia, 1815.

A New System of Banking, developed and exemplified on a New Scheme to establish a Merchants' Bank of General Deposits ; and also on a Scheme to establish a Grand National Bank. By Peter Stephen Chazotte. Philadelphia, 1815.

twenty-four, and those of Baltimore at thirty. No Southern bank-notes were to be seen. Treasury notes were not worth seventy-five cents on the dollar. A one-hundred-dollar United States six-per-cent. bond would not bring more than sixty.

Philadelphia merchants and traders who dealt largely with the West and the South were so affected by these rates of exchange that meeting after meeting was held in April, 1815, to discuss the serious inconveniences they suffered. At last a committee was chosen to seek a remedy, and made a report full of interest. The evil, it told the meeting, was deeply seated, and the remedy was not in the hands of the community at large. Want of a circulating medium was the true source of the difference of exchange between different States. Absence of specie put them in the position of foreign countries, the value of whose money was regulated by the balance of trade. States against which a balance arose would have their paper depreciated in the State to which they were indebted. This was precisely the condition of the South and the West with regard to Philadelphia. They were in debt. The balance of trade was against them, and nothing but the restoration of a national circulating medium could bring relief. How far the National Government should attempt to accomplish this was not, the committee said, for it to say.

Had the banks been the only sufferers for the want of a circulating medium, they would have waited long for Government aid. But they were not. Every day the Secretary of the Treasury felt the need of such a medium. Goods, wares, and merchandise were coming into the ports from foreign lands, in quantities such as had never before been known. Yet not a cent of the duty paid on them could be moved from the city at whose custom-house it was collected without heavy charges for exchange. In hopes of stopping this, and forcing the banks to resume the payment of specie, the Secretary gave notice, in June, 1815, that on and after August first the collectors would not receive the notes of banks which did not pay specie, and did not take and pay out Treasury notes at par. Some, whose depositors did a large custom-house business, or in whose vaults was Government revenue, reluctantly yielded. But so many important banks did not accede that on August

fifteenth a new circular was issued.   The purpose of the proposition made to the banks by the Treasury in the circular of
June was, the Secretary said, to secure a circulating medium,
both local and general.   The local medium was to be made up
of State bank-notes, Treasury notes, and cents, which the mint
was to issue at once.   The general medium was to consist of
Treasury notes, to be taken at par all over the country, and
so afford a ready means of making remittances from place
to place.   This proposition, he was glad to state, had been
generally accepted by the State banks.   Two in New York,
one in Connecticut, and one in Georgia had flatly refused
to comply.   Eight in New York, two in New Jersey, two in
Pennsylvania, and two in Ohio had made no answer.   Notice
was therefore given that, after the first day of October, 1815,
the notes of these banks would no longer be received in payment of duties or taxes due the United States.   This was
vigorously protested against.   No wonder, it was said, that
New York banks will not receive and issue Treasury notes at
par, while those in the South do.   When the New York city institutions suspended specie payments, they solemnly agreed not
to extend their loans above the amount then out.   To this they
adhered strictly, and by so doing kept the value of their paper
steady, while that of Southern banks went down.   When the
Secretary made his proposition, Treasury notes sold at three-
per-cent. discount in New York, and at three-per-cent. premium
in Baltimore.   In New York, therefore, taking Treasury notes
at par was a tax of three per cent., while in Baltimore it was a
bonus of three per cent.   But this was not all.   Bills of the
Baltimore banks which accepted the Secretary's proposition
were taken in payment of custom-house bonds, though the
bills were seven per cent. below Treasury notes.   In Boston,
Treasury notes were cheaper than bank bills.   The rate of
duty being the same, a Massachusetts importer would therefore pay in a currency seven per cent. more valuable than the
Baltimore merchant.   On goods carrying a duty of twenty-
five-per-cent. *ad valorem* this was equal to two per cent., and
two per cent. was enough to pay the freight and insurance
from Baltimore to Boston.   If a merchant in each of these
cities had imported five million dollars' worth of hardware and

crockery, woollens and linens, the one in Baltimore would have paid three hundred and fifty thousand dollars less revenue than his fellow in Boston.

Nevertheless, the notice was effective, and seven of the banks which had failed to comply in July complied before the first of November. By that time the people were growing weary of the refusal to resume, and of the flood of paper money poured out on the community by individuals, counterfeiters, and by associations having no charters. At a meeting, made up of the merchants, tradesmen, and citizens of Albany, resolutions were passed not to accept any change bills other than those issued by the corporation of the city, nor any bank-notes which did not pass current at the city banks. A citizen of Richmond, having collected ten one-hundred-dollar notes of the Bank of Virginia, presented them and demanded silver. He was refused; and, on seeking counsel to bring suit, he could not find a member of the Richmond bar who would take the case. He thereupon went to the office of the clerk of the Superior Court and took out a summons against the president and directors of the bank. When rule day came, as they failed to appear, a *distringas* was issued. Still the bank would not obey, and, on the president refusing to submit peaceably, the sheriff summoned a posse, shut the doors of the banking house, and carried him off. In a few days, however, he was doing business in his old quarters, and in open contempt of the court.

Shortly after this affair the Virginia Legislature took up the matter, and placed on the statute-book three laws concerning the currency: One required every bank in the State to resume specie payment by November fifteenth, 1816. The penalty for not doing so was a writ of execution, to issue in ten days, and costs and six per cent. interest on the bill from the day specie was refused in exchange for it. In order to comply with this law, the banks began to call in loans, stopped discounting, and so deranged business that tobacco and produce fell off in price from five to twenty per cent. This led a grand jury to present the law as a daring attempt to infringe the constitutional rights of the people, and a violation of that section of the Federal Constitution which limits the powers of the States. "Should the Legislature," said the jury, "attempt to enforce the law, and pronounce absolute judgment of confiscation, its action may furnish a proper occasion for a popular revolution." The second law provided that in all cases of debt, or of money due on execution, deed of trust, judgment, or mortgage, not an article should be sold unless, ten days before the sale was to take place, the persons to be benefited should write on the execution their willingness to take such notes of the chartered banks of Virginia, of the neighboring States, and of the District of Columbia as were current in the county where the sale was to be held. It was then made the duty of the judges of the courts of the counties and of the corporations to decide each month what bills were current within their jurisdiction, and to fix the rates of depreciation as compared with the notes of the Farmers' Bank and the Bank of Virginia, the only chartered institutions in the State. The third law fixed a date whereon the notes, bills, and tickets of unchartered banks and corporations should cease to be currency, and after which to issue or receive such bills or tickets would be a misdemeanor.

In each case the remedy was again worse than the disease. In each case the law failed to accomplish its purpose, was assailed with bitterness, and in time suspended.

At the court of hustings held for the corporation of Staunton the judges flatly refused to execute the law. At a court for Augusta County the judges declared that the paper of the chartered banks of Virginia, Maryland, Pennsylvania, District of Columbia, and of the State Bank of North Carolina should be taken at par, and that no other bank paper should be current. The court of hustings sitting at Richmond ordered that notes of the Bank of Virginia and of the Farmers' Bank should be rated at par; but that Philadelphia paper should pass at seven and a half per cent. discount, Baltimore paper at ten, and that of the District of Columbia at twelve and a half. Rulings such as these put an end to business. Notes which in Augusta County the people were forced to take at par, the citizens of Richmond were forbidden to take at all. Bills which at Richmond were, by order of the Court, received at a discount of ten per cent., were, for the same reason, current at Fredericksburg at their face value.

To make matters worse, the associations and companies doing an unchartered banking business began to call in their paper, in order to comply with the law aimed directly at them. These companies were of two classes, were to be found in the valley rather than in the tide-water region of Virginia, and owed their existence to the bad system of State banking. In 1803 and 1812 the Legislature had chartered banks, had given to them power to establish branches in certain towns, and, since the establishment of these two, had granted no other charters. Exercising its powers, the Bank of Virginia had opened branches at Norfolk, Fredericksburg, Petersburg, and Lynchburg. The Farmers' Bank had branches at Norfolk, Petersburg, Lynchburg, Fredericksburg, and Winchester. In each case the parent bank was at Richmond.

The great and fertile region lying west of Richmond was thus left without any money-loaning institution. But it was into this region that immigration had long been pouring, and it was to meet the needs of these immigrants that two classes of companies had grown up. In the one class were the associations known by such names as the Bank of Winchester in Virginia, Bank of Martinsburg, Bank of the South Branch of the Potomac, the Virginia Saline Bank, the Farmers' and Mechanics' Bank of Harper's Ferry, and a host of others, which, without charters, did a regular banking business, made loans, discounted notes, received deposits, and issued paper money. In the other class were the exporting companies, the companies for the encouragement of agriculture and manufactures, and the farmers' companies, all of them great buyers and shippers of produce, who paid their debts in paper of their own issue, which soon became the circulating medium of the country. The efforts of these two classes to obey the law carried financial distress into regions where bank bills were almost unknown. By the middle of the summer the whole State was clamorous for a special session of the Legislature to repeal the banking and currency laws. A special session was accordingly held in November. The law requiring the banks to resume specie payment was suspended, first for one month, and then for seven; and fifteen unchartered banking institutions were given till the last day of August, 1817, to call in their paper and comply with the law. To please the people of the mountain region two new banks were created. One, called the Northwestern Bank of Virginia, was to be at Wheeling, with branches at Wellsburg, Morgantown, and Clarksburg; the other, named the Bank of the Valley in Virginia, was to be at Winchester, with two branches to be located in the neighboring counties, provided sufficient subscriptions were made.

The experience of Virginia was the experience of every State. In the Pennsylvania House of Representatives an attempt was made to instruct the committee on banks to inquire into the expediency of revoking the charters of every one within the Commonwealth that refused to pay specie. But their friends rallied, and succeeded in changing the motion to one bidding the committee report on the cause of suspension and the remedy. The causes, the committee declared, were too many banks and an enormous issue of paper. The forty-one chartered in 1814 had not added one dollar to the specie in the State. Yet each one had put out paper far beyond the limit required for its own safety, or the good of the public, or the ability of the community to redeem in specie. The remedy was, the committee reported, a law providing that if any bank in Pennsylvania should on demand refuse to pay its notes in coin after January first, 1817, interest at eighteen per cent. should begin from the time the demand was made, and continue till it was fully satisfied. But if any bank, after January first, 1818, refused to resume specie payment, its corporate rights should instantly become null and void.

After hearing the report, the friends of the banks, under the lead of James Buchanan, moved a substitute which gave very different reasons and suggested a very different remedy. During the war, they said, the ports of the Southern and Middle States had been strictly blockaded, while those of the East had been open. Foreign merchandise, even when intended for the South and Middle States, came in therefore through the Eastern ports. As it could no longer be paid for in produce it was paid for in specie, which began to flow steadily eastward. But more than this: New England had made small subscriptions to the Federal loans—so small that they were far less than the Federal expenditures in that region; and to make up this difference more specie was drawn from the Middle States. Just at the time this was going on the people in the interior of Pennsylvania, seeing that all the profits of banking were monopolized by the citizens of Philadelphia, and becoming displeased at the behavior of the branch banks, which were sending all the coin in the State into the vaults of the parent banks at Philadelphia, came forward in a body and demanded that the Legislature establish banks in the interior. This was done, and the new institutions, drawing on Philadelphia for their specie capital, steadily lessened the gold and silver in that city, and forced the banks to suspend. With peace many of these disturbing causes ceased. But new ones took their places, for the importation of foreign goods so exceeded the exportation of American products that specie still continued to be sent abroad to settle the balance. This was the condition at the present time, and under such circumstances it was unwise to adopt measures forcing the banks to resume. As the result of these conflicting views, consideration of the report was postponed.

In North Carolina, likewise, the Legislature felt called on to interfere, and ordered that no individual and no corporation should, under heavy penalty, issue bills, orders, tickets, promissory notes, or due bills, to be used as small change, or draw and pass a check for a sum under one dollar. That the people might have change of some sort, the State Treasurer was commanded to have eighty thousand dollars in Treasury notes printed. The denominations of the notes were five cents, six and a quarter, ten, twelve and a half, twenty, twenty-five, thirty-five, forty, fifty, and seventy-five cents. They were payable to bearer, were numbered, signed, and dated by the Treasurer, and paid to the cashier of the State Bank as part of a debt due from the State. The bank used them as currency.

South Carolina chose May first, 1817, as the day on which all bill and promissory notes under one dollar, issued as currency by corporations or individuals, should become void, and named January first, 1817, as the day after which it would be illegal to draw such bills for less than five dollars. Georgia took similar action, and commanded her banks to resume specie payments under five dollars on February twentieth, 1817, and over five dollars whenever the banks of the adjoining States set the example.

Like attempts to drive bank paper out of circulation failed in New York and Maryland. In Ohio, in Indiana Territory, in Kentucky, notes of unchartered banks were declared illegal. On the other hand, those of chartered banks were so highly protected in Kentucky that when an execution issued, and the plaintiff wrote across the face of the writ the words "Notes on the Bank of Kentucky, or its branches, or notes on any other incorporated bank of this State, or notes on the Treasury of the United States, will be accepted in discharge of the whole of this execution," the defendant had but three months within which to replevy. Should the plaintiff refuse to accept paper money, the defendant might replevy at any time within a year.

To the evils produced by so debased a paper currency, coming from more than four hundred sources of issue—from banks with charters, from banks without charters, from cities, from towns, from individuals, from importing companies and exporting companies, from factories, and from the Treasury of the United States—must be added yet other evils which sprang from the opportunities afforded rogues and sharpers. Men without consciences printed their change bills on paper so bad that it fell to pieces in the pockets of the takers. Counterfeiters plied their shameful trade so successfully that hundreds of thousands of dollars of false notes were soon afloat in the country. One gang made its headquarters in Indiana Territory. Another had its presses somewhere on the Hudson. Four members of the Western gang, who were captured at Harrisburg, had in their valises three hundred and fifty thousand dollars of counterfeit notes of the Miami Exporting Company of Ohio. A member of the Eastern gang, when caught, had with him counterfeit notes of every important bank along the seaboard, from Savannah to Albany. The largest and most carefully organized of them all carried on its operations along the great highways between Philadelphia and Reading and Pittsburg. The paper on which its notes were printed was made in Virginia; the press-work was done in a hut in the Alleghany Mountains, in Bedford County, Pennsylvania; the engraving was executed by old counterfeiters in a camp at Pine Grove Furnace, on South Mountain, Adams County, Pennsylvania; and the bills, when ready, were put into circulation by travelling gamblers and by a gang of thirty teamsters who drove freight wagons between Philadelphia and Pittsburg. The newspapers all over the United States were full of notices of false bank notes, and, what was quite as bad, of notes of banks which had no existence. These wildcat institutions were the creation of a class of men who would have thought counterfeiting infamous. Two or three of them would associate, select a name and a city, have plates engraved in the best and most artistic manner, print bills of all denominations, and sell them to the exchange brokers, or pass them off in cities far away from the place where the bank was supposed to be located. New York, as a great commercial centre, was a favorite spot, and in it many such imaginary institutions were located. One, taking the name of the City Exchange Bank and claiming to have two million dollars of capital, scattered tens of thousands of dollars in notes all over the South. Another, called the Merchants' and Mechanics' Exchange Company, victimized the people of Augusta, of Fayetteville, and of Charleston. Notes of a third, the Ohio Exporting and Importing Company, appeared at Trenton, at Philadelphia, and in western Virginia. They were engraved in the best manner possible by a firm of reputable bank-note printers, who, finding that they had been deceived by a gang of cheats, gave public notice of the fraud, and declared that upward of half a million dollars of the counterfeit bills had been sent to Cincinnati. That city was so flooded with them that the local banks appointed a committee to investigate and report, and soon published the names of thirteen persons whose chief occupation seemed to be passing wildcat money. The owners of a fourth, known as the Commercial Bank, did a thriving business from Cooperstown to Buffalo. The president of one of the best known of the city banks happening to be a gentleman named Bayard, a swindler who called himself Haskins hunted through the army-lists till he found a soldier of the name of Bayard, and, having obtained from him a power of attorney to sign his name to money bills, began to issue notes in imitation of those of the Bank of America. They were drawn on the Agency and Exchange Bank; but when returned to New York for redemption, nobody had ever heard of such an institution.

But this prosperity was not to endure; for, in spite of State banks, exchange brokers, and sharpers, the day for the resumption of specie was near at hand. Congress had established the second Bank of the United States for the express purpose of regulating the currency, and had, by resolution, instructed the Secretary of the Treasury to see to it that, after February twentieth, 1817, the revenue was paid in legal currency.

Madison, in his message to Congress, had touched on the state of the currency and on the pressing need of finding a remedy for the disorders that beset it. The hoarding of the precious metals would, he believed, be temporary. But till such time as they were again the general medium of exchange it behooved Congress to find a substitute. If the State banks could not do this, the ability of a national bank to regulate the currency ought to be considered. These vague remarks of Madison were sent to a select committee, of which Calhoun was chairman. That a bank charter of some kind would be reported was well known. No surprise, therefore, was manifested when, early in January, the committee brought in a bill to establish a national bank based on a plan outlined by Dallas. The life of the institution was to be twenty-one years; the capital was to be thirty-five millions of dollars, of which the Government was to own seven millions. One quarter of the remainder was to be subscribed for by corporations and individuals in gold and silver, and three fourths in funded debt of the United States. The parent bank was to be at Philadelphia; was to have power to establish branches in the States; was to issue notes receivable in all payments to the United States; was to receive and transfer the public money from place to place; was to have no rivals, and was to pay for its charter a bonus of one million and a half of dollars, payable in equal instalments at the end of two, three, or four years.

A bill to execute the newly-made commercial treaty with England, the revision of the revenue laws, and a host of minor matters hindered the House from considering the question for a month. Then it was taken up and discussed elaborately. Much that was said may be passed by unnoticed. But the records made in that debate by three men of growing reputation —Webster, Calhoun, and Clay—must not be disregarded.

Calhoun opened with a strong plea for the bank. The doubtful state of the currency was, he said, a strain on public and private credit. By the Constitution Congress was given sole power to regulate the currency. But, in point of fact, that duty was done by the banks, for, gold and silver having disappeared, there was no currency but paper money beyond control of Congress. The right to make money, which was an attribute of sovereignty, was exercised, not by the Government, but by two hundred and sixty banks scattered over the Union, and not responsible to any power whatever for the issue of paper. The plain duty of the Government was to restore specie payments, and as such a restoration could only be effected through the agency of a national specie-paying bank, it was clearly within the power of Congress to establish one.

Clay took the same view, and, leaving the Speaker's chair, came down on the floor, where in a long speech he explained his new position. An explanation was necessary, for in 1811 nobody had been more eager to destroy the old bank, and in 1816 nobody was more eager to found a new one. In 1811 he had opposed a recharter because, he said, he had been instructed to do so by his State Legislature, because he believed the old bank had meddled in politics, and because the power to create a bank was not expressly granted, and did not then seem necessary to carry out any power which was specifically given. But times had changed. The Legislature of Kentucky showed no hostility to the proposed charter; the fate of the old bank would be a warning to a successor, while the general suspension of specie payments which deprived the Government of the control of the currency, a condition which did not exist in 1811, now made a bank indispensably necessary. He saw scattered over the United States three hundred financial institutions, under no direct control of the Government, issuing paper money which was the actual currency of the country. He saw them exercising what had ever been considered an attribute of sovereignty—the power of regulating the circulating medium. He saw this paper, which the Treasury was forced by circumstances to receive, obstructing the operations of that department, for it accumulated where it was not wanted, and could not be used where it was needed without a ruinous and arbitrary brokerage. He saw every man who paid money to the Government pay as much less than he ought to have done, as was the difference between the medium he offered and specie. In this state of affairs it appeared to him to be the duty of Congress to apply a remedy, and that remedy was a national bank. He knew this statement would subject him to the charge of inconsistency. But he would rather sacrifice the pride of consistency than the interests of his country.

Of the great triumvirate, Webster alone opposed the bill. That a national bank should be created to regulate the currency was, he said, a mistaken idea. No nation in the world had a better currency than the United States. It was gold and silver, had been established by the Constitution as the only legal money, could not be disestablished by any act of Congress, and it did not need to be regulated or reformed. It was true that alongside of the constitutional currency there had sprung up in the States a paper medium issued by the banks with a promise to redeem in specie—a promise they were unable to perform. But Congress had not created these banks; they were State institutions. How, then, could Congress control them? To his mind there was but one way, and that was by forbidding the Custom-House collectors and receivers of taxes to take State bank notes in payment of duties and taxes.

Opposition was useless. The bitter experience of three years had taught the Republicans many things, and on March fourteenth the House, by a majority of nine, passed the bill. The Senate approved, and on April tenth Madison signed the act and made it law.

But it was not on the exertions of the new bank and its branches that Calhoun and his supporters solely depended for the speedy return of specie payments. The needs of the Treasury in this respect were imperative, and in hope of bringing it coin before the bank could go into operation, Calhoun inquired of Dallas * if the taxes could not be collected in gold; silver, Treasury notes, and notes of banks paying specie. The Secretary replied that it would be possible and most desirable, and sketched a plan for a law requiring such payments to be made, which Calhoun, in April, presented. After the last day of December, 1816, no collector of revenue or receiver of taxes, the bill provided, was to take anything but gold, silver, copper, such foreign coins as were current by law, and Treasury notes; though the Secretary might, if he thought proper, receive notes of specie-paying banks. After December thirty-first no public revenue was to be deposited with any bank or banker whose notes were not redeemed in coin, while on that day such nonconvertible notes were to become subject to new and heavy stamp taxes. The opposition was strong. A cry was raised that the bill was fraught with partiality, with ingratitude, with cruelty, and with injustice. Members were reminded that the banks had stood bravely by the Government and loaned it money many a time when the people would give it nothing. They were told that the paper so borrowed had been paid out by the Government to the people, and they were asked if it were just for the Government, now that it was rid of the notes, to refuse to take them back again for taxes. Yet the supporters of the measure carried the bill through all its stages up to the moment when the Speaker asked, "Shall the bill pass?" Then the opposition triumphed, and by one vote defeated it.

Next day Webster took up the matter, and easily obtained a joint resolution which, as it came from the hands of the President, bade the Secretary do his best to have the duties, taxes, and debts due the United States paid at an early day in coin, Treasury notes, notes of the Bank of the United States, or of banks redeeming their bills in legal money, and fixed Feb-

---

* March 15, 1816.

ruary twentieth, 1817, as the day on and after which nothing but such currency would be taken by officers of the United States.

The law creating the Bank of the United States prescribed that on the first Monday in July, 1816, subscription books should be opened in twenty of the great towns and cities scattered over the country from Portland to New Orleans, and be kept open for twenty days—exclusive of Sundays, when they were to be shut. At each place named in the law, three commissioners, appointed by the President, were to receive the subscriptions, which were to be paid in three instalments six months apart. Each share cost one hundred dollars, of which thirty were to be paid down when the subscriber entered his name. Of this thirty all might be, and at least five must be, in gold or silver coin of the United States, Spain, or the dominions of Spain, and twenty-five in the funded debt of the United States. As specie then commanded a premium of five per cent., and as the rate at which the Government stock could be taken by the commissioners was fixed by law, it was feared that the State banks, the brokers, and the stock-jobbers would combine and force up the price of stock and the premium on specie. This would have made subscription too costly and would have defeated the bank, an event which the State institutions would gladly have seen happen. Luckily, it could not be done, and when the twenty days elapsed but a little more than three of the twenty-eight millions of stock offered remained unsold. This was at once taken by Stephen Girard, of Philadelphia, whereupon preparations were begun for the election of directors and the organization of the bank and its branches. From the statistics of the subscription books some facts of more than passing interest may be gathered. The number of share-holders was thirty-one thousand three hundred and thirty-four; but fifteen thousand six hundred and ten of them subscribed at Baltimore and were believed to be inhabitants of Maryland. The amount of their subscriptions was four millions, which was twice as much as twenty-six hundred and forty-one made in New York, and nearly four times as much as twenty-four hundred and seventy-four made in Middletown, Connecticut. All New England furnished but three thousand share-holders and took but a trifle over four millions of stock.   Philadelphia, on the other hand, gave a hearty support and contributed nearly nine millions of dollars to the capital of the bank.

While the five commissioners at Philadelphia were busy organizing the mother bank, Dallas was doing all he could to bring about the resumption of specie payments.   The injunction to do this was imperative, and in obedience to it he addressed a circular letter on the subject, late in July, to all the State banks in the country.   In it he reminded them that there were then three kinds of currency in existence.   There was, in the first place, the lawful money of the United States, gold, silver, and copper coin, which had been made legal tender by the Constitution in all cases whatsoever, and which was the only kind of money possessing that quality.   There were, in the second place, certain quantities of Treasury notes, and the notes to be issued by the Bank of the United States, which had, by particular acts of Congress, been made receivable in all payments to the United States.   And there were, in the third place, the notes of State banks, which, because of the suspension of specie payments and because of the depreciation of Treasury notes, both the people and the Government had been forced to take and pay out as a national currency.   When the suspension of specie took place the banks, Dallas said, had excused their acts as necessary, and had again and again asserted that they would soon resume.   But they had not resumed, and the belief had become current that the profit made by irregular banking was so great that they never would return to metallic money unless forced to do so.   Under these circumstances a speedy and simultaneous resumption would, he believed, not only restore gold and silver to circulation, but would revive public confidence.   As a step toward this end, Congress, in April, had passed the resolution requiring and directing him to adopt such measures as would cause all taxes, duties, and debts due the United States to be paid in coin, in Treasury notes, in notes of the Bank of the United States, or in those of banks which, on demand, redeemed them in specie.   In order to discharge this duty in a way as convenient for the banks as possible, he had framed a draught of a circular which he enclosed.   If the banks approved, he would issue it in official form.   If they did not approve, then they must remember that after February twentieth, 1817, the notes of non-specie-paying institutions would no longer be taken by the United States.

The substance of the circular was that after October first bank-notes of five dollars and under should not be received by collectors of the revenue unless convertible on demand into coin ; that if any bank refused to cash its notes under five dollars, none of its bills of any denomination should be taken by Treasury officials ; and that after February twentieth, 1817, all duties and taxes must be paid in legal currency.

On receipt of this letter the chartered banks of Ohio met at Chillicothe and sent Dallas word that they would resume as soon as the institutions on the seaboard did, but that it would not be safe for them to do so sooner.   The country banks of Pennsylvania, in convention at Harrisburg, came to a like decision.   But those of New York, Philadelphia, and Baltimore declined to resume for one year.   It did not seem likely, they declared, that the Bank of the United States and its branches would be in operation before July, 1817.   Until they were in operation a return to specie payments by the State banks would be inexpedient, and the best that could be done was to recommend that the first Monday in July, 1817, be agreed upon as the time for a general resumption throughout the country. As Dallas knew that, if the State banks refused to release their coin, the people could get none wherewith to pay their taxes, he gave up the attempt to hasten an early resumption and announced that no further effort would be made to collect the revenue in legal currency till the twentieth of February, 1817, when the law would surely be enforced.

To this threat the State banks gave little heed at the time. But a course of events they had not carefully considered very soon forced them to yield.   The eight millions necessary to enable the Bank of the United States to begin business was all paid in September.   The president and directors were elected in October, and notice sent to Washington that the mother bank at Philadelphia would open her doors for business on the first day of the new year.   But what was more important still, the people of New York city lost their patience and rejected all bills issued as small change. At a meeting of grocers in September it was resolved that after the first of October no change bills under one dollar should be taken in payment of groceries unless issued by banks promptly redeeming them in specie. The Exchange Bank thereupon gave notice that it was ready to do so at once. Twenty-two exchange brokers in return signed a paper pledging themselves not to buy or sell specie under half a dollar. The bankers followed, and promised to pay all sums under one dollar in silver and copper coin; the butchers imitated the action of the grocers; the city corporation began to call its change bills, and it then appeared that what had been so long wanted was some one to make the first move. In Poughkeepsie, in Albany, in Newark ticket money disappeared as if by magic. In Philadelphia the brokers agreed not to buy small change, and by the end of the first week in October the "silver age," as the people called it, had come again. For months past, moreover, specie had been pouring into our seaports from all parts of Europe. Not a week had passed during this time but thousands and hundreds of thousands of dollars in gold and silver had come from London, from Lisbon, from Antwerp, from Rotterdam, Amsterdam, and South America. Coin was sent in to be invested in our stocks. Some belonged to the emigrants flocking by shiploads to our shores, but much was imported by merchants, who found specie more marketable than merchandise.

Under these favorable circumstances Crawford, who by this time had succeeded Dallas as Secretary of the Treasury, made a new appeal to the banks. He informed them that on the first of January, 1817, the Bank of the United States would begin business and be ready to receive the Government money then in their vaults. If they persisted in their determination not to resume specie payments till July, he would promptly order the deposits to be transferred. If they would resume on February twentieth, he would not move the deposits, and till July first would draw on them as little as possible.

This threat, joined to the fact that the bank actually began business in January, brought the State institutions to terms, and by agreement those in New York city, in Philadelphia, in Baltimore, in the District of Columbia, in Virginia, and two in Ohio resumed specie payments on the twentieth of February, 1817. The day was looked forward to with no little anxiety. The belief was general that the eagerness of the people to again hear the "yellow boys" jingling in their pockets would produce a general run. The banks at New York therefore made great preparations, and when their doors were opened at ten o'clock on the eventful day their counters were piled high with specie. To the surprise of every one, but little was wanted, and in the afternoon the porters carried the bags of coin back to the vaults; and this was the experience everywhere. The crowds in the Philadelphia banks were large, but the amount of specie they took away, over and above what was wanted for change, was very small and no greater than had been usual in days before suspension. Nowhere was anything resembling a run experienced.

Yet it must not be supposed that paper money by any means disappeared. There was very much less of the notes of good banks; but, just in proportion as the sound institutions reduced their discounts and called in their bills in order to meet the demand for specie, the illegal, unchartered, and wild-cat banks put out more paper. Indeed, a new kind, called "bank facilities," was created to meet the emergency. They were notes issued by the country banks and paid out over their counters, not to be received on deposit, or redeemed, or even taken by the banks of issue except in payment of a debt due it. As such debts would always be for less than the amount of the facilities, the new paper became irredeemable. From the report of the Treasurer of Pennsylvania it appears that on the first of January, 1817, there were in that State forty-eight legal and chartered banks, twenty-two unlawful and unchartered banks, and thirty-nine private individuals issuing notes from five cents to two dollars in value. The unchartered banks were bridge companies, turnpike companies, town councils, trading companies, and associations of individuals. In the West the condition of affairs brought about by this rage for paper money was dreadful, and is well illustrated by the case of Zanesville, where more than thirty kinds of paper were passing from hand to hand. There were bills of the Canton

Bank, the Owl Creek Bank, the Virginia Saline, the Granville, the Perryopolis, the Mansfield and New Philadelphia banks, and the Saddlebag Bank, as that at Parkersburg was nicknamed from the fact that all its capital had been carried in a saddlebag from Pittsburg to Parkersburg. But most plentiful of all were the "shinplasters" issued by bridge, turnpike, and manufacturing companies, city authorities and borough authorities, merchants, tavern-keepers, barbers, and shoeblacks, and ranging in value from three cents to two dollars.

CHAPTER XXXI.

THE TARIFF OF 1816.

IN the outburst of joy and thanksgiving which spread over the land in the spring of 1815, no toasts were so often drunk to as " Peace and Plenty," " Peace, Commerce, and Prosperity." Here and there some croaker's voice was indeed raised to warn the people against the illusion contained in their favorite toasts. They were told not to be amazed if commerce, instead of being attended with expansion and prosperity, was narrowed and shut within a little compass; if its profits fell off; and if, in place of the plenty which was enjoyed when the war in Europe made them the carriers for the world, they now found it harder to gain one dollar on the ocean than they did before the war to make ten. They were reminded that, since the day when France declared war on Great Britain and opened her West Indian ports to the world, three-and-twenty years had gone; and that during these years business of every sort had been completely revolutionized. Generations of farmers, shippers, and merchants who, when Louis was guillotined, were youths, boys, children scarce able to prattle, had grown to manhood and entered business without ever in their lives knowing a time when business was not conducted on a war basis, and such a war basis as never could be known again. Was it likely that such men—and they were in the majority—could easily and quickly adjust their ideas to the new state of affairs? Greatly mistaken would those be who looked on a ship as the prelude to a fortune, or who believed the dashing merchant of the past would continue to be a money-making man. Henceforth traffic would be precarious, profits would be small, and the old plodding times of pounds, shillings, and pence would return again.

Happily, the forebodings of the croakers were signally con-
founded. The change from the interests of the past to the
wholly dissimilar interests of the future was not only made,
but was made with a suddenness and rapidity simply marvellous. Had a stranger landed at any of our seaports in April,
he would have found it hard to believe that for almost three
years the people had been fighting the most powerful of nations. Save the earthworks thrown up hastily to defend the
harbors, not a trace of war remained. The truth is no people
had ever before fought so ·long a war at so small a sacrifice
of life, property, and money. Never at any time were there
more than thirty thousand fighting men in the army. Never
were there actually engaged in any battle as many as four
thousand regulars and militia. From such returns and statistics as are trustworthy it seems that the number of men killed
in all the land fights was under sixteen hundred, and the number wounded less than thirty-five hundred. Indeed, it is safe
to say that the total of killed and wounded was not far from
five thousand. How many perished on the sea can never be
known, for no returns were ever made by the privateers.

More astonishing still is the trifling amount of property
destroyed. The Niagara frontier, it is true, was harried.
Part of Maine was in possession of the enemy for several
months. The shores of Chesapeake Bay and the coast of
Georgia were plundered. Nevertheless, the harm done was
small, for those regions were far from rich and populous, and
did not contain a town of the first order. No large town, and
no city of importance save Washington, was ever in the hands
of the British for one day. Behind the seacoast the affairs of
daily life went on more actively during the war than before it.
The soil was tilled, the crops were raised, flour was made, and
the business of transportation carried to an extent never before known. The blockade stopped commerce ; but the stoppage of commerce transferred capital from ships to manufactures, which, unhampered by foreign competition, developed
amazingly. The rice, the cotton, the tobacco, the flour, the
lumber, the harvests of two bounteous seasons, were still largely
in the hands of the producers. But the very moment the
blockade was lifted, this mass of domestic produce poured

forth on the markets of Europe, which had long been waiting to receive it. In the palmy days before the embargo the
highest monthly average of exports reached in any year was
four millions of dollars; in 1815 it went over five millions.
From the first day of March to the last day of September more
than forty-six million dollars' worth of domestic produce left
our ports and gave employment to more than eight hundred
and fifty thousand tons of American shipping.*

Sure that a time of prosperity was coming, the merchants,
before the contents of the treaty were known, before the Senate
had received it, before Madison had read a line of it, began to
prepare for an immense trade. Crews were engaged, ships were
chartered, cargoes were advertised for, and calkers, riggers, and
sail-makers were in such demand that four dollars for ten hours'
labor was freely offered in the great cities. The water fronts
presented such a scene of activity as drew the citizens there
by thousands, and no sight was so much enjoyed as the lifting of "Madison's nightcaps." To preserve the masts of the
ships laid up by the war it was customary to cover the top of
each with a tar-barrel, and these barrels had been called Madison's nightcaps. Now, the report that they were to be lifted
from a ship would bring a crowd to the wharf at any time of
day to watch the sailors as with a cry of " Have a care below,
off comes Madison's nightcap!" they would toss the barrels to
the ground, where a crowd of boys and sailors would seize and
consign them to the flames.

When at last the treaty was ratified and made public it appeared that trade was not to be restored at once. As some
time must pass before the war ships and the privateers of the
two nations could be notified of peace, various periods were
named in the treaty during which captures might continue to
be made. Thus the coasting trade could not be safely resumed
till twelve days after the ratification, which would be March
second. That to the West Indies, Great Britain, France,
Spain, and Portugal would be safe after March twentieth;
and that to the North Sea, the Baltic, and the Mediterranean
ten days later. Trade south of the equator was liable to

---

* American State Papers, Commerce and Navigation, vol. ii, p. 647.

interruption till May nineteenth, and to other parts of the world till June eighteenth.

March second thus became a white day in the commercial calendar. As it drew near, the sailors began to crowd the streets; the coffee-houses and the exchanges began to wear their old-time look; the signs " For Rent," " To Let," began to disappear from the shops and counting-houses, and the list of advertisements of brigs and sloops for sale, for charter, or seeking a cargo, began to grow longer and longer in the newspapers.

When at last the day came, a vast fleet of merchantmen put out to sea from Boston, from New York, from Philadelphia, from Baltimore, followed by the cheers and good wishes of a happy people who crowded the wharves to see them depart. On that day the marine insurance companies opened their doors for business, on that day sea risks began to run, and clearances at the custom-houses to assume their accustomed places in the columns of the daily newspapers. But the event looked forward to with the deepest interest was the sailing ·of the European fleet toward the middle and end of the month, and the arrival in this country of the fleet which about the same time would sail from Europe. The war, the blockade, the serious interruption of commerce, had left the markets of every port without a crate or a box of the many kinds of foreign goods which the people had come to look on as necessities. Patriotism and the bitter feelings aroused by the French decrees and British orders in council had done much to make American manufactures popular. Nobody was ashamed to wear cotton cloth or woollen cloth produced from native fibre by the mills and factories of New England. But silks and satins, muslins and brocades, hardware and hollow ware, edged tools, Madeira, molasses, coffee, tea, and a thousand articles of household use, must still be had from abroad or gone without.

Toward the end of May and the beginning of June they began to come, and they came not in a few ships, but in great fleets, and in such quantities as had never been known in the experience of the oldest merchants. Yet great as was the quantity, the demand was greater still. The seaports literally swarmed with buyers eager and ready to pay almost any price the importer asked. In times past the business of importing and selling had been conducted in an orderly way. The importer would send to the foreign maker orders for such goods as suited the home market, and for such a quantity as he was sure he could vend. On removing his consignment from the ship he would sell in original packages to another class of merchants, who sold by the piece to retailers and country shopkeepers, who in turn disposed of the goods to the consumer. But now all was changed. British manufacturers, finding European and South American markets closed, had, without waiting for orders, emptied their warehouses on the United States. Needing money very badly and seeing the cities full of buyers, the supercargoes and captains in charge of the goods hurried them to the auction-block, where enormous prices were secured in consequence of the buyers bidding against each other. Thus one hundred and eighty-three crates of earthenware, costing eleven hundred and six pounds, ten shillings sterling, sold at auction in Philadelphia for twelve thousand and thirty-one dollars, or ten dollars and ninety cents per pound sterling, which was three hundred and eight per cent. advance. Another cargo from Liverpool, consisting of seven thousand bushels of salt and four hundred crates of earthenware, sold in the same city for sixteen dollars per pound sterling, which was five hundred per cent. advance. The total of one week's auction sales of British goods exceeded four hundred and sixty thousand dollars. During the same week the receipts from auction sales of imported hardware and groceries, earthenware and dry goods, in the three cities of New York, Philadelphia, and Baltimore, was one million three hundred thousand dollars. In New York city the duties paid at the Custom-House during April, May, and June amounted to three million nine hundred and sixty thousand dollars. During three days in August sixty-five vessels came into the port from foreign countries laden with cargoes worth in several instances fifty thousand pounds sterling. On November fourteenth the value of property entered at the Custom-House was more than twice as great as had ever before been entered in one day. The goods were brought by a fleet of twenty square-rigged ships, which, favored by wind and tide, came up the bay together. Five days later fifteen ships and eight brigs arrived in twenty-four hours.

What took place at New York took place in every importing city. On one occasion the Charleston Courier was so crowded with advertisements of British goods for sale in packages, and of auctions soon to come off, that of the sixteen columns the journal contained, but two and a half were given to news. In another issue are eleven auction notices and fifty-three advertisements of package sales. Yorkshire cloth and Scotch muslins, flushings, fearnaughts, plushes, taffetas, levantine silks, jaconet muslins, bombazettes, kerseys, saggathys, windsor soap, grantines, and London Duffel blankets, cut nails, salt, bed-covers, tacks, pencil-cases, toy watches, tooth-brushes, pins, grindstones, cast-iron pots, cart-boxes, teakettles, iron bolts, axes, broad hoes, spades, ploughshare-moulds, lightning-rods, zinc, stoves, jugs, iron, wool, and negro pipes—such were a few of the articles Americans then found it necessary to have from abroad. Every package of them was sold at the block in South Carolina, to the great profit of the State, which laid a tax on sales at auction.

As the summer wore away and the eagerness to buy began to subside, a stimulant was applied in the form of credit. Purchases under five hundred dollars in value were paid for in cash before the goods were delivered; but on sums greater than five hundred dollars a credit of sixty days, ninety days, four, five, and six months was given, according as the amount of the bill was small or large, and the buyers became more eager than ever.

The beneficiaries of this system were the English manufacturer, the British ship-owner, the auctioneer, and the State and Federal Governments, which made great gains by the taxes on auction sales and the duties on imports. The chief sufferers were the American importer, the wholesale merchant, the American manufacturer, and the country merchant, who, buying on credit, purchased far more goods than he was ultimately able to sell or pay for.

But as the war duties were high and the people well disposed toward American manufactures, there did not seem to be any immediate cause for alarm. In many parts of the country, and chiefly in those where no mills existed, there was, it is true, a strong feeling against them. A favorite argument with men so disposed was, that the country was new that the West was yet to be settled, that the Government had vast tracts of land for sale, and that no steps ought to be taken toward the establishment of any industry which, by gathering men and women in towns and villages, stopped the purchase of public lands and hindered the movement of population toward the Mississippi. Others of the same mind looked on the employment of girls and young children in mills as ruinous to good morals and education. Yet, withal, the sentiment of the country was toward the encouragement of manufactures. A feeling was widespread that, as the people of the United States were independent of Europe politically, so they ought to be industrially, and that the present was the very time to become so. The long period of commercial restrictions and the war had turned capital from ships and commerce to mills and factories. The return of peace in Europe, by diminishing commerce and the carrying trade, would divert still more capital, and to employ it a home market was all that was necessary. Why should Americans toil early and late in order that they might send fifty millions of dollars to Great Britain, there to buy tapes and crockery, hardware and dry goods, which could just as well be made at home with a very little assistance? This assistance was to be derived from the patriotic determination of every man to wear none but American-made clothes, eat off none but American-made dishes, and use in his calling none but American-made tools and implements. Toward the accomplishment of such an end fashion could do much, and to set the fashion it would be well for the President, the secretaries, the senators, and members of the House to appear clothed from head to foot in goods of domestic growth and manufacture. A few went so far as to urge an amendment to the Federal Constitution giving Congress power to tax raw materials exported. But no suggestion was yet made of a tariff for protection. For that the manufacturers were responsible.

By the early autumn of 1815 the fleet-loads of English goods which had been hurried into the country and sold at auction, for prices in many cases much higher than the home manufacturer would have dared to ask, had completely prostrated the wool and cotton industry. A few months of peace proved to the makers of such goods that neither patriotism nor costliness were sufficient to allay the thirst for English wares. If, then, they were not to go down in ruin, prompt and vigorous aid must be rendered by the Government, and this aid they resolved to seek.

The position taken by these men was that during a time of great distress, caused by the interruption of commerce, they had, at much cost of time and money, begun the manufacture of cotton goods. The scarcity of men fit to superintend such operations, the enormous pay demanded by the few who were qualified, and the high rate of wages, had as yet prevented their undertakings becoming lucrative. This was to be expected, and was an evil inseparable from any attempt to set up new industries. But if a free and unrestricted importation of cotton goods was to be allowed, their factories would not only never yield a reasonable return, but would be shut, and every cent of capital so invested would be lost forever. Such a disaster would be widespread and deeply felt, for, not only were the establishments numerous and important, not only had they furnished the people and the Government, during the long period when trade was interrupted, with cotton goods better in quality and lower in price than could be had elsewhere, but they had also given a livelihood to thousands of women and children for whom agriculture afforded no opportunity, and had helped the South by using annually thousands of bales of cotton which, during the war, could not be exported, and, if the American mills were shut, would again be forced to seek a foreign market. "Is it wise," they asked, "to destroy such an industry, when it can be saved by so simple an act as the prohibition of the importation of foreign cotton fabrics of coarse texture? These fabrics are made in countries lying beyond the Cape of Good Hope, are shamefully manufactured, are not paid for in native products, and are thus trebly harmful to the country. Their importation discourages the growing of cotton, and so injures the South. They are of such poor quality that to sell them is a fraud on the innocent buyer, and they have on that account been shut out of almost every country in Europe and ought to be from America. They are, moreover, rapidly draining the country of its specie. A fine illustration of this has lately occurred at New York. A British ship arrived there in June from Calcutta, Madras, the Cape of Good Hope, and St. Helena, with nine hundred bags of sugar, indigo, spices, saltpetre, pepper, and nearly six hundred tons of piece goods, selected for the American market. At the liberal allowance of four ounces to the yard, six hundred tons would make about five million yards, which, at the current price of twenty-five cents per yard, would yield twelve hundred thousand dollars. One ship, and she a foreigner, was thus enabled to draw from the stock of industry of the United States a vast sum of money, which, under other conditions, might have been kept at home and expended for home-made goods."

The prohibition of India cottons, the manufacturers admitted, was contrary to one of the fundamental doctrines of political economy as then expounded by the best writers. Trade, these teachers held, should be left free and unrestrained. Heavy imposts and prohibitive duties on foreign commodities with a view to encourage domestic manufactures were, they said, ruinous to the interests of the people. In theory this was sound. But its reduction to practice supposed two conditions which had never yet existed. One was, that free trade should be accepted and acted on by every nation with which the United States had commercial relations. The other was, that freedom of commerce should never be hindered by war, nor by the watchful jealousy of rivals. "Is there any sign in Europe of the adoption of such a policy? Is there not much in the experience of the United States during the last ten years to show the folly of a nation adhering to a theory which makes it dependent on a foreign market for articles of universal and necessary consumption? England can send us woollens, India can send us cottons; let us, therefore, eat our sheep and make desert places of our cotton-fields, was once our cry. And what came of it? We subjected ourselves to an absolute dependence on Great Britain, were compelled to submit to indignities and insults, to orders in council, and to retaliatory French decrees, and drew down on ourselves all the sufferings of war by resisting her ungenerous and galling outrages. Every nation whose government has been wisely administered and whose physical condition did not prevent has always labored to put those articles on which it depended for subsistence or defence beyond the reach of accident or war by encouraging their home production at every sacrifice and at any expense. Whatever may be the policy of the United States toward other industries, this is the true policy toward the manufacture of cotton and woollen goods. It is greatly to the interest of England to continue the control she has so long held over our markets, and keep us in that condition of commercial dependence it is now in our power to throw off. From this purpose no prospect of present loss will deter her. By pouring in upon us during the current year a flood of goods at reduced prices she will endeavor to crush our infant manufactures, and without the prompt interference of the Government she will succeed."

As the autumn came on, these sentiments began to find expression in open appeals for legislative aid, in which the cotton and woollen manufacturers of Morris County, New Jersey, led the way, and when the Legislature met in October, petitioned for the removal of the State tax on their mills and on the spindles used in them. A committee of the Assembly recommended that the prayer be granted, and gave as a reason the belief that if these young industries were suffered to languish and droop under the powerful competition of European rivals our country would be independent in name only.

About the same time the cotton spinners of Providence met and, having decided to appeal to Congress, drew up a memorial and sent copies of it to manufacturers in all parts of the country with a request for like action. The memorial, after explaining the circumstances which induced the petitioners to engage in the business, and after narrating the hardships laid on them by the war, set forth the importance of the industry by the aid of statistics. There were, it seems, within a radius of thirty miles of Providence one hundred and forty factories, spinning each year twenty-nine thousand bales of cotton, which, when turned into cloth, would make twenty-eight millions of yards, worth six millions of dollars. To turn the raw cotton into the finished fabric would require the steady labor of twenty-six thousand persons, and yield them as wages near two and a half millions of dollars. But in truth a vastly greater number of men and women were employed, for the coloring was done, not in the factories, but in a thousand farm-houses by thousands on thousands of persons partially engaged in other pursuits. When to these were added the uncountable throng busy in occupations indirectly dependent on the manufacture of cotton—the sailors who manned the ships that carried the cotton up from the South, the draymen who carted the bales to the factory door, the artisans who made the machinery used in the mills, the farmers who supplied the spinners with food and drink, and the men who placed the finished product on the market for sale—the industry assumed an importance and an extent which, the petitioners believed, justified them in asking for protection. Let all cotton fabrics, nankeens excepted, made at places beyond the Cape of Good Hope be absolutely shut out by laws prohibiting their importation, and let heavy duties be placed on goods of coarser texture brought from other lands, and the petitioners would be content; their business would be saved from ruin, and the riches and prosperity of the nation greatly increased. In precisely the same strain were the memorials which came from Brunswick in the District of Maine, from New Hampshire, from Massachusetts, Connecticut and New York, from New Jersey, from Philadelphia, from the mill-owners on the Brandywine in Delaware, and from Baltimore.

Monday, December the fourth, was the time for the assembling of Congress, and on that day both branches were organized in the old Patent-Office. It was with real pleasure, however, that the members learned that new and more convenient quarters had been made ready for them during the summer. A number of citizens, greatly pleased that Congress had decided not to remove the Capital, and knowing that some years must elapse before the new buildings just beginning to rise from the ruins of the old would be fit for use, had formed a company, had applied to Latrobe for a plan, and in five months had erected a new capitol, which they now offered to Congress. It stood on Capitol Hill, on the corner of First Street, East, and Maryland Avenue. On the fourth of July the site was a cabbage-garden. Not a brick afterward used in the structure had then been baked, every stick of timber was then on the stump, and not a piece of stone had been taken from its quarry-bed. But such had been the energy of the builders that on December fourth the rooms were almost ready for occupation. That for the Senate was on the first floor, was about twenty-five by forty-five feet, and some fifteen feet from floor to ceiling. The chamber of the House was over that of the Senate, was forty-five by seventy-seven feet, and twenty feet in the clear from floor to ceiling. Each had a gallery and plenty of committee-rooms and offices. As soon as the House had organized by electing Clay Speaker, a joint committee was appointed to examine the new building, and made so strong a report in its favor that a bill granting the President power to rent it was rushed through both Houses without an hour's delay. Madison approved, and after a week spent in the old quarters, Congress moved into the new.*

Madison in his message alluded to the ending of our quarrel with Algiers, to the conclusion of a commercial convention with England, to the pacification of the Indians, to the difficulties of reducing the army to a peace establishment, and asked that provision be made for the veterans and invalids who had not been kept in the service. He reminded Congress of the state of the revenue, of the desperate condition of the Treasury, of the disorders of the currency, of the want of a circulating medium, and of the increase of the national debt, which on the first of October was one hundred and twenty millions, and told it that the time had now come to consider very seriously whether it would not be well to establish a national bank, protect domestic manufactures, begin a system of internal improvements, and found a national university in the District of Columbia. Each suggestion was sent to a committee; but the business of the session did not get well under way till the Committee of Ways and Means reported in January, 1816. Dallas, in his annual report, had suggested that the double duties on imports, which must expire by law in February, should be continued till the end of June; that the war rates on refined sugar, stamps, sales at auction, and on postage be retained; that the direct tax be reduced from six to three

---

* December 11 and 13, 1815.

million dollars; that the furniture tax, the watch tax, and the tax on certain articles made in the United States be repealed; and that a national bank be established.

The system of taxation which the Secretary thus proposed to destroy in part had been built up in the closing months of the war, and had been the subject of loud and bitter complaint during the summer and autumn of 1815. From the opening of the year to the middle of April hardly a month and sometimes not a fortnight went by without the imposition of a new tax or duty. On January first the tax on carriages and harness not used solely for farming purposes or for the transportation of goods and wares became law. Before the month ended a new direct tax of six millions was apportioned to the States; an annual duty was laid on household furniture, on gold and silver watches, and on certain goods, wares, and merchandise made within the United States. On the first of February the law providing for additional duties on spirits distilled within the United States and its Territories and on the license which every man must take out before he ventured to distil spirituous liquors went into effect. That same day existing duties on sales at auction were doubled, those on licenses to retail liquors were greatly increased, and rates of postage on letters made larger by fifty per cent. Later in February gold, silver, and plated ware and jewellery and paste made in the country were taxed. In March the direct-tax law was amended, and on the first of April the assessors and their assistants began the work of making lists of property subject to the tax. But the dark day was the eighteenth of April; for then it was that the manufacturers' tax, the household-furniture tax, and that on gold, silver, jewellery and watches went into force.

To the rates very serious objection was raised; but that which made the laws most offensive to the people was the burden imposed by the manner of collection. A farmer of the well-to-do class, having an estate worth three thousand dollars, a chaise, a watch, and using a minimum amount of tea and coffee, sugar and molasses, salt, and clothing subject to taxation, would, it was estimated, have his yearly expenses increased thereby at least forty-six dollars. A tradesman of the middle class, with a family of the ordinary size, and living in his own house, or owning his shop, would be taxed at least one hundred and eighty-six dollars by the Federal Government over and above all taxes laid by the State.*

If the tax payer were a small manufacturer of certain kinds of goods and wares; if he were a tallow-chandler, or brewed beer, ale, or porter; if he ground snuff, or made hats of leather, wool, or fur worth more than two dollars each; if he were an ironmonger, a saddler, a paper-maker, a shoemaker, a goldsmith, a jeweller, a tobacconist, a manufacturer of umbrellas or parasols, he must, in addition to his direct tax, his furniture tax, and the long list of taxes on the food he ate and the clothes he wore, take out a license to ply his calling, and give bonds with two sureties to pay the Government from five to eight per cent. on the value of all articles he made, if above the value of two or three dollars. Having secured his license, he must furnish the collector with a correct list of every implement, utensil, vessel, and machine used in his work, state the quantity and real value of material consumed in his business, and

---

* These taxes were distributed as follows:

Direct tax on house valued at \$2,000	\$10 00
Shop tax	37 50
Chaise	2 00
Watch	1 00
Furniture	1 00
	\$51 50
1 pair boots or 3 pair of shoes	2 00
1 hat	1 00
40 lbs. sugar, at 4 cts. duty per lb	1 60
80 lbs. candles, at 3 cts	2 40
Duty on leather paid by tanners and added to rent of shop	1 00
365 lbs. sugar, at 5 cts. lb. tax	18 25
20 lbs. hyson tea	12 80
10 gals. molasses	1 00
100 lbs. coffee	10 00
20 gals. spirits	10 00
12 " wine	7 20
No. 200 of European goods	60 00
No. 10, raisins, lemons, foreign fruit	4 00
No. 10, spices	4 00
	\$186 75

write down in a book full particulars of the exact denomination and quantities of the articles made, the number sold, the price, and the name of the buyer. These books must be open every day from sunrise to sunset to the inspection of the collectors, and each quarter the entries must be verified under oath.

The wrong and injustice of the tax were made plainer by the experience of a cigar-maker. Between the nineteenth day of April, when the tax began to run, and the twentieth of May, he had manufactured a quantity of plug tobacco and cigars, of which the market value was four hundred and twenty-five dollars. The cost of raw material and workmanship was three hundred and thirty-five dollars. This added to eighty-five dollars, the twenty-per-cent. tax on the market value of the article, made his outlay four hundred and twenty dollars, and left him five dollars profit on a month's work. In the face of these facts, he asked if any fair-minded man could deny that it was oppressive to tax him eighty-five dollars a month while his neighbors, the soap-boiler, the upholsterer, the cabinet-maker, the brush-maker, the brass-founder, and the coppersmith, were hammering away without having to pay one cent for the liberty of following their trades.

Another, a bank cashier in New York, gave the public an account of the way the furniture tax was assessed, and how, on his refusal to make a return of his furniture, because the value of it being less than two hundred dollars it was not taxable, the collector broke open his house-door and insulted his family. A shoemaker set forth his case, which was that of every cobbler and small dealer the country over. As the law required, he had taken out a license, had found two sureties to sign his bond, had purchased a book and in it had entered a record of each pair of shoes made, with the cost, price for which it was sold, and name of the buyer. He had then made the journey to the town of Keene, where the collector lived, to render a quarterly return. As no returns were required of sales amounting to less than ten dollars, he had but one pair of boots to account for, and on them paid a tax of forty cents. The expense of the journey to him was two dollars. But, as he must go four times each year and his sureties go once, the travelling expenses entailed on him by the odious tax in the course of a twelvemonth was fourteen dollars. Still another declared that he had paid a tax of seventy-four cents, and that to do this he had been forced to write out four quarto pages, take three oaths, sign the paper five times, and see the collector countersign three times.

That complaints such as these should weigh far more with the members of the House than with the Secretary of the Treasury, and that the Committee of Ways and Means should urge the repeal of every kind of internal tax, is not surprising. Ever since the days of John Adams and his stamp tax, his direct tax, and tax on household furniture, to hate all systems of internal revenue had been sound Democratic doctrine with the great body of voters. The committee, therefore, did no more than yield to the popular demand when, in a long report, they not only endorsed the plan of Dallas but asked, also, for the repeal of the taxes on sales at auction, on licenses to retail liquor, on spirits distilled in the United States, and for a reduction of the rates of postage. As this would produce a deficit, an increase of forty-two per cent. in the current rates of customs duties was asked for. The difference between the plan of the secretary and that of the committee so far as revenue was concerned was trifling ; * but the difference in principle was great, for the committee proposed that a sum of seven millions † of dollars, which would be lost by abolishing the internal taxes, should be made up by a heavy increase in the tariff, and this increase was but another name for protection. Each plan was to serve as a permanent peace establishment, and to produce a surplus revenue of nine millions and a half,‡ which the committee suggested should be used to increase the sinking fund # for the payment of the national debt, and to afford means for national defence and internal improvements.

As it seemed certain that questions of no common sort, involving principles of great weight, were likely to arise, the minority before the debate came on made an earnest effort to get rid of the previous question. The opportunity was af-

---

* The plan of Dallas was reported to yield a net revenue of $25,278,840, that of the committee $25,369,500—a difference of $90,660 in its favor.

† $7,064,340.

‡ $9,590,831.   # From $8,000,000 to $13,150,000.

forded by the report of the Committee on Rules and Orders and by the House going into the Committee of the Whole to consider it. But the effort failed; the committee rose without coming to any decision, the rule remained, and the debate on the new revenue system began. For a month and more it went on day after day, and most distinctly marked the opening of a new era. The opponents of the system—and they were very close in numbers to the majority—insisted that there should be no surplus, no internal taxes, no direct tax, and a reduction of customs duties to such rates as would yield just enough money to pay the expenses of a government economically administered. The friends of the plan insisted that the experience of the past should be the guide for the future, and gave it as their firm conviction that experience had shown the folly of longer adhering to the principles of government which belonged to the period before the war. "No taunt," it was said, "was so often uttered during the late struggle as that charging the Government with rushing hastily and unprepared into the contest. That we were unprepared is true; but it is now the intention of all patriots that such a condition shall never exist again. A part, and a large part, of the money to be raised by the new revenue system is therefore to be spent on national defence, or, as some gentlemen will have it, on a standing army and perpetual navy. We need a navy to defend our enormous coast line and to attack an enemy where she is most vulnerable, and that spot is in her commerce. It is true that we are now at peace with Great Britain. But three great points of difference are yet unsettled: She still holds Eastport and the islands in Passamaquoddy Bay; she is daily driving our fishermen from Nova Scotia and Newfoundland; she has not renounced the right of search, impressment, and paper blockades; and while these things remain unsettled, peace may not be of long duration. We need a regular army to defend our frontier and to garrison our coasts, to create a force ready to meet an enemy at a moment's notice and form the nucleus of an army around which the militia may gather. The militia is, indeed, the bulwark of our liberties. But dare we forget how the New England Governors refused to furnish militia; how the Governor of

Vermont recalled the few he sent; nay, how the militia stood debating on the banks of the Niagara River while their fellow-countrymen were taken at Queenston? We need an army, it may be, to punish the growing insolence of Spain. Our true policy is to maintain the army, increase the navy, fortify and strengthen points shown by experience to be vulnerable, provide in the amplest manner depots for the munitions and implements of war, and build military roads and canals that men and supplies may be easily carried from places where they exist to places where they are wanted. In short, let us act seriously, effectively, and on the great principle that it is wise in time of peace to prepare for war. Led on by Calhoun and Clay and William Lowndes, the new school Republicans carried the day, and the plan was adopted. A million a year for eight years was voted to the navy for ship-building; the duties on licenses to retail wines and liquors were diminished; the taxes on sales at auction, on spirits distilled within the United States, on household furniture, on gold and silver watches, and on certain goods of domestic manufacture were repealed; the rates of postage were reduced, and the direct tax made three instead of six millions.

The first part of the plan of the committee having been adopted, and a revenue of seven millions swept away by the abolition and reduction of internal taxes, the second part, providing for an increase in the import duties, followed of necessity. Some sort of tariff revision was imperative, for, as many of the double duties laid at the opening of the war were to stop one year after the war, and as peace was proclaimed in February, 1815, the House of Representatives of the Thirteenth Congress just before it dissolved instructed the Secretary of the Treasury to report a new tariff to take the place of the old. But Dallas in obeying this command had made a strong plea for protection. While performing the task assigned him he had, he said, been ever mindful of the fact that the United States had always regarded the establishment of home manufactures as a chief object of its policy. In the earliest acts of the Congress of 1789 the raising of revenue to pay the debts had been expressly connected with the policy of protecting manufactures. In 1790 Hamilton had been called on to report a plan for making the United States independent of foreign nations "for military and other essential supplies." In 1810 so great was the solicitude to know how far the country had become industrially independent that a census of manufactures had been taken. But it was during the time of the restrictive system and of the war, when the country scarcely knew where to turn for clothing, for blankets, for weapons, and for munitions; when the market was a scene of gambling and extortion, and when an illicit traffic with the enemy went on openly by land and sea—that the importance of domestic manufactures came home to the mind of every statesman and every patriot. In the preparation of the new tariff he had therefore been careful to so arrange the duties as to encourage and protect the manufactures which existed and which experience had shown were greatly wanted. These could be placed in three classes, according as they had been long established and could fully supply the home market, or had been recently set up and could but partially supply the market, or were just being introduced and left the country still dependent on foreign sources. For the first class he would have prohibitory duties, for the second a protective tariff, and for the third a tariff for revenue.

The suggestions of the Secretary were referred to the Committee of Ways and Means, and while before it the Committee on Commerce and Manufactures—to which had gone a bundle of petitions from wool manufacturers in Connecticut, New Jersey, Pennsylvania, and Delaware, representing an investment of twelve millions and an annual production worth nineteen millions of dollars—submitted a report in favor of protecting woollen goods by a heavy *ad valorem* duty.* Though the report was laid on the table, it was in effect an instruction to the Committee of Ways and Means, which reported a tariff bill, a few days later, providing for an *ad valorem* duty of twenty-five per cent. on imported cotton and woollen goods of all descriptions.† March twentieth the House went into Committee of the Whole and took it into consideration. In the debate which followed, no member of any note, save John Randolph, who had returned to the House, failed to

---

* Annals of Congress, March 6, 1816, pp. 1701–1711.   † March 12, 1816.

declare himself in favor of protection ; but the greatest diversity of opinion existed as to the amount of protection necessary. There were those who, led on by Webster, described themselves as friendly to such manufactures as then existed, but not friendly to any course of action by the Government which would produce manufactures. They were not anxious, as Webster said, to hasten the day when the great mass of American laborers should no longer find employment in the field, when the young men of the country should be forced to close their eyes upon the heavens and the earth and confine themselves in close and unwholesome workshops, when they should shut their ears to the bleatings of their own flocks on their own hills, that they might open them in dust and smoke and steam, "to the perpetual whir of spools and spindles, and the gratings of rasps and saws." The restrictive system and the war had never been undertaken for the purpose of creating manufactures. Yet they had been called into existence by these measures, and as they were in existence they should be protected. There were those again who, led on by Ingham, of Pennsylvania, declared that revenue was only an incidental consideration ; that a principle of national policy was at stake ; that the question was not the raising of dollars and cents, but the industrial independence of America ; the establishment and the encouragement of manufactures of every sort. There were those, in the third place, who claimed that protection should be limited to such manufactures as produced articles absolutely necessary in time of war and of the very first importance in time of peace ; and there were those who did not want protection in any form. In numbers this class was in the minority ; but it was a most formidable minority, and again and again in the course of the debate came within three or four votes of defeating motions.

Though the bill was intended to establish a tariff based on the broad principle of protection, the manufactures to be chiefly benefited were those of cotton and woollen goods and sugar. It was about these, therefore, that the debate centred. As the majority in the House was in favor of protection in some form, the two questions which arose were, How much shall be given ? and Shall it be permanent or for a short time ?

The suggestion of Dallas was that all imported goods of which cotton was the chief material of value should be charged with an *ad valorem* duty of thirty-three and a third per cent., and if they cost less than twenty-five cents per square yard, should be deemed to have cost that much and be taxed accordingly. For fabrics of which wool was the chief material of value he suggested a duty of twenty-eight per cent. The Committee of Ways and Means, thinking the rates too high, reduced both to twenty-five per cent.; but Clay, to see, as he said, how far the House was ready to carry protection, moved that the duty on cotton goods asked for by Dallas be restored. This was too much, and, the Committee of the Whole having rejected it, Clay moved that the duty be thirty per cent. This was carried; but Webster destroyed half its value by securing a limitation of the rate to a period of two years, after which it should be twenty-five per cent. for two more years, and then be twenty per cent. permanently. Yet even this was further than the majority, on second thoughts, was willing to go, and before the bill went to the Senate the rate was changed to twenty-five per cent. for three years, after which it was to drop to twenty per cent.

As passed, the bill was partly the work of the Secretary and partly the work of the House. It provided, as Dallas suggested, for prohibitory duties on cloths and foreign articles of which a full supply could be made at home; taxed at twenty per cent. *ad valorem* those of which a full supply could not be manufactured in the United States; and laid a tariff for revenue on a class of articles consumed in large quantities and almost entirely made abroad. There were five rates of *ad valorem* duties, instead of eight, as Dallas wished. There was a schedule of one hundred and nine articles on each of which a separate and specific duty was imposed. There was a free list, a discriminating duty on goods, wares, and merchandise brought in vessels not owned in the United States, and a continuation of the bounty and drawbacks on pickled fish and sugar exported. The vote, both yea and nay, was well distributed. But the strongest opposition came from New England, and the warmest support from the South. New England resisted, lest a falling off of imports should injure her shipping and commercial interests. The South approved, because she made sugar, raised cotton, and consumed a great quantity of coarse India cotton cloth, which was not paid for in native products, but drew away specie and threatened to ruin her banks. To protect the banks of the South on the one hand, and the Northern manufacturers on the other, the " principle of the minimum " was introduced, and the law provided that after June thirtieth, 1816, all fabrics of cotton—except nankeens direct from China—the cost of each square yard of which at the place whence imported (with twenty per cent. added if that place were the Cape of Good Hope or beyond it, and ten per cent. if elsewhere) was less than twenty-five cents, should be considered to have cost that much and the duty be imposed accordingly. The effect was to double and treble the rates and stop the importation of low-priced India or negro cloths, which thenceforth were produced in this country.

Unhappily for the friends of domestic manufactures, the framers of the tariff had utterly ignored the importance of an agent destined not only to break it down, but to destroy the manufactures it was intended to protect, prostrate the importing and retailing business, send tens of thousands of men into idleness and want, and involve the people heavily in debt. The overthrow of Bonaparte at Waterloo had been followed by a lasting peace, and the consequent exclusion of British-made goods from many of the ports and countries of the Continent. Thus deprived of lucrative markets in Europe, the English manufacturers turned their attention to the United States, and in the spring of 1816 began a second time to send over shiploads of their products, the larger part of which had not been ordered. The prospect of disposing of them in a legitimate way was poor, for the people, allured by the auction credit system of 1815, had bought far more than they could use or pay for, and, deep in debt, were not disposed to continue buying ; the tariff which became law on the last day of June had greatly increased the duties, and there was everywhere in the North and East a strong feeling in favor of domestic goods and a home market. Yet the British shippers were not discouraged, and in six months' time had triumphed over every obstacle. The disbanding of the British army threw out of employment thousands of men who, to earn a livelihood, were forced to rush into the ranks of labor, where competition with those already there lowered wages and put it in the power of the manufacturer to make his fabrics cheaper than heretofore, and sell them at prices most tempting. By the auction system he was enabled to destroy the business of the American importer and retailer, just as by false sales and invoices he was enabled to break down the American tariff. His plan for " getting under the tariff " was ingenious. He would send two agents to some city, as New York or Boston, and to one of them, purposely kept in ignorance of the value of the goods, he would pretend to sell them at a price very much less than the cost of manufacturing. The invoice setting forth this false statement of sale would then be presented to the American Consul at the port of shipment and, after endorsement by him, would be that on which duties were charged at our Custom-House. This broke down the tariff. But the goods were no sooner through the Custom-House than they were sold by the first agent to the second agent, who had in his possession a true statement of the cost and whose duty it was to place the articles on the market. All these men were out of reach of the law ; for the owner lived in a foreign land, the first agent had no knowledge of the value of the goods except the false invoice ; and the second agent was not a party to the entry at the Custom-House.

But the advantage these men had over the Americans, who paid current market rates abroad, and therefore more duty at home, did not end here. In the first place the Englishman hurried his packages to the auction block, and so avoided store rent, clerk hire, and the merchant license tax,* and secured an immediate sale.

In the second place, when an American merchant wrote an order for such goods as suited a particular market, and for such a quantity as could surely be vended, the British manufacturer would duplicate it in kind and quality and ship his own goods, invoiced at reduced prices, to America by the very same vessel

---

* For these facts I am indebted to a very interesting memorial of the American Society for the Encouragement of Domestic Manufactures to Congress.

that brought the merchant's, and by the aid of the auctioneer sell it before the importer had his packages in his store.* The importer usually sold by package to another class of merchants, who disposed of their goods by the piece to retailers and country shopkeepers, from whom they were purchased by the consumer. The country merchant always bought on credit and gave like credit to the farmer, who in turn paid in produce, which the store-keeper sold to the exporter, and with the proceeds paid his debt to the retailer and got new credit. But this trade was now utterly ruined. Not only were goods sold in their original packages at auction, but it became a common, every-day usage to sell them by the piece, by the gross, nay, by the yard. So far was this carried, that there was in New York city an establishment known as " The Ladies' Retail Auction Room," where, day after day, the women would assemble to bid against each other for a yard of lace, a pair of gloves, a dozen buttons, or a spool of thread.

In the third place, the auction encouraged a new kind of fraud. When the goods or wares in their original packages were under the hammer, the invoice could not be seen or their quality examined. Knowing this, the British makers had begun to turn out articles bad in quality though fine in appearance, and so defrauded the consumer. Goods were made to sell and not to wear.

After submitting to this state of affairs till it was impossible to submit to it any longer, the merchants and traders of New York city met at the City Hotel one day in December and petitioned the Legislature to put a stop to the retail auctions by taxing them out of existence. There ought, they believed, to be a duty of five per centum on all sales of broken packages—that is, on articles sold by the piece, the dozen, gross, or hundred, and a duty of ten per centum on sales of merchandise in less amounts. If this could not be, then every man ought to be allowed to vend his goods at public sale, and the monopoly of the business then enjoyed by twenty auctioneers abolished. Auctions, again, should be limited to

---

* Address of the American Society for the Encouragement of Domestic Manufactures to the People of the United States, p. 24.

the hours of nine to two, and should not be suffered to run on till candle-light.

There were then in New York twenty-nine licensed auctioneers, who in 1816 paid a State tax of one hundred and ninety-five thousand dollars on sales equal to thirteen millions of dollars. As their commission was two and a half per cent., the income derived was three hundred and twenty-five thousand dollars, of which one firm got fifty thousand. It may well be supposed, therefore, that the action of the merchants alarmed these men, who likewise petitioned the Legislature. The evil, they said, was temporary and would soon pass away. It was caused by the war and the sudden and extraordinary change in the condition of Europe. Taxes would not cure the trouble, but would agitate it by driving auction sales to other cities not so impolitic as to follow the action of New York. This argument had great weight with the Legislature, and no taxes were laid.

While the retailers and the auctioneers were thus contending before the State Legislature the importers carried their case to Congress. They dwelt long on the iniquity of false invoices, and auction sales, and on the need of building up American manufactures. They reminded Congress that when the war began the country was dependent on the enemy not only for powder and shot, but for clothing for the troops; that the demand for these articles led to an illicit trade along the frontiers which drew away specie, extinguished patriotism, and degraded national character; that patriotic citizens, knowing the needs of the ·country, had then embarked in domestic manufactures which had since absorbed capital to the amount of one hundred millions of dollars; that England, seeing her danger, had attacked this splendid industry, and by the auction and the false invoice was fast accomplishing her purpose. They asked, therefore, that the tariff of 1816, in place of being limited to two years, be made permanent; that the importation of cotton goods from beyond the Cape of Good Hope be prohibited, that smuggling by false invoices be stopped, and that foreigners be not allowed to become sureties for duties; that a tax of ten per cent. be laid on all foreign goods sold at auction; and that the officers of the army and the navy and all civil officials of the United States be asked to use American fabrics.

The merchants of Baltimore called for the appointment of inspectors to examine imported goods and see that false invoices were not used; for severer laws against smuggling; for a duty of ten per cent. on auction sales of foreign linens, cottons, woollens, silks and on articles made of metal; and a recommendation that every official of the United States, from the President down to the humblest seaman in the navy, and every official of each State, wear nothing made outside the United States.

At Pittsburg the manufacturers were in such distress that a committee was appointed at a meeting of citizens in December and charged with the duty of inquiring into the state of manufactures in and about the city. They did as requested, and reported that the makers of cotton and woollen goods, flint glass, and the finer articles of iron had suffered a most alarming depression in their business. One cotton factory, which used steam and occupied a three-story building, was closed, and all hands discharged. Two others had but half their usual force. The owners of a flint-glass factory which had done a business of one hundred and thirty thousand dollars a year could now with difficulty sell a fourth of their output. A wire-mill, a butt-hinge factory, and a currycomb factory were shut. As about two thirds of the population of Pittsburg were engaged in manufactures of some kind, the depression was strongly felt by the farmers for miles around. Indeed, while prosperity lasted, the consumption of all sorts of produce was so large that very little of the flour of western Pennsylvania went down the Ohio, while whole cargoes of bacon were imported from Kentucky, and a great fish trade was established between the seaboard, the lakes, and Pittsburg. But this prosperity the committee believed was rapidly declining. " The tariff of duties established by the last Congress," they said, " is wholly inadequate to stop the influx of British goods. They have continued to pour in upon us, drawing off our money, stopping our mills and factories, and piling up such a balance of trade against us that all the specie in the land cannot discharge it. Even Britain—that old, that im-

placable enemy of our manufactures—is satisfied and triumphant. Brougham, in a late speech in Parliament, after noticing the great losses suffered by the immense exportation of
goods to the Continent, said : ' The peace with America has
produced somewhat of a similar effect; though I am very far
from placing the vast exports which it occasioned on the same
footing with those to the European market the year before,
both because the Americans will pay—which the exhausted
state of the Continent renders very unlikely—and because it
was well worth while to incur a loss upon the first exportation
in order, by the glut, to stifle in the cradle those rising manufactures in the United States which the war had forced into
existence contrary to the natural state of things.' In the face
of this open avowal from the ablest of English statesmen, can
any one doubt that the policy of Great Britain is the extermi-
nation of American manufactures? Can any one doubt that
the present depression is the result of her policy and the ease
with which our own laws enable her agents to carry that policy
into effect?" When the meeting had listened to the report
it was ordered that a copy should be sent to Congress.

Appeals, memorials, petitions to Congress were well enough
in their way; but it was to the State Legislatures that the
manufacturers looked for the relief which, to be efficacious,
must be speedy. That auction sales were ruinous and ought
to be stopped was universally admitted; but it was also admitted that if one State taxed auctions out of existence, some other
State would surely encourage them, and in consequence no
Assembly responded to the calls for anti-auction legislation.
The only hope of the friends of domestic manufactures, therefore, was in the establishment of a home market and in such
limited protection as it was within the power of a State to
afford, and this they succeeded in getting. The General Assembly of Connecticut, four fifths of whose members wore
nothing of foreign make, resolved that, inasmuch as the cotton and woollen factories established within the State were,
from causes believed to be temporary, subjected to embarrassment, it was expedient that the people of Connecticut should
buy and use American cotton and woollen fabrics in prefer-
ence to those of any other land, and encourage and protect by

legal measures the factories set up among them. The joint Committee on Manufactures of the New York Legislature, after reciting the effects of peace on the European market of Great Britain and the efforts of England to get control of that of the United States, recommended that the senators be instructed and the representatives be requested to do their best to secure higher and permanent duties for the protection of the infant manufactures of the United States, and particularly those of woollen and cotton cloths; that the members of the Legislature, all State officers, and the delegation in Congress, be urged to wear American-made clothes; that no taxes be laid on the buildings and plant of cotton and woollen mills; and that manufacturers be exempt from militia service, labor on the highways, and jury duty in suits to the value of twenty-five dollars and under. In Pennsylvania the Senate, after deeply regretting that the State government could afford no adequate protection, called for a law exempting factories from taxation and workmen from duty in the militia, and bade the members of Congress do all they could to obtain such measures as would really protect and encourage home manufactures. The New Hampshire Legislature recommended that a society for the encouragement of agriculture and domestic manufactures be formed in each county in the State, and offered each so formed one hundred dollars to be used as premiums.

But the importers and the manufacturers were not the only men who found business dull. The shippers had the same complaint to make. As soon as the Treaty of Ghent was signed, the American commissioners addressed a note to those from Great Britain on the subject of commercial intercourse. Receiving no answer, the Americans supposed the ministry was waiting till the treaty had been ratified by the United States. But when news of the ratification came and still no reply was sent, our commissioners left Ghent and repaired to London. Even then three weeks passed, and an intimation of their intention to quit England was made before Castlereagh could find time to attend to them. Matters then went on rapidly, and on July third, 1815, a commercial convention was framed, and ratifications exchanged the following December.

The first part related to trade with the European possessions of Great Britain, and provided that neither power should lay a discriminating duty on the products or the ships of the other. The second part related to the British West Indies and North American possessions, and left each party free to regulate this trade as it saw fit. The third part had to do with Madras, Bombay, Calcutta, and the Prince of Wales Island, and specified that trade must be direct.

The stipulation forbidding a discriminating duty made it necessary to repeal the act imposing higher duty on vessels and goods brought in British vessels than on ships and goods brought in ships owned in the United States. When an act to do this came down to the House from the Senate a violent opposition arose. The limitation on the treaty-making power, the question how far the House was forced to carry out treaty stipulations, the question whether the treaty did not itself repeal the law, were discussed as they had never been discussed since the day, twelve years before, when the House was called upon to authorize the issue of stock to pay for Louisiana. The bill, by a small majority, was passed, and in a few months the country began to see and the shippers to feel the consequences. No branch of New England commerce was then more valuable than the transportation of plaster of Paris from Nova Scotia and New Brunswick to the Middle States, where it was chiefly consumed. But when the convention went into force the merchants and shippers of St. John's petitioned their Legislature to so regulate the trade that no plaster could be delivered in any port east of Boston in such a way as to enable an American coaster to carry it to the place of consumption. The prayer was granted and laws were passed, both by New Brunswick and by Nova Scotia, laying an export duty of twenty shillings a ton on plaster of Paris if delivered at any port east of Boston, and fifteen thousand tons of American shipping became idle.

But even this was not all. Great Britain, being free under the convention to regulate her colonial trade as she saw fit, returned to her old-time colonial policy, shut American ships out of the West Indies, and limited the carriage thither of American flour, pork, lumber, rice, corn, horses, mules, cattle, poultry, potatoes, peas, and beans to vessels owned by British subjects. The value of our products thus exported was six millions of dollars annually, and to carry them required eighty thousand tons of shipping. The enforced idleness of so many ships was bad enough ; but, what was worse, it gave advantage to English ships engaged in the trade between the British Islands and the United States which made it tenfold more ruinous. A merchantman laden with 'dry goods or hollow ware, with china or hardware, would come over from Liverpool to Boston or New York, would land the packages, and, after taking on a cargo of flour or lumber, would sail for the British West Indies. There she would load with sugar, rum, or molasses, and either return to the United States for cotton, or go directly home. The profits of this triangular voyage enabled her to bring British goods, wares, and merchandise from England to the United States for much less than the actual cost of transportation on an American vessel, which could not make a similar voyage. An English merchant-carrier could even afford to bring goods from Liverpool to New York at an actual loss, inasmuch as he could easily recover on the voyages from New York to the West Indies, and from the West Indies back to Liverpool, on neither of which could American competition affect him. In the hope of doing to American shipping what false invoices and auction sales had already done to American importers, manufacturers, and retailers, the direct trade between England and America was carried on by Englishmen so much below the cost of the voyage that during the summer of 1816 beef and tallow, butter, hams, and potatoes were actually brought from Galway and Newry to New York, where they undersold our home products.* Indeed, companies were formed to continue their importation. Thus the one trade which by the convention seemed to be on a basis of equality was in reality conducted in a way wholly favorable to England.

A few months of such reciprocity, added to the loss of the West Indian trade, sufficed to prostrate the shipping interests

---

* Advertisements of these importations may be seen in the newspapers, as the New York Evening Post, May 1, 13, and June 3, 7, 1816.

and bring back to memory the days of the long embargo. Half the tonnage owned along the seaboard and engaged in the coasting and foreign trade was said to have been laid up. The number was greatly overestimated; yet there was no seaport where many ships could not be seen dismantled and literally rotting at the wharves, while American sailors sought occupation abroad, and American shipwrights went off to New Brunswick to cut timber and build vessels to carry it to Europe or the Indies. Once more all branches of trade connected with ship-building languished, and thousands of mechanics were thrown out of employment.

When winter came the condition of the unemployed and their families in the great cities was such as to call for public assistance. There had never been a time when idleness and rum had not in every city produced a feeble-spirited and dependent class for whose relief charitable people had made provision. Some by their wills would bequeath to their native city a few hundred or a few thousand dollars, the interest of which was to be expended for bread, flour, or wood, to be given at stated times to the deserving poor. But the usual method was the organization of a relief society for the accomplishment of some definite purpose. Thus in the city of Philadelphia there were at that time the Society for the Relief of Widows and Young Children, the Humane Society, the Society for the Promotion of Industry, the Female Society of Philadelphia for the Relief and Employment of the Poor, the Female Hospitable Society, and the Society for supplying the Poor with Soup, which opened its doors about the middle of December of each year and doled out daily quarts of soup and loaves of bread to such needy persons as on investigation were found to be deserving. But the society had no sooner begun its good work in December, 1816, than its room was too small to hold half the applicants. Before a week had passed three hundred and five families were registered and supplied each day. As the number continued to increase, the managers early in February made an appeal to the public for donations of bread, vegetables, and money, which came in most liberally. But it was then so manifest that the distress was too widespread to be relieved by any single association, that a town meeting was held at the City Hall to take into consideration the distressed state of the poor. After listening to a few speakers and adopting a few resolutions, a committee was appointed for each ward in the city and for the adjoining district of Southwark, the East and West Northern Liberties, Kensington, Moyamensing, and the townships of Spring Garden and of Penn, to collect money and distribute supplies.

At New York like causes had produced like effects. A few kind-hearted citizens having opened a soup-house on the first of February, twelve hundred applicants were fed in twenty-four hours. Arrangements were then made to supply double the number on the following day; but again the demand exceeded all expectation, and a call was made for meat, vegetables, and money. The response was so hearty that another step was taken and a public meeting held at the City Hotel, where ward committees were chosen and more than nine hundred dollars subscribed by those present. The next day three thousand were given soup and bread, and from that time the number steadily increased till the first of March, when six thousand six hundred and forty persons were on the roll for a daily supply. At Philadelphia one of the soup-houses distributed between January and April twenty-four thousand quarts of soup to ten thousand and twenty-nine persons. Another had charge of seventeen hundred people.

CHAPTER XXXII.

POLITICAL REFORMS.

The many grave questions of a domestic character which thus occupied the attention of the people during 1815 dwarfed the interest they would otherwise have taken in another contest with Algiers. In one sense it was but a part of our struggle with Great Britain, for without the assurances of her agent that the American flag would be swept from the ocean, that our navy would be annihilated, that our arsenals would be burned, and our commerce ruined, the Dey would never have made war. No provocation whatever existed. But when the Dey heard that war had really been declared against England he went seriously to work to stir up strife, and found a provocation in the laws which regulate the motions of the earth and the moon. During seventeen years past the United States had been paying an annual tribute to the Dey; but as the Moors computed time by the moon, while all Christian people reckoned it by the sun, the Moorish year was the shorter, and this difference in the course of the seventeen years amounted to some six months in favor of the Dey. According to his mode of measuring time, he was therefore entitled to twenty-seven thousand dollars more than he had received, and for this sum a demand was made, and instantly complied with by Mr. Tobias Lear, the American Consul. It now became necessary to find a new cause of complaint, which the Dey accordingly did. The stores, he said, sent by the United States in place of money were bad in quality, and notified Mr. Lear to depart at once. The Consul might possibly have quieted the Dey even on this point; but, unhappily, two ships loaded with cables and anchors, powder and shot, and naval stores, a present from Great Britain, reached Algiers, and the Dey sent forth his corsairs, armed and equipped by England, to prey on American commerce in the Mediterranean. There was little to be destroyed, yet they made prize of the brig Edwin of Salem, sold the crew of ten men into slavery, and dragged an American citizen from the deck of a Spanish vessel. While the war with England lasted these outrages had to be endured; but, five days after peace was proclaimed, Madison asked that war be declared against Algiers. Congress willingly complied, and two fine squadrons, in charge of two gallant seamen, were soon assembled at Boston and New York. Captain William Bainbridge commanded that in the port of Boston. Captain Stephen Decatur commanded the fleet at New York. He was first to get under way, and with ten vessels, mounting two hundred and ten guns, put to sea on May twentieth. A short run across the Atlantic by way of the Azores brought the squadron off the coast of Portugal, where a sharp lookout was kept for the enemy. The foe was indeed not to be despised, for the Algerian fleet consisted of five frigates, six sloops of war, and a schooner, carrying, all told, three hundred and sixty guns. The crews were well drilled and thoroughly trained. The vessels were well equipped with every appliance of modern naval warfare and, what was quite as important, were commanded by Rais Hammida, the terror of the Mediterranean. Though every ship fell in with was spoken, nothing was heard of the enemy till June fifteenth, when Tangiers was reached, and Decatur learned from the American Consul that the Algerian admiral had passed the straits two days before in the forty-six-gun frigate Mashouda. Not a moment was lost in giving chase, and that same day the fleet anchored off Gibraltar, where Decatur was told that the vessels he sought were to be found off Cape Gata. As one despatch boat had been detected making for the cape to notify Rais Hammida of the presence of the American squadron, and another had been seen making all sail toward Algiers, Decatur again weighed anchor without loss of time, and, standing up the Mediterranean before a good breeze, sighted the Mashouda in the early dawn of June seventeenth. She was lying to off the coast, and as everything about her showed that her commander had no suspicion of the character of the squadron, Decatur gave the order, "Do nothing to excite suspicion," and bore steadily down upon her. But the order was misunderstood by the officers on the Constellation, who, when about a mile from the enemy, hoisted the American flag. Every other ship instantly displayed the English colors; but the Moor was not deceived, and crowding on all sail he made for Algiers, till the Constellation, which happened to be nearest, opened fire at long range and placed several of her shot upon his deck, when he came about and headed for Cartagena. Decatur in the Guerrière then bore down to close with him, and, reserving fire till his ship just cleared the yard-arms of the Mashouda, he poured in two broadsides in quick succession. The slaughter was dreadful. Rais Hammida was killed and the deck covered with dead and wounded. Yet the Moors would not surrender, but, putting up the helm, made every effort to escape. In doing so they crossed the path of the gun brig Épervier, which, though vastly inferior in size and armament, fired broadside after broadside till the Mashouda struck her flag. She was sent to Cartagena while the fleet sailed on in search of the remainder of the Algerian squadron supposed to be near at hand. No enemy was seen, however, till June nineteenth, when a sail was descried not far from Cape Palos and chased. A hard run of three hours' duration brought the stranger into water so shallow that none but the Torch, the Spark, the Spitfire, and the Épervier could follow, and as these kept on in hot pursuit, the Moors ran their brig aground and took to their boats. The prize, which was floated off and sent to Cartagena, proved to be the Estido of twenty-two guns and a crew of one hundred and eighty men, of whom eighty-three were taken prisoners.

As enough had now been done to make the Dey listen to reason, Decatur led his squadron toward Africa, and on the twenty-eighth of June sighted the glittering pile of houses which formed the city of Algiers. By the little fleet which approached it, the place would have seemed to an onlooker to be impregnable. The artificial mole which made the harbor bristled with two hundred and twenty heavy guns. Almost three hundred more were mounted on a wall of immense thickness which surrounded the city. Decatur, however, paid no attention to the dangers of the task he had to perform, but sailed boldly in with a white flag at the foremast and a Swedish flag at the main, and in a few hours had the Swedish Consul and the captain of the port on board. "Where," said Decatur, addressing the Algerian, "is your squadron?" "By this time," was the answer, "it is safe in some neutral port." "Not all of it," was the reply, "for we have captured the Mashouda and the Estido." At first the captain of the port would not believe it. But when the lieutenant of the Mashouda stepped forward and confirmed the news, he asked what were the terms of peace, and proposed that those charged with the duty of concluding it should land and begin negotiations. His purpose was so plainly to gain time that Decatur stoutly declared that peace must be made on the deck of the Guerrière or not at all, and the Moor went back to consult his master.

Next day he returned with full powers to negotiate, and was informed of the terms. The Dey must renounce all claims to future tribute; must set free all American prisoners without ransom; must repay in money the value of the goods and property taken from them; must pay ten thousand dollars to the owners of the Edwin, and guarantee that the commerce of the United States should never again be molested by Algerian corsairs. The agent of the Dey protested that the terms were too hard; declared that it was the late Dey, Hadji Ali, and not his master, Omar Pasha, who began the war; and claimed, now that Hadji Ali was dead, that Omar was not to blame. His protests and his arguments were of no avail, and, finding that Decatur would abate nothing, he asked for three hours' delay. "Not a minute," said Decatur, "not a minute"; and the captain of the port hurried ashore with the understanding that if the Dey accepted the terms he would return with a white flag in his boat.

When he had been gone about an hour, an Algerian ship of war loaded with Turkish soldiers was seen approaching the harbor. At the sight of the ship the Guerrière was cleared for action and was on the point of getting under way when the boat of the captain of the port was descried coming rapidly toward the Guerrière, with a white flag in her bow, and in a few minutes the treaty and the ten liberated prisoners, doomed to a yet more terrible fate, were on board. With as little delay as possible the men, rejoicing in their new-found liberty, were transferred to the Épervier, which, with a copy of the treaty, sailed for the United States. Lieutenant John Templar Shubrick was in command, and on July twelfth passed the Straits of Gibraltar, never to be seen again. The British West Indian fleet reported having seen a brig of her description during a very heavy gale, in which it is believed she foundered. But when and how she met her fate is still a mystery.

After the departure of the Épervier, Decatur sailed for Tunis and dropped anchor before the town on July twenty-sixth. During the war the American privateer Abellino had sent prizes into Tunis, a neutral port. But the Bey had suffered the British cruiser Lyon to retake them, and for this Decatur demanded the payment of forty-six thousand dollars within twelve hours. The terms were accepted, the money was paid, and Decatur went on to Tripoli, which he reached August fifth. Tripoli had doubly offended. The Bashaw had suffered the British cruiser Paulina to take out two prizes sent in by the Abellino, and had forced the American Consul to lower his flag. Decatur therefore demanded thirty thousand dollars for the lost prizes and a salute of thirty-one guns to the flag. The Bashaw blustered, refused, gathered an army of twenty thousand men, manned the batteries, and threatened to declare war. But when he saw Decatur taking soundings, he recalled the bombardment of 1804 and made peace. The money indemnity was reduced to twenty-five thousand dollars, and in consideration of this the Bashaw released ten Christians held as slaves. Two were Danes and the others Sicilians.

As all differences with the Barbary powers now seemed honorably settled, Decatur repaired to Gibraltar and joined the squadron under Bainbridge. Lest a withdrawal of all the ships should be followed by a renewal of the war while the Dey, the Bey, and the Bashaw were still smarting under their punishment, the squadron was divided. Part returned with

Bainbridge and Decatur to the United States. Part wintered at Port Mahon.

The precaution proved to be a wise one. During the winter and early spring of 1816 the Dey of Algiers saw many reasons for disliking the treaty. Flatterers and agents of all sorts were very busy persuading him that it was disgraceful to so humble himself before Christian dogs. The brig Estido, which Decatur had promised should be returned to him, and which was actually delivered to his officers, had been seized by the Spanish authorities as a ship captured within their waters, and for this the Dey blamed the United States. But more than all was the treaty made with Lord Exmouth by which Great Britain was forced to pay four hundred thousand dollars for the liberation of twelve thousand Neapolitans and Sardinians held in captivity. Decatur had secured the release of captives without paying a dollar. When, therefore, the squadron left Port Mahon in April and anchored off the mole at Algiers, and the American Consul presented the treaty duly ratified by the Senate, it was returned by the Vizier with such insolence that the Consul hauled down his flag and took up his abode on the Java.

Captain John Shaw, who commanded the fleet, instantly put his ships in position to bombard the mole, arranged his boats in two flotillas to attack the land and water batteries, selected the night for the attack, and was about to move when the commander of a French frigate discovered his preparations and sent word to the Dey, who at once submitted. A visit to the Bey of Tunis ended the naval operations on the Mediterranean, and in October all the ships save four sailed for home. The task was thoroughly done. At last our flag was respected, not merely by the Barbary powers, but by the nations whose dominions lay along the north shore of the Mediterranean Sea.

To our countrymen of that day, however, the work of Decatur seemed little more than the punishment of a horde of pirates. They were indeed proud of his success, and dined him and toasted him repeatedly. But they soon forgot the significance of his victories in the press of interest nearer home and apparently of more importance, for the summer and autumn of 1816 was a time of no little excitement, both political and industrial. The Secretary of the Treasury was required by law to do his best to force the banks to return to specie payments. The merchants and manufacturers were to adjust their business to the new tariff. The people were to choose presidential electors, and the members of Congress were to justify two acts of an odious character—the Compensation Bill, and the caucus nomination of President and Vice-President.

The law which, till 1816, regulated the pay of congressmen was that passed in 1789 by the first Congress that ever assembled under the Constitution. Though there were in that body numbers of men whose talents would in our time enable them to hold at the bar, in the business world, or as managers of great corporations, positions which would bring them many thousands of dollars yearly, their services as senators and as members of the House were thought by themselves to be amply compensated by mileage and six dollars for each day on which they attended during the session. The Speaker received twelve dollars per day and was the envy of members who, after spending six months at the capital, away from their homes and families, were paid, mileage included, nine hundred dollars.

But times had changed greatly since 1789. Board, lodging, food, clothes, rents, everything, had increased in price. Sugar had risen from twelve to twenty-five cents a pound, coffee from eighteen to thirty-seven, beef from eight to fifteen, pork from nine to twenty, and bacon from fourteen to twenty-five. The average salary for clerks, which had once been six hundred dollars, was then one thousand dollars. Not a little of the increase, it is true, was owing to the depreciated State bank paper which then formed the circulating medium of the country. But when every allowance had been made, the fact still remained that while the cost of living, daily wages, yearly salaries, all had risen, the pay of the member of Congress was still what it had been twenty-seven years before. This of itself was reason enough for a moderate increase. But a very different and much worse one was given for changing the manner and amount of compensation.

The House had been in session upward of three months; yet such grave questions as the establishment of a national bank, the protection of American manufactures, and a host of minor matters remained to be disposed of. In truth, but seven bills had been sent to the President, though the session was in its tenth week. As the Fourteenth Congress was eminently a Congress of reform, this slowness in the despatch of public business was felt to be discreditable. There was no reason, in the opinion of the reformers, why two hundred and eighteen gentlemen should give up six months or more of every year to the transaction of business which could just as well be done in three, and after casting about for the cause of the evil and for a remedy, they found both in the manner of compensation of members. The daily pay of six dollars, it was believed, had much to do with the slothful habits of the House and its long sessions, and a change from a per diem to a fixed yearly sum was suggested. On the fourth of March, 1816, accordingly, Richard Mentor Johnson asked for a committee to consider the matter. Such a change would, he said, be beneficial for three reasons : It would shorten the session; it would give members greater compensation if they acted with industry; and it would save money to the Government, for the shorter the sitting, the less the cost of fuel, stationery, and attendance. The sum need not be large ; indeed, it need not be a cent more than was then paid each member for being present during six months. Randolph supported the motion. " The present manner of payment," said he, " is disgraceful. Is it wonderful that we are considered by the people at large as no better than day laborers when we are willing to come here and work for something less than a dollar an hour, which is something more than you pay a man for sawing wood ? There should, too, be another change made. A member should be paid whether he attends or not. Is it to be presumed that because he is out of his seat he is idle ? Is the only diligent member the one who comes each day, writes and franks so many letters, reads so many newspapers, stitches together as many documents as he chances to find on his table, and adjourns when the clock strikes four ? " When Randolph had finished his characteristic speech the motion was carried and a committee appointed.

Two days later a bill was reported changing the pay from six
dollars a day to fifteen hundred a year for each member, and
to three thousand each for the Speaker and the Vice-President
or, if there were none, president *pro tem* of the Senate.

Those who opposed it were moved by all manner of considerations. Some would not support it at all, and declared it
to be utterly wrong. Some would approve it if the yearly
sum were reduced to one thousand dollars; others if the law
were not to apply till the meeting of the next Congress. But
the majority stood firm. Fifteen hundred dollars was not too
much. Should Congress sit nine months—and such sittings
were not unknown—each member would at the present rate
receive nineteen hundred and twenty dollars. Nay, there
were members on the floor at that moment who had been paid
fifteen hundred dollars for attending one session. Six dollars
per day in 1789 would go further than eighteen dollars per day
in 1816. The result was that men of talent and genius, the
men most wanted in Congress, could not afford to come unless blessed with private riches or willing to make great sacrifices for the good of the country. How many brought their
families? How many saved one cent of their pay? The
Speaker declared that, though he was given twice as much as
any other member, he for one could never make both ends
meet. The opposition answered that an increase of pay would
not be followed by the appearance of one more family at
Washington. Extravagant members would spend more, eco-
nomical members would take more home in their purses.
The very highest price asked for board and lodgings in Washington was fifteen dollars a week for a gentleman, four for a
servant, and eight for two horses, or twenty-seven in all, which,
taken from the weekly pay, left a surplus of fifteen. What
more did they want? Moderation, frugality, and economy
were the safeguards of men in public life. It ought not to be
supposed that in ordinary times any salary that might be
offered would bring to Congress the best talent in the country. Great crises might induce them to sacrifice their private
interests; but not such pay as the House could give. Randolph heartily approved of the bill, but did not believe the
new plan would shorten the session by a day. Members would

still have to be roused from slumber to hear the question and
to vote on bills concerning the merits of which they knew
nothing; the House would still at times be prevented from
adjourning because such men had not finished their letters or
sent off the last newspaper; debates would still be swelled to
great length by the inattention of members who would never
be attentive, while the House continued to be a bookbinder's
shop. Calhoun declared that he would like to see the sum
made twenty-five hundred. The extent, the population, the
wealth of the country made a strong Executive necessary.
The framers of the Constitution accordingly had given it the
preponderance in the Government by constituting it a branch
of government and bestowing on it all the patronage. The
sole check on an undue executive power was an able, intelligent, and experienced House. But such a House could not
be had unless the pay was enough to draw men of ability into
its seats and keep them there.

The House passed the bill within forty-eight hours after
its introduction, and, though the Senate was less hasty, it met
with small opposition and in two weeks was a law. That
some grumbling and complaint would be called forth was
fully expected. But that every man who voted for it would
be denounced from one end of the country to the other was
not expected. The newspapers, it is true, began to cry out
almost as soon as the law was known; but when constituents
and legislatures, grand juries and public meetings, joined in
the demand for the choice of men who would repeal the law,
the matter became most serious. The excitement was out of
all proportion to the interests concerned. Early in May a
grand jury drawn from the seven counties of the North Carolina district of the Circuit Court of the United States protested
against it as costly and ruinous in its tendency; for who,
said the jurors, will tug out a six months' session of Congress
when he will receive the same pay if the session be but one
week? Public business will be neglected or hurried through
without due and careful consideration. The change from
daily wages to a salary is a change "from the simple habits of
republicanism into the emoluments of power." At a meeting
of voters of Putnam County, Georgia, a "handsome compli-

ment" was paid to Mr. Benjamin Huger, who voted against the bill, and an effigy intending to represent its supporters was burned amid loud acclamations. In New York the constituents of Mr. Throop made such an outcry that he resigned and indignantly refused to sit out his term. The Legislature of Rhode Island described the increase of pay as wholly inconsistent with the economy of Republican institutions and with the dignity of the representative, as it raised the doubt whether he accepted his place from a sense of duty to the people or was "allured to it by the emoluments of office," and called for the repeal of the law. At Lynchburg a petition was framed and passed about for signatures. It was addressed to Congress, and told the members frankly that they were not forced into their seats; that they had sought their places and the votes that put them there; and that if they did not like the wages they ought not to have undertaken the work. A grand jury of Wilkes County, in Georgia, following the example set by that in North Carolina, presented the conduct of the supporters of the law as deserving universal detestation, and called on the voters to return no man to Congress who was not hostile to the measure. A great meeting of citizens of Nashville demanded that every member of the Tennessee delegation in Congress who voted for an increase of pay should instantly vacate his seat. Once started, the opposition spread rapidly through the States. Indeed, it was soon almost impossible for fifty men to gather together for any purpose, civil or political, without condemning the salary act. For years past it had been the custom for patriotic citizens to meet on the fourth of July and toast the illustrious characters and the famous events in our history. But when they assembled in 1816 they all, without regard to party, found room in their list of toasts for one consigning to private life "the fifteen-hundred-dollar characters" who had so well cared for themselves. At a fourth-of-July meeting the citizens of Jackson County, Georgia, adopted a long preamble denouncing their congressmen, and in a set of resolutions declared their intention not to return the present members, and called on the new candidates to make known their views on the Compensation Law in the Georgia Journal.

How deep and widespread this detestation was began to be apparent when the returns came in from the August and September elections. Among the States where congressmen were chosen at that time of year was Kentucky, in whose delegation of ten were two men of national reputation—Johnson, who made the motion which brought the matter of compensation before Congress, and Henry Clay, who spoke and voted for the bill. Yet each was now bitterly reproached by his constituency. "Wherever I went," said Clay to the House of Representatives, some months later, "I do not recollect to have met with one solitary individual of any description of party who was not opposed to the act; who did not, on some ground or other, think it an improper and unjust law." Benjamin Hardin, of the same State, declared that hatred to the law was the one sure road to office and popular favor. If a man came into a county court to be appointed a constable or a road surveyor, nothing would do but he must enter his solemn protest against the Compensation Act. If a demagogue wanted to get into the Legislature, the first thing he did was to put up in the inn or tavern frequented by his constituents a statement of his dissent. Clay and Johnson did, indeed, come safely through, and were re-elected ; so, too, did Desha, who had voted against the bill. But Hardin and six others were not returned to Congress. Philip P. Barbour, of Virginia, another member who, like Desha, opposed and spoke against the law, declared that when he went back to Virginia he found there a "fixed and settled discontent at the measure." Georgia sent back but one of the old members, South Carolina but three out of nine, Maryland but four out of nine, and Pennsylvania thirteen out of twenty-three. From Ohio, from Delaware, from Vermont, not one was returned. Connecticut re-elected two out of seven. When the House met again in December it was found that nine members had resigned in disgust, and that new men, all hostile to the compensation law, had been appointed in their stead. The punishment was unreasonable, and, as is so often the case in great outbursts of popular anger, was harmful, for, of all the Congresses which up to that time had assembled under the Constitution, the ablest and the most useful was that so ruthlessly swept away.

Side by side with the election of congressmen went the choice of presidential electors. The question, " Who shall follow Mr. Madison in the presidential chair?" had been generally asked as early as the close of the war, for it was known that, according to what was fast becoming established usage, a nomination would be made by a caucus of Republican congressmen early in 1816. The friends of each aspirant began, therefore, at once to work in their chief's behalf. Madison himself leaned strongly toward Monroe, who, his supporters declared, had retired from the contest in 1808 with a more than tacit understanding that he was to be the next President. But the jealousy and hatred nursed by a portion of the New York Republicans had by no means died out. It had spread to the most popular and influential leaders of the party. The time had come, in their opinion, for the Virginia dynasty to end. There ought again to be a Northern President. But, as New England was Federalist in politics and in their view disloyal, the choice should be confined to the Middle States, or, in other words, New York. A quiet and earnest effort was therefore made during the summer of 1815 to prepare the Legislature to urge and the State delegation to support the claims of Daniel Tompkins, then Governor of the State. As Congress met before the Legislature, some assemblymen who were friendly to Tompkins made a canvass of such Republican congressmen as were likely to attend the congressional caucus. To their delight they found that discontent with the Virginia dynasty was quite as strong south of the Potomac as north of it; but to their chagrin the Southern members flatly refused to support Tompkins because he had never been in national politics, and brought forward William Harris Crawford. The appearance of Crawford as a possible candidate really narrowed the contest to himself and Monroe. Nevertheless, the Republican members of the Legislature of New York went through the form of requesting the Republican congressmen of the State to present and support the Governor's name in the general caucus at Washington. But a State convention in Rhode Island and a legislative caucus in Pennsylvania came out so strongly in favor of Monroe that all hope of securing a Northern President was given up, and the opposition united on Crawford. The next step was to call the meeting, which was done by sending a written notice through the mail to every Republican member of the two Houses of Congress. The circular bore neither date nor signature, but fixed the twelfth of March, at seven o'clock in the evening, as the day and hour for a caucus to consider the propriety of nominating candidates for President and Vice-President. The opponents of Crawford, seeing in this the hands of his friends, instantly took it up, and in an editorial in the National Intelligencer, a Republican journal published at Washington, forbade the meeting. The authors of the call, said the editor, are unknown. No one owns it or appears to know anything about it. It is certain that it did not originate with the friends of Mr. Monroe, and they surely will not attend on such an invitation.* The meeting, in consequence, was postponed four days lest the revolt of the followers of Monroe should reduce the caucus to a small minority. The intervening time seems to have been spent in smoothing over the trouble, and on Saturday evening the members met in the chamber of the House of Representatives. The question first to be considered was whether or not a nomination should be made. To decide it, Clay moved that it was not expedient to make any recommendation. On the vote being taken, it was found that the nays had it. A New York member then moved that the practice of naming candidates for the offices of President and Vice-President by members of Congress was expedient, and ought to be continued. This passed, and in a little while Monroe was chosen the presidential candidate over William H. Crawford by a majority of eleven votes. As every one knew that Crawford would never consent to run for the vice-presidency, which was still looked on as an office of no importance, the two nominees were Governor Tompkins, of New York, and Governor Snyder, of Pennsylvania, and Tompkins was chosen.

From this famous caucus twenty-nine Republican members stayed away. Five sent proxies and were counted as present. Twenty-four flatly refused to attend. But this symptom of

---

* National Intelligencer, March 12, 1816.

discontent gave small indication of the general displeasure, not over the choice, but over the manner of the choice. Journals and men, who never for a moment intended to vote against Monroe, vented their anger upon the caucus. The Constitution, it was said, declares that no member of Congress shall be appointed an elector. But when a nomination is equivalent to an election, and that nomination is made by congressmen, are they not in reality the electors? The poor people seem to have nothing to say in the matter. Their masters have directed, and they must obey. Our servants have usurped our places. They have seized on the drawing-room and parlor, taken the keys and the plate, and thrust us into the kitchen. Nine seems to be the lucky number. It gave Dallas the bank on a Thursday, and Monroe the Presidency on a Saturday.

To this the Republican journals, as the mouthpieces of Republican voters, made answer: We deprecate the caucus method of nomination. We admit that it has much the appearance of an unwarrantable assumption of the rights of the people. But it is not. The congressmen meet as citizens, acting in the interests of union and harmony, single out one man and bring him to the attention of the electors. The electors are not bound, though they are asked, to support him. They are quite at liberty to choose some one else. The caucus system, moreover, has grown out of the nature of our free institutions. In a country where all are free to nominate, this piece of political machinery is necessary, in order to prevent a dozen men being put in nomination and defeat thus assured. Only when the people waver in their choice does the caucus become dangerous. In this case the people have not hesitated. They are all for Monroe. The East sees in him one of the last of that glorious band of patriots of the Revolution from whom no man should ever be allowed to take the presidency. The West remembers him as the man so instrumental in the purchase of Louisiana. The South recalls with gratitude his efforts to open the Mississippi. He is the choice of the people. We may, then, wave all question as to the manner of his nomination. The end has fully justified the means.

So far as the people were concerned this was strictly true. Everywhere Monroe's nomination was approved. Even in New England, when the spring elections came, great Republican gains were made. In New York the Legislature, which had been Federalist in 1815, became Republican in 1816, and this in spite of the fact that the Republicans, led on by Martin Van Buren, had by an infamous proceeding stolen the Assembly but a few weeks before. There were then one hundred and twenty-six members of the Assembly, but so close had been the election of 1815 that each party secured sixty-three. But ere the Legislature met, one Republican had died, another had gone abroad for his health, and, as one Federalist was too ill to attend, the numbers of the two parties were : Republicans sixty-one, Federalists sixty-two. It happened, however, that the seat of Mr. Allen, the Republican from Ontario County, was contested by Mr. Fellows, the Federalist, who, though he received seven more votes, was refused a certificate by the county clerk because some of the ballots were cast for Hen. Fellows, when, according to law, they should have been cast for Henry Fellows. As this gave the Republicans a majority of one, the announcement was made openly that when the House met they would elect a Speaker and Council of Appointment—an announcement which so incensed the Federalists that on the first day of the session they refused to attend, stayed out in a body, and prevented a quorum. On the second day, fearing their constituents would not approve such conduct, they all attended, and, despite every effort they could make, a Republican Speaker and clerk were elected. It was then moved to expel Mr. Allen instanter ; but the Republicans defeated the motion and proceeded to choose a Republican Council of Appointment by the casting vote of the Speaker, and having thus secured the patronage of the State by the aid of the vote of Mr. Allen, they unanimously unseated him and gave his place to Mr. Fellows.

As one of the duties of the Council of Appointment was to appoint the clerks of the counties, the opportunity for repeating this fraud to any extent seemed to have been secured by the Republicans. The Federalist members of the Assembly therefore made a long address to the people, reciting the facts and calling on them to make their decision accordingly.* This the people did, and at the election held in 1816 made the Assembly Republican by a large majority.

In Maryland, where the election was sure to be close, the Federalists in their turn attempted to resort to fraud, and selected the town of Annapolis as the place of their operations.

Under the Constitution of Maryland the State Senate was chosen every five years by a body of electors sent from the counties. But it so happened that the number of these men had nothing whatever to do with the population of the districts they represented, and that the city of Baltimore, where some six thousand votes were cast, and the city of Annapolis, where the voters were never more than two hundred and sixty, each chose one elector. Now the Federalists wanted but one more elector to secure a Federalist Senate for five years; and as Annapolis was Republican by about thirty majority, they decided to colonize the city and carry it. But no citizen could vote in Maryland who had not resided for six consecutive months in one city or county. During the last days of February and the first week of March, therefore, the people of Annapolis were not a little surprised to notice groups and bands of laborers and mechanics flocking to their city till some forty men had arrived and put up at the taverns. They said they were in search of work. But when it was seen that—though no work was to be had—they still lingered at the taverns, paying their bills and showing very little concern that none of them were busy, the party leaders of the Republicans suspected it was politics and not work that caused the singular migration, and soon unearthed the plot. Indeed, they proved that the pretended laborers were hired, for twenty dollars a month and their board, to go to Annapolis, acquire residence, and vote for the Federalist ticket. Such an outburst of indignation followed this discovery that the men were discharged and the attempt abandoned. Party spirit in Maryland ran high; yet the Federalists suffered badly in consequence of their efforts to colonize, and when the presidential election took place they chose but three of the eleven

* American Daily Advertiser, February 21, 1816.

electors. With this they had much reason to be pleased, for, save in Massachusetts, Connecticut, and Delaware, not another electoral vote was secured by their party. The admission of Indiana into the Union added three more members to the Electoral College and raised the number of votes to two hundred and twenty-one; but as one member did not vote in Delaware, and the three Federalists in Maryland refused to attend at the State Capitol, but two hundred and seventeen ballots were cast, and of these, Monroe and Tompkins each received one hundred and eighty-three. Thirty-four were given to Rufus King, the Federalist candidate for the presidency, and the same number scattered among four apparent candidates for the vice-presidency.* On February twelfth the votes were counted in the presence of the Senate and House, and Monroe and Tompkins declared President and Vice-President for the next four years, beginning March fourth.

The widespread condemnation of the caucus system of nominating candidates afforded an excuse for again introduc-

---

* The electoral vote by States was :

STATE.	PRESIDENT.		VICE-PRESIDENT.				
	Monroe.	Rufus King.	Tompkins.	J. E. Howard.	James Ross.	John Marshall.	R. G. Harper.
New Hampshire...........	8	..	8				
Vermont................	8	..	8				
Massachusetts...........	..	22	..	22			
Rhode Island............	4	..	4				
Connecticut............	..	9	..	..	5	4	
New York..............	29	..	29				
New Jersey.............	8	..	8				
Pennsylvania............	25	..	25				
Delaware...............	..	3	..	..	..	..	3
Maryland...............	8	..	8				
Virginia................	25	..	25				
North Carolina..........	15	..	15				
South Carolina..........	11	..	11				
Georgia................	8	..	8				
Kentucky..............	12	..	12				
Tennessee..............	8	..	8				
Ohio..................	8	..	8				
Louisiana..............	3	..	3				
Indiana................	3	..	3				
Total..............	183	34	183	22	5	4	3

ing in Congress an amendment to the Constitution which had often been proposed both by individuals and by States. The mover on this occasion was Israel Pickens, of North Carolina, who laid before the House a joint resolution providing that the Constitution of the United States should be so amended that in each State both members of the House and electors of President and Vice-President should be chosen in districts.

Pickens, and those who supported him, took the ground that their proposition introduced no new principle into the Constitution, but merely defined the mode of using a most important one already there; that steadiness and uniformity in the exercise of it was greatly to be desired; and that uniformity could only be secured by a constitutional amendment. "So long," said they, "as the States are free to change the mode whenever they please, all will be fluctuation and uncertainty. We shall see, as we have seen, in the same State, now a general ticket; now a resort to the district system; now a choice by the Legislature, according as the needs of the ruling party will be best served. The disgraceful struggles which cost New York her electoral vote in 1789, and almost deprived Pennsylvania of hers in 1800 and Massachusetts of hers in 1812, and the sudden change in New Jersey on the very eve of an election, are but so many cases in point. If it be asked why the district system is recommended to be made the uniform system, we answer, because it is equitable, just, and democratic. To choose representatives by a general ticket and electors by State Legislatures is contrary to the spirit of our Government, which is essentially a popular one. The voice of the people expressed at the polls is the only sovereign and independent use of authority known to this nation. By the district plan the voters are enabled to know something of the candidates. They can judge by their own knowledge who is entitled to their support. They do not need the interference, the dictation of a caucus. They are not hampered by a general ticket of many names, some of whom they may not know and others of whom they may not like. The elections, confined to narrow limits, will be free from intrigue, corruption, and public excitement."

"Pray, Mr. Chairman," said those who answered these

arguments, "why is uniformity desirable? Of what consequence is it to New York that in Virginia electors are chosen
by general ticket, or to Virginia that in New York they are
chosen by the Legislature? It is, to be sure, a fancy, rather
pretty than otherwise, that the whole Union should be marked
off into lots thirty miles square, and that on the same day and
in the same manner the men of each district should vote for
electors or representatives. But does anybody suppose that
uniformity is then obtained? Not at all; for in Virginia none
can vote but landholders, while in Maryland any man over
twenty-one may have a voice in the election. Does anybody
suppose the districts will be laid off without regard to the political ideas of their inhabitants?"

"Mr. Chairman," said a member, "I had the honor of a
seat in the Legislature of New York when that State was last
divided into districts for the purpose of electing members of
this House; and how were they laid off? Why, with the
sole view of returning supporters of the administration, and
for this purpose counties were cut and slashed in every direction; districts of every shape were manufactured; cities were
sundered, and parts whose political character was not of the
right sort were joined with counties a hundred miles away;
towns were torn out of the very heart of one county and
annexed to others—in short, no device, however shameful,
was omitted to secure the result, and the result was secured.
Gentlemen, we have heard of the senatorial districts of Massachusetts, and of the name to which one of them gave rise,
and how, in Maryland, in order to get a Republican elector of
President and Vice-President, the county of Montgomery was
most unnaturally divided and a part, strongly Federalist, joined
to the city of Baltimore by a narrow strip which runs the whole
length of the county of Anne Arundel. With these facts full
in view, can we hope for any good from the districting plan?
Sir, the source of all the evils of which we are complaining is
the legislative caucus. And will districting stop the caucus,
prevent State intrigue, palsy executive influence, prevent executive interposition?" Before voting, the resolution was
divided, and though each part was carried in the Committee
of the Whole by a handsome majority, it was so apparent that

the support of two thirds of the members could not be obtained that the House laid the resolution on the table.

While still smarting under the punishment administered for the Caucus and the Compensation Bill, the members of the Fourteenth Congress had gathered in their hall on December second in no amicable frame of mind. So indignant were they that when a Virginia member, who had taken care to be out of the House in March when the yeas and nays were ordered on the bill, moved that the Committee on the Judiciary be instructed to report a bill to repeal the Compensation Law, the House refused to consider it. Nevertheless, when Johnson asked for a special committee to inquire into the expediency of repeal, the request was granted. On the committee, besides Johnson, were Daniel Webster, William Findley, the father of the House, Timothy Pitkin, now gratefully remembered as the most accurate and painstaking statistician of his time, and three others of lesser fame. Webster wrote the report which defended the act and recommended a return to daily wages. Debate was put off till after the holidays in order that all the members might be in their seats; but when it began, no other business was considered for nine days. During that time every phase of the question—the depreciation of money; the rise in the cost of living; the purchasing power of six dollars in 1789 and in 1816; the duty of the representative to bow before public opinion; whether tirades in the newspapers and resolutions of public meetings could be considered as the expression of public opinion; the right of constituents and legislatures to instruct or request—was under discussion. At length, when debate was over, the House decided to take the money, repeal the act after the close of the session, and leave the matter of pay in future to be settled by the Congress elected on that issue.

The Compensation Law put to rest, the House, about the last of January, turned once more to public business, and with characteristic energy placed eighty-one acts and resolutions on the statute books before the fourth of March. All were important, but a few were especially so. One authorized the people of Mississippi to form a State constitution. Another organized the new territory of Alabama. A third admitted the State of Indiana into the Union. A fourth regulated the trade in plaster of Paris and stopped its importation from any country from which it could not be brought in vessels of the United States. The act was, of course, in retaliation for the plaster laws of Nova Scotia and New Brunswick. A fifth, the Navigation Act, was aimed directly at Great Britain and Sweden, and provided that, beginning on October first, no goods, wares, or merchandise should be imported into the United States from any foreign port or place except in vessels of the United States, or in such foreign ships as truly belonged to the citizens or subjects of the country in which the goods, wares, or merchandise were grown, produced, or made. Yet another—an " act more effectually to preserve the neutral relations of the United States"—was the most lasting and important of all, as it defined the attitude toward warring nations we have so carefully maintained ever since. The subject of neutral relations was brought up by the complications growing out of the revolutions in Spanish America.

It will be remembered that the invasion of Spain by Napoleon and the accession of his brother to the throne was the nominal cause of a general revolt of the Spanish viceroyalties and the establishment of juntas to rule in the name of Ferdinand VII in America. But the fall of Napoleon and the restoration of the Bourbons in the person of Ferdinand had not been followed by a return of the provinces to their ancient allegiance. A taste of even such liberty as they enjoyed was enough, and one of the first acts of the King after regaining his throne was to attempt to reduce Buenos Ayres, Cartagena, and Mexico by force. In the struggle which ensued, not a little help in men, money, and supplies was drawn by the rebels from the United States. Ship after ship, armed and equipped for fighting, cleared from the Custom-Houses at Baltimore and New Orleans as merchantmen, and, after touching at some port specified in the papers, would hoist the flag of New Granada, or the United Provinces of Mexico, and begin to rob, plunder, and destroy the commerce of Spain. Some, without going through the form of entering the port for which they had cleared, would throw off their merchant character the moment they were on the high seas, would mount their guns, raise their flag, and prey on the commerce of a nation at amity with the United States. In other instances ships from the revolted provinces, with the flags of their governments at their mast-heads, would enter our ports and buy guns, powder, and food, enlist men for the armies, and even take on board as passengers citizens of the United States who were to serve in the army of the insurgents.

As soon, therefore, as diplomatic relations were renewed with Spain, in 1815, a demand was made upon the administration that such violations of neutrality should be stopped. The demand would have been made long before were it not for the fact that since 1808 no diplomatic relations of any kind had been held with Spain. She was then engaged in her struggle with Napoleon, whose brother Joseph occupied the throne, and was governed by the Supreme Central Junta, which claimed to act in the name of the deposed Ferdinand VII. This junta in 1809 sent out Don Luis de Onis to be Envoy Extraordinary and Minister Plenipotentiary to the United States. But on his arrival, in October, 1809, he was assured that, much as the United States applauded the efforts of the Spaniards, eager as we were to maintain a good understanding with Spain, he could not be received as Minister from the provisional government. So long as the crown was in dispute the United States would be neutral. During six years, therefore, he remained in this country, entering protests against the action of the Government in Florida affairs that never were answered, writing for the press under an assumed name, and gathering a curious mass of matter out of which he constructed in after times a statistical account of our country, called a " Memoir upon the Negotiations between Spain and the United States of America which led to the Treaty of 1819." At last, in December, 1815, as no doubt existed in the mind of Madison as to who was to have the Spanish crown, Don Onis was received as Minister, and began at once to press for the prosecution of the men concerned in breaches of neutrality. He reminded the Secretary that it was a well-known fact that "a factious band of insurgents and incendiaries" had long continued to infest Louisiana, and especially New Orleans and Natchitoches; that under the lead of José

Alvarez de Toledo and José Manuel Herrera, who had issued some fifteen hundred commissions, troops were being openly raised and armed within the United States for the purpose of " lighting the flame of revolution in New Spain " and robbing the peaceful subjects of the King, his master. He complained that ships under the insurrectionary flag of Buenos Ayres, Carthagena, and the Congress of Mexico had been allowed to enter the ports of the United States and land and sell cargoes of goods plundered from Spaniards on the high seas, and he asked that these practices be broken up, that the men engaged in them be punished, and that the ships of the revolting provinces be shut out of our ports.* Monroe replied that the United States was under no obligation to surrender any inhabitant of Spain or her provinces on the demand of the Spanish government; that no such inhabitant could be punished in the United States for acts done out of it, and that, in the present disorganized state of many countries, where government repeatedly succeeded government, the President had ordered collectors of the ports not to make the flag of any vessel the criterion of its right of entry.   Nevertheless, that all the facts might be known, the complaints of Don Onis were referred to the United States District Attorney in Louisiana, who denied that troops had been openly enlisted in Louisiana, but admitted that attempts had often been made to arm and fit out ships, and that while some of these failed, others had been successful.   Indeed, he sent a long list of men prosecuted, ships libelled, and Spanish property seized and restored since the peace under the act of June, 1794.† The attorney at Baltimore furnished like information, and Madison, taking up these two letters, made them the subject of a special message as soon as Congress assembled. The message was referred to the Committee on Foreign Relations, whose chairman called on the Secretary of State for information as to what was needed to make the laws effective. Monroe answered that when the character of a vessel was suspected, bonds should

---

* The Minister of Spain to the Secretary of State, December 30, 1815.   American State Papers, Foreign Relations, vol. iv, pp. 422, 423.

† Letter of John Dick, Esq., to the Secretary of State, March 1, 1816.   Ibid., pp. 104, 105.

be required, and that when the presumption of an intent to violate the neutrality of the United States was strong the collector should have power to seize and hold the vessel.   As the law then stood, it was in two parts.   The first, the law of 1794, called forth by the conduct of Genet, provided that no citizen of the United States could accept a commission from any foreign power, or enlist or cause others to enlist in the service of a foreign power, or fit out vessels within the United States to cruise against or set on foot military expeditions to fight against friendly nations.   The second part, the law of 1797, forbade a citizen to go without the jurisdiction of the United States and do any of the acts the law of 1794 prohibited him to do within the United States.   There was nothing, however, to prevent a citizen and a foreigner doing together what neither could do alone.   Indeed, to avoid the law, it was merely necessary for an American to build, arm, and equip a vessel in any of our ports and sell it to a foreigner, who could take it out of our waters and use it to plunder the commerce of friendly nations.   Moreover, the President had no power to interfere to prevent the commission of offences.

The bill which the committee presented provided, therefore, among other things, that whoever fitted out or armed a vessel to be used for cruising against the subjects of a power at peace with the United States, or sold such a vessel knowing that the purchaser intended to so use it, should be fined and imprisoned; that the owners of armed vessels should give bonds not to employ them against friendly nations; and that collectors of the ports should seize and detain suspicious craft till the will of the President was known, or the owners gave bonds not to be guilty of a breach of neutrality.   The bill was eminently wise and proper.   But Spain was to be greatly benefited by it, and the recollection of the many injuries suffered at her hands raised up a strong opposition.   Her demand for the Mississippi valley at the end of the war for independence, her refusal to recognize the boundary line of thirty-one degrees, her long occupation of our soil, her refusal to open the Mississippi, the reluctance with which she made the treaty of 1795, her refusal to pay for spoliations committed on our ships and commerce in her ports, her protest against the purchase of Louisiana, and the dispute which had so long been raging over the limits of Florida and Louisiana, were not forgotten. Of all foreign nations she was undoubtedly at that moment the most hateful to the great mass of the people in the South and West, and their dislike was plainly reflected in Congress. Indeed, the majority in favor of the bill, which on principle ought to have received every vote, was but thirty-four in a House of one hundred and fifty-four. Of the sixty nays, thirty-two were given by men from States south and west of Pennsylvania. Every vote cast by Ohio, Kentucky, Tennessee, and Louisiana was against the bill, for Spain had no friends in the valley of the Mississippi. In the whole New England delegation she had but three enemies.

Among the bills which failed was one creating a fund for a general system of internal improvements, which Madison vetoed in the last hours of his term of office. The ceremonies which attend the inauguration of his successor were performed in the open air in 1817, for the first time since 1789. Monroe had informed the president of the Senate that, according to custom, he would take the oath of office in the chamber of the House of Representatives, and the Senate committee had drawn up an elaborate order of exercises. The President-elect, attended by the heads of departments, the marshal of the district, the marshal of the day, and the mayors of the district, was to have been met at the door of the House by the Senate committee of arrangements and escorted to the Speaker's chair. On the right was to sit the president of the Senate, with the ex-President and the Speaker on either hand. To the left of the chair were to have been the foreign ministers and their suites, while the justices of the Supreme Court were to sit at a table in front of the chair. Behind them were to be, first, the senators, then the members of the House, and then as many ladies as space would allow. The gallery was to be open to the public. Unhappily, before the day came, a quarrel arose between Clay and the committee, and the use of the chamber of the House was refused. The enemies of Clay declared that he was angry because Monroe had not selected him to be Secretary of State, a post then looked on as that of the "heir apparent to the presidency." His friends declared

that he did not think the floor of the room was strong enough
to support so great a crowd.   But the truth seems to be that a
serious disagreement existed concerning the use of the furniture belonging to the House, and that, as Clay would not yield,
the committee erected "an elevated portico" in front of the
Congress hall, and on this Monroe delivered his speech and
took the oath of office in the presence of "an immense concourse of officers of the Government, foreign officers, strangers,
and citizens."   Such a concourse, it was said, "had never before been seen in Washington, the number of persons present
being estimated at from five to eight thousand."   When the
speech was ended and the oath taken a single gun announced
the fact; salutes followed at the navy yard, at the Battery, at
Fort Warburton, and from some pieces of artillery on the spot,
after which the President was escorted to his house by a long
cavalcade of militia and citizens on horseback and in carriages.
That night there was a fine ball at Davis's Hotel.

That Clay was deeply offended was shown by his conduct,
for of all the distinguished men in Washington on that day,
he alone did not attend the inauguration.   The place which
he so much coveted was given to John Quincy Adams.   The
secretaryship of the Treasury went to William Harris Crawford.   John C. Calhoun became Secretary of War, and B. W.
Crowninshield Secretary of the Navy.

The selection of these men was a matter of several months,
and before appointing them Monroe announced his intention
of visiting all the forts and posts along the seaboard from Baltimore to Portland, and from Portland westward to Detroit.
About the end of May, accordingly, he set out, spent the first
Sunday in June at Baltimore, visited the battle ground where
Ross was killed, examined Fort McHenry, inspected the militia,
and, after receiving and replying to some fulsome addresses,
took the steamboat for Philadelphia.   His intention was to
make the journey a tour of duty.   Congress, as he told the
people of Baltimore when they invited him to a public dinner,
had voted large sums of money for the fortification of the
coast and inland frontier, and for the building of ships and
naval dockyards, and had made the executive largely responsible for their faithful construction.   That he might carry out

this trust he must see the works in process of building, and
for this purpose—and for this purpose alone—he had undertaken the journey. He could, therefore, "·assume no style in
regard" to his countrymen other than that of a fellow-citizen.
But the people were determined to treat him not as he wished
to be treated, but as the chosen ruler of a great and prosperous
nation. Since the days of Washington no President had ever
shown himself to the people. Since the days of Adams no
President had ever entered New York or New England, nor,
indeed, so much as crossed to the north bank of the Potomac
save to go to Washington. The appearance, therefore, of
Monroe in the cities of the Middle and Eastern States aroused
an outburst of enthusiasm which turned his tour of duty into
a triumphal progress. The old prejudice against him as a
Southern man, as a member of the Virginia dynasty, as a
President inimicable to the interests of the North and the
East, disappeared instantly. Men of both parties joined in
giving him such a welcome as had never been extended to any
of his predecessors. At Philadelphia, at Trenton, at New
Brunswick his approach was heralded by the discharge of
cannon. He was met at the outskirts of the towns by the
municipal authorities, by the militia, and by crowds of people,
all eager to behold a President, and escorted through the streets
to the sound of ringing bells and what was then called a "*feu
de joie.*" While at New York he visited the Battery, Harlem
Heights, West Point, the forts in the lower bay, and the State
Arsenal, where a salute was fired from two guns taken by the
corps he commanded at the battle of Trenton. Stern Democrats were somewhat disgusted at the stress which the Mayor
in his address laid upon the fact that "the Chief Magistrate
of the nation" had come to the city "in the capacity of a private citizen," and by the request of the aldermen that "His
Excellency" would sit for a portrait. But this was nothing
to what was to come, for the farther east he went the greater
became the enthusiasm which he excited. At New Haven, to
which place he travelled by steamboat, he won the hearts of
the people. It was not, said a newspaper in describing his
reception, the sound of artillery, nor the ringing of bells, nor
the splendid procession that expressed the feelings and senti-

ments of the people, but the general spirit of hilarity which showed itself in every countenance. "The demon of party for a time departed, and gave place to a general outburst of national feeling." At Hartford he was addressed as the "political father and guide" of the people, and congratulated "that the spirit of party, with its concomitant jealousies and misrepresentations, no longer render alien to each other those who ought to be bound together by fraternal affection." When Bristol was reached he stopped for a few hours "at the splendid mansion of George De Wolf" to "partake of refreshments." But as he drew near to the house he noticed that the entrance was strewn with roses, and when he departed the ladies showered them upon him. From Bristol he went by steamboat to Providence, where he held a public reception, and then hurried on to Pawtucket, where he was shown the first Arkwright machine ever erected in this country. After bidding farewell to his Rhode Island friends, Monroe crossed the boundary into Massachusetts, was met at Dedham by one of the Governor's aides, and was escorted with the utmost ceremony to Boston neck, where the municipal authorities, the grand committee of reception, squadrons of cavalry, foot militia, and thousands of citizens on horseback and in carriages awaited his coming. With these for an escort he entered the city and passed through streets lined, it was said, with fifty thousand people. There might easily have been that number, for every inhabitant of Boston, from the school children to the Governor, seemed determined to do their utmost to entertain the President. The six days of his stay were marked by an uninterrupted succession of breakfasts, dinners, receptions, excursions, salutes, congratulatory addresses, and every kind of civic and military honor. But the effect on the people was most astonishing. In no city in the land had party hate been so savage as in this stronghold of Federalism. Friendships had been embittered, families had quarrelled, society and whole neighborhoods had been parted because of differences of opinion on political questions. With the arrival of Monroe, however, the community suddenly realized that peace had removed old causes of animosity, and that issues which two years before had been vital were then extinct. "The visit of the President," said the Chronicle, " seems to have wholly allayed the storms of party.   People now meet in the same room who, a short while since, would scarcely pass along the same street.   If no other effect is produced by the President's visit, this alone will be an ample remuneration to him for the journey.   It is found that citizens of opposite parties are not so unworthy of reciprocal respect as before they were thought to be."   Another journal spoke of the visit of Monroe as " an event which has a more direct tendency than any other to remove prejudices, harmonize feelings, annihilate dissensions, and make us indeed one people, for we have the sweet consolation that the President will be President not of a party, but of a great and powerful nation." A third remarked that ever since Monroe's arrival " party feeling and animosities have been laid aside, and but one great national feeling has animated every class of our citizens." The Centinel observed that during the " jubilee many persons have met at festive boards, in pleasant converse, whom party politics had long severed."   What took place in Boston was but an example of what had already taken place everywhere. When, therefore, the Boston Centinel dubbed the times " the era of good feelings," the whole country recognized the fitness of the epithet, and used it, and the eight years of Monroe's administration have, in consequence, ever since been known by that name.

From Boston, Monroe pursued his way eastward through Lynn, Salem, Beverly, Newburyport, York, Dover, and Kennebunk to Portsmouth, where he turned westward, and, crossing New Hampshire and Vermont, went down Lake Champlain by steamboat to Plattsburg, and so to Ogdensburg, which he reached late in July.   From Ogdensburg he went by water to Sackett's Harbor, whence a naval vessel carried him to Fort Niagara.   A short visit to the Falls and to Buffalo followed, after which another sloop of war took him to Detroit.   There his westward journey ended, and, turning homeward, he entered Washington in September, and was escorted by the citizens to what has since been known as the White House.   It was still far from completed; but it was habitable, and in it Monroe took up his abode—a wiser man than when he left the Capitol.

CHAPTER XXXIII.

THE ROUTES OF TRANSPORTATION.

THE extraordinary events which attended the tour of Monroe through New England proved to him that he was more truly than any of his predecessors the president not of a party, but of a great and united people. What he saw across the mountains must have convinced him that the questions he would have to deal with would be of home, not of foreign, origin; and that in settling those questions the West would have a most decisive influence. During the last three years the growth of the West had been phenomenal, and had taken place at the cost of the East. There had never been a time for thirty years past when the population of the country had not been moving westward. But over and over again the rate of movement had been decreased or accelerated by the general condition of the people. In good times it was slow; in bad times it was rapid. The long period of distress which followed the Revolution and continued till after the adoption of the Constitution sent the people westward in such numbers as threatened to depopulate the Atlantic States. But with the outbreak of the French revolution; with the opening of the French and Dutch West Indian ports to neutral commerce; with the demand for American flour and grain, lumber and fish, pork, and produce of every sort; and with the employment of thousands on thousands of American ships and sailors in the carrying trade between the French, Dutch, and Spanish possessions in America and the parent countries, flush times returned. Once more all classes found employment. Once more the wild rush westward was checked, and the people held on the seaboard or turned into the valleys of the Mohawk, the Genesee, and the Susquehanna, whence produce could easily be floated to a market. The influence which this state of affairs had on the movement of population is well illustrated by the history of the settlement of Kentucky and Tennessee as compared with that of Ohio. The allurements which from 1787 to 1791 brought so many New Englanders to Marietta and to Cincinnati, having been destroyed by the Indian War and the better opportunities afforded by central New York, the population of the Territory of the United States Northwest of the River Ohio almost ceased to grow. But that of Kentucky and Tennessee, coming from a region little benefited by the commercial prosperity of the Eastern and Middle States, went on increasing steadily, and after 1796, when the Spanish treaty opened the Mississippi river to trade, multiplied so fast that in 1800 there were two hundred and twenty thousand people in Kentucky and one hundred and five thousand in Tennessee. In that same year the Government adopted the system of selling land in Ohio on credit, and this, coupled with the return of peace in Europe and the consequent decline of business in the agricultural and commercial States, sent another wave of population into Ohio which enabled it in 1803 to enter the Union as a State. Such was the rush that for the moment it seemed as if Indiana must soon follow Ohio. But in 1803 war was renewed in Europe, and trade and commerce received such an impetus as was never known before or since in the history of our country. The demand for sailors, for shipbuilders, for artisans, for mechanics of every sort, for farm produce, for lumber, was astonishing. No inducements any longer existed to go beyond the mountains, and emigration to Ohio again diminished only to be again increased by the commercial depression which began with the long embargo and continued till the end of the war. Burdened with taxation, deprived on a sudden of all means of support, in debt, and liable at any moment to be imprisoned for being in debt, farmers, artisans, mechanics, tradesmen who had long been held on the seaboard by the flush times which preceded the war, now sold their possessions for whatever they could get, and, quitting the Atlantic States forever, hurried away to find new homes along the shores of the Great Lakes or on the eastern slope of the Mississippi valley.

Unhappily, no records of this movement in any sense complete are now to be found; but from such information as can be gathered from town documents and newspapers, toll-gate returns, and private letters, it is certain that till 1812 the stream of emigrants travelling westward along the great highways was steady and large in volume, and that the class of people was such as no State could afford to lose. Thus a letter from Robbstown, in Westmoreland County, Pennsylvania, a village lying directly on the western highway to Pittsburg, announces that in one month, toward the end of 1811,* two hundred and thirty-six wagons, with men, women, and children, and six hundred Merino sheep, passed through on their way to Ohio. Four of the wagons were attended by sixty persons, but, as it was then customary to consider eight as the average in such cases, it is probable that not far from eighteen hundred persons were concerned in this migration. Yet the record is confined to one month and to one town. The Indian uprising and the war did much to retard emigration in 1812; but dull times, the coast blockade, the taxes, and the disorders of the currency so accelerated it that in the winter of 1814 the exodus from the seaboard States became alarming. Old settlers in central New York declared they had never seen so many teams and sleighs loaded with women, children, and household goods travelling westward, bound for Ohio, which was then but another name for the West. One account describes the roads passing through Auburn as thronged all winter long "with flitting families from the Eastern States." Another, from Newburg, in New York, declares that during one day in July six wagons with seventy persons, all from Massachusetts, entered and left the village for the Ohio, and that scarcely a week passed without its citizens "witnessing more or less emigration of the same kind."

As the year wore away the belief was expressed that when autumn came it would be found that the worst was over, and that the good times it was expected would follow peace would

---

* October 6 to November 6, 1811.

keep people on the seaboard. But the good times did not return. The condition of trade and commerce, of agriculture and manufactures grew worse instead of better, and the western movement of population was more pronounced than ever. Reports from Lancaster state that one hundred moving families had been counted going through the town in a week, and that the turnpike was fairly covered with bands of emigrants. At Zanesville fifty wagons crossed the Muskingum in one day. Ohio, which in 1810 contained a population of two hundred and thirty thousand, was believed to have four hundred thousand in 1816. Indiana increased the number of her inhabitants during the same period from twenty-four thousand to seventy thousand. The census of 1810 gave Kentucky four hundred and six thousand inhabitants, but a careful estimate in 1816 fixed the number at more than half a million; yet Kentucky had made no small contribution to Missouri. It was said, with much truth, that it seemed as if Virginia and Carolina, Kentucky and Tennessee had agreed to pour their citizens into Missouri and Illinois for the purpose of making them States. Day after day every ferry on the Ohio and the Mississippi was crowded with passing families and their negroes, wagons, carts, and carriages. Both in North Carolina and in Virginia the removal of so many people was felt seriously, and measures to stop it were urged in their Legislatures. That of North Carolina, during the session of 1815, appointed a committee to consider the matter of inland navigation. Apparently, this had little to do with the migration of her citizens. But when the committee reported they declared that want of inland navigation was depopulating the State. With an extent of territory, said they, sufficient to maintain a population of ten millions of souls, we can boast of but something less than six hundred thousand, and it is plain that this number, under present conditions, is not likely to be much increased. Within twenty-five years two hundred thousand people have removed to the waters of the Ohio and the Tennessee, and it is mortifying to see that thousands of rich and respectable citizens are still moving West each year, to be followed by thousands of poorer citizens who are literally driven away by the prospect of poverty. In the Virginia

Legislature a Committee on Roads and Internal Navigation attributed a like condition to the same cause. "While many other States," said the report, "have been advancing in wealth and numbers with a rapidity which has astonished themselves, the ancient dominion and elder sister of the Union has remained stationary. How many sad spectacles do her lowlands present of wasted and deserted fields, of dwellings abandoned by their proprietors, of churches in ruins! The fathers of the land are gone where another outlet to the ocean turns their thoughts from the place of their nativity, and their affections from the haunts of their youth."

Fed by this never-ending stream of new-comers, the West was almost transformed. Towns grew and villages sprang up with a rapidity which even in these days of rapid and easy communication would be thought amazing. Mount Pleasant, in Jefferson County, Ohio, was in 1810 a little hamlet of seven families living in cabins. In 1815 it contained ninety families numbering five hundred souls, had seven stores and three taverns, a meeting-house, a school-house, a market-house, a machine for spinning wool, a factory for making thread, and forty artisans and mechanics representing eleven trades. Within a radius of six miles of it were nine merchant mills, two grist-mills, twelve saw-mills, a paper-mill, and a factory for fulling woollen cloth. The town of Vevay, Indiana, was laid out in 1813, and was not much better than a collection of huts in 1814. But in 1816 the traveller down the Ohio who stopped at Vevay found himself in a flourishing county seat, with court-house, school-house, and public library, stores, taverns, and seventy-five dwellings, occupied by a happy population who boasted of having among them thirty-one mechanics of various trades; of receiving three mails each week, and of supporting a weekly newspaper called the Indiana Register. Forty-two thousand settlers are said to have come into Indiana in 1816, and to have raised her population to one hundred and twelve thousand. That so many made their abiding place on her soil and not in Ohio was due to better opportunities for acquiring land and to the admission of Indiana into the Union as a State.

Letters from New York describe the condition of that

State west of Utica as one of astonishing prosperity. Log cabins were disappearing and frame and brick houses taking their places. Villages were increasing in population at the rate of thirty per cent. a year. The pike from Utica to Buffalo was almost a continuous village, and the country for twenty miles on either side was filling up with an industrious population. Auburn, where twenty years before land sold for six shillings an acre, was the first town in size and wealth west of Utica, and land within its limits brought seven thousand dollars an acre. Fourteen miles west was Waterloo, on the Seneca river, a village which did not exist in 1814 and which in 1816 contained fifty houses. Rochester, the site of which was a wilderness when the war closed, had a printing-house, a book-store, and a hundred houses.

With the approach of winter the rush westward, for the first time in our history, suffered but little decline, and put on an aspect it had never before worn. Farmers and men well to do were in the minority, and artisans, mechanics, professional men, merchants' clerks, and representatives from the very poorest ranks of society were greatly in the majority. Despair of better times and the wild stories which came back from the West seem to have inspired them with a hope of acquiring a competence in the new land beyond the mountains, and to see men and women making the journey thither on foot became a common sight, and at times a most pitiful one. A family of eight, on their way from Maine to Indiana, walked all the way to Easton, Pennsylvania, which they reached late in February, dragging the children and their worldly goods in a handcart. A blacksmith from Rhode Island made his way in the dead of winter across Massachusetts to Albany. In a little cart on four plank wheels a foot in diameter were some clothes, some food, and two children. Behind it trudged the mother with an infant at the breast and seven other children beside her. The father and a boy of twelve pulled the cart. A family of seven passed through Bridgeport, Connecticut, in March. They had come down from Three Rivers in Canada, the men drawing a small cart on four plank wheels, and the women and larger children following on foot. Yet another family, consisting of man, wife, and five children, passed through Woodbury, New Jersey, with all their household goods in a wheelbarrow. They were walking to Ohio. Still another couple with seven children were so destitute that the man carried his property on his back.

These, it is true, were extreme types; but they were fair examples of the class that was to follow, and which a few months later began to choke the ferries and crowd the western highways. Early in the spring families set forth from almost every town and city along the seaboard. Their departure excited no comment, for in general but few went from any particular locality. But the moment they struck the great highways in New York and Pennsylvania their aggregation produced an almost continuous stream of wagons, carts, and foot parties. A traveller who had occasion to go from Nashville to Savannah in January, 1817, declares that on the way he fell in with crowds of emigrants from Carolina and Georgia, all bound for the cotton lands of Alabama; that their place of meeting was Burnt Corn Springs; that he counted the flocks and wagons, and that, carts, sleighs, gigs, coaches, and wagons all told, there were two hundred and seven conveyances, twenty-nine herds of cattle, twenty-seven droves of hogs, and more than three thousand eight hundred people. At Haverhill, in Massachusetts, a train of sixteen wagons with one hundred and twenty men, women, and children from Durham, Maine, passed in one day. They were bound for Indiana to buy a township, and were accompanied by their minister. Within thirteen days seventy-three wagons and four hundred and fifty emigrants had passed through the same town of Haverhill. At Easton, Pennsylvania, which lay on the favorite westward route for New Englanders, five hundred and eleven wagons with three thousand and sixty-six persons passed in a month. They went in trains of from six to fifty wagons each day. The keeper of Gate No. 2 on the Dauphin turnpike, in Pennsylvania, returned two thousand and one families as having passed his gate bound west between March and December, 1817, and gave the number of people accompanying the vehicles as sixteen thousand. Along the New York route, which went across the State from Albany to Buffalo, down the lake to Westfield, and on by way of

Chautauqua Lake to the Alleghany, or across New York and by land to the Alleghany river, the reports are just as astonishing. Two hundred and sixty wagons were counted going by one tavern in nine days, besides hundreds of people on horseback and on foot. The editor of the Genesee Farmer declared he met near the town of Hamilton a train of some twenty wagons and one hundred and sixteen persons on their way to Indiana, and all from one town in Maine. That they were the party from Durham already mentioned is not unlikely.

Mingled with these emigrants as they hurried westward were little bands of a religious sect which arose no one knows when or where, and, after flitting across the country and attracting public attention for a time, disappeared somewhere on the prairies of Missouri. They called themselves "Followers of the true Christ," whose prophet had come from some place in Canada, and was described by them as a man of most austere habits, who rejected surnames, forbade marriage, allowed his followers to cohabit promiscuously, and had not changed his clothes in seven years. The men ate standing, made a virtue of uncleanliness, declared that their sick were never healed nor their dead buried, and frequently did penance for their sins. The women when they prayed fell prostrate on the ground face downward. One such band with five wagons full of household goods, and followed by some fifty men, women, and children, passed down Cherry Valley. Another crossed New Jersey. Others were noticed elsewhere on the western route leading to Indiana; but all seemed to have started in Vermont and to have grown in numbers as they went.

The migration from the seaboard had become so great by 1817 that its effects were visible. Towns and cities ceased growing. Some were almost depopulated. Others made but trifling gains. In New York the increase of population between 1810 and 1816 was but thirty-six hundred, and had it not been for the thousands of emigrants that came in from the Old World the depopulation of the Atlantic States would have been yet more perceptible. The distress which followed the pacification of Europe, the disbanding of the armies and navies, the enormous war taxes, and the general depression of trade and agriculture, sent the middle classes of England, Ireland, and Germany to our shores by thousands. During 1815 hardly a ship came over from France or Ireland without a score or two of emigrants. As is always the case under such conditions, the best men came first, so that in 1816 the British journals began to lament the departure of the tillers of the soil. It was a shame to see hundreds of farmers and mechanics, the editors complained, hurrying to America to increase her wealth by their labor in times of peace, and help defend her by their arms in time of war. One newspaper cited the case of some Lincolnshire farmers who sold their stock, and, quitting four thousand acres of good land, sailed for America with the curate of their village. The middling orders, said another, endeavoring to save something of the wreck of their fortunes, are collecting in various parts of the kingdom with a view to exportation. In three English villages public meetings were held, where the idea of going to America was discussed and heartily approved. As they were all farmers, they desired to continue as such in the United States. But they had heard of the high price of labor, and, considering this a serious obstacle, it was decided to article some young laborers out of employ for two years, give them a fixed salary, and take them to America. But when it was announced, the difficulty was not in engaging but in selecting the men from the crowd that offered.

The general demand of the press was for parliamentary action to stop what was called a " ruinous drain of the most useful part of the population of the United Kingdom," for all over it the people were preparing to depart by neighborhoods and by parishes. Meantime all manner of falsehoods were spread abroad by the newspapers in hopes of checking emigration. Business, trade, and commerce were declared to be dull. Englishmen who had emigrated, it was said, were in a deplorable state. Upward of a thousand of them had actually applied to the British Consul at New York to be sent home as distressed British subjects ; but no effect seems to have been produced by these idle tales. Every week the arrivals at the seaports from Newry, from Belfast, from Dublin, from Gal-

way, from Londonderry, from Bristol, and London continued
to bring so many carpenters, masons, weavers, and blacksmiths
that before the middle of 1816 six thousand emigrants were
said to have left Ireland. The report that two hundred and
twenty-nine emigrants from Great Britain had landed at New
York in one week, that a vessel had been seized on the Thames
for attempting to carry off two hundred and thirty persons
when her tonnage permitted her to take but one hundred and
seventy-four, and that upward of sixteen hundred people had
engaged passage for America, was declared by the English
press to be a very serious matter.

It was, indeed, a serious matter, for none but the well-to-
do could pay for a passage, and they could ill be spared. As
no ship was allowed to carry more than two passengers for
each ton, vessels which used to come with from two hundred
and fifty to three hundred were now suffered to have but
seventy or eighty emigrants. This restriction raised the passage rates and absolutely prevented the emigration of that
class of laborers and peasants which with difficulty earned its
daily bread. Yet with this hindrance to contend with the
emigrants continued to come in steadily increasing numbers.
A newspaper published at New York and called The Shamrock contained a list of four hundred Irishmen who landed
at New York from five ships between the tenth and the seventeenth of August. During the week which ended on the
twenty-third of August, fifteen hundred natives of Great
Britain are known to have arrived at the five ports of Boston,
New London, New York, Amboy, and Philadelphia. In the
course of the next week the number fell to eight hundred,
but rose again during the third week to one thousand and
twenty-seven.

For so many new-comers to find employment at once, and
in a time of general business depression, was impossible, and
some, finding their dreams of prosperity were not instantly
realized, lost heart and went back. But these were few in
number, for at Philadelphia the Society of United Irishmen
and at New York the Shamrock Friendly Association took
the strangers in hand, secured places for such as wished to
stay in the cities, and furnished such as wished to go west-

ward with all the necessary information as to outfit and routes. Many of them as they travelled inland through the rich farming regions of Pennsylvania and Ohio were amazed at what they saw, and expressed their surprise in unstinted terms. " This be a main queer country," said a Yorkshire-man who with his family was on his way to Zanesville. " This be a main queer country, for I have asked the laboring folks all along the road how many meals they eat in a day, and they all said three and sometimes four, if they wanted them. We have but two at home, and they are scanty enough. And only think, sir, many of these people asked me to eat and drink with them. We can't do so in Yorkshire, sir, for we have not enough for ourselves."

Such comments might well have been considered flatter-ing ; yet there were those who saw in the sentiments expressed a cause for alarm, and who looked with no favor on the new-comers. " Let us not forget, before it is too late," they would cry, " what motive brings these people to our shores. Let us remember that it is cheap lands, high wages, food in plenty, and freedom from military service ; not a love for our institu-tions, or a belief that our form of government is better than that they have. Let us remember that they come with all the prejudices which are the result of race and early training, and that in welcoming what seem to be the oppressed of other lands we may really be taking an adder into our bosom." *

There were others, however, who scouted these fears as unworthy of Americans ; who asked, " Who are we that we should talk of foreigners ? " and took umbrage at a very inno-cent circular which went out from one of the departments of Government. A resolution of Congress bade the President lay before that body, at stated intervals, a list of the names of all officers of the Government, with their salaries and places of birth ; and the Postmaster-General, in obedience to it, called on the postmasters, to inform him in what state or country each of them was born, and to furnish a list of his clerks and the places of their nativity. But no sooner was it made pub-lic than it was set upon as a gross insult to foreign-born citi-

---

* American Daily Advertiser, July 26, 1817.

zens, and as an attempt to sift and classify the people. The postmaster at Canandaigua wrote in reply that he would not obey ; that he considered it a " firebrand of discord " between the native and the naturalized citizen, and a request for information Congress had no constitutional power to make. The editor of the Ontario Messenger announced that as a printer of the laws of the United States he would not comply, and in this determination both he and the Canandaigua postmaster were followed by many others. In the West in particular the feeling was strong against the circular, and the emigrant was assured that this attempt at discrimination found no favor with the people. Come, it was said, and partake with us of the blessings of liberty. Come and help us cut down our forests, bridge our streams, dig our canals, clear our water-courses, and reap rich harvests where now the buffalo ranges. Our flag is large enough to cover both you and us. We have land to spare, and need you.

Had the invitation been actually accepted, the stream of emigrants could not have been much larger. Thirty thousand were believed to have come during 1817. Near fifteen thousand are known to have arrived during the year at Philadelphia and New York, and almost as many more during 1818. Upward of a half were Irishmen who, having but little means and no idea how to make a livelihood in America, were quickly stranded on the seaboard, and in many instances became a charge on the community. With a hope of eradicating this growing evil, and with a sincere desire to help their suffering countrymen, citizens of Irish descent formed the Hibernian Society of Baltimore, the Irish Emigrant Association in New York, and like societies in Philadelphia and Pittsburg, and began seriously to seek a remedy. Each body reached the conclusion that the emigrant should be encouraged, and when necessary assisted to go West into one of the new States or Territories and settle, and after an interchange of letters decided to call on Congress for aid.

The call was in the form of petitions which were presented early in 1818, and asked for a land grant. The subscribers, who signed in behalf of their societies, set forth that they had often beheld with pity the hardships endured by Irish emigrants on their arrival in America. Unlike the Swiss and the Germans, who usually migrated in companies, the Irishmen came singly, without concert, and with no intention of settling at any particular place. The port to which the ship brought them was in general all they knew of the geography of the country destined to become their future home, and there they remained, tormented with doubt and uncertain which way to turn till their scanty funds were consumed and abject poverty stared them in the face. The educated emigrant might be able to bear up with fortitude against such adversity, but experience proved that the ignorant rustic could not. After loitering for a while about the seaport to which fate had sent him, he might perhaps find employment during the summer, but with winter would come idleness; and then, lacking the moral courage which education gave, he would yield to despair, fall into vice, waste the hard earnings of the summer, and in the spring would be utterly unfit to resume his wonted labors. Yet with a little help, a little careful advice and direction, these unhappy men might have been saved from misery and turned into prosperous, happy, and useful citizens. It was with the intention of doing this, the petitioners said, that they had formed their emigrant societies. But the thousands of men who poured in from Ireland rendered it utterly impossible to aid half the strangers who needed assistance, and forced them to ask for the help of Congress.

This help should be extended in two ways: In the first place, a tract of unsold land in Illinois should be set apart for settlement by emigrants from Ireland, and by no one else. In the second place, a credit of fourteen years should be given each settler on the tract. The advantages of colonization were believed to be many. Thousands of suffering men and women, who, deterred by the discouraging falsehoods circulated by the British press, were hesitating and doubting whether to endure want and oppression in the Old World or seek liberty and opulence in the New, would make up their minds at once when they heard that a great area where land was cheap and credit long had been reserved for their especial use in America. The good news would spread from village to village with the rapidity of lightning, and fifty thousand Irish

families settling together would raise up a new and happy
Erin in the bosom of the West. Illinois was selected because
it was on the frontier, where settlers were wanted; because
land was more likely to be granted there than elsewhere; because the climate was not very different from that of Ireland;
because its great stretches of prairie, interspersed with patches
of woodland, closely resembled their own cleared and cultivated country, and could easily be worked with the implements of husbandry to which they were used; because the
societies were acting for persons who never saw a slave; and
because Illinois, lying west of the falls of the Ohio, enjoyed
an unobstructed navigation to New Orleans.*

The terms and conditions of the grant, as mentioned in
the memorials, were very general; but the agents who represented the societies at Washington offered six specific propositions to the Committee on Public Lands. They asked that the
Secretary of the Treasury should be authorized to set apart a
certain number of townships east of the military bounty line in
Illinois; that each alternate section of the townships should
be sold to emigrants from Ireland; that no man should be
permitted to buy more than a square mile; that the price
should be two dollars per acre, payable one third after four,
one third after eight, and the rest at the end of twelve years;
that the settler must cultivate twenty out of each one hundred
acres he bought, erect a suitable tenement, and if he did not
comply with the three conditions of settlement, improvement,
and payment, he should be dispossessed when the twelve years
were out.

Unhappily for the scheme, the committee could see no
reason why a man who came from Ireland should be able to
buy land on easier terms than a man who came from Connecticut or Pennsylvania, and advised that the prayer of the petitioners be not granted. At a time when land was selling at
public sale in Alabama at seventy-three dollars an acre and at
forty dollars in Mississippi, it did not seem to be good policy
to dispose of great tracts in Illinois at two dollars an acre on

---

* See the Petitions of the Hibernian Society of Baltimore and the Irish Emigrant Societies of New York and Philadelphia.

long credit.   Nor was the House inclined to consider Illinois
so near the frontier as the petitioners believed, for that Territory was about to be admitted into the Union as a State.

Six years had indeed made astonishing changes in the
frontier.   Detroit, when Hull surrendered it, was but little
more than a military post.   Now it had much the character
of Pittsburg in 1800. . It was the centre of a lake commerce
of no mean dimensions.   Its streets were beginning to be
crowded with a miscellaneous population of Indians and half-
breeds, frontiersmen, Canadians, and Americans of every sort,
from trappers and hunters to men who laid claim to wealth
and refinement.   In its storehouses were piled up bales of
Indian blankets, bundles of trinkets suited to the needs of the
fur trade, and packages of such stuffs as are in demand in
flourishing and cultivated communities.   In St. Louis the
population exceeded three thousand souls.   Emigrants were
hurrying up the Missouri river in such numbers that in
August the first sale of public lands took place in the Territory, and forty thousand acres were disposed of fifty miles
west of St. Louis.   Before the year closed, the territorial Legislature marked off a vast area, asked Congress to admit it as
a State, and so brought on that protracted dispute which ended
in the Compromise of 1820.   South of St. Louis the frontier
crossed Arkansas and passed far to the west of Alexandria,
where, at the Falls of the Red river, a flourishing town existed.   In 1817 there were not one hundred families above the
" raft "; in 1818 there were more than eight hundred families,
with ten thousand acres of land planted in corn.

The favorite place for Southern emigrants, however, was
Alabama.   When Jackson entered the Territory in 1813 it
was a wilderness overrun by Creeks and Seminoles.   Not one
American in a thousand had then, in all probability, ever heard
of Fort Claiborne, which stood on the banks of the Alabama,
sixty miles from Fort Stoddart, and which, so late as 1816, had
but one settler's log cabin near it on the spot where in 1818
was a village of twenty-seven hundred souls.   The site of the
town called Blakely in 1817 was covered with a heavy forest.
But in 1818 Blakely boasted of eighty dwellings, of ten warehouses, of five hundred inhabitants, and of the largest hotel in

Alabama.   Between January and June, 1818, six hundred thousand dollars' worth of goods, a printing-press, one hundred brickmakers, and fifty ship-carpenters left New York for this rising settlement.   Ship-building bade fair to be a leading industry.   Since the beginning of the year forty-eight ships had loaded and unloaded at the town, a brisk West Indian trade was established, and three steamboats were in course of construction.   Two were to ply between Blakely and the up-country; one was to connect the town with New Orleans.   Such was the demand for town lots that at a sale at Florence two hundred and eighty-four lots brought two hundred and twenty-six thousand dollars.   One sold for thirty-five hundred dollars. Township Four, Range Seven, West, was bid off at more than half a million, which was something more than twenty-two dollars an acre.   A company buying a town site for speculation paid two hundred and fifty-one dollars an acre for one half of a quarter-section, and one hundred and fifty dollars an acre for the other half-quarter.   At a sale at Huntsville a planter bought a quarter-section of cotton land at one hundred and twenty-seven dollars an acre.   More than three millions of dollars were realized from Alabama land sales at one public auction.

Many of these purchases were fraudulent.   The law required that every acre of public land should be put up at auction and, if possible, sold to the highest bidder.   If no bids were made, or if the bidder did not pay for his purchase, the land became subject to private entry.   This enabled dishonest men to evade the law.   A band of speculators would select a township or section, and when the day came for offering it at auction they would send agents to make bids so extravagant that honest purchasers could not compete.   But when the auction was over and the time arrived to make the first payment the bidders had disappeared.   The principals would then come forward and take the land at a trifle more than the lowest sum for which the Government agent was permitted to sell it.   Nevertheless, the genuine sales were enormous in extent, and yielded prices which seemed fabulous. A census taken during the year showed a free population of forty-five thousand and a slave population of twenty-one thousand.

The rapid removal of hundreds of thousands of people from the seaboard to the Mississippi Valley gave a new impulse to internal improvements.   No one was so blind as not to see the splendid field for commercial enterprise opened up by the new West.   The market was no longer, as it had once been, in prospect; it now existed, and unless it was speedily supplied from the East, it would surely be supplied by way of the Mississippi river.   Not only to the manufacturers, to the shippers and importers, but to the people of the East in general, therefore, the question of cheap transportation of freight became one of serious importance.

The men of the seaboard, who up to this moment had, as it were, been looking toward Europe, now on a sudden veered around and faced the Mississippi Valley.   Every old scheme of inland communication by turnpike, canal, or steamboat was at once revived and urged with a seriousness hitherto unknown. Enterprises which in 1812 were thought to be only fit for private corporations to undertake if they pleased to waste money were now brought forward as public necessities, and the cry raised that the State should build them.   State after State heard the cry, and an era of internal improvements opened which did far more to cement the Union and join the East and West inseparably than did the Constitution and the laws.

No characteristic of that remarkable era is so noteworthy as the development of steam navigation.   As late as 1812 the use of the steamboat was confined to the Hudson and the Delaware.   East of New York city not one existed, but such was the commercial importance of that city that eight found employment in administering to the wants and conveniences of its citizens.   Three of them—the Paragon, the North River, and the Car of Neptune—belonged to the Fulton-Livingston Company, ran between Albany and New York, and were undoubtedly the finest specimens of their kind afloat. For that day they were swift, could make five miles an hour against the tide, and rarely spent more than thirty-two hours in going from one city to the other.   Each was thus enabled to accomplish one round trip a week, and as at least two nights had to be passed on the river, enough berths and sofas were provided to afford sleeping accommodations for one hundred passengers.   North-bound steamers left New York each Tuesday, Thursday, and Saturday afternoon at five o'clock ; the south-bound left Albany the same days at nine in the morning and stopped at all the large towns along the river banks from Kinderhook to West Point and Newburg.   Way passengers paid five cents a mile ; through passengers were charged seven dollars ; but no fare, however short the distance, was less than one dollar.

A fourth steamer, not much larger than a modern tug, called the Fire Fly, plied between New York and Newburg, stopping on the way at Sing Sing, Verplanck's Point, and West Point.   The others were ferry-boats.   Two of them, the Jersey and the York, replaced the sail boats, which till July, 1812, were on the ferry from New York to Paulus Hook.   One was advertised to start each half hour during daylight, and lest travellers, misled by ill-regulated clocks or watches, should lose a boat, the management announced that the clock in the steeple of St. Paul's Church should mark the time.   In structure these vessels were not unlike a modern catamaran.   In place of one large hull there were two small ones, each ten feet beam and eighty feet long, placed ten feet apart, and fastened in that position by strong beams which, covered with plank, formed a deck thirty by eighty feet.   Between the two hulls was the paddle wheel, while on deck over the open space stood the boiler, the engine and the machinery, leaving ten feet on either side for horses, carriages, cattle, and passengers. The space reserved for horses and cattle was uncovered, but that set apart for passengers was sheltered by an awning under which were benches.   There was also a narrow passage and stairway leading to a cabin five feet high in the clear and placed over the machinery.   Into this when it rained or when the weather was cold the travellers crawled to warm themselves at a stove.   For convenience in getting on or off the boat there was in each slip a bridge one end of which was fastened by hinges to the bulkhead of the dock, while the other rested on a framework floating on the water.   By this means the bridge rose and fell with the tide and was always exactly even with the end of the boat.   Fifteen minutes was the schedule time of crossing; but wind and waves and tide frequently combined to prolong the fifteen minutes to an hour.

Till the summer of 1813 the boats on the Paulus Hook ferry, and the steamboat Raritan, which ran between New Brunswick and New York, carried all the travellers, all the teams, and all the freight that passed between Boston and Philadelphia; but in 1813 Governor Ogden, of New Jersey, built a steamer which he called the Seahorse, and opened a rival ferry from Elizabethtown Point to New York. For that time the Seahorse was remarkable. Her speed was described as "incredible," as she easily made four trips a day, and repeatedly came up from the mouth of the Kills to the Battery, a distance of nine miles, in an hour, "with her awnings down and a strong wind and strong tide against her." For this piece of enterprise Governor Ogden was promptly attacked by Fulton and Livingston, who enjoyed the sole right to navigate the waters of New York State by steam, and in time was forced to yield.

Once at Paulus Hook, New Brunswick, or Elizabethtown, travellers were carried by stage across New Jersey to some place on the Delaware, down which any one of six steamboats was ready to convey them to Philadelphia. The Camden and the Phœnix ran from Trenton and, stopping at Bordentown and Burlington, made connections with the stages for Mount Holly and Long Branch. The Bristol—which the public were assured had been built at the joint expense of the citizens of Bristol, Burlington, and Philadelphia, without any idea of profit and merely to accommodate travellers—and the Eagle left Burlington and made the round trip each day.

The New Jersey plied between Whitehill and Philadelphia, touching at Burlington and Bristol, and made her trips on Sundays, Tuesdays, and Thursdays, because on those days the other boats did not run. By her the through fare from Philadelphia to New York was but three dollars and a quarter. This in time was increased somewhat by the necessity of passing the night at New Brunswick or South Amboy. Yet such was the persistence with which travellers held to the old ways of travel that the proprietors of the stage which ran through in one day raised the fare to ten dollars and still had their vehicles always full.

The Phœnix, having now become an old boat, was taken off the regular line to Trenton in the autumn of 1813 and her place given to the Philadelphia, a new boat, "furnished in a style of superior elegance." With her appearance the Phœnix ran no higher up than Bordentown.*

Below Philadelphia there were no steamboats on the Delaware. South and west of Philadelphia much had been attempted, but little had been done. The Legislature of Pennsylvania had just granted the exclusive right to use steam on the east branch of the Susquehanna, from Wilkesbarre to Tioga Point, to a man named James Barnes, provided he placed his boat on the river within three years. The efforts of John Stevens to establish a line of steamboats on the Chesapeake had led to the formation of a company; but no boats were on the bay. The grant which he had obtained from North Carolina of the exclusive right to navigate the waters of the State by steam had excited Livingston and Fulton to an unusual degree, and every possible effort was being made by them to prevent the use of it. Public warning was given in the newspapers that the law making the grant was illegal, null and void. It was contrary to the laws of the United States under which a patent had been issued to Livingston and Fulton, and whoever conspired with Stevens to invade their rights would surely be prosecuted. But, lest this should not be enough, an agent was sent South, and soon had three steamboat companies organized. One was to connect Elizabeth City, at the head of the Pasquotank river, with New Berne, on the Neuse river. A second, the Robert Fulton Company, was to run a boat from Beaufort to Wilmington, while the vessels of a third, the Charleston Steamboat Company, were to ply between Wilmington and Charleston, South Carolina. There was also to be a steam ferry across Albemarle Sound, from Edenton to Plymouth, and a line of boats on the Cape Fear river, connecting Fayetteville with Wilmington. Every share of stock in

---

* American Daily Advertiser, October 29, 1813.

each company, it is said, was taken in the spring of 1813. But the war and the blockade of the coast made further operations impossible.

For some time past a clumsy flat-bottomed steamboat, called the Columbian, had been used on the Potomac to carry grain and wood to Washington. It was at best a small affair, but it served to arouse a desire for something better, and in January a company was organized and application made to the Virginia Legislature for an act incorporating the Potomac Steamboat Company. But two years passed before the first of its boats appeared on the river. Beyond the mountains there was but one steamboat, the New Orleans, which went back and forth between Natchez and New Orleans. That steam could ever be used on the Mississippi had been doubted even by Livingston and Fulton, and to put the doubt at rest Nicholas J. Roosevelt made a voyage down the Ohio and the Mississippi, from Pittsburg to New Orleans, in 1809. He gauged and sounded the rivers, determined the velocities of their currents in the dry season and in the wet, examined their banks with a view to a cheap supply of fuel, and came back to New York in 1810 with so favorable a report that he was promptly sent to Pittsburg to build a steamboat.

Once at New Orleans, her work as a trader began, and for more than a year she ran regularly between the two cities, earning in that time, it is said, some twenty thousand dollars; and well she might, for the fare up the river was twenty-five dollars, and that down was eighteen. In 1814 she was snagged and lost near Baton Rouge.

Meanwhile rivals appeared on the river to compete with her. The successful trip of the New Orleans, and the news of her performances at Louisville and Cincinnati, aroused the liveliest interest at Pittsburg, and three steamers were at once put on the stocks. The first to get off was the Comet, a stern-wheel boat of twenty-five tons, which left Pittsburg in 1813, and early in 1814 began to run between Natchez and New Orleans. But after two trips her owners, finding that she could not compete with the New Orleans, sold her, and the purchaser used her machinery to run a cotton-gin. Ere this the Mississippi Steamboat Company, an organization which dated back as far as 1811,* had one boat on the river and a second under way. The first, named the Vesuvius, steamed away from Pittsburg in the spring of 1814, and was followed a year later by the Ætna, which soon became famous as the first steamboat that ever made the trip up the Mississippi from New Orleans to Louisville.† The second was the Enterprise. She was built at Brownsville, and, after making two trips between Pittsburg and Louisville, was sent down to New Orleans in December, 1814, with a cargo of ammunition for Jackson. The war over, she went up and down the river towing vessels from the Balize to New Orleans, made one trip to the rapids of the Red River, and after a few voyages to Natchez started up the Mississippi, bound for Louisville. Her safe arrival there in twenty-five days was hailed with delight, for the city was fast becoming a steamboat centre, and was already the terminus for three prosperous lines. Indeed, it was noted with pride that on one and the same day there were made fast to the river bank the Enterprise from New Orleans, the Despatch from Pittsburg, and the Kentucky Elizabeth from the upper Kentucky, and that at last the time had come when Pittsburg and the heart of Kentucky were joined by steam with New Orleans, and when it was possible for the farmers and the planters of the Mississippi valley to exchange their flour and their cotton, their beef and their pork, for the liquors, the spices, and the merchandise of Europe and the West Indies.

The event was indeed most significant. Yet things just as great had been done in the East. At New York, in 1814, the Fulton, a steamer intended to ply between New York and New Haven, was launched, and, as the Sound was blockaded, ran up and down the bay with pleasure parties. The great steam war-ship bearing the same name went off the stocks that same year, but too late to be of any service. But most noticeable of all was the serious effect which the monopoly Livingston and Fulton held over the waters of New York was

---

* Cramer's Magazine Almanac for 1811.

† The American Daily Advertiser of December 9, 1815, notes that in November the Ætna, from New Orleans, passed Natchez for Louisville with a cargo of foreign merchandise.

producing on the commerce of that great State. Unwilling to pay the royalty demanded by the monopolists for a license, and well aware of the many advantages of machine boats over sail boats for ferry purposes, enterprising men had begun to look about for some other motive power than steam, and had found a temporary substitute in the horse. The credit of the invention of the Teamboat, as it came to be called, was ascribed to Moses Rogers, who built the first one and put it on the ferry between New York and Brooklyn. Like the York and the Jersey on the Paulus Hook ferry, it was a twin boat with a wheel between the two hulls, that it might not be injured by floating ice. Motive power was supplied by eight horses walking in a circle on deck and turning a crank.*

Primitive as the machinery was, it drove the boat across the East river in from eight to fifteen minutes, and made a type of boat which came rapidly into use. No steam, no boiler, no fuel, no sails—so dangerous when the wind was high—were required, and, what was quite as important to every ferry owner in the State of New York, there were no license fees to be paid to Fulton. No such consideration weighed with the proprietors of the Brooklyn ferry, for the Legislature had just incorporated them as a steam ferry company, and by joining with Fulton they had been enabled to put on a steam ferry-boat, which they called the Nassau. But the consideration did weigh with others, and before the summer ended a second teamboat was on the ferry from Corlear's Hook to Williamsburg,† while a third met the Seahorse as she came up from Elizabethtown Point. In his efforts to prevent the Seahorse entering the waters of New York Fulton had been successful, and Governor Ogden had been compelled to resort to the expedient of sending "a safe ferry-boat, impelled when necessary by oars," from New York to meet the steamer at a point within the jurisdiction of New Jersey. This vessel left Marketfield Street wharf daily at ten in the morning and three in the afternoon and ran down to the flats near Ellis Island, where the Seahorse met it, and after exchanging passengers the two would return to the

---

* New York Gazette, April 8, 1814.   † Ibid., August 5, 1814.

places of departure.* But after the teamboat came in Ogden procured one, and toward the end of the summer of 1814 the teamboat Substitution took the place of the safe ferry-boat impelled by oars, and met the Seahorse near Bedloe's Island.† Horses, carriages, and freight were carried on a sail boat.

On the Delaware the steamboat Camden was no longer running. The venture had ceased to be profitable, and the boat had been sold " to close a concern." But new enterprises were being pushed on rapidly. One association of capitalists, taking the name of the Shrewsbury Stage and Steamboat Company, obtained a charter from New Jersey and began to make preparations to run a ferry on the Delaware. Another, the Pennsylvania and New Jersey Steamboat Company, was granted a charter by each State, and began a ferry from Southwark to Kaighn's Point, New Jersey. A third had long been ready to connect Philadelphia and Baltimore by steam the moment the war ended. The return of peace, indeed, was the occasion for a most astonishing development of steam navigation. The Fulton, which for a year past had been running to Albany and back, was instantly put in readiness, and in March commenced her trip to New Haven. In May the Washington steamed past Sandy Hook, went to sea, and, to the surprise of the doubters, in fifty hours was riding in the harbor of Norfolk.‡ She was the property of the Potomac Steamboat Company.

In June the Eagle was taken from the Delaware, and in her turn sent by sea to Baltimore, to ply between that city and Elkton. The Vesta was then put on the Delaware from Philadelphia to Wilmington, and, save for the few miles' land carriage from Wilmington to Elkton, and from New Brunswick to Trenton, it was now possible for the traveller to go by steam from New Haven to Baltimore. But a greater thing yet was meditated, and in September subscriptions were opened at New York for a steamboat to join that city and Charleston. One hundred thousand dollars were needed. Such a venture, it was claimed, could not fail to pay. The boat could easily

---

* New York Gazette, July 20, 1814.

† Ibid., October, 1814.

‡ Norfolk Herald, May 24, 1815; New York Evening Post, May 27, 1815; National Intelligencer, June 1, 1815.

make forty single trips a year, and with fifty passengers each trip at fifty dollars apiece, her earnings would be one hundred thousand dollars. Interest, repairs, and running expenses would consume forty thousand, and leave a very handsome bonus for the shareholders. As to the possibility of navigating boats by steam in rough water, that was settled. The Fulton, on her way to and from New Haven, had often been caught in a gale. The Eagle, on her trips down Chesapeake Bay, had many a time gone safely and speedily through rough water and high seas.* That the last shadow of doubt might be removed, six experts were asked for their opinion and answered that if a vessel to carry nothing but passengers had her machinery and her ballast so placed that wind and sea could not upset her, and had air-chambers so arranged as to make her insubmergible when seas broke over her, she would be safe.†

The experiences of the captains of the steamboats on the Sound and on the Chesapeake went far toward establishing the belief that such vessels, if properly built, could navigate great bodies of water in safety. Little surprise, therefore, was expressed when it was announced that the freight-moving firm of Porter, Barton & Co. were constructing a steamer to run between Buffalo and Detroit, and that it was their determination to make communication between these two growing cities as safe and speedy as that between Albany and New York.

Undertakings such as these soon brought out warnings from patentees and privilege holders, whose rights and monopolies the enthusiastic boat-builders had put at defiance. In the East, Nicholas J. Roosevelt notified the public that the vertical wheel then in use on every steamboat in the country was his invention. He had secured a patent on it, and every one who used it must get his license so to do or be prosecuted under the law for damages equal to the profits of the boat. In the South, Ferdinando Fairfax, of Virginia, took the broad ground that it was the Constitution of the United States and the acts of Congress that secured to each inventor certain rights

---

* New York Evening Post, September 28, 1815.
† Ibid., November 15, 1815.

and privileges; that the Constitution and the laws made under it were the supreme law of the land; and that any act of any State which tended to infringe patent rights was null and void. He then announced that, as the only surviving member of the John Fitch Steamboat Company of years ago, he was the holder of the oldest steamboat patent in the United States, and that without his license no man could legally move boats by steam in any State or Territory. This privilege he declared he was ready to defend, and was about to go to law in order to test the right of any State to create a monopoly of steam navigation on its waters. In the far South, Edward Livingston, as the owner of Fulton and Livingston's sole right to use steam on the waters of Louisiana, was making trouble of a more serious kind. He was actually seizing steamboats that came down the Mississippi, and in the case of the Despatch from Pittsburg forced her to go without the jurisdiction of the State. This so alarmed the people of Ohio, where a company had been formed to send steamboats to New Orleans for the purpose of exchanging the pork and grain of Ohio for the products of Europe and the West Indies, that the Legislature was called on for help. But when the Legislature looked into the matter it found it impossible to give any aid. The Assembly therefore passed a resolution to the effect that the citizens of Ohio were deprived of the advantages arising from steamboat navigation in consequence of the threatened suits and the conflicting claim of inventors, and the act of Louisiana, and bade the State delegation in Congress seek a judicial decision on two points: Did recent improvements to a discovery long in use entitle the discoverer to the benefits of a patent? Had not Louisiana gone beyond her constitutional power in giving Livingston and Fulton their exclusive privilege? Later in the year the rights of Livingston, which dated from the time Louisiana was a territory, were tested, and his monopoly set aside by the District Court, as one a territory had no power to create.

Despite the monopolies, the licenses, and the threats, the use of the steamboat continued to spread rapidly. On the Sound a new steamer began to ply between New York and New London, stopping at New Haven. The boat had originally been intended for a trip to Russia and was the first built with the lines of a sea-going vessel. On New York Bay a swifter boat took the place of the old Raritan to compete with the Seahorse, which now ran from Brunswick and South Amboy. From Philadelphia two rival lines struggled for the Baltimore trade—one by way of Wilmington and Elkton, and one by way of Newcastle and Frenchtown. In the far South a steamboat plied from Charleston to Sullivan's Island and towed vessels in and out over the bar, where in other days they had not uncommonly been forced to wait from five to forty days for wind.* Yet farther south Savannah and Augusta were joined by a steamer which carried not only passengers but freight.† Another made the trip from Charleston to Savannah in thirty-one hours.

The spread of steam navigation, combined with the system of turnpike roads, on which the Federal Government, the States, and private corporations had been pouring out money for ten years past, revolutionized travel. The dangers, the inconveniences, the tedious delays of twenty years before were gone forever.

Private enterprise combined with State aid had covered the seaboard with a network of turnpike roads and bridges, over which coaches of the newest pattern rolled along at the rate of six miles an hour. It was still the custom to begin stage journeys at three or four o'clock in the morning; but it rarely happened that they were prolonged after six at night, nor were more than six or seven passengers suffered to ride in a coach. Between New York and Philadelphia, where the travel was heaviest and competition greatest, nothing was spared that could make the traveller comfortable. Five lines of stages ran each way daily, and assurance was given the public that the horses were sound and the drivers sober and civil, "which," said one advertisement, "is the most difficult and dangerous part of the business of running stages." Books were to be found at each house where a stop was made, that patrons might enter their complaints if the drivers were rude, or the

---

* New York Evening Post, June 22, 1816.
† New York Gazette, April 26, 1816.

coach late, or more than six passengers were taken on by the driver. Baggage—and each person was now allowed to carry twenty-eight pounds instead of fourteen as of old—was chained on some lines and watched on others lest it should be stolen. On none was the coach left for a moment without a guard on the box to hold the horses. Favored by the hard roadways, good bridges, frequent relays, and the light loads carried, these vehicles sped along at a rate which twenty years before would have seemed marvellous. Two days were now sufficient for the traveller to go by coach from Boston to New York. There, after resting overnight, he could board the Seahorse at five in the morning and at the end of fifteen hours * alight at the best tavern in Philadelphia, enjoy a comfortable night's sleep, and in fifteen hours more be put down at Gadsby's Hotel in Baltimore. Within thirty hours after leaving Philadelphia he could, if he wished, be standing on Capitol Hill, Washington, or be listening to a debate in the House of Representatives. Four days and a quarter were all that need be spent on the road between Boston and Washington, and of this time one day and a half were consumed sleeping at the taverns. The cost in money was but thirty dollars. From New York the trip could be made in two and a half days.

That city, in fact, had become the centre of the entire system of inland communication. By the boats on the Hudson river she had been brought within twenty-four hours of Albany, and within thirty-six hours of Whitehall, and by the steamboats on Lake Champlain and the St. Lawrence within eight days of Quebec, of which time three days were spent at Whitehall and Montreal waiting to make connections, and five in actual travelling. The cost of such a journey was forty-seven dollars. †

By the close of 1816 the great seaboard routes for the transportation of passengers had thus been so improved, by bridging and turnpiking and the use of steam, that travel from Boston and Quebec to the banks of the Potomac was a matter of little time, expense, or discomfort. But the same improve-

---

* The trip through in fifteen hours (5 A. M. to 8 P. M.) was made in spring and summer, but not in winter.

† Albany Argus. American Daily Advertiser, August 1, 1816.

ment had not been made in the transportation of freight. No coach could take anything but passengers, mail, and baggage. No steamboat, either on the Hudson or the Sound, the Delaware or the Chesapeake, would carry sacks of grain or bales of goods in any quantity. Merchandise was still moved from place to place by packet-boats or lumbering wagons, dragged slowly along the roads by four or five horses. Nevertheless, the war had done much to increase both the speed and facilities of such movement. The first effect of the arrival of British fleets on our coast and the blockade of our harbors was to stop all interstate commerce between the North and the South. The tar and pitch, the cotton and tobacco, which it had always been customary to bring North by sea; the Yankee notions, the teas and spices, the cotton cards, the foreign goods, which had till then been carried South by sea—were forced to find new routes by land. The exemption from blockade which New England enjoyed filled the ports of Boston and Salem and Marblehead with foreign goods, brought thither under the neutral flags of Sweden and of Spain, and by British ships falsely carrying those flags. To the same ports, again, came all the produce, all the lumber, all the cotton and tobacco our farmers and planters were eager to send away in neutral ships. In a little while, therefore, every road from the South and the West to New England was literally choked and worn out by long trains of heavy wagons transporting goods. Then was it that the importance of Gallatin's plan of internal improvements came home to the people with a meaning it had never possessed before. The steamboats at New York enabled the wagon trains to cross that dreadful ferry with safety and speed. But the want of such a means on the Chesapeake and the James turned them aside at Philadelphia and forced them to cross the Susquehanna and the Potomac, and so lengthened the journey that to send a wagon from Boston to Savannah was a matter of one hundred and fifteen days, and an expense of nearly a thousand dollars.

With the cessation of hostilities the ox and horse marine disappeared and the packet sloop once more began its voyages. But the lesson and effects were lasting. The demand for quick transportation over long distances, and the immense quantity of goods to be carried, had led, during the war, to the consolidation of shippers and handlers of freight and to the formation of what, in our day, would be called trunk-line routes. Lines of sloops soon began to run from Albany and from New Haven to New Brunswick, where the Union Transportation Company took the freight in charge and delivered it in Philadelphia, Baltimore, or Pittsburg.   By thus passing New York the cost of carriage was lessened twelve and a half cents the hundred pounds, and the old expense of cartage and storage at that city was entirely avoided.   The enormous importation of British goods which followed peace continued to give these southern routes plenty of business; but when the wares and merchandise were to be sent westward the need of better and closer connection with the West was felt most keenly.   Indeed, it had become a business necessity, for cotton and sugar had been brought up from Louisiana to Pittsburg by steamboat, and had been transported by wagons to the Atlantic cities and sold at a profit; and the day seemed near at hand when the merchants of Ohio and Indiana, Kentucky and Illinois, would cease to buy from the importers at New York and Philadelphia, and when New Orleans would become the emporium of their trade.   The country would thus be parted by the mountains into two sections, each independent of the other commercially, and it might be, in time, politically, unless these two sections were speedily united by a good system of internal improvements national in character.

Madison referred to the subject in his message to Congress when it met in December, 1816, and the committee to whom his remarks were referred recommended, in substance, the plan of Gallatin.   They reminded the House that four short canals, across four necks of land which did not aggregate one hundred miles, would enable ships to go by an inland or shore route from Boston to St. Mary's river.   They advised a national turnpike through the seaports and large towns and along the chief post routes from Maine to Louisiana.   They advocated less costly roads leading over from some point on the great turnpike in New York to the military and naval stations at Sackett's Harbor and on the lakes; from Pittsburg to the frontiers of Pennsylvania, Ohio, and Michigan; from Detroit to St. Louis; and from St. Louis to New Orleans.   They approved of aiding in building the Erie Canal, of joining Lake Erie with the Ohio below the falls, and of good roads over the mountains to connect the head waters of the chief rivers of the Atlantic slope with those flowing into the Mississippi.

None of these great enterprises should, the committee thought, be undertaken solely by the United States.   Federal aid should consist of subscriptions to the stock of private corporations chartered by the States to carry out the many parts of the general plan.   As petitions for such aid had already been presented, a second report was made by the committee, strongly recommending assistance, and presenting a bill authorizing the Secretary of the Treasury to subscribe to the stock of the Delaware and Chesapeake Canal, and to the Dismal Swamp Canal, which, in a rude and humble way, had already been constructed.   But neither the reports, nor the bill, nor a memorial from the Erie Canal Commissioners, received any consideration.

The attention of the House was wholly engrossed by a bill from a select committee appointed on motion of Calhoun. He had, he said, in introducing his motion, heretofore opposed all plans of internal improvement at Government expense, because he believed them ill-timed.   The want of funds and the embarrassed state of the finances made them unreasonable. But now that peace had returned, and revenue was abundant, it seemed quite proper to look into these plans most carefully, for they were all-important.   He asked, therefore, for a committee to consider the expediency of setting apart, as a fund for internal improvement, the bonus and the net annual dividends to be paid by the Bank of the United States.   The motion was carried, and the committee soon reported a bill providing that the million and a half of dollars exacted from the bank as the price of its charter, and the dividends on the seven million of its stock owned by the United States, should be set apart and pledged as a fund for building roads and canals.   Little disposition, however, was shown to take up the bill, and the session was fast closing before Calhoun could persuade the House to go into a Committee of the Whole and consider it.   When at last the House did so, he began his speech with an elaborate statement of the many advantages of good roads and canals. " What," said he, " can add more to the wealth, strength, and political prosperity of our country than cheapness of intercourse ?   It gives to the interior the advantages of the seaboard. It makes the country price, whether in the sale of raw product or in the purchase of the article to be consumed, come near to the price of the commercial town, and it benefits the seaboard by enlarging the sphere of demand. Were the pecuniary gains of the farmer or the merchant the only consideration, it might well be doubted whether a system of good roads and canals should not be left to individual enterprise.   But there are far higher motives. The strength and political prosperity of the republic are concerned in it. No country enjoying freedom ever occupied as great an extent of territory as that possessed by the United States.   One hundred years ago the most profound philosopher did not suppose it possible that a pure republic could exist on even so small a scale as Great Britain.   Yet what was then considered chimerical we have, and so happily are the powers of the States and the General Government blended, that much of our political prosperity is drawn from the very extent of our territory. Let it not, however, be forgotten—nay, let it forever be kept in mind—that our vastness exposes us at the same time to the worst of all calamities—dissension. We are great, and rapidly, I was about to say fearfully, growing. This is our pride and our danger, our weakness and our strength. The strongest of all cements, it is true, is the wisdom, the justice, the moderation of this House. Yet good roads and canals will do much to unite us. Those who know the human heart know well how powerfully distance tends to break the sympathies of our nature. Nothing, not even differences of language, so estranges man from man. Let us then bind the republic together with roads and canals. Am I told that the Constitution does not give Congress the necessary power, and that we can not expend public money save for the execution of enumerated powers? I answer, I am no advocate of refined arguments on the Constitution. That instrument was not intended as a thesis for the logician to exercise his ingenuity on. It ought to be construed into plain good sense, and what can be more explicit

than the Constitution on this very point? Congress shall
have power, says the Constitution, to establish post-offices and
post-roads. It is true that this is usually said to mean the
designation of the roads over which the mail shall be carried.
But does not the word 'establish' comprehend something
more? Congress, again, has power to lay and collect taxes,
duties, imposts and excises; and for what purpose? In order
to pay the debts and provide for the common defence and
general welfare of the country. It is commonly contended
that the paragraph contains three distinct grants of power:
laying taxes, providing for the common defence, and doing
what is necessary for the general welfare. This is a wrong
interpretation, and, as roads and canals will contribute to the
general welfare, Congress may lay taxes and duties to pay
for them."

When he finished speaking, Timothy Pickering rose and
denied the justness of such interpretation. To put such a
meaning on the words "general welfare" was to render useless the long enumeration of powers which followed. It was
from the express grant of the right to regulate commerce with
foreign nations, and among the States, and with the Indians,
that Congress must get authority to build roads and canals.
To aid commerce and make it safe by sea, light-houses, beacons,
buoys, and piers have been built and the coast survey established. Yet who had questioned the right to do these things?
Why not, then, in order to facilitate commerce by land, build
roads and canals? The discussion now became general. One
member moved to limit the expenditure of money to canals. If, said he, we must interfere with the rights and sovereignty of the States, let us do so as little as possible. Constructing roads is a municipal regulation. Except in great
leading roads, the convenience of country, of town, of neighborhoods is chiefly consulted. Not so canals; they may, as
in the case of the proposed canal in New York, join distant
States, and unite remote parts of the Union in bonds so strong
that no Hartford Convention can ever break them. When
the motion was voted down, another member moved that the
money be distributed among the States on the basis of representation, to be used by them for such internal improvements

as they thought proper. A third suggested that Congress should designate the objects and the States spend the money, and the bill so amended was reported to the House.

In the debate which followed, the questions of constitutionality and expediency were again discussed. To remove all doubts as to the right of Congress to use revenue for internal improvements, Pickering offered an amendment, which in the end was accepted. The bonus and the dividends were to be set apart as a fund for constructing roads and canals, and improving the navigation of watercourses, "in order to facilitate, promote, and give security to internal commerce among the several States, and to render more easy and less expensive the means and provisions necessary for their common defence." But no such works were to be begun in any State till its consent had been obtained. This secured the support of three classes of men—those who, with Calhoun, believed the common defence a good reason for building roads and canals; those who, with Pickering, believed the power was vested in that of regulating commerce; and those who, with Ross, of Pennsylvania, held that to engage in such works without leave of the State was destructive of the rights of the State. In the end the amendment prevailed, but it was expediency and sectional interest that carried the day.

When the yeas and nays were called, one hundred and seventy members responded to their names. Leaving out of consideration the Territorial delegates, who had no vote, there were, therefore, but eight voting members absent. This was an unusually full House, and as no other important measure of that session—not even the Compensation Bill, in which every member was directly interested—brought out so heavy a vote, it is fair to suppose that the large attendance was due to the deep interest every section of the country took in the question of internal improvements. Indeed, the sectional character of the vote shows this to have been the case. New England was bitterly opposed to the scheme, because there the West was hated, there the feeling was strong that nothing should be done to encourage the migration westward that was fast depopulating the seaboard, and there the people looked with dread on the admission of Western and Southern States into the Union. Of her forty-one representatives, therefore, thirty-four said No and six Yes. One was absent. Delaware, Maryland, and Virginia gave eight affirmative and twenty negative votes. The Carolinas were divided. New York, Pennsylvania, and Ohio, with fifty-six votes in the House, cast fifty-one in favor of the bill, which was pre-eminently a Middle and Western State measure, and which passed by the slender majority of two. In the Senate the yeas were twenty and the nays fifteen, every senator from New England save one voting No. It was on the first of March that the bill passed the Senate, and the third when it reached Madison. As his term of office was about to expire, he might have suffered the act to die unnoticed; but he promptly sent it back to the House with his veto and the statement that, on constitutional grounds, he could not approve it. An attempt to pass the bill over the veto failed miserably.

But the great work of developing communication with the West was not delayed in consequence. The time for it had come at last, and four months after Madison sent the "Bonus Bill" back to the House of Representatives the first shovelful of earth was dug for the Erie Canal at Rome. When the canal commissioners returned from Washington in 1812 and advised the Legislature of New York to waste no more time seeking aid of Congress and the sister States, the advice was taken, and the commissioners were authorized to go seriously to work on the task assigned them. They were to contract conditionally for the purchase of the interest of the Inland Lock Navigation Company, chartered in 1792 for the purpose of connecting Albany and Oswego; were to borrow five millions of dollars on the credit of the State; and, if a competent and experienced engineer assured them, after actual examination of the ground, that the canal was practicable, they were to commence construction. But the war opened almost immediately, and all thought of canal building was given up till peace returned. Nevertheless, the commissioners were not idle. As required by law, they applied to land-owners along the route for gifts of land, and received a hundred thousand acres; they attempted to borrow money in Europe, and sent to England for an experienced canal engineer, and in 1814 reported these facts to the Legislature. The war was then at its height, and the State using every resource to keep the enemy from her soil. To continue the power which the commission enjoyed of borrowing five millions of dollars seemed, therefore, an extravagant if not a ruinous policy, and it was quickly taken away. Thus stricken down, the commissioners made no report in 1815. But the promoters of the canal were not discouraged, and when peace returned made an appeal directly to the people. The first step was taken in New York city, where, in the autumn of 1815, a long memorial,* written by De Witt Clinton and addressed to the Legislature, was submitted to a meeting of citizens at the City Hotel. It was a strong and well-written appeal, setting forth the many advantages of internal communication by means of canals, and the great benefit the State would derive by joining the waters of Lake Erie with the Hudson.

The meeting endorsed it most heartily, and ordered copies to be printed and scattered broadcast over the State. The effect was immediate. Men of influence, who before had cared little for the project, now became its fast friends. Great meetings in every town of importance, from Albany to Buffalo, approved it; the corporation of New York city seconded it; and when the Legislature met in 1816 the document was laid before the Senate and Assembly with such a public support as had rarely been given to any measure. Thus beset, the Legislature yielded, and in April, 1816, appointed five new commissioners,† gave them twenty thousand dollars with which to explore canal routes from Albany to Lake Erie and from the Hudson to Lake Champlain, bade them seek aid of Congress, of the neighboring States, of the owners of land through which the canals were to go, of all bodies politic and corporate, public or private, and of all citizens of the United States, and, when the Legislature met again, report plans, estimates of cost, and the terms on which money could be borrowed on the credit of the State.

---

* Memorial of the Citizens of New York in favor of Canal Navigation between the Great Western Lakes and the Tide-waters of the Hudson.

† De Witt Clinton, Stephen Van Rensselaer, Samuel Young, Joseph Ellicott, and Myron Holley.

In a month's time the new board organized, made De Witt Clinton president, and began work so energetically that when the summer was ended four hundred and forty miles had been, explored, surveyed, and levelled; the centre line of the canal had been staked out; and maps and profiles carefully drawn. The report was most convincing, and, despite the delays caused by members who opposed canals, the business of the commission progressed so smoothly that early in March Clinton was called on by a joint committee of the two Houses for a plan for raising money, just as word came that Madison had vetoed the Bonus Bill. The blow was a heavy one, for the share of New York would have been ninety thousand dollars a year, and would have been a grant of a million and a half for the canals. But the effect was not serious. Disappointment gave place to determination, and on April fifteenth, 1817, "an act respecting navigable communication between the great western and northern lakes and the Atlantic Ocean" became a law.

This authorized the commissioners to begin the construction of the middle section of the Erie Canal, stretching from the Mohawk to the Seneca rivers, and bade them commence digging the northern canal to join the Hudson with Lake Champlain. They were empowered to raise two hundred and fifty thousand dollars by taxing the lands and farms lying along the routes of the two water ways and within twenty-five miles of them, and were to extinguish the rights of the Western Inland Lock Navigation Company. Moreover, a canal fund was created, and given in charge of a board of commissioners, who were to borrow as much money on the credit of the State each year as, with the income of the fund, would not exceed four hundred thousand dollars. To pay the interest and redeem the principal of the money so borrowed, a duty of twelve and a half cents a bushel was imposed on all salt made in the eastern district; and a tax of one dollar laid on each person who travelled more than one hundred miles, and of fifty cents on each one who travelled more than thirty miles by the Hudson river steamboats. Lest this should not be enough the proceeds of all lotteries drawn in the State; the toll from the canals when built; all the proceeds of the State

interest in the Western Inland Lock Navigation Company ;
all grants and donations for the purpose of building the canals ;
and all duties on sales at auction save the thirty-three thousand five hundred dollars already set apart for other purposes
—were made over to the fund.   The commissioners were furthermore permitted to hire out the convicts in the State prison
to the contractors, in order that the work might not be delayed
for want of laborers.

Some time was necessarily spent in levelling, staking out
the cuts and fills, sampling the earth and rocks, marking off
the sections, and preparing the details of the contracts.   But
on June twenty-seventh the first contract was signed, and on
July fourth, in the presence of the commissioners and a crowd
of citizens, ground was broken at Rome, and the greatest
piece of engineering up to that time attempted in the United
States was fairly started.

The energy thus displayed by New York, joined with the
experience gained during the war, aroused the people of New
Jersey to seriously consider the building of a second link in
Gallatin's national system of internal improvement.   For thirty
years past the idea of a canal from the Raritan to the Delaware had been before the people.   Once, in 1804, a company
incorporated to dig the canal had gone so far as to locate the
route, run a line of levels from Lamberton on the Delaware,
by way of Assanpink Creek, Stony Brook, and the Millstone
river to the Raritan, and even open subscription books at
the chief towns between New York and Philadelphia.   But,
partly because of the great number of improvements then in
course of construction, partly because of the belief that the
plan of using the beds of the rivers was bad, and partly because it was usual to declare that the country was too young
to engage in works so costly and so extensive, few shares were
purchased.   Time and experience, however, had removed
these objections.   No one now proposed to use the river bed.
The sight of thousands of wagons passing to and fro during
the war between the Hudson and the Delaware, and the immense sums expended on transportation of goods, had convinced the most incredulous that a canal would pay, and pay
handsomely.   The Governor, therefore, when he met the

Legislature in January, 1816, made an earnest appeal for the canal, and secured, from a committee chosen to consider the matter, a hearty approval.   From data not to be doubted, they had ascertained, the committee told the Assembly, that during the war almost two millions of dollars had been paid for the cartage of produce, goods, wares, and military stores across the State from Trenton to New York.   Had a canal existed, more than half would have been saved, and this half would have paid the cost of building.   They asked, therefore, that a commission be appointed and empowered to employ scientific men to select and level the best route for a canal and report the cost to the next Legislature.   A commission with the power suggested was appointed; but when the Legislature assembled, in October, it was not ready to report.

Nor was Pennsylvania one whit behind her neighbors. The policy adopted in 1811—when, during one session of the Legislature, eight hundred and twenty-five thousand dollars were appropriated for opening roads and building bridges—was never for a moment abandoned.   Neither the evils of war, nor the disorders of the currency, nor the low state of trade and commerce, could check her liberality.   The cost of the war to her had been nine hundred and nineteen thousand dollars.* Yet between 1812 and 1816 there were taken from her treasury and expended on schools and on academies, on turnpike roads and on common roads, on bridges, rivers, and creeks, eight hundred and seventeen thousand dollars more.†   Once free from the burdens of war, her interest in internal improvements was again displayed, and in 1817 five hundred and thirty thousand dollars were appropriated, raising the sum so expended in six years to two millions and a quarter.‡   Meantime her citizens had laid out five millions in like enterprises. She had now a thousand and forty-two miles of turnpike roads, and not a few of the finest specimens of bridge engineering the world could produce.   In boldness of design the United States then led the world; but Pennsylvania led the United States.   The longest arch in all Europe was in the Wearmouth

---

* Report of the Committee of Ways and Means.   ‡ $2,198,435.
† $816,885.

Bridge, in England, and had a span of two hundred and thirty-six feet; but in Pennsylvania there were three bridges with arches of far greater length. At the request of Maryland, commissioners had been appointed to join others named by her to examine the Susquehanna with a view to improving the navigation of the river and opening up the heart of Pennsylvania to settlement by providing an easy way to market. The report set forth that twenty thousand dollars would clear the river and its branches from Harrisburg to Tioga Point, and urged legislative action.

The report was read with pleasure by thousands of Philadelphians who had become seriously alarmed at the vigorous efforts made by New York and Baltimore to secure the trade of the West. "Geographically considered," these men would argue, "no city is so favorably situated as Philadelphia for commanding the whole inland trade of the continent. Astonishing as it may seem, seventy-five miles of canal are all that is necessary to give water communication between the Market Street Bridge over the Schuylkill river and the Pacific Ocean at the mouth of the Columbia. To reach central New York we have but to clear the Schuylkill from Philadelphia to its upper branch, dig a canal twenty-three miles long to the Susquehanna at Berwick, go up the North Branch to the Tioga river, up the Tioga to Elmira, and thence by canal to Seneca Lake. Should New York carry out the proposed canal from Canandaigua outlet to Great Sodus Bay, we shall have boat connection with Lake Ontario. But even if she does not, we shall tap the salt and plaster trade of central New York, the lumber trade of the upper Susquehanna, and send back to the lake counties of New York the iron and coal of Pennsylvania." So promising did this scheme appear that the Legislature ordered an examination to be made of the route of the canal from Elmira to Seneca Lake,[*] and, with the consent of Governor Clinton, the survey was made in 1817.[†]

"Once at Berwick," the friends of inland lock navigation would continue, "the way to Pittsburg and Lake Erie lies be-

---

[*] Act of March 22, 1817.
[†] Journal of the House of Representatives, 1817–1818, p. 394.

fore us. A journey down the North Branch and out the West Branch of the Susquehanna to the head waters of Sinnemahoning Creek, will bring us to a point but twenty-three miles from the Alleghany. A canal across this strip of country will open communication with the Alleghany, which is the highway to the valley of the Mississippi and the Great Lakes. The river to the Conewango, the Conewango to Chautauqua Lake, the lake to its head, and a canal nine miles long to Lake Erie, is an easy route to Buffalo, to Erie, to Cleveland, to Detroit, to the fur-bearing regions of the Northwest. Down the Alleghany to Pittsburg is the way to the Ohio. But while the people of central New York and northern Pennsylvania will send their salt, their plaster, and their grain by this waterway, there is a better one for the merchants of Philadelphia. It leads up the Schuylkill to Reading, and then by canal to Middletown on the Susquehanna ; up the Susquehanna to the sources of the Juniata, and on by a canal fourteen miles long to the Alleghany. And what a trade is then ours! More than two thousand rafts, more than three hundred arks, innumerable boats, carrying two hundred barrels of flour or seven hundred bushels of wheat, go down the Susquehanna river each year. Is it too much to expect that all this will come to Philadelphia ? Fifteen hundred flat-bottomed boats and five hundred barges floated down the Mississippi from the upper country to New Orleans during the year 1817. On that river and its tributaries in another year will be thirty steamboats, laden with the produce of what in time will be the garden spot of our country. But every ton of it will go on to New Orleans if we do not bestir ourselves. Yet with inland navigation Philadelphia may have it all; for, with the few openings the physical features of Pennsylvania invite us to make, a ton of goods may be brought by water from the Mandan villages on the upper Missouri to Philadelphia—thirty-two hundred miles—at less than it now costs to send the like weight to Pittsburg. The trade of the Great Lakes, of the Ohio, of half the Mississippi, of all the region drained by the Missouri, of three fourths of Pennsylvania, and one third of New York, lies within our reach. We can and we must baffle the attempts of our neighbors to get it.

No neighbor was more eager to get it than Baltimore, where the merchants were already demanding free pikes to Cumberland, to the Susquehanna where it crossed the State line, and for a canal from the Chesapeake to the Delaware. Across the Potomac, Virginia, attributing her depopulation to the lack of internal improvement, created a fund and appointed a board of control to expend it. Into the fund went all bank, turnpike, and navigation company stocks owned by the State, all dividends paid on such stock, and such bonus as might at any time thereafter be paid for a bank charter. On the board were the State Treasurer, the Attorney-General, and ten citizens—three from the region west of the Alleghany Mountains, two from the counties between the Alleghany and the Blue Ridge Mountains, three from the country between the Blue Ridge and the head of tide-water, and two from the tide-water region. North Carolina appointed a commissioner to examine and report on the practicability of improving the navigation of the Tar, the Yadkin, and the Neuse rivers, and called on Congress to open direct communication from the ocean to the waters of Albemarle Sound. When the books of the Cape Fear Navigation Company were opened for subscriptions to a stock issue of ninety-four thousand dollars, more than two hundred thousand dollars were subscribed. The report that a company was to be formed for the improvement of navigation on the Roanoke river put up the price of land along its banks twenty per cent., and spread dismay over Petersburg and Lynchburg, which had long disposed of the produce of the fertile region drained by the Roanoke and the Dan.

When such a spirit for internal improvements was abroad in the country, it was inevitable that Congress should again be called on to lend a helping hand. The veto of the Bonus Bill was not thought to be a serious matter. The man whose official act had destroyed it had, a few hours later, become a private citizen. His successor was believed to be an executive who would not stand in the way of progress; who would not in 1818 hold with stubborn tenacity to constitutional opinions formed in 1789, but, admitting that the framers of the Constitution could not foresee the future, would change his old-time idea to meet the changed condition of the country. A little surprise was felt, therefore, when, in his first message to Congress, Monroe frankly declared that he did not believe Congress had a right to use public money for internal improvements. No such power, he said, was expressly granted, nor was it incidental to the proper use of any power that was specifically granted. That Congress should engage in such enterprises was, he admitted, desirable; but if they were to be undertaken by the Government, the Constitution must be amended and the power expressly given to Congress.*

His words were referred to a special committee, which made a most remarkable report. A careful examination of the acts of past Congresses and past executives convinced it that power to construct roads at the cost of Government had in some instances been used. The right could not, therefore, in all cases be denied; and as there were at least a few kinds of public works which Congress could order to be built, the committee determined what they were, and arranged them in three classes. The Government might, the report stated, lay out, construct, and improve post-roads through the States, provided the State through which the roads passed consented. It might open, build, and improve military roads with the assent of the States interested, and it might, under the same conditions, cut canals to promote interstate commerce, and for the transportation of military stores in time of war.

In support of this position the committee declared it would not resort to a liberal construction of the Constitution, though such would be justifiable. Where the authority claimed was oppressive in its character, dangerous in its tendencies, and was asserted without deference to the assent of the State; where it tended to aggrandize the Union and depress its members, there was indeed good reason for holding Congress to the letter of the law. But where the power to be used was beneficent in its effects, was not to be exercised till the State consented, and was far more likely to increase the wealth and power of the States than to aggrandize the Union, a free construction of the Constitution was surely justifiable. That the

---

* Monroe's Message, December 2, 1817.

expenditure of Government money for roads and canals was neither dangerous in its tendencies nor calculated to injure the States was certain, for the President had asked that such power be granted by a constitutional amendment.   Happily no liberal interpretation, no amendment, no resort to the general-welfare clause was needed.   Under the power to establish post-offices and post-roads Congress, with the consent of the States, was free to act.   There were not wanting, it was true, those who held that "establish" meant nothing more than a mere designation of particular roads over which the mails were to be carried.   Such an interpretation would make it impossible for the Postmaster-General to perform the duty assigned him. In many a State the judge of a county court could shut a road at his discretion, and if it so happened that the highway was a post-road, the carriage of letters and papers would be stopped on that route till Congress met and "established" another.   If "establish" meant designate, then how could Congress keep a ferry over a deep and rapid river, or punish with twenty years' imprisonment any ferryman who detained or hindered the passage of the mail?   With the power to establish post-roads and the sole power to carry the mails goes the duty of doing whatever is "necessary and proper" for their quick and easy transmission.   Surely, then, Congress has the right, if the States consent, to build bridges over streams and rivers, remove obstructions from highways, level hills, fill up morasses, and, where necessary, construct roads.

By a like process of reasoning the committee deduced the right to build military roads from the positive injunction to provide for the common defence, and the right to cut canals from the power to regulate commerce between the States and with the Indians.   Those who doubted whether or no the Federal revenue could be used for such purposes were reminded that money was constantly spent for objects not mentioned in the Constitution.   Were not bounties granted to fishermen and protection to manufacturers?   Were not trading houses established with the Indians?   Were not piers and light-houses and beacons built?   Was not the coast surveyed? Were not paintings and books bought for the Capitol?   Had not charity been dispensed to foreigners, a bank chartered, and roads made through the different States? Yet not one of these laudable objects could have been undertaken if Congress had searched for express power to do it. The plain intention of the framers of the Constitution was to give Congress wide discretionary power in the expenditure of the revenue. No human foresight could foresee, no human industry could enumerate, the infinite variety of purposes to which public money might wisely and properly be applied. This the framers of the Constitution had recognized, and had limited the use of the revenue by no other restrictions than were contained in the words " provide for the common defence and general welfare of the United States." It was to be noticed again that the term " general welfare " ended the clause which gave Congress authority to raise and use revenue, and not the clause which concluded the enumeration of powers. A distinction was to be drawn, therefore, between power to vote money for roads and canals and power to construct them. Money could be spent for the " general welfare," but canals could not be dug for the " general welfare." The power was not expressly granted ; it belonged therefore to the States, and only with the assent of a State could the Government engage in internal improvements within her jurisdiction. The report ended with a resolution that the dividends on the bank stock owned by the United States should be set apart as a fund for internal improvements to be carried on with the assent of the several States concerned.

The report was understood, and undoubtedly was intended to take issue with the President on the question of internal improvements. Monroe had in substance served notice on the House that if money was to be spent on roads and canals, the Constitution must be amended. The committee had declared that internal improvements were expedient and necessary, and that the Constitution gave Congress ample power to undertake them. But was the House ready to support the committee, and support it in so handsome a manner as to override a veto? To frame a bill, spend whole days in discussing its features, and then pass it through all its stages by less than a two-thirds vote would be ruinous, the friends of internal improvements felt, to their cause. It would destroy all hope in the breasts of the people of obtaining any aid from the Government during the four, and it might be the eight, years of Monroe's term. The report and the resolution were therefore sent to the Committee of the Whole, where it was determined a test vote should be taken. But it was March, 1818, before the committee was ready to consider the matter, and when it did, new and more troublesome constitutional questions were raised and debated. Is the consent of a State, it was asked, necessary? If it is, how can it be obtained? A State most surely may engage in road building and canal construction. But how can it delegate that right? When the people give to their Legislature the power to do a certain act, the Legislature becomes the agent of the people, and must either do it or not do it, as seems best. But it cannot transfer to the Federal Government the power to do it. A transfer of a new power from the States or the people to the Federal Government can be made in no other way than by a Constitutional amendment, which requires the consent of many States. The broad-constructionists answered these arguments so successfully that four resolutions were carried in the Committee of the Whole. Congress, it was resolved, did have power to build post-roads and military roads; could construct canals for military purposes; could build such roads and canals as were necessary to facilitate commerce between the States, and was empowered to appropriate money for any of these public purposes. But when the resolutions were considered by the House, all save the last were defeated.

By the people in the Middle States the result had been awaited with interest. The rivalry between the three great cities of New York, Philadelphia, and Baltimore, for the monopoly of trade with the new West, was assuming a most serious aspect. Already an Albany firm owning a Hudson river packet line were advertising to move freight from New York to Pittsburg for six dollars, and from New York to Sandusky or Detroit for four dollars and fifty cents per hundred pounds. The appearance of Walk-in-the-Water, the first steamboat that ever floated on Lake Erie, and her successful trip to Detroit, would, it was believed, lower these rates to four dollars per hundredweight. That New York was already in control of the trade of that great northern belt which stretched from

Albany to Detroit, and into which people from New England and New York were moving by thousands, was beyond dispute. Might she not also get control of the trade of the Ohio valley? Already her shippers and traders were upon the head waters of the Alleghany, and at the mouths of every river that entered Lake Erie from Ohio. Her sole competitors were Philadelphia, Baltimore, and New Orleans. Near as Philadelphia was to Pittsburg, and rich as was the trade between the two, the people of Pennsylvania, with a most singular apathy, were suffering it to slip from them. During 1817 goods to the value of three and a half millions of dollars were carted across the State and deposited at Pittsburg for shipment down the Ohio. The cost of carriage was ten per cent. of the value. Not a little of this cost had been distributed along the way for tolls on the turnpikes and bridges, for food at the taverns, and to blacksmiths and wainwrights for shoeing horses and mending the huge Conestoga wagons. Yet with two neighbors eagerly competing for this richly paying traffic, the people of Pennsylvania were making no vigorous efforts to retain it. In 1817, indeed, some Philadelphia merchants concerned in the Western trade met, discussed the situation, and decided to unite and establish a line of wagons to Pittsburg, and, if successful, secure a charter of incorporation. Thirty-five thousand dollars were soon obtained; sixty wagons, enough for two lines, were purchased, and contracts entered into with teamsters to haul them back and forth across the State. It was intended to begin on the first day of April, 1818, but the roads were so bad that three weeks passed before two of the company's wagons rolled over Market Street bridge on their way to Pittsburg. Thenceforth two set off each week day from Philadelphia and Pittsburg, and made the journey in twelve days. Eight other vehicles, owned by private individuals, also left Philadelphia for the West daily; yet, despite them, the company succeeded in lowering the freight rates from nine dollars and a half per hundred pounds in the summer of 1817 to six dollars and a half in the summer of 1818. At its next session the Legislature granted a charter, and, under the name of the Philadelphia and Pittsburg Transporting Company, the proprietors called upon the public to aid by purchasing thirty thousand dollars more of their stock, and met with a very small response.

On the Western carrying trade of New York, the Philadelphia enterprise had no effect whatever. One of its rules required every Western merchant who bought goods in Philadelphia to pay in advance for their transportation to Pittsburg. Another disavowed all responsibility of the company for losses or damage by the way. Western merchants, therefore, still continued to buy in New York, where the shippers and carriers of freight paid damages for injury to goods, were content to collect freight charges when the goods were delivered to the owner, and charged for the service one dollar and a half per hundred pounds less than was asked by the Philadelphia and Pittsburg Transporting Company. Yet neither the inducement thus held out to Western buyers, nor the line of swift packets which joined New York and Liverpool and sent a vessel regularly once a month from each city, nor the preparations making in New York for a steamship line to New Orleans, nor the three thousand men hard at work on the Erie Canal, nor the loud complaints of the press,* could rouse the people of Pennsylvania to such activity as was necessary to enable them to keep abreast of the times.

In the West no spur was needed. There all was bustle and hurry. Pittsburg became the greatest distributing centre in the country. On one day in June several thousand emigrants, and goods worth three millions of dollars, were in the city, waiting for the water of the Ohio to rise that they might be floated down the river. A part of the goods was destined for New Orleans. But some were loaded on a new kind of conveyance, and were to be peddled down the river from farm to farm and from hamlet to hamlet. In appearance it resembled a floating house, but within were counters and shelves piled high with clothing and hardware, furniture and kitchenware, china, crockery, hoes, shoes—with every sort of article and utensil of use in the household or the field. As the store floated slowly along, the owner, when he espied a farm-house or

---

* Pittsburg Gazette, May 22, 1818; Crawford Weekly Messenger; Aurora, June 25, 1818.

came within sight of a new settlement or a little village, would begin to blow a horn. At the sound of it men and women would hurry to the river bank, where the store was made fast, and barter pork, flour, and produce for such goods as they needed or were tempted to buy. The produce received from the settlers was easily sold by the store-keeper at Louisville or Cincinnati.

Louisville had become a great shipping port, and often had as many as eight steamboats lying along the river front. Near by, in the autumn of 1818, seven more were building. But the chief centre of steamboating was New Orleans, where eighteen were trading regularly. Commercially, no city, not even Pittsburg or New York, had then before it a brighter future.

CHAPTER XXXIV.

THE SEMINOLE WAR.

THE conquest of the Creeks by Jackson in 1814 was followed by the treaty of Fort Jackson, whereby the Indians gave up to the United States several millions of acres. As the land was purposely so chosen as to cut off the possessions of Spain in Florida from the Indian settlements in Georgia and Alabama, it was confidently believed that peace and quiet in that quarter was assured to citizens of the United States. So indeed they would have been had not that part of the Creek nation which scouted the treaty of Fort Jackson and which claimed to be still unsubdued, fled over the border to Florida and taken refuge with the Seminoles, whose chief was Billy Bowlegs. There they became the allies of Great Britain, and as such fully expected that when peace was made, their powerful friend would see to it that the lands taken from them by the United States were restored. In this they were encouraged by the reappearance after the peace of Colonel Edward Nicholls. Claiming to be " on his Majesty's service," he concluded a treaty of offensive and defensive alliance between the Seminoles and Great Britain, rebuilt an old fort on the Appalachicola sixty miles below the mouth of the Flint, called it the British Post on the Appalachicola, and made a demand on Colonel Benjamin Hawkins for the arrest of certain persons charged with murder by Bowlegs, and for the evacuation of the Creek lands, according to the ninth article of the treaty of peace. Hawkins sent the complaint of Bowlegs to the Governor of Georgia and an account of Nicholls to the Secretary of War. Madison therefore instructed Adams to remonstrate with Bathurst. But early in the summer of 1815 Nicholls with his troops, the prophet chief Francis, and some Creeks, set sail for London. In the fort he left seven hundred and sixty-three barrels of cannon powder, twenty-five hundred muskets, casks of gunpowder, and hundreds of carbines, pistols, swords, and accoutrements.

Now there were in Florida besides the Indians upward of a thousand negroes who had been so happy as to escape from the slavery of Georgia planters. They were commanded by chiefs and captains, we are told, and had farms and grazing lands that stretched fifty miles up and down the Appalachicola from the British Post. Seeing the post abandoned by Nicholls and the Seminoles, these negroes naturally took possession, and, being well supplied with arms and powder, soon began to plunder the frontiers of Georgia. They harried the country, drove off cattle, fired on boats going up and down the river, enticed negroes to run away, and, joined by the hostile Creeks, made the Negro Fort, as the post was now called, the terror of the region for miles around. As something must be done to abate the evil, Jackson, who commanded the Southern Division, was ordered by the Secretary of War to call the attention of the Spanish commander of Pensacola to the subject, and demand that he suppress the nuisance.* The demand was promptly made, coupled with the assurance that if Spain did not destroy the fort and scatter the banditti, the United States would.†

Meanwhile General Edmund P. Gaines had been ordered to take possession of the new purchase, build block-houses and forts where necessary, and protect the surveyors engaged in running out the township and section lines. On this errand he despatched Lieutenant-Colonel D. L. Clinch, of the Fourth Infantry, early in March. But as Colonel Clinch moved down the Chattahoochee, Gaines, feeling uneasy over the Negro Fort, wrote to Jackson for authority to build a post on the Appalachicola close to the boundary,‡ in order

---

* Crawford to Jackson, March 15, 1816. State Papers, Second Session, Fifteenth Congress, No. 122, p. 5.

† Jackson to the Governor of Pensacola, Ibid., p. 8.

‡ Gaines to Jackson, March 20, 1816. State Papers, Second Session, Fifteenth Congress, No. 122, pp. 14, 15.

to overawe the negroes, and received it in the fullest terms. "The growing hostility of the Indians," said Jackson, "must be checked by prompt and energetic measures. Half peace, half war, is a state of things which must not exist. I have no doubt that this fort has been established by some villains for the purpose of murder, rapine, and plunder, and that it ought to be blown up regardless of the ground it stands on. If you have come to the same conclusion, destroy it, and restore the stolen negroes and property to their rightful owners." * The new post—afterward called Fort Scott—was accordingly ordered to be built not far from where the Flint and Chattahoochee join and form the Appalachicola. To supply it by land would be so costly and hazardous that Gaines determined to attempt to bring his rations from New Orleans by sea. This would necessitate passing the Negro Fort; and fearing an attack on the boat, he asked Daniel T. Patterson, commanding the New Orleans station, to provide a convoy of gun-boats.† He complied willingly, and Sailing-Master Jairus Loomis was commanded to take two gun-boats, rendezvous at Pass Christian, and be ready to escort two transports laden with ordnance and provisions to Fort Scott. Late in June the schooners General Pike and Semilanto were loaded at New Orleans, and, dropping down the Mississippi to Pass Christian, joined the gun-boats and set sail for the mouth of the Appalachicola, where the fleet arrived on July tenth. There Loomis was met by an express from Colonel Clinch at Fort Scott. Gaines, hearing that the Indians were dancing the war dance and drinking the war medicine, felt sure that the passage of the fleet would be hindered at the Negro Fort, and had ordered Colonel Clinch to go down the river with troops, take his station near the fort, and, if the fleet was fired on, raze the post to the ground. The messenger accordingly requested Loomis not to enter the river till Clinch had reached the Fort. But a week passed before Clinch was ready to move; and during this week a boat-crew, while seeking fresh water, was attacked by the negroes, and three of the men

---

* Jackson to Gaines, April 8, 1816.

† Gaines to Patterson, May 22, 1816. State Papers, Second Session, Fifteenth Congress, No. 122, pp. 118, 119.

killed and one made prisoner. At last, on the sixteenth of July, Clinch embarked at Fort Scott, and, as he floated down the river, fell in with a negro-hunting party of Seminoles. They had heard of his mission, and hoping to regain possession of their fort, joined him, and, on nearing the place, captured a negro with a white man's scalp at his belt. By this prisoner the story of the fate of the boats was narrated to Clinch, who instantly pushed forward and invested the fort. A demand of the Seminoles for its surrender was followed by the hoisting of a red flag with the English Union Jack above it, and by a discharge of cannon. Clinch thereupon sent word to Loomis to come up with the boats, which early on the morning of the twenty-seventh came within range and opened fire. Finding the ramparts much too strong to be battered down by the light guns of the vessels, Loomis determined to destroy them by fire, and after discharging a few cold shot to get the range, a ball made red-hot in the cook's galley was put in the gun and sent screaming over the wall and into the magazine.* The roar, the shock, the scene that followed, may be imagined, but not described. Seven hundred barrels of gunpowder tore the earth, the fort, and all the wretched creatures in it to fragments. Two hundred and seventy men, women, and children died on the spot. Of sixty-four taken out alive, the greater number died soon after. Among the living was Garçon, the leader, and a Choctaw chief. But, learning that the members of the boat-crew captured by the negroes had been tarred and burned alive, Garçon and the Choctaw were delivered over to the Seminoles and put to death.†

For some months all was peace and quiet along the frontier. The negro power was gone. The Seminoles seemed awed by the strength and vigor of the Federal power. The garrison at Fort Scott was greatly reduced in the spring of 1817, and as the day seemed near when Florida would become part and parcel of the United States, a wild speculation in Pensacola lands was started by Tennesseeans. But Florida was

---

* Jairus Loomis to Daniel T. Patterson, August 13, 1816. State Papers, Second Session, Fifteenth Congress, No. 119, pp. 15, 16.

† Ibid., p. 17.

not long to enjoy her state of quiet. The Seminoles were far from pacified. Their ancient grievances continued to rankle and fester, and while they in the West only waited a leader and a new provocation to take the war-path, a swarm of pirates and vagabonds, adventurers, patriots, privateersmen, and filibusters descended once more on the Island of Amelia in the East.

Their leader was an erratic Scotchman of rank and fortune named Gregor MacGregor, who, after helping the Spanish provinces of South America in their revolt against Spain, appeared in Baltimore for the avowed purpose of gathering another band of patriots to " wrest the Floridas from Spain." To gather such a band of filibusters in that city was an easy matter, and in the month of June, 1817, his fleet of one brig, one ship, and a few small schooners were on their way to Florida. On the morning of the twenty-ninth he landed on Amelia Island with fifty men, and, after a ten-mile march across the swamps, reached the town of Fernandina. Announcing himself as " Gregor MacGregor, commander-in-chief of all the forces, both naval and military, destined to effect the independence of the Floridas, duly commissioned by the constituted authorities of the republics of Mexico, Buenos Ayres, New Granada, and Venezuela," he demanded and received the surrender of the garrison, arms and munitions of war from Don Francisco de Morales, the civil and military commandant on the island.* Elated by his success, he began to make war by proclamation, and produced a series of documents almost equal to those of General Smyth. In one, each conqueror was bidden to wear on his left arm a shield of red cloth with the words " Venredores de Amala " and a wreath of oak and laurel leaves embroidered in yellow silk.† In another, the soldiers were assured that he would soon " plant the Green Cross of Florida on the proud walls of St. Augustine," and notified all Royalists that his motto was " Victory or Death." ‡ By a third he laid a blockade on the whole coast of Florida from Amelia Island to the Perdido.# Yet he did not thrive. Dis-

---

* Aurora, July 14, 21, 1817.

† Ibid., July 21, 1817.

‡ Ibid., September 5, 1817.

Ibid., September 5, 1817.

ease and desertion thinned his ranks. Provisions were hard to get. His paper money was not willingly taken. The expedition to St. Augustine did not take place, and in September MacGregor went off to New Providence in search of friends, money, and troops. But he had not been very long away when another filibuster of a very different stamp came to the island and took command. He bore the name of Louis Aury, and, according to his own account, had gone to Cartagena to shed his blood, and, if need be, give his life in the cause of liberty. But the Spanish fleet and troops in command of Morillo descended on the coast. Cartagena fell, and Aury, with a few ships and followers, ran the blockade and made for the island of San Domingo. After laying in stores and provisions he and his men began, as he said, " to look around whither to direct their steps in order to offer their services and to spill their blood in the cause of American independence and freedom." Naturally enough, their attention became fixed on Texas, where Cardenas and Gutierrez were struggling for liberty, and they started for Galveston Bay. On arriving there, Aury wrote to Don Manuel de Herrera, Minister Plenipotentiary from the Republic of Mexico to the United States, who was then at New Orleans. Herrera hailed him with delight, repaired to Texas, and on September twelfth, 1816, acknowledged and declared Galveston Pueto Habillitado of the Republic of Mexico. Aury was made military governor. Letters of marque were issued ; courts of admiralty were established, and a band of vagabonds quickly assembled. To him flocked negroes, mulattoes, smugglers from the gulf coast, refugees from Barataria ; French and Italian mariners, and freebooters, a dozen years of commercial restrictions and war had gathered and stranded at New Orleans. Finding the patch of sand on which he had made his establishment far from convenient, Aury abandoned it in April, 1817, and, having burned the huts and cabins, sailed away to Matagorda, leaving no one behind with authority to form a government. None was needed, and ten days after his departure some thirty sailors and freebooters, from all parts of the earth, who remained behind or came after Aury was gone, set up a government of their own with governor, admiralty judge, collector, notary public, secretary, and all the other functionaries of state. The sole object of these men was the capture of Spanish ships and property. Concerning the Republic of Mexico they knew and cared nothing.* They did not have and did not wish connection with any power on earth. They were in reality a piratical crew, bent on plundering every sort of property found on the high sea, without much regard to its nationality. But property so obtained was of little value without a market, and to get a market they raised the flag of Mexico, declared they were acting under the authority of that republic, and in their courts of admiralty condemned the ships and cargoes brought in by the pirates as good prizes. Once condemned, the goods were hurried to New Orleans, where the market was soon flooded with jewellery, laces, silks and linens, muslins, britannias, seersuckers, china, crockery, glass, and slaves smuggled over the border. Indeed, more than one merchant of New Orleans owned ships especially fitted out to make the captures.

At Matagorda, meantime, Aury was as dissatisfied as at Galveston, and, hearing of the arrival of MacGregor at Amelia Island, he again broke up his establishment, and with one hundred and fifty followers sailed for Fernandina, to find Mac-Gregor gone and one R. Hubbard, lately sheriff of New York city, installed as governor. Appeals were at once made to Aury for help. But he positively refused all aid unless the Green Cross flag was lowered, the Mexican flag raised in its place, and he made governor and commander in chief. There was nothing to do but submit, and on October fourth Amelia Island was formally declared a part of the Republic of Mexico and passed into the hands of Aury. But his rule was short. The capture of the island by MacGregor had alarmed the President, who, acting under the joint resolution of January, 1811, ordered troops and ships to go down and expel the invaders. No resistance was made, and early in 1818 Aury and his crew departed, the flag of the United States replaced that of Mexico, and Fernandina was a second time garrisoned and held by United States troops in trust for the King of Spain.

---

* Testimony of John Ducoing, the Admiralty Judge. American State Papers, Foreign Relations, vol. iv, p. 137. Also that of Richard Espagnol, the notary public and secretary. Ibid., pp. 137, 138.

Next to be dealt with were the Seminoles. Failure to recover the lands lost by the treaty of Fort Jackson had made
them sullen and savage. The building of the forts in their
ancient domain and the appearance of white settlers had greatly
excited them, and had aroused a determination on the part of
a few to come back and take their territory by force. During
the spring and summer of 1817 the debatable strip had in consequence been the scene of a series of acts of violence. Cattle
were run off, men, women, and children were murdered, cabins
were burned, and preparations of every sort made by the Indians for war.* One settlement of some forty warriors, known
as Fowltown, and which stood fifteen miles east of Fort Scott
and near the boundary, became especially excited. The red
war pole was erected, the war dance was held, and a warning
sent to Major Twiggs at Fort Scott "not to cross or cut a
stick of timber on the east side of the Flint." † He paid no
attention to the threat; but when General Gaines, thinking the
conduct of the Indians along the frontier a little threatening,
came down to Fort Scott with more troops, he sent for the
Fowltown chief to come to him.‡ The answer was a defiance.
Gaines then sent Major Twiggs with two hundred and fifty
men to bring the chief and his warriors, or, if they resisted, to
treat them as enemies. On reaching Fowltown at daylight
one November morning, Twiggs was fired on by the Indians,
returned it, and in a few minutes held possession of the place
and opened the Seminole War.

While the Indians took refuge in the swamps, Twiggs
built a rude stockade near the town and waited for orders
from General Gaines, who came in person and burned the
village. Upon this the whole country rose. At a meeting of
Indians held in one of the towns some time before—a meeting at which it was thought twenty-seven hundred warriors
were present—a decision was reached to attack the troops the
moment they crossed the Flint.# Gaines having crossed the
Flint, it now remained for the Indians to carry out their

---

* American State Papers, Military Affairs, vol. i, pp. 681–685.
† Ibid., p. 685.
‡ Ibid., p. 686.
# Gaines to the Secretary of War, November 9, 1817.

agreement, which they did most signally. It happened that while the soldiers were sacking Fowltown a large open boat, with seven women, four children, and forty United States troops, under the command of Lieutenant Scott, was being slowly warped up the Appalachicola river toward Fort Scott. He knew nothing of the affair at Fowltown, but he had been warned that his passage would be opposed, and had sent to Gaines for help.* All went well, however, till a place was reached where, in order to avoid the current, the boat came close to the shore of a swamp densely covered with trees, when, on a sudden, a volley of musketry at point-blank range was fired upon the party. At the first discharge Lieutenant Scott and almost every soldier was killed or wounded. But the savages fired again, and then boarding the helpless craft, began an indiscriminate butchery. Children were taken by the heels and their brains dashed out. All the women save one were cut down and scalped. The dead were mutilated. Of the entire party, none escaped death save one woman, carried into captivity, and four men, who leaped overboard and swam to the other bank. †

Scott and his party had been sent down the river to assist Major Muhlenburg, who was coming up with three boats laden with military stores from Mobile. His call for help was at once responded to, and two covered boats with forty men were despatched to meet him. But it was too late; and passing the scene of the massacre in the night, the party reached Major Muhlenburg just in time to aid him in a battle with the Indians. During four days the boats were forced to lie at anchor in mid-stream, because no man dared raise his head above the bulwarks. At last they were rescued by troops from Fort Scott.‡

A report of these outrages was duly sent to Washington by Gaines. But almost at the same moment Calhoun, expecting no trouble from the Indians, wrote to Gaines, ordering him to go to Amelia Island and take part in the opera-

---

* Scott to Gaines, November 28, 1817. American State Papers, Military Affairs, vol. i, p. 688.

† Ibid., p. 687.

‡ Ibid., vol. i, pp. 690, 691.

tions against the filibusters. As the two letters passed each other on the way, Gaines was compelled to hasten to Fernandina, while the Secretary of War, by the seriousness of the situation about Fort Scott, was forced to replace Gaines by Andrew Jackson.

The order to Jackson bidding him go to Fort Scott, assume command of the forces, call on the governors of adjacent States for militia, if necessary, and end the war, was dated December twenty-sixth, and was passed on its way south by a letter from Jackson to Monroe. He was well pleased, he wrote, to know that Amelia Island was to be seized. The order he thought ought to be executed at all hazards, and, at the same time, the whole of East Florida should be taken and held as indemnity for the outrages of Spain on the property of the citizens of the United States. Such an act would put down all opposition, secure full indemnity, and could be executed without in any way implicating the Government. " Let it," said he, " be signified to me through any channel (say Mr. J. Rhea) that the possession of the Floridas would be desirable to the United States, and in sixty days it will be accomplished." *

On the sixth of January, 1818, the letter was delivered to Monroe, and concerning what then happened two different and utterly irreconcilable stories are extant. One, of which Monroe was the author, sets forth that when the packet came the President was sick ; that he did not read it, but, seeing it was from Jackson, handed it to Calhoun, who happened to come in ; that the Secretary returned it with the remark that it would require an answer ; that Monroe next showed it to Crawford, who in like manner read and returned it, but without comment ; and that it was then put aside and forgotten, till the serious events to which it led had almost brought the country into war. The other story, which is that of Jackson, sets forth that Monroe did read the letter ; did send for Mr. John Rhea, a member of Congress from Tennessee ; did ask him to answer it and say the suggestion was ap-

* Jackson's Exposition of his Conduct in Florida, in Benton's Thirty Years' View, vol. i, p. 170.   Parton's Life of Jackson, vol. ii, pp. 433, 434.

proved; and that Rhea's letter reached Jackson before he arrived at Fort Scott.

The order to go to Fort Scott was received at the Hermitage on January eleventh, and gave Jackson power to call on the governors of the adjacent States of Georgia and Tennessee for militia. But the Georgia militia had been called out by Gaines just before he started for Amelia, and Jackson, not considering them enough, determined to get a thousand more from Tennessee. Unhappily, Governor Slaughter was off in the Cherokee country, no one knew where, and, as time was passing, Jackson took the responsibility and called on the officers of the volunteers of the last Creek campaign to meet him at Nashville. They promptly agreed to act with him, and in twelve days' time two regiments of mounted men, numbering more than a thousand, gathered at Fayetteville ready to march without a word from the Governor.* With twenty days' rations they started for Fort Jackson, while the general with two companies set off post haste for Fort Scott. At Hartford he met General Gaines with a new quota of Georgia militia, and heard from Fort Scott that unless food reached the troops by a certain day the post would be abandoned. To prevent this, Gaines, with twelve men, took boat and started down the river, but Jackson and the Georgians went by land,† and on the evening of March ninth entered Fort Scott. To his amazement, Gaines and his twelve men had not arrived, nor had any intelligence been received from the Tennessee volunteers. Gaines had been wrecked on his voyage, and, after wandering for days through the woods, came in cold, half starved, and with no clothing but a pair of pantaloons.‡ The Tennesseeans, after reaching Fort Mitchell, ought to have gone to Fort Gaines, but such positive assurances were given their commander, Colonel Hayne, that Fort Gaines was almost starved out, that they went off into Georgia in search of supplies.

Thus situated at Fort Scott, Jackson formally assumed command on the tenth of March, ordered all the cattle killed, and with one quart of corn per man and three days' rations of meat

---

* Jackson to Calhoun, January 25, 1818. American State Papers, Military Affairs, vol. i, p. 696.

† Ibid., p. 698.   ‡ Ibid., pp. 698, 699.

he started down the eastern bank of the Appalachicola River in search of food.   At Prospect Bluff, where the Negro Fort had once stood, he halted and began to build a new work to protect his supplies when they came.   This was named Fort Gadsden, and while there late in March the provision ships, with an armed escort commanded by Lieutenant Isaac McKeever, of the navy, entered the bay.*

And now Jackson began to make war.   The Rhea letter, according to his account, had been received when four miles out of Hartford on the road to Fort Scott, and within twenty-four hours after the arrival of the fleet he was on his way to St. Mark's.   A letter of instruction to McKeever explains the movement.   " It is reported to me," wrote the general, " that Francis and Peter McQueen, the prophets who excited the Red Sticks, are now at work near St. Mark's exciting the Seminoles. With them are Woodbine, Arbuthnot, and a motley crew of brigands made up of slaves enticed or stolen from their masters during the last war.   They will, as the army approaches, attempt to escape to the sea islands.   You will therefore cruise along the coast and seize all sorts of persons—black, white, and red—with their goods, chattels, effects, ships, craft, and vessels, and hold them for adjudication.   Spaniards going in their ships to St. Mark's may be allowed to enter the river, but none are to pass out unsearched.   In eight days I shall be at St. Mark's and will communicate with you in the bay."

While Jackson by land and McKeever by sea were thus closing in upon St. Mark's a third personage, whose name is forever linked with that of Jackson, was riding slowly along on horseback toward the same place.   He was Alexander Arbuthnot, a Scotchman of education and ability, who came to Florida in 1817.   He had long been a merchant on the island of New Providence, and had been attracted to Florida by the fine prospect of Indian trade.   The monopoly of that trade till he came was enjoyed by a firm named Forbes & Co. But the Indians, claiming that their skins and beeswax had been greatly undervalued and the goods they purchased sold at an exorbitant price, turned from the old firm to the new-

---

* American State Papers, Military Affairs, vol. i, p. 699.

comer, and found in him a friend. That his bargains were more just and less grinding may reasonably be doubted, for he was withal an Indian trader. But he gladly undertook to do what he could to keep others from plundering and oppressing them. He wrote long letters, at the request of the chief, to the Governor of the Bahamas,* to the British Minister at Washington,† to Colonel Nicholls,‡ at London, to the governors in Florida, to the officers commanding the United States fort,# to General Mitchell, of Georgia,‖ and to the Governor-General of Havana,△ and received from the Creek chief a power of attorney to act for him in all matters concerning the nation.◊ The burden of these letters was the same. The Americans were violating the terms of the treaty of Ghent by not restoring the Indians to the lands taken by the treaty of Fort Jackson. Edmund Doyle and William Hambly, once clerks to Forbes & Co., were the fomenters of all the troubles. The backwoods Georgians were killing and robbing the Indians. The British Government ought to send out an agent to keep the British Minister informed of what the Americans were doing in Florida.

Thus engaged in befriending the Creeks and Seminoles, Arbuthnot traded back and forth between Nassau and the Indian towns for more than a year, when, in April, 1818, an evil fate turned his steps toward St. Mark's. As he entered the fort he heard for the first time of the approach of the army of Jackson and of the arrival of the fleet of McKeever. Without losing a moment he wrote to his son, then in charge of his schooner lying at anchor in the Suwanee river just below the towns of Billy Bowlegs, bade him get his goods over the river to a place of safety, or, if possible, hurry them on the schooner and sail for Cedar Keys Bay.

Jackson, after leaving Fort Gadsden, moved directly for St. Mark's, and when five days on the road fell in with a regiment of Tennesseeans and had a sharp brush with the Indians. They were quickly routed, and General Gaines, following them,

---

* American State Papers, Military Affairs, vol. i, pp. 722, 723.
† Ibid., p. 723.   ‖ Ibid., p. 729.
‡ Ibid., pp. 724, 725.   △ Ibid., p. 726.
# Ibid., p. 682.   ◊ Ibid., p. 726.

entered Fowltown the next day. There he found the red pole decorated with scalps standing in the square, took a few prisoners, on one of whom was an army coat once the property of a murdered soldier, and, having secured three thousand bushels of corn and a thousand head of cattle marked with the brands of Georgians, he set fire to the town and destroyed it. Resuming the march, the army reached Fort St. Mark's on April sixth, and while it halted near by, Jackson sent in his aide-de-camp to demand admittance. To prevent the recurrence of such gross breaches of neutrality as had happened in the past, it was necessary, the Governor was told, that St. Mark's should be garrisoned by United States troops and held till the end of the war. Don Francisco Casa y Luengo replied that he would write for authority to admit the troops. But Jackson was in no mood for delay, and, hearing that Alexander Arbuthnot was in the fort, he despatched Twiggs to seize it. At the gate Arbuthnot was found in the act of mounting his horse, and was arrested. The soldiers, entering, pulled down the Spanish flag, raised the Stars and Stripes, and took possession of the barracks. Down the harbor, meantime, two more prisoners had been taken by Captain McKeever, who entered the bay with the English flag at his masthead, and by this ruse lured on board his ship the Indian prophet Francis or Hellis Hajo and his friend Hemollemico, who had attacked Lieutenant Scott and his party and had tortured the survivors most barbarously. The two Indians had come, supposing the ship contained the long-expected supply of arms, ammunition, and blankets from England, and, on being enticed into the cabin, were seized and bound. Next day they were sent up to the fort, where, by order of Jackson, they were hung.

After a halt of forty-eight hours at St. Mark's the army resumed its march for Suwanee, the town of Boleck, or Bowlegs, and the refuge of negroes, half-breeds, and runaway slaves. The way led for one hundred and seven miles across a flat and swampy wilderness covered with trees and great ponds and destitute of food for man or beast. Some Indians were met and some fighting done on the march ; but on the afternoon of April seventeenth the troops came to a large pond which the guides said was six miles from Suwanee. Expecting to find the town occupied and the Indians and negroes in force, Jackson formed his army in three divisions, and, pushing on, reached the place about sunset and found it abandoned. Arbuthnot's letter to his son had been read to Bowlegs, and the chief, crossing the Suwanee with his women and children, had disappeared in the swamp and inaccessible retreats so plentiful in the region. A small band—three hundred or less—of Indians were indeed encountered by one of the divisions and driven over the river; but a deserted town, a few horses and cattle, and twenty-seven hundred bushels of corn were the sole fruits of the campaign. As the sacking and burning of the town would require a day or two, the army encamped on the bank of the river. But, at midnight on April eighteenth, it was suddenly aroused by the sentinels, who had detected four men attempting, as they supposed, to enter the camp. The party, when seized and brought in, proved to be two negroes and two white men who, knowing nothing of the presence of the troops, had come unexpectedly on the camp while on their way to Suwanee town. On one of the negroes was found the letter of Arbuthnot to his son. From one of the white men, Peter B. Cook by name, it was learned that this letter had been read to the negroes and Indians, and was the cause for the evacuation of the town; that the other white man was Robert C. Ambrister, and that his headquarters were on board Arbuthnot's schooner, then at the mouth of the Suwanee river. Lieutenant Gadsden was thereupon sent off to seize the vessel, and did so.

As the war was now over, Jackson began to break up his army, and, after sending the Georgia militia home to be disbanded, and dismissing McIntosh and his Indians, he, with the Tennesseeans and the regulars, went back to St. Mark's. It may well be supposed that his feelings toward Arbuthnot were far from kindly. The letter of the trader had enabled Bowlegs and his horde to escape, had turned aside the crushing blow he meant to deal the Indian power, and had made the march of two hundred miles all but fruitless. Indeed, that he did not, on reaching St. Mark's, at once hang or shoot Arbuthnot with as little ceremony as he had shot Francis and

Hemollemico, is a sure sign of an earnest effort on his part to act calmly and justly. Arbuthnot and Ambrister, whom Jackson regarded as no better than an accomplice, were handed over to a court-martial convened to decide on their guilt or innocence, and what punishment, if any, should be inflicted.

Arbuthnot was the first to be tried. Of all tribunals yet invented by man, the court-martial is undoubtedly the least likely to dispense justice. The men who form it are not selected because of any special fitness for the work to be done, nor because they possess in the smallest degree the qualities of a judge. But of all courts-martial, it would be hard to find one which went farther astray than that over which Gaines presided and before which Arbuthnot was now forced to plead. The charges against him were three in number: He had excited the Creek Indians to war against the United States; he had acted as a spy, had aided and comforted the enemy, and had supplied them with munitions of war; he had urged the Indians to murder William Hambly and Edmund Doyle. This last charge was so absurd that the court declared it had no jurisdiction over the matter, and it was withdrawn. But on the others two thirds of the court declared him guilty and sentenced him to be hung.

Ambrister was charged with aiding and comforting the enemy and with waging war on the United States, was found guilty and sentenced to be shot. But a member of the court secured a reconsideration of the sentence, and the prisoner was then doomed to receive fifty lashes on the bare back, and be confined, with chain and ball, to hard labor for one year. This Jackson heartily disapproved, and ordered the finding and first sentence carried out. Early in the morning of April twenty-ninth, accordingly, Arbuthnot was hung from the yard-arm of his own schooner Chance. On the same day Ambrister was shot.

Having by these means restored peace and good order in East Florida, Jackson and his Tennesseeans marched back to Fort Gadsden, where, toward the end of May, most astonishing information reached him. Five hundred and fifty Indians, he was told, had gathered at Pensacola, were fed by the Governor, and in the course of several forays had murdered and

plundered citizens of the United States. Again he was on
fire, and taking a small detachment of regulars and militia he
hurried off for Pensacola. As he marched along, an express
from the Governor of the town met him and delivered a
summons to quit West Florida or meet force with force. To
threats, even when accompanied by a show of force, Jackson
had never in his life given heed. This one served but to urge
him on, and without the slightest opposition he entered Pensacola on May twenty-fourth. The Governor, as he drew near,
fled to Fort Carios de Barrancas, and there attempted to make
resistance. But Jackson brought up two guns, opened on the
fort, and before the sun went down had the Governor, the
garrison, the Barrancas, and Pensacola in possession of his
troops. Leaving some soldiers to hold the place, he started
homeward five days later, more than ever the idol of the army
and the people of the Southwest.

Long ere this the fame of his doings had reached the ears
of Don Luis de Onis. His Excellency was still busy protesting most justly against the bold and impudent use of our
ports by the privateers of Buenos Ayres, and was still complaining that parties of filibusters sailed from them to wage
war against Spain, when he read in the newspapers the circum-
stantial accounts of Jackson's campaign against St. Mark's.
That every word was true he never doubted; yet he waited
till the story of the Governor of West Florida reached him,
and then entered a vigorous protest, demanding that St. Mark's
be delivered to the Spanish commander with all the arms and
warlike stores, and insisted that indemnity be made for damages done by the army in Florida, and that the troops be withdrawn.* This note had scarcely been written when, taking
up a copy of the National Intelligencer, he read of the attack,
assault, and capture of Pensacola. As the Intelligencer was,
in his language, "the Government paper," the news seemed
reliable enough to justify prompt action, and he at once asked
Adams to tell him "in a positive, distinct, and explicit manner" just what had occurred.†

---

* Don Onis to the Secretary of State, June 17, 1818. American State Papers,
Foreign Relations, vol. iv, p. 495.

† Ibid., June 24, 1819, pp. 495, 496.

Before Adams could answer, fuller and better accounts came up from Florida confirming the first report, and Don Onis once more protested.* " It seems," said he, " that under the pretence of chasing and punishing the Seminoles, General Jackson not only violated Spanish soil, but actually possessed himself by force of arms of the bay and fort of St. Mark's, and sent the garrison as prisoners to Pensacola, the capital of West Florida. Not satisfied with this, he next demanded Pensacola, just as if war existed between Spain and the United States. When delivery was refused he marched in, surrounded the castle of Barrancas, bombarded, assaulted, and carried it, sent the Governor off to Havana, and raised the American flag over every fort in West Florida. Against these acts of hostility and invasion I protest most solemnly in the name of the King, my master, and I demand a prompt restitution of St. Mark's, Pensacola, Barrancas, and all other places wrested by General Jackson from the Crown of Spain. I demand the delivery of all artillery, stores, and property, both public and private, indemnity for all injuries and losses, and the punishment of the general and his officers."

Two weeks passed before an answer was returned, for Monroe and his advisers were utterly unable to agree on just what to say. Calhoun was sure Jackson had disobeyed his instructions and had attacked Pensacola in hopes that a Spanish war would follow and he be sent into Mexico.† Crawford was afraid that if Pensacola was not at once restored, and the act of Jackson disavowed, war would follow; that our ships and commerce would become the prey of privateers sailing under the Spanish flag from all parts of the world, and that the administration would not be sustained by the people.‡ Monroe was confident that Jackson had acted not only without, but against his orders, and had waged a war on Spain that ought to be disavowed immediately. At meeting after meeting of the Cabinet the sole friend and defender of the general was Adams. The argument of the Secretary of State was, "there is no real, though there is a seeming violation of orders. Jackson was

---

* American State Papers, Foreign Relations, July 8, 1818.
† Memoirs of John Quincy Adams, vol. iv, p. 107.
‡ Ibid., vol. iv, p. 109.

authorized to cross the Spanish line in pursuit of the Indian enemy. This was a perfectly proper order, because, as Spain could not police her own territory, the observance of an imaginary line, such as the thirty-first degree of north latitude, would afford no protection to the frontier of the United States, while it would make Florida a refuge for the Indians. It was necessary, therefore, to cross the line and punish the enemy even on Spanish soil in order that the Indian war might end. This Jackson had done. His purpose in going over the boundary was not to wage war on Spain, but to put an end to the Indian war, and Fort Barrancas was captured and Pensacola held merely because the Spanish Governor threatened to drive him out of the province." Against this the Cabinet, led by Calhoun, contended that the taking of Pensacola was not necessary to self-defence ; that it was therefore both an act of war and a violation of the Constitution ; that if the administration approved it, the blame would rest on the President, and give Spain cause for war; that if it was disavowed, the blame would rest with Jackson, and Spain have no cause for war. At last Monroe made a draft of a note to Onis which, in the end, became the basis of Adams's reply.* A newspaper paragraph was then written by Attorney-General Wirt and given to the editor of the National Intelligencer for publication.†

The answer of Adams reminded Don Onis that by the fifth article of the treaty of 1795 both Spain and the United States were solemnly bound to keep peace along the frontier. Neither power was to allow the Indians dwelling on its soil to cross the boundary and molest the subjects or citizens of the other. Notwithstanding this compact, Spain had suffered the Seminole Indians and bands of negroes to sally from her territory, rob, plunder, massacre, and destroy the property and lives of American citizens, and return in safety to the dominions of his Catholic Majesty with all the horrid fruits of their crimes. When Jackson, in 1816, in accordance with the treaty, called on the Governor of Pensacola (Mauricio de Zuniga), to break

* Memoirs of John Quincy Adams, vol. iv, p. 114.
† Ibid., pp. 112, 116.

up this horde of savages and runaway slaves, the Governor admitted the obligation, but pleaded inability to destroy the Negro Fort.*   Remembering this, the President, when hostilities broke out in 1817, had given Jackson authority to cross the boundary and attack the Indians in Florida if it became necessary, and provided they did not find shelter under a Spanish fort.   The seizure of Pensacola and St. Mark's were Jackson's own acts, made necessary by the immutable principles of self-defence and the open hostility of Governor Mazot. Conduct so contrary to the treaty justified the United States in demanding the punishment of all Spanish officers concerned. Confident that this would be granted by Spain, the President was ready to deliver Pensacola to any one authorized to receive it, and to give up St. Mark's when a force large enough to hold it against the attack of hostile Indians was provided.†

An account of the situation in Florida had been sent to Spain by Don Onis, and a few days after Adams wrote his answer, Don José Pizarro, who had succeeded Cevallos as Secretary of State, began to make inquiries of Mr. George W. Erving, our Minister at Madrid.   As despatch after despatch brought fuller details, Pizarro became more and more urgent for an explanation, till in August, by order of the King, all negotiations with the United States were stopped.‡   They were soon resumed,# however, and Adams, taking up the complaint of Pizarro, answered it in one of the finest state papers he ever wrote.

He began with the landing of Colonel Nicholls and his British troops in Florida in August, 1814; he described the capture of Barrancas by Nicholls, cited his invitation to Lafitte and the Baratarians to join him, gave a copy of the proclamation to the people of Louisiana, told of his flight at the approach of Jackson and of his building of the fort on the Appalachicola, of the abandonment of the place, and of the events which finally led to its destruction with the English

---

* Jackson to the Governor of Pensacola, April 23, 1816; Governor Zuniga to Jackson, May 26, 1816.

† Adams to Don Onis, July 23, 1818.

‡ Pizarro to Erving, August 29, 1818.

Don Onis to Adams, October 18, 1818.

flag flying from its staff. He told of the arrival of Arbuthnot, whom he described as the successor of Nicholls, and as a foreign incendiary instigating the Seminoles and outlawed Red Sticks to hostilities against the United States, and laid great stress on the fact that his arrival was followed by all the horrors of savage war. He said nothing concerning the blowing up of the Negro Fort, alluded only incidentally to the capture of Fowltown, but justified the action of Jackson in crossing the line and seizing Fort St. Mark's, and the arrest of Arbuthnot, "the British Indian trader from beyond the sea, the firebrand by whose touch the Negro-Indian war against our borders has been rekindled." He declared that in St. Mark's councils of war had been held by the savage chiefs and warriors ; that Spanish storehouses had been appropriated to their use ; that cattle known to have been taken from the citizens of the United States had been sold in open market, and bought by officers of the garrison ; that from the fort a letter had been sent to the Indians by Arbuthnot giving full information as to the strength and movements of the American army, and that Jackson was therefore, by every law of neutrality and of war, by prudence, by humanity, justified in anticipating his enemy by the friendly or, if necessary, the forcible occupation of the fort. He next declared that the capture of Pensacola was right and proper for precisely the same general cause —the hostility of the Spanish Governor.

Turning from his narration of the events of the war to the complaints of Pizarro, Adams answered his charges in detail. Pizarro had spoken of "the sanguinary executions on Spanish soil of the subjects of powers in amity with the King." Adams sent him such a mass of documents, and such a picture of the doings of Nicholls and Woodbine, MacGregor, Arbuthnot and Ambrister, and of the horrors of Indian warfare as silenced him. Pizarro had described the march of Jackson as "a shameful invasion of his Majesty's territory." Adams asked him what was the character of Nicholls's invasion, and where was his Majesty's indignation over that. Pizarro had complained that his Majesty's forts and places had been violently seized on by Jackson. Adams reminded him that Nicholls had not only seized on them, but had blown up the largest of them; nay, had actually built one on Spanish soil, and asked "where was his Majesty's profound indignation at that? Has his Majesty suspended formally all negotiations with the sovereign of Colonel Nicholls? Has his Majesty given solemn warning to the British Government that these were incidents 'of transcendent moment, capable of producing an essential and thorough change in the political relations of the two countries'? If ever a whisper of expostulation was wafted from Madrid to London, it was not loud enough to be heard across the Atlantic, nor energetic enough to transpire beyond the walls of the palace from which it issued and to which it was borne." He closed the paper with the statement that the duty of the United States to protect the lives and property of its citizens was imperative; that "it must be discharged"; and that if it ever again became necessary for the United States to seize Spanish forts and places in Florida, another unconditional surrender would not be made.

Mr. Adams was still at work on his answer when November eighteenth came and the Fifteenth Congress began its second session. Both in the House and in the Senate the remarks of Monroe on affairs in Florida were sent to committees. That of the House presented two reports: one from the majority, condemning the proceedings on the trial and execution of Arbuthnot and Ambrister, and one from the minority, declaring that while they saw much in the conduct of the campaign to praise, they saw little to censure, and that when they recalled the incalculable benefits resulting to the nation from the ending of the Seminole War, they believed that Jackson and his officers deserved the thanks of the nation.

In good time the majority report was taken up in Committee of the Whole; and the resolution "That the House of Representatives of the United States disapproves the proceedings in the trial and execution of Alexander Arbuthnot and Robert C. Ambrister" being under consideration, William C. Cobb, of Georgia, opened the debate. In the course of his speech he moved three amendments: One instructed the Committee on Military Affairs to report a bill forbidding execution of any captive of the army of the United States in

time of peace, or in time of war with any Indian tribe or
tribes, unless the President approved.   Another declared that
the House disapproved of the seizure of St. Mark's, Pensacola,
and the Barrancas as contrary to orders and the Constitution.
The third instructed the committee to frame a bill prohibiting
United States troops marching into foreign territory unless
ordered to by Congress, or when in hot pursuit of an enemy
beaten and flying for refuge across the border.   With the
speech of Cobb the debate began in earnest, and went on for
twenty-seven days without interruption and to the exclusion
of all business.   No attack which up to that time had been
made on any public man—not the trial of Samuel Chase, not
the trial of Aaron Burr—had so interested and aroused the
country.   A man of the people; a bold, energetic, and determined soldier; a general, uniformly successful in the field,
and whose triumph on the swamps below New Orleans was
the pride and glory of the country, was in danger of being
censured for acts done in the course of a campaign of singular
vigor against an enemy deserving no quarter, and aided and
comforted by a power never friendly to the United States.
Both among the upholders and the detractors of his behavior
were the finest orators, the ablest debaters, the shrewdest
politicians and statesmen that generation produced.   The
display of oratory would of itself have sufficed to fill the
room where the House sat; but the interest felt in the result—the belief that on it might possibly depend a war
with Spain—when joined to the fine speaking, "filled the
galleries," in the language of the newspapers, "to suffoca-
tion."

After Mr. Holmes, of Massachusetts, had answered Mr.
Cobb, and defended Jackson and the President, Clay resumed
the attack in a speech greatly and justly admired.   Conscious
that his well-known disappointment at the failure of Monroe
to appoint him Secretary of State, that his flings at the President and his steady opposition to the administration would
lead even honest men to suspect his motives, he began with a dis-
claimer.   "All inferences of unfriendliness to the Chief Magistrate of the country, or to the illustrious military chieftain
whose operations are under examination, will be," he said,

" wholly unfounded. Toward that distinguished captain who has shed so much glory on our country, whose renown constitutes so great a portion of its moral property, I never had—I never can have—any other feelings than those of the most profound respect and of the utmost kindness. I know the motives that have been and will again be attributed to me in regard to the other exalted personage alluded to; but they have been and they will be unfounded. I may be again reluctantly compelled to differ with him, but I have formed no resolution, come under no engagements, and never will form any resolution or contract any engagements for systematic opposition to his administration or to that of any other chief magistrate."

With this painful excuse for an opposition, in which he was unquestionably sincere, he began his speech with a fierce attack on the treaty of Fort Jackson. The occasion which produced it, the dictatorial spirit we showed, the four-times-repeated words, " The United States demand," the call for the surrender of the Indian prophets, especially excited him. Strangely ignorant of Indian life, he mistook the prophets for religious leaders, and in a fine burst of eloquence pleaded for religious toleration. " When," said he, " did even conquering and desolating Rome fail to respect the altars and the gods of those whom she subjugated? Let me not be told that these prophets were impostors who deceived the Indians. They were their prophets. The Indians believed and venerated them, and it is not for us to dictate a religious belief to them. We leave to the humane and benevolent efforts of the reverend professors of Christianity to convert these unhappy nations yet immersed in gloom. But spare them their prophets! Spare their delusions! Spare their prejudices and their superstitions! Spare their religion, such as it is, from open and cruel violence!"

Though this wicked treaty was the cause of the Seminole War, he acquitted Jackson of all blame save the little that attached to him as negotiator. But he was loud in his denunciation of the snare by which Francis and Hemollemico were captured, and of the unceremonious way in which they were hung under cover of retaliation for the enormities their follow-

ers had committed. He waived, he conceded, for the sake
of argument, the guilt of Arbuthnot and Ambrister; but he rejected with scorn the argument of Jackson that an individual
of one nation making war on the citizens of another, the two
nations being at peace, forfeits his allegiance and becomes an
outlaw and a pirate. He claimed that whatever might be the
character of men waging private war, the principle of Jackson
was utterly wrong when applied to men fighting under a power, whether Indian or civilized, and capable of waging war and
making peace. He showed that such doctrine would make
every alien serving in our armies an outlaw and a pirate. He
asked what jurisdiction, and how acquired, the military power
had over pirates, robbers, and outlaws, and why, if such had
been captured, they had not been handed over to be dealt with
according to law. He likened the treatment of Arbuthnot and
Ambrister to the execution of the Duc d'Enghein by Bonaparte; he compared the seizure of Pensacola and St. Mark's to
the bombardment of Copenhagen and the capture of the Dan-
ish fleet by England, and while he " cheerfully acquitted "
Jackson " of any intention to violate the laws of the country
or the obligations of humanity," charged him with doing acts
above and beyond the law. He charged Jackson with violating his orders and assuming not only the right to judge what
Spain was in duty bound to do, but the power of deciding what
should be the penalty for her failure to do it; he accused him
of seizing forts and so usurping the power of making war
which belonged exclusively to Congress, and warned the people
to beware of the military hero covered with glory. " We are
fighting," said Clay, " a great moral battle for the benefit not
only of ourselves but of all mankind. The eyes of the whole
world are fixed upon us. One—the larger—part, is gazing with
contempt, with jealousy, and with envy. The other part with
hope, with confidence, and with affection. To us belongs the
high privilege of transmitting unimpaired to posterity the fair
character and the liberty of our country. Can we expect to
execute this high trust by trampling or suffering to be trampled
down law, justice, the Constitution, and the rights of other people? Beware how you give a fatal sanction in this infant period of our republic, scarcely yet twoscore years old, to mili-

tary insubordination. Are former services, however eminent, to protect from even inquiring into recent misconduct? Is there no limit, no prudential bounds to national gratitude? I hope gentlemen will deliberately survey the awful isthmus on which we stand. They may bear down all opposition. They may even vote the general public thanks. They may carry him triumphantly through this House. But if they do, in my humble judgment it will be a triumph of the spirit of insubordination, a triumph of the military over the civil authority, a triumph over the powers of this House, a triumph over the Constitution of the land. And I pray most devoutly to heaven that it may not prove in its ultimate effects and consequences a triumph over the liberties of the people."

The speech was indeed a great one, and it may well be believed that the splendid diction, the stirring appeals, delivered with all the fire of the speaker, strongly affected the House, while the reasoning, the illustrations, the charges, and the glowing peroration roused the undying hate of Jackson.

But Jackson was not without defenders in the House. Johnson and Tallmadge and Poindexter, and Alexander Smyth, of Virginia, who had himself felt the pangs of wounded vanity, and Barbour, and a host of others set upon Clay and tore his speech to pieces. Clay had laughed at the doctrine of Jackson that Arbuthnot and Ambrister had forfeited their allegiance and become outlaws. But Vattel and Martens were cited to prove that Jackson was right. Clay had denied the right of a general to retaliate for acts of cruelty done by the enemy. But he was overwhelmed with instances proving he was wrong. The case of Captain Huddie and the resolutions of Congress concerning it; the case of Colonel Hayne and the order of General Greene thereon; the case of Major André and the conduct of Washington, were cited over and over again by the speakers. So many spoke, and the speeches were so long, that it was not till the eighth of February that the votes were taken on the amendments and the resolution. In each case Jackson was sustained both by the Committee of the Whole and by the House.

In the Senate the message and documents relating to the

Seminole War were sent to a committee early in December; but no report was made till February twenty-fourth. The document then submitted condemned his conduct at every point, and, after being ordered to be printed, was laid on the table, where it remained when the second session of the Fifteenth Congress ended on March fourth.

CHAPTER XXXV.

THE FISHERIES AND BOUNDARIES.

WHEN the news reached Washington that Jackson had put to death British subjects and had seized a Spanish town, two important treaties were under way with Great Britain and Spain. It was feared at first that his conduct would delay, if indeed it did not prevent, their ratification. But no such evil consequences followed, and each was soon brought to a happy conclusion. That with Great Britain grew out of the interpretation placed by her on the third article of the definitive treaty of 1783—an article which recognized the right of the people of the United States to a share in the Northeastern fisheries.

As the question of right which then arose is still, after the lapse of nearly eighty years, a vexed one, it is well worth our while to recall how that article came to have a place in the treaty. To say that the fisheries played a great part in the commercial life of colonial New England is but feebly to express their true position. No citation of statistics, no statement of the quintals of fish caught and dried, of the number of ships and men employed, of the thousands of pounds sterling which, in one form or another—in rum, in molasses, in bills of exchange, or in packages of English goods—came each year to the seaports of New England in exchange for cod and herring, affords any adequate conception of the real importance of this industry. That it was of truly vital importance is abundantly proved by two well-known incidents in our history : by the excitement, the violence, the protests, the remonstrances which followed the passage and enforcement of the Molasses Act in 1764, and by the attempt of Lord North

to reduce the rebellious colonies to obedience in 1775 by restraining their commerce and destroying the fisheries. In
the list of parliamentary acts which did so much to bring on
the Revolution there is none so infamous as that aimed at the
fisheries. Its purpose was to limit the trade of the four New
England colonies to England, Ireland, and the British West
Indies, cut off the great fish trade with France, Holland,
Spain, Madeira, Paramaribo, and Brazil, and stop all fishing
on the banks of Newfoundland. Though witness after witness was examined at the bar of the Commons, though each
one testified that the bill would work irreparable injury, that
the fisheries were the life-blood of New England, that the
colonies could not subsist three months without them, that
the loss of them would strip six thousand fishermen of Massachusetts of a livelihood, and force ten thousand others to seek
employment elsewhere, it was the Lords and not the Commons who were impressed by its infamy. The bill did indeed
pass by a great majority; but twenty-one peers entered a
solemn protest against it. " We dissent," said they, " because
the attempt to coerce, by famine, the whole body of the inhabitants of great and populous provinces is without example
in the history of this or, perhaps, of any civilized nation." Nor
were Lord North and the Parliament alone in the belief that
the act must be fatal to New England. Even Vergennes shared
it, and a year later, when Silas Deane was seeking French aid
in Paris, the subject on which the Minister most wanted assurance was the ability of the rebellious colonies to subsist without the fisheries. When at last that aid was given, and the
day seemed at hand when independence would be secured,
Congress also became most anxious for the preservation of
the ancient fishing privileges. This concern was expressed
now by a resolution that the fisheries must not by any treaty
be given up; now by an instruction to Adams that it was
essential to the welfare of the United States that her people
should enjoy, in peace and quiet, the right to fish on the
banks of Newfoundland and in the seas of North America;
and now by a resolution that if, after peace was made, England should obstruct the people of the United States in
the use of their common rights in the fisheries, such action

would be considered a cause of war, and the force of the Union would be used to secure redress for the injury inflicted. Again it was an instruction to Franklin to propose to the French King an article binding France and the United States to make common cause against England for the protection of the fisheries. Unhappily, when the time came to test the sincerity of these high-sounding resolutions, Congress yielded, and in July, 1781, resolved that the guarantee to an equal right in the fisheries with Englishmen was not an ultimatum of peace. That such rights were finally obtained is due to the zeal of John Adams and the firmness of his fellow commissioners, who made it a condition of peace.

As defined in the treaty of 1783, these rights or liberties were three in number: that of deep-sea fishing; that of inshore fishing; and that of using the shores of certain bays, creeks, and harbors for the purpose of drying and curing the catch. As to the first, it is agreed, said the treaty, that the people of the United States shall continue to enjoy unmolested the right to take fish of every kind on the Grand Banks, and on all the other banks of Newfoundland, in the Gulf of St. Lawrence, and at all other places in the sea where the inhabitants of both countries used at any time heretofore to fish. As to the second, it was provided that Americans might take fish of every sort on such parts of the coast of Newfoundland as was free to British fishermen, and on all other coasts and and in all other harbors, bays, and creeks of his Majesty's dominions in America. But the only places where fish could be dried and cured were the unsettled shores of the harbors, bays, and creeks of Nova Scotia, of the Magdalen Islands, and of Labrador.

During the period which elapsed from the signing of the treaty to the adoption of the Constitution the fishing industry was prostrate. It did, indeed, give employment to five hundred and forty ships and thirty-three hundred seamen. But the business had steadily declined till, in 1789, the average yearly earnings of each vessel was two hundred and seventy-three dollars, and the average yearly expense four hundred and sixteen dollars. Under the Constitution Congress came to the relief, and, first by a bounty on dried and pickled fish, and then by an annual allowance for each ton of the ship, did not a little toward reviving the industry. The war in Europe and the opening of the French West Indies did more; and with the incoming of the new century the British colonists began to cry out that the Yankees were ruining them. Unable to get help from the mother country, they seemed to have taken matters into their own hands; and in 1806 our fishermen, in their turn, complained to Congress. If their accounts are to be trusted, they were stopped and searched when going to and returning from the Grand Banks; were fired on; were forced to pay toll as they passed through the Gut of Canso; and, if they dropped anchor in any bay, were made to pay light money and anchorage.

From this hated competition the British fishermen were relieved by the long embargo. It was, indeed, but a temporary relief. But it was so much to their liking that when the war opened Englishmen engaged in the Newfoundland fisheries besought the mother country never again to grant such liberties to America. At a meeting held at St. John's, in 1813, a memorial was prepared and delivered to their Governor in which it was asserted that by the concession great national benefits had been lost. A door had been opened to illicit trade to the injury of the revenue and the morals of his Majesty's subjects. Fifteen hundred American ships had been known to be fishing at one time on the coast of Labrador. These brought with them teas, coffees, spirits, and other contraband goods, which, as the vessels passed through the narrow Gut of Canso, were smuggled ashore. Coming in such great numbers, the Americans overawed the British on the fishing grounds, and tempted them to emigrate to the United States. Under the influence of notions imbibed from these men, the small planters and catchers of fish would first become dissatisfied with their supplying merchants, who could not meet their foreign competitors on equal ground, would then fail to pay their debts, and finally, growing disobedient and insubordinate, would emigrate, to the great loss of the colony. Nor did the evil stop here. It followed the British merchant into the markets of Europe and the West Indies, where the Americans undersold him; because in the United States men, provisions, and outfits were to be had on much better terms than in the British colonies. For these reasons and for many more, the petitioners prayed that foreigners might never again be suffered to fish in colonial waters.*

The publication of this memorial aroused no little sectional feeling. In New England the cry became "No peace without the fisheries." But the conduct of New England during the war had won her no friends; and when it was known that the English commissioners had made the surrender of the fisheries a condition of peace, the sentiment in the Middle and Southern States was, as a newspaper expressed it, that "peace was better than codfish." Unhappily, the treaty said not a word about the fisheries, and this the colonists construed to be an abrogation of all fishing rights. The war, they held, had ended the treaty of 1783. The liberty of fishing in British waters was granted by that treaty, and was therefore a thing of the past. Toward the end of May, therefore, a rumor reached Boston that the collector at Halifax had declared that he would send out ships and drive the Americans from the Nova Scotia coast if they attempted to fish there. It was not believed that he would. But in July a sloop entered Boston with a Halifax newspaper which announced that the British sloop of war Jaseur had returned from a cruise with eight American vessels caught fishing on the western coast of Nova Scotia. After a detention of forty-eight hours their papers were endorsed forbidding them to fish within three miles of the western coast. They were then released. Almost at the same time a fishing vessel entered the port of Barnstable. She had been visited when forty-five miles from Cape Sable by an officer of the Jaseur, who wrote on her enrolment and license the words, "Warned off the coast by his Majesty's sloop Jaseur. Not to come within sixty miles." † On reaching port the captain reported these facts and showed his license to the collector at Barnstable, who promptly notified the Secretary of the Treasury, who informed Monroe, who lost no time in demanding an explanation from

---

* Niles's Weekly Register, June 11, 1814.

† Monroe to Sir Anthony St. J. Baker, July 18, 1815. American State Papers, Foreign Relations, vol. iv, p. 348.

Sir Anthony Baker, the British Chargé. He was assured that the act of the captain of the Jaseur was not authorized by the British Government.* It mattered little, however, for, as every ship the Jaseur fell in with was ordered off the coast, the summer fishing season was a failure.

As soon as Monroe had despatched his note to Mr. Baker, he wrote and sent off one to John Quincy Adams, who had recently become United States Minister at the Court of St. James. After reciting the warning of the Jaseur to American fishermen not to come within sixty miles of the coast, Monroe defined the position of the United States, declared that every fishing right acknowledged by the treaty of 1783 was still unimpaired, and instructed Adams to give the subject his earnest and prompt attention. An interview was accordingly sought and had with Lord Bathurst, and three subjects of serious complaints—the surrender of Michilimackinaw, the conduct of Colonel Nicholls in Florida, and the warning of the Jaseur—duly presented. Lord Bathurst then stated that despatches on all these matters had just been received from Mr. Baker, and that the act of the captain of the Jaseur had been promptly disavowed.

Great Britain, he said, would not deprive American fishermen of any of the rights enjoyed under the treaty of 1783 during 1815 ; but after 1815 it was her intention to exclude them from fishing within one marine league of the shores of her North American possessions, and from drying and curing fish in the unsettled parts of those territories, and from such parts as had become settled since 1783. It was not her intention, however, to hinder them at any time from fishing in the open sea, or anywhere without her jurisdiction of one marine league. Mr. Adams expressed the hope that no final determination would be reached till he had time to present the views of the United States. His lordship answered that the document should be carefully read, and shortly afterward received it.

Mr. Adams began by reminding him that from the planting of the English colonies in America until their separation

---

* Sir Anthony St. J. Baker to Monroe. Ibid., pp. 348, 349.

from Great Britain, in 1776, the liberties of catching, drying, and curing fish had been enjoyed by them in common with other subjects of the Empire; that they had, indeed, been the original discoverers and improvers of the fisheries, had used the grounds more than had the men of any other part of the Empire, and had borne their full share, and more than their full share, in conquering the French provinces on whose coasts the fisheries were situated. "Doubtless," said Mr. Adams, "it was for these reasons that in the treaty of 1783 an express stipulation was inserted, recognizing the rights and liberties the people of the United States had always enjoyed in the fisheries, and declaring that they should continue to enjoy the right of fishing on the Grand Banks and have the liberty of catching, drying, and curing fish wherever they used so to do while subjects of Great Britain. These rights and liberties were in no sense grants from King George to the United States. The stipulations of the treaty are simply the acknowledgment of them as rights and liberties existing when the United States were colonies, and which it was agreed should continue after the United States became an independent power. On neither side were the stipulations intended or understood to be grants from one sovereign state to another; yet such seems to have been the view of the British Government when, in August, 1814, her plenipotentiaries at Ghent informed those of the United States that Great Britain 'did not intend to grant to the United States gratuitously the privileges formerly granted by treaty to them of fishing within the limits of British sovereignty and using the shores of the British territories for purposes connected with the British fisheries.' To this the American representatives made answer that no authority had been given them to discuss any of the rights and privileges the United States enjoyed in the fisheries, and that from the nature of these rights and from the peculiar character of the treaty of 1783, by which they were recognized, no further stipulations were necessary. The treaty did not create them, but merely recognized them as already existing. They could not therefore be in any wise impaired by the declaration of war in 1812, nor by the declaration of the British plenipotentiaries in 1814, that the rights would not be renewed. All the stipulations in the treaty of 1783 are permanent, and Great Britain cannot say this one is perpetual and that one is abrogated. Yet this is just what she is doing. In that document is an acknowledgment that the United States are free, sovereign, and independent States, and a description of their boundaries. Suppose Great Britain had announced at Ghent that she did not intend gratuitously to again acknowledge our independence or to again gratuitously grant the same boundary line she did in 1783; would not the proper answer have been that we need no new acknowledgment of our independence; that we need no new grant of a boundary line; that these provisions are permanent; that they cannot be forfeited or lost without our consent? By what right, then, can Great Britain select one article and say this particular stipulation has been forfeited by the war, yet hold all the others to be lasting? Did she consider her right to navigate the Mississippi, as secured by the treaty of 1783, was lost by the war of 1812? * "

"You contend," said Lord Bathurst in his reply, "that the treaty of 1783 was of a peculiar character, and that because it contains an acknowledgment of American independence it cannot be abrogated by a subsequent war. To a position so novel as this Great Britain cannot accede. She knows no exception to the rule that every treaty is put an end to by war between the two parties. She cannot give to her diplomatic relations with one state a permanency she does not give to such relations with other states. She cannot consider any one state at liberty to give to a treaty with her such a peculiarity of character as shall make it an exception to all others. It is true that the United States does not need a new boundary; but the war did not arise out of a contested boundary, and Great Britain did right in treating with the United States as unchanged in this respect save so far as the *jus belli* had interfered. It is true that the independence of a state is acknowledged, not created, by a treaty, and that when once acknowledged it cannot be revoked. That would be destruction of the thing itself; therefore the power to revoke is neces-

---

* Mr. Adams to Lord Bathurst, September 25, 1815. American State Papers, Foreign Relations, vol. iv, pp. 352–354.

sarily renounced when the acknowledgment is made. But the nature of the right to fish within British limits is essentially different from the right to independence in all that respects duration. It has the aspects of a policy temporary and experimental, and depending for its continuation on the use made of it. When, therefore, Great Britain, admitting the independence of the United States, denies the right of its citizens to catch, cure, and dry fish within her limits, it is not that she selects from the treaty articles, or parts of articles, and says, at her own will, this stipulation is subject to forfeiture by war, that stipulation is irrevocable, but that she holds that one article differs from another because they are founded on grants of a totally different character. The very language of the treaty proves this. The United States had the *right* to catch fish on the Banks of Newfoundland, from which Great Britain does not claim the right to exclude any nation. But the United States had only the *liberty* to cure and dry fish in certain unsettled places within his Majesty's territory. Throughout the treaty the word right is used as applicable to what the United States were to enjoy in virtue of recognized independence; but the word liberty applies to what they were to enjoy as concessions, as grants arising from the treaty itself. While Great Britain could not recognize the claim of the United States to enjoy these liberties as matter of right, she was quite willing to negotiate for a modified renewal of the liberty.* "

A long illness prevented Mr. Adams answering this note till the close of January, 1816,† by which time Lord Castlereagh had resumed his duties as Secretary of State for Foreign Affairs. In an interview with him Mr. Adams was again assured that Great Britain was willing to treat, and, as no power had been sent to the American Minister to enter into negotiations, full power to do so was sent to Mr. Charles Bagot, the new British Minister at Washington.

In opening the subject to Monroe, Bagot offered the liberty of drying and curing fish on the unsettled parts of the coast of Labrador, from Mount Joli, opposite the eastern end of Anti-

---

* Lord Bathurst to Mr. Adams, October 30, 1815.

† Mr. Adams to Lord Bathurst, January 22, 1816.

costi, eastward to the bay and isles of Esquimaux near the western entrance to the Straits of Belle Isle, and insisted that all
claims to fish or cure within the maritime limits of any other
of the coasts of British North America should be abandoned.
Before replying Monroe consulted the fishermen of Marblehead
and Salem, and, finding that it would be more advantageous to
have no eastern limit, but extend the liberty through the straits
and indefinitely up the coast of Labrador, suggested such a
modification.   Mr. Bagot declined to consider it, and offered
as an alternative the south coast of Newfoundland from Cape
Ray eastward to the Rameau Islands, or longitude 57° west
from Greenwich.*   Once more the fishermen were consulted,
and, as they declared that the Newfoundland coast was as little
used as that of Labrador, Monroe rejected each proposition.†
Mr. Bagot then tendered both coasts, ‡ but the offer was declined
on the ground that they were not used by American fishermen.#

Meantime Great Britain was maintaining her position with
a show of force.   During the summer of 1816 the ship
Menai, of sixty-four guns, scoured the waters of the Bay of
Fundy and the Gulf of St. Lawrence, and wrote on the license
of every American fisherman she overhauled the words,
" Warned from fishing in the ports, harbors, creeks, or bays
within the jurisdiction of his Britannic Majesty's North
American colonies, or using any part thereof for any purpose
connected with fishing."   Seven vessels belonging to Kittery
and three owned at New Castle, a little fishing port not far
from Portsmouth, in New Hampshire, were captured, while
fishing three leagues from land, by the barges of a gun-brig.
After holding them four days, the commander of the brig
warned, and released them.   The American fishermen, though
unaided by their Government, were not disposed to give up
the struggle, and, when the fishing season of 1817 opened, a
fleet of twenty fishing vessels sailed from the ports of New
England and made for the western banks.   Some got safely
to the grounds, others were overtaken by storms and sought

---

* Mr. Bagot to Mr. Monroe, November 27, 1816.
† Mr. Monroe to Mr. Bagot, December 30, 1816.
‡ Mr. Bagot to Mr. Monroe, December 31, 1817.
# Mr. Monroe to Mr. Bagot, January 7, 1817.

shelter at Ragged Island, not far from Shelburne light-house. There, according to the story told by the men, their boats were boarded by an officer of the customs, who, though they had entered port in distress, demanded and was paid light money, after which they went on to the banks.

While the American fleet was thus engaged, Sir David Milne, commander of the North American station, despatched the Dee, Captain Samuel Chambers, to cruise between Sambro Light and Cape Sable. "You will," said his orders, "protect the fisheries on the coast against the encroachment of foreigners. On your meeting with any foreign vessel fishing or lying at anchor in any of the harbors or creeks in his Majesty's North American province, you will seize and send her to Halifax for adjudication, unless it should appear that she has put in there in distress." On reaching the fishing grounds, the captain of the Dee heard nothing of any foreign ships till June third, when, happening to be off the Isle Maten, he was informed that the whole of the banks were fished by American schooners, that they constantly entered the creeks on the coast to catch bait, clean fish, and get wood and water, and that the harbors of Cape Negro and Ragged Island were favorite places for passing Sunday. Captain Chambers, on hearing this, put into Shelburne, and despatched the boats of the Dee into Ragged Island harbor, where nine American fishing vessels were found at anchor with their nets set, and were ordered to Halifax. The gig and cutters were next sent to Cape Negro, where nine more were seized and taken to Halifax, where, after a delay of many weeks, they were brought to trial. The Advocate-General, in his argument before the judge of the Vice-Admiralty Court, laid great stress on the fact that the war had abrogated the fishing liberties granted the Americans by the treaty of 1783. To this the judge assented. But as American fishermen had so long enjoyed that liberty, as no specific prohibition had been made public by Great Britain since the treaty of Ghent, as none of the men before the court were taken in the act of fishing or trading with the inhabitants, but had merely put in for shelter, he refused to condemn the ships, and ordered them restored on their owners paying costs.

By this time Mr. Adams had come home to be Secretary of State, and Richard Rush, who had been chosen his successor, was about to depart. The instructions Rush took with him when he sailed in November bade him conclude a commercial treaty to take the place of the commercial convention of July, 1815. But he had not been very long in London when the refusal of England to open her colonial trade to American merchants produced the Plaster-of-Paris Act, the Navigation Act, and a change in his instructions. He was now to propose the immediate negotiation of a commercial treaty, offer a continuation of the convention of 1815, and ask a settlement of such old grievances as were fast growing serious. Among these were our fishing rights, the demand for indemnity for slaves carried off by British officers at the end of the war, the boundary line from the Lake of the Woods westward, and our title to the little settlement at the mouth of the Columbia river. Should Great Britain agree to negotiate, Gallatin, who was then our Minister to France, was to join Rush at once. Great Britain did agree, and on the twenty-seventh of August Gallatin and Rush, on the part of the United States, met with Frederick John Robinson and Henry Goulburn, on the part of England, and formally opened a conference, which closed on the twentieth of October with the signing of the Convention of 1818.

Power had been given to the American plenipotentiaries to agree to an article stripping the inhabitants of the United States of the liberty to take, cure, and dry fish within British jurisdiction generally, provided that liberty was secured to them forever along the south coast of Newfoundland from the Rameau Islands to Cape Ray, and along the coast of Labrador from Mount Joli through the Straits of Belle Isle and northward indefinitely. But they did more than was expected of them, and by the first article of the convention four things were agreed upon: In the first place, it was provided that inhabitants of the United States might forever catch fish on the shores of the Magdalen Islands, on the coast of Newfoundland from the Rameau Islands to Cape Ray, and from Cape Ray to the Quirpon Islands, and on the shores of Labrador from Mount Joli eastward through the Straits of Belle

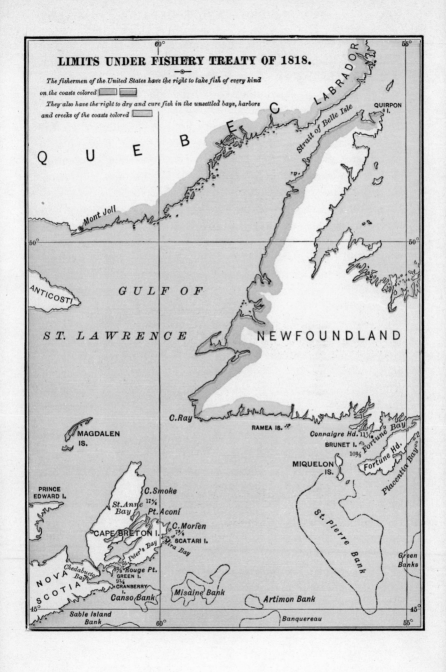

LIMITS UNDER FISHERY TREATY OF 1818.

The fishermen of the United States have the right to take fish of every kind on the coasts colored

They also have the right to dry and cure fish in the unsettled bays, harbors and creeks of the coasts colored

Isle and northward indefinitely. In the second place, it was provided that American fishermen might forever dry and cure fish in any of the unsettled bays, harbors, or creeks of New-foundland from Rameau Islands to Cape Ray, and of Labrador from Mount Joli eastward and northward indefinitely. In the third place, it was agreed that, in consideration of this liberty, the United States renounced forever the claim of its inhabitants to take, dry, or cure fish within three miles of any other of the coasts, bays, creeks, or harbors of his Britannic Majesty's possessions in North America, but that they might enter any of these bays, creeks, or harbors for the purpose of seeking shelter, mending damages, buying wood, or obtaining water, and for no other purposes whatsoever.

The instructions of the American plenipotentiaries, again, bade them secure a northern boundary for the United States from the Lake of the Woods as far westward as possible. The old treaty of 1783 had defined the boundary to be a due west line from the most northwestern point of the Lake of the Woods to the Mississippi, which was then supposed to rise in British America; but, as the possibility of drawing such a line soon became doubtful, the treaty of 1794 called for a joint survey of the Mississippi from one degree below the Falls of St. Anthony to its source or sources, and the establishment, if necessary, of a new line. The joint survey, however, was not made, and when Rufus King concluded his convention in 1803 it was stipulated that the boundary should be the shortest line from the northwest corner of the Lake of the Woods to the Mississippi. That convention was never ratified, and its rejection was most fortunate, for the purchase of Louisiana a few months later, when joined to our claim to the Columbia, gave a new value to our possessions in the Northwest. At the next treaty-making with Great Britain in 1806 the question was once more seriously considered and three propositions were made. Great Britain asked for the forty-ninth parallel from the Lake of the Woods to the Stony, or, as we know them, the Rocky Mountains. Monroe and Pinkney, not feeling sure that the parallel in question would touch the lake, offered a line beginning at the most northwestern point of the lake and running due north or due south till it did meet the forty-ninth parallel, and then along it to the mountains. The boundary finally chosen was that offered by Monroe, with the Stony Mountains stricken out and the provision "as far as the respective territories of the parties extend in that quarter" inserted. But this treaty was repudiated by Jefferson—was never even sent to the Senate—and the boundary was still unsettled when the peace commissioners met at Ghent.

In the interval, however, the claim of the United States to Oregon had been yet further strengthened by the enterprise of her citizens. When the agent of Mr. Jefferson received the formal surrender of upper Louisiana in March, 1804, the centre of the great Northwestern fur trade was St. Louis. From the day when Laclede obtained the monopoly of the Indian trade and founded the little frontier post of 1764, St. Louis became and remained the Montreal of the Mississippi. With this its geographical position had much to do. Northward and westward lay the Mississippi and the Missouri, with their immense network of beaver-hunting streams, and the great plains over which roamed countless herds of buffalo and deer. To transport such bulky furs from the regions of the Northwest by lake and river, stream and portage, to Lake Superior, and on by Michilimackinaw, Lake Nipissing, and the Ottawa to Montreal, consumed half their value. But the easy water routes which joined St. Louis with the fur regions on the one hand, and with New Orleans and a market on the other hand, gave to her an advantage over the old route which the fur traders were quick to seize. To it, therefore, resorted the most adventurous and daring of the *voyageurs* and *coureurs des bois*. Long after the United States acquired it three fourths of its population were hunters and boatmen, while all derived their livelihood from the trade in furs. St. Louis traders pushed their ventures in every direction, put up trading posts on the Arkansas, the St. Francis, and the Red, opened the Santa Fé trail, and even gathered peltry on the waters of the Osage, the upper Missouri, the Des Moines, and along the shores of upper Michigan. When, therefore, Lewis and Clark came back in 1806 from their explorations in the far Northwest, the most enterprising of these traders saw a new and yet unused hunting ground open before them, and, under the lead of Manuel Lisa, Pierre Chouteau, and Governor William Clark, the Missouri Fur Company was quickly formed to occupy and use it. With the capital of this company and under its direction, before two years passed, several trading posts were established on the upper Missouri and another built far beyond the Rocky Mountains, at the head waters of the Lewis river. It was a veritable outpost, and was in all probability the first ever formed by white men within the region drained by the Columbia river. As such it met the fate which so often befell like undertakings. The Indians around it were bitterly hostile. It was far from any source of supply, and in consequence was abandoned in 1810.

But just as the Missouri Fur Company was about to withdraw from Oregon, a rival which had sprung up in the East was preparing to make a foothold. This rival was called the Pacific Fur Company, founded by John Jacob Astor, of New York. It was indeed little more than in name a company, for though one half its shares were held by Canadians and Americans familiar with the fur trade, and Scotchmen who had long been in the service of the British Northwest Fur Company, it was Astor who furnished the capital and directed the enterprise. His purpose was to establish a network of trading posts on the Pacific coast, on the Columbia, and on the head waters of the Missouri, and supply them either from St. Louis by the latter river or from a factory at the mouth of the Columbia.

To this factory were to be brought the furs gathered at the interior posts, and such goods, sent out annually from New York by ship, as were necessary for trade and sustenance. After landing the supplies the vessels were to take on board a cargo of furs, sail for Canton, and there exchange them for tea and silk, which were to be brought back to New York city. Mr. Astor was to remain in New York, but the partners were to conduct the business in the West and share one half the profits. All being in readiness, some, with the clerks and minor officials, set sail in the ship Tonquin from New York in September, 1810. The rest, under the lead of the general agent, left St. Louis in January, 1811, on an overland journey to the Pacific coast. The Tonquin reached her destination first, and in March, 1811, landed her goods and passengers at the mouth of the Columbia, where, on the south bank of the river, some eight miles from the ocean, a spot was chosen as the site of the factory, which was named Astoria, in honor of the man whose money maintained the venture.

This done, the Tonquin sailed away to the northward in search of furs, leaving the partners to put up the building, plant the gardens, and open trade with the Indians. While so engaged they were surprised by the arrival in July of a party of Englishmen sent out by the Northwest Fur Company to take possession of the country and occupy the mouth of the river. On the way down from British America they had therefore put up rude huts and raised their flag as evidence of the ownership of Oregon by Great Britain ; but they reached the mouth of the river too late, and went back frustrated for the time being.

Meantime the party from St. Louis went up the Missouri to the great bend that river makes in what is now the State of Iowa. There, leaving the river, they struck westward across the prairies, passed through the Black Hills, went over the Rocky Mountains, at about the parallel of forty-five degrees, and, after suffering untold hardships from cold, hunger, and fatigue, reached the Salmon river, down which they passed to the Columbia and by it to Astoria, where they arrived in the spring of 1812.

So far all had gone well, but now disaster followed hard upon disaster. First came news that the Tonquin, while in one of the inlets of Nootka Sound, had been attacked by savages, that the crew had been overpowered, and that when most of them had been massacred, the survivors, who had taken refuge in the hold, had blown up the ship and perished with their Indian enemies. Next came word that war had been declared by the United States against Great Britain. Finally, a body of men in the service of the Northwest Fur Company appeared at Astoria one day in the early autumn with the alarming intelligence that a frigate and an armed ship were on their way from England to take possession of the mouth of the Columbia, that the Atlantic coast of the United States was blockaded by English squadrons, and when they had terrified the partners with these statements offered to buy them out. They consented, and on October sixteenth, 1812, all the buildings, furs, and property of the Pacific Fur Company were sold to the Northwest Company for forty thousand dollars in bills on Montreal. Six weeks later the British sloop of war Raccoon entered the Columbia and anchored off Astoria. Her captain had come in hopes of securing a rich booty by the seizure of the furs and goods of the Americans. He found much of it had already been floated up the river toward the Canadian posts of the British company, and was forced to be content with raising the English flag over the factory and changing the name from Astoria to Fort George.

The capture of the factory and the sale of the property of the company were unknown to the peace commissioners when they met at Ghent. Each party, therefore, brought forward the line offered in 1806; but to the British offer was added the new condition that her subjects should have access across the territories of the United States to the Mississippi, and the free navigation of that river to the Gulf. This made the acceptance of the British line impossible, and as her commissioners would not separate the question of the boundary from the question of the use of the Mississippi, no conclusion was reached.

By the first article of the treaty it was further agreed that all territory and places taken by either party during or after the war should be restored without delay. Monroe accordingly notified the British Chargé in July, 1815, that the President intended to reoccupy Astoria immediately, a threat so slowly carried out, that more than two years were allowed to pass before the Ontario sailed from New York in October, 1817, on a voyage around the Horn for the purpose of taking possession of the mouth of the Columbia. Her departure called out a remonstrance from Mr. Bagot and the statement that the country adjacent to the Columbia " was considered as part of his Majesty's dominions." But Bathurst did not sustain it, and by his orders Astoria was quietly surrendered to the American commissioners on October sixth, 1818.

Meantime the question of ownership was temporarily arranged at London. At the conferences held there in 1818 the

American plenipotentiaries proposed a line due north or due south from the most northwestern point of the Lake of the Woods to the forty-ninth parallel, and westward along it to the Pacific, with the provision that west of the Stony Mountains the inhabitants of each nation should enjoy the free navigation of all the rivers and the free use of all the ports and harbors within the territory of the other. Great Britain, of course, put in a counter project which accepted the line as far as the Stony Mountains, but required that the country west of the mountains and lying between the forty-fifth and the forty-ninth parallels should be held in joint occupation. The result was a compromise by which the boundary became a line from the most northwestern point of the Lake of the Woods due north or due south to the forty-ninth parallel and westward along it to the summit of the Rocky Mountains. The country beyond the mountains, claimed or possessed by either, was to be held in joint occupation for ten years. The trade convention of July third, 1815, was likewise continued for ten years, and the question of damages for slaves carried off at the end of the war was submitted to arbitration.

The settlement of a boundary between the United States and the British possessions in America on the north was very quickly followed by the establishment of a boundary between the United States and the possessions of Spain on the south. On the renewal of diplomatic relations with Spain in December, 1815, Don Onis made a demand for the surrender of so much of West Florida as Madison took possession of under the act of 1811.* He was answered by Monroe that when the United States purchased Louisiana in 1803 she bought it, as France owned it prior to the treaty of 1763, when the Perdido was the limit on the one side and the Rio Grande on the other, and that to the territory within these rivers she considered her title to be established.†

From this Don Onis dissented. The country from the Mississippi to the Rio Grande, he said, had been under the Crown of Spain ever since the discovery and conquest of

---

* Don Onis to Monroe, December 30, 1815.
† Monroe to Don Onis, January 19, 1816.

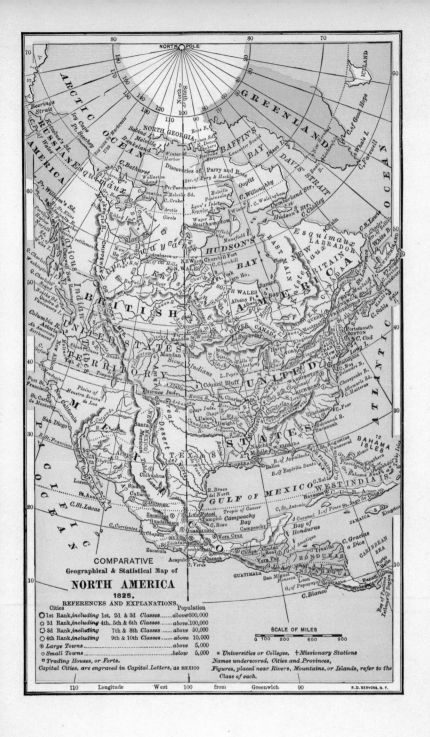

COMPARATIVE
Geographical & Statistical Map of
NORTH AMERICA
1825.

REFERENCES AND EXPLANATIONS.

Cities   Population
⊘ 1st Rank, *including* 1st, 2d & 3d *Classes* ...... above 300,000
⊘ 2d Rank, *including* 4th, 5th & 6th *Classes* ..... above 100,000
⊘ 3d Rank, *including* 7th & 8th *Classes* ..... above 50,000
○ 4th Rank, *including* 9th & 10th *Classes* ...... above 10,000
● Large Towns .... above 5,000
○ Small Towns .... below 5,000
▫ Trading Houses, or Forts.
Capital Cities, are engraved in Capital Letters, as MEXICO

* Universities or Colleges, † Missionary Stations
Names underscored, Cities and Provinces,
Figures, placed near Rivers, Mountains, or Islands, refer to the
Class of each.

SCALE OF MILES
0   100   300   600   900

Longitude   West   100   from   Greenwich   90

R. D. SERVOSS, N. Y.

Mexico, and had never at any time belonged to any other nation. As to West Florida, France ceded it to England in 1763; by England it was held till 1783, when, by the valor of Spanish arms, it was conquered and came under the dominion of his Catholic Majesty, who owned it still, for when in 1800 he receded to France what France had given him in 1763, he could not and he did not give up what he had conquered from England. How, then, could France have sold it in 1803 ? *

" If," said Monroe, " West Florida was not ceded to France in 1800, why was not the fact so stated in the treaty? Why did the treaty, on the other hand, distinctly declare that the province of Louisiana is ceded by Spain 'with the same extent that it now has in the hands of Spain, and that it had when France possessed it' ? Why this distinction between the 'extent it now has' and the extent 'it had when France possessed it,' unless for the very purpose of including in the cession that part obtained from England, and which you claim was not part of it 'when France possessed it' ? As to the country west of the Mississippi, the discovery of the river, as far down as the Arkansas, by Frenchmen in 1673, the further exploration of the river to its mouth by Frenchmen in 1682, the founding of settlements on its banks, on the bay of St. Bernard, and on the Colorado at a time when the nearest Spanish port was at Panuco, prove conclusively that it was French soil and passed to the United States when that nation sold Louisiana." †

At this point a new difficulty arose. Monroe in his note expressed regret that Don Onis should continue to bring up these old troubles when he had no authority to settle them, and told him that full power to do so had been sent to George W. Erving, Minister of the United States at Madrid.

But Cevallos, having no intention of being troubled with such a negotiation,‡ gave Don Onis full power to treat, and referred the whole matter to Washington. Early in January of 1817 the discussion was accordingly resumed and an offer

---

* Don Onis to Monroe, February 22, 1816.

† Monroe to Don Onis, June 10, 1816.

‡ Erving to Monroe, September 27, 1816.

made by Monroe of so much of Texas as lies between the Rio Grande and the Colorado in exchange for the two Floridas. Don Onis answered that the soil in question was already in the possession of Spain, and could not be made the basis of exchange, and that, furthermore, he had no instructions covering the entire cession of the two Floridas.* Thereupon Monroe abruptly closed the negotiation on the matter of boundary, † while Don Onis despatched the Secretary of Legation to Madrid for definite powers.

The arrival of the Secretary was made the occasion for a proposition by Don José Pizarro, the successor of Cevallos, that the negotiation should again be transferred to Madrid and carried on by Erving and himself.‡ To this Erving consented, and, after a month spent in exchanging notes, Pizarro submitted the outline of a treaty, by one of whose articles Spain was to cede the Floridas in return for every inch of territory the United States owned or claimed west of the Mississippi from its source to the Gulf of Mexico.# When this was rejected, the secretary of Don Onis was at once sent back with instructions, and the negotiation again transferred to Washington. ‖

In the interval John Quincy Adams had become Secretary of State, and with him in December, 1817, the Spanish Minister renewed the discussion. After an exchange of notes reciting with great fulness the history of the discovery, exploration, and occupation of the Mississippi Valley, Adams offered to accept the two Floridas in satisfaction of the claims of the United States on Spain for damages, and suggested the Colorado from its mouth to its source and a line due north to British America as the western boundary.△ The only result was to bring on another long, elaborate, and tedious discussion of the grounds on which each rested its claim ◊—a discussion

---

* Don Onis to Monroe, January 16, 1816.
† Monroe to Don Onis, February 20, 1817.
‡ Pizarro to Erving, July 16, 1817.
# Pizarro to Erving, August 17, 1817.
‖ Pizarro to Erving, August 31, 1817.
△ Adams to Don Onis, January 16, 1818.
◊ American State Papers, Foreign Relations, vol. iv, pp. 464–486.

which ended at last with the statement from Don Onis that the demand of the United States for the Colorado as a boundary was so extraordinary that he must again send a messenger to Madrid for instructions.*

Once more carried back to Spain, the negotiation was resumed by Pizarro and Erving, till the end of July, when the messenger set out on his return. In October Don Onis informed Adams of the arrival of the new instructions, and offered as the boundary a line from the Gulf of Mexico between the rivers Mermenteau and Calcasieu, to the Red river at latitude thirty-two degrees, thence due north to the Missouri, and along that river to its source.† This first sign of yielding on the part of Spain was followed by the first concession on the part of the United States, which, abandoning the Rio Grande, proposed the Sabine from its mouth to thirty-two degrees; a line due north to the Red river; the channel of that river to its source in the mountains, then to the summit, and along the crest to latitude forty-one degrees, and by it to the Pacific. Don Onis accepted the Sabine, but, pleading no authority to go to the Pacific, Adams withdrew the offer and declared that the United States stood by the Rio Grande. Nothing more was heard of the matter till January, 1819, when Don Onis, announcing new instructions, offered the old line to the source of the Missouri, with a new one thence to the source of the Columbia and so to the sea. This was the beginning of the end, and as each receded gradually, the two met at last on the boundary defined in the treaty which they signed on Washington's birthday, 1819. The moment the papers were signed and sealed and the copies exchanged, Adams went over with one to the President's house. The message and documents were already prepared, and these with the treaty were at once sent to the Senate.

---

* Don Onis to Adams, March 23, 1818.

† ". . . a line beginning on the Gulf of Mexico between the rivers Mermenteau and Calcasieu, following the Arroyo Hondo, between the Adaes and Natchitoches, crossing the Rio or Red river at the thirty-second degree of latitude and ninety-third degree of longitude from London, according to Melish's map, and thence running directly north, crossing the Arkansas, the White, and the Osage rivers, till it strikes the Missouri, and then following the middle of that river to its source." Don Onis to Adams, October 24, 1818.

Some remarks against the treaty, and especially against the boundary line, appeared next day in one of the Washington papers, and was believed to have been written by Clay. But his opposition had no effect, for on February twenty-fourth the treaty was unanimously approved, and on the twenty-fifth the ratification was proclaimed by the President.

But the treaty was one of amity and settlement, as well as of limits. After defining the boundary, therefore, it provided for the cession of the two Floridas, for the incorporation of their inhabitants into the Union, for the renunciation of all claims for damages, suffered by either party from the other up to the time of signing the treaty, and for the payment in consequence of this renunciation by the United States of five millions of dollars, to such of her citizens as had claims against Spain.

But now a new difficulty arose and delayed the ratification by Spain for almost two years. In February, 1818, while the negotiation for the cession of the Floridas was under way, Mr. Erving wrote from Madrid that the King had just made three huge grants of land in Florida. One was to the Duke of Alagon, captain of the body-guards; another was to the Count of Punon Rostro, one of his Majesty's chamberlains; and the third, which it was believed contained every foot of land in Florida and the adjacent islands not already given away, was to Don Pedro de Vargas, treasurer of the household. The intention of the King, beyond all doubt, was to deprive the United States of any benefits that might arise from the ownership of land in the province in case it was ceded to her. All this was duly noted by Adams, and in October, when discussing the basis of a treaty offered by Don Onis, he inserted in one of the articles a provision that all grants made since 1802 in the territories to be ceded should be null and void. Don Onis suggested as an amendment that all grants made since January twenty-fourth, 1818, should be null and void, that being the date when Spain first expressed her willingness to part with Florida. Adams in the end accepted this date, and, as he did not know exactly when the grants mentioned by Erving had been made, he distinctly stated that he did so with the understanding that the grants to the Duke of Alagon, the Count of Punon Rostro, and Don Pedro de Vargas were void.* That no doubt might exist on this point, Mr. John Forsyth, when he went to Spain as Minister from the United States in March, 1819, received special instructions to deliver a written declaration to that effect when he exchanged ratifications of the treaty.†

On reaching Madrid in May, he accordingly applied to the Marquis Casa Yrujo for the appointment of a day when the ratifications might be exchanged, and after waiting two weeks and receiving no reply wrote again, ‡ reminding the Marquis that the sloop of war Hornet had long been lying in the harbor of Cadiz; that the time was near when she must depart, and that if she went without the ratified treaty a most unfavorable impression would be created in the United States. He was now told that the great interest and importance attaching to the treaty made it necessary for the King to deliberate; # that before a decision was reached several explanations must be made with the United States; and that a person high in the confidence of his Majesty would be despatched to Washington for the purpose. ‖ As August twenty-second was the last day on which, according to the treaty, the ratification could be exchanged, Forsyth, on the twenty-first of August, served formal notice on Spain that matters were in precisely the same condition as they were before the convention was made, and that the United States was free to enforce and maintain her claims as she saw fit.

But the Hornet meantime had reached the United States, and at the very time Forsyth wrote to Don Manuel Gonzales Salmon, new instructions were on their way to Spain. He was now to announce that although the sixth month had expired, the ratification by Spain would still be received on two conditions. It must be made within one week, and it must be accompanied by the avowal that the three land grants were null and void. But no sooner was this demand explicitly

---

* American State Papers, Foreign Relations, vol. iv, pp. 651–684.
† Adams to Forsyth, March 10, 1819.
‡ Forsyth to the Marquis Casa Yrujo, May 18 and June 4, 1819.
# Don Manuel Gonzales Salmon to Forsyth, June 19, 1819.
‖ Ibid., August 10, 1819.

stated * than the note was returned to Forsyth with the statement that it could not possibly be laid before the King.†
Forsyth thereupon insisted that it be received,‡ and wrote
home to Adams that if it were not he should surely leave
Madrid. #

The situation now became so serious that Count Bulgary,
the Russian Chargé d'Affaires, was sent to explain matters and
ask that the returned note be withheld, and to say that a minister would at once be sent to the United States to ask for certain explanations. The person chosen was the Mariscal-de-
Campo Don Francisco Dionisio Vives, and with his selection,
Forsyth was informed, all discussion of the difficulty must
cease at Madrid.

In order that as much time might be consumed as possible,
Don Francisco Dionisio Vives travelled by easy stages from
Madrid to Bayonne, from Bayonne to Paris, from Paris to
England, and reached the United States in April, 1820. The
first letter he addressed to Adams made known the cause for
delaying the ratification of the treaty. Such a scandalous system of piracy had been carried on from the ports of the
United States against Spain and her possessions, and such a
spirit of hostility had been displayed everywhere over the
country, that his Majesty could not, with a due regard to his
dignity, ratify the treaty till the United States had given assurances that these things would be stopped. He must have a
pledge that no more armaments should be fitted out in the
ports of the United States; he must be assured that no more
expeditions would be allowed to go out to attack or invade the
dominions of Spain in North America, and the United States
must promise not to recognize the independence of the revolted
South American provinces. ‖

He was told, in the reply, that the stories his Government
had heard of the hostility of the people, the courts, and the
administration were unfounded. The United States had con-

---

* Forsyth to the Duke of San Fernando and Quiroga, October 18, 1819.

† The Duke of San Fernando and Quiroga to Forsyth, November 12, 1819.

‡ Forsyth to the Duke of San Fernando and Quiroga, November 20, 1819.

Forsyth to Adams, November 27, 1819.

‖ Don Francisco Dionisio Vives to Adams, April 14, 1820.

stantly avowed and had faithfully maintained an impartial neutrality. Old laws, when found defective, had been strengthened by new ones; Spanish property illegally taken had been restored, and even life itself had not been spared when individuals were found guilty of piracy against Spain. It was true that a wretched band of lawless men had moved into a territory to which his Catholic Majesty had no acknowledged right other than that conferred by the yet unratified treaty. When that treaty was ratified, a boundary line established, and Texas the acknowledged property of Spain, then the United States would respect the line and take care to prevent transgressions of it. But she would not commit herself to any line of conduct regarding the revolted provinces of Spain in South America.*

With the answers of Adams to the first and second demands General Vives declared himself satisfied. But the reply to the third was so unsatisfactory that he felt constrained to ask Mr. Adams to wait while the answer was referred to Spain, especially as the adoption of the Constitution of 1812 would limit the power of the King and make the ratification of the treaty no longer dependent on his will. This called forth a tart reply from Adams, in which he proved by citations from Vattel and from Martens the absolute obligation of the King to ratify, and notified the Minister that the correspondence should at once be laid before Congress, to whom it belonged to decide whether the United States could submit to any further delay.

On the ninth of May, accordingly, the secretary of the President, bearing a message and the letters, repaired to the building where Congress sat and delivered the papers to the House and Senate. Neither took action, for the day of adjournment was but one week distant; so the matter went over to the next session. In the House, however, much had been said about the treaty, and several attempts had been made to arouse vigorous action. On one occasion a member from Virginia, possessed with the idea that Don Onis had been authorized to cede far more territory than he did, moved that

---

* Adams to Don Francisco Dionisio Vives, May 3, 1820.

the President be asked to inform the House how much soil
the Spanish Minister was authorized to cede.   On another occasion the Committee on Foreign Affairs reported a bill authorizing the President to take possession of East and West
Florida and use the army, the navy, and the militia, if necessary.   But neither the motion nor the bill received any attention, and, as the House showed a strong disposition to do
nothing, Clay came forward and made a vigorous attack on
the treaty.   He began by submitting two resolutions, which
were referred to the Committee of the Whole.   The first set
forth that, by the Constitution, Congress had power to dispose
of the territory belonging to the United States, and that no
treaty purporting to alienate any part of it was valid unless
Congress approved.   The second declared that as the equivalent offered by Spain for so much of the territory of the United
States as lay west of the Sabine was inadequate, it would be
inexpedient to renew the treaty.

In defending his first resolution Clay declared that it was
not his intention to revive the old discussion of the treaty-
making power.   Yet he felt sure no one would assign to that
power a boundless scope.   He presumed that it would not be
contended by anybody that in a Government which was limited
there was a functionary which was not limited.   He was certain that wherever there were in the Constitution specific
grants of power to Congress, they limited or controlled, or at
least modified, the action of the treaty-making power.   Now,
as Congress had " power to dispose of " the territory of the
United States, it followed, from his view, that no treaty which
undertook to dispose of a large piece of the territory of the
United States was valid without the consent of the House as
well as of the Senate.   He would not contend that a treaty
may fix the limits of the territory of the United States without
the intervention of the House.   The treaty with England in
1794 had done so in the case of the river St. Croix.   The
treaty with Spain in 1795 had established the parallel of thirty-
one degrees as the boundary between us and Florida, just as
the late treaty of Ghent provided for commissions to determine
the northeastern boundary of Maine.   Yet the House had not
felt called on to interfere.   Nor was there any need.   These

documents merely made plain what was before uncertain. They did not trace out a new boundary; they proclaimed where the old line was. Not so the Florida treaty. The whole correspondence showed that the question was not, Where are the limits of Louisiana? but, Where shall they be? Now it was the Mississippi; now the Missouri; now a river east of the Sabine; now the Sabine; and at last a new and perfectly arbitrary line, with a large cession of territory to Spain—a cession which could not be made without consent of the House.

The second resolution asserted, that the equivalent granted by Spain was inadequate. "What do we get?" said Clay. "We get Florida loaded and encumbered with land grants which leave scarcely a foot of soil for the United States. What do we give? We give Texas free and unencumbered; we pay five millions of dollars, and we surrender all our claims on Spain for damages not included in that five millions of dollars."

Several speakers answered him, and told him that Texas had always been disputed territory; that our claim to it had never been clear and unquestionable; that it had been given up for that reason, and that reason alone; and that such a construction as he placed on the treaty-making power would prevent any question of limits ever being settled without consent of the House, inasmuch as such questions always involved the cession of territory by one party, and generally by both. In the end his resolution failed to pass the committee, and the matter for the time being was dropped. Monroe, in his message transmitting the correspondence with General Vives, had asked that no action be taken till Spain had once more been heard from. With this Congress willingly complied, and the summer of 1820 was spent by Mr. Foster in earnestly endeavoring to secure the ratification by Spain before Congress should meet again. In this most happily he succeeded, and on the fifth of October the Cortes, after annulling the three land grants, advised the King to ratify the treaty, which he did nineteen days later. The period of six months, during which the document was to have been approved by the King, having long since expired, it became necessary to again send the treaty to the Senate, which a second time consented to its ratification on the nineteenth of February, 1821.

CHAPTER XXXVI.

HARD TIMES AND ANTI-BANKING.

WITH the opening of the year 1818 the hard times which, twelve months before, were felt by the manufacturers and traders, began to be felt by the people. They, too, had engaged deeply in speculation, and, carried away by the flush times of 1815, had anticipated the growth of the country by many years. Sure that the distressed state of Europe would for years to come afford a ready market for American products, they had hurried to get into debt, and were now about to gather the fruits of their folly. Farms yet uncleared had been mortgaged, crops yet unsowed had been pledged, and the money squandered on foreign goods now contemptuously described as the gewgaws and trappings of luxury. That money could so easily be borrowed on such doubtful security was due to the vast number of chartered banks, wildcat banks, and corporations which, from one end of the country to the other, were struggling to put their notes into circulation. The inducements which they offered were too tempting to be withstood. The people yielded, and the enormous profits which flowed into the strong-boxes of the owners of the bank served but to incite still others to seek for charters. The disorder of the currency, which was the chief cause for the establishment of the Bank of the United States in 1816, taught no lesson. In the very face of it State after State set up new banks, till, in 1818, three hundred and ninety-two were doing business in twenty-three States and Territories. Pennsylvania and Kentucky led with fifty-nine each, which was just seventeen more than were scattered over the rich and populous State of New York.* Yet, rich and prosperous as she was, the facilities which they offered to borrowers and the shameful methods to which they resorted to keep their notes in circulation brought on such widespread distress that Governor Clinton, in his annual message, called loudly for legislation. Great numbers of them had been incorporated at places where there was neither commerce, trade, nor manufactures. As the patrons of such a bank were few in number, and their deposits small, its profits depended chiefly on the currency of its notes, which were put into circulation by liberal discounts, by loans to the farmers on easy terms, and by agents who went about exchanging its bills for those of rival institutions passing current in the neighborhood. So long as the rivals did not strike back all went well. But when at length banks whose notes it had driven out of circulation began in turn to gather its bills and present them for redemption, nothing was left but to call in the loans and exact partial, or it might be full, payment of the debts. Then the community, reduced to desperation, would cry out for a new bank, which, if chartered, would in the end only increase the rivalry, the loss of commercial confidence, and the public distress. To these mischievous institutions the Governor traced the banishment of metallic money, the deceitful show of fictitious capital, the increase of crime, the multiplication of civil prosecutions, the rise of prices, and the dangerous extension of credit which must end in general bankruptcy. His charges were indeed serious. But the committee to whom they were referred substantiated them in every respect. The

---

* New Hampshire	12	South Carolina	3
Vermont	5	Georgia	3
Massachusetts	38	Ohio	28
Rhode Island	35	Indiana	3
Connecticut	10	Kentucky	59
New York	42	Tennessee	3
New Jersey	14	Louisiana	3
Pennsylvania	59	Michigan	1
Delaware	8	Missouri	2
Maryland	25	District of Columbia	15
Virginia	17		—
North Carolina	7	Total	392

State banking system, as then carried on, was declared by the committee to be one of the great evils of the day. Not only did the banks by their rivalry hinder the transmission of money from one part of the State to another ; not only did they, by engrossing the whole circulation in their neighborhood, impede internal commerce, but they enabled the unprincipled speculator to so steep the industrious, honest, and unsuspecting part of the community in debt by means of borrowed notes and indorsements as to secure its property at sheriff's sale. Hardly a fraud of any kind could be mentioned of which the banks had not been guilty. Some, to get their notes in circulation, would deposit a small sum in specie with a distant bank for their redemption. The fact would be loudly proclaimed, and when their bills had risen to par in that locality and were passing freely, a special issue would be made and signed with ink of an unusual color. The far-away bank would then be instructed not to redeem notes signed with the colored ink, and all persons who had taken them would thus be subjected to heavy losses. Others would issue " facility notes," which they would not receive on deposit, nor take in any way save in payment of a debt due the bank. Still others would give large accommodation to individuals on condition of their keeping a specified sum in circulation for a specified time. Others were given discounts provided they would pay their notes when due in the bills of other banks. This would force the borrower to collect and lay by the paper of rival institutions. If he had not secured enough when the note fell due, the loaning bank would then sell him the bills he needed at a premium of fourteen, and even twenty per cent. Often the terms of a loan or a discount required that one half the sum should remain on deposit while the note ran, or that the borrower should buy from the loaning bank the notes of other institutions, pay a heavy premium for them, and then exchange them at par for the bills of the bank he was dealing with. On one occasion a board of directors made a rule that no discounts should be given to any man who traded at a certain store in the village. The owner, who was a depositor, had presumed to ask for " good current money " with which to pay a debt in New York. It was high time, the committee said, that these practices were brought to an end ; and that the Legislature might have full and substantial evidence on which to act, it asked for the appointment of a joint committee charged with the duty of examining the conduct of the incorporated banks. It was to find out if improper means had been used to force their paper into circulation ; it was to report if any of them had refused to redeem notes in specie, or had used its funds for usurious or oppressive purposes ; and it was to look carefully into the conduct of officers and directors and see if they had been guilty of fraud or usury.

The Eastern and Southern States, into which no emigrants were going, escaped most of the evils of bad banking. But from New York and Pennsylvania westward to the Mississippi and southward to Tennessee a state of general bankruptcy prevailed. The rush of emigration into this belt had been followed by a wild fever of speculation. In their eagerness to gratify it the people had borrowed from each other and from the banks. The banks, to gratify the people, had issued five times as much paper as they could ever redeem. The depreciation which ensued destroyed commerce and credit, and left the people utterly unable to pay even a part of their debts. The signs of this distress were everywhere. At Carlisle, in Pennsylvania, the sheriff advertised twenty-seven tracts of land for sale at one time. The owner of each one of them was in debt to the banks. At Lancaster a public meeting was held to discuss what should be done to stop the evils flowing from the overabundance of bank paper. After due deliberation an agreement was drawn and signed by one hundred and fifty citizens, declaring that they would receive no notes not at par in Philadelphia and Baltimore unless heavy discounts were made.* At Bedford, also, the people met and came to a like decision. They had hardly done so when the Allegheny Bank, which did business in the borough, suspended specie payments till January, 1819. The stockholders were then to meet and consider if it ought not to cease business. In Ohio the banks were in such a condition that the land agent at Cincinnati was ordered to take nothing

---

* Pennsylvania Gazette. Aurora, November 17, 1818,

but United States notes and specie in payment of land sales. When this was known, and when the United States Branch Bank at Cincinnati, in obedience to orders from the mother bank, called for the settlement of a debt due it by the State banks, they instantly suspended. Those of Dayton, Lebanon, Urbana, and Zanesville followed; and at a meeting of bank delegates from middle and western Ohio it was agreed to petition the Legislature to take back their charters and repeal the bonus law.

In this state of affairs a few voices were raised to tell the people that the banks were not to blame for the general distress and bankruptcy. It is not, it was said, the pistol of the highwayman that perpetrates the robbery; it is not the knife that commits the murder. Why, then, should the banks be held responsible for the hard times? They did not create themselves. How came they to be? Who created them? Who borrowed from them after they were created? Who, to be sure, but the very men who are now so loud in denouncing them? As the people have by their own act produced the cause of the evil, so they have in their own hands the remedy. Let them not speculate; let them stop importing the needless trappings of luxury from abroad; let rich men spend their surplus on home manufactures; let the middling class live within its means; let young men live by labor, and not by their wits; let the Government issue Treasury notes to merchants, and stop the exportation of American coin and of every sort of specie; let the banks enlarge their discounts and no longer draw their balances from one another in specie, and the times will soon be good enough. But such reasoning was of no avail. The people had made up their minds that the banks were to blame for bad times. They were in no condition to be reasoned with, and, enraged by their losses, they turned on the banks with a fury which threatened to destroy them. Niles, in his Weekly Register, suggested that every candidate for Congress or the State Legislatures should be required to pledge himself to oppose the establishment of any bank during his term of office. Other journals took up the idea, and in a little while candidates were pledging themselves unasked. In Pennsylvania, where almost every bank west of the mountains had suspended specie payment, the people demanded that the Legislature should repeal the charter of such as did not pay specie. Had the demand been extended to such as could not pay in specie if pressed, hardly a bank in the State would have escaped. None were sounder than those of Philadelphia. Yet by the statements made by them to the State Treasurer in November, it appears that not one could have met a tenth of its specie liabilities. One had twenty-seven thousand dollars in gold and silver with which to redeem three hundred and ninety-five thousand dollars of notes. Another had thirty-seven thousand dollars in coin, and debts amounting to three hundred and sixty-five thousand dollars. A third had thirty-five thousand dollars in specie, and five hundred and thirty-four thousand dollars of debts. All the banks chartered in 1814—" the litter," as they were now called—had nearly four millions of notes in circulation and but seven hundred and fifty thousand dollars in coin. This condition was no worse than it had always been since 1814. But the people were now against banks, and beset the Legislature with petitions for relief. One asked for the repeal of the charters of all banks save those of the city and county of Philadelphia. A second asked that every bank charter be annulled, and that a tax be laid on the Bank of the United States and its branches. The men of Centre County declared that the influence of banking institutions had become dangerous and oppressive, and prayed for laws to remedy the evil. From Mifflin County came another, asking that the banks " be compelled by law to pay for their notes in specie." Others wanted the number of banks reduced ; or their charters taken away if they suspended specie payment ; or a law passed forbidding notes under five dollars to be issued. To satisfy this widespread demand, the Legislature, before it rose, annulled the charters of ten banks for refusing to pay specie, and gave them five years in which to go out of business.

As the spring of 1819 advanced the signs of general distress took on a new form. Public meetings began to be held in all parts of the distressed belt, and resolutions adopted setting forth the evils felt and the remedy demanded. In May a Grand Jury of New Castle County, Delaware, ascribed the hard times to an unfavorable balance of trade resulting from excessive importation of foreign goods over and above our exports; to the drawing away of specie; and to the depressed value of real estate. The remedy was economy in personal expenses; a retrenchment in the use of foreign goods and imported luxuries; a steady attention to the improvement of agriculture; and the building up of a home market by fostering and protecting domestic manufactures.

Later in the summer a number of citizens of Delaware County, Pennsylvania, "friendly to promotion of national industry and economy," met in Upper Providence township and addressed their countrymen. The ease, said they, with which we have heretofore obtained paper money from the banks has led us into extravagance, speculation, and indulgence in foreign luxuries we can no longer support. Vast importations from Europe are draining us of our specie, are creating an immense debt to foreigners, are destroying the manufactures already existing, and preventing others from springing up. Let us reverse this and follow the example set by Great Britain, where no article of foreign make is allowed to come in competition with one of home manufacture. Let us combine for the support of domestic industries, and appeal to Congress to protect our workshops by a further duty on foreign fabrics. At the same meeting "The Society of Delaware County for the Promotion of National Industry and Economy" was formed.

At Philadelphia a call was issued for a meeting in the county court-room one Saturday afternoon in August of all citizens interested in the support and encouragement of American manufactures. So many came that the meeting was held in the State-House yard, where, after appointing committees to report on the condition of manufactures in Philadelphia in 1814 and 1816, and to draft a memorial to Congress and frame a plan for a society for encouraging manufactures, an adjournment was taken till the fourth of September. The reports presented on that day resulted in the formation of the Pennsylvania Society for the Encouragement of American Manufactures and in the circulation of a memorial to Congress. After passing in review the policy of Great Britain,

France, Spain, Austria, and Russia, the writers of the memorial took up and answered one by one the current objections
to the encouragement of manufacture : That labor was too high
to enable us to compete with foreign countries ; that mills and
factories demoralized the people ; that it was a pernicious policy to entice capital from farms and agriculture to workshops ;
that high tariffs encouraged smuggling ; that it was unjust to
tax the many for the benefit of the few ; and that commerce
would surely be ruined. They then presented some advantages that would, in their opinion, surely follow from the
adoption of a policy of protection, repeated the maxim, " Buy
where goods can be bought the cheapest," and ended with the
prayer that Congress would revise the tariff in such manner as
would revive the drooping manufactures and afford effectual
protection to national industry.

The report of another committee was relied on to prove
that manufactures were really drooping. Though far from
complete and confined to the city of Philadelphia, it should
have been most convincing, for it showed that thirty branches
of business which in 1816 employed nine thousand six hundred and seventy-two workmen, had discharged seventy-five
hundred of them in 1819 ; and that if each workman fed two
other mouths, twenty-two thousand human beings were deprived of support. Such stagnation had its effect on real
estate, and of eighty-five business houses, on six squares of
Market Street, which in 1818 rented for eighty-eight thousand
dollars a year, forty-nine were unoccupied in 1819, and the
annual rent of the others but thirty-five thousand dollars. On
looking over three fourths of the city, the committee found
four hundred houses unoccupied as the result of hard times.

The picture of idleness and business depression thus drawn
in the report was no exaggeration. That manufactures were
steadily declining was manifest everywhere ; and as the people were in a dissatisfied mood, and particularly receptive of
arguments in favor of reform, it became an easy matter to
interest them in the movement for a new tariff. The old
custom, so successfully used in 1808, of forming patriotic societies for the encouragement of domestic industry by consum-
ing none but American-made goods, was revived, and all over

the seaboard States, from Maryland eastward, such associations sprang up and began to flourish.   To join a society for the encouragement of domestic industry and economy became the proper and patriotic thing to do ; and once a member, it was necessary to wear American-made clothing and lay all the ills of the times on bank paper and the low tariff.

The measures taken by Congress in 1816 were believed at the time, the friends of national industry would say, to have been ample ; but the vast and unexpected increase of cotton in the markets of Europe ; the immense accumulation of goods in consequence of the use of labor-saving machines operated by people content to live on potatoes, rice, and water ; the exclusion of British goods from the markets of Europe and European goods from the markets of England—made it necessary for English manufacturers to seek our open market, where they have been only too well received.   Their goods and wares, cheaply made, and evading our tariff by fraudulent means, have been sold at the auction block at prices which distance all competition and have been paid for with depreciated bank paper which the auctioneers have exchanged for specie, which the foreigners have taken away to the injury of our finances. The ruin of our banks and of our manufacturers will soon be followed by the ruin of our farmers and the decline in the value of land ; for, now that hundreds of thousands of persons who consumed provisions, liquor, fuel, forage, but raised and made them not, are out of employment, where will our farmers find a vent for the cotton, grain, tobacco, and produce they have been raising in rapidly increasing quantity to supply a home market ?

The presence of idle workmen in the great cities, the dull times, the disorders of the currency, and the activity of the friends of industry gave to these arguments an extraordinary force, and it soon became impossible for any body of men to assemble for any purpose without issuing an appeal in some form for the exclusion of British goods.   Grand juries presented it as a grievance.*   Political conventions called on

---

* Grand Jury of Essex County, New Jersey, September 22, 1819. Grand Jury of the Circuit Court of the United States for the Eastern District of Pennsylvania, October 30, 1819.

the people to withhold their support from congressmen who would not vote for it.   Public meetings were called to discuss it.   As the time drew near for the assembling of Congress petitions went round in every manufacturing city and community, and delegates from Massachusetts, Rhode Island, Connecticut, New York, New Jersey, Delaware, Pennsylvania, Maryland, and Ohio gathered at New York.   Taking the name of a Convention of Friends of National Industry, they called on their friends in every State to form societies, hold State conventions, find out the true history of the rise, progress, and decay of American manufactures, and send representatives to a national convention to meet at New York in January, 1820.

The appeal was hardly necessary, for all over the North and East the people were meeting, complaining, organizing, and petitioning Congress and their State Legislatures.   At Harrisburg they called for a reduction of Federal and State salaries and heavy duties on foreign goods.   In Ontario County, New York, they petitioned for a law to stop the sale of real estate at auction in satisfaction of an execution.   If the personal property of the debtor were not enough to pay the debt, then only so much of his real estate should be transferred to the creditor as, in the opinion of three freeholders, was enough to make up the deficiency.   The manufacturers at Providence, Rhode Island, represented that the flood of foreign goods sold at auction for less than cost had destroyed their business, that their buildings and machinery were falling into decay, and that numbers of families of industrious artisans had been driven away to seek where they could for a livelihood and to occupations for which they were not fitted.   The Republican electors of Woodbridge, New Jersey, asked for a total prohibition of the importation of all merchandise from beyond the Cape of Good Hope, save drugs and spices ; for a like prohibition of all articles of luxury from any country that would not receive our cotton, grain, tobacco, flax, hemp, bread-stuff, meat, fish, and lumber, with an *ad valorem* duty of not over twenty-five per cent. ; for a total stoppage of the importation of such goods as could be made at home ; for more tonnage duty on ships employed in foreign commerce,

and for a uniform bankruptcy law. At Pittsburg, at New
Haven, in the western counties of Pennsylvania similar memorials were framed.   Estates, it was said, are being sacrificed, families are being ruined, agriculture is declining, foreign goods have banished the precious metals, establishments
that gave employment to thousands are idle, and the whole
country is overspread with despondency and gloom.

With these appeals to Congress went petitions to the State
Legislatures, all of which responded in some way.   Ohio declared it to be her belief that the pecuniary embarrassments of
the country were in a great degree caused by the want of encouragement and protection of American industries, and asked
for such a change in the tariff as would stop the importation
of foreign goods, and such an appropriation of money or
lands by Congress for the building of roads and canals as
would promote the general welfare of the nation.   Vermont
forbade imprisonment for debts under fifteen dollars.   In
Pennsylvania a petition from Northumberland County declared that the currency was so debased as scarcely to be usa-
ble ; that the produce of the farms had never been so cheap ;
that the larger part of the people, even with the utmost
economy, could hardly obtain the very necessaries of life ; that
debts were unpaid, creditors dissatisfied, and the jails full of
honest but unfortunate persons whose wives and children had
thereby become a burden on the township.   The people of
Wayne County stated that by the fall in the market price of
produce and the scarcity of money they were reduced to dire
want, and saw their property daily passing into the hands of
rich speculators.   The citizens of Pike County asserted that
their property was constantly being sold by the sheriff for one
fourth its value, and that the banking system, instead of becoming a blessing, was like the scorpions among the children
of Israel, a curse to the people.   Sundry inhabitants of Hunt-
ingdon County represented that their property taken for debt
was selling so low that even the fees of the law officers were
not realized, and that the evil times were only beginning.
Some wanted an act to force creditors to take the estates of
debtors at an appraised value ; others asked that property
taken on execution might not be sold for three years ; a few

—and the Governor was one—asked for a loan office.   The committee to whom the petitions went disapproved of each, and recommended protection to all branches of industry by the Federal Government, the beginning of public improvements at the expense of the State, and the education of the rising generation in sound principles of economy.

The Senate committee in their report on the causes and extent of the general distress drew a most dismal picture. Look where they would, the signs of hard times stared them in the face.   Landed property was daily sacrificed at sheriffs' sales for a half, a third, nay, a quarter, of its value, and hundreds of industrious farmers thereby deprived of their homes and the fruits of years of labor.   Merchandise, household goods, farming stock, would not bring at forced sale one half the cost of production.   Bankruptcies were numerous both in the mercantile and agricultural portions of the community. Money was so scarce that it had become impossible for husbandmen and owners of real estate to borrow on landed security, though they offered usurious interest.   Laborers were idle. Factories were shut.   Business was limited to the sale and purchase of the necessaries of life.   The prisons were overflowing with debtors confined for trifling sums.

As a means of relieving this suffering the committee recommended that money be voted for internal improvements; that the banks chartered in 1814 be forbidden to buy property sold under their own judgments or mortgages; and that a loan office be opened and one million and a half of dollars be distributed among the counties, to be loaned to farmers and manufacturers on land, in such small sums and for such a period of years as would do the greatest good to the greatest number.   The loan office seemed for a time to be most popular, and, despite the adverse report in the House, a bill was introduced, debated, and lost by a tie vote.   A bill to prevent usury was referred to the next Legislature.   In New Jersey an act against usury was passed, and seven per cent. was made the lawful rate of interest.

That the Bank of the United States should escape the storm which was fast overwhelming the State institutions was impossible.   Indeed, it was charged, and not unjustly, with a

large part of the responsibility for the depressed financial condition of the country. When it first opened its doors for business in January, 1817, it undertook to accomplish two things
—to force the State banks to resume specie payments, and to
provide the country with a paper medium which would circulate in every State and Territory and be redeemable on demand in specie. To secure this latter result seven million
dollars in gold and silver were imported, and the notes issued
by the parent bank and its eighteen branches scattered over the
land from Portsmouth to New Orleans were cashed wherever
presented. As soon, therefore, as a branch was opened in any
region where specie was scarce, and began to issue its notes,
they were sold at a premium, paid for with State bank-bills,
hurried by the takers to some other branch in a region where
specie was plenty, were there redeemed, and the coin carried
back to the place of scarcity. The bills so redeemed were
then returned to the branch which issued them, to be again
emitted. Now there was little coin in the South and West
and much in the North and East, and, as a consequence, it
was not long before there was a steady stream of notes from
the branches in the South and West to those in the North, and
a steady stream of specie and redeemed bills from branches in
the North to those in the South and West. The result was inevitable, and in eighteen months' time the bank was forced to
begin a rapid curtailment of business in the Southwestern
offices, which in eight months amounted to six and a half millions of dollars. As the branches began to stop discounts and
press the local banks to redeem their paper, they in turn began to press the people, who were deeply engaged in reckless
land speculation. A general bankruptcy followed, and the
debtors in their distress turned upon the bank and its branches
as the cause of all their misery. In Congress a desperate effort
was made for a repeal of its charter. The State Legislatures,
having no such power, were beset with demands that they
should tax its branches out of existence. To this North Carolina yielded, and laid a tax of five thousand dollars a year on
the branch at Fayetteville. A committee of the Assembly of
South Carolina reported that a tax was not expedient. In
Pennsylvania the question was referred by one Legislature to

the next. This was simply a reference to the people, and when the State elections came on, candidates were required to give a solemn pledge to support a State tax. In Maryland, Ohio, Kentucky, and Tennessee heavy taxes were laid and in each case resisted. In two instances—in that of McCulloch *versus* the State of Maryland, and in that of the Auditor and State Treasurer of Ohio *versus* the branch bank at Chillicothe —the resistance has become historical.

In 1818 the State of Maryland laid a tax on all banks and branches of banks doing business within her bounds and holding charters which she had not granted. For the purpose of collecting the tax easily the law provided that corporations subject to it should issue notes of no other denominations than five, ten, twenty, fifty, one hundred, five hundred, and one thousand dollars, and must print them on stamped paper provided by the treasurer of the western shore. If, however, the foreign corporation preferred, it might relieve itself from the use of stamped paper by paying fifteen thousand dollars annually in advance.

With these requirements, which went into force on the first of May, the branch of the Bank of the United States at Baltimore refused to comply. The directors would neither pay the stipulated sum in advance, nor buy the stamped paper, nor receive it when offered by the treasurer. Indeed, they continued after the first of May not only to print notes on un-stamped paper, but to issue them over their counters. Some of these, on a certain day in May, were paid by the cashier, James William McCulloch, to George Williams in return for a promissory note which the bank had discounted. Because of this transaction McCulloch was sued in the Baltimore County Court for debt by John James, treasurer of the western shore, and, on judgment being given for the State, carried his case to the Maryland Court of Appeals, which affirmed the decision of the lower court and suffered the case to be brought by a writ of error to the Supreme Court of the United States.

The questions discussed were, Has Congress power to incorporate a bank? Has the bank when incorporated a right, on its own authority, to open branches in the several States? and Have the States power to tax such branches?

The opinion of the Court, from which no member dissented, was that Congress did have power, under the Constitution, to charter the bank; that the bank did have power to establish branches in the States without their consent, and that the States could not tax them.

This famous decision was handed down on March sixth, 1819, and was immediately defied and set at naught by Ohio. In the spring of 1817 the bank had opened an office of discount and deposit at Cincinnati, an act which aroused much bad feeling throughout the State, where all the profits of banking were wanted by the State institutions. On the meeting of the Legislature in December this ill feeling found vent in a resolution calling for a report on the expediency of taxing such branches as were or might be in the State. The report was adverse, but the House rejected it and passed a resolution declaring the right of the State to tax and the expediency of doing so. When, however, the bill imposing the tax was read it was laid over till December, 1818. Meantime the bank, instead of heeding the warning and leaving the State, gave more offence by opening another office at Chillicothe in the spring of 1818. This was too much, and in February, 1819, Ohio laid the long-threatened tax, and fixed the amount to be paid by each office of discount at fifty thousand dollars a year. On September fifteenth the Auditor was required by the law to charge this sum against the banks, and immediately draw a warrant commanding anybody he pleased to enter any office of the Bank of the United States in Ohio and demand payment. Should it be refused, the agent was empowered to levy on any specie, bank-notes, goods or chattels he might find in the room. Should the amount so taken be less than the tax, he was to open every vault, room, closet, drawer, and box, search them, and seize whatever they contained. Lest he might not even then have property enough to satisfy the debt, he might, if necessary, summon the bank officers to appear in Court and account for the bank property.

A few weeks after the passage of the law the Supreme Court rendered its decision in the case of McCulloch *versus* the State of Maryland. But, as the law was mandatory, the Auditor of Ohio, Ralph Osborn, was forced to obey. The bank, therefore, on September eleventh, exhibited a bill in chancery before the Circuit Court of the United States then sitting at Chillicothe, and obtained a subpœna in chancery restraining Osborn from collecting the tax. Instead of taking from the clerk a copy of the order and a writ of injunction, the counsel for the bank sent a copy of the bill with a subpœna to answer. These were duly served on the Auditor on September fifteenth, but, not considering them to be an injunction, he issued his warrant to John L. Harper, commanding him to collect the tax. On the evening of September seventeenth, just as the branch at Chillicothe was about to close its doors for the day, Harper, duly provided with horse, wagon, and men, appeared at the bank and demanded the tax. The money was refused, and Harper, entering the vault, seized such specie and bank-notes as he found, loaded them on the wagon, and carried the money to the Bank of Chillicothe.

Next day a second writ was issued by the Court against Osborn and Harper, restraining them from paying over the money or making a report of its collection to the Legislature. The writ was served on Harper while on his way to Columbus with the money in his wagon. But he again disregarded the writ and paid over the cash to the State Treasurer.*

For this act Harper and Thomas Orr, who aided him, were arrested by a deputy marshal on a *capias* for a trespass *vi et armis* in taking the money out of the vaults, and, in spite of an effort to secure a release on a writ of *habeas corpus*, were held prisoners. Their trial came on before the Circuit Court sitting at Chillicothe early in January, 1820, when a motion was made for the discharge of the defendants Harper and Orr from the custody of the marshal. It was shown by the defendants that they were arrested on October eighteenth by a person acting as a special bailiff for the marshal, by virtue of a few words written on the back of an old letter; that they were confined in prison in Chillicothe while the bailiff sent for the marshal, who came on the twenty-first and made the return as if he had arrested the men on the twenty-second. The Court held that the marshal could not make a special bailiff,

---

* Belmont Journal; also Zanesville Express. Aurora, October 11, 1819.

but only a deputy, pronounced the arrest illegal, and discharged the two men.

The Bank of the United States now made a demand on the Franklin Bank at Columbus, where the money had been deposited, for its delivery, and when it was refused filed a second bill in chancery against the Auditor, the Treasurer, Harper, Orr, the Bank of Chillicothe, the Bank of Franklin, and the persons who acted as guard to Harper when he carried the cash from Chillicothe to Columbus. This suit was afterward dismissed.

For having delivered the money to the Franklin Bank, the United States Circuit Court granted a rule against Osborn and Harper to show cause why an attachment should not issue against them for contempt of court. The case came on for argument early in 1820, but was continued till September, when the attachment issued. It was returnable on the first day of the January term of the Court, 1821.

At this stage of the dispute the Legislature of Ohio met, in December, 1820. The report of the Auditor concerning his proceedings under the " crowbar law " was at once sent to a special committee, from which came some remarkable advice.

" The question," said the committee, " whether the Federal courts are the sole expositors of the Constitution or share that power with the States themselves, has been settled by an authority from which there can be no appeal—the authority of the people themselves. As early as 1798 the passage of the Alien and Sedition Laws, and certain decisions in the Federal courts recognizing the obligatory force of the common law, made an expression of popular opinion on this question necessary, and such an expression was sent forth by Kentucky and Virginia. These famous resolutions and the answers of the co-States were a direct and constitutional appeal to the States and to the people on the great question at issue. The co-States did, indeed, dissent. Two of them even declared that the Federal judiciary were the only expositors of the Constitution. But the people in 1800 reversed this and affirmed the doctrines of Kentucky and Virginia by effecting a total change in the administration of the Federal Government. Such high authority, and the clear right in the case, impose a duty on

Ohio from which she cannot shrink without dishonor. So long as one single constitutional effort can be made to save them, she ought not to surrender her rights to the encroaching pretensions of the Circuit Court.

"It is said that after the decision in the case of McCulloch *versus* Maryland—a decision made between the passage of the law and the day it went into effect—the duty of the State and her officers was to acquiesce. But neither in theory nor in practice is this the necessary consequence of a decision of the Supreme Court. There are cases in which the will of that tribunal has not been regarded. In the case of Marbury *versus* Madison the Supreme Court of the United States decided that William Marbury was entitled to his commission as Justice of the Peace for the District of Columbia, and that the keeping back of the commission by President Jefferson was a violation of Marbury's vested right. Yet Marbury never obtained his commission, the person appointed in his place continued to act, his acts were valid, and Jefferson retained his standing in the estimation of the American people.

"So, again, in the case of Fletcher *versus* Peck, the Supreme Court decided that the Yazoo purchasers from the State of Georgia were entitled to their lands. But the decision availed them nothing. Are not these two cases evidence that in great questions of political right and political powers a decision of the Supreme Court is not conclusive of the rights decided by it? If Jefferson stands justified in withholding a commission which the Supreme Court adjudged to be the party's right, if the United States retained possession of the Yazoo lands after the same Court had decided they belonged to the purchasers from Georgia, surely the State of Ohio ought not to be condemned because she did not abandon her solemn legislative acts as dead letters on the mere expression of an opinion by that same tribunal."

With such examples before them, it was the plain duty of the State, the committee held, to go on and defy the Supreme Court, "and ascertain distinctly if the executive and legislative departments of the Government of the Union will recognize, sustain, and enforce the doctrine of the judicial department." As a means of making this test it was therefore recommended that the Legislature should declare the Bank of the United States and its branches to be outcasts beyond the pale of the law.   Every jailer should be forbidden to receive into his custody any person committed at the suit of the bank, or for any injury done to it.   Every judicial officer should be prohibited to take acknowledgment of conveyances when the bank was a party, and every recorder from receiving and entering them.   Notaries public should be prevented from protesting bills or notes held by the bank and made payable to it; and justices of the peace, judges, and grand juries should no longer take cognizance of any wrong committed on the property of the bank, though it were burglary, robbery, or arson.*

Shameful as this suggestion was, the Legislature approved it, and passed "an act to withdraw from the Bank of the United States the protection of the laws of this State in certain cases." †   If the bank gave notice to the Governor of its willingness to stop the suits against the State officers, and to submit to a four-per-cent. tax on its dividends, or leave the State, the Governor might suspend the law by proclamation. But the bank showed no such willingness, the suits were continued, the law went into effect in September, 1821, and the bank became an outlaw in Ohio.

In the end the Circuit Court decided against Osborn, and required him to pay back not only the one hundred thousand dollars, but also to pay interest on so much of it as was in specie.   From this he appealed to the Supreme Court of the United States, where, in 1824, in the famous case of Osborn *et al. versus* The President, Directors, and Company of the Bank of the United States, the decision was affirmed, except as to so much as related to the payment of interest.‡

But the committee went further still and reported a set of resolutions which the General Assembly adopted.   These declared that with respect to the powers of the General Government and the powers of the several States the doctrines asserted by the Legislatures of Kentucky and Virginia in 1798

---

* Journal of the Nineteenth General Assembly, pp. 98, 117.
† Laws of Ohio, Chapter LXI, January 29, 1821.
‡ 9 Wheaton.

and 1800 were sound and true; that the General Assembly protested against the action of the Circuit Court as a violation of the eleventh amendment to the Constitution of the United States; that the General Assembly asserted and would maintain the right of the States to tax the business and property of any private corporation chartered by the Congress of the United States, and doing business in any State; and that the General Assembly further protested against the doctrine that the political rights of the separate States, and their powers as sovereign States, could be settled by the Supreme Court of the United States in cases between individuals and in which no State was a party direct.

Among the people two opinions were current concerning the conduct of the Legislature in its struggle with the bank. What separate and sovereign rights had Ohio as Ohio, the people of the East asked, before the formation of the Constitution? None. She took her very being from the General Government, and nothing can be more ridiculous than for that State to pretend that an institution emanating from an act of Congress can be a usurpation of the rights of Ohio whose land titles and school endowments have issued and continue to issue from the United States. That the people of Ohio will approve the action of their Auditor, particularly as some of the cash carried off belonged to the United States, is not likely. But the people of Ohio, was the answer, do approve. They have yet to learn that because the United States own stock in a bank the whole stock is exempt from taxation. If the United States were to buy one half of the town of Chillicothe, would the other half be free from State taxes? To charge them with resisting the Federal Government is absurd. They resist the shaving shops of a club of foreigners located among them without their consent, and until some competent authority declares the Federal Government and the bank one and indivisible, they will continue to tax the branches and collect the money. Ohio claims the right to expel any corporation located within her bounds by any other than her own laws, or force them to submit to such penalty as will stop their operations. This doctrine, it is true, is dangerous to the General Government. But it is subversive of State rights

to suffer Congress to create corporations with stock unlimited
in amount and place them in a State to whose laws they are
not amenable. Is it more ruinous to the principles of constitutional government for a State to tax them out than for Congress to force them in? A State must be allowed to make a
hard struggle before it can be expected to protect persons and
property over which it has no control. It cannot willingly
submit to a monopoly of banking or of commerce within its
jurisdiction. Let it be remembered, moreover, that the
branches are not the creatures of Congress, but of the bank.
The charter authorizes, but does not create or locate them.
Two of them were placed in Ohio. In one the revenue of the
United States was deposited. In the other it was not. The
Farmers' and Mechanics' Bank of Cincinnati and the bank at
Steubenville were the agents of the Government for receiving, keeping, and paying out the revenue. The branch at Cincinnati was merely the agent of the mother bank at Philadelphia; was engaged in ordinary banking transactions, and
had not a dollar of United States revenue in its boxes. Now
if, according to the ruling of the Supreme Court, the bank
and the branches engaged in the collection of the revenue are
to be exempt from taxation, then the Cincinnati branch is very
properly taxed by Ohio.

The reports from Kentucky revealed a condition of depression and desperation in the West quite as bad as that in
Pennsylvania and Ohio. The rush of emigrants into the
State and the appearance of the steamboat on the Ohio and
the Mississippi had produced a time of wild speculation, of
reckless borrowing and debt. The contraction of bank discounts and the reduction of bank currency brought on the
day of settlement, which the people were not ready to meet.
In Kentucky, as in the East, the branches of the Bank of the
United States were clearly responsible for the stoppage of
loans and the contraction of the currency, for they gathered
up large quantities of State bank-notes and presented them
for payment. It was against the branches, therefore, that the
wrath of the people and the Legislature was directed when
during the session of 1818–'19 a law was passed imposing on
each a monthly tax of five thousand dollars. In February,

before the first instalment was collectible, the United States
District Attorney applied to the United States Judges for an
injunction to stop the execution of the law.   The application
was made in behalf of the United States as a stockholder, and
of the branch at Lexington.   The ground taken was that
Kentucky had violated the act of Congress incorporating the
bank ; that her law did not lay a tax, but imposed pains and
penalties, as it was on its very face intended to drive the
bank out of the State.

The judges refused to consider the constitutionality of the
law, because, they said, a case intended to settle that point
was at that moment pending before the Supreme Court of
the United States.   But they granted a temporary injunction
restraining the collection of the tax by the State, and required
the bank to give security, in the sum of forty thousand dollars,
not to take its funds out of Kentucky till further orders.   The
injunction was to hold till May, when the Circuit Court would
be in session.

From this decision, and from that rendered a week later
by John Marshall, it appears, said the Kentucky Herald, that,
notwithstanding the wishes of the people of the West, this
monster of iniquity is to be saddled upon us.   We are to be
taxed by a corporation unknown to the Constitution, and
known to us only by its oppressive and vindictive acts.   We
know it as the means by which the bread of industry has been
taken from the poor and given to the rich ; by which our
manufactories have been paralyzed, foreign luxuries brought
in, our specie transported across the mountains, and the best
of our banks driven to add to the ruin and devastation it has
made by calling in their debts or sacrificing their own credit
for the public good by ceasing to redeem their notes on demand.   In this strait the people of this State looked to the
Legislature for aid.   The Legislature laid a tax on the
branches.   The Supreme Court has declared that the States
have no right to do this.   If the bank may tax us without
our consent, may locate branches among us without our consent, and if these branches are to be free from State taxation,
we had better give up our Constitution and return to the condition of a Territory.

Overcome by distress, the inhabitants of Franklin County gathered, in response to a public notice, at the church at Frankfort and took into consideration the desperate condition of their worldly affairs. The scarcity of money, the pressure of the banks upon individual debtors, the pressure of these debtors on those indebted to them, the difficulty of raising very moderate sums of money even by enormous sacrifices of property, the usurious rates of interest demanded for the use of money, the general embarrassment of the commercial world, were, they believed, hastening a general suspension of specie and the utter destruction of social order and happiness. Taken together, these causes threatened to bring suddenly into the market, at forced sales at auction, a large part of the most valuable property in the country, as well the products of the soil, as the real and personal estate of the people. The many sales and the few bidders without competition must shift this property from the many to the few, entailing poverty and wretchedness on the husbandman, on the journeyman, on the apprentice, on the master and the servant, and leaving a heart-broken, dispirited population in a desolated land. Neither justice nor humanity required nor should permit such ruin and devastation if a peaceable remedy could be found, and it could be found if the banks would only do their duty. They had, indeed, to a great degree brought on the evil times. They had induced the extravagant importation and use of foreign luxuries by furnishing the means; they had gathered specie in large quantities by dealing in credit, money, and exchange, and, by giving their own notes as a circulating medium at home, had made specie accessible to exporters and foreign dealers in money, and had enabled the Bank of the United States—that great dealer in foreign exchange—to open a sluice-way by which the coin of the western country flowed to the seaboard and from the seaboard to the East Indies. Pressed itself, it in turn pressed the State banks, which, forced to stop discounts and reduce notes in circulation, had distressed and ruined the people.

The duty of the banks, then, was to suspend specie payments at once, stop their calls, and issue more paper on good security. The Legislature should next meet and prescribe the

amount of paper each bank might issue and the kind of security individuals should give. A committee was then appointed
to invite the other counties to join in a call for a special session of the Legislature.*

A few days after the people had passed their resolutions
and gone home, delegates from the Bank of Kentucky, from
the two branches of the Bank of the United States, from the
Farmers' and Mechanics' Bank, and the Commercial Bank met
at Frankfort to consider the distressed state of the country and
find a remedy. Before they parted they agreed in the name of
the institutions they represented not to suspend specie, and to
render all the aid in their power to individuals by loans.† The
other banks could make no such promise, and before the first
of December seventeen of the State institutions had suspended
specie payments, and forfeited their charters by so doing.‡

This threw the State into great excitement. The debts
due the banks were upward of ten millions of dollars. Five
were owed to the Bank of Kentucky and its branches, three to
the United States Bank, and two to the independent banks,
as the " litter " was called. In their excitement the people
resorted to county meetings, where the favorite remedy was a
suspension of specie payments, more paper money, and an
extra session of the Legislature. At many of these assem-
blages the question was flatly put whether or not the Bank of
Kentucky should be encouraged to suspend specie payments.
Sometimes the decision was in the negative, but generally
a suspension was recommended. The bank accordingly suspended, for the directors were sure that, in the face of such a
public approval, the Legislature could not but sanction their
action.

Meanwhile, the tax laid on the branch banks by the Legislature—the collection of which the district court had enjoined
—remained unpaid, and became the subject of some strong
remarks by Governor Slaughter when he met the Legislature
in December. He was sure, he said, that much of the embarrassment felt by all good citizens had been caused by the
branches of the United States Bank collecting and cashing the

---

* Aurora, June 4, 1819.   † Ibid., June 17, 1819.   ‡ Ibid., December 14, 1819.

bills of the State bank and its branches, thereby hindering that freedom of banking which the commercial condition of the State required. If so, it was the duty of the Legislature to inquire if this baleful influence could not be counteracted. He was aware of the decision of the Supreme Court, but it behooved them to inquire how far it was compatible with the supreme power of the State to be manacled, restrained, or propelled by persons clad with authority by the nation; for, if one department of the national Government could usurp the sovereignty of the States and another department consecrate the usurpation by declaring it constitutional, State sovereignty was a fit subject of derision.

The Legislature responded by instructing its senators and requesting the representatives to do all in their power to have the branch banks removed from Kentucky and by repealing the act of 1818, which chartered the "litter" of independent banks. But these measures, violent as they were, would not relieve the great body of the people, whose farms and plantations were in imminent danger of passing into the hands of the sheriff. To help the debtors, therefore, a law was enacted by the Legislature suspending all sales under executions, decrees, and replevins for sixty days after the passage of the law if the defendant gave bonds that the goods levied on would be produced at the end of that time.* The acting Governor refused to sign it. He did not believe, he said, that a law should delay or deny justice. But the Legislature passed the act over his veto, gave permission for the introduction of a bill to declare void all sales made under any execution issued in favor of the Bank of the United States or its branches, and just before the expiration of the sixty-day stay law passed a replevin act of a most shameful character. Thenceforth, when any execution issued, on any bond, judgment, or decree, from any court or justice of the peace, the plaintiff had the privilege of writing on the bill the words, "Notes of the Bank of Kentucky or its branches will be accepted in discharge of this execution." If he made this indorsement the defendant could replevy but for one year. Should the defendant fail to replevy, the property

---

* Laws of Kentucky, Chapter CCCCLVI, December 16, 1819.

was to be sold on credit for one year for what it would bring. Should the plaintiff refuse to make the indorsement, the defendant might replevy for two years.*

The law seemed so iniquitous and such a flagrant violation of contracts that the right of the State to pass it was tested before the United States Circuit Court sitting at Frankfort. To the astonishment of many, the Court affirmed the right of the State to pass a replevin law, and affirmed the constitutionality of the provision requiring an indorsement that Kentucky paper would be taken, but declared so much of the law as permitted property seized under execution to be sold on credit was unconstitutional and void.

Across the Mississippi in the newly-made State of Missouri the condition of the people was, if possible, worse than in Kentucky. During four years they had been deeply engaged in a wild speculation in land and in the reckless issuing and borrowing of bank paper. In the days before the war the circulating medium of the territory had been furs of every sort, lead, tobacco, and cut money, or bits of Spanish dollars, made by cutting that coin into halves, quarters, and eighths. But, with the rapid growth of population which followed the war, a better currency was demanded, and before 1817 the Bank of St. Louis and the Bank of Missouri were chartered and an era of paper money opened. In that same year the General Pike, the first steamboat that ever stemmed the current of the Mississippi north of the Ohio, reached St. Louis. She was indeed a clumsy craft, and more than once on the voyage was helped along by the crew, who polled and bushwhacked as if she had been a common barge. But her arrival opened new possibilities of trade and commerce. St. Louis was now connected with the East and the South; money was easy to get; emigrants were coming by thousands, and to borrow, buy, and sell again to the new-comer became the rage. The merchants imported more goods than ever before, the farmer planted more acres, the land speculators laid out towns and farms all over the territory, and sold on credit to whoever would purchase. The people were seized with a terramania.

---

* Laws of Kentucky, Chapter DXLIV, February 11, 1820.

The questions asked were not, Is the claim a good one? Is the title clear? but, Does the land lie along the route the emigrants are taking? If so, the bidders were many and eager. On one occasion a tract of which no other description was given than that it was thirty miles north of St. Louis was put up at auction and promptly bid off. On another, the whole of St. Charles County was sold under a grant which had never been confirmed. On yet another, a piece of land was offered by two rival claimants and easily disposed of.

In the midst of this seeming prosperity came the hard times and the day of reckoning. The banks suspended, and, as their paper had driven out specie, no circulating medium existed. The taxes were not paid. Debts were not settled, and neither land, labor, nor produce was salable. Happily for the people, Missouri at this crisis became a State, and, as its acts were no longer subject to revision by Congress, the Legislature gave speedy relief. Stay laws were passed, and a State paper money created. The Federal Constitution forbids the issue of bills of credit, yet two hundred thousand dollars of certificates were issued in sums from fifty cents to ten dollars, and loaned to the citizens. No State, says the Federal Constitution, shall make anything but gold or silver a legal tender. Yet Missouri made her bills receivable, not only for taxes and debts of every kind due the State, but for salaries and fees of all officers, and for salt sold by the lessees of the Salt Springs.

While the Legislatures of the States were thus defying the Supreme Court, and seeking by stay laws and replevin laws to restore good times, Congress was being urged to act vigorously by the merchants. Hardly had it assembled in December, 1819, when its tables were piled high with long memorials and remonstrances from every class of business men the country over. Never before had the people as a body manifested so deep an interest in manufactures or spoken out so plainly in behalf of free trade. First to be presented was the memorial from the convention of "Friends of National Industry." They had assembled at New York city to consider the prostrate situation of our manufactures, and were so convinced that a serious crisis was at hand that they determined to appeal to Congress to apply a remedy. Looking over the country, they were distressed to see that the United States—though possessing every advantage of climate, soil, and production, though inhabited by a people intelligent, industrious, and enterprising to a degree never approached by any nation—was in a state of business depression which involved every class of citizens. Commerce was prostrate ; shipping had sunk to one half its value ; real estate had depreciated ; merchants, manufacturers, and farmers were reduced to bankruptcy. Though we had sent to foreign nations as much of our surplus as they would buy, we were still deep in their debt. Though our manufacturers were ruined ; though our workmen were destitute ; though our factories were falling into decay, and our water-powers unemployed, our cities and towns were full of the manufactured products of other nations, by which the people were daily drained of their wealth. Such general distress in a time of profound peace, the petitioners were convinced, could only mean that there was something unsound in our polity, and as a remedy suggested three measures. These were : Abolish credits on import duties ; lay a restrictive tax on sales at auction ; and increase the duties on imported goods. No greater evil existed than the unrestrained sales of foreign-made goods at auction. Originally such sales had been confined to damaged articles, to the effects of bankrupts, or to property taken in execution. But now great quantities of silk, woollen, and cotton goods were made in Europe and the East Indies expressly for sale at auction in the United States. These goods were shorter in length, less in breadth, and more flimsy in quality than the goods they represented, yet so well dressed and highly finished that the fraud escaped detection till the silks and cottons reached the consumer. In the city of New York, during 1818, fourteen millions of dollars' worth of merchandise of this description were sold at auction. In the United States the amount must have reached the prodigious sum of thirty millions.

Nobody supposes, said the memorial of the " American Society of the City of New York for the Encouragement of Domestic Manufactures," that legislation can restore that part of our commerce which was lost by the pacification of Europe,

nor create foreign markets for those surplus productions of
our soil of which a superabundance is yielded in every land.
But legislation can restrain the excessive influx of foreign
products, which has made us so dependent on foreign markets, by abolishing the credit given on bonds at the custom-
house and by taxing auction sales of imported goods, and can
build up our struggling industries by an increase in the tariff.

To these views the Chamber of Commerce of New York
took exception. The ten-per-cent. duty asked for on sales at
auction was, it said, too much. It would amount to a prohibitive tax and stop such sales altogether. The abolition of
the credit system, and the establishment of cash payment of
duties, would be the overthrowing of a system in successful
operation for thirty years, would draw money from commerce, agriculture, and manufactures, would disturb the deposits of State banks, and would inflict untold injury to the
commerce of the country, by subjecting it to all the evils of a
change from a system which was well understood to one whose
operations were uncertain and unknown.

The United Agricultural Society of Virginia, composed of
five societies, protested against any increase in duties. Protection to manufactures, it declared, was highly dangerous
in its tendencies. It gave one class peculiar privileges and
immunities at the expense of others, was inconsistent with the
principles of justice, and incompatible with the spirit of our
free institutions. The merchants and inhabitants of Salem, in
Massachusetts, were not prepared to go so far in their condemnation of protection; yet they, too, protested against an
increase of duties as ruinous to shipping. On the other hand,
the book manufacturers of Philadelphia earnestly sought for
protection. Their business, they asserted, had of late years
increased to an unexpected extent. Some idea of the magnitude of what they were doing might be had from the fact
that five family Bibles and numerous Testaments and small
Bibles were constantly standing in type; from the fact that a
Latin Dictionary had been stereotyped in Philadelphia and an
English Dictionary in New York; and from the fact that
Ree's and Gregory's and the Edinburgh Encyclopædias, the
Edinburgh and Quarterly Reviews, three editions of Hume's

England, two editions of Gibbon's Rome, the British Classics, the British Poets, Ramsey's Universal History, and a list of other great works too long to mention, had been reprinted or were in course of publication in the United States. Yet all this had been accomplished without the aid of heavy duties, and might have gone on growing without their aid were it not for the state of affairs in England. There the book business was so bad that publishers had turned to the United States, and had sent out enormous quantities of books to be sold by subscription, deliverable in numbers. Hawkers travelled the country from end to end persuading the people they could get Bibles at far less cost from them than from any one else, and were securing subscriptions by thousands. Indeed, between seven and eight hundred thousand numbers of a family Bible sold in parts to subscribers had recently been imported to supply this demand. Not only was the business of the regular trade thereby injured, but the Government was defrauded. If a work were in a series of volumes, each volume would be sent to a different port, would pass the custom-house as a defective book, and be taxed at little more than waste paper. If the publication were in numbers the same fraud was resorted to. They begged, therefore, that the duty of fifteen per cent. on books be changed to thirty-three and a third cents per pound; and that, when books were imported in sheets and bound in this country, the binding be taxed at fifty per cent. The Society of Paper-makers of Pennsylvania and Delaware asked for a duty of twenty-five cents a pound on all writing, printing, and copper-plate paper, and fifteen cents a pound on all other kinds. From the women of Providence came a petition asking for protection for the manufacturers of straw goods.

Fear that a heavy duty might be laid on molasses aroused the shippers and rum-makers of Boston to remonstrate. It is, said they, the distillation of Jamaica rum in New England that enables the West Indian planter to buy our fish, our produce, our manufactured goods, and pay for it in an article bulky enough to give employment to thousands of tons of shipping. No less than sixty thousand hogsheads of molasses are brought to our ports each twelvemonth. But if this raw material is to be taxed, while skins and hides, copper and brass, dyewoods and rags come in free, a deadly blow will be given to the lumbering, fishing, and coasting trades of New England. From the Chamber of Commerce of Philadelphia came a remonstrance against high duties on the wines and liquors of Portugal and Spain, and the statement that the duties then existing had shut the ports of those countries to the consumption of our corn and our flour. From some people in Connecticut, from New York, from western Pennsylvania, from Delaware, from Maryland, from New Hampshire, and from Kentucky came other memorials praying for the protection of home industries.

Thus beset from every quarter, the House went seriously to work on the revision of the tariff before the session was three days old. Hitherto such matters had always been referred to the Committee on Commerce and Manufactures. But the friends of manufacture now insisted that the House should amend its rules, make a standing committee on manufactures, and carried their point by a good majority.

The chairman of the new committee was Henry Baldwin, of Pennsylvania, and by him a new tariff bill was reported in April, 1820. The committee, said he, in framing this bill have not been guided by any consideration of private interests. If the bill, either in its general principles or its details, cannot be supported on national principles, then let it fall. We have thought that this nation can never be flourishing, can never be independent, unless it can supply from its own sources its food, its clothing, and the means of defence. We have thought that to be dependent on foreign nations for the articles essential for these purposes is not our true policy, and that the system which makes us thus dependent must be radically changed. But to decide what this change should be was hard, for many things have occurred to embarrass the committee. At an early day in the session the House called on the Secretary of the Treasury to report what effect the prohibition of iron, woollens, and cottons would have on the revenue, and he answered that the effect would be a decrease in the revenue and an increase in smuggling. As he had already reported a deficit of five millions in the receipts of the year,

and as the Committee on Ways and Means positively refused
to recommend any way to fill the Treasury, nothing was left
but to assume the responsibility and report a bill for the general revision of the tariff.

The revision consisted in the main in a change of *ad
valorem* duties from seven and a half and fifteen to twelve
and a half per cent.; in raising twenty-per-cent. to twenty-five-
per-cent. duties; in increasing the tax on woollens and cottons
eight per cent., and that on silks from India fifty per cent.;
in laying an additional duty on hemp of twenty dollars a ton;
and in such an adjustment of other rates as would give manufactures in general a fair protection.

The bill was one of great importance and far-reaching in
its consequences. Yet a week was thought sufficient in which
to debate it and come to a vote. It then passed by a majority
of thirteen. Every member from Rhode Island, New York,
New Jersey, Delaware, Ohio, Indiana, Illinois, and all but one
from Connecticut and Pennsylvania, voted Yea. Indeed, from
the twelve States north of Maryland and the Ohio river—a
region which, when the vote was taken, had one hundred and
eight representatives on the floor—there came but fifteen
Nays. The opposition was strong in the South and the
Southwest, which cast but eight yeas to fifty-four nays. In
the Senate the opposition triumphed, and, by a vote of twenty-
two to twenty-one, postponed it till the next session. Nor did
any other remedy demanded by the people fare any better,
for the bill to require cash payment of duties was defeated in
the House, and that laying a tax on sales at auctions was lost
in the Senate.

Thus was the question sent down to the people and sent
down on the eve of a Presidential and Congressional election.
Yet it had no influence whatever in that election, which, so
far as the choice of a President was concerned, is the most
remarkable in our annals. Early in April, 1820, some members of Congress, who felt uneasy because no candidate had
been formally named for the Presidency, urged the chairman
of the caucus of 1816 to name a time and place for another,
which he did. The call was very mild and apologetic. It
began with a statement why it was made, and ended with an

invitation not only to all Republicans, but to such "other members of Congress as may think proper to attend." *   On the appointed Saturday night a few came, and promptly resolved that it was not necessary to proceed to the recommendation of suitable persons to fill the offices of President and Vice-President of the United States, and adjourned.   As the Federal party had by this time become almost extinct, even in Massachusetts and Delaware, no candidate was named by it.   The choice rested therefore with the electors, who, everybody knew, would re-elect James Monroe and Daniel D. Tompkins.   It has, in consequence of this, been generally asserted that the second election of Monroe was not even contested; but this is very far from being the case.   He had been guilty of what was undoubtedly the most famous act of his life. In the face of petitions and remonstrances from public meetings, and of resolutions from State legislature, he had signed the bill which drew the line 36° 30′, and established slavery beyond the Mississippi.   Of this many, very many, of his warmest friends in the free States did not approve.   Some in Philadelphia denounced him, and called for a meeting of citizens opposed to negro slavery and to the electoral ticket formed by the friends of James Monroe and Daniel Tompkins.   They met in the mayor's court-room one day in October, but, as not half the crowd which attended could get in, an adjournment was taken to a neighboring tavern, where a committee was selected to frame a ticket of electors of President and Vice-President in opposition to that formed at Lewiston in favor of Monroe.

The party was wholly and entirely anti-extension of slavery. " At no time since the Declaration of Independence," its members held, " have the dearest interests and the essential rights of freemen been so seriously threatened.   The extension of slavery accomplished by the Missouri Bill has recognized slavery as incorporated in our Constitution, and the recognition has been carried under the auspices, by the influence, and with the approbation of James Monroe.   As President of the United States Mr. Monroe is the adviser of Congress.   He is possessed

---

* National Intelligencer, April 5, 1820.

of a mass of patronage and influence sufficient at any time to give him a powerful control over the acts and deliberations of the National Legislature. He has, moreover, a veto with which he can, if he will, defeat any act of Congress. It is not our intention to charge Mr. Monroe with all the guilt which attaches to the passage of the Missouri Bill. But there is a peculiar responsibility which belongs to him as President. He was elected as the guardian and protector of the rights and liberties of the States, and has betrayed both by assenting to a bill which carries slavery into a region where it need not ever have existed. In the South this deed has been extolled as the most brilliant act of his life, and the black plume has been exultingly placed in his political bonnet. Whoever, therefore, votes for Monroe, votes for the extension of slavery. He is the candidate of slavery, and is taken up and supported by the slave States. But will the friends of humanity, freedom, and virtue support him? What are we to think of men who, in the very face of their boasted freedom, extend the boundaries of slavery through an immense region of new country and give their sanction to the traffic in human flesh? What would we think of England if she were to do such a thing as this? We do not expect, it would be foolish to expect, to unseat Mr. Monroe at the present time. But we do expect that the people of Pennsylvania will enter their solemn protest against remaining any longer submissive vassals to a slave aristocracy." *

It was no secret that the candidate of the antislavery Republicans was De Witt Clinton. On election day, therefore, which happened to be Friday, the third of November, two electoral tickets, one headed Monroe and one headed Clinton, were voted. In the late contest for choice of a Governor forty-seven hundred votes had been polled in Philadelphia. Now but two thousand were polled, and of these the antislavery ticket received nearly eight hundred.† Hundreds, it was said, kept away because they would neither oppose their party nor support its slavery pretensions.

Elsewhere not the smallest opposition was made. Where

---

* Aurora, October 23, 26, 27, 28, 30, 31 ; November 2, 3, 1820.

† American Daily Advertiser, November 4, 1820.

the choice of electors was by popular vote the people did not take the trouble to attend the polls.   Indeed, it is said that in Richmond but seventeen votes were cast.   Monroe, as a result, secured the electoral vote of every State in the Union.   But when the day came for the electoral colleges to meet in their respective States, an elector in New Hampshire voted for John Quincy Adams.   It was due to the memory of Washington, he explained, that no other man should share with him the honor of a unanimous election to the Presidency.

No such apathy and indifference, however, was shown regarding the tariff.   The action of the Senate, and the close vote by which that action was taken, both encouraged and excited the opponents of revision.   All over the country, during the summer of 1820, they held meetings, passed resolutions, drew up remonstrances, and sent memorials around for signature.   At an anti-tariff meeting in Faneuil Hall, before which Webster appeared and spoke, it was resolved that manufactures were desirable when they grew up naturally, and undesirable when fostered by bounties and protection; that taxes should be laid for revenue, but when imposed for the benefit of one class of men they were unconstitutional and impolitic; that the idea that the country was dependent on foreign nations for articles of subsistence and defence, and would be till a new tariff was made, was fallacious and fanciful; and that such a tariff as that lately proposed in Congress would diminish industry, impede prosperity, and corrupt the morals of the people. A convention of free-traders from the seaboard States met at Philadelphia, passed resolutions of a like kind, and petitioned Congress.   The Legislature of Georgia unanimously approved the vote of her senators and representatives against the Tariff Bill in May.   When the Legislature of South Carolina met, a member introduced a set of State rights resolutions so violent in tone as to call forth the condemnation of the House.   It did not, it said, believe in a tariff.   Protection to manufactures was premature and pernicious; was a wretched expedient to repair losses incurred in commercial districts by improvident and ill-directed speculation; was an unwarrantable attempt to compel those parts of the Union which were still flourishing to contribute, even to their utter ruin, to fill the coffers of a

few monopolists elsewhere.   Yet, when it considered that the
States had expressly given Congress power to regulate commerce, and, above all, when it considered the consequences
likely to result from the practice, already too common, of
arraying the States as distinct and independent sovereignties
against the General Government on questions of national
policy, it became its duty to protest against so mischievous a
tendency and to adhere to the wise, liberal, and magnanimous
principles by which South Carolina had always been so proud-
ly distinguished.*

The fruit of all this excitement was not apparent, however, till Congress met and the petitions again came pouring
in.   With scarcely an exception they were remonstrances from
the agricultural societies and planters of the South and the
shipping interests of the North.   Manufactures, said the
Southern men, have protection enough.   Twenty-five per cent.
duty is given by the present tariff.   Freight, insurance, and
commissions add fifteen more.   Conditions in Europe raise
this to eighty per cent. ; yet the manufacturer is not satisfied.   But it is high time to look out for the farmer and
shipper.   More tariff will injure our commerce, reduce the
revenue, encourage smuggling, stop ship-building, tax the farmer for every article he consumes, and rob us of that market
for raw cotton which Great Britain has hitherto afforded.
Our conditions are not those of Great Britain.   Burdened with
a surplus population, with one person in every seven a pauper,
her people must manufacture or emigrate.   But we have no
surplus population to provide for.   With vast and limitless
stretches of vacant land—to be had almost for the asking—
there is a livelihood within the reach of every man who will
but till the soil.

As the remonstrances came in they were sorted and sent
to either of two committees.   Those from the agricultural societies went to the Committee on Agriculture, composed of
anti-tariff men.   Such as were sent in by chambers of commerce, by the auctioneers, by people in the towns and cities,

---

* Report of the committee to whom was referred the preamble and resolutions
of Pleasant May, Esq., on the subject of the tariff, December, 1820.

were referred to the Committee on Manufactures, which, during the last session, had reported the Baldwin Bill. The result might easily have been predicted. In time each presented a long, elaborate, and exhaustive report; the one against, the other for, a new tariff; the one an earnest plea for the manufacturers, the other an earnest plea for the farmers.

"It is a matter of little consolation," said the Committee on Manufactures, "that, after being thirty years in operation, the Government has not brought the country into a more prosperous condition. The debt has increased twenty millions. The revenues are insufficient to meet expenditures. The national domain is impaired, and twenty million dollars of its proceeds gone. Thirty-five millions have been drawn from the people by internal taxation, and three hundred and forty-one millions by tariff duties; yet the Treasury depends on loans. In a time of profound peace the country is embarrassed with debts; real estate is shrinking in value; the markets for manufactures and the yield of the farm are declining; commerce is struggling not to retain the carrying trade of other lands, but of our own. Not one national interest is thriving. Why are these things so? The sea, the earth, the forest, yield their abundance. Pestilence and famine commit no ravages. Peace smiles on us. Plenty blesses the land. Whence, then, this burst of distress? History affords no other example of a people impoverished while in the full enjoyment of health, peace, and plenty. Elsewhere an overflowing Treasury indicates national prosperity. With us the two years of greatest revenue form the epoch which has consummated our embarrassments. The reason is plain. In other lands, taxes are drawn from the surpluses of the people. In ours, revenue depends on the markets and consumption of the people, and both of these depend on foreign interests and power. Our prosperity is in a ratio inverse to that of Europe. When Europe is convulsed we rise to greatness. When Europe is in repose our interests are shaken to their foundations. It is true that five years of European peace have taken from the resources of the people more than was acquired in twenty-two years of European war. We adapted our system of revenue to a state of war in Europe, and have not changed it to suit a time of peace.

" From the estimates of the Treasury Department, it appears that between 1816 and 1820 the currency of the country was contracted from one hundred and ten millions to forty-five millions ; and why ? Because the business of the country required no more. Business, then, has fallen off fifty-nine per cent. in three years. But what kind of business ? Not that of importing, which was never so great. Not that of remittance abroad, which is still in full activity, requiring not only specie, but bank stock, public stock, bonds, judgments, notes, and sheriff's sales to pay the balance against us. But the business of making profits—this has been taken from us by foreigners. Foreign agriculture supplies the materials, and foreign industry the labor which produces for the American people their clothing, their utensils, their means of defence."

As the committee had no fondness for foreign importations, either of goods or opinions, it most heartily urged the adoption of those sound American principles of protection to American industries which had been approved by our greatest statesmen ; which had been used by the Government when it began its operations ; which led to prosperity when pursued, and had left us in adversity when abandoned.

It then went on to answer the many objections to a protective system : That it was not constitutional ; that it injured morals and bred pauperism ; that it increased smuggling ; that it was a tax on the many for the benefit of the few ; that it destroyed revenue, ruined commerce, injured agriculture, and that the country had enough of it already.

The report of the Committee on Agriculture was presented a few days later. It was a long and careful argument in support of everything the Committee on Manufactures had condemned, and closed with the resolution that the increase of duties proposed in the bill reported by the Committee on Manufactures are not compatible with the interests of agriculture and the community generally, and ought not to be adopted. In the end their wish was attained, for Congress expired four weeks later without having taken any action on the tariff.

CHAPTER XXXVII.

PAUPERISM AND CRIME.

THE serious consequences which the hard times I have attempted to describe produced in the seaboard States were displayed in a most interesting manner by the census of 1820. Indeed, no counting of the people which, up to that time, had been made in this country is so well deserving of careful examination, for in it are the results of a migration westward the like of which was not seen again for many years. The entire population now numbered more than nine and a half millions. One million and six hundred thousand of these lived in New England, two millions and seven hundred thousand in the Middle States, two millions and nine hundred thousand in the Southern States, while more than two millions and a quarter dwelt beyond the Alleghany Mountains. In every one of the Atlantic States from Maine to Georgia the ratio of the increase of population had fallen save in Connecticut and South Carolina, and even in them the increase was but a fraction of one per cent. In Delaware the census takers could find but seventy-five more people in 1820 than were in the State in 1810. Virginia was no longer first in rank. New York was now the most populous State in the Union, and had added four hundred and thirteen thousand human beings to her inhabitants. No other State had approached this. Ohio came next in increase with an addition of three hundred and fifty-one thousand, which raised her from thirteenth to fifth place. Massachusetts, which ten years before was fifth, had become seventh. Kentucky was sixth with one hundred and fifty-eight thousand more people than in 1810. Tennessee had one hundred and sixty-one thousand

MAP
Showing in Five Degrees of Density, the
Distribution within the Territory East
of the 100th Meridian of the
POPULATION
OF THE
UNITED STATES
EXCLUDING INDIANS NOT TAXED.
Compiled from the Returns of Population
at the Fourth Census, 1820.

NOTE.
★ Centre of Population 39°5.7′N.
78°33′W.

Cities over 8,000 inhabitants in solid color, in circles proportionate to population.

Under 2 inhab. to the
Sq. Mile

2–6 inhab.to the Sq.Mile   I

6–18   "   "   II

18–45 inhab.to the Sq.Mile   III

45–90   "   "   "   IV

90 and over   "   "   "   V

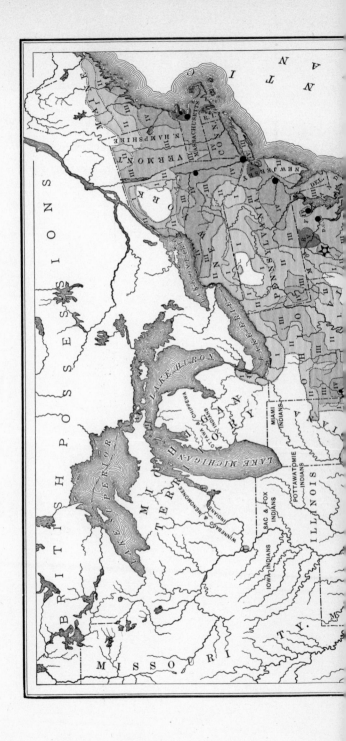

more; but both these States had contributed largely to swell the population in Indiana, Illinois, and Missouri.

In passing westward the people followed the three great highways of emigration as heretofore. The northern stream has now traversed all Ohio, has joined Cleveland with Detroit, and has populated the entire southern shore of Lake Erie. The middle stream, pushing down the valley of the Ohio, has peopled all the southern half of Ohio, and much of the southern part of Indiana and Illinois has crossed the Mississippi and moved up the Missouri almost to the western boundary of the United States. The third stream—which, unable to cross the country of the Creeks and Cherokees in Georgia, had for thirty years past been moving down the Cumberland and the Tennessee, and had just reached northern Mississippi in 1810—has gone down the Mobile river and its branches, leaving a wide strip of populated country across Alabama from its northern border to the Gulf and has entered southern Mississippi. Indiana, Illinois, Alabama, Mississippi, and Missouri have become States in the Union, and raised the number to twenty-four.*

East of the mountains three States † had each over a million of people, and, taken together, had almost as many inhabitants as thirty years before were to be found in the whole United States. Not a little of this increase in the case of New York was due to migration from other States and from abroad. The Erie Canal, now half-way toward completion, was visibly attracting settlers to the interior of the State. Within ten years, and despite the war, three hundred and fifteen new towns and one hundred and sixty-one new villages had sprung up, and eight new counties had been established. The city of New York had become the favorite spot for landing emigrants from England and Ireland, and, as most of those who came went no farther, the growth of the city since the war had been portentous. During the first half of the decade, when her trade and commerce were gone, her bay

* Indiana was admitted December 11, 1816; Mississippi on December 10, 1817; Illinois on December 3, 1818; Alabama on December 14, 1819; Missouri on August 10, 1821.

† New York, 1,372,111; Pennsylvania, 1,047,507; Virginia, 1,065,117.

blockaded and the business of her merchants ruined, she had almost stopped growing. A census taken for municipal purposes in 1816 returned but forty-two hundred more people than were reported by the census of 1810. But with the return of peace strangers came streaming in from every quarter and added twenty-three thousand * to her population in four years. In no other great city in the Union did the increase approach these figures. Some added far less to the number of their inhabitants from 1810 to 1820 than they did from 1800 to 1810. In Boston the increase was eight thousand during the one decade and eleven thousand in the other.† In Albany the gain fell from four thousand in the first to three thousand in the second decade,‡ and in Baltimore from twenty thousand to seventeen thousand.# Philadelphia, which in 1810 had a population about equal to that of New York gained but twelve thousand between that time and 1820. But most remarkable of all was the depopulation of Charleston, where there were but eighty more inhabitants in 1820 than there were in 1810.‖ War and the hard times had checked the growth of the great seaboard cities. During no other census period has the population of the cities failed to increase at a much more rapid rate than the population of the rural districts; but between 1810 and 1820 the ratio of increase was precisely that of the period preceding, which was four and nine tenths per cent.

Although the population of the seaboard had grown but slowly, the pauper, dependent, and petty criminal classes had multiplied with what seemed alarming rapidity. Some declared that the war, and above all the general idleness which followed the war, had demoralized the lower classes. All admitted that crime, profaneness, desecration of the Sabbath, intemperance and pauperism, prevailed everywhere to an ex-

---

* In 1810 the population was 96,372; in 1816 it was 100,619; and in 1820 it was 123,700.

† Boston in 1800 had 24,000; in 1810, 32,000; and in 1820, 43,000.

‡ Albany had 5,000 in 1800, 9,356 in 1810, and 12,360 in 1820.

Baltimore had 26,000 in 1800; 46,000 in 1810; 63,000 in 1820.

‖ The Federal census gave a population of 24,700 in 1810; a local census in 1817 gave 23,950; and the Federal census of 1820 returned 24,780.

tent which called loudly for public interference.   As early as
1813 a Society for the Suppression of Intemperance had been
formed in Massachusetts, each member of which pledged himself to discountenance the use of liquor at entertainments,
funerals, and auction sales, and on no account to furnish laborers with grog during haying time, as was then the custom.
So too the Presbytery of Cayuga, in New York, in 1813 urged
the formation in the different counties of moral societies for
the enforcement of the laws against Sabbath-breaking, swearing, and tippling.   But it was not till the distress produced
by the hard times of 1816 caused such general misery among
the idle and dependent classes that the people went earnestly
to work to seek for the causes of pauperism.   As might
have been expected, they found them in intemperance and
in ill-regulated and ill-advised charity, and at once began an
attack on each.   In the great cities, where the suffering was
most keen, the citizens had been called on to come to the
aid of such charitable organizations as existed, and in response had contributed winter after winter in the case of New
York and Philadelphia as much as ten thousand dollars for
the relief of the destitute.   That such calls might be prevented in the future, the committees intrusted with the use of
the money were asked to investigate the condition of the poor,
find out, if possible, the causes conducive of pauperism, and report a remedy.   At Philadelphia the Committee of Superintendence addressed the ward and district committees and asked
them to ascertain what kind of persons were most improvident; what they alleged to be the cause of their poverty;
how much liquor, pawnbrokers, and soup societies contributed
to it; if the poor could be induced to deposit their surplus
earnings in savings-banks; how many children industrious
parents could support; how many were willing to go into
the interior of the State in search of work, if assisted; and
how many indigent parents were willing to bind their children to tradesmen or send them out to service in families,*
and with the information so gathered made a most interesting

---

* Circular of the Committee of Superintendence, Philadelphia, February 21,
1817.

report. They found that a radical change in the mode of administering charitable relief was most imperative. The number and variety of benevolent associations which Philadelphia supported were so great that, when joined to the provision made by law for the care of the poor, they made the city a veritable "emporium of beggars." Not only was a dependent pauper class created thereby at home, but a temptation was actually offered to every idle vagabond in the neighboring counties of the State to come in and live on the city. Nothing could stop this but a better system of granting relief; the judicious care of orphans from their infancy; the education of indigent children at county expense; the discouragement of the use of liquor, and a rigid execution of the law against dram-shops and tippling houses. That such desirable results might be secured it was necessary to keep public attention ever on them, and to do this it was suggested that a society be formed for the sole purpose of improving "the condition of the poor, and removing or preventing the causes that produce mendicity." Before the meeting which listened to this report and suggestion adjourned, a committee was chosen to propose by-laws and a constitution,* and so founded the Pennsylvania Society for the Promotion of Public Economy.† Among its many committees was one to suggest such methods of effecting savings in the diet, fuel, and clothing of the poor as should lessen consumption and tend to avert the evils of poverty; another was to report on the suppression of tippling houses and the promotion of sobriety and industry; a third was to examine the poor laws; a fourth was to concern itself with the management of prisons; while a fifth was to ascertain if the laws establishing public schools were properly administered, and if not, report such improvements in the mode of educating the poor as might seem worthy of public indorsement. The Constitution of Pennsylvania enjoined it on the Legislature to see to it that, "as soon as conveniently may be," schools should be "established throughout the State in such a manner that the poor may be taught

---

* American Daily Advertiser, May 10, 1817.
† Ibid., May 22, 1817.

gratis." But although the Constitution had been law for more than twenty-six years, the Legislature had never obeyed the injunction. Large sums had indeed been voted to endow " seminaries of learning," and in 1809 it was made lawful for parents who could not pay for the education of their children to send them to the most convenient school, and have them taught at the cost of the county.* Three years' experience under the law proved so burdensome to the tax payers of Philadelphia that in 1812 the city and county were exempted from its working, and the select and common council given authority to establish public schools.† But the war opened and nothing had been done when, in 1817, the Society for the Promotion of Public Economy appointed its committee on public schools. A plan, based on the system of Lancaster, was quickly prepared by the committee ; an appeal was made to the Legislature ‡ by the society, and the law secured which made the city and county of Philadelphia the first school district of Pennsylvania, and established in it public schools.#

The action of the people at New York was almost identical with that at Philadelphia. Hard times had produced destitution and want far beyond the means of the benevolent societies to relieve. A public meeting was therefore called, money raised, soup-houses opened, and a committee appointed to examine into the causes of the increase of pauperism. The cause was not far to seek, and the committee soon came to the old conclusion that nothing was so fruitful a source of poverty as rum. A careful examination of the reports on the condition of the poor for ten years past revealed the alarming fact that paupers were increasing more rapidly than population. Fifteen thousand, or one seventh of the population of the city, were actually living on charity. About one sixteenth of them were worthy persons reduced to poverty by the depressed state of commerce. Another sixteenth were paupers from a variety of causes. But seven eighths were people reduced to abject poverty by the inordinate use of liquor. As far back as 1809

---

* Act of April 4, 1809.
† Act of March 31, 1812.
‡ Journal of the Pennsylvania House of Representatives, 1817–'18, p. 69.
# Act of March 3, 1818.

the Humane Society found eighteen hundred licensed dram-
shops scattered over the city retailing liquor in small quantity,
and offering every inducement to the poor to drink.   Supposing the number of such tippling houses had not decreased and
that each sold two dollars and a half worth of rum every day,
the enormous sum of one million six hundred thousand dollars* would, in the course of a year, be paid down by the laboring classes for drinks.   If laid out in flour at ten dollars a
barrel this would buy one hundred and sixty thousand barrels,
or more than enough to supply the entire population of the city
with bread for a year.   Should the receipts of the dram-shops
average three and a half dollars a day, the money expended in
these annually would buy not only all the bread, but all the fuel
consumed in New York city in a twelvemonth.   Facts such
as these were sufficient, the committee thought, to convince
anybody that eighteen hundred dram-shops scattered over a
city of a hundred thousand people, and drawing from the poorest and most dependent classes several millions of dollars a year,
was an evil so portentous as to require instant and serious attention.   To go on year after year contributing food, clothes,
money, was idle.   It increased pauperism, which could only be
lessened by reforming the method of dispensing charity, by
stamping out grog-shops and corner groceries, and by educating the children of shiftless and worthless parents in houses
of industry.   All this required public support, persistent effort,
a careful study of the existing conditions of the poor, and
money, and was very properly the work, not of a committee,
but of a society which, it was earnestly recommended, should
be formed at once.   Such a body, known as The Society for
the Prevention of Pauperism in the City of New York, was
accordingly formed early in 1817 with a large number of well-
known citizens for managers.

As soon as the managers were appointed they organized,
and chose nine standing committees to report on idleness and
sources of employment, on intemperance, on lotteries, on houses
of ill fame, on pawnbrokers, on charitable institutions, on gambling, and on ignorance.   But when the committees had gath-

---

* $1,642,500.

ered all the information they could and the managers had
digested it in a report, the causes especially conducive of pauperism were declared to be drink, lotteries, pawnbrokers, and
the many charitable institutions of the city. Drunkenness was
singled out and described as the cause of causes. More than
sixteen hundred licensed groceries then existed in the city, in
any one of which any human being of any age could buy liquor
in small quantities. If each one of these sixteen hundred dealers sold two hundred and fifty cents' worth each day, the amount
of money so wasted in a year would be nearly one million five
hundred thousand dollars,* a sum large enough to build fifty
churches worth twenty thousand dollars apiece, and still leave
enough to erect school-houses and pay for the education of
every child in the city.

The lotteries were almost as bad as the dram-shops and
tippling houses. The time spent in making inquiries regarding them and in attending at the lottery offices, the feverish
anxiety that seized on the adventurer from the day he bought
his ticket, the depression and disappointment that so invariably followed the drawing, diverted the laborer from his
work, weakened his moral tone, consumed his earnings, and
soon brought him to pauperism. But worse than the authorized lottery were the self-created lottery insurances, where
young and old were enticed to spend little pittances under the
delusive expectation of a gain, the chance of which was as low
as it was possible to conceive.

To place the many noble charitable institutions with which
the city abounded in the same category with lotteries, dram-
shops, and pawnbrokers, was most unfortunate. They had
been founded by the purest motives of true philanthropy, and
had unquestionably relieved thousands of human beings from
pinching want, cold, hunger, and even untimely death. But
was it not true that all of this good was offset by the evils that
flowed from the expectations they aroused, by the relaxation
of industry their display of benevolence produced, and by encouraging a reliance on charitable aid in evil days which
ruined, in the minds of the laboring classes, that wholesome

---

* $1,460,000.

anxiety to provide for the future which alone can save them from a state of absolute dependence on the community?

As a means of checking these evils, the managers suggested that street begging be stopped, that the petty dram-shops be closed, that houses of industry be established, that more churches be built and more Sunday-schools opened in the outer wards of the city, and that the poor be encouraged to invest their money in savings-banks, benefit societies, and life insurances.*

The public, as was to have been expected, turned a deaf ear to the report. But the managers persevered, and in the course of another year founded a Saving Fuel Fund Society, and a savings-bank—the first in New York and the third in the United States—secured new regulations from the city regarding pawnbrokers and lottery offices, and aroused the Common Council to call on the Mayor for information on the subject of grog-shops and tippling houses. His report showed that there were then in the city nineteen hundred licensed grog-shops, and at least six hundred where rum was sold without a license. Each of these twenty-five hundred was frequented by the poorest and most vicious classes, and, what was worse, by the very men and women who as street beggars and out-door poor were themselves dependent on public charity for support. That such a condition of affairs existed in a country so vast in extent, so easily cultivated, with a population so thinly spread, where taxes were so light, where rank was unknown, where industry was so richly rewarded, and where all were eligible to the highest offices in the Government—must be due, the managers believed, to a radical defect in the laws and institutions. Year after year, therefore, they continued to call for the stoppage of street begging by the refusal of the public to yield to applications for relief, for the arrest of beggars and for their removal to houses of industry.

While the two societies were hard at work at Philadelphia and New York, a general movement in behalf of temperance and better morals swept over the Atlantic States. At last the

---

* First Annual Report of the Managers of the Society for the Prevention of Pauperism in the City of New York, February 4, 1818.

people seemed to be aware that of the hundreds of wretches who filled the poorhouses and workhouses or were supported by taxation as " out-door poor," the larger part were habitual drunkards. The newspapers began to print long communications on the cost of intemperance, on the vast sums spent each year for liquor, and on the good the thirty-three millions of dollars so wasted annually would do in founding churches and libraries, schools, seminaries, and starting in life young men of correct habits. The Portland Society Auxiliary to the Massachusetts Society for Suppressing Intemperance reported that out of eighty-five persons in the workhouse, seventy-one became paupers through drink. In another town forty-nine out of fifty-one tenants of the workhouse were habitual drunkards. The people of Waldoboro, Maine, in town meeting assembled, gave it as the sense of the town that drunkenness prevailed to an extent which was ruinous to morals and destructive to health ; that a speedy check must be put to it, and instructed the select-men to enforce the laws against taverners. A grand jury at Albany drew a picture of their city quite as dismal, and presented the immense number of dram-shops and corner groceries where liquor was retailed by the cent's worth as an evil and a nuisance to society. Members of the jury could recall a time when not a dram-shop or corner grocery existed ; but so common had they become since the war that they were fast destroying good morals and religion, and reducing a large class of the community to beggary and dependence on public support.* The farmers of upper Providence township in Pennsylvania met in the school-house just before harvest time and agreed not to give liquor to their field hands, nor to use it in the hay-field or during the harvest, nor to allow any one in their employ to use it.† When the local elections took place in Philadelphia an earnest call was made on the voters to attend the elections of constables, as they were the men whose duty it was to suppress unlicensed dram-shops and tippling houses.‡ In Baltimore a citizen petitioned the Legislature

---

* Albany Gazette, June 13, 1817. Presentment made June 11.
† American Daily Advertiser, June 20, 1817.
‡ Ibid., March 21, 1817.

for relief. Within the bounds of Baltimore there were, he
said, some five hundred tippling houses, each holding out
every sort of allurement to the laborer to spend his earnings
for rum. To them went not only laborers, both black and
white, but servants of both sexes, and even apprentices.* The
Legislature gave his petition no attention, but public sentiment was aroused and the Mayor in a message to councils
urged them to establish a house of industry as a remedy for
pauperism and vice.† The Moral Society in the Pendleton
district of South Carolina insisted that the justices of the peace
should execute the laws providing for the punishment of curs-
ing, swearing, and Sabbath-breaking.

Had the times improved, public interest in the reformation
of morals would undoubtedly have subsided. But the times
grew worse, and with each succeeding winter the people in the
cities were required over and over again to make contributions for the relief of the destitute. These repeated drains
upon their pockets kept them ever mindful of the suffering of
their less fortunate fellow-men, and did not a little to convert
what might have been a temporary effort on the part of a few
kind-hearted gentlemen into an important part of a great
humanitarian movement. The five years which followed the
war were most favorable to such a movement. Never in the
history of our country had the sufferings of the dependent
and unfortunate classes been so forcibly and persistently
brought to the attention of the public, for never before had so
many worthy citizens been reduced to want. Under such circumstances it is not surprising that one of the first manifesta-
tions of a kindlier spirit was lessening the severity of the laws
for the imprisonment of debtors. No class of the community
deserved consideration more. For years past they had been
treated with a cruelty and barbarity disgraceful to the humanity of our ancestors. For the smallest debt possible to
contract, though it were but a cent in value, the body of the
debtor, whether man or woman, would be seized by the credit-
or and cast into jail. By an old law, which went back to the
days when Pennsylvania was a colony, magistrates were allowed

---

* New England Palladium, January 31, 1817.   † Federal Gazette.

cognizance, without appeal, of debts under forty shillings or
five dollars and thirty-three cents in amount.   When the indebtedness exceeded that paltry sum the debtor was entitled
by law to a stay of execution.   But no such happiness awaited
the poor wretches who owed a sixpence or a shilling, and who
each year were dragged to prison by thousands on what were
truly called "spite actions."   Once behind the prison walls they
were consigned to a fate harder than that which awaited the
worst criminal.   Murderers and thieves, forgers and counterfeiters, were fed, clothed, and cared for at the expense of the
State ; but for the unhappy man whose sole offence was his
inability to pay a trifling debt of a few cents no such provision
was made.   The food he ate, the shreds that covered him,
the medicine he took—nay, the very rags he wrapped about
his sores *—were provided, if provided at all, by his friends,
by the public, or by some Humane Society, or Society for
alleviating the Miseries of Public Prisons.   The room in
which he was confined with scores of other offenders was
utterly without furniture of any sort.   In it were neither beds,
nor cots, nor tables, nor chairs, nor so much as a bench or
stool.   He sat on the floor, ate off the floor, and at night lay
down to sleep on it like a dog, without mattress, blanket, or
covering ; and this misery he endured till he died, or his debt
was paid, or his creditor released him.   Against this at length
humanity revolted, and in 1792 a change for the better was
ordered.†   "Whereas," says the law then enacted, "many persons confined for debt in the prison called the debtors' apartment, in the city of Philadelphia, are so poor as to be unable
to procure food for their sustenance, or fuel, or covering in
the winter season, and it is inconsistent with humanity to suffer
them to want the common necessaries of life," the State must
come to their relief.   It was then ordered that the inspector
should provide fuel and blankets for such debtors as, by reason
of their dire poverty, could not get them ; and should make
an allowance of seven cents a day for food, and charge this

---

* See, for instance, the appeals in Baltimore Federal Gazette, February 25,
1804, and November 9, 1804.

† Act of April 4, 1792.

against the creditors. If any creditor refused to pay after ten days' notice, his debtor was to be discharged. For twenty-two years the community seem to have thought that this mild concession was all that humanity required, for no further change was made till 1814.* Then was passed the "Bread Act," under which each prisoner whose debts did not exceed fifteen dollars was entitled to a discharge after an imprisonment of thirty days. Such as were destitute were to have a daily food allowance of twenty cents, payable every Monday morning by the creditors. On failure to pay it for a space of three days, the debtor could apply to the judge of the Court of Common Pleas for his release. All this seemed fair enough. But the duty of carrying the petition was assigned to no one in particular, and as a fee of one dollar and a half was exacted for fulfilment of the process, many a prisoner was detained long after his spiteful creditor had ceased to feed him. From documents presented to the Senate of New York in 1817, it appears that the keeper of the debtors' jail in New York city certified that during 1816 nineteen hundred and eighty-four debtors were confined, and that upward of six hundred were always in the prison or on its limits. The sheriff of the county certified that eleven hundred and twenty-nine were imprisoned for debts under fifty dollars ; that of these, seven hundred and twenty-nine owed less than twenty-five dollars each, and that every one of them would have starved to death but for the kindness of the Humane Society. Indeed, he had more than once been forced to buy fuel out of his own pocket to keep them from freezing. One man who had been confined for a debt of fifty dollars remained in the jail three years before death ended his misery, and during this entire time was fed by the Humane Society. Another had been imprisoned six years and supported by charity.

In the face of such evidence the Legislature relented, and in 1817 forbade the imprisonment of debtors for sums less than twenty-five dollars. This led the way, and State after State followed. In 1818 New Hampshire exempted her inhabitants from arrest for debts under thirteen dollars and

---

* Act of March 26, 1814.

thirty-three cents. A year later Vermont abolished imprisonment for debts under fifteen dollars. Pennsylvania and Kentucky were not ready to go so far; yet each amended her laws and exempted women.* When the new States in the West framed their constitutions prior to admission into the Union, each one of them made it part of the fundamental law of the State that no citizen should be imprisoned for debt unless he refused to give up his estate.† The relief afforded, the misery averted, by this humane legislation cannot now be truly appreciated. Nothing done by the States since they provided for the gradual or complete abolition of slavery did so much to alleviate human suffering, unjustly and often maliciously inflicted, as the abolition of imprisonment for petty debts.

But nothing which philanthropy had been able to devise had tended in the least to suppress pauperism or diminish its great cause—intemperance. Statistics of the cities, and indeed of the populous counties, revealed a condition of affairs which was getting worse instead of better. Year by year the inmates of workhouses and almshouses increased at a far more rapid rate than the inhabitants of the cities. Winter after winter the same demands were made on the public for contributions to keep the destitute from starvation. In the cities the children of the pauper and dependent classes had now become so numerous as to seriously threaten the peace of the community. Bands and gangs of young boys and lads roamed the streets, stealing, destroying, and insulting passers-by. At last, in Philadelphia, matters were brought to a climax by the hard winter of 1820–'21. The distress exceeded anything ever before experienced. The Northern Soup Society; the Southern Soup Society; the Western Charitable Association; the Indigent Widows' and Single Woman's Society—all the innumerable charitable societies were taxed to their utmost. Yet the number of paupers seemed greater than ever, and brought out the usual earnest appeals to the humane for help. Farmers

---

* Laws of Pennsylvania, Chap. XXXII, February 8, 1819. Laws of Kentucky, Chap. DCXXXIX, February 14, 1820.

† See the Constitutions of Indiana, 1816; Mississippi, 1817; Illinois, 1818; Alabama, 1819.

who came to the city with food for market were urged to give flour, meat, and vegetables. Citizens of New Jersey and Delaware were asked to remember how much they had benefited by the trade of Philadelphia, and contribute liberally to her distressed poor. But the destitution was too great for such slow means of relief, and once more a general call went forth for a meeting of citizens at the City Hall to take steps for the relief of the suffering poor. In some of the wards such meetings had already been held, and committees had been appointed to receive and solicit donations of food, wood, and clothing. But at the public meeting committees for each of the fourteen wards and the adjoining districts and townships were chosen, and a general system of collection begun.*

As the work of relief went on it was found that no charges which the committees had to meet were heavier than those for fuel. More than twenty-five hundred dollars was expended for wood alone.† As not a little of the destitution arose from improvidence, it occurred to those concerned in affording relief that this item of expense could be greatly reduced by the formation of a Fuel-saving Society. Its purpose was to furnish the poor in winter with wood bought with funds provided by themselves. Every workingman and woman was to be encouraged to deposit a small sum each week with the society, and receive in winter as much fuel as the money so deposited would buy at the low rates for which the society as a wholesale purchaser could sell it.‡ The public gave the scheme a hearty approval, and the society went promptly to work.

But the criminals and habitual paupers were yet to be cared for. The question of pauperism seemed so hard to deal with that the Legislature was appealed to, and a law secured which bade the Governor appoint a committee of nine to investigate the causes of pauperism in Philadelphia, and report to the next Legislature. While these gentlemen were at work another series of public meetings was called to devise a plan for improving the morals of a certain class of the youth of the city.#

---

* American Daily Advertiser, January 31, 1821.
† Ibid., June 13, 1821.
‡ Ibid., May 15, 1821.
# American Daily Advertiser, June 18, 25, 27, 1821.

It was not a little surprising, the call said, that no association had been formed to save young children from falling into vicious ways. The great number of idle boys who frequented the wharves on Sunday playing pitch and toss and other games destructive of morals, and who during the week spent their time in pilfering goods landed on the wharves from the ships, was an evil as serious as any which had received public attention. It ought to be stopped, and as a few citizens were determined to make the attempt to do so, all who were like minded were asked to meet them at the Mayor's office on a certain day in June.* So few attended that it was thought best to renew the call, and at the same time to state the evils complained of, which were breaches of the Sabbath, and the means by which they were effected. The first thing we hear, it was said, on the Sabbath morning is the ringing of bells on the steamboats on the Delaware river, to invite our youth to go to Camden, where they may engage in every sort of mischief and dissipation. Gardens and places of public resort are kept open, and oyster cellars and dram-shops, which are so many receptacles for the worthless and profligate of all descriptions.†

At the adjourned meeting it was resolved to urge the people in the wards and districts to take up the matter, investigate it, and send delegates to a general meeting where some plan for curing the evil might be considered and digested. Never, it was said, had the increase of vice and immorality been so alarming. Not one person in a hundred is aware of the frightful extent of juvenile crime among us. The number of children whose constant occupation is theft is enough to make one shudder. There is very good reason to believe that many of the fires which afflict our city so often are kindled by these youthful villains. The Mayor has done wisely to call on the people to investigate this subject for themselves, and the people will do wisely to follow the advice of the Mayor. That the citizens should act in a body was impossible. The promoters of the investigation, therefore, made a formal call for ward meetings to elect delegates to a general convention,‡ to which the

---

* American Daily Advertiser, June 5, 1821.

† Ibid., June 12, 1821.

‡ Held July 9, 1821.

Mayor addressed a most interesting letter. He called attention
to the great number of children and apprentices thrown out of
work by the hard times, who roamed the streets and wharves,
picking up and carrying away every article their strength and
adroitness enabled them to secure, and stated that he alone in
the course of three months had sent twenty boys of from ten
to eighteen to prison for larceny. He complained of the
second-hand shops and pawnbrokers where stolen goods were
sold for a tenth of their value. He pointed out the dangers
of the tippling houses and corner groceries, where liquor was
sold by the cent's worth to children of five years old, and paid
for often with stolen goods, and asked for a serious consideration of the flagrant breaches of the Sabbath.

This letter the meeting referred to a committee which reported a month later.*

The authors of the report earnestly advised that the community, in place of being content with the punishment of
crime when committed, should go further and seek to destroy
the sources of crime, which were six in number. At the very
head and front stood the tippling houses. With an audacity
that was simply unparalleled they fixed themselves in the
places of greatest resort, and in open violation of the law conducted their unlicensed business. They preyed not only on
the laboring class, whose savings were needed for the support
of families, but on servants, on young men, and even on children. They encouraged idleness, fraud, and vice; tempted
men to waste their earnings, reduced families to beggary, and
inflamed those passions which led straight to crime.

Almost as dangerous were the oyster cellars. As a city
institution they had but lately come in. Early in the century
the lover of oysters was forced to get a supply on the oyster
boats at the wharves, or seek the oyster man, who drove his
wagon up one street and down another, and, provided with
crackers, salt, and pepper, fed his customers at the street corners with oysters opened at the cart's tail. As population increased and the city spread, this primitive method was too
slow. The cartman was unable to supply the demand and

---

* August 6, 1821.

gave place to a host of wheelbarrow-men, who occupied the
street corners in the busy hours of the day and tempted every
passer-by. But to this method, in turn, there were objections,
for the streets were often hot and dusty and the business entirely interrupted in times of severe cold and rain. These considerations finally induced one of the oyster men to take up his
quarters in a cellar, and, finding that he succeeded, the whole
fraternity followed. Once there, the business quickly under-
went a change, and the oyster cellar became the club-house, the
tavern, the exchange of apprentices, serving men, and idlers.
Liquor was sold without license, and acts were done which for
very shame would not have been allowed in a tippling house or
a tavern. Under the pretence of a fondness for oysters, young
men—from the school-boy to the clerk in the counting-house
—resorted to these places and learned to drink, to smoke, to
swear, and to gratify their sensual passions.

Next were the shops for the purchase and sale of second-
hand articles. In them everything from a brush, broom, or an
old bottle to a jewel of the first water were bought at a great
undervaluation and without asking a question. They became
in consequence the receptacles of that unlawful business which
the pawnbrokers could not transact. They were open markets
for the sale of stolen articles and a great incentive to pilfering
and petty thefts.

But of all the sources of youthful crime none was so prolific
as the neglect of education. Crowds of idle and disorderly
boys infested the streets, wharves, vacant lots, and ponds, where
they engaged in games, sports, and mischief to the ruin of
their morals and the annoyance of the community. They swore
and drank, resorted to oyster cellars, formed parties for the
redress of each other's wrongs, and stole in open day.

The best remedy for these evils was, the committee thought,
a stricter enforcement of the laws and the establishment of an
asylum where the mechanical arts should be taught to boys.
The advice was heartily approved by the meeting, and a committee appointed to draft a law and submit it to the next
Legislature.

However effective this remedy might be in the future, it
could do nothing for the suppression of the evils of the present,

which were fast becoming unbearable. House-breaking, till-robbing, assaults on peaceable citizens were of almost daily and nightly occurrence. With the opening of the new year, there-fore, the young men had a public meeting and chose seven of their number for each city ward and assigned to them the duty of rousing the people to take vigorous "measures to suppress the alarming nightly depredations on the persons and property of our citizens." * As the men engaged in these depredations were believed to be usually negroes, the African Methodist Church called a meeting of colored people, who pledged them-selves to aid the Mayor in his efforts "to detect and suppress the villanies and vice carried on in this city." †

The time had come, it was evident, for a reform in the gov-ernment of large cities. Philadelphia was attempting to con-trol a population of a hundred thousand by the same primitive methods which had been in use when she did not contain twenty thousand. She had grown to be a city without ceasing to be a village, and what was true of her was true of her neighbors. At New York the Society for the Prevention of Pauperism found thirteen thousand paupers in the city main-tained by public charity. Prostitution was so rife that the women formed a society and opened a home for girls, between five and ten years of age, whose parents were drunkards, taught them to read, write, and sew, and, when old enough, sent them to service with respectable families, or bound them to a trades-man. At Providence, where the cost of the poor was twenty thousand dollars a year, a town meeting ordered a committee to devise a plan for providing paupers with work and not with free livings. New Hampshire required the select-men of each town to post the names of tipplers in every tavern and fined anybody ten dollars who sold them liquor.

From such earnest efforts to prevent pauperism and crime there sprang most naturally a discussion and revision of the means then employed to reform criminals and lessen the rep-etition of crime; in short, of the criminal codes and peniten-tiary systems in use in the States. Imperfect as they were,

---

* American Daily Advertiser, February 18, 1822.
† Ibid., February 16, 1822.

our ancestors might well have been proud of them, for barbarous as they now seem there was then no other country on
the face of the earth where they were so mild, so rational, and
so wisely suited to their ends.   The earliest attempt at a reform in penal jurisprudence in America was made by William
Penn, a name that ought never to be mentioned without a
grateful recognition of his many noble efforts to lessen the
burdens and promote the happiness and comfort of mankind.
The charter which was given him by Charles distinctly required
that the penal laws of Pennsylvania should be like those of
England; but, with a courage that did him honor, Penn put
the injunction at defiance; abolished forfeitures in cases of
suicide; abolished the deodands that followed murder; abolished capital punishment for robbery and burglary, arson and
rape; forgery and levying war upon the Governor; substituted imprisonment with hard labor, and sent to England a
code so humane that Queen Anne and her council promptly
vetoed it.   A feeble and unavailing struggle followed, and
down to the opening of the Revolution sixteen species of crimes
were punishable with death in Pennsylvania.   But with independence a better era began, and in 1786 and again in 1790
and 1794 Pennsylvania reformed her code, swept away every
trace of English cruelty, made treason and murder alone punishable with death, built the State Prison at Philadelphia, and
with it began the penitentiary system of the United States.
New York was next to feel the humane spirit of the new era.
There, too, for any one of sixteen crimes men and women
might be put to death.   But in 1796 * her Legislature abolished
capital punishment in fourteen cases and ordered State prisons to be erected at Albany and New York.†   Thenceforth
no period of four years elapsed but some State followed these
happy examples, ‡ and in doing so they imitated not only all
that was good, but all that was bad in the system of Pennsylvania.   The prisons were usually huge buildings cut up into
cells of two sizes.   Those for the use of convicts doomed to
solitary confinement were eleven by eight feet, were heated

---

* Law of March 26, 1796.   † That at Albany was not built.

‡ Virginia in 1800; Massachusetts in 1804; Vermont in 1808; Maryland in
1811; New Hampshire in 1812; Ohio in 1816.

by stoves placed without the grated doors, were lighted by little windows, and provided with necessaries, for no prisoner once within his cell ever crossed its threshold till he was pardoned or had served out his term. Those for the use of convicts whose sentence did not require solitary confinement were often twenty by eighteen feet in area, and into them were crowded every night boys and men without discrimination. The sexes were indeed kept apart. But with this all attempt at classification ended, and murderers awaiting sentence, thieves and highwaymen, swindlers and poor debtors, boys convicted of petty larceny, men held as witnesses—were all herded together in one common crowd. These little rooms had originally been designed to accommodate six or eight prisoners. But so crowded had the jails become that as many as thirty and even forty were to be found in each of them. The New York prison, which was intended to hold three hundred, had seven hundred, and the Governor was actually forced to pardon old convicts in order to make room for the new.* During 1818 two hundred and eighty were turned out in order that three hundred might be admitted.†

Evidence of the dreadful condition into which the prisons all over the country had long been sinking is abundant. As far back as 1809 the Humane Society of New York sent a committee to visit the Bridewell, or City Prison, and report what they saw. The picture which they drew is indeed a horrid one; but it is well to present it as evidence of what then went on in half the jails and penitentiaries of the country. In a room used as the women's apartment seventy-two prisoners guilty of twenty different crimes—vagrants and prostitutes, thieves and drunkards, offenders sentenced for sixty days, paupers who had misbehaved at the almshouse, women committed on suspicion or held as witnesses, black and white, old and young—were indiscriminately mingled together. Some, destitute of garments of every kind, went about with nothing but a dirty blanket wrapped around them. All were very ragged, all were very dirty, and, having no beds, were forced to

---

* Report of a committee to the New York Senate, March 7, 1817.

† Report of the Committee on Criminal Law and the Employment of Criminals on the Canals, to the New York Senate, 1822.

sleep on the floor.   Their food consisted on three days in the week of meat and potatoes, and at other times of mush and molasses.   The mush was brought in a great tub around which the prisoners gathered and fed themselves, some with spoons, some with tin cups, some with their hands, while one of the number, armed with a whip, was appointed by the keeper to maintain order.

The men's apartment was worse, for the inmates were as foul and destitute as the women and far more brutal.   In one of the rooms, where blacks and whites were confined, the captain—the man chosen by the jailer to keep order—was a negro, who told the committee that he was often forced to strip and beat his companions into obedience.   As he spoke he pointed to a corner where lay a prisoner heavily chained by his orders. But the worst case of all was that of a wretch who for more than ten years had been confined in the dungeons on the ground floor; yet neither keeper nor turnkeys could tell for what offence.   He was blind and insane, and so ragged that the committee remarked on it, and were assured that as often as a shirt was given him it was eaten by the rats.*

Aroused by this report, some unknown citizen visited the debtors' jail and drew of that a picture almost as dreadful. The building consisted of four stories and a cellar cut off from each other by strong doors.   Underground in the cellar were the damp, unwholesome dungeons, unventilated and unlighted, save by little openings high up in the wall near the ceiling. Into these were thrust such wretches as were condemned to solitary confinement, and, from time to time, such unhappy women as could not find lodgings in the women's apartments. The ground, or first floor, was occupied by the families of the jailer and the turnkeys, and by the bar, where liquor was sold to the prisoners at a high price.   The second or middle floor was given up to well-to-do debtors who could contribute to a stock purse for cleaning, lighting, and whitewashing the hall,

---

* Report of a Committee of the Humane Society appointed to inquire into the Number of Tavern Licenses; the Manner of granting them; their Effect upon the Community; and other Sources of Vice and Misery in this City; and to visit the Bridewell.   Prefaced with an Address to the Citizens of New York.   December 27, 1809.

and by so doing made themselves members of the "Middle Hall Society." On the third floor was the great mass of debtors, most of whom were supported by the Humane Society, for neither State nor city made any provision for giving them so much as a crust of bread. Their hall was without light at night, and often without fire in winter. Yet in it, during 1809, were confined eleven hundred and fifty-two persons, not one of whom owed twenty-five dollars.* During 1808, the Embargo year, when trade and commerce were much depressed, upward of thirteen hundred debtors had been imprisoned, and were fed and clothed by the Humane Society.†

The prisons and the discipline in force in them had not kept pace with the growth of population and the spirit of the times. The history of the New York penitentiary so well illustrates this fact, and is so closely resembled by that of every similar institution then in the land, that it is well worth while to follow it. From the reports made by those in charge it appears that down to 1803 the ends for which it was established were accomplished. But in that year the report contained the ominous words, "There will soon be a want of room." This was the first sign of coming trouble, and thenceforth for eighteen years the record is one of growing failure. In 1804 it fell into debt, and the cost of keeping the prisoners was eleven thousand dollars more than the product of their labor. In 1805 the debt increased, and overcrowding of the convicts began. A year later the effects of overcrowding is noticed; complaint is made that "lessons of vice are inculcated"; that no reform is seen; and the suggestion is offered that no offenders be sent to the prison whose term of confinement is under five years. During 1807 and 1808 the vices of the system were yet more fully developed. The cells are packed; the hospital is crowded with sick; numbers of convicts are in for second offences; and twenty thousand dollars are wanted to make up the deficit in expenses. Alarmed at this

---

* 591 for debts under $10.00.
　235 "　　"　between $10.00 and $15.00.
　326 "　　"　　　"　　15.00 "　25.00.

1,152

† Theophilanthropist, No. 3, March, 1810.

steadily growing debt, the visiting judges and the Governor begin the vicious practice of making the number of discharges equal to the number of commitments, and in 1810 one hundred and thirty are pardoned in order to make room for one hundred and seventy-one admitted. But even this afforded no relief. The deficit and the number of convicts went on increasing, and in 1814 it was found that old offenders who had been pardoned were in again for second and even third offences. Then was it that the Legislature, for the first time in many years, gave serious attention to the state of the prison, ordered a new one to be built at Auburn, and in 1816 appointed three men to investigate and suggest reforms. They told the Legislature that want of room and the consequent necessity of pardon was the greatest evil of the system; they described the prisoners as corrupting and being corrupted by each other; asserted that men left the prison more confirmed in their vicious propensities than when they entered it; and admitted that the penitentiary had failed to accomplish the great object for which it had been created. Between 1810 and 1815 seven hundred and forty had been released by pardon, and only seventy-seven by the expiration of their sentences. Of all who, in that period, had been incarcerated for a second or third offence, more than two thirds were men who had been pardoned.

The experience of New York was not extreme. Wherever the penitentiary system was in use the same complaints were heard. Whoever was in any way concerned in prison discipline—judges, grand juries, governors, lawyers, secretaries of state, societies for the suppression of crime, committees of investigation—all agreed that the penitentiary was a failure. Indiscriminate herding had defeated reform, and turned what ought to be an institution for the betterment of morals into a seminary of every vice. Culprits came out more depraved and desperate than when they went in. The young were advanced in the path of guilt; the old were hardened in their baseness; morals were destroyed; conscience was blunted, and the ranks of the criminal classes steadily recruited.* It was

* Report of the Committee on the Penitentiary System to the Pennsylvania Senate, 1821. Report on the Penitentiary System in the United States, prepared

from such associates and in such surroundings that the young
learned to commit the fearful crime of sodomy; to make
molds for counterfeiting small coin; to pick locks and construct skeleton keys; to alter banknotes, and become skilful
in the art of picking pockets.

Great results had been expected from the penitentiary
system. Failure to realize them was therefore followed by
astonishment, by disappointment, and by a complete revulsion
of public feeling. A belief now prevailed that the kind-
hearted and benevolent gentlemen who had persuaded the
community to mitigate the severity of the penal code had been
led astray by their benevolence; that the system was wholly
wrong; that nothing but evil had come of it; and that it
could not be too soon abolished. Some in their disappointment cried out for a return to the barbarous practices of
twenty years before, and declared that they longed for the
day when malefactors would again be pelted in the stocks and
flogged at the whipping post, and when the number of criminals would be lessened, not by reformation but by hanging.
Others were for the transportation of criminals—for a Botany
Bay—and when asked where it should be, invariably answered,
At the mouth of the Columbia river in Oregon. But wiser
counsels prevailed. State legislatures, prison discipline societies, societies for the suppression of vice, well-known philanthropists, took up the matter, and, guided by their reports and
pamphlets, public opinion gradually settled to the belief that
reformation of a criminal was not impossible, that a return to
capital punishment was a step backward, and that solitary confinement, by day and by night, of men whose sentences were
not for life was an expedient worth trying.

It was at this time that the tread-mill, a device borrowed
from England, was introduced into the prisons. A hot con-
troversy was waged by the physicians over the question of its
effect on the physical organization of man; but it held its

---

under a resolution of the Society for the Prevention of Pauperism in the City of
New York, 1822. I have borrowed largely from this. On the Prisons of Philadelphia, by a European, 1796. Statistical View of the Operation of the Penal
Code of Pennsylvania, to which is added a view of the present state of the Penitentiary and Prison in the city of Philadelphia, 1817.

place for many years.   Societies for the reformation of juvenile delinquents; prison-discipline societies; houses of refuge;
public schools; new prisons, constructed in accordance with
humane ideas—appeared in many States, and the first quarter
of the nineteenth century closed with a serious effort for the
prevention of crime and the education and reformation of
criminals.

Again the cry for the abolition of imprisonment for debt
arose in the Eastern States, and a flood of literature setting
forth the cruelty and barbarity of the system was poured
forth on the community.   The cause now found friends even
in Congress, where, session after session, efforts were made to
secure the abolition of imprisonment for debt by process from
a United States court.   The speech made by R. M. Johnson,
on one occasion when the subject was under debate in the
Senate, was considered so fine an effort that the Society for
the Relief of the Distressed in Boston published it with an
appendix full of information concerning the sufferings of
debtors.   From this statement it appears that between the
first day of January, 1820, and the first day of April, 1822,
three thousand four hundred and ninety-two persons were imprisoned for debt in Boston; that two thousand of them were
deprived of liberty for sums less than twenty dollars; that
four hundred and thirty were women; and that the suffering
and distress occasioned to the families of the persons imprisoned involved more than ten thousand human beings.   One
brute had a woman, who owed him twelve dollars, dragged to
jail with an infant at her breast.   There she and her child
remained in a crowded room for twenty days, by which time
the infant had become insane and was carried away by a
stranger to breathe its last, while the miserable mother remained in confinement.   Nothing short of the payment of
the debt would induce the creditor to release her.   Yet
another creditor imprisoned a woman for a debt of three
dollars and sixty cents, and forced her to leave two children
under two years of age behind her in what had once been
her home.   An instance, the Society declared, was known
to them of a man who was lodged one bitter winter night
in the Cambridge Jail, where he froze to death before morn-

ing ; * and another of a debtor imprisoned for thirty years. When his case was brought to light his friends had utterly forgotten him ; but they came nobly to his relief, and raised the three thousand dollars necessary to pay the jail fees which had accumulated during the long period of confinement.

The one region of our country which showed no signs of moral awakening was the District of Columbia. In it when the quarter century closed were the most barbarous criminal code and the foulest prison in the United States. On the Virginia side of the District thirty crimes were punishable with death, and on the Maryland side fourteen. A white man who broke into a storehouse, warehouse, or tobacco house, and stole to the value of five shillings, or escaped from jail when confined under charge of felony, could, under the law, be put to death. But a slave who maliciously burned a house, though it were a privy, not only could but must be hung, and when dead have his head cut off, his body quartered, and the fragments displayed in the most public places in the District.

The jail was as bad as the code. Through the middle of it, from end to end, ran a broad passage with eight cells on a side. Under each cell was an arched sewer. With this sewer the cell was connected by a hole which was cut through the brick floor and served as a privy. In these sixteen rooms, not one of which was over eight feet square, the marshal of the district was often forced to confine seventy and even eighty persons ; the innocent with the guilty ; the old with the young— nay, not infrequently the witness with the criminal against whom he was to testify. A member of Congress who visited the prison declared, in his place in the House, that in one cell there were seven persons—three women and four children ; that they were almost naked ; that they had neither bed nor chair, nor stool, nor any other of the common necessaries of life, and were compelled to sleep on the damp brick floor without any other covering than a few dirty blankets.

Nothing, perhaps, illustrates the neglected state of the prisons so fully as the fact that no effort worthy of mention had

---

* Appendix by the Society for the Relief of the Distressed to a pamphlet edition of the speech of R. M. Johnson, on a proposition to abolish imprisonment for debt, delivered in the Senate, January 14, 1823.

been made toward giving their inmates moral and religious instruction. In New Jersey, in Pennsylvania, in Maryland, and Virginia no chaplain was provided by the State, and not a cent was expended for religious services even on Sunday. Now and then some society, or some individual, shocked at this state of affairs, would see to it that the Bible was read a few times and a few sermons preached. But periods of three and five months would pass without a service. New Hampshire, whose penitentiary was a source of revenue, and often paid from one to five thousand dollars a year into her treasury, spent twenty-five dollars annually for religious instruction. Massachusetts appropriated two hundred dollars. Vermont set apart one hundred dollars, and made a weavers' shop of the prison chapel.

Such indifference is the more remarkable because at that very time great religious activity was displayed in every part of the country. The missionary societies were flourishing and busy. Bible societies were being formed in towns and cities; a National Bible Society was in existence, and money was being freely given to send Bibles and teachers into the West, where there was far less need of them than in the prisons of the East.

CHAPTER XXXVIII.

AMERICAN BIBLE AND COLONIZATION SOCIETIES.

THIS earnest desire to do something for the moral welfare of the people of the great West was largely the work of Samuel John Mills, a young man whose name is closely connected with almost all the missionary enterprises of his day. He was a native of Torringford, in Connecticut, was the son of a minister of that town, and while still a boy, according to his biographers, exhibited a strong religious bent. We are told that when a lad of sixteen he announced a wish to spend his days in teaching the Gospel to the heathen; that this wish grew stronger and stronger till, ripening into a purpose, it drove him at twenty-three to abandon his farm and seek an education with a view of becoming a missionary. In 1806, therefore, he entered Williams College, interested a number of students in his purpose, and soon organized a society for making inquiries and forming plans for foreign missions. No such thing as a foreign missionary society then existed in the United States. The New York Missionary Society, the Connecticut Missionary Society, the Massachusetts Missionary Society, the New Jersey Missionary Society, the Massachusetts Baptist Missionary Society, the Western Missionary Society at Pittsburg, were all devoted to work at home, on the frontier and among the Indians. The establishment of the Serampore Mission in Bengal had, indeed, attracted no little attention, and since 1805 had drawn from the Cent Societies, the Female Mite Societies, and the benevolent of every sect, as much as three thousand dollars a year. But no missionaries had been sent to the Old World, for it was home, not foreign, missions that received the support of the people.

The purpose of Mills and his band of fellow-students in founding their society was to arouse public interest, persuade people to give money and induce young men to volunteer as missionaries. They began therefore by publishing missionary sermons and spreading them broadcast. They next visited distinguished clergymen and sought to interest them in their cause, and finally sent some of their number to reside at Middlebury College, and to arouse the students at Dartmouth, Union, and Yale. Success came slowly and it was not till Mills entered the Divinity School at Andover that he found three young men ready to go on foreign missions, and with them made an appeal to the General Association of Massachusetts. Their minds, they stated, had long been deeply impressed with the duty of personally attempting a mission to the heathen, and they now begged to know whether they should abandon their object as visionary and impracticable, or go on. If they went on, should they labor in the Old World or in the New, and should they look for support to a missionary society in America or Europe? The Association bade them hold fast to their purpose, and immediately formed " The Board of Commissioners for Foreign Missions," and assigned to it the duty of finding ways and means "for promoting the spread of the Gospel in heathen lands."

Two years passed before the Board, with much hesitation, ventured to send out its first missionaries, and by that time the Massachusetts Missionary Society and the Connecticut Missionary Society had employed Mills and John F. Schermerhorn to labor in the West. They were to make a tour through the Western and Southern States and Territories, preach the Gospel to the destitute, explore the country, examine the moral and religious state of the people, and promote the establishment of Bible societies wherever they went. They began their labors the moment they crossed the Alleghany Mountains in Pennsylvania, explored that State from the mountains westward, traversed New, or, as we know it, West Virginia, entered New Connecticut, as the Western Reserve was sometimes called, crossed Ohio, passed over Kentucky, Tennessee, and Missouri, reached New Orleans in March, 1813, and brought home a most graphic report on the religion and

morals of the people of the Mississippi Valley. Wherever
they went they found great tracts of country inhabited by
from twenty to fifty thousand people in which there was not
a preacher of any sect. Where there were any they were
almost invariably Methodists. Occasionally they were Baptists, but rarely Presbyterians. The discipline of the Methodists was especially well suited to the state of the West. Population was scattered. The people were poor and not at all
inclined to form societies and incur the expense of maintaining
a settled minister. A sect, therefore, which marked out the
region into circuits, put a rider on each and bade him cover it
once a month, preaching here to-day and there to-morrow, but
returning at regular intervals to each community, provided
the largest amount of religious teaching and preaching at the
least expense. This was precisely what the Methodists did,
and this was precisely what the people desired. Such men
and women as made any profession of religion were therefore very generally Methodists; but the West was too vast a
region to be Christianized by any one sect, and the great body
of the people were in a state of indifference.

The sole competitors of the Methodists in their good work
were the Baptists. From the Presbyterians they had little to
fear. The General Assemblies and the Cumberland Presbytery did indeed send a few missionaries each year into certain parts of Ohio and Kentucky and Tennessee. But their
labors ended in six or eight weeks, and the good work they
did was easily undone in the ten months which elapsed before
they came again, or its fruits were gathered by other sects.
The strongholds of the Presbyterians were the large towns
and villages, in each of which was generally to be found one
small congregation in charge of a man who was its preacher
rather than its pastor. He was not uncommonly of Eastern
birth and the graduate of some seminary of learning, and
made his living by farming, by teaching school, or practising
what passed for medicine. His religious duties were sec-
ondary matters, and were defined in the contract which he
made from year to year with the congregation. His dis-
courses were extemporaneous, and were exhortatory rather
than doctrinal. The catechising of children, the distribution

of tracts and Bibles, the visitation of the family, the instruction of the weak, the confirmation of the doubtful, the building up of churches in new settlements, were affairs in which he never meddled.

Taking the country in general, Mills and Schermerhorn found it, in spite of all that had been done, in a state of spiritual darkness. The most respectable part of the West, in their opinion, was Ohio, though it contained a greater variety of sects—New Lights, Halcyons, Swedenborgians, Infidels, and Universalists—than any other equal area of our country. This was attributed to the influence of New England men and institutions. Yet it was admitted that there was much room for improvement. Everywhere, but especially in the Ohio river towns, the Sabbath was polluted by visiting, feasting, hunting, fishing, and by a gross neglect of religious duties, and the people disgraced by drunkenness and profane swearing. Across the river in Kentucky the people added gambling, duelling, and horse-racing to the sins of their brethren in Ohio, and their towns are described by the two missionaries as sinks of iniquity, and the mass of the inhabitants as ignorant and vicious, and utterly destitute of Bibles and religious books. One hundred of the five hundred Bibles committed to their charge by the New York Bible Society were left for distribution with the Kentucky Bible Society, which they had helped to reorganize at Lexington. Fifty more were left at Franklin, Tennessee.

At this latter place Mills and Schermerhorn were introduced to General Jackson, and accompanied his troops on their famous expedition to Natchez. There another Bible society was founded and a hundred Bibles sent it for distribution. Resuming their journey, they went on by flat-boat to New Orleans, which seemed to them the most sinful city they had ever beheld. The entire population of Louisiana, as they expressed it, was utterly ignorant of divine things, as they had been taught nothing save to attend mass and count their beads. There were no schools, no Bibles, no religious instruction. Sunday was a high holiday. The mass over, every man and woman in the city seemed bent on pleasure. The theatres and billiard-rooms were open ; parties of pleasure were made up, and the visiting, the dancing, the gambling, and the feasting continued till far into the night. More actual sin, Mills declared, was committed there on Sunday than in all the other days of the week taken together. Three fourths of the inhabitants, as far as could be judged, had never seen so much as the back of a Bible. A society for the distribution of Bibles in French and English was accordingly formed, and one hundred and fifty copies of the book left with it.

The account of the wickedness of the land brought back by Schermerhorn and Mills was spread broadcast among the Bible and missionary societies of the East and aroused them to new efforts, which resulted in sending Mills on a second missionary tour to the West. He set out, in company with a young man named Daniel Smith, in the summer of 1814, fairly loaded down with religious literature. To his care were intrusted seven hundred English Bibles, five thousand copies of the New Testament in French, fifteen thousand tracts, and great bundles of sermons and pamphlets—all contributed by the Bible and tract societies of New England and the Middle States. But as they went westward, founding Bible societies and distributing their books, they were appalled at the magnitude of the work that lay before them. What had been bad before was daily growing worse, for emigration had now set strongly toward the West, and thousands of new settlers, as destitute as the old, were pouring into the Territories each week. After going over the field a second time, Mills gave it as his calm and deliberate opinion that there were in 1815, between the Alleghany Mountains and the Mississippi river, seventy-six thousand families destitute of the Bible. This number was increasing yearly, and as the supply sent each twelvemonth by the Eastern societies was less than the increase, some mighty effort must be made if the West was not to become as ignorant of God's Word as the heart of Africa.

When Mills came back from his second tour in the summer of 1815 he urged on the societies of the East the duty of forming a national society with branches in every city and town. In New Jersey his appeal was heard, and from the Bible Society of that State a plan went out in 1815 to the sister societies for concurrence. But the New York Society suggested a convention of delegates from the seventy Bible societies then in the United States, and asked the New Jersey Society to name the day and the place, which was done, and a call for a convention to meet in New York city on the eighth of May, 1816, was duly published in the newspapers. A constitution was then prepared and, bound up with a pamphlet " on the subject of a General Bible Society for the United States," * was spread broadcast.

On the appointed day delegates from twenty-eight societies attended, and these, with a host of laymen and preachers friendly to the movement, founded the American Bible Society and adopted the constitution suggested in the pamphlet. Strangely enough, a violent opposition arose to it. Some declared there was no need for such an institution ; that it was a castle in the air ; that it could not exist in our country ; that it would become the instrument of a party and promote the interests of a particular sect ; that it would draw money away from other worthy institutions ; and that Americans ought to join with the British and Foreign Bible Society and not set up one of their own. The Episcopalians were especially hostile. Bishop White would give it no support. Bishop Hobart attacked it in a bitter " Address." Yet despite all this it thrived. Auxiliary societies sprang up everywhere till, when it was five years old, there were two hundred and thirty-nine of them. By that time more than one hundred and forty thousand Bibles, Testaments, and parts of Testaments had been given away.

But it was not merely the spiritual destitution of the whites in the South and West that appealed so strongly to the Christian people in New Jersey and New York and led them to take the steps which founded the American Bible Society. The report of Mills on the condition of the blacks was most shocking. The census takers had returned a million and a half of them in 1810. Some were free ; the vast majority were slaves ; but, whether slave or free, they were as a class in the South as destitute of teachers and preachers as the whites were of Bibles. Their condition was therefore as proper a

---

* A Memoir on the Subject of a General Bible Society for the United States of America. By a Citizen of New Jersey, 1816.

subject for betterment as that of their owners and oppressors, and became the occasion of an overture laid before the Synod of New York and New Jersey by the Committee of Overtures in October, 1816. It was proposed that a school should be established in which young men of color should be educated and fitted to become the teachers and ministers of their race, not only in the United States, but elsewhere.

The Synod had no funds to apply for so laudable a purpose. But with the understanding that it must look to the public for support, the African school was established, and in March, 1817, received two negro students on probation. Toward this prompt action the Synod, it was afterward said, was moved by the belief that before very long an effort would be made to colonize free negroes by themselves, either in America or abroad; that teachers of color would then become indispensable, and that in opening the school it was making a wise provision for a coming event.*

The idea of colonization was an old one, and, like every other movement in behalf of the negro, it was slow in taking form. As early as 1777, when the "rights of man" were in everybody's mouth, the Legislature of Virginia appointed a committee to revise the laws of the Commonwealth. The chairman was Jefferson, and under his lead the committee went so far as to report a bill for the gradual abolition of slavery. Every child born of a slave mother after the passage of the act was to remain with the parent to a certain age, when the State was to step in and educate it. If a female, it was to be instructed in household arts till eighteen. If a male, it was to be taught farming, or the arts and sciences, till twenty-one, at which ages both male and female were to be colonized at such places as seemed best. War and the miseries of war prevented even an attempt to carry out the idea. Ten years later, however, just as the English philanthropists were about to land their colony at Sierra Leone, William Thornton offered to lead a colony of blacks from Rhode Island and Massachusetts to the west coast of Africa.

---

* A View of the Exertions lately made for the Purpose of colonizing the Free People of Color in the United States, in Africa, or Elsewhere. Washington, 1817, p. 19.

This time lack of funds defeated the effort, and colonization was forgotten for a period of thirteen years. At length, in 1800, just after the outbreak in Richmond of what was feared would be a great slave insurrection such as had swept over San Domingo a decade before, the Legislature of Virginia met in secret session to take measures for the public safety. Much of the danger which seemed to beset the slave-owner was then attributed to the presence, side by side in the same community, of free negroes and slaves, and to get rid of the former the Legislature resolved to recommend colonization. The Governor, therefore, was instructed to correspond with the President on the subject of buying lands without the limit of Virginia, to which, in the language of the resolution, "persons obnoxious to the laws, or dangerous to the peace of society, may be removed." A later resolution selected Africa as the proper place for such colonization. But after a few half-earnest attempts to secure land for the colony, first at Sierra Leone and then in other places, this plan shared the fate of its predecessors, and for sixteen years remained buried up in the secret journals of the Virginia House of Delegates. There, however, in 1816, the proceedings were discovered by Charles Fenton Mercer, a member of the House, who immediately made them public, and at the next session of the Legislature secured the passage of a new resolution on colonization.

The Governor was once more instructed to correspond with the President, for the purpose of obtaining land on the coast of Africa, or on the shores of the North Pacific, or at some other place, not in Virginia, nor in any of the States, nor in any of the Territories of the United States, to serve as an asylum for such persons of color as were free, and desired the same.

The resolution was most timely, for the general sentiment of the country, even in the free States, was strongly in favor of the colonization of free blacks. The enthusiasm which at the close of the Revolution led the people of the Northern States to provide for the gradual abolition of slavery had died out. But the laws had remained, and under their working thousands of negroes whose parents were slaves had, on attaining a certain age, become free. In general they settled in the great seaports, where their rapid increase was looked on with dread. In the city of New York, in 1790, the number of whites to free blacks was as twenty-five to one; but in 1800 it had declined to fifteen to one, and by 1810 had fallen to ten to one. In Philadelphia, which was known through the South as the paradise of negroes, the white population was to the free negro population as twenty-four to one, in 1800 as ten to one, and in 1810 as nine to one. At Baltimore, in 1790, the ratio was thirty-three to one, and eleven to one in 1810. What was true of these great cities was true of the States in which they were, and of the free States in general. Enormous as had been the increase of white population, that of the free negroes had surpassed it. According to the first census, there were but a trifle more than fifty-nine thousand free negroes in the country to nearly four millions of population,* or as fifty-three to one. When the census was taken for the third time, the population of the United States was more than seven and a quarter millions, and the number of free negroes one hundred and eighty-six thousand,† or as thirty-one to one.

Great as this increase was, it would have excited little attention were it not for the fact that the negroes, in spite of their freedom, were a despised, proscribed, and poverty-stricken class. Nowhere was their lot as happy a one as in Pennsylvania. Save for the requirement that none but "free, able-bodied white males" should be liable for military duty, neither the constitution nor the laws of Pennsylvania made any distinction between the free white man and the free black. In the eye of the law every black freeman was the political equal of every white freeman, had every right of citizenship, could vote, and was eligible to any office from the humblest in the borough to the highest in the State. The Legislature, the bench, the Governorship, were open to him. Yet no black man ever attained to either of them. No assessor of a county rate would return him as a "taxable inhabitant." Unless so returned he was not taxed, and unless he paid a county

---

* Population, 1790, 3,929,326; slaves, 697,697; free negroes, 59,481.

† Population, 1810, 7,239,903; slaves, 1,191,364; free negroes, 186,446.

or State tax he could not vote. He could, indeed, if he demanded it, compel the assessor to insert his name in the county book. But few ever had the spirit to do so.

As the free negroes, as a class, cast no votes, they were never candidates for office, were never employed in public affairs, were never summoned on a jury, and took no part either in the making or the administration of law. In Philadelphia, where seventeen thousand of them were crowded into a few narrow and filthy alleys, they were as much a class by themselves as in any slave-holding city of the South. They worshipped God in their own churches, under the lead of ministers of their own race. Negro physicians attended them in sickness; and their children, when they went to school at all, were taught by negro teachers.

As their numbers increased, the question, What should be done with them? thus became as troublesome in the North as, for a very different reason, it had long been in the South. That they should not be admitted to a political and social equality with the whites was taken for granted. But with this, disagreement began. Some who read prison statistics and followed the course of crime declared that nearly half of the criminals convicted at the quarter sessions and the Mayor's courts were negroes (though the ratio of whites to free negroes was as thirty-one to one), and cried out that they were a burden on the community—a source of moral corruption that must be removed.* Some cited the history of the Helots to prove that the republic was not safe while such political discrimination existed between two portions of the same people, and hinted that they ought in some way to be scattered. The moment, therefore, that a serious and deliberately prepared

---

* Statistics for 1820:

STATE.	Population.	Colored.	Convicts.	Colored convicts.
Massachusetts	523,000	7,000	314	50
Connecticut	276,000	8,000	117	39
New York	1,372,000	39,000	637	154
New Jersey	277,000	20,000	74	24
Pennsylvania	1,049,000	30,000	474	165

plan of colonization was brought forward the public gave it a hearty support.

The originator of the movement was Doctor Robert Finley, of Basking Ridge, in New Jersey. He had long cherished the idea of an American colony in Africa, or on the Pacific coast, similar to the English colony at Sierra Leone. "Our fathers," he would say, "brought the blacks here, and we, the sons, are bound, if possible, to repair the wrong done by our fathers. Could the plan be carried out, could the free negroes be sent back to Africa, a threefold benefit would arise : we should be cleared of them ; we should send to Africa a partially civilized and Christianized population ; and we should have our own negroes in a much better position." * But it was not till the autumn of 1816 that he put his scheme to the test and gathered a few men of note at Princeton, where a memorial was prepared praying the Legislature of New Jersey to use its influence with Congress to adopt some plan for the colonization of free blacks. That such a memorial would produce no effect whatever was well known to Dr. Finley, who almost immediately went to Washington to agitate for the formation of a National Colonization Society with senators and congressmen for leaders. With the help of his brother-in-law, Elias Boudinot Caldwell, a number of leading men in the House and Senate were enlisted in the cause, and a public meeting called to discuss the question of the practicability of colonizing free negroes in the United States, and of forming an association for that purpose.

Justice Bushrod Washington, of the Supreme Court, had promised to be present. But in his absence Henry Clay was put in the chair, and explained the object of colonization to the meeting. The lot of the free negroes was, he said, a peculiar one. They neither enjoyed the immunities of freemen nor were subject to the incapacities of slaves, but partook to some extent of both. From their condition and the unconquerable prejudice which sprang from their color they never could amalgamate with the whites. It was desirable, there-

---

* Memoir of the Rev. Robert Finley, D. D.   By Rev. Isaac V. Brown, A. M., 1819, p. 77.

fore, both for them and for the rest of the population of the country, to drain them off. This could be done by colonizing them on some part of the west coast of Africa. There was a peculiar, a moral fitness in restoring them to the land of their fathers. But he wished it distinctly understood that the meeting was not called on to touch in the slightest degree on any question connected with abolition or emancipation.

John Randolph, of Roanoke, followed Clay and spoke at length on this matter. "It seems to me," said he, "that the fact that there is nothing in the colonization of free negroes which touches even in the remotest degree on the question of negro slavery has not been sufficiently insisted on. It ought to be insisted on, and with a view to secure the support of all the citizens of the United States it ought to be made known that the colonization scheme tends to secure the property of every master to, in, and over his slaves. It is a notorious fact that the existence of free negroes is looked on by every slave-owner as one of the greatest sources of insecurity to slave property. They excite discontent. They act as channels of communication not only between different slaves, but between slaves of different districts. They are the depositories of stolen goods and the promoters of mischief. Aside from all questions of a moral kind, the slave-owner, from worldly motives, is interested in casting out this population from the bosom of the people." After Randolph and a few others had spoken, some resolutions were adopted as expressing the wish of the meeting.* The situation of free people of color has always been, the resolution set forth, a matter of grave concern to the people of the United States. But the difficulties and dangers which beset us when an infant nation, and the dreadful convulsions in Europe for a quarter of a century past, have made any national effort to provide a remedy impossible. But the present time is most auspicious. The powers of Europe are at peace. The rights of man are better understood. That government is founded for the benefit of man is generally acknowledged, and an ardent zeal for the

---

* National Intelligencer, December, 1816. American Daily Advertiser, December 27, 1816, January 2, 1817.

good of man is felt everywhere. It is well, therefore, to seize the opportunity and help on the great work of civilization by forming an association to assist in the Colonization of Free People of Color in the United States. Committees were then appointed to collect information, frame a constitution, and memorialize Congress.

The constitution which was adopted a week later named the association "The American Society for the Colonization of the Free People of Color of the United States," and declared its one object was to promote and execute a plan for the colonization (with their consent) of free blacks in Africa, or wherever else Congress deemed most expedient.* On January first, 1817, the organization was completed by the choice of Bushrod Washington as president, and of thirteen well-known men as vice-presidents.

At these proceedings the free people of color took alarm, and such as were near Washington met at Georgetown a few days later.† The sense of those present was that while they were willing to colonize, the place must be in the United States and not in Africa; that Congress should be petitioned to assign a spot on the waters of the Missouri, and that a great national association of negroes should be formed with branches reaching into every county, town, and district in the land.

The resolutions passed at this meeting, together with copies of the memorial to Congress, were sent to all the chief cities, and in Philadelphia aroused great feeling. At a gathering of free blacks held in the Bethel Church a remonstrance was drawn up and a committee chosen to correspond with Joseph Hopkinson, who represented Philadelphia in Congress. " Our ancestors," said the blacks, " were, though not from choice, the first cultivators of the wilds of America, and we, their descendants, claim a right to share in the blessings of her luxuriant soil which their blood and sweat manured. We read with deep abhorrence the unmerited stigma, attempted to be cast on the reputation of the free people of color, that ' they are a dangerous and useless part of the community.'

---

* American Daily Advertiser, January 3, 1817.   † January 6, 1817.

We declare that we will never be separated from the slave population of this country; that to thrust the free people of color into the wilds of Africa without a knowledge of the arts and sciences, and without a government of any kind, is to send them into perpetual bondage." *

As Dr. Finley passed through Philadelphia on his way home a few days later, he sought out the leaders of the movement, attempted to calm their fears,† and seemed to have succeeded, for no further opposition was publicly made for several months.

Meantime the Colonization Society presented its petition to Congress. In the House it was referred to the Committee on the Slave-Trade, which approved of the idea of colonization and proposed and answered three questions. The first was, Should the colony be planted within the limits of the United States? to which the answer was emphatically No. The second was, Should Africa be the site? and to this the answer was Yes. To the third, Will it be expedient to establish a new colony in Africa, or ask Great Britain to receive emigrants from the United States into her colony of Sierra Leone? the answer was a joint resolution proposing many things. In the first place, the President was authorized to negotiate with all the governments where ministers of the United States were to be found for the total and immediate stoppage of the slave-trade. In the second place, he was to ask Great Britain to receive into her colony of Sierra Leone such free negroes from the United States as were willing to go there. Finally, if Great Britain would not open Sierra Leone to settlement, he was to obtain from the various maritime powers of Europe a stipulation guaranteeing the permanent neutrality of any colony of free negroes which might be founded on the African coast under the auspices of the United States.‡

No further action was taken by the House during that session. But the Society was much encouraged, and in July the Board of Managers announced that they were about to enter on the prosecution of the object they had so much at heart. Their

---

* January, 1817.   † Memoir of Robert Finley, pp. 100–102.

‡ Joint Resolution presented to the House of Representatives, February 11, 1817.

first duty was, of course, to obtain information regarding the best place for beginning a settlement. With this end in view, therefore, they had decided to send an agent to visit Sierra Leone and explore the coast of Africa. For this money was needed, and it was hoped the friends of colonization would respond liberally.* In support of this effort, societies auxiliary to the American Society were at once formed in the large cities, and among them was one at Philadelphia.† The appearance of this society, and of the vigorous movement of which it was a part, again aroused the free blacks, who met a second time and protested. They renounced, they said, and disclaimed all connection with it, and would not in any way take part in it. The final abolition of slavery in the United States, with God's help, was steadily going on. Each year saw the release of many victims of oppression; but if emancipation should, when colonization went into effect, be attended with transportation to Africa, and was to be granted on no other condition, then it was better that it should cease forever. A colony so founded, without arts, sciences, and industries, and made up of people unused to provide for their wants, must become the home of vice and misery.‡ In spite of this opposition, the Society continued to grow, and by November had gathered sufficient money to despatch Samuel J. Mills and Ebenezer Burgess to find a suitable spot on the west coast of Africa. In England they were warmly received by the members of the African Institution, were introduced to Bathurst, Secretary of State for the Colonies, and were given letters to the officials at Sierra Leone, which they reached in March, 1818. The letter from Bathurst secured them civil treatment; but they were given so plainly to understand that no negroes from America were wanted that they went on down the coast as far as Sherbro Island. As the natives promised to sell them land, they chose that place as the site of the American colony, and in May, 1818, started home. Mills died at sea; but Burgess reached the United States in safety in October, with so glowing an account of the trip that the Society determined to begin colonization at once.

---

* See the Appeal in American Daily Advertiser, July 10, 1817.

† American Daily Advertiser, August 5, 12, 1817.   ‡ Ibid., 12, 1817.

Two things—money and emigrants—were needed, and of these the Society had neither. That money could be raised was not doubted; but that free negroes could be persuaded to emigrate to Africa was still in doubt, when a law of the State of Georgia placed a number of emigrants at the Society's disposal. The United States statute of 1807 which forbade the importation of slaves into any State or Territory, made no provision for the disposal of such slaves as might be seized in the attempt to smuggle them into the country in spite of the law. The States were left to say what should become of them, and, exercising the power, Georgia ordered them to be sold into slavery for the benefit of the State. From time to time thereafter great numbers of them were so disposed of till 1817,* when Georgia provided that if, previous to the sale of such negroes, the Colonization Society would agree to export them to Africa and pay all costs incurred on their account by Georgia from the time they were captured and condemned, it might have them. Now it happened that early in 1819 another batch of poor wretches were seized, condemned, and advertised for sale by Georgia, and that a copy of the advertisement cut from a Georgia newspaper by Secretary Crawford, who was a vice-president of the Society, was sent to the Secretary. No finer chance to begin its work could be wanted. The directors, therefore, embraced the opportunity, despatched the Reverend William Mead to Milledgeville to secure the release of the negroes, and called on the humane to contribute the sum necessary to reimburse Georgia for the cost of maintaining them. George Washington Parke Custis offered the use of an island he owned near Cape Charles as a place of refuge for them till a place could be made ready for them in Africa. The Governor of Georgia postponed the sale, that the redemption money might be raised, and the Society called on Monroe to use the new power given to him by an act of Congress passed at the close of the session in March, 1819. It was called " an act in addition to the acts prohibiting the slave-trade," and contained three important provisions. The first authorized the President to make such arrangements as

---

* December 19, 1817.

he thought fit for the safe-keeping, support, and removal beyond the limits of the United States of such negroes, mulattoes, or persons of color as might be seized under the act for the suppression of the slave-trade.   The second authorized him to send an agent to reside in Africa, and receive such negroes and mulattoes as might be taken from the decks of slavers by commanders of United States armed vessels.   The third set apart one hundred thousand dollars to carry the law into effect.

Thus empowered to act, Monroe selected Samuel Bacon and John P. Bankson to be United States agents, resident in Africa; chartered the brig Elizabeth to carry out such free negroes as the Society were ready to send away; set apart thirty-three thousand dollars to pay for tools, implements, and the cost of transportation, and ordered the United States armed ship Cyane to act as escort.

Meantime some free negroes in Philadelphia and New York applied to the Society for transportation to Africa, and in their behalf the Society appealed to the people of the two cities for money, food, clothing, and implements,* and brought down on it the indignation of the free blacks.   At a public meeting in Philadelphia † the appeal was described as the work of obscure and disgruntled strangers eager to be made presidents and governors in Africa, and not an expression of the wishes of free people of color.   Among them there was but one sentiment, and that was a decided disapproval.   Colonization in Africa could lead to nothing but the perpetual establishment of slavery in the United States, and for this reason they protested most solemnly against it.

That the protest had some effect in checking emigrants is quite likely.   In December, when the Society advertised that the ship Elizabeth was lying at the foot of Liberty Street, New York, and would receive emigrants, it was announced that one hundred and seventy had engaged to embark.   But when the Elizabeth, escorted by the Cyane, dropped down the harbor of New York on the sixth of February, 1820, she had on board but eighty-six men, women, and children.

---

* November 15, 1819.   † November 16, 1819.

An uneventful voyage of five weeks brought the pilgrims to Sierra Leone, whence they soon set sail for Sherbro Island. There good fortune deserted them. The natives had changed their minds, disavowed the promise made to Mills, and refused to sell the colonists one foot of land. While parleying with the Africans the rainy season set in, and the three agents and twenty colonists fell victims to fever, bred by bad water, a bad climate, and the marshes on which they were forced to dwell. On the death of the agents the command of the party passed into the hands of one of the colonists, named Daniel Croker, who led his sick and disheartened countrymen back to Sierra Leone.

But the Society and its auxiliaries were not discouraged, and early in 1821 twenty-eight colonists, in charge of Ephraim Bacon and J. B. Winn, sailed in the brig Nautilus from Norfolk and landed at Freetown in March. While Winn collected the scattered members of the first colony and settled them with the new-comers, Bacon went southward, and on the Grain Coast of Guinea, found a high, fertile, and healthful tract of land, which seemed in every way suited to his purposes. This tract was Cape Montserado. At first the natives were well disposed, and the negotiation for the purchase of the cape went on smoothly, till the agents began to insist on the abolition of the slave-trade as a condition of purchase, when it instantly ceased. To the Africans the traffic in slaves was most valuable, as it was the only means by which they could obtain rum and the many articles of European manufacture they prized so highly. Bacon thereupon returned disheartened to Sierra Leone, whence, Winn having died, he went back to the United States, leaving the affairs of the struggling colony in the hands of Wittberger.

Once more the Society was not discouraged by these reverses, but incited to new activity, and in the fall of 1821 sent Dr. Ayres to Sierra Leone. There he was soon joined by Lieutenant Richard F. Stockton, in the United States schooner Alligator, and with him went off to Cape Montserado to make one more effort to buy it. Success attended them, and a document was finally drawn up and signed by King Peter and five African chiefs on the one part, and by Ayres and Stockton on the other, by which, in consideration of goods and

trinkets worth three hundred dollars, a tract of land was secured for the colony.

To this tract the colonists now hastened in high hopes,
and landed on two small islands just within the mouth of the
Montserado river.   They had intended to take possession of
their cape, but the fickle King Peter and his chiefs had
changed their minds, and would not give up the territory.
The firmness of Stockton and the persistence of Ayres, in the
end, induced the chiefs to again consent to the purchase, and
on April twenty-second, 1822, the colonists took possession of
the cape and began the building of a town.   While this work
was under way, a British vessel, full of recaptured Africans,
while stopping off the cape for water, parted her cable and
drifted ashore.   Almost at the same time a French slaver, in
search of a cargo, appeared off the coast.   These two events
so excited the natives that they attempted to take the negroes
from the British ship by force ; but the colonists rallied in
her defence, and in the struggle that followed two natives
were killed.

This act brought the colony to a desperate plight.   The
rainy season had set in.   Supplies were running low.   Fever
had long been decimating the little band.   But when to
these was added the hostility and treachery of the natives,
Dr. Ayres lost heart and offered to lead the colonists back to
Sierra Leone.   Many would surely have gone had not Elijah
Johnson, a negro emigrant from New York, come forward,
stoutly declared he would never quit the cape, and so aroused
his fellows that they remained and struggled bravely on under
their negro leader.   After the departure of Ayres and a few
followers in June, 1822, the condition of those who remained
grew steadily worse.   Indeed, they would surely have perished
had not relief come unexpectedly from the United States.   At
length the Government had secured possession of ten recaptured negroes, and placing them in charge of the Reverend
Jehudi Ashmun, it sent them to Africa in the brig Strong.
With Mr. Ashmun went thirty-seven emigrants, collected by
the Colonization Society, and a quantity of stores.   Ashmun
had no authority from the Society to act as agent, and had expected to return in the Strong.   But when he reached the

little colony in August he found it in such desperate straits that he decided to remain. A visit to the neighboring chiefs convinced him that they meditated the extirpation of the colony, and led him to prepare for an immediate attack. The means of defence were small indeed. Twenty-seven men able to bear arms made up his army. One brass field-piece and five dismounted and rusty iron guns constituted his armament. But he went resolutely to work, and, despite the rains, the fever, and the scanty supply of food, drilled his men, put up earthworks, and cleared away the trees and underbrush in front of them. The work was begun in the very nick of time, and at daybreak on November eleventh eight hundred Africans rushed from the forest, seized the outworks, and were carrying all before them, when the colonists manned the brass field-piece and opened a fire which drove back the assailants. The state of the colony was now worse than ever, for both food and ammunition were exhausted, and the enemy was preparing for a second attack. But it was not destined to perish. An English captain, happening to touch at the cape, most generously gave the colonists stores and food. The next night the Africans attacked the town a second time. Again they were beaten off, and again unexpected succor saved the colony. The sound of heavy cannonading at midnight attracted the attention of the captain of an English colonial schooner laden with military stores. He at once put in to investigate, and gave the negroes every assistance in his power. Stores and munitions were landed, a peace was concluded with the natives, and when he sailed, his midshipmen and eleven sailors volunteered to remain and help the exhausted colonists. This event marked the turn in the tide, and thenceforth, despite internal bickerings, Liberia, as the Colonization Society named the territory, and Monrovia, as it called the town on the cape, went steadily forward on a prosperous career.

CHAPTER XXXIX.

SLAVERY BEYOND THE MISSISSIPPI.

ON the twenty-sixth of March, 1804, the newly acquired territory of Louisiana was cut into two parts by act of Congress. The dividing line was the thirty-third degree of north latitude. To so much as lay south of it was given the name Territory of Orleans; but that almost boundless region which stretched away northward and westward to the Rocky Mountains and the possessions of Great Britain was called the District of Louisiana. Orleans was given a government of its own; but Louisiana was attached to the Territory of Indiana. Against this the people protested so vigorously that Congress yielded, granted their prayer, and on July fourth, 1805, it became the Territory of Louisiana, with a governor, judges, and secretary of its own.* Seven years later, when the Territory of Orleans was admitted into the Union as the State of Louisiana, the name Territory of Louisiana was dropped and Territory of Missouri substituted. The census of 1810 had given it a population of twenty thousand souls—a number which, according to precedent, entitled it to some local self-government. By the same act which changed the name it was therefore raised to a Territory of the second grade and given a House of Representatives elected by the people, a Legislative Council of nine chosen by the President from a list of eighteen names sent him by the Territorial Legislature, and a delegate to Congress.

At the time of the purchase of Louisiana the population of Missouri was confined to a few thousand souls who lived in the old French settlements close to the west bank of the

---

* History of the People of the United States, vol. iii, pp. 29, 30.

Mississippi. They were Creoles from Louisiana; Frenchmen and Spaniards from the Old World; half-breed Frenchmen from Canada; *voyageurs* and *coureurs des bois*, and negroes brought from every kraal on the coast of Congo and of Guinea. But in the westward march of population down the eastern slope of the Mississippi Valley a small contingent began to enter Missouri at an early day, and when the census was taken, in 1810, had increased the population to twenty thousand. These people then occupied a strip of country twenty miles wide along the Mississippi, from the Arkansas to a point some miles north of the mouth of the Missouri. A few hundred were engaged at "the diggings" or lead mines, and had scattered their cabins along the Big river, Terre Bleu, and the Mineral fork in the heart of the county of St. Genevieve. Some lived by agriculture, and were already pushing their farms and settlements up the Missouri. Others —and they were chiefly in St. Louis—carried on an extensive fur trade with the Indians; while still others—as the inhabitants of St. Charles—were renowned as Mississippi boatmen. With the opening of the war with England the tide of emigration diminished in volume. But when the hard times, which came with the return of peace, began to drive people westward by hundreds of thousands, the stream that poured into Missouri was enormous. As a Territory where slavery was permitted, it became a promised land for every slave-owning emigrant from Virginia and North Carolina, Kentucky and Tennessee, and thither they went.

A humble chronicler, who was himself one of that countless throng, has preserved for us a living picture of what he saw.* He had come from Massachusetts and had taken up his residence at St. Charles, a little town on the north bank of the Missouri twenty miles above its junction with the Mississippi. The place was directly on the route to northern Missouri and through it, he declares, as many as a hundred persons would pass in a day, and this for days together. Standing on the Mamelles, a succession of regular cone-shaped bluffs that rise from the prairie, and looking toward the Mamelles Ferry

---

* Recollections of the Last Ten Years passed in Occasional Residences and Journeyings in the Valley of the Mississippi, etc. Timothy Flint. Boston, 1826.

on the Mississippi, he had seen the plain dotted with nine six-horse wagons, each followed by cattle, hogs, horses, sheep, and from three to twenty negro slaves. Sometimes a dozen such wagons could be counted at the ferry waiting for a chance to cross. "The whole appearance of the train—the cattle with their hundred bells; the negroes with delight in their countenances, for their labors were suspended and their imaginations excited; the wagons, often carrying two or three tons, so loaded that the mistress and the children are strolling carelessly along at a gait which enables them to keep up with the slow travelling carriage—carried me back to the pastoral pursuits of those ancient races whose home was in a tent wherever their flocks found range. Just about nightfall they come to a spring or a branch where there is water and wood; the pack of dogs set up a cheerful barking; the cattle lie down to ruminate; the team is unharnessed; the huge wagons are covered so that the roof completely excludes the rain; the cooking utensils are brought out; the blacks prepare a supper which the toils of the day render delicious." All are bound for Boon's Lick. "Ask one of them," says Flint, "whither he was moving, and the answer was, 'To Boon's Lick, to be sure!'"

The arrival of these settlers in such numbers was followed by a steady demand for a new change in the form of government. As early as 1816 Congress had consented that the Council should be elected by the people and should consist of one member for each county. But this was not enough. In three years' time the Territory had doubled its population, the frontier had moved westward almost to the Indian boundary line, and nothing would now satisfy the settlers but the same kind of local government they had left behind them in the States. The admission of Indiana into the Union in 1816, of Mississippi in 1817, and of Illinois in 1818, served but to make this feeling stronger till, at the close of 1817, it found expression in petitions to Congress for leave to form a State Government and come into the Union. Little attention was paid to them, as they seemed to be the work of individuals and not the setting forth of public opinion. But one which came from the Territorial Legislature was sent to a select committee of which John Scott, the Missouri delegate, was chairman. A bill in accordance with the petition was soon reported, read twice and sent to the Committee of the Whole, where it was when the House adjourned for the summer. When it reassembled in November, 1818, the Speaker presented a second petition from the Legislature ; and Mr. Scott another from the people of what is now Arkansas, asking for a division of the Territory. The usual routine was again gone through with ; the petitions were referred, a bill to enable the people of Missouri to form a State Constitution was reported, and after a month's delay was taken up in Committee of the Whole.* But the discussion had hardly opened when James Tallmadge, Jr., moved an amendment which threw the committee into confusion. He asked two things : that the further introduction of slaves into Missouri be forbidden, and that all children born after the admission of Missouri should be free, but might be held to service till twenty-five years old.†

It may well be supposed that he was instantly set upon from all sides. Such a restriction, said those who opposed it (and among them was Henry Clay), is unconstitutional, unwise, and not possible to carry out. It is unconstitutional because Congress has no power to lay any restriction on any State as a condition of its admission into the Union ; because, by the treaty of purchase, Congress is pledged to form Louisiana into States and admit them into the Union on the same footing with the original States ; because Missouri will not be on an equal footing with the original States if forced to abolish slavery before coming into the Union ; and because the citizens of each State are entitled to all the rights, privileges, and immunities of the citizens of the several States. One of these rights is that of going wherever a man listeth with his property—a right which will be most seriously impaired if the

---

* February 13, 1819.

† Provided that the further introduction of slavery or involuntary servitude be prohibited, except for the punishment of crime whereof the party shall have been duly convicted ; and that all children born within the said State after the admission thereof into the Union shall be free, but may be held to service until the age of twenty-five years. Journals of the House of Representatives, Fifteenth Congress, Second Session.

citizens of the slave States are forbidden to settle in Missouri
with that kind of property which consists of slaves.

Such a restriction would be unwise, because it would shut
the Southern emigrant from Missouri and open that splendid
region to free State men alone; because such a diminution of
emigrants would lessen the number of purchasers of land;
because a decrease in the number of purchasers would be followed by a fall in the price of public lands, and this, in turn,
by a serious lessening of the public revenues.

Such a restriction could never be carried out, for, though
the people of Missouri did accept the condition and did come
into the Union as a free State, they could, whenever they
pleased, mend their Constitution and re-establish slavery—an
act no one who knew them could for a moment doubt that
they would commit.

Threats and arguments such as these had little weight, and
the committee, by a vote of seventy-nine to sixty-seven, agreed
to the Tallmadge amendment, and the bill so amended was
reported to the House. In the House it found more friends
than when before the committee, and by a vote of ninety-seven
to fifty-six nays it was ordered to be engrossed and read a
third time. Of the nays, six came from States north of the
Mason and Dixon line and the Ohio river.

In the Senate the matter was quickly disposed of. As the
session was drawing rapidly to a close, the bill was read a second time by unanimous consent; was hurried to a committee
having in charge a memorial from Alabama; was promptly
reported with the Tallmadge amendment stricken out, and in
this form was passed on the first day of March. The House,
however, by a majority of two, refused to concur, and sent
the bill back to the Senate. But the Senate voted to adhere
to its amendment, and returned the bill to the House, which
now a second time voted to adhere, and the bill was lost for
want of agreement.

But the struggle for free soil beyond the Mississippi was
not confined to Missouri. The petition from sundry inhabitants in the southern county of Missouri for a division of the
Territory and a separate territorial government for that part
in which they dwelt had been followed by a bill creating the

Territory of Arkansas. This bill came up in Committee of the Whole one morning in February,* when John W. Taylor moved an amendment in all respects similar to that of Tallmadge to the Missouri bill. A short and sharp struggle followed. Clay accused the free-soil members of "Negrophobia," of a desire to coop up their brethren of the South, and demanded what they had done that they should be proscribed. A member from North Carolina asked if the South was to be deprived of all part and lot in the territory west of the Mississippi, and the people of Arkansas of the natural and constitutional right of legislating for themselves, by imposing on them a condition they might not accept. These two arguments had much weight. Members were not willing to hinder the slave-owning emigrant from going across the Mississippi with his slaves, and the amendment failed. That part which forbade the future introduction of slaves failed by a vote of sixty-eight to eighty. That part which declared all children born in the Territory after the passage of the bill to be free, and prohibited them being held to service after they became twenty-five years of age, was lost without a division. Next day the bill came up in the House, when Taylor again moved his amendment. Once more the first part was lost by one vote; but the second part, in the words "all children of slaves within the said Territory shall be free, but may be held to service until the age of twenty-five years," passed by two votes. An attempt to secure a reconsideration then failed by two votes, which so alarmed the slavery extensionists that they laid the bill on the table.† On the morrow at noon it was taken up, and on a motion to send it to a select committee with instructions to report it with the gradual abolition clause, the vote was a tie. The Speaker then gave his casting vote, and the motion was carried. The select committee was instantly appointed, the bill reported at once without the amendment, and the report immediately concurred in. Taylor thereupon offered new amendments, which the House rejected, till, finding some concession necessary, he moved that slavery should not thereafter be introduced into any of the Territories north of thirty-six

---

* February 17, 1819.   † February 18, 1819.

degrees and thirty minutes.* For this the House was not ready; and Taylor, seeing that no line of demarcation was likely to be accepted, withdrew the amendment, and the bill was ordered to be engrossed. On the following day it passed.† No opposition was encountered in the Senate, and before the session closed the act had been signed by Monroe.

This ended the first struggle for free soil beyond the Mississippi. So far it had been confined to Congress; but now, when Congress laid it down, the people took it up. The times were hard. Distress and discontent were everywhere. The subjects which absorbed the attention of the people were stay laws and relief systems, the evils of banking, the pressure of debts, auction sales, the tariff, and the protection to be given to American industries. But from the moment the Fifteenth Congress expired on the fourth of March, leaving the question, raised by it, of freedom or slavery in the Territories undecided, the whole North, without distinction of party, was roused for action. In that section the status of slavery had long been regarded as settled. No one supposed for a moment that another slave State would ever be added to the Union. The antislavery societies, which had once been so flourishing, had fallen into decay. Between 1808 and 1814 the annual convention of delegates from them was not held. Even the literature of antislavery ceased to appear. The moral awakening which followed the war did indeed arouse a feeling that slavery was wrong; but the action this feeling developed was confined almost entirely to the South. In the long list of vice-presidents of the Colonization Society the only names of national repute—Bushrod Washington, Henry Clay, William H. Crawford, Andrew Jackson, John Taylor, of Caroline—were Southern men and slave-owners. The only antislavery newspaper then in existence in the United States, the Philanthropist, was edited by a Southern man, and circulated in the South. The only antislavery societies that were really active were the manumission societies of the Southern States.

---

* "That neither slavery nor involuntary servitude shall hereafter be introduced into any part of the Territories of the United States lying north of thirty-six degrees and thirty minutes north latitude."

† February 20, 1819. On March 2, 1819, the President signed it.

The apparent listlessness of the North was due wholly to the belief that the status of slavery was settled. The sentiments of the people on this matter had undergone no change. The moment, therefore, the Missouri struggle brought up the question of the further extension of slavery the North was violently excited. The moral iniquity of such an act, the political wrong of such an act, became proper themes for sermons, for Fourth-of-July toasts,* and for pamphlets without number. Newspapers attacked it. Politicians pointed out that the North would never be rid of Southern presidents and Southern rule if the slave-holding States were increased in number. Unhappily, a congressional election had just taken place and a new Congress was about to meet.. The question could not therefore be settled by an appeal to the voters; but it might possibly be settled or postponed by an appeal to Congress. Toward the close of the autumn, therefore, public excitement, which during the summer had been rising higher and higher, began to find vent in meetings and resolutions. In response to a call, hundreds of citizens from New Jersey met at Trenton to consider the subject of slavery in the States hereafter to be admitted into the Union. The sentiment of all present was that the true policy of the United States was not only to prevent the further importation of slaves, but also to promote the abolition of slavery. Slavery, however, could not be abolished, nor the importation of slaves stopped if the Federal Legislature lent itself to measures intended to extend and perpetuate the institution by opening markets for slaves in the new States. It was the duty, therefore, of the senators and representatives of New Jersey in Congress to do their utmost to prevent the establishment of slavery in Missouri and in any other State hereafter to be admitted.

A great meeting held in the Boston State-House declared that Congress had ample power under the Constitution to prohibit the admission of slavery into any new State created beyond the limits of the original territory of the United States, that it could make a prohibition of slavery a condition of ad-

---

* Bedford, Orwigsburg (Pa.), Trenton, Troy, Windsor (Conn.), Charlestown, Salem.

mission into the Union, and that in the case of Missouri it was expedient to do so. The Philadelphia meeting took the ground that the slavery of human beings was the greatest evil in the United States; that it was at variance with the Declaration of Independence, and with the principles of universal liberty and human rights on which the Constitution was founded; and that, in view of these facts, it was inconsistent in principle and unwise in policy to allow States hereafter to be created to set up or tolerate slavery within their jurisdiction. At Baltimore the citizens gave expression to like sentiments.

At New York a meeting was held one evening in November. Two thousand were estimated to have been present, and after a fine speech on the horrors and cruelty of slavery by Mr. Peter A. Jay, the usual resolutions and addresses were adopted. Slavery was described as a political and moral evil, derogatory to the character of the American people, dangerous to the public welfare, and opposed to the benign spirit of Christianity. That Congress had power under the Constitution to prohibit the admisison of slavery into any State or territory hereafter to be formed was indubitable. It was indeed true that Congress had authority to admit new States into the Union. It was equally true that the treaty by which Louisiana was acquired stipulated for "the admission of the inhabitants into the Union according to the principles of the Federal Constitution." But it did not by any means follow that their right of admission was absolute, and the power of Congress limited to the single inquiry into the form of government.

These resolutions of the great cities were re-echoed by county meetings, by grand juries, and by town meetings all over the States from Maryland eastward, and in time by legislatures. New York instructed her senators and requested her representatives in Congress to oppose the admission into the Union of any State not comprised within the original bounds of the United States unless slavery was forbidden therein, and to make this a condition of admission. New Jersey expressed her opinion in a long set of resolutions and sent them to her delegation in Congress. Delaware told her senators and representatives that it would give great pleasure to the Legislature if they could in conscience oppose the introduction of slavery into Missouri. Pennsylvania, after denouncing slavery in a long preamble, went further than any and called for the abolition of slavery. Not only were her delegates requested to vote against the admission of any Territory into the Union as a State unless the further introduction of slavery, or involuntary servitude, except as a punishment of crime, was prohibited, but they were to insist that all children born of slaves after the admission of the State into the Union should be free, but might be held to service till twenty-five years old.

South of Pennsylvania and Delaware public sentiment changed, and with Maryland the instructions began to be of a very different sort. Her representatives were bidden to use their utmost endeavors to secure for new States when about to be admitted, not only all the rights and privileges of the old States, but to see to it that the prohibition of slavery was not made a condition of admission. Virginia assumed a threatening tone. Congress, according to her view, had no authority to dictate to the people of Missouri what principles should govern them in the formation of their constitution. On the other hand, it was bound by the treaty of 1803 to admit Missouri into the Union on equal terms with the other States. The General Assembly would therefore "support the good people of Missouri in their just rights and admission into the Union, and would co-operate with them in resisting with manly fortitude any attempt which Congress might make to impose restraints or restrictions as the price of their admission." Kentucky declared the attempt to restrict slavery was an attack on State rights, and demanded the admission of Missouri with or without slavery as her Constitution might provide. Ohio and Indiana declared in favor of never allowing slavery to cross the Mississippi.

While the people and the States were thus arraying themselves on opposite sides the Sixteenth Congress opened its first session in the building which we now know as the Capitol, and which the British had burned five years before. It consisted at that time of two large rectangular structures united

by a long wooden passageway, for the rotunda had not then
been commenced.   The soft freestone of the buildings which
had been chipped and cracked by the fire had been carefully
repaired, and the smoke-stains obliterated by a coat of white
paint.   The Hall of the House of Representatives in the south
building, the chamber now given up to the most hideous collection of statues ever gathered together in any land, was
semicircular in form, and was considered the finest of its
kind in America.   But there, as in many another public room,
use had been sacrificed to architectural adornment, and to the
last day of its occupancy the voice of many a member was
lost in the vast dome which formed the ceiling, or was destroyed by the long line of columns and recesses which ran
along the semicircular wall.   These columns of pudding-stone
supported what was then the gallery, and between them, in
the hope of destroying the echoes, were hung great crimson
curtains.   Over the Speaker's chair and resting on four posts
was a huge canopy of crimson silk, while curtains of the
same color shut out not a little of the light and air which
might have come from the windows in the rear.   On the
Speaker's desk stood immense candlesticks—for those were
still the days of the candle and the lamp—and before him on
the floor of the chamber were desks and chairs for one hundred and eighty-five members and two Territorial delegates.
Eighty-four of these men had never before been members of
Congress.   Fifty-six of the eighty-four came from the free
States.   New York sent twenty-three new men in a delegation
of twenty-seven, Connecticut sent six in a delegation of seven,
and Pennsylvania ten out of twenty-three.   Rhode Island
completely changed her representation.   This was indeed a
serious matter, for it left the division of the House on the
Missouri question in doubt.

As it was the great question of the hour, the House had
no sooner organized and made Clay Speaker than John Scott
moved that the memorials sent by Missouri to the last Congress be referred to a select committee.   Strong, of New York,
thereupon gave notice that he would on the following day ask
leave to introduce a bill prohibiting the further extension of
slavery within the Territories of the United States.   At the

same time a memorial was presented from Maine asking admission as a State before the last day of January, 1820.

The appearance of Maine as an applicant for admission, and the great part which her application played in the struggle which followed, renders this a proper place to narrate the history of her separation from Massachusetts. The earliest public discussion of the expediency of separation seems to have been carried on in the Falmouth Gazette of 1785. Though a host of writers argued against it, the public mind seemed so ready that in September, 1785, a call was formally made in the Falmouth Gazette for a conference of such inhabitants of the three counties as would attend. Quite a number came, and these, after choosing Peleg Wadsworth chairman, appointed a committee to write to the towns and invite them to send delegates to a convention to consider the expediency of separation. At that convention, which met in January, 1786, at Falmouth, or, as the place is now called, Portland, a committee was ordered to draw up a list of grievances and report the cost of a State government. Regarding the cost nothing was said ; but the grievances were many. The mode of taxation was unjust. The system of representation was unequal. The excise and impost acts, the duty on deeds, and the regulation of trade were burdensome and injurious in the extreme. As the records of the Supreme Court were kept at Boston, every suitor must go there for all papers to be used in evidence, thereby greatly increasing the cost of justice. But most serious of all was the impossibility of Massachusetts ever understanding the interest of Maine.

On the matter of separation the convention said not a word, but asked the towns to send delegates to another convention to meet in September. Meantime the General Court met, and, the Governor having in his speech mentioned the attempt at separation, a committee was ordered to report a bill declaratory of the allegiance the people of the District owed the Government, and the evils of dismembering the Commonwealth. Nothing more was done, and before the General Court met again the convention a second time assembled at Falmouth. This time a petition to the Legislature praying for separation was prepared, and the town urged to act on the matter one way or the other. It then adjourned till January, 1787. The returns from the appeal were so few and meagre that the committee having charge of the petition did not present it till 1788. But the Legislature would do nothing, and, as public interest died out so rapidly that the adjourned meetings of the convention were rarely attended by more than the president, the secretary, and the Falmouth members, the first attempt at separation expired.

The second effort began in 1791, when the senators and representatives for the District, after failing to secure favorable action on the old petition of 1786, addressed the people. They had ascertained that the tax paid to Massachusetts by the District, not a cent of which was spent in Maine, would support a State government. If separation took place then, Maine would go off without any debt and with one tenth of the public lands. Her population was nearly double that of Rhode Island or Delaware, was greater than that of Vermont, and about equal to that of the whites in Georgia. Once more public attention was aroused, and that the sense of the people might really be tested, the General Court in 1792 fixed the first Monday in May as the time when the people in the several towns should vote for or against separation. When the returns were completed two thousand and seventy-four were found to have voted yea and twenty-five hundred and twenty-five nay, and the second attempt failed as miserably as the first.

The third attempt began in 1793, and a new series of conventions were held till 1797, after which time the matter rested till 1807, when the Maine delegates once more persuaded the General Court to submit the question to the people. On this occasion one hundred and fifty towns voted, and defeated the attempt by a vote of nine thousand to three thousand. No more was then heard of separation till 1815. The exodus to the West was then under full headway; the people were alarmed lest the District should become depopulated and in the hope of checking migration agitation for statehood began for the fifth time. Meetings were held, societies were formed, pamphlets were written, and so many petitions sent to the General Court that it yielded, and once more submitted the question to popular decision. This time the yeas

were ten thousand and the nays six thousand; whereupon
the General Court ordered delegates to be chosen for a convention to meet at Brunswick. If when they were assembled
it appeared to them that the votes in favor of separation (which
was to be voted on when the delegates were chosen) were to
those against it as five is to four, they were to frame a State
constitution, and not otherwise. But the convention, when it
met, fell to quarrelling, and Massachusetts declared its powers
revoked. Three years later the final and successful effort was
made, and in October, 1819, a convention met and framed a
constitution which the people accepted just as the application
for admission was made to Congress.

The memorial was sent to a select committee, and on the
last day of the year a bill to admit the State of Maine into the
Union was considered in the Committee of the Whole. On
the question being put that the committee rise and report the
bill, Clay took the floor and resisted it. His speech was long
and bitter; but the substance was that he would never give
his assent to the admission of Maine while a restriction of any
sort was imposed on Missouri. "A State in the quarter of
the country from which I come," said he, "asks to be admitted
into the Union. What say the gentlemen who ask the admission of Maine? Why, they will not admit Missouri without a
condition which strips her of one essential attribute of sovereignty. What, then, do I say to them? That justice is due
to all parts of the Union. Equality is equality, and if it is
right to make the restriction of slavery the condition of the
admission of Missouri, it is equally just to make the admission
of Missouri the condition of that of Maine."

The friends of Clay gave another reason. Nothing, they
pointed out, had been said regarding the representation of
Maine in the House. True it was that many supposed that the
seven gentlemen who then represented the District of Maine
would continue to represent the State of Maine. But it was
not clear that this could be. The House knew nothing of the
District of Maine. The seven gentlemen on the floor who
happened to live in that District were known to the House as
seven members of the Massachusetts delegation which by law
was fixed at thirteen. Could Congress diminish that number

by seven and give the seven cut off to Maine ? Could Massachusetts by her consent give Congress power so to do ? If she
could, how was that consent to be expressed ? By the Legislature ? By the whole people ?

After an excited debate the bill was reported to the House,
which ordered it engrossed and read a third time, and on the
next day passed it.

Once in the Senate, it was referred to the Committee on
the Judiciary, and soon reported back with an amendment,
made by taking a wafer and with it fastening the bill to
admit Missouri, without restriction as to slavery, to the bill to
admit Maine. A senator from Pennsylvania now moved to
recommit it, with instructions to separate the two bills. On
this the debate began in earnest.

The action of the committee was declared, on the one
hand, to be irregular, extraordinary, and unjustifiable, as it
united in one bill two subjects totally distinct. Maine was a
part of one of the old original States. Her constitution was
framed. She had the consent of the State from which she
was about to be separated. There was no dispute about her
boundaries, her population, or the justness of her claim to be
admitted. Very different was the condition of Missouri.
Her population was guessed at. Grave doubts existed as to
the wisdom of giving her such bounds as she asked. She had
small claims to be made a member of the Union. Her application was so objectionable as to excite the whole country
in a way it had never been excited by the admission of any of
the nine States that had come into the Union since the Constitution was adopted. The Maine bill simply asked the consent of Congress to her admission and operated instanter.
The amendment, or Missouri bill, was prospective, and had to do
with several acts to be performed in the future—with the calling of a convention, with the election of delegates, with the
formation of a constitution on certain principles yet to be defined, with the submission of that constitution to Congress,
and with its acceptance or rejection by Congress and the
President, acts which must delay the admission of Missouri to
at least the next session of Congress. By the terms imposed
by Massachusetts, Maine must be admitted before the fourth

of March.   This was necessary because the annual election of State officers took place on the first Monday in April, and the Legislature of Massachusetts, then in session, must make ready for that election if Maine was admitted.   There must be a re-districting of the Commonwealth for counsellors and senators, and a marking out of new circuits for her Supreme Court.

We do not, was the answer, admit that this union of the two bills is improper.   The purpose of each is to admit a State.   That they differ in detail is true; but differences in detail is no ground for separation.   Their union is expedient—nay, necessary—for without such union one State is not likely to be admitted.   That her claim to be admitted is a strong and just one is certain.   Indeed, if the claim of the one State is any better than that of the other, the difference is all on the side of Missouri.   Congress may or may not admit Maine, for the language of the Constitution is, "New States may be admitted by the Congress into this Union."   But Congress must admit Missouri, for a treaty is the supreme law of the land, and in the treaty by which Louisiana was acquired are the words, "The inhabitants of the ceded territory shall be incorporated into the Union of the United States and admitted as soon as possible."   The terms are imperative, and no conditions are annexed.   No hardship again can be inflicted on Maine by keeping her out.   She may almost be said to be partially in the Union; for, as a part of Massachusetts, seven men represent her, speak for her, vote for her in the House of Representatives.

By a vote of twenty-five to eighteen the Senate * refused to separate the two bills, whereupon Roberts moved † to add to the Missouri bill the proviso that the further introduction of slaves into that State should be absolutely and irrevocably forbidden.   During three weeks senator after senator rose in his place and discussed it; yet in all that was uttered, it would be hard to find one new argument.   We are not, said the friends of Missouri, advocates of slavery.   We lament that it

---

* January 16, 1820.

† Provided, that the further introduction into said State of persons to be held to slavery or involuntary servitude within the same, shall be absolutely and irrevocably prohibited."—Journal of the Senate, January 17, 1820.

exists. We know it is an evil, and have always supported with unanimity every proposition which had for its object the suppression of the slave-trade. The question before us, however, is not Shall slavery be diminished, but shall slavery be confined to its present limits; shall it be diffused over a wide-spread country, and the slaves by the smallness of their numbers be brought within the reach of a humanizing policy, or shall it be concentrated in a little area till the blacks so out-number us that we shall be driven from the country? A restriction which tends to do this is unjust, inexpedient, unconstitutional, and contrary to the terms of the treaty of cession.

It is unconstitutional because powers not expressly granted are reserved to the States or to the people. " New States," says the Constitution, " may be admitted into this Union." But there is no statement that they may be admitted into this Union on such conditions as Congress may see fit to impose. The right to impose conditions, therefore, is expressly reserved. Congress may admit or reject; if it admits, then the new State comes in possessed of all the sovereignty, freedom, and inde-pendence retained by the original States, and one of these sovereign rights is that of fashioning her government accord-ing to the will and pleasure of her people.

The Constitution, again, guarantees that " the citizens of each State shall be entitled to all the privileges and immuni-ties of citizens in the several States." But if you say to the emigrants from Virginia, Kentucky, or South Carolina, You cannot take your slaves with you into Missouri, yet do not require the emigrant from New York, New England, or Pennsylvania to leave his black ox or his black horse behind, do you not violate the guarantee? Is the citizen of the slave State who cannot take all his property to Missouri possessed of all the privileges of the citizen of the free State who can? But we are told that this power to forbid the removal of slaves from one State to another is derived from the words, " the migration or importation of such persons as any of the States now existing shall think proper to admit shall not be prohibited by the Congress prior to the year 1808 "; that 1808 is long passed and that Congress may prohibit the migration and importation of such persons. Never were words more misconstrued.

Importation refers to slaves brought into the country from Africa or Europe or the Indies by water. Migration refers to slaves brought in by land from the possessions of foreign powers. Neither has anything to do with interstate migration. We are told that Congress has power to make all needful rules and regulations for the government of the Territories. Undoubtedly it has; but the restriction to be imposed on Missouri is unjust and arbitrary, and in no sense needful, and is to be laid on a State and not on a Territory. Nay, more; by the language of the treaty of cession, such a restriction cannot be enforced. "The inhabitants of the ceded Territory," says that instrument, "shall be incorporated in the Union of the United States, and admitted as soon as possible, according to the principles of the Federal Constitution, to the enjoyment of all the rights, advantages, and immunities of citizens of the United States." In the face of this solemn promise, how can Missouri be refused admittance into the Union, much less required to forbid slavery, when it is one of the rights of a citizen of the United States to own slaves?

But the two great speeches which stood out before all others, and were regarded as masterpieces of their kind, were delivered, the one, in defence of slavery and the South, by William Pinkney, of Maryland, and the other, on behalf of freedom and the North, by Rufus King, of New York.

Pinkney was a native of Annapolis, Maryland, where he was born on the seventeenth of March, 1764. On the completion of his education he thought for a while of studying medicine, but turned to law, and while yet a youth raised himself to sufficient prominence to be elected a delegate to the Convention of Maryland which ratified the Constitution of the United States. From that day forth he was never out of public life. For seven years he sat in the Legislature of Maryland; for seven more he was a commissioner under the Seventh Article of Jay's treaty with Great Britain; now he was Attorney-General of Maryland, and now Minister for the United States to Great Britain. In 1811 Madison appointed him Attorney-General of the United States; in 1815 the peo-

ple of Baltimore sent him to Congress; in 1816 he was despatched on a mission to Russia. There he remained two
years, and on his return was chosen a Senator of the United
States by the State of Maryland.

When Pinkney took his seat early in January, 1820, he
was without exception the finest orator the House or Senate
could produce. At no time during that long and exciting debate were the halls and galleries of either House without a
crowd of listeners. But the announcement that Pinkney would
speak would fill the floor and gallery of the Senate to suffoca-
tion, and pack the halls, the lobbies, and the stairways with such
a gathering as came thither on no other occasion. Members
of the Cabinet would desert their offices. Foreign ministers
would gladly make their way through the crowded lobbies to
the places set apart for them; and on the day of his great
speech the House of Representatives, it is said, adjourned
early that the members might attend. A fair listener, to whom
we owe a lively picture of the scene, declares that on one of
these occasions not less than a hundred women could be seen
on the floor of the Senate. Vice-President Tompkins in an
unguarded moment had invited a party of young women with
whom he was dining to take seats on the floor of the Senate.
All gladly availed themselves of the unusual privilege; but
scarcely were they comfortably seated on the sofas and provided with warm footstools than the women in the gallery, seeing them there, came down in a body and entered the room,
surrounded the senators, and crowded out the representatives and foreign ministers. The Vice-President was greatly
dismayed, and that afternoon fastened a notice on the doors
shutting out all women not introduced by one of the senators.*

When the arguments of Pinkney and King had been made
and answered, the Roberts amendment was voted on and defeated.† On the following day, ‡ however, the restrictionists

---

* The scenes and incidents in Washington at that time are delightfully described in the letters of Mrs. Seaton, in William Winston Seaton, of the National
Intelligencer. A Biographical Sketch, Boston, 1871, pp. 146, 147.

† February 1, 1820.   Yeas, 16; nays, 27.

‡ February 2, 1820.

came forward with a new amendment, which was moved by Senator Burrill, of Rhode Island. It provided that "the three first articles of compact in the ordinance of July thirteenth, 1787," should be added to the Missouri bill. But on the next day * he withdrew it to make way for a very different amendment, moved by Senator Thomas, of Illinois. The debates in the Senate and the temper of the two sections of the country, as expressed at public meetings, made it certain that nothing but a compromise could succeed, and this compromise was offered by Thomas. He proposed that in all that tract of country ceded to the United States by France, under the name of Louisiana, which lay north of thirty-six degrees and thirty minutes north latitude, except so much as was included in the intended State of Missouri, there should be no slavery. But a few days later,† and before the Senate had begun to consider his amendment, he withdrew it in order to present it in another form. This left nothing before the Senate save the amendment reported by the Judiciary Committee uniting the Maine and Missouri bills in one. Another week was then spent in useless debate before the yeas and nays were taken and the amendment carried by the close vote of twenty-three to twenty-one.‡ Every senator was present.

As soon as the chairman of the Committee of the Whole had announced the result, Thomas rose and moved that the sixth article of the Ordinance of 1787 should apply to all that tract of country ceded by France to the United States, under the name of Louisiana, which lay north of thirty-six degrees and thirty minutes, except so much as was to be included in Missouri. The moment he sat down Barbour, of Virginia, moved to amend the amendment by striking out thirty-six and a half and putting in forty degrees north latitude. A great majority voted this down. Senator Eaton then offered a substitute for the amendment, which was declared out of order. Mr. Trimble, of Ohio, next attempted to so amend the Thomas amendment as to make it apply to all the country west of the Mississippi except the States of Louisiana and Missouri. This, too, was lost, and the Senate adjourned with the Thomas

---

* February 3, 1820.　　† February 7, 1820.　　‡ February 16, 1820.

amendment still pending.   Next day * Thomas withdrew it and moved in its place the one he withdrew ten days before, and this, by a vote of thirty-four to ten, was passed.†   The bill, as thus amended, was hurried through all its stages, and reached the House of Representatives on the nineteenth of February.

After passing the bill to admit Maine, which now came back to it with the bill to admit Missouri as an amendment, the House had taken up a Missouri bill of its own,‡ and had debated it hotly ever since.   The free-soil party began their opposition with a motion to postpone consideration of the matter for a week with a view to awaiting the action of the Senate.   When this was lost Henry Storrs, of New York, moved that there should be neither slavery nor involuntary servitude, save in punishment of crimes, north of thirty-eight degrees and west of the Mississippi, except in Missouri.   But the House was not ready for a compromise, and the motion passed in the negative.#   John W. Taylor, of New York, thereupon moved as an amendment to the bill a new section, which forbade slavery to exist in Missouri, but provided that persons there held to service should not thereby secure either civil rights or freedom.   This was still under debate when the Maine-Missouri bill, with the Thomas compromise amendment, came down from the Senate.   Taylor at once moved that the House disagree, and Scott, of Missouri, that the bill be sent to the Committee of the Whole.   This latter motion was lost,‖ and the former debated for three days before the House stripped the Missouri rider from the Maine bill, voted down the Thomas amendment to the Missouri bill by an immense majority,△ and went back to the consideration of its own bill to admit Missouri.   The Senate, however, would not recede,

---

* February 17, 1820.

† "*And be it further enacted*, That in all that territory ceded by France to the United States, under the name of Louisiana, which lies north of thirty-six degrees thirty minutes north latitude, excepting only such part thereof as is included within the limits of the State contemplated by this act, slavery and involuntary servitude, otherwise than in the punishment of crimes whereof the party shall have been duly convicted, shall be and is hereby forever prohibited."   Then followed a provision for the return of fugitive slaves.—Journal of the Senate.

‡ January 24, 1820.   ‖ Yeas, 73; nays, 93.
# January 26, 1820.   △ Yeas, 18; nays, 159.

and sent its secretary with a message that it insisted on its amendments. But the House stood firm, insisted on its disagreement, and bade its clerk so inform the Senate. He found that body on the point of adjourning for the day; but his message had no sooner been delivered than all thought of rising vanished, and after an angry debate it was voted to ask for a conference. To this, on the following day, the House consented.

While the conferrers were busy, the representatives went back once more to their bill for the admission of Missouri, passed it with the restriction amendment of Taylor, sent it to the Senate, and within twenty-four hours received it again with Taylor's amendment cut off and Thomas's tacked on. By this time the Committee of Conference had completed a report, which was presented the moment the clerk had finished reading the message of the Senate. It recommended three things. These three were that the Senate should give up its attempt to unite the Maine and Missouri bills in one, and that Maine should be admitted; that the House should no longer insist on the exclusion of slavery from Missouri; and that both Houses should agree to pass the Senate bill which admitted slavery to Missouri, but shut it from all the rest of the territory ceded by France to the United States north of thirty-six degrees and thirty minutes. To yield was hard; but three stayed away, four changed their votes, and when the clerk had finished calling the roll the Speaker announced that the yeas were ninety and the nays eighty-seven. Of the members who on that memorable day voted yes, fifteen came from States whose Legislatures had solemnly protested against the admission of slavery into Missouri, three more came from Northern States which had made no protest, and it was to these eighteen that John Randolph in course of the debate applied the term " doughface," a term which thenceforth for forty years was used to describe a Northern man with Southern principles. Thus was it that by three votes the great principle for which those early free soilers had struggled so sturdily during two sessions was abandoned, and Missouri given leave to form a constitution without excluding slavery from her domain.

On the following morning, when the journal of the preceding day had been read, John Randolph rose and expressed a wish to move for a reconsideration of the vote by which the House concurred with the Senate in striking out the restriction from the Missouri bill.   The Speaker was greatly alarmed, for the bill was still in his possession, and nothing was more foreign to his wishes than a reopening of the question.   He therefore declared Randolph out of order.   The gentleman from Virginia must wait till the business of the morning, as prescribed by the rules, had been disposed of.   Randolph appealed to the House, which sustained the Speaker.   The business of receiving and referring petitions then went on till Virginia was reached, when Randolph moved for the retention of the Missouri bill till the proper time for a reconsideration was reached, but was again declared out of order.   When that time did come, Clay announced that the bill had been carried to the Senate by the clerk, and was out of the possession of the House.   While the petitions were being presented Clay had signed the Missouri bill and sent it off post haste to the Senate.*   For that piece of trickery Randolph never forgave him.   The breach which had opened between them a few weeks before was now vastly widened, and they became henceforth mortal foes.

As the news of the passage of the Missouri bill swept over the Northern States, the first feeling of grief and disappointment gave way to outbursts of rage.   Fullerton, of Pennsylvania, was burned in effigy by the angry citizens of Carlisle.†   James Lanman, of Connecticut, suffered like treatment at Hartford.‡   Henry W. Edwards, of Connecticut, one of the three absentees when the vote was taken, was accused of skulking, and defended himself in a long public letter.   He had been in his place in the House, he said, all day without a morsel to eat, and toward night had seized the opportunity when Mercer rose to speak to slip out and get his supper.   But Mercer, too, was exhausted, and fainted in the middle of his

---

* Annals of Congress, 1819–1821, pp. 1588–1590.   Memoirs of John Quincy Adams, vol. v, p. 4.

† National Intelligencer, March 28, 1820.

‡ Ibid., February 26, 1820.

speech; whereupon, before Edwards got back—nay, almost before Mercer had recovered his senses—the question was taken and the bill passed.* The position of the three who changed their votes was set forth in the speech of one of them, Charles Kinsey, of New Jersey. " On this question, which for nearly six weeks has convulsed this House, I have," said he, " voted with the majority. But I am convinced, should we persist in rejecting the olive-branch now offered, the most disastrous consequences will follow. Do our Southern brethren demand an equal division of this widespread fertile region—this common property purchased with the common funds of the nation? No; they have agreed to fix an irrevocable boundary beyond which slavery shall never pass, thereby surrendering to the claims of humanity and the non-slaveholding States, to the enterprising capitalist of the North, the Middle, the Eastern States, nine-tenths of the country in question. In rejecting so reasonable a proposition we must have strong and powerful reasons to justify our refusal. Should we now numerically carry the question, it will be a victory snatched from our brothers. It will be an inglorious triumph gained at the hazard of the Union. Gentlemen of the majority have treated the idea of disunion with ridicule; but to my mind it presents itself with all the horrid, gloomy features of reality." †

When Monroe heard that the Maine and Missouri bills had passed he summoned his Cabinet and asked for their opinion, in writing, on two questions. The first was, Has Congress a constitutional right to prohibit slavery in a Territory? To this Adams, Crawford, Calhoun, and Wirt unanimously answered Yes. The second was, Does the section of the Missouri bill which interdicts slavery forever in the territory west of the Mississippi and north of thirty-six degrees and thirty minutes apply to the territorial state alone, or is it binding on the States formed out of that Territory? On this a lively debate followed and brought out the fact that while Crawford, Calhoun, and Wirt regarded the injunction as applying only to the territorial condition, Adams believed it to be applicable

---

* National Intelligencer, April 11, 1820.

† Annals of Congress, 1819–1821, vol. ii., p. 1579.

to a State as well. Calhoun then suggested that the question be changed and put in the form, " Is the eighth section of the Missouri bill consistent with the Constitution ? " Monroe consented, and a few days later each of the secretaries answered the two questions in writing, and the bill was signed.*

The passage of the Maine † and Missouri ‡ bills and their approval by the President seemed to end the struggle ; but in truth a third contest more bitter and desperate than either of its predecessors was yet to come.#

The convention authorized by the Missouri bill met at St. Louis and adopted a constitution which was laid before Congress in November. With the recollection of all that had so lately taken place fresh in their memory, the men who framed that instrument of government would have been wise had they done no more than establish slavery and provide for its protection. But they went further, and inserted two provisions which aroused all the old feelings and renewed the old strife. The one forbade the Legislature to ever pass a law emancipating slaves without consent of their masters. The other made it the duty of the General Assembly to forbid free negroes or mulattoes ever to enter the State on any pretext whatever. On this the free soilers fell with redoubled fury. They reminded the pro-slavery members that there were States where negroes were free men and citizens, that to shut such men out of Missouri was a violation of that clause of the Constitution which provides that " the citizens of each State shall be entitled to all the privileges and immunities of citizens of the several States," and that Missouri ought not to be admitted till she struck this odious discrimination from her constitution.

To this it was answered that Missouri was already a State in the Union ; that the only condition laid on her by Congress

---

* The Memoirs of John Quincy Adams, where they touch on this discussion deserve to be read. Vol. v, pp. 5–12, 13–15. " It is a singular circumstance that when, in consequence of the publication of this passage, search was made in the Department of State for these papers, nothing was found but what appeared to have been an envelope referring to them as enclosed." Memoirs, vol. v, p. 15, note.

† March 3, 1820.   ‡ March 2, 1820.
# Yeas, 90 ; nays, 87.

was that she should form a State government; that she had done so, and, having thereby become a State, was of consequence in the Union; that each State had a right to exclude obnoxious persons, and that the laws and constitutions of the States were full of the kind complained of. Some would not permit certain persons to vote; others would not allow them to serve in the militia. In Tennessee no minister of the Gospel could sit in the Legislature, nor could a man who denied the being of a God and a future state of rewards and punishments hold a civil office. In Maryland no Jew could vote. In Massachusetts no black could marry with a white. Connecticut would not allow a free negro to travel without a pass from the select-men or the justices, and gave her town authorities the power to seize a citizen of any of the United States and send him to the State whence he came. New York provided that if a stranger were entertained in the dwelling-house of a citizen for fifteen days without giving notice to the overseers of the poor, he should be fined fifteen dollars. Were not these, it was asked, restrictions on the citizens of other States? The House was not convinced that they were, and by a vote of ninety-three to seventy-nine rejected a resolution declaring Missouri to be a State in the Union.

This brought up the question, If Missouri is not a State what is she? Congress by an enabling act, it was argued, has authorized her people to form a constitution and a State government, and they have done so. She has a Governor, a Legislature, a judiciary, and senators and representatives to Congress. Does not this make her a State? Undoubtedly it does, for Congress can only admit States, and if it were not for the clause in her Constitution she would be admitted. She is then a State either in or out of the Union. If out, then in what relation does the Government of the United States stand to her? How about the public lands, the navigation of her rivers, the collection of the revenue? To bring this issue clearly before the House, a Virginia member moved that the Committee on the Judiciary be instructed to inquire into the legal relation of Missouri to the United States. But the resolution was tabled.

A few days later a member presented three memorials

from the Senate and House of Representatives of Missouri.
Seizing on this, the pro-slavery men, when the journal was
read on the following day, attempted to insert the words "the
State" before Missouri in the record, and make it read "Mr.
Lowndes presented three memorials from the Senate and
House of Representatives of the State of Missouri," and were
only prevented by the casting vote of the Speaker, John W.
Taylor. Attempts were then made to secure the insertion
of the words "the Territory of," and, finally, "the late Territory of"; but each failed, and the House adjourned in confusion.

A lull of two weeks now occurred before a member ventured to move a resolution declaring Missouri admitted on
condition that the objectionable clauses were expunged from
her constitution.

But the House was not yet in a yielding mood, voted it
down,* and heard no more of Missouri till the Senate sent in
a proposition to admit her coupled with a most discreditable
proposition.† "Nothing herein contained," the resolution
read, " shall be so construed as to give the assent of Congress
to any provision in the constitution of Missouri (if any such
there be) which contravenes that clause of the Constitution of
the United States which declares that the citizens of each State
shall be entitled to all the privileges and immunities of citizens of the several States." It was a cowardly shirking of the
very responsibility the free soilers were attempting to force
Congress to assume, and never for a moment had a chance of
passing; yet it stirred up again the old sectional strife, and
was debated day after day till Clay, in alarm, succeeded in
carrying a motion that it be referred to a committee of thirteen.‡

On that committee were men from every section of the
country, and holding every shade of opinion. Eight were
from the free States, five were from the slave States. One had
contended that Missouri was already in the Union; another
believed that she was a State without the Union, and, by the
refusal of the House to declare her admitted, had been dis-

---

* January 24, 1821.   † January 29, 1821.   ‡ February 2, 1821.

charged from all obligations to the Union. Another had once moved to admit her if she would expunge the objectionable clause from her constitution. Yet another had argued that a Territory did not become a sovereign and independent State by the mere formation of a constitution, and that Missouri was not a State till the people of the United States through their representatives had examined and approved her constitution. Over them all, as chairman, was the great conductor of compromises, Henry Clay.

From a committee so constituted and so led nothing but compromise was to be expected, and any attempt of such a character was sure to fail. The committee, however, presented its report,* and named two conditions on which Missouri should be declared admitted. In the first place, no law was ever to be passed which prevented any description of persons who were or might be citizens of any of the States from coming to or settling in Missouri; in the second place, her Legislature was to agree to this by a solemn act which was to be transmitted to the President. This done, Monroe was, by proclamation, to declare Missouri a State in the Union. Still, the majority would not yield, and the Senate resolution, with the amendment offered by the committee of thirteen, was defeated by three votes.†

The excitement at this stage was intense. Members who were absent when the roll was called rose from their sick-beds, hurried to the Capitol, and asked to have their votes recorded. But this required unanimous consent; and, as it could not be secured, a struggle for a reconsideration began, and continued till the motion was defeated by a majority of six ‡ on the eve of the day fixed for counting the electoral vote.

Missouri, using the right which she claimed to be hers as a State, had chosen electors who had cast their vote and had sent a certified copy in the usual way to the President of the Senate.

As the time drew near when this vote must be canvassed, yet the struggle over her admission was as far from a happy

---

* February 10, 1821.

† Yeas, 80; nays, 83. February 12, 1821.

‡ Yeas, 82; nays, 88. February 13, 1821.

settlement as ever, the House and Senate agreed upon a plan which it was hoped would prevent contention. Whether her vote was or was not counted, the election, as was well known, would not be affected, and Monroe would still be President. It was decided, therefore, that if the reception of the vote of Missouri was objected to, the President of the Senate, when he rose to announce the ballot, should state first what the result would be if her vote was counted, then what it would be if not counted, and should finally declare, "but in either case A. B. is elected President of the United States." * .

At the hour appointed for this ceremony the Senate, with its President at its head, and attended by its Secretary and Sergeant-at-Arms, entered the Hall of Representatives and took the seats assigned. The President was then escorted to the Speaker's chair; sat down, with the Speaker on his left hand; rose after a few moments' pause, and opening the ballots of the States, handed them one by one to the tellers, who in loud tones read each twice while the Secretary of the Senate and the clerk of the House recorded them. As the order was partly geographical and partly that of admission into the Union, Missouri came last on the list. But the President had no sooner opened and read her vote and handed the paper to the tellers than a member called out, " Mr. President and Mr. Speaker, I object to receiving any votes for President and Vice-President from Missouri, because Missouri is not a State in this Union." A great clamor instantly arose from every part of the room. Some called Order! Order! Some seconded the objection. At length the voice of a senator was heard above the din calling on the Senate to withdraw. Amid the confusion the President put the question, declared it carried, and leaving the House to wrangle as it pleased, the senators hurried away to their own chamber.

---

* Resolved, That if any objection be made to the votes of Missouri, and the counting or omitting to count which shall not essentially change the result of the election, in that case they shall be reported by the President of the Senate in the following manner:

"Were the votes of Missouri to be counted, the result would be, for A. B., for President of the United States, ――― votes; if not counted, for A. B., as President of the United States, ――― votes; but in either case A. B. is elected President of the United States, and in the same manner for Vice-President."

After the departure of the Senate the disorder in the House went on for an hour before the members, hoarse and exhausted, quieted down. Floyd, of Virginia, then moved "That Missouri is one of the States of this Union, and her votes for President and Vice-President ought to be received and counted." But Clay succeeded in getting this tabled, and long after the candles were lighted the clerk was sent to inform the Senate that the House was ready to go on with the count. The Senate thereupon returned; the certificates of Missouri were opened; her vote was read; * the tellers made their reports, and the President of the Senate began to announce the result in the manner agreed on by the two Houses. But as he was about to utter the words "I there-

* The electoral vote in 1821:

STATES.	PRESIDENT.		VICE-PRESIDENT.				
	James Monroe, Va.	John Quincy Adams, Mass.	Daniel D. Tompkins, N.Y.	Richard Stockton, N.J.	R. G. Harper, Md.	Richard Rush, Pa.	Daniel Rodney, Del.
Maine	9	..	9				
New Hampshire	7	1	7	..	..	1	
Vermont	8	..	8				
Massachusetts	15	..	7	8			
Rhode Island	4	..	4				
Connecticut	9	..	9				
New York	29	..	29				
New Jersey	8	..	8				
Pennsylvania *	24	..	24				
Delaware	4	..	..	..	..	..	4
Maryland	11	..	10	..	1		
Virginia	25	..	25				
North Carolina	15	..	15				
South Carolina	11	..	11				
Georgia	8	..	8				
Alabama	3	..	3				
Mississippi *	2	..	2				
Louisiana	3	..	3				
Kentucky	12	..	12				
Tennessee *	7	..	7				
Ohio	8	..	8				
Indiana	3	..	3				
Illinois	3	..	3				
Missouri	3	..	3				
Total	231	1	218	8	1	1	4

* One elector in each of the States of Pennsylvania, Mississippi, and Tennessee died after appointment, and before the meetings of the electors.

fore declare," he was interrupted by Floyd, who demanded of the Speaker, whether the votes of Missouri had or had not been counted.   Loud cries of Order! Order! drowned his voice, and before he could go on, Randolph rose and was addressing the Speaker, when he too was stopped by the shouts of his fellows.   The Speaker, as soon as he could make himself heard, requested Randolph to be seated.   A third member protested, and was loudly called to order.   Mr. Floyd was next declared out of order, and amid some murmuring on the part of the House the President went on to pronounce James Monroe President and Daniel D. Tompkins Vice-President of the United States for the next ensuing term.

On the day following this shameful scene another effort was made to admit Missouri on condition that she would expunge the clause in dispute from her constitution, and failed. This was on the fifteenth of February.   As Congress must adjourn on the fourth of March, if anything was to be done for Missouri it must be done quickly.   Yet no further efforts were made for a week, when a new and unexpected phase of the question was presented in a motion for a repeal of the enabling act.   Missouri said the mover has not been admitted. The compromise based on her admission is therefore void, and so much of it as lays antislavery restrictions on the territory of the United States north of thirty-six degrees thirty minutes must be repealed.   The price promised for this restriction has not been paid.   This new attack again alarmed Clay, who now came forward with a last proposition for settlement, obtained a committee of twenty-three to take into consideration the question of admission, and laid before the House a report very like the one presented by the committee of thirteen and rejected.   Missouri was to be admitted on one "fundamental condition," which was: that nothing in her constitution should ever be construed to authorize the passage of any laws, and that no laws ever should be passed by which any citizen of any State should be deprived of any of the privileges and immunities to which he was entitled under the Constitution of the United States.   When the State Legislature by its solemn act had given assent to this "fundamental con-

dition " * the President was to declare her admitted.† This
was the end. The House, after another conflict, accepted it ‡
late in the afternoon of February twenty-sixth, and the long
struggle over Missouri passed into history.

---

* It did so June 26, 1821.
† The proclamation was issued and dated August 10, 1821.
‡ Yeas, 87 ; nays, 81.

INDEX TO VOL. IV.

END OF VOLUME IV.